GOWER HANDBOOK OF QUALITY MANAGEMENT

Gower Handbook of Quality Management

Edited by

Dennis Lock

Consulting Editor

David J. Smith

Gower

© Gower Publishing Company Limited 1990

Published by
Gower Publishing Company Limited
Gower House
Croft Road
Aldershot
Hants. GU11 3HR
England

Gower Publishing Company
Old Post Road
Brookfield
Vermont 05036
USA

British Library Cataloguing in Publication Data
Gower Handbook of quality management.
1. Industries. Quality control
I. Lock, Dennis, *1929–*   II. Smith, David J.
658.562

ISBN 0 566 02770 4

Reprinted 1991

Printed in Great Britain by
Billing & Sons Ltd, Worcester

Contents

Part One POLICY AND ORGANIZATION

Part Two QUALITY-RELATED BUDGETS AND COSTS

Management-controllable variation — Worker-controllable variation — Managing organizations and people: when quality participation does not work — The need for statistical control techniques — Further reading.

Part Seven QUALITY PLANNING FOR MANUFACTURE

Part Eight QUALITY FUNCTIONS IN MANUFACTURING

Tables

Figures

Notes on Contributors

Trevor C. Ashton (National and International Engineering Design Standards) is employed by GEC Measurements Limited, Stafford. He has worked on standardization for over twenty-five years, including preparation of the full range of company standards for design, manufacture, purchasing and quality assurance in the light electronics and electromechanical field. In his early career he served an apprenticeship with the former English Electric Company and spent ten years in the mechanical design of protective relays and household meters. Mr Ashton is an active member of the British Standards Society, and has chaired both its Midland Region and Electronics Group as well as serving on the management committee. He lectures for the British Standards Society and is a principal contributor to the booklet PD 3542 *Operation of a Company Standards Department* published by the British Standards Institution.

Dr Jim Bell (Metrology) came to the National Physical Laboratory (NPL) as a Physicist in 1962, following his Doctorate at the Queen's University of Belfast. He has published some 50 papers and articles on atomic physics, and on the spectroscopy and microstructure of glasses. Dr Bell has been associated with the field of quality assurance since 1978, when he became a founder member of NPL's National Testing Laboratory Accreditation Scheme (NATLAS). He has been responsible for drafting many of the basic requirement and procedure documents for NATLAS and its successor the National Measurement Accreditation Service (NAMAS). Dr Bell is currently head of NPL's International Liaison Office.

Darek Celinski (Training for Quality) operates at home and overseas as a freelance training consultant, and has over thirty years' experience of training and development in industry. Previously he was with

Coventry Management Training Centre, which he joined in 1972. In addition to running personnel and general management courses he specialized in the training of trainers (training managers, training officers, training advisors and similar people from commercial and industrial organizations). Before that, he was training manager at Herbert-Ingersoll. His earlier appointments in training were with the Aviation Division of Smiths Industries and with the South Wales Division of the British Steel Corporation. Mr Celinski is a Fellow of the Institute of Training and Development.

Dr Barrie Dale (Just-in-time and Supplier Development) is Director of the UMIST Quality Management Centre. The centre is involved in four major activities: research into total quality management; the centre houses the Ford Motor Company Northern Regional Centre for training suppliers in total quality excellence and SPC; the operation of a Quality Management Multi-Company Teaching Programme involving at any one time, eight industrial collaborators; and total quality management consultancy, including the Q-share initiative. He is co-editor of the International Journal of Quality and Reliability Management and has co-written a book on managing quality.

John Edge (Quality-related Costs; Common and Special Problems; Quality Improvement; Lessons for Management; Quality Improvement Activities and Techniques; Essential Quality Procedures) has over 15 years experience in the software and computing industry and the last 10 have been spent in quality and project management of software based developments. These have included: commercial industrial and manufacturing systems; military and off shore real-time, and computing services. As a quality consultant he advises companies seeking ISO9000 quality management certification, as part of the Government's 1992 European strategy on quality and market competition and is particularly interested in the quality initiative managed by the Production Engineering Research Association (PERA) for the DTI. He has also been involved in computing companies' certifications against the commercial/industrial standard BS 5750/ ISO9000 and the military standards 05/21 and AQAP. Mr Edge has his own quality consultancy – Assured Systems And Products (ASAP) and currently provides consultancy to the Systems Development Group, Siemens PLC.

Peter Foyer (Product Reliability) is a principal consultant with Ingersoll

Engineers which he joined in 1975 and has over 28 years of experience in the manufacturing and transport industry, with emphasis on advanced manufacturing technology, applications and financial disciplines. Since joining Ingersoll he has participated in and managed projects for the heavy engineering, aerospace and automotive industries. His specialized knowledge of robotics and manufacturing strategy has resulted in his leading the production of a well-publicized report to the government on industrial robots. Mr Foyer is active in the Institution of Production Engineers and is a member of the Council of the British Robot Association.

Don Harrison (Quality Organization and Programmes) started his industrial career as an Engineering fitter in an aircraft factory. Following a short spell in the Royal Navy Fleet Air Arm, he joined Pedigree Petfoods, a Mars Group Company. He worked in Engineering, Production and R&D, and was Quality Manager for many years. He is a member of the Institute of Statisticians. Now a management and quality consultant, he is best known for his forward control approach to quality achievement, getting across the basics of statistical process control, and for preaching the importance of people training and attitude in getting quality right.

John Hunt (Budgeting for Quality) has professional quality assurance experience gained in client and supplier roles, including electronics; medium power engineering; guided weapons; aircraft systems; oil and gas exploration and production and computing systems. This experience embraces the application of military and civilian QC, QA and quality system standards ranging from that of stockist to design and production, post design support and major construction projects.

David Lascelles (Just-in-time and Supplier Development) is Chief Executive of Q-MAS Ltd., a total quality management consultancy operating under the auspices of the UMIST Quality Management Centre. Prior to this he was a lecturer in the Manchester School of Management at UMIST, and has held positions in sales, marketing and project management in the mechanical engineering and steel stockholding industries. His research interests include the motivational causes of quality improvement, strategic issues of TQM and supplier development. Dr. Lascelles received the 1989 European Quality Award for best European doctoral thesis on quality management.

Geoffrey Leaver (Functional Testing) is the Principal of G.L. Consultants, an independent consultancy specialising in quality assurance systems and quality management. Mr Leaver, who holds a masters degree in metallurgy is a Chartered Engineer and a Lead Assessor and Fellow of the Institute of Quality Assurance. He has been involved in technical and quality fields for over 20 years, initially in heavy engineering and fabrication followed by quality management within the Philips Electrical Industries Group. Mr Leaver established G.L. Consultants in 1983 and, as a consultant listed under the U.K. Department of Trade and Industry Support for Quality Scheme, currently offers a comprehensive service to industry and commerce covering all aspects of quality assurance and quality management.

Dennis Lock (Editor; Control of Engineering Changes and Design Modifications) after beginning as a qualified electronics engineer went on to amass an exceptionally wide management experience in industries ranging from the manufacture of subminiature electronic devices to giant machine tools and mining enginering. Mr Lock has carried out consultancy assignments in Europe and the United States and is now a freelance writer specializing in management subjects. He has written or edited numerous books, including The Gower Handbook of Management, Project Management, and many other successful books for Gower.

David Newton (An Introduction to Statistics for Quality Applications; Process Capability; Control Charts: 1. Shewhart Charts; Control Charts: 2. Cusum Charts) commenced his industrial career as an apprentice with Smiths Industries Ltd., during which time he also studied for the London University external degree in Mechanical Engineering. He continued at Smiths in various appointments in quality assurance and reliability until he entered academic life in 1968. He was initially a research fellow, and later a lecturer in the Department of Engineering Production at Birmingham University, being particularly involved in quality assurance education, including a period as course director for the postgraduate course in quality and reliability engineering. He left the University in 1989 to pursue a career as a freelance lecturer and consultant. He holds Bachelor's and Master's degrees in engineering and is a Chartered Mechanical Engineer. He is a fellow of the Royal Statistical Society, the Institute of Quality Assurance and the Institute of Statisticians.

Robin Plummer (Design Objectives; Quality Control of Design;

Quality of bought-out material; Quality of bought-out services; Inspection) is a management consultant specialising in operations, services and quality. After working for short periods in the electro and defence industries, and the construction industry, he joined British Telecom in 1973, gradually becoming fully involved in project management of multi-million pound, advanced technology installations. His main responsibility was in the quality assurance of suppliers' software. Later, as part of a large consultancy team, he was seconded to Libya as senior electrical, telecommunications and building engineer on the $600 million Libyan Coaxial Cable Project. During this time he was held for nine months as a political detainee and later released by Mr Terry Waite. More recently, Mr Plummer has been quality assurance manager for a section of British Telecom, and has been at the forefront of implementing total quality management in a service environment within his own section and at the premises of dozens of suppliers. Mr Plummer has recently presented courses on total quality management at Cambridge and provided guidance to companies across a wide spectrum of industries on a range of quality matters, in his capacity as a management consultant. He is a Chartered Engineer, a Member of the Institution of Electrical Engineers, a Fellow of the Institute of Quality Assurance and a Registered Lead Assessor of quality management systems.

Frank Price (The Quality Concept and Objectives) is a Fellow of the Institute of Quality Assurance and a member of the Association of Management Education and Development. He has spent more than thirty years initiating and implementing quality control systems in a variety of manufacturing companies, and has written and lectured widely on the subject. He studied statistics at Leicester College of Technology and industrial psychology at Nottingham University. From 1957 to 1963 he was a Quality Control Manager at Pilkington, then left to run a successful company of his own. He re-entered the world of industry when invited to set up a QC function for a new electronic enterprise, and similar assignments soon followed. He is currently an independent consultant in the field of quality management and cultural change in the work organization.

David J. Smith (Quality-related Costs; Statutory Provisions and Obligations; The Traditional Approach to Software Quality; Quality Software through Formal Methods; Essential Quality Procedures) has spent the last 25 years in a number of senior positions in both quality and reliability management. He has written five successful works on quality, reliability, maintainability and statistics and during that time has been directly concerned with this branch of engineering in the telecommunications, electronics and control and oil and gas industries. He has assisted a number of companies from the very large to the very small, in obtaining MOD and British Standards quality systems approvals. He is best known for his many seminars and courses on reliability engineering, its contract implications and other related topics. At the time of going to press, he is chairman of the Safety and Reliability Society, whose journal he edits.

Ray H. Spencer (Managing Non-Conformances) has gained broad international experience in the field of quality, having worked in Europe, the United States of America and Asia. Following roles in manufacturing engineering and project management, he became Supplier Quality Assurance Manager with Rank Xerox Ltd. He was involved with the development and implementation of supplier quality strategies, which resulted in a significantly reduced supplier base and enabled direct to line shipment of materials. The role not only provided the opportunity of developing systems within Rank Xerox, but also to help many suppliers improve performance by re-assessing their systems and employing techniques for increasing capability and control. Mr Spencer then crossed over the supply line, to become a Quality Manager with STC Components, supplying electronic components to professional, defence and consumer markets. The experience gained proved invaluable when he moved to the consumer electronics industry, becoming Divisional Quality Manager within Thomson Consumer Electronics' European TV Division. This experience has afforded an excellent opportunity for examining and selecting a proven approach for the management of nonconformance.

Gordon Staples (Quality audits and reviews) is widely experienced in quality, having worked worldwide in quality management consultancy in company-wide programmes, IQA Lead Assessor training, quality circles and quality systems. He currently leads the Quality Management Services Division of AMTAC in Manchester, and worked prior to consultancy in the gas industry, auditing and assessing vendors and subcontractors in all types of industry. He also presented training courses in quality management and assessment. He was QA Manager for a valve and desuperheater supplier to the nuclear industry with previous working experience in design in the computer and machine tool industries.

Eric Wallbank (Product Reliability) is a Senior Consultant with Ingersoll Engineers, having joined in 1985. Previously he spent 10 years in the product areas of a variety of industries, but mainly working in domestic electrical goods, commercial electronics and defence systems. During this period he progressed from practical design and development work to responsibility for the mechanical engineering group in a large product design and development department. Since joining Ingersoll, he has worked on a broad range of projects, mainly concerned with product strategy, design and evaluation, covering many industry sectors.

Abbreviations

ACARD	Advisory Council for Applied Research and Development
ACMH	Advisory Committee on Major Hazards (HSC)
AGREE	Advisory Group on Reliability of Electronic Equipment (US Defence Department)
ANSI	American National Standard Institute
AQAP	Allied Quality Assurance Publications (NATO)
ATE	Automatic test equipment
BS	British Standard
BSI	British Standards Institution
CAD	Computer aided design
CAE	Computer aided engineering
CAI	Computer aided inspection
CAM	Computer aided manufacturing
CAR	Corrective action request
CAT	Computer aided testing
CCITT	International Telephone and Telegraphic Consultative Committee
CEC	Commission of the European Communities
CECC	CENELEC Electronic Components Committee
CEE	International Commission for Conformity of Electrical Equipment
CEN	European Committee for Standardization
CENELEC	European Committee for Electrotechnical Standardization
CIE	International Commission on Illumination
CIM	Computer integrated manufacturing
CIMAH	Control of Industrial Major Accident Hazards Regulations
CWQI	Company wide quality improvement
DCCC	Document configuration and change control
DEF	Ministry of Defence standards

DTI	Department of Trade and Industry
DIN	Deutsche Normenausschuss
DTI	Department of Trade and Industry
EEA	Electrical Engineering Association
EEC	European Economic Community
EFTA	European Free Trade Association
EUROMET	European Collaboration on Measurements Standards
FMEA	Failure mode and effect analysis
FMECA	Failure mode, effect and criticality analysis (extended version of FMEA)
FMS	Flexible manufacturing system
FTA	Fault tree analysis
HPP	Homogeneous Poisson process
HSC	Health and Safety Commission
HSE	Health and Safety Executive
IAEA	International Atomic Energy Authority
IEC	International Electrotechnical Commission
IECQ	IEC system for electronic component assessment and certification
IEE	Institution of Electrical Engineers
IEEE	Institute of Electrical and Electronics Engineers (US)
IFAN	International Federation for the Application of Standards
ISO	International Standards Organization
JIT	Just-in-time
KISS	Keep it silly simple
MAD	Mean absolute deviation
MIL	United States Military
MoU	Memorandum of understanding (as issued by NAMAS and others)
MPI	Magnetic Particle Inspection
MRB	Material review board
MRI	Master record index
MTBF	Mean time between failures
MTTF	Mean time to failure
MTTR	Mean time to repair
NACCB	National Accreditation Council for Certifying Bodies
NAMAS	National Measurement Accreditation Service
NATO	North Atlantic Treaty Organization
NDT	Non destructive testing
NEDO	National Economic Development Office
NIGs	National Industry Groups (HSE)

NMR	Nonconforming material report
NPL	National Physical Laboratory
PES	Programmable electronic system
PQA	Programmable quality assurance
PROM	Programmable read only memory
QA	Quality assurance
QAD	Quality assurance department
QC	Quality circle
QIP	Quality improvement programme
R&D	Research and development
REM	A remark entry in a computer program
RPI	Relative precision index
SD	Standard deviation
SPC	Statistical process control; *also used for* Stored programme controlled telephone exchanges
STACO	Standing Committee for the Study of Principles (ISO)
SQA	Supplier quality assurance
THE	Technical Help to Exporters (BSI)
TPM	Total productivity maintenance
TQC	Total quality control
TQM	Total quality management

Preface

Not very long ago the quality of purchased goods was mainly a subjective attribute. Although certainly seen as a desirable aim for manufacturers it was nevertheless ill-defined and difficult to quantify. The buyer might associate quality with a particular brand name and perhaps (often mistakenly) with a high price tag. Manufacturers' attitudes to quality relied at best on inspection and testing to weed out manufacturing flaws and faulty components or, at worst, on accepting that goods might fail in service so that customers would have to return them for exchange or repair.

As technological complexity increased it seemed that there was more to go wrong, and reliability became more of a problem. Buying could be regarded as something of a lottery, and faults in many goods were regarded as inevitable. An extreme example was the case of early computers, built with thermionic valves before the days of transistor microchips. Valves deteriorated in use and occasionally burned out when switched on. The probability of component failure in such a computer increased so seriously with size and complexity as to be a serious constraint on building larger machines.

Many factors have combined to bring about a dramatic change in both the perception and achievement of quality. Purchasers have become more discerning and thus have higher quality expectations. Modern materials and manufacturing techniques have allowed great improvements to be made in component reliability and in the consistency of dimensions and performance. A comprehensive framework of legislation and engineering standards now imposes a quality discipline on manufacturers. Above all, there is now a greater awareness of and commitment to quality by designers and manufacturers than ever before. They both realize that quality is not simply a desirable goal, but is indeed essential for economic survival.

This particularly follows the challenge set by the Japanese, once regarded merely as cheap imitators of the West but now seen as formidable competitors who are continually setting new world quality standards.

During the 1980s an awareness spread throughout the industry that quality assurance techniques are important not only for hardware, but also for the computer software on which the safe and reliable operation of so many plant installations and products depends. Contemplation of hazardous incidents arising from software errors has stimulated this interest, so that the importance of software quality is now widely recognized.

Achieving high quality demands total management commitment, but it also needs appreciation and application of appropriate methods and practices. Our contributors have devoted the greater part of their working lives to the attainment and teaching of these aims and this handbook has been compiled so that readers can benefit from sharing their experience.

Dennis Lock
St Albans, 1990

Part One
POLICY AND ORGANIZATION

1 The Quality Concept and Objectives

Frank Price*

Quality: the latest buzzword?

'Quality'; the word itself must have been used more in the last ten years than in the preceding ten centuries, yet the more we hear it the more confusing its meaning seems to become.

At one time the word was defined as 'conformance to specification', until it was realized that specifications sometimes do not exactly and explicitly match a particular customer need and that, though some article or service might indeed meet its specification, it still failed to result in customers' satisfactions. So the operational definition of quality evolved, in the light of this potential incongruence, into 'meeting the customers' expectations'. This seems to be as useful a definition as any, provided that the 'customers' expectations' which are supposed to be met are clearly and unambiguously understood by the one who sets out to meet them and so provide the 'quality'. This is not always the case.

This definition has undergone further honing into: 'Quality is the supplying of goods which do not come back, to customers who do'. Although there is a certain slickness about this definition it does embody a commercial truism, but it depends upon actually *achieving* perceived quality requirements, with consistency and regularity; this is not easy.

The quality function is an information gathering service; from the mass of data which is available in every production process and every service activity in the complex world of commerce, quality extracts that which is most meaningful from that which is less so, and by analysis of such process data sets out to control the future behaviour of the process towards even greater customer satisfaction — towards better and better quality. Because all modern business systems generate such colossal amounts of data, quality makes use of the mathematics of big numbers — statistical methods — to distill useful meaning from the daunting mega-heaps of data. So the belief has arisen that quality is little more than applied statistics; this is on a par with averring that Chippendale furniture making is little more than the applying of chisels to wood. Quality makes use of statistical thinking purely as a tool of convenience, because there is no other tool as appropriate to the task as that provided by mathematical statistics. This tends to put people off, memories of the blank incomprehension occasioned by the algebra of schooldays shroud the subject in veils of mystery. It all seems too complicated, and best left to the specialist practitioners who have mastered its mysteries. Often these 'experts' themselves foster this mystification by speaking in their own esoteric tongue which is unintelligible to the rest of us. This leads us to ask what has all this fancy mathematics to do with quality in the workaday world, to which the answer is not much. Maybe this is one of the reasons why quality used to be a despised discipline done by despised people, whereas nowadays, thanks in large measure to Japan on the one hand and the Ford Motor Company's quality training initiative on the other, quality is a highly respected discipline. Done by despised people.

This is one of the reasons why we in the west are, generally speaking, not as smart at quality as we could be — it is still looked upon in the corporate culture as a low-status activity of sufficient unimportance to be entrusted to low calibre people, to those unsuited to the more rewarding and demanding jobs of financial jiggery-pokery or marketing manipulativeness. This statement is not a mere opinion, it is borne out by the most cursory survey of the job advertisements in the 'quality' newspapers; see which jobs are held in highest esteem as measured by salaries offered, note where quality comes in the pecking order. In these 'quality' newspapers the prestigious positions (financial management being the most highly regarded, presumably because it is assumed that anybody who can correctly count money can also earn it for the company — a belief with zero basis in reality) offer the highest pay, plus a 'quality' motor car. Note the misuse of language here. What is a 'quality' car? One which fulfils its intended purpose. So to an itinerant window cleaner a fuel-thrifty Robin Reliant van with a roof rack to carry his ladders is a 'quality' car. To a successful rag-and-bone gatherer who is privately ashamed of his scavenging way of life such a vehicle would demean his self-image so he buys a Rolls-Royce to park on the gravel drive in front of his mansion. His is a different 'intended purpose' from the window cleaner's.

Quality is fitness for purpose, it has nothing whatever to do with status, or grade, or class. Yet this wrong interpretation of the word is an endlessly recurring source of trouble, it causes so many misunderstandings. 'We cannot afford the luxury of quality', decrees the boss of a small outfit making modest earthenware drinking mugs, 'we are not in the Wedgwood or china porcelain end of the business'. No, but whoever buys the mugs expects them to hold the tea without leaking, expects them to fulfil their intended purpose; expects, in a word, *quality*.

Perhaps another of the reasons why we in the west are still not quite as smart about quality as we could be lies in the paradox that when it is present, quality is, in fact, invisible. What do we mean by that, *invisible?* Pray consider the following paraphasing of a famous advertising jingle:

A million housewives every day open a can . . . and *throw it away!*

After having emptied its contents of baked beans into the saucepan, of course. In the act of throwing the emptied can away without a second thought these housewives are collectively paying a daily million tributes to the *quality* of the tin can which brought them something to go with their breakfast bacon — *by ignoring it*. The quality of these cans (which is to say the way they fulfil their intended purpose) is so superlatively good that it may safely be taken for granted. Not once, not twice, but a million times a day. Now *that* is real quality! An invisible input. Achieved by a succession of invisible people, employed in the once-despised but lately respected calling of quality control, right back up the supply chain which ends when the emptied can is tossed absent-mindedly into the garbage bin. Achieved by the men and women in the cannery who control torrents of output streaming along the production lines at hundreds of cans per minute, at these vast output rates it is not possible to make a *little* mistake. So, very few mistakes are made. Achieved by their counterparts in the can-making plant; by those upstream in the tin plate mill; by those further back in the steel casting and rolling mill . . . an unremitting application of statistical method and quality skill which culminates in an emptied can, its purpose fulfilled, being casually tossed onto the rubbish dump — by the million, and rarely does a dud appear. (When did you last see a can with its ends domed-out, blown?) The rare defectives are not counted even in parts per million, they occur in ones per several million, if at all.

To sum up the foregoing:

Quality is: Giving the customer what he wants today,
At a price he is pleased to pay,
At a cost we can contain,
Again, and again, and again,
And giving him something even better tomorrow.
Quality is: The degree of congruence between expectation and realization.

Or, to put this into plainer words:

The matching of what you wanted with what you got.
Expectation versus fulfilment.

Quality is: Invisible when it is good,
Impossible to ignore when it is bad.
An *invisible* input.
Quality is NOT: Mathematical statistics.
Quality is: The application of simple statistical method.
Quality is NOT: Status, grade or class.

Quality: is it important?

Important? The answer to this question depends, as answers so often do, on the questioner's standpoint. Seen through the listless eyes of a Polish housewife with a purseful of useless zlotys, in a butcher's shop emptied of everything except a trio of surly assistants, a foraging party of disappointed bluebottles and a few scraps of darkening offal, the bulging displays of a British supermarket must take on the aspect of a fevered dream, a tantalizing glimpse into a Gomorrah of gluttony supporting a *quality* of life so rich it must be part of a different universe. As far as she is concerned it is a case of never mind the quality, I'll take whatever is available. Quality is relative. It is to a large extent dependent on economics, to the inexorable law of supply and demand.

Whenever there is an excess of money pursuing a shortage of goods or services to spend it on, quality is of secondary importance to mere availability.

In a free market economy such a famine of consumer goods is not permitted to exist for very long; market forces, in the form of entrepreneurial capitalism, respond to the imbalance of too much cash chasing too few goods. The balance is redressed. Soon there is an abundance of goods available to sop up the cash in the economy. The system overbalances in the other direction, and an excess of goods bloats the market, rival brands competing for the consumers' spending power. Now quality, which mattered not at all when things were scarce, matters more than anything else now they are plentiful. So quality is a function of supply, once sellers' markets have given way to buyers'. Of the three factors governing purchasing decisions — price, service and quality — at a time when goods were scarce service was the be-all and end-all, 'make it . . . sell it' was the order of its day. This is how things used to be in the halcyon days of western manufacturing, before a quality revolution exploded out of the east to shatter complacency for evermore. As soon as goods became plentiful price became the arbiter, but price wars are too costly to support for too long, so *quality* inevitably becomes the *primary purchasing determinant*, to use the language of the buying officer. This fact is borne out by formal research, as well as by general observation and historical awareness.

This economic context emphasizing the importance of quality, as it is used as a marketing competitive edge external to the manufacturing (or servicing) enterprise, is symmetrically balanced by an equal stress on the economics of quality within the enterprise. Quality is, as well as an information gathering agency, a *discipline of thrift*, a doctrine of frugality in the use of available resources.

Resources . . . what are the resources at the disposal of the manufacturer? There are four — raw materials, machinery, time and people. The 'trick' of manufacturing management is to make the best use of time and machinery, through the capabilities (or, as they are called these days, 'competencies') of people, in order to transform 100 per cent of the bought-in raw materials into saleable finished goods. Sounds simple enough. It is. But it is not easy. This conversion ratio — the proportion of raw materials entering the plant which eventually departs from the plant as finished goods (as opposed to scrap or returned product) is a valid measure of the effectiveness of management. This must be why a good many companies are unable to quote it. The maximization of this conversion ratio is the job of quality.

You might at this point choose to step into that ancient and cloying swamp of semantics by asking that hoary old conundrum 'who is *responsible* for quality?', and then going on to suggest that the quality function cannot be 'responsible' for quality, since its practitioners do no more than measure it. You might then go on to suggest, as so many others before you have suggested, that since quality is not the responsibility of quality it must therefore be the responsibility of production. Your thinking, if you have pursued this route, is now well and truly bogged down in the mire of meanings. You are now committed to a silly sectarian squabble about who is responsible for quality, and it will go on and on and you will never escape the swamp. Save your breath. It is *the process which is responsible for quality*. The job of the people in the quality department is to measure the capability of the process, to balance the see-saw on one end of which sits the customers' needs, while on the other is perched the measured capability of the process to meet those needs. The 'responsibility' for quality belongs to the process and therefore to those in whose stewardship the entire process of wealth-generation rests, whether they are called 'production' or 'quality' or whatever. They are collectively the custodians of the resources whose purpose is the generating of wealth by the adding of value, through the activity called 'work'.

Work, from an economic standpoint, is identifiable as one of two kinds:

- Work which adds *value*.
- Work which adds *cost*.

To demonstrate this crucial difference, consider (using the following example) what research in the UK shows to be typical of manufacturing performance.

A hypothetical manufacturer buys £100's worth of components — his 'raw materials'. He processes them through his lathes and his grinders, to turn them into saleable goods. He has done work which adds value. Their value is now £200. Well, it would be, but for the distressing discovery that 30 per cent of the finished goods are incorrect to specification, so these are rejected to be reworked. So only £70's worth of the original lot have achieved saleable status. These now have a value of £140. The remaining components, costing £30 but now having a *nominal* value of £60, are consigned to rework. This costs money in machine time and wages. This work is now *adding cost*. If all are salvaged, their value will still be £60, but their cost will be considerably higher. This would be a bad enough state of affairs, but there is worse; half of the 30 per cent reworked components are found to be irredeemably defective *after* the rework costs have been added, these are now scrapped. Money is now pouring down the plug hole. All hope of any profit is lost. Company cash is added to that Danegeld which collective quality incompetence extorts from British manufacturing industry, every year to the tune of a staggering figure somewhere between £10 000 million and £20 000 million. These are statistical estimates of the awful reality, they are figures of unimpeachable pedigree, elicited by university research (Lockyer and Oakland, Bradford UMC). The hypothetical company (Hypothetical? Don't you believe it!), which is the subject of this tale of woe, might argue 'So what! It is *our* money we are losing'. True, true yet false; it is ultimately the *nation's* wealth they are squandering through their wasteful mismanagement of the resources that society entrusts to their stewardship. Their private loss is our public loss in their frittering away of irreplaceable resources. Perhaps they seek to excuse their inexcusable misconduct by citing another of the convenient managerial cop outs of our times and claiming 'you cannot have quality and quantity'. Again they are wrong, the truth is:

The higher the quality the *less* it costs.

This is very obvious, when you think about it. Making duds sops up just as much machine capacity as making OK output does, so to improve quality is to bring more productive capacity into profitable employment. You would wonder why it is necessary to state such an obvious truth, alas, it is often necessary to do so.

So this thing we call quality, which is about satisfying the needs of the customer and doing so at an economic cost, is a subject well worthy of consideration at the highest level. Quality, used for a generation and more by Japan as a key element of manufacturing and marketing strategy, offers us the chance to create a strong competitive edge. Quality, once the Cinderella of the organization, is about to become a royal bride. Unless we get it wrong, and it becomes just another ugly sister instead. So how do we get it right?

Quality: leadership through commitment

There is an old Chinese benediction which goes 'May you be so fortunate as to live in uninteresting times'. The idea of it being, one supposes, that the even tenor of life should never by upset by the arrival of the unexpected, there must be no surprises. This is a not inappropriate tenet of faith for anyone engaged in the supply of goods or services of specified quality — never disturb the equanimity of the customer by *surprising* him, especially by making a delivery of sub-standard output. This is not to confuse 'uninteresting' with 'boring', there is no boredom to be found in consistently delivering high quality product, but 'interest' — even shock — is generated by the delivery of the rejectable. Like the housewife who disposes of the empty can with utter disinterest (she would only find it of interest if it had failed in its purpose) the customer has no wish to find your product 'interesting' because it is contaminated with troublesome duds. After all, what is it that you are *really* selling? This is not a trivial question, it is central to the whole commercial thrust. Elizabeth Arden, of cosmetics fame, asked and answered this question; when someone made the observation 'Ah, Miss Arden, I see you are selling cosmetics', she is said to have replied 'No I am not selling cosmetics, I am selling the hope of beauty'. There is a world of difference. What is the can manufacturer selling to the cannery which puts the beans into the cans which are bought by a million housewives? Empty tin cans? Ends to be seamed on to the cans once they are filled? No, he is selling the certitude of trouble-free running to the canner who will use his product at the rate of over a thousand a minute. He is selling *peace of mind*. He is selling 'uninteresting times'. This notion might be pushed even further, by suggesting that it is in the interest of the manufacturer to attend to all the interesting quality requirements of his product, in order to deprive his customer of the interesting discovery that they are not to specification. The customer will have enough problems controlling his own quality, and will feel completely disinclined to add to his burden by accepting yours. Customers are people, and after all, in our mechanistic scheme of things people are generally perceived to be nuisances; this is a legacy of our rationalist and scientific culture, this is the motivation behind the millennial dream of the 'workerless factory' from which people have been exiled by automation. Trouble is though, that the achieving and sustaining of high process and product quality is the direct result of the application of creativity, imagination, analysis, synthesis, willpower — *people* things. This is where quality leadership has its roots, in the vision of quality which is the essential precursor of its attainment.

This is not to suggest that there is no place for managerial systems and advancing technology, these are essential. But on their own they cannot be enough. The best system of quality management, BS5750, is a fine system. But that is *all* it is, a system, a scaffolding within which people must transform the pile of bricks it embraces into a house. Any system is all form and no content, the latter must be supplied by people. Many managers set great store by systems, and it is easy to oversystematize, to fall into the trap of assuming that because there is a system for dealing with every eventuality then every eventuality will be dealt with; disappointment and frustration sometimes ensue. Systems sometimes help us to generate the right answers to the wrong questions, whereas quality is about *asking the right questions*. Systems are concerned with administration, quality is to do with inspiration. This is the most important gift the quality function can make to the organization, a vision of success to which it is feasible to aspire, to say 'this is where we are aiming, this is our strategic goal'; and then to provide the means of achieving it, the techniques of quality, saying 'this is how we get there', this is the tactical support.

In this way the quality function will finally free itself from the stigma of being a despised discipline. It will have earned respect. And quality, of world-class leadership, is achieved through education, which is what this handbook is all about.

2 Quality Organization and Programmes

Don Harrison

Quality and value for money are inseparable. Design quality that meets consumer needs can be achieved by setting key organizational objectives.

Good quality achievement depends upon setting the right standards, and creating an organization such that these objectives will be achieved. Effective organization is achieved by matching responsibility with authority.

Good quality control is achieved by recognizing that the current process capability and natural variability set the basis for operating standards. Quality programmes based on effective control loops, formal and informal, short and long term, involve everyone in the organization. The ultimate goal is to achieve the target design quality.

Organizing for design quality

Design quality is the degree to which the design standards for a product or service meet the needs of the customer and the market. Value for money is inseparable from quality, and it is at the design stage where the basics of quality and value for money are decided.

As the customer always looks at product, service and value for money in relation to competitive offerings, there must be examination

13

of the competition whenever customer perception of a product is examined. Departmental organization for design quality will vary with the size and nature of the product. Nevertheless, there are some elements of organizational objectives that are essential for the success of any enterprise. These key elements are:

1. The identification of customer needs for quality in relation to value for money.
2. The definition of main competitors in the market.
3. Measurement of the customer's view of product compared with the competition.
4. The identification of trends or changes that might affect competitive position.
5. Regular assessment of performance in the market place to measure the quality present when used.
6. Formal customer complaint procedures. To address customer dissatisfaction, and to generate data on product performance.
7. Where complaint data is scarce, taking positive steps to get customer response.
8. Setting a target to achieve and maintain an element of superiority in quality and value for money over the competition.

Achieving these objectives is usually a research and development (R&D), marketing or product development department responsibility.

Implementation of product design

To implement the product or service design, product descriptions, product specifications and quality operating standards must be prepared.

Product descriptions and *product specifications* are technical documents that specify the best technical capability for achieving product design.

Quality operating standards set targets and limits for specific attributes of materials, processes and operations.

This activity generates the working documents to specify design targets for:

1. The buying of raw materials.
2. Purchase and maintenance of equipment.
3. Production methods and operations.

They represent the current methods for achieving the target product design, and are the criteria against which quality performance is measured. Used effectively, with good control systems, they help to provide a product that performs consistently, meeting customer's expectations.

The job of generating product design standards and product descriptions is usually the responsibility of R&D in cooperation with the marketing department. The job of setting operating standards must involve the production department. Without their input unachievable standards may be set for production.

It is at this stage that the process capability must be considered. Process capability is the quality level and variation that can be achieved when the raw materials, process, and operations are normal.

Process capability limitations may prevent the achievement of product design. In this case it is vital to base production operating standards on the process capability. In addition, identifying any shortfalls of raw materials, equipment, people or operations, warts and all, will indicate clear objectives for improvement in process capability. Operating standards must also reflect variation in quality due to normal variation. This requires the application of statistical method, in the form of statistical process control (SPC) procedures.

The use of arbitrarily tight, or 'ivory tower' standards for process control will not improve quality. Adjusting the process when it is achieving process capability will make things worse, not better.

Quality organization for setting operating standards based on the process capability must involve the production department. They are responsible for output and cost, and are the only people who actually control the output process, hence the process capability, hence quality.

However never forget that the product design is the ultimate standard. No one should hide behind operating standards! Achievement of the product design should be the ultimate company goal.

It is the job of production to achieve operating standards, with the objective of narrowing performance within tolerances. This also forms part of the programme of improvement for suppliers, operating and development departments.

We are now entering into the area of conformance quality.

Formal organization for conformance quality

Conformance quality is the degree to which manufactured quality or the service provided meets the design standards.

Good organization is essential for achieving conformance quality goals. Everyone quotes that 'quality is everyone's job', and so it is. What a pity it is that many organizations see quality as a completely separate function. They often place complete responsibility for quality with one department. Although specific quality jobs are necessary to achieve quality targets, care must be taken to make sure that these jobs do not diminish other people's quality responsibilities. How can this be done?

By making sure that any quality responsibility is matched by the appropriate authority.

The quality department and historical problems

The old concept of a quality department, independent of production, which was totally responsible for quality, is rapidly disappearing. It was never a valid responsibility, since the control of production quality has always actually rested with those responsible for making the raw materials, and running and maintaining the process. The so-called independent quality department can never have these authorities. Some quality departments still have authority over quality decisions, such as release of finished product. This provides the luxury of having authority without responsibility. Such an organization can also lead to a somewhat bureaucratic quality department, making complicated rules for product disposal, auditing operations and similar policing activities.

Any independent quality department given responsibility for output quality is put in a difficult situation. If quality is bad they get the kicks, but have no real authority to put things right in production. This leads to strained relationships between production and the quality department. The quality department begins to set tighter operating standards and heavier sampling procedures in a vain attempt to put a safety net between the production line and the customer to catch all the bad quality. This is not effective. Operating standards that are too tight in relation to the process capability lead to unnecessary adjustments that make things worse, not better. The safety net can never be 100 per cent effective and relies upon spotting bad product after it's made, rather than prevention by good control and improvement. Visible signs of this type of organization are:

1. Unnecessary bureaucracy.
2. High scrap rates.
3. Lots of product 'holds'.

4. A 100 years' war between production and quality departments.
5. High quality costs.
6. Long lived, chronic quality problems.
7. Concentration upon sorting out bad quality after manufacture at the expense of quality improvement.

The same situation can develop in the area of raw material if an independent quality department is made responsible for incoming raw material quality. They neither buy nor manufacture the raw material, so have no associated authority. Their only defence is to set up the safety net between the supplier and goods-in, with similar results!

Example: A department within R&D in a large manufacturing industry was given the job of deciding whether output was fit to ship or not. They were made responsible for outgoing quality. They were called the quality assurance department (QAD). The justification for this organization was that R&D were independent. Not being subjected to demands of cost or output, they would be unbiased in their decisions. To achieve their objective QAD set up sampling schemes for finished product, operated by themselves and the production departments. When customer complaints arrived these were seen as a failure by QAD, who were asked to improve their performance. They tried to do this by setting up larger sample sizes and tighter operating standards. Procedures for finished product acceptance decisions became more complex. Product rejections increased. So did customer complaints. What was wrong?

The responsibility and authority for quality were sitting in two different departments. Production were the only people with the authority to control manufactured quality. To protect themselves QAD placed emphasis on finished product inspection, tying up production resources that should have been used to control and improve quality.

The systems used by QAD were statistically sound. The problem was that product defects were, as usual, running at a roughly constant level. No sampling system can discriminate between batches when all batches are about the same.

Eventually the organization was changed. Responsibility for product quality control and disposal was given to production. They now had full recognition of their responsibility for output, cost and quality. They had always had the authority over output, cost and quality, since only they could adjust processes, stop lines or initiate improved process capabilities.

A group of people was formed into the production quality department, which reported to the production manager. This group included former members of the quality assurance department, and its people were skilled in statistical process control (SPC). This group now had responsibility for control systems, identifying the cause of quality problems and working with production management to set up action programmes to improve quality. *They were not responsible for quality.* This was the producing department's responsibility.

Within a year of the reorganization customer complaints had been reduced by over 70 per cent. Rejection and scrap costs were down by 80 per cent. This was achieved by a permanent improvement in manufactured quality performance. A 25 per cent reduction in the total company quality department strength was achieved by delegating the responsibility for quality measurement and control to the production operators as part of their job. A continual plan of production quality improvement was generated with the ultimate objective of achieving product design. This involved every department in the company.

All this was achieved simply by aligning quality responsibility with authority. This alignment is the most important principle of quality organization.

Some companies give authority for stopping production lines to an independent quality department. This is said to give proper authority to the department. The results for quality may improve, but the problem now becomes one of cost and output. Taking action decisions without considering output and cost leads to low outputs and high costs. Quality may be adequate, but not value for money. And unless they perceive both quality and value for money in a product, customers will buy elsewhere. Production cannot feel responsible for output and cost if another department is making stop decisions.

Using the above example and arguments, the ideal organization for conformance quality control is to establish responsibility for manufactured quality firmly with the production department.

This means that all decisions about product quality rest with production, together with full accountability for quality. The quality department responsible for designing the SPC systems and operating standards based upon the process capability, although not responsible for quality, are part of the production team, reporting to the production manager.

All quality measurement in the production process is a production responsibility. This measurement is not carried out by the quality department but by the production operator team. The production quality department has the following responsibilities:

1. Measurement of process capability.
2. The design and maintenance of quality control systems, and operating standards using SPC methods.
3. The analysis and presentation of long term results from the records generated by production from the SPC systems.
4. Generation of other quality management information, such as product hold rates, scrap rates and other quality costs.
5. Cause analysis: using data generated by production to identify causes of quality problems, leading to quality improvement action programmes.
6. Assisting production in carrying out trials and tests of improved operating methods.

Benefits of this organization are:

1. R&D are not longer saddled with the responsibility for output quality. The main quality job is determining design standards.
2. Production now have full responsibility and accountability for quality output and cost, the three-legged stool of production. (Three-legged stools never rock, but the legs must be balanced if one is to sit comfortably!)
3. Production quality control department is part of the production team. Better for relationships.
4. Responsibility for quality measurement, decisions and actions can be delegated as far down the production organization as possible, limited only by ability.
5. The production quality department becomes a small team responsible for systems, control information and quality trials. This leads to economies in quality manpower requirements.

Vendor assurance

Vendor assurance is working with suppliers to ensure that delivered raw materials meet requirements. Only the supplier can control raw material quality. Vendor assurance is usually the responsibility of R&D or some other technical department. Certainly it should not be a production responsibility. They usually have no authority over raw material quality. Anyway their place is in the plant. If R&D are made responsible for incoming raw material quality, then all they can do is to try to set up a safety net between the supplier and goods-in. The pitfalls of this approach have already been demonstrated. Developing the same argument used for production, then the buying department should be responsible for vendor assurance.

The buying department is always responsible for cost and delivery. When it comes to quality this is usually someone else's responsibility. Yet with any product quality, cost and delivery are inseparable. (The three-legged stool of buying!)

Giving responsibility for vendor assurance to a department independent of the buying function is another case of failure to align authority with responsibility. The ideal solution would be to make the buying department responsible for vendor assurance. Although this is the organization in a few companies, this does not seem to be the current trend. Yet where the buying department are responsible for raw material vendor assurance the matching of responsibility with authority works well.

Informal organization for conformance quality

Everyone has a responsibility for quality. The benefits from the meeting of these responsibilities are often not fully realized. This results in failure to achieve the achievable in quality performance, stemming from a failure to organize effective quality control loops. A quality control loop is a circle of actions. To be effective the circle must be complete. Figure 2.1 shows the control loop diagram. The key activities are:

1. The measurement of quality at a key point.
2. Deciding whether quality meets standard or not. (SPC methods)
3. Reporting if quality is not to standard.
4. Deciding what action to take.
5. Taking the action.
6. If quality is OK, repeating the cycle.

Quality control loops can be formal or informal. Formal loops are part of the written quality control procedures, including:

1. Frequency of sampling and measurement method.
2. Decision limits and corrective actions.
3. Individual responsibilities for specific activities.
4. Auditing and system review procedures.

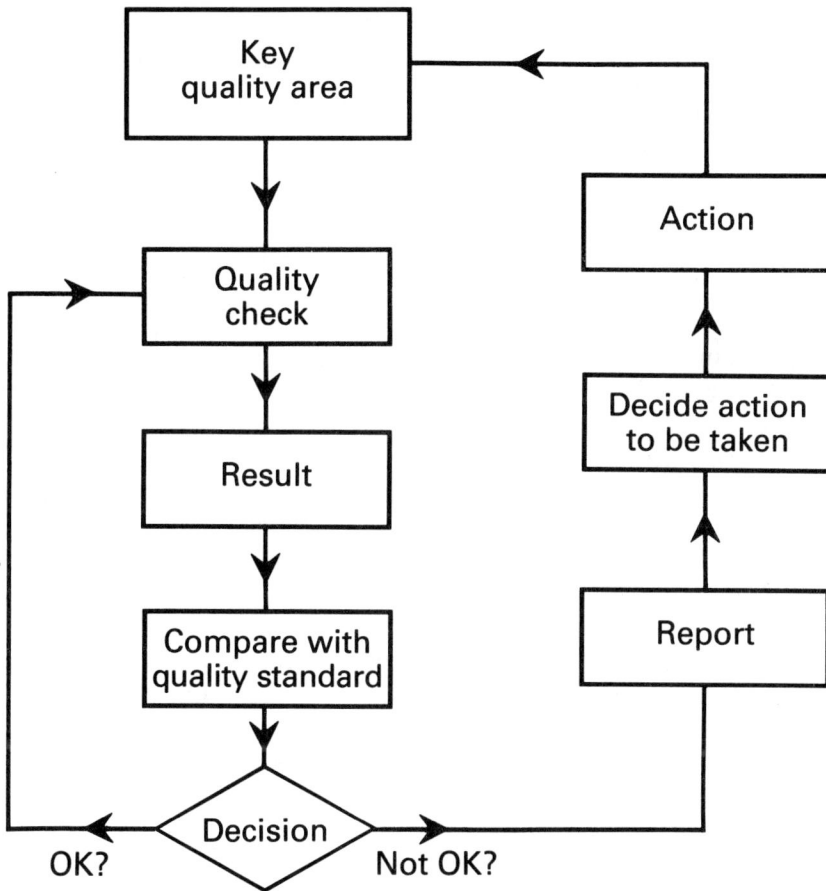

- A quality control loop is a circle of activities
- The circle must be complete for effective control

Figure 2.1. A quality control loop. This shows a quality control loop diagrammatically, illustrating the need for a continuous loop of information, decisions and actions

Formal systems are usually operated well, limited only by ability and motivation.

Informal systems are not written down. They are nevertheless very effective.

Example: A labelling machine is checked every 15 minutes for output quality using a formal system. Shortly after the last check, which was OK, the operator hears a slight clicking noise from behind the machine. He decides to check it out and finds every label is being torn by a crashed package trapped in the machine. He stops and fixes the problem. He then keeps an eye on the area for the next hour or so to make sure everything is all right.

Example 2: A raw material manufacturer isolates a batch of powdered raw material for oversize lumps due to sieve failure. The batches are isolated and resieved. He rings the customer and tells him of the problem, and asks him to 'eyeball' the raw material, 'just in case'. The customer finds one batch with lumps, and sends it back to the supplier.

Example 3: The colour of a process material is checked every 30 minutes using a formal system. During the shift raw material from a different supplier is introduced. Remembering problems with this supplier the last time it was used, the operator runs an immediate check, which is OK.

Example 4: An operator reports a process temperature reading outside control limits using a formal system. The manager authorizes a process adjustment. Although the thermometer is checked regularly he has it checked out as well. The thermometer is found to be in error. The manager had remembered that the thermometer had been replaced 2 days ago.

The beauty of informal systems is that they are not written down, and so have complete flexibility. They rely upon people using their eyes, ears, nose, memory, process knowledge and common sense. Because of their flexibility the concentration of effort can be varied to hit likely problem areas. They always operate on the most up-to-date knowledge of conditions.

People need to be organized and motivated so that the full value of these informal systems can be realized. This is a job for management. Giving full responsibility for control over manufactured quality to production is the starting point. Delegation of quality measurement and control to the production operators builds quality responsibility into the operator's job. Most operators intuitively operate informal quality control loops. The full benefits can be realized through training. The key elements of this training are that everyone:

(a) understands the contribution of quality towards business success;
(b) has basic knowledge of the key quality features of the product;
(c) knows what can go wrong with materials, processes and products;
(d) knows the consequences of these failures for the product, the customer and the business;
(e) recognizes the importance of informal control loops, and the jobs of operator and manager in making them work;
(f) has sufficient process knowledge of cause and effect in process and quality control.

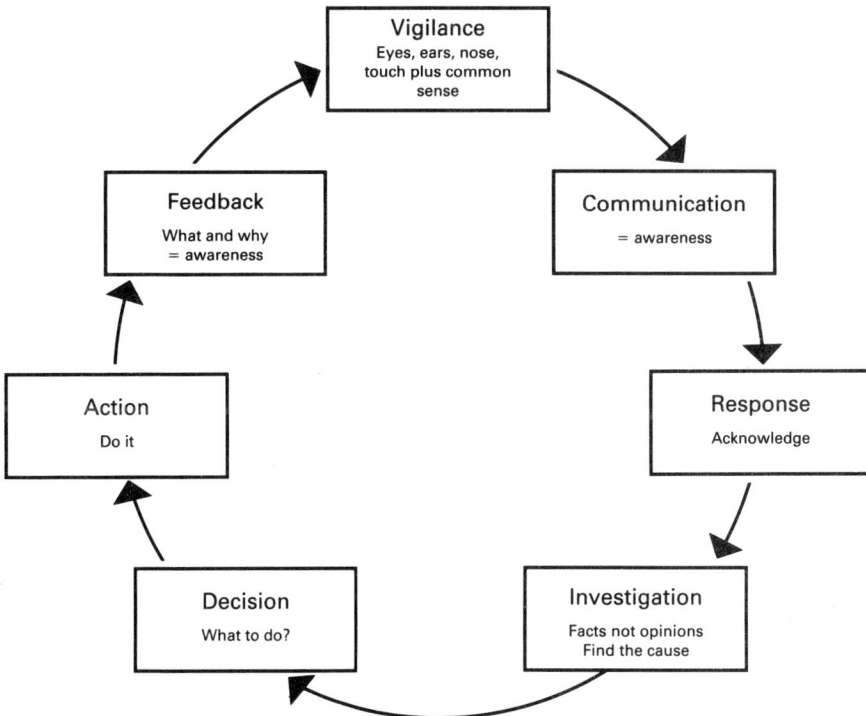

This loop can:
• Prevent problems
• Find problems
• Eliminate problems

Figure 2.2. An informal quality control loop. This informal quality control loop is shown from the point of view of individual awareness, response and communications.

Informal quality control loops require specific contributions from both the operator and the manager for success:

1. Vigilance: using ears, eyes, nose and common sense to identify any anomalies.
2. Communication: the reporting of any anomalies to the appropriate person.
3. Acknowledgement of communication.
4. Ensuring effective investigation using facts, not opinions.
5. Good decision-making about the necessary action.
6. Making sure the action is completed.
7. Feed back about what was done, reasons why and the results of the action.

Figure 2.2 shows the activities involved in an informal control loop. Which of these are management and which are operator contributions depends upon the organizational responsibilities. It is therefore vital that individual responsibilities and authorities in informal control systems are clear to everyone. Verbal agreement is all that is required.

Failure in informal control usually results from failure to train, or vague responsibilities.

The beauty of informal control loops is that they are informal. This gives participants freedom and authority to concentrate on those areas which they feel will most benefit quality. With this freedom and authority comes the responsibility to make the key contributions necessary for the loop to be effective.

Establishing a quality programme

The opportunities for starting a quality programme from scratch are very rare. Usually they involve established organizations that want to revitalize their quality performance for particular reasons:

1. To deal with acute or chronic quality problems.
2. Changes in quality policy due to marketplace pressures.
3. Realization of the potential benefits of better quality performance.
4. Opportunities for change with new processes products or plants.
5. Striving for new levels of excellence.

It is a mistake to think of a quality programme as a separate activity which can be completed. Quality is a never-ending job. Still there is the need for change. The programme of changes necessary to improve quality performance begins with a new quality policy.

Quality policy

Quality policy reflects the intentions of top management with respect to design and conformance quality. The golden rule of quality policy is not to make any statement that will not have the backing of words, deeds and resources necessary for its achievement. Policy statements are nothing without this backing. Empty policy statements will not fool the customer, and can alienate the workforce. The most important policy decision is defining the position of design quality in the market place. The positional scale has milestones:

1. Design quality leadership.
2. Competitive design quality.
3. Adequate design quality.

There should be a policy to put design quality somewhere on this scale. Design quality less than adequate is not recommended! Apart from this there is no element of best or worst in this scale. A good policy selects the position for design quality best suited to the product, target market and business.

The key elements in the policy statement are:

1. Reasons for the new policy statement.
2. Identifying the design quality target position in the market.
3. Describing the basic approach to achieving the chosen design quality position.
4. Stating objectives for conformance quality.
5. Defining basic quality responsibilities.
6. A statement of commitment to achieving the policy.

Organizing change with control loops

The change in quality policy will be backed up by changes in quality control. These are best considered as changes or additions to control loops. Formal and informal control loops used by production for immediate control have already been discussed. An extension of the loop principle to longer term control can provide an effective tool for organizing change as part of a quality control programme.

Where longer term loops are in place then they can be reviewed as part of the quality programme, using the new quality policy as a basis for change.

If longer term loops are not in place then their introduction will be the key to achieving new or existing quality goals.

Good control loops operate in several layers, each successive layer usually involving a higher level of management and a longer time scale. This enables each level of control loop to do its job without the intervention of higher management, but ensures that they do get involved in time.

In the event of serious or chronic problems then appropriate management involvement may be necessary in the short term, but the control loop procedures provide an effective framework for this. The exception is forward control, an activity which involves all departments, and is a continuous process.

The control loops are:

1. Forward control.
2. Instantaneous control.
3. Short term control.
4. Long term control:
    (a) weekly;
    (b) monthly.
5. Business quality plans.
6. Quality aspects of capital projects.

Forward control
Forward control comprises those company-wide activities which ensure that all the conditions needed to achieve good quality are satisfied in advance. These are:

1. The right design quality.
2. The right raw material quality.
3. Good and well-maintained processes.
4. Good operations.
5. Effective control systems.

If successful this guarantees that product quality will be satisfactory, and if things go wrong, that they will be picked up and fixed.

The forward control systems may be formal or informal. Because of the wide scope of forward control activities, there is usually no formal review of the activity as a whole, but forward control is one of the factors checked out as part of the operation of the other control loops.

Instantaneous control
Instantaneous control of the manufacturing process is that achieved

by the process equipment and the plant operators. With forward control, it is probably the most critical phase of the control of output quality, and yet it operates mainly by informal systems. This is supplemented by any automatic feedback about the process or output condition. In the absence of any such automatic feedback, objective results of output quality are unknown until samples are taken and measured to determine quality performance. This is the formal short term control loop.

What in many operations is called instantaneous control, are the routine, formal systems for the evaluation of output quality, which are actually short term control since they are never instantaneous, but operate at the time interval set for the routine sampling procedures.

Short term control
Short term control is the first level of the formal quality control systems. At the set interval, samples are taken, measured and the necessary control parameters calculated. These results are usually plotted on SPC control charts so that good decisions can be made about the process or product performance in relation to standards. This activity should be part of the production operator's job. He is running the process and so is controlling the continuing output, cost and quality. It makes sense that he should operate the short term quality control loop. The standards are based upon the process capability. An out-of-control condition indicates that the process capability is not being achieved. By definition the process can be achieved when everything is normal, so there must be a cause. The objective then is to remove the cause and quality will return to normal process capability.

As part of the short term loop, any out-of-control condition is:

(a) recorded;
(b) communicated.

Reporting is to the person responsible for the decision about what action (if any) will be taken in response to the out-of-control situation. This will usually be first line operating management, although the responsibility for this decision may be given to the operator. Both the reporting and the decision are formally recorded, so that this information is available for longer term control activities.

These records include information about the specific out-of-control condition, action taken or reasons why no action was taken. The cause is also recorded.

The quality control system repeats itself, indicating whether any action was successful or not, and maintaining the short term loop.

The short term control loop just described is often the only formal control system. It is assumed that short term control is sufficient, and often the only follow-up comes in the event of poor overall quality results, excessive levels of scrap, product holds or customer complaints. A longer control loop is necessary to:

1. Determine whether the short term loop is working properly.
2. Measure the efficiency of the quality control system.
3. Measure the overall quality performance against standards.
4. Identify trends or changes in performance.
5. Carry out analysis for maintenance decisions (adjustments, overhaul or modifications).
6. Identify any chronic or recurrent problems needing long term action.
7. Measure the reliability of the production process. (How often does it go out of control?)

All that is necessary is to carry out simple analysis of routine results and get the commitment of people to examine and discuss the outcome, and agree and carry out necessary actions.

The weekly meeting
An important part of the long-term control loop is the weekly meeting. When the latest results are available, management from the appropriate departments meet to look at results and decide what action, is to be taken. This action is in addition to the continuing short term control actions, and is necessary to correct conditions which are not responding to short term control.

The quality department is responsible for organizing this meeting, and for preparing the items and information to be discussed. Inputs from other departments, engineering, R&D, etc., will also be necessary, but the quality department should 'drive' the proceedings.

The results of this meeting include the agreed actions. The minimum requirement is that the agreed actions are logged. Effective logging requires a simple list of:

1. Item for action.
2. Action agreed.
3. Expected results of this action.
4. Who is responsible for getting the actions done.
5. The agreed completion date.

This simple format imposes considerable discipline on the meeting, avoids unspecified action or vague expectations, and insists upon agreed completion dates and responsibilities. Identifying the expected results of an action minimizes the 'let's collect some more results' approach.

This list is reviewed and modified at each subsequent meeting. The management time involved in the weekly meeting should not be excessive, it is often possible to meet 'standing up' around the weekly charts.

The monthly quality review

This is a short review of overall performance, presented by the quality department and attended by higher management. Results are presented by exception. If it's OK it is not raised. The objective of this meeting is to keep management aware of quality performance, acute and chronic quality problems, and associated difficulties. Identified quality opportunities are raised at this review.

Management are in a position to allocate the necessary priorities and resources to improve performance. A log of actions is generated similar to that set up at the weekly meeting. Again the amount of management time committed to this meeting should not be excessive. If the results are properly prepared and presented then a short but effective meeting is all that is necessary. The objective should be to avoid long protracted discussions. It helps if attention is focused upon causes, not blame, and on the necessary action, not excuses. Achieving this last objective can be difficult with higher management.

Business quality plans

The business quality plans review is carried out by top management, usually annually. The review covers the business quality objectives and plans, with inputs from all divisions of the company. The items considered at this review include:

1. Quality projects.
2. Quality or quality cost improvement plans.
3. Quality organization review.

The overall quality performance for the previous year is examined at this time, and the output from this review is the business quality plan, which sets the company quality objectives and plans for the coming year.

Typically business quality plans may be two or three paragraphs reviewing achievement against previous plans, and listing the broad company quality objectives for the coming year, and the people or departments responsible for achieving these objectives. These quality plans are then reviewed at the monthly quality review.

The mechanism of generating a company quality plan ensures that quality is regularly and formally reviewed at top level alongside the other business parameters. Its publication demonstrates overall company commitment to quality, as well as committing resources to realizing quality opportunities.

Quality aspects of capital projects

Another business level quality control loop is in the field of capital projects. The project raising system should include a requirement for the 'effect upon quality' of the project to be considered, and included in the project proposal write-up. This can identify and so avoid any adverse effects upon quality that may result from project activity. There is also the chance to identify quality opportunities in projects which may otherwise be missed. This requirement has a significant motivational impact, leading to more quality awareness in the project engineering area. The inevitable involvement of the quality department at the project design stage is another valuable result.

The requirement for 'effect upon quality' to be a formal part of project activity is another visible demonstration of the commitment of top management to quality.

Involvement and commitment

The setting up of a quality programme through the review or introduction of quality control loops involves everyone. The activity is not a one-off exercise however, but sets up a continuous quality management activity.

This then is the control loop activity. From forward and instantaneous control through the short and long term there is a feedback loop. These loops have as their backbone the review of performance against targets, setting of new targets and effective planning to deal with deviations from plan. They not only ensure that acute and chronic quality problems are effectively identified and dealt with, but that quality opportunities can be realized. These quality control loops will involve every department in the company in the quality control activity. Their ultimate goal is the setting of good product quality design and achievement in production of this design.

They involve the whole company at all levels in the identification of cost-effective ways of improving quality performance, and in reducing quality costs. This is known as quality breakthrough.

Good control means making sure that the product is the best that can be made given the process design and raw materials, i.e. maintenance of process capability.

Breakthrough means that product quality is cost-effectively improved, setting new and higher standards of excellence.

In principle these methods are simple. However that does not mean they are easy. Walking a tightrope is a simple concept, but is not easy. It takes commitment and practice.

To succeed, these methods need commitment from top management. Without this commitment they will fail. With the right commitment they cannot fail to succeed.

3 Training for Quality

Darek Celinski

Training for quality, just like any other kind of training in organizations, should be provided only when there is a clearly defined need to be satisfied. In all, there are just three kinds of needs that can be identified in organizations under the heading of training for quality. These three needs are:

1. The need to improve the general quality of products or services.
2. The need to improve a specific aspect of quality, for example to reduce (by the amount specified) the scrap and rework on the XYZ product.
3. The need to learn to use a quality control or a quality improvement system.

The recommended methods and procedures that are the most effective in satisfying each of the above needs are described below under the appropriate headings. Each description begins with a brief explanation of the principles and processes involved in satisfying that need.

Improving the general quality of products and services

A critical contribution to satisfying the need to improve quality is to increase the general competence of the people who work in the organization. The only method for achieving this increase and maintaining it at the new high level is by using a system of departmental trainers. Departmental trainers are able to provide much more effective on-the-job training than the alternative arrangement, where training is carried out by managers and supervisors.

The function of departmental trainers

A departmental trainer is an experienced, non-managerial and non-supervisory employee who likes to train others and has volunteered to work as a part-time trainer in his or her own department. Being a part-time trainer means doing one's own usual job and providing instruction only as and when a need for it arises within the section or department.

The term 'system' with reference to departmental trainers is used to mean an arrangement capable of being centrally monitored and controlled to ensure that their standards of instructions are maintained at a uniformly high level and that there is always at least one fully qualified trainer in every section and department within the organization.

Instructional technique

It is an essential requirement that, after being officially appointed, every departmental trainer is trained to use an *instructional technique*. Thereafter the trainers are encouraged to use this technique whenever they are conducting training of any kind. They must be discouraged from taking any shortcuts or attempting simplifications.

When using an instructional technique, trainers work through two steps in sequence. The first step can be called 'How to get ready to instruct' and the second is 'How to instruct'.

How to get ready to instruct

Trainers have a choice from a number of different approaches that they can use when 'getting ready to instruct'. One of these that is particularly effective starts with finding out who in the department produces an especially high quality of work. With his or her help and cooperation, the trainer then observes the work being done, and records the methods and procedures that are being used on *job instruction breakdown* sheets. This enables the trainer to train others to use exactly the same methods and procedures as the best employee, and thus attain the same high level of competence. When this method of approach is applied to satisfy every training need that arises within the organization, the general quality of products and services is certain to be high.

How to instruct

The second step when using an instructional technique, 'How to instruct', requires the trainer to use a four part procedure. The four stages are:

1. Prepare the learner.
2. Present.
3. Try out.
4. Put to work.

During the 'present' stage the trainer follows closely the relevant job instruction work breakdown sheets, and instructs clearly, completely and patiently. During the third, 'try out' stage, the learner practises in front of the trainer for as long as it takes him/her to become confident that the learner has completely mastered the job.

Learning and the effectiveness of training

In all there are just four situations which require departmental trainers to conduct training in their sections and departments. These four situations are:

1. Whenever a newly recruited employee joins the department.
2. Whenever an employee is transferred to do a new (to him or her) job — this may be either a transfer within the department or from a different department.
3. Whenever any changes are being introduced that require an employee to do some aspects of his or her job differently.
4. Whenever the department's manager or supervisor decides that some specific aspects of an employee's current job performance should be improved.

When the above training is conducted by departmental trainer who use an instructional technique, the learning is at least twice as fast as when it is conducted by managers and supervisors, and at least 10 per cent higher quality of work is produced.

Learning, whenever any of the above four situations arise, is unavoidable. For example, absolutely every employee on joining a department has to learn his or her new job. Even when no training at all is provided, because his or her job depends on this, the employee concerned usually manages to learn to do it by personal effort and by trial and error. The problem with this form of learning is that it is slow, inefficient and invariably results in low quality of work.

The effectiveness of learning is only slightly improved when the required training is provided by managers and supervisors. Although they willingly accept that it is their proper duty to train those who work in their sections and departments, and report to them directly, in practice, almost without exception they are found to be far too busy to do it properly. Even brief observation of managers and supervisors at work usually shows that they are often interrupted, spend a good deal of their time away from their sections and departments, and have many other urgent jobs to do. Because of this, they invariably lack the time to prepare, which is essential for giving good instruction and to give later their undivided attention that is necessary to make it effective. Often they are simply not available to instruct and therefore, other experienced employees, who have their own jobs to do, are asked to help.

In view of these pressures it cannot be surprising that training by managers and supervisors is often fragmented, haphazard and piecemeal. Because of this, the employees concerned have invariably no alternative but learn whatever they are required to do by their own personal effort,and by trial and error. The need for this is completely removed when the necessary training is conducted by departmental trainers. This increases substantially the level of competence of the people who work in the organization, and thus improves the general quality of its products or services.

Need for a training specialist

An organization which decides to introduce the system of departmental trainers needs a training specialist who is able to make it fully effective. There is no problem if a suitably qualified training manager or training officer is already employed in the organization. Otherwise an employee who is interested in this type of work can be trained in operating the system, or an appropriately qualified trainer can be recruited from outside.

Statement of training policy

Once the right person has been found to operate the system, the first step in introducing it is to design the system so that it suits the needs of the organization. This involves formulating a training policy statement.

The policy statement will detail who is responsible for doing what and how it is to be organized, conducted, monitored and controlled. When completed, this document is initially just a proposal, to become official policy only when it has received approval from the organization's chief executive. Continuing interest from the chief executive after the system has become fully operational will help ensure that it is maintained at the highest possible level.

Details given in policy statements vary a great deal between different organizations. This is because factors like size, structure, even products or services have to be taken into account. Thus the example given in Figure 3.1 is just an illustration of the type of information that policy statements contain.

These policy statements indicate that in order to operate the system of departmental trainers successfully, the training officer needs a good deal of willing cooperation from the organization's managers and supervisors. How much cooperation is eventually obtained, depends to a large degree on the care taken during the early stage of its introduction. People usually resist change. Therefore the benefits that the system is likely to bring to them need to be carefully explained. Thus, as soon as a decision has been made to introduce the system, all managers and supervisors should be kept fully informed and consulted frequently. Also, figures and measurements generate greater trust and confidence than general promises and assurances. Whenever possible, therefore, it is important that the improvements foreseen from the training programme are quantified by estimates or calculations.

Improving specific aspects of quality

The work on improving any aspect of quality within an organization should always begin with getting the facts about the particular situation, including finding out the reasons why it is unsatisfactory. Years of experience show that this is usually due to one of two possible reasons. The first of these is that the people involved in doing the particular work are not sufficiently competent and hence produce a high incidence of scrap, rework, corrections, mistakes, delays, failures of all kinds and many other such inefficiencies. The second main cause is shortcomings in the work structure and its organization. The above two causes can be found at every stage of any organization's operations — that is, in the quality of products or services delivered

---

Darcelinski Products PLC

Statement of Training Policy
— Departmental Trainers

Date issued:

Aim: To contribute to product quality improvement through a system of on-the-job training operated by departmental trainers.

The policy is:

1. That the training manager is responsible for the operation and the effectiveness of systematic on-the-job training within every department within the organization.
2. That a specialist training officer is responsible for the effectiveness of the on-the-job training within every section and department throughout the organization.
3. That the specialist training officer trains all departmental trainers in using an instructional technique.
4. That departmental managers and supervisors cooperate with the training officer and seek his specialist help and advice on all matters related to the effectiveness of their trainers.
5. That all on-the-job training within every department is conducted by departmental trainers who are required to use an instructional technique when instructing.
6. That departmental trainers work as part-time instructors, that is they do their usual work and instruct only when there is a need for it within their own departments.
7. That departmental trainers are selected and trained in accordance with the appendix to this policy statement, which is given below.
8. That departmental trainers remain directly responsible to their departmental managers and supervisors, and are subject to the same conditions of employment as other employees within the department.
9. That departmental trainers are paid wages and salaries that apply to their main job, without any special additions for their instructional duties.
10. That departmental managers and supervisors provide adequate facilities for their trainers to enable them to instruct properly and accept instructing as a priority over all their other work.

Figure 3.1   Example of a company training policy statement for a system using departmental trainers.

11. That departmental managers and supervisors keep their trainers informed about any plans or developments that are likely to give rise to training needs within their departments.
12. That departmental managers and supervisors take interest in the results that their trainers produce and inform the training officer whenever they consider that there is a need for improvement.
13. That departmental managers and supervisors maintain adequate numbers of fully qualified departmental trainers to cover all foreseeable eventualities and inform the training officer whenever any additions or replacements are required.

Appendix: Training of departmental trainers (see item 7, above)

The policy is:

1. That vacancies for departmental trainers are formally advertised within the departments in which they arise.
2. That applicants interested in the vacancies, before being placed on the list of applicants, are given the policy statement on systematic on-job-training and this appendix to read.
3. That every applicant who, after reading both policy statements, wishes to be considered is interviewed by the departmental manager or supervisor with the training officer and no more than a few days later is informed whether successful or not.
4. The selected applicants are allowed by their managers or supervisors to attend an internally run course in instructional technique.
5. That the course is run by the training officer and its duration is ten days: four consecutive days during the first week and two days during each of the three subsequent weeks.
6. That ideally, each instructional technique course should be attended by eight participants.
7. That a sufficient number of courses is run each year to meet the needs of all departments.
8. That departmental trainers are encouraged to seek help and advice from the training officer and communicate to him any suggestions for improvement.
9. That the training officer monitors the results achieved by departmental trainers and provides further training and coaching when these appear to be necessary.
10. That departmental trainers can be relieved of their instructional duties when they wish, by giving appropriate notice to their managers or supervisors.

to customers, as well as during the work that takes place within every section and department within an organization.

Training is the only method available to organizations for improving quality by increasing the competence of the people involved. This is by far most effective when it is conducted on-the-job, and an instructional technique is used. However, people whose job is to deal with their organizations' clients and customers cannot be trained on-the-job, and therefore their training has to be off-the-job. The problem with off-the-job training is that it is usually difficult to transfer the newly acquired learning to on-the-job applications. Managers and supervisors of the people who receive off-the-job training should be aware that this difficulty exists and assist with its transfer.

Organizations have a choice of a number of approaches towards improving shortfalls in quality that are due to shortcomings in the work structure and its organization. The most straightforward of these is when a training specialist is asked to organize and carry out the necessary work. Another method of approach that is most beneficial to organizations is to set up management and supervisory development teams, and to ask then to carry out the work. The third method of approach is to allocate this work to specially set up task teams (for example, quality circles).

Whichever of these approaches is used, it is important that nothing about the situation which is to be improved is assumed, and everything about it is measured and quantified. This means that all the work, as well as any training in operating improved methods and procedures, are carried out within the organization. This is likely to produce the best improvements when the following five-stage procedure is used:

1. State and define in writing the specific aspects of quality that the organization wants to improve.
2. Analyse and quantify the situation that is to be improved and identify the causes of the particular quality shortfall.
3. Design the improved work structure/organization/methods/ procedures, as appropriate, and design the required training.
4. Conduct training and implement/install the improved methods.
5. Measure the results as often as necessary to ascertain that the required quality improvement has been achieved and is being maintained.

Probably the best method of explaining how to work in accordance with the above procedure is to describe an actual example.

Example: Improvements in meeting contractual delivery times

This particular example concerns a company which designs and manufactures transfer machinery for the automotive and other high volume engineering production industries. The term 'transfer' means the machinery which accepts at one end a rough casting (for example, an engine block of a motor car) and then transfers it automatically from one machining station to another, until it eventually comes out at its other end fully machined and ready for assembly.

A typical transfer machine is some hundreds of yards long, and carries out hundreds of different operations. The machine itself is electrically controlled, machining operations are carried out by electric motors, and all other movements are produced hydraulically. Each hydraulic movement is produced by a separate hydraulic cylinder; these are regarded as the 'muscles' of the machine.

When negotiating new orders with customers for transfer machines, delivery dates constitute an important part of each contract. Thus this particular company was greatly concerned a few years ago when every machine was delivered substantially later than specified in the appropriate contract. This was especially worrying as most of the contracts were subject to penalty clauses for late deliveries. The usual pressures from management were applied on various sections and departments demanding improved efficiency. Many meetings were held each year in order to decide what to do to improve the situation but it all made very little difference. Eventually the company training manager was asked whether some kind of training could help. In the event this proved to be the best solution as the principal causes for failing to deliver on time became removed.

The work that produced this result was conducted in accordance with the above-mentioned five-stage procedure.

When initially discussing the problem with management, the improvement that was wanted by the organization was stated as:

> To design a training scheme that will help the company to improve on its past record and deliver at least 4 of the 5 transfer machines that are at present on order on the dates stated in the respective contracts.

This statement ended by specifying the reference number of each of the five transfer machines with the names of the customers and the delivery dates.

When working through stage two in the procedure, that is analysing the situation in order to identify the causes of the problem, the earlier suspicions that the hydraulic cylinders were responsible for the delays were confirmed. Although they were known in the past to be a problem area, no methods of improving the situation had been found. Each machine requires several dozen of such cylinders. They are ordered from their manufacturers in a wide range of sizes, lengths of stroke, rod lengths and diameters, piston construction, air bleed positions, accessories and all other features. Many of them are 'specials' which are not quoted in makers' catalogues and are therefore especially expensive.

Whenever an incorrect cylinder was ordered this did not become apparent until it was being fitted on to the machine. Then the cylinder had to be sent back to the suppliers with the details of required modifications. Each such instance not only attracted additional costs but also delayed delivery of the machine to the customer.

The procedure for ordering hydraulic cylinders was that the engineer who was designing a machining station decided what was required. He then completed a separate order form for each cylinder which was afterwards passed on to the purchasing department for a formal order to be placed with the suppliers. An analysis of a number of forms received by the suppliers showed quite a significant proportion of them to be incorrectly completed. Further investigations revealed that the engineers found the forms to be difficult to complete, as their layout lacked any particular logic and some of the terms used were not clear to them.

Stage three in the procedure was to design a new order form. A very experienced engineer was invited to help in this. By observing the sequence in which he worked when deciding what exactly was required, the form was laid out for these decisions to be recorded in the same sequence. The new form required much less work to complete as most features were listed as a multichoice, so that a circle had only to be drawn round the appropriate word to indicate what was needed. Additionally, a very simple but detailed procedure was drawn up, giving step-by-step explanations and listing the preferred range of features that should be used whenever possible.

Stage four in the procedure, which is to conduct training and install the improved method, consisted of a session where the engineers 'learned by doing'. This meant that a small group of engineers (about eight at a time) were given a number of assembly drawings, blanks of the new cylinder sheets and a copy of the newly drawn-up procedure. Without any kind of teaching, they worked unaided to complete the forms. In each case, their actual results were compared to ensure that each form was completed exactly as it should be.

When the time arrived for stage five in the procedure, that is to measure the results, it became apparent that substantial improvements were being achieved. Although the originally stated requirement that at least four out of five machines on order at the time would be delivered on their contract dates was not satisfied in full (only three of these were actually ready) the company was well satisfied with the improvements that were produced.

The total costs of obtaining these improvements were quite typically insignificant. About one man-week was taken up in the investigations, drawing up the new procedure and the cylinder order sheets, and in preparation to conduct training. A three-hour session per engineer was an insignificant price to pay for such an important improvement.

Quality improvement from project-based management and supervisory development

Attendance at management and supervisory development courses is by far the most widely used form of management and supervisory development. During these courses managers and supervisors learn by listening to lectures, working on case studies, role-playing and carrying out other kinds of exercises.

Continued popularity of these courses is no doubt due to the managers' and supervisors' complimentary comments about their value and the usefulness of the learning that they provide. However, these comments are difficult to justify as all formal investigations conducted to date show that their attendance makes no difference to the managers' and supervisors' subsequent job effectiveness and that the organizations which do not support this kind of development are likely to be as successful as those that do a great deal of it.

Because of these findings, organizations which wish to increase the effectiveness of their managers and supervisors, instead of using this kind of course, run project-based form of management and supervisory development. Out of a wide range of projects that can be selected for this purpose, those concerned with quality improvements tend to produce the best results.

When conducting a quality improvement project-based management and supervisory development, the same five-stage procedure that is described on the previous pages is used. Although the general approach to running a project-based management development is very similar to project-based supervisory development, there are some recognizable differences between these two systems. In each case,

---

Darcelinski Products PLC

Statement of Training Policy
— Supervisory Development

Date issued:

Aim: To enable experienced supervisors to build on their existing knowledge and experience to develop further, and thus to increase their supervisory effectiveness.

The policy is:

1. That work problem solving approach is to be used for developing experienced supervisors.

2. That the supervisory training officer plans, organizes, coordinates and controls every phase of supervisory development activities.

3. That every supervisor and equivalent from every section and department is eligible to participate, but strictly on a voluntary basis.

4. That in November each year a memo is sent to all those eligible offering them opportunities to participate in the next year's supervisory development programmes.

5. That the supervisor who wishes to participate discusses this with his or her immediate manager and attends only if the permission to do so is given.

6. That two supervisory development programmes per annum are run and the membership of each programme is limited to 12 participants.

7. That two weeks before the start of each programme its participants are briefed about selecting projects on which they will be working during the programme.

8. That supervisors aim to work on the projects in which successful solution they have a vested interest and which involve wider issues than their everyday responsibilities.

9. That supervisors discuss the subject of the proposed project with their immediate managers and encourage their interest and support.

10. That supervisors, within the framework of the whole programme, can work on their projects as individuals, in pairs or in threes.

Figure 3.2   Example of a company training policy statement for project based supervisory development.

11. That the maximum duration of each programme is four months, consisting of ½ day per week when any formal inputs are given to the whole group and ½ day per week for project teams to work on their own.

12. That the supervisory training officer assists and helps whenever asked to do so but never imposes his ideas or interferes with work progress.

13. That supervisors prepare a brief written report about their project which details their findings/conclusions/recommendations.

14. That each programme ends by its participants making a formal verbal presentation to their managers that aims at obtaining their approval for the implementation of the proposals and recommendations.

15. That if an approval cannot be given during the presentation, a decision about it is made within the subsequent two weeks and is communicated to the supervisor concerned.

when introducing any of these systems, the first step is to decide precisely how it is to be run, who will be responsible for what, and where and when the relevant activities will be taking place. It is usual that all such decisions are recorded in a suitable policy statement. An example is given in Figure 3.2.

Value engineering and value analysis in quality improvement

Sometimes, the quality of products or services supplied by an organization is so low that they cannot be considered to represent good value to customers. When this is the situation, the only way that the quality can be improved is to redesign the product or fundamentally improve the service. This is when value engineering or value analysis, as appropriate, should be used.

Value engineering is the technique that is used when designing new products and when improving designs of the existing products. In either of these two cases the following five-phase procedure is used:

1. *Orientation phase* Define the real boundaries of the design task.
2. *Information phase* Obtain customer requirements and design requirements; define primary functions and secondary functions of each design feature.
3. *Creative phase* Conduct a formal 'brainstorming' session with a small team of people (say five or six) to generate many ideas of how each of the primary functions can be satisfied.
4. *Analytical phase* Evaluate ideas produced during the brainstorming session so that the lowest cost idea that fully satisfies primary and secondary functions is selected.
5. *Proposal phase* Formulate final proposal; prepare drawings/ sketches/procedures; complete 'value engineering proposal' form; design an action plan for implementation of the proposal.

Any design that is carried out in compliance with the above procedure is much better than when this procedure is not used. When it is not used, the designer concerned usually works without any clearly defined plan to follow. Therefore his or her work is often unstructured, disjointed and piecemeal. Furthermore, the quality of the design is completely dependent on the particular designer's own ideas, past good and bad experience, and judgement. When using value engineering, a small team is assembled for a brief brainstorming session so that their creative powers can be combined and many ideas produced. By careful review of these ideas much better and more cost effective solutions are found than those by designers when working on their own.

After being value engineered, existing products usually become simpler and need fewer manufactured parts. The effect of this is to reduce manufacturing costs and improve reliability. The products also become easier to service and maintain. The customer therefore receives better value. None of this has to be assumed or guessed at because the cost benefits can be calculated, allowing the value of improvements to be expressed in real financial terms.

When value engineering is applied to new products there will probably be no comparison possible to show how much better the new designs are than if the technique had not been used. There is, however, some evidence to show that, when the same value engineering procedures are used for new product design as for improving existing products, similar benefits are obtained. The only proven difference that value engineering produces in the case of new designs is that the total design hours needed are substantially reduced.

Value analysis uses appropriately modified but essentially the same five-phase procedure that is used when conducting value engineering. Its actual uses are much less clearly defined than those of value engineering. As a general rule, this technique is effective when an organization wishes to find some ingenious and creative ideas about improving the value of its non-engineering products or services that it provides to customers. Sometimes value analysis can be used to reduce costs and improve the quality of an organization's internal processes and procedures.

Organizations which wish to use either or both value techniques frequently employ their own 'value engineer'. It is never his or her duty to carry out the actual work, but to help the people who are required to do it to carry out each phase in the correct manner. Organizations which wish to use either or both of the value techniques occasionally, usually invite a specialist consultant from outside to provide the required training. This is most effective when conducted in the form of a short training workshop which enables its participants to learn about value engineering and value analysis by actually using these techniques. For this purpose participants of the workshop are asked to bring with them information about the problems that they would like to improve. The consultant then leads the workshop through all the stages in the procedure with its participants working on their problems, until an acceptable solution has been produced. This is the most convincing method of demonstrating to the management and the organization's senior staff that value engineering and value analysis can make massive improvements in the quality of products and services.

After completing value engineering or value analysis work, the next stage is the implementation of the solutions produced. This is in practice a very difficult task to carry out and, for all kinds of reasons, many ideas are never implemented. Thus the organizations concerned deprive themselves of benefiting from the ideas produced. The best known method of avoiding this happening is when an organization's senior manager or even a director is made responsible for implementing all the accepted ideas produced during the value engineering and value analysis workshops.

Training to use quality control and quality improvement systems

Instructional technique is the most effective training method available to organizations. When this technique is used, people learn whatever they are required to do quickly and efficiently. Thus organizations will derive the greatest benefits from any quality control or quality improvement system when the training required is conducted in accordance with an instructional technique. A brief explanation of the approach to instructional techniques was given in the first main section of this chapter.

Sometimes it is found that the instructional technique cannot be used when new quality control or improvement procedures are being introduced. Then there is no alternative to using a training course, which may be internal or external. When no suitable external course is available, or if there is a large number of people to be trained, it is usual for organizations to run the course internally. This begins with the work of designing the course.

The process of designing and conducting a training course embodies a number of risks, and the result may be that the participants are not brought up to the required standard of performance in their particular work. This may happen because the course content is not particularly relevant, or because it does not provide sufficient practice to produce learning, or because there are no opportunities for applying the newly acquired learning in the job environment. In order to avoid such risks, there are modern training practices which include methods and procedures which practically guarantee the required levels of competence.

The most fundamental requirement when using these methods and procedures is that, before starting to design a training course, a written statement is formulated which defines *precisely what its participants will be required to do on its completion that they were not able to do before.* This statement is a prerequisite of an effective training course because:

1. It indicates that there is a real training need to be satisfied. If such a precise statement cannot be made, it indicates that there is no need for training and therefore no effective training is possible, and the intention of running the course should be abandoned.
2. It is needed when designing the course content — by analysing the work that leads to producing the required results, every item of skill and knowledge used is identified and thus a strictly relevant course is designed.
3. It is needed during the course — it provides a means for monitoring the progress of learning until it can be ascertained that the participants can perform, in the course environment, the work specified.
4. It is needed on return to work after the course — knowledge of precisely what people should be able to do after the course provides a means for managers and supervisors to assist in the transfer of learning from learning to the work performance environment.

Probably the most difficult quality improvement system that various organizations attempt nowadays to implement is called total quality control. In order to illustrate how to use the above procedure, an example of a course that was designed for implementing such quality improvement system is described below, in the sequence in which it was carried out.

The first step after deciding to introduce total quality control was to define precisely every detail of its operation, including stating who was to be responsible for what. After some considerable amount of thought and discussion these decisions were eventually formulated as a policy statement. In practice it was so detailed that it could be used as a manual, and it was ten pages long.

After explaining that the purpose of the statement was 'to detail the courses of action that the organization decided to take on all matters related to operating its total quality control (TQC) system', the main sections were:

1. What is TQC?

2. Why is the system needed?
3. When to initiate a TQC project?
4. Who can work on TQC projects?
5. How to conduct TQC projects?
6. Where is the TQC work to be carried out?

The next step was to define the terms 'TQC project' and 'TQC project team' and to list the duties and responsibilities of the 'project leader' and 'project facilitator' as follows:

(1) A TQC project is all the work that is carried out from the identification of a customer's need for increased satisfaction to its achievement.
(2) A TQC project team is a small group of employees who have been invited to work together on a single project.
(3) A TQC project leader is an employee who has identified a customer's need for increased satisfaction and is automatically in charge of the project. Thus, it is his or her duty to plan, organize, coordinate and control all project work until its completion.
(4) A TQC project facilitator is an employee who is skilled in using statistical and analytical 'tools' of the TQC. As these tools are necessary for conducting successful projects and as most project leaders, who are actually responsible for the projects, do not possess these skills, facilitators help and advise.

Following the above definitions, there were 17 tasks of a project leader listed. The list of duties and responsibilities of a TQC project facilitator consisted of eight items. On completion of this work all the paperwork needed to run TQC projects was designed.

When the work on designing the TQC system was completed, the work on designing the required training could begin. It was decided that this was to be in the form of in-company run courses. Analysis of the training needs showed that three different courses were necessary. One of these was to be for the managers. This was to enable them to encourage and support setting up of TQC projects in their sections and departments. The second course was to be for the facilitators. This was to enable them to use analytical and statistical tools of the TQC. The third course that had to be designed was to be called 'The TQC Skills Course'. This was to enable its participants to work as members of TQC project teams and, when required, as their leaders.

Each of these courses was designed using the same methods and procedures. In each case this started with stating in writing precisely what the course participants should be able to do on its completion that they could not do before. For example, in the case of the TQC Skills course this was stated as:

> To enable the course participants to carry out each of the 17 tasks that are listed in the document called 'TQC Project Leader's Duties and Responsibilities'.

Task No. 1 on the above list was:

> Completes Part 1 of the 'TQC Project History Sheet' (TQC 01/3) that describes the customer's need for increased satisfaction that he or she had personally identified.

The last task listed, No. 17, was:

> Convenes the final meeting of the team in order to formally close the project.

The work of designing the course was carried out in three stages:

1. Compile the *job specification;* this was not a formal document, just a helpful set of notes which specified every item of skill and knowledge needed to carry out each of the above 17 tasks.
2. Formulate *instructional plan;* this document detailed how every item of skill and knowledge listed in the job specification was to be learned, including the content of the *explanation* to be provided, what kinds of *demonstrations* would be presented and precisely what the participants would be doing when learning through *practice.* When formulating an instructional plan it is necessary to ensure that just 10 per cent of the total course time is allowed for *explanation,* 25 per cent for *demonstration* and 65 per cent for *practice.*
3. Construct the *training programme;* this was the master document for running an effective course, it stated its total duration, its aims, its objectives and their methods of evaluation during the course and on return to work on its completion. This was the information that the course participants needed at its beginning, as a reference document throughout its duration and to ensure its proper evaluation.

On completion of the course design work and preparation of the training materials to be used, the course itself could be conducted.

It is sometimes surprising to find that the time taken to design a course using the procedure described above is usually much less than when this procedure is not used. An additional benefit of using it is the certainty that the course is strictly relevant, that nothing is assumed and no item needed to perform a task is omitted, or time is wasted on providing something that is not necessary. Thus, a course designed using the above procedure practically cannot fail to be fully effective.

The effectiveness of such a course is ensured by its participants learning one task at the time by actually doing it until it has been properly mastered. Because of this, instead of using the familiar course assessment forms which require its participants to judge such abstract concepts like quality of the tutors, relevance of the course content, standards of training materials, proper course evaluation forms can be used. This was formulated as follows:

Evaluation of the TQC Skills course.

The *AIM* of the above course was stated as to enable you to do the following on return to work:

(1) To work as a member of the TQC project teams operated within the company.
(2) To lead TQC project teams in accordance with the company's policy statement.

It is important for the future effectiveness of the TQC Skills course that you answer the following two questions:

(1) Do you feel that you are now able to work as a member of the TQC projects teams?
(2) Do you feel that you are now able to lead TQC project teams in accordance with the company's policy statement?

If your answer to both these questions is an unqualified 'Yes' there is no need for you to provide any further explanations. However, if the answer to either or both of these questions is 'No', please describe as fully as possible why. What improvements do you feel are required?

The TQC Skills course participants should have no problem in completing the above form because during its last two days they will be working on a real project. They will thus be able to judge for themselves their ability to do the above work.

Conclusion

Training for quality uses exactly the same methods and procedures as any other training provided by organizations. It is by far the most effective when it is on-the-job and the instructional technique is used. When it cannot be on-the-job, but the instructional technique can be used in an off-the-job situation, it is still preferred to a training course. If it is unavoidable that a training course is used, then the disciplined approach to its design and subsequent conduct is certain to produce far superior learning than when it is based on assumptions and is unstructured.

Part Two

QUALITY-RELATED BUDGETS AND COSTS

4 Quality-related Costs

John Edge and David J. Smith*

It is essential that every industrial company knows the cost of quality, and that this awareness permeates the whole organization. A company might survive if individual projects or products failed to meet requirements, but if the most senior management fail to appreciate that costs must be identified and measured in relation to quality as part of company-wide policy, then the company will cease to trade competitively, and will eventually cease to trade at all.

To survive and compete, companies must provide products and services that not only satisfy requirements but often exceed them in terms of quality, cost, product variety and time of production. Consumer protection and product liability legislation is reinforcing the social and individual necessity to meet these criteria.

In order to satisfy these conditions and provide 'value for money' it is absolutely vital for companies to identify, measure and control all quality costs related to production. Every company needs to establish a quality cost system. This system will very often have to collect costs across the whole life cycle of the product or service to include user and operational failure costs. Only this approach (discussed later) will give the total cost of quality across all the activities of the company and its clients.

When the total cost of the lack of quality is realized by management it is soon appreciated that the cost of improving quality is small compared to the cost of not having a quality cost system. This appreciation leads to the allocation of more resources and better trained personnel with greater emphasis on the four Ms (men, machines, methods and materials), and the general need for value and value-added engineering and production.

Quality costs should be regularly monitored and reported to management; the quality cost system itself should be monitored and reviewed regularly for its effectiveness.

Types of quality-related costs

The need to identify the costs of quality is not new, although the practice is not widespread. Attempts to budget for the various types of quality-related costs are rare, and planning activities to identify, measure and control these costs is even rarer.

Quality can be described as one of two types:

1. Operating quality costs.
2. External assurance quality costs.

These types, and their sub-types, are summarized in a recent international standard (International Standards Organization, 1987):

> Operating costs are those costs incurred by a business in order to attain and ensure specified quality levels. These include the following:
>
> (a) prevention and appraisal costs (or investments)
> * prevention: costs of efforts to prevent failures
> * appraisal: costs of testing, inspection and examination to assess whether specified quality is being maintained.
> (b) failure costs (or losses)
> * internal failure: costs resulting from a product or service failing to meet the quality requirements prior to delivery (e.g. product service, warranties and returns, direct costs and allowances, or product recall costs, liability costs).

External assurance quality costs are described as follows:

> External assurance quality costs are those costs relating to the demonstration and proof required as objective evidence by customers, including particular and additional quality assurance provisions, procedures, data, demonstration tests and assessments (e.g. the cost of testing for specific safety characteristics by recognized independent testing bodies).

These two types will be discussed, within the quality cost system of a manufacturing organization.

Quality cost type analysis

A good example of operating quality cost subtypes is given in Smith (1988) and is shown in Figure 4.1. This figure shows a generic breakdown of operating quality costs for a six-month period in an organization which manufactures and assembles electronic equipment.

The total quality cost is £171 200 and sales for the six-month period are £2000 000. The ratio of quality costs to sales is the usual way of expressing the relationship. The ratio is then converted into a percentage, to give the cost of quality as a percentage of sales.

In this case the result is 8.75 per cent. It is well known, however, that the reported costs of quality are very frequently markedly lower than the actual costs of quality. It is not uncommon for the cost of quality to be as high as 25 per cent of sales.

Returning to Figure 4.1, the activities described below must be performed to minimize quality costs.

Prevention costs

Design reviews Reviews of engineering designs at various stages in the evolution of a product prior to the release of drawings to production; once released, production reviews must be held regularly to ensure conformance to specifications.

Quality and reliability training The quality department needs to be staffed by those with an understanding of not only quality control but also of quality assurance and quality management. The quality department may include personnel with qualifications in a specific discipline (reliability engineers, for example).

Vendor quality planning All vendors must be able to satisfy product or service requirements; where they do not, the manufacturing company will produce inadequate products and both it and its vendors will suffer. A vendor's ability to meet requirements will be evaluated by assessments, surveillance reports, meetings with clients of the vendors, questionnaires, product and company appraisals and audits.

Audits Audits can be internal to the manufacturing company, carried

1 January — 30 June 1984
(sales £2000 000)

	£'000	% of Sales
Prevention costs		
Design review	0.5	
Quality and reliability training	2	
Vendor quality planning	2.1	
Audits	2.4	
Installation prevention activities	3.8	
Product qualification	3.5	
Quality engineering	3.8	
	18.1	0.91
Appraisal costs		
Test and inspection	45.3	
Maintenance and calibration	2	
Test equipment depreciation	10.1	
Line quality engineering	3.6	
Installation testing	5	
	66.0	3.3
Failure costs		
Design changes	18	
Vendor rejects	1.5	
Rework	20	
Scrap and material renovation	6.3	
Warranty	10.3	
Commissioning failures	5	
Fault-finding in test	26	
	87.1	4.36
Total quality cost	171.2	8.57

Figure 4.1   Operating quality cost subtypes.

out by its own quality personnel or independent auditors. Audits can also be external on the company's vendors and these audits can be performed by the manufacturing company's quality personnel or independent auditors.

Installation prevention activities   These can include a wide range of activities which must be fulfilled if contract conditions are to be satisfied. For example, availability of proper tooling, equipment and instrumentation, manuals, drawings, other documents and data. All these activities need to be reviewed, planned and often audited.

Product qualification The testing of the evolving product against its engineering specifications to ensure conformance to the specifications under different operational modes and stress conditions. Only when tested satisfactorily against its engineering specifications, should the product's drawings be released to manufacturing.

Quality engineering The preparation of quality manuals and quality plans relating to a product or service. Quality standards and procedures and work instructions are also included.

Appraisal costs
Test and inspection During production the product must be regularly tested and inspected against production specifications and quality engineering documentation. This will be done by manufacturing personnel and not quality department personnel. They have different reporting lines and overhead rates. Rework and idle time are excluded (see later).

Maintenance and calibration These are the costs of labour, subcontract and items needed to ensure the correct calibration upkeep, usability, availability and repair of all test and inspection equipment.

Test equipment depreciation Much test and measure equipment and instrumentation is capital-expensive and will depreciate over accounting periods. It will also 'age' as technology advances.

Line quality engineering Besides documentation preparation, many questions regarding the implementation and interpretation of quality documentation will arise. This is a time-consuming process and time spent on it needs to be properly reported and costed.

Installation testing The installation and commissioning of products in many high technology environments requires careful planning by suitably qualified personnel.

Failure costs
Design changes Any defects found in manufacturing (or indeed later)

will result in design changes. Some or even all the activities detailed under prevention costs will have to be addressed as the defect is traced through the engineering and production process. In fact, traceability back to user specifications and even the contract might be needed and in the worst case right back to the marketing quality conditions.

Vendor rejects   Purchased items which are found to be defective must be reworked, worked around, reclaimed from the vendor or written off. Procedures and standards for purchasing, receiving, storing and handling vendor's items and services are essential to minimize failure costs.

Rework   With each rework or work around, production costs are incurred. Design changes might result from work arounds. With all reworks, testing will be needed. Reworks will often result in idle time on other parts of the shop floor, which must be costed.

Scrap and material renovation   The difference between the cost of purchased items which are found to be defective and any reclaim from the vendor.

Warranty   Any products recalled under warranty must be carefully investigated. Losses associated with a poor product or service and a falling reputation are difficult to quantify in the short term. Depending on the nature and complexity of the problem many of the headings of preventive costs might have to be addressed. All labour and part costs must be accurately recorded.

Commissioning failures   These failures can be particularly costly where delays result in deadlines not being satisfied and revenue lost. Specialist labour is often needed during installation; there will also be rework, spares and testing costs.

Fault-finding in test   Production personnel will usually 'bunch' test products and if easily modifying faults are found, will correct them. However, where less easily modifiable defects are found, whether by production personnel or test personnel, they need to be included under this heading. The cost of investigating these faults must be carefully recorded.

External quality assurance costs
External assurance quality costs should be lower than operating

quality costs since most quality costs will have been incurred before the involvement of external quality assurance personnel. Ideally, external assurance personnel should be involved with both the product and the company, and this should be at the end of production but before the product is released.

An example of external assurance would be an independent testing organization which would test the product against its specifications. This approach is increasingly common with high technology products, using computer-based emulators and simulators to mimic the real world accurately in the test environment. Independent testing is vital to establish the credentials of any product which, if it failed, could have product liability implications for its producer.

Another example of external assurance would be an independent assessment organization. It would perform a detailed and in-depth study of all areas of a company's activities which may affect the quality of its products or services.

The company must demonstrate that it has the capabilities for supplying products and services which are of the required or implied quality. The company must consistently achieve the required or implied quality by its implementation of a quality management system which must satisfy specified minimum requirements stipulated by the independent assessment organization. Such organizations in the United Kingdom include: the British Standards Institution, Lloyds Register Quality Assurance and the Ministry of Defence.

Checklists
Checklists covering quality cost types and subtypes, together with comments on them, are detailed in BS6143 (1981). These are particularly applicable to the more traditional engineering and manufacturing environments. They need considerable reworking if they are to be used in computing or software organizations.

Life cycle costs

So far, this chapter has only considered the costs of the producer. There are costs, however, which arise outside the production organization once the ownership of the product or service has been transferred to the user. The client has costs associated with acquiring, operating and maintaining the product or service. These are the total life cycle costs. The client's costs can be described as follows:

Acquisition costs The capital expenditure in acquiring the product (or service) and adapting the client's facilities to the new product.

Ownership costs The day-to-day costs of keeping the product operational. These will include modifications and enhancements to the product as well as preventive and corrective maintenance. This will mean maintenance and support contracts to minimize mean times between failure and repair, especially in critical systems. Special test/ diagnostic instruments might have to be purchased. Idle time costs and all revenue losses must be recorded.

Operating costs The day-to-day costs of spares, consumables and energy. There could also be costs in educating and training operators and providing suitable personnel back-up.

Administration costs The need to keep records, logs and other product documentation. This could entail the storage of electronic and paper media under controlled conditions, for long periods, especially where safety is involved.

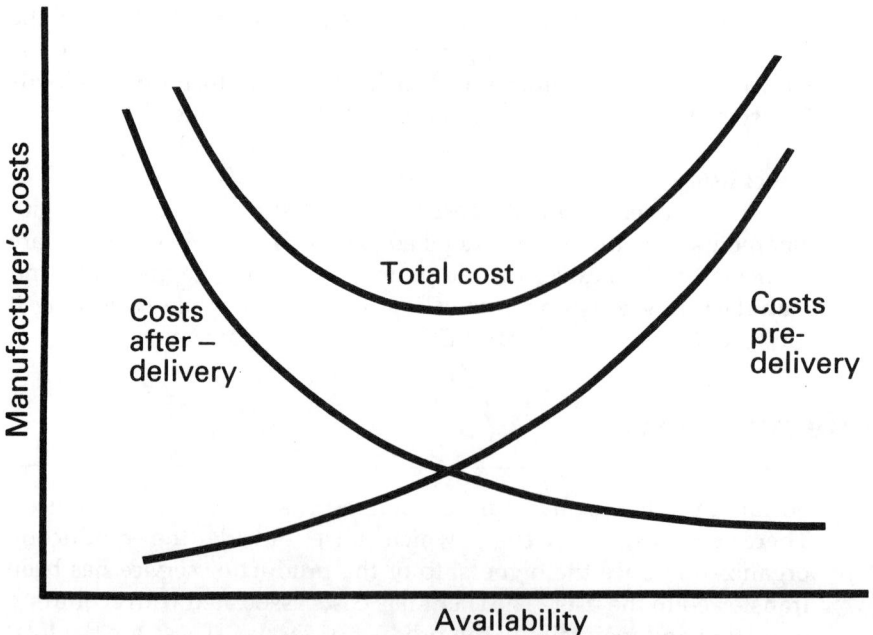

Figure 4.2. Availability and cost in manufacturing.

Life cycle quality costs will be reduced by reliable, available, maintainable and safe products only if the activities associated with these quality parameters have been performed. It is necessary to find the optimum set of parameters which minimize the total life cycle costs. Figures 4.2 and 4.3 (taken from Smith, 1988) show the relationships graphically. Each curve represents cost against availability (which is calculated from reliability and maintainability).

Figure 4.2 shows the general relationship between availability and quality costs. The manufacturer's pre-delivery costs increase with product availability. His after-delivery costs decrease as product availability improves. The total cost curve, in which pre-delivery and after-delivery costs are summed, indicates a trade-off point for availability with the minimum total cost.

In Figure 4.3 the total quality cost curve has been replotted from the point of view of the user's total costs. The price of the product to the client or user will be related to this total quality cost. In this figure, the user's quality costs must include any losses and expenses which he has to bear owing to the product's failure. The result is an optimized

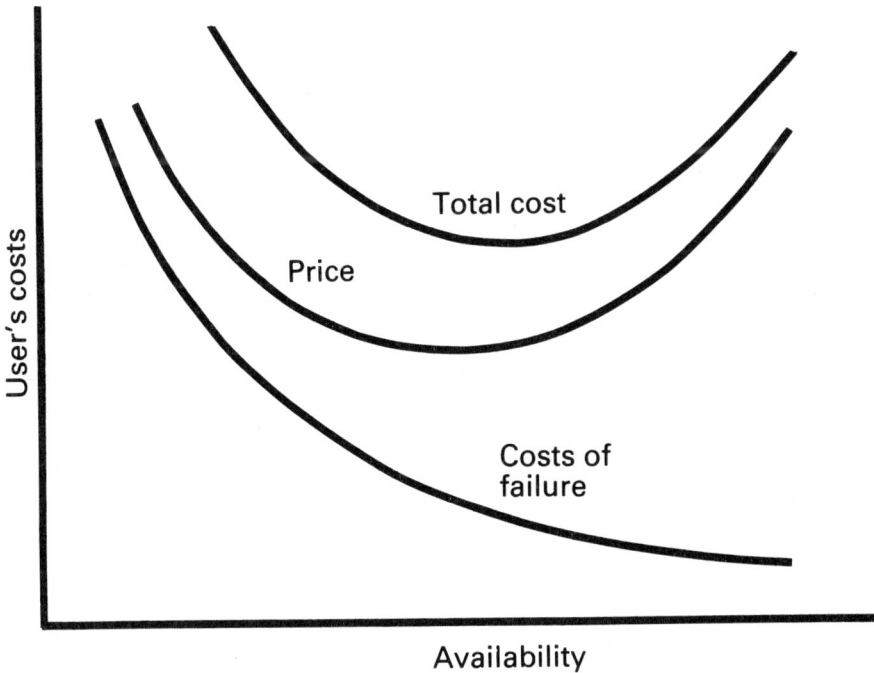

Figure 4.3.   Availability and cost for the user.

price curve, which shows the trade-off relationship between availability and cost.

Figures 4.2 and 4.3 illustrate that where cost is minimized by seeking enhanced availability (which is derived from reliability and maintainability), the savings from the enhancements exceed the initial expenditures.

Escalating life cycle costs

Life cycle costs escalate where there is a lack of management commitment to quality; this attitude flows down through the organization, to the shop floor. All products (and services) go through life cycle phases approximating to: initial conception, feasibility, system requirements definition, engineering system design and detailed design, manufacturing/production, component and integration testing, system and client acceptance testing, operations and maintenance, and withdrawal from service.

As we move through these life cycle phases the cost of correcting defects and failures increases dramatically. In an electronics manufacturing company, with machining, assembly, wiring and functional test activities, the following costs will be incurred for defects found at various life cycle phases:

- a component at incoming inspection and before it is used in engineering, 1 cost unit;
- the same component used in detailed engineering design pre-production prototypes, 10 cost units;
- this component in the integrated product, undergoing system testing, 100 cost units;
- component failure when the product is in operational use in the field, 1000 cost units.

Thus when the defect is found in operational circumstances failure costs are punitive. For the cost activity implications of failures in the field, see earlier headings on failure costs and prevention costs.

Companies using the most up-to-date technology (e.g. computer-aided design, engineering and manufacturing, computer-integrated manufacturing, flexible manufacturing systems) still find the cost of the lack of quality crippling. It is not uncommon in the high technology industries that for every 1000 cost units spent on product development, 700 cost units are then spent on maintaining the product in the field.

Even these product quality costs can be overshadowed. If there is an omission by upper management to think through the consequences of new policies and developments — a product brought late to the market place or a contract broken — there is not just a product failure but a company failure.

The lessons of the cost of lack of quality do not seem to be learned. It was estimated by the Department of Prices and Consumer Protection (1978) that the turnover for UK industry was £105 billion. As quality costs were estimated at between 4 and 15 per cent, the average was taken as 8 per cent. Related to the total turnover, this amounted to £8.4 billion. Since failure costs account for about half of the total quality cost, it was therefore costing industry some £4.2 billion in failures and defects. If a 12.5 per cent reduction in failures could have been achieved, an extra £500 million would have been released into the economy for this period.

Several later research studies have been funded by the government in the United Kingdom on the economics of quality control practices and the implementation of statistical process control (Followell and Oakland, 1985). The findings were not encouraging. The main conclusions were that there was a lack of understanding of how the practices and processes could lessen quality costs; there was little management commitment and inadequate attention to training.

In a second study (Plunkett, *et al.* 1985), it was claimed that very many managements had little idea of what quality-related costs their organizations were incurring. This study put quality-related costs at between 5-25 per cent of an organization's sales turnover. It also found that very very few companies used statistical techniques to monitor and control costs.

Software now has an impact on the operational and administrative functions of many companies. Software quality-related costs are huge. A 1988 Price Waterhouse study for the Department of Trade and Industry reported that:

> Poor software quality results in substantial costs to both suppliers and users. These 'failure costs' include costs of correcting errors before and after delivery of the software, overruns and unnecessarily high maintenance costs.
> At a conservative estimate, UK users and suppliers currently suffer failure costs of over £500 million a year. This figure includes domestically produced, marketed software only; if we were to include imported software and software produced in-house, failure costs would be much higher. There are in addition indirect costs, which are clearly substantial but which we were unable to quantify. These costs represent the potential benefits to be achieved from improving software quality. (Price Waterhouse, 1988)

This figure is just for domestically-produced marketed software. If we could quantify over the other areas mentioned plus any costs incurred due to hardware/electronics, the high technology industries alone probably have quality-related costs of well over £1 billion a year.

Introducing a quality cost system

Only by knowing where costs are incurred and their order of magnitude, can managements monitor and control them. Quality costs must be collected and recorded separately, otherwise they become absorbed and concealed in numerous overheads. Regular financial reports to management are vital if there is to be management visibility into quality-related costs.

> Quality costs should be regularly reported to and monitored by management and be related to other cost (ratio) measures, such as 'sales', 'turnover', or 'added value' so as to
>
> (a) evaluate the adequacy and effectiveness of the quality management system;
> (b) identify additional areas requiring attention;
> (c) establish quality and cost objectives. (ISO, 1987)

Point (a) is essentially the regular review of the quality management system and the associated quality cost system. Only with the availability of regular financial reports is it possible for managements to identify critical quality-related cost areas. A Pareto analysis of the vital few from the trivial many quality-related cost areas, will enable management to concentrate resources and allocate priorities.

As quality-related costs can arise in any part of a company, there must be company-wide management commitment to the introduction and continuous supporting of a company-wide quality cost system. Only where managements understand the magnitude of quality-related costs can there be progress; this usually begins to happen with an understanding of the very much smaller cost of introducing and supporting both a quality management system and a quality cost system.

With this continuing commitment, management will make it possible for quality cost procedures to be implemented and for quality cost action teams to be established. Members of the team will usually need training, but once trained will promote quality cost awareness throughout the company; this is best done by participative means, e.g. quality circles, which are discussed elsewhere in this Handbook.

In operating a quality cost system, data should be drawn from the existing accounting system; accounting practices should not be changed until proper analysis of cost allocations and responsibilities are known. This will often entail input from engineering and other technical personnel.

The steps to be gone through in successfully introducing a quality cost system in a traditional engineering and manufacturing environment are well described in BS6143: 1981. This recommends that the first step is a pilot study to determine the scope of work and the creation of quality cost types. There are then comments on these, on a checklist.

Then when the quality cost types have been identified, the collection of data against them can begin. The following steps are suggested: (a) and (b) are prevention and appraisal; (c) to (e) are failure costs.

(a) Step one is to calculate those costs which are directly attributable to the quality function.
(b) Step two is to identify costs that are not directly the responsibility of the quality function (e.g. stores, purchasing) but which should be included as part of the total quality costs of the company.
(c) Step three is to identify internal failure costs for which budgets were allocated, e.g. planned over production runs where failures were anticipated.
(d) Step four is to identify internal failure costs for unplanned failures, e.g. reworks, scrap.
(e) Step five is to identify the cost of failures after the change of ownership, e.g. warranty claims.

Sources of quality cost data will be varied in most companies, from payroll/time sheet analysis to material review boards. For the data to be collected consistently, tabulated data sheets are needed, addressing each of the quality cost types identified.

Further reading and references

BS6143: 1981, *Guide to the Determination and Use of Quality Related Costs*. The British Standards Institution, Milton Keynes.
Department of Prices and Consumer Protection, *A National Strategy for Quality*. Her Majesty's Stationery Office, London 1978.

Followell, R. F. and Oakland, J. S., *Research into Methods of Implementing Statistical Process Control.* Quality Assurance, 1985 Vol. 11, No. 2.

International Standards Organization (ISO), *Quality Systems, Section 0.2, Guide to Quality Management and Quality System Elements.* ISO9004 and BS5750, 1987: *Part 0: Section 0.2* The British Standards Institution, Milton Keynes.

Ministry of Defence Procurement Executive, *The Planning and Cost Management of Major Development Contracts*, DEFCON Guide No. 1, Ministry of Defence, London 1975.

Plunkett, J. J., Dale, B. G. and Tyrell, R. W. *Quality Costs.* Department of Trade and Industry, London 1985.

Price Waterhouse. *Software Quality Standards: The Costs and Benefits:* A review for and published by the Department of Trade and Industry, London 1988.

Smith, D. J. *Reliability and Maintainability in Perspective,* 3rd ed, Macmillan, London 1988.

The Consumer Protection Act 1987. Her Majesty's Stationery Office, London.

5 Budgeting for Quality

John Hunt*

This chapter is concerned with the establishment of budgets for resourcing the quality function. This is the group of one or more individuals in the organization who are to provide independent advice, policy directives and services to management and customers for assuring that quality objectives are met and quality problems are resolved. The approach of this chapter is to deal principally with the subject of estimating the effort needed to fulfil these quality activities. Conversion of these estimates into quality budgets then becomes a matter of applying salary rates and overhead allowances according to the circumstances of the particular organization.

This chapter concentrates on the provision of the means for carrying out quality tasks rather than discussing the reasons for the tasks or the benefits to be obtained from them. These other aspects will be found elsewhere in this book, and in the writings of such authors as Kitchenham (1985), Juran (1978), Crosby (1978) and others. Where the resourcing effort is placed determines not only the efficiency of the organization, but who benefits in the shorter or longer term. The curves in Figure 5.1 suggest that a balance is needed between the minimum cost to the supplier and the minimum cost of ownership to customers in order to maximize market share, rather than attempting

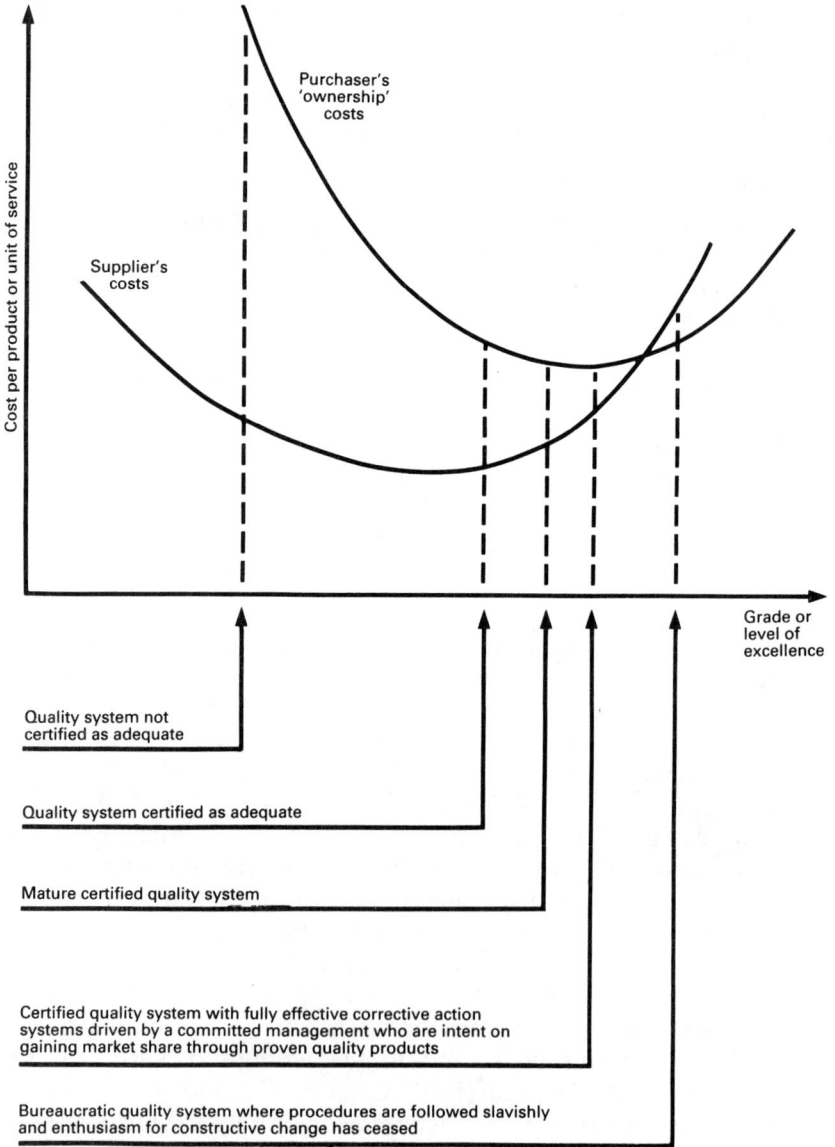

Figure 5.1. Quality economics. These curves illustrate the contrast between costs to the supplier and to the customer. The customer's cost is largely determined by the supplier's product or service reliability. This is a function of the supplier's attention to detail, and of the intensity of his corrective action.

simply to beat the competition by minimizing the direct costs to the supplier.

The historical and organizational background

The terms quality assurance, quality system and quality function are relatively new to our vocabulary. The all embracing term 'quality assurance' first came to the professional journals as a 'new' term around 1967, and entered the titles of standards and guides, (principally US Military Standards and the NATO allied quality assurance publications) to direct attention at management control systems rather than product inspection control. Prior emphasis had been on the effectiveness of inspection. As a consequence a new breed of quality professionals emerged. As a result the power of inspection departments withered over the years as they came alongside new quality audit departments, with both departments, (among others) coming under the umbrella of a quality assurance manager or quality manager.

Inspection departments grew into or became subsumed by larger quality departments in the early 1970s. Then, during the late 1970s as responsibility for quality was pushed back down to the actual producers of goods and services, so inspection activities and other functions were also pushed back to them. The net effect has been a general decrease in the size and scope of quality functions headed by quality managers within organizations. An increased emphasis on limiting the role to that of quality audit or assessment is now apparent.

Quality systems and quality functions

Just as quality assurance is defined as embracing all activities and functions concerned with the attainment of quality, so the 'newer' term quality system is defined as the organizational structure, responsibilities, procedures, processes and resources for implementing quality management.

A quality system provides a structure that facilitates the creation and monitoring of quality. All organizations therefore have a quality system. What distinguishes one from another is its level of formality in terms of whether the structure and facilities have been planned and documented, and the thoroughness with which it expends effort.

A quality system when 'formally' documented is designed to achieve quality through a hierarchy of requirements: policies and general requirements which have been expanded as detailed actions to be taken, and records which demonstrate that these have been implemented. This process of formalizing, and hence expending effort over and above what appears to be the minimum to get the job done, can help to improve both internal and external customer satisfaction by reducing the frequency and magnitude of failure to satisfy quality requirements. One side-effect of this is an overall reduction in costs.

Thus, quality systems are management systems, with the word 'quality' replacing the word 'management' to emphasize that the systems should be planned, designed and implemented with quality in mind, and not just come about by evolution or chance. The hope is that if they are planned then they are more likely to support the organization's stability through anticipation of problems rather than reacting to their unexpected arrival.

Quality systems can be regarded as consisting of three main elements:

1.   Organization-wide procedures and company ethos;
2.   Quality control as applied to specific tasks;
3.   Quality assurance, as used in the title of a department, i.e. the quality function.

Organization-wide procedures include the general methods and approach to be adopted for design, production and development control techniques, including training to develop the 'right' ethos and 'testing' to confirm that each method employed and step taken satisfies quality requirements.

Quality control applies to the above by identifying specific measures to be taken to meet specific quality requirements and thus is concerned with the selection of appropriate measures to be taken (planning) and checks to be made (reviews, tests) geared to the individual unique task. They are the operational techniques and activities that are used to fulfill requirements for quality.

The three elements identified above can be related to the human resource needs of the quality function as follows:

1.   Procedural and ethos issues are the direct responsibility of line management, but these are often delegated to the quality function.
2.   Quality control is the direct responsibility of project and departmental management, but much of the planning element is often delegated to the quality function.
3.   Quality assurance, while management's responsibility, is invariably delegated to the quality function. The monitoring part

is seen as belonging to the quality function by tradition, as many customers prefer their supplier to have a pseudo-independent body within its organization to monitor performance, with sufficient independence and authority to be able to safeguard the customers' interests.

The quality function is invariably classed as indirect (overhead). It will probably comprise a quality manager (or similarly titled person) plus a number of other quality staff linked to the manager either through a direct line organization or functionally.

The structure of a quality function

Quality functions can be organized in many ways. They often have a board representative in the form of a part-time quality director whose primary interests lie in other areas, and hence usually acts more as a figure-head for the quality function. Under the quality director will be a decision-making head for day-to-day purposes who may also be part-time with primary duties elsewhere, but is usually referred to as the quality (assurance) manager. Under this manager, directly or indirectly, will be people responsible for:

1. Technical standards and work procedures.
2. Specialist calibration of inspection and test equipment.
3. Laboratory test facilities (although these are increasingly coming under the control of other departments such as design and development).
4. Inspection and testing of in-house and bought-out products.
5. Inspection and test records analysis and corrective actions, where these are handled separately from 4.
6. Independent quality audits and assessments for the regular review of internal compliance with procedural requirements and, often under a separate manager, for the review of the quality systems of suppliers and their compliance with special subcontract quality requirements.
7. Certification engineers, or product liability or safety specialists, where these are necessary (e.g. petrochemical, oil-gas and nuclear industries).
8. Reliability or hazard assessment specialists, the former for aerospace, and both for oil-gas and nuclear industries and similar.
9. Project quality, for assisting in or producing a specific-to-contract project quality system (usually documented as a 'quality plan')

and/or monitoring the compliance of project teams with their 'tailor-made' quality systems.

10. The latest 'non-gimmick' project for changing the company quality ethos, quality orientation, quality image or similar. This is often by the introduction of 'new' quality tools such as statistical sampling techniques and quality circles under the banner of such titles as QIP, TQM, CWQI (quality improvement programme, total quality management, company-wide quality improvement) etc.

Surprisingly, yet appropriately, the last of these is often directly managed by a top level director or manager using an external 'quality' consultancy for support, with little or no contribution being made by the internal quality manager.

Quality auditing and contract project quality management remain the most popular activities coming under the direct influence of the organization's quality manager, next to standards maintenance. The remaining functions above are increasingly coming under the direct influence of other managers, principally technical and production management. The emphasis of this chapter therefore reflects these changing patterns in the scope of the quality function.

In addition to specific roles such as contract-related project quality management, laboratory or calibration management, etc., specific additional low key activities are placed on these managers more than on other members of line management simply because they are in a quality function. The most noticeable additional workload elements are likely to be:

1. Contribution to organization-wide quality system standards and procedures, and the coordination of comments on them.
2. Participation in organization-wide and subcontractor audits, assessment and quality planning.

These activities tend to be overlooked when estimating the workload of these managers, and should be taken into account to reduce the stress on them.

Quality function: parametric or global estimates

Examples of quality function costs are scarcely to be obtained in the literature. What does exist is generally unreliable and based largely on qualitative opinion and crude estimates. This is because most record-keeping arrangements are not suitable for the collation of data relevant to this chapter, and so actual cost or manpower data is generally not available.

Major influences

Quality costs are determined principally by the size of the organization, management style, level of technology and the level of management commitment to quality.

To some extent major clients can influence system-wide arrangements, by insisting that the organization as a whole will comply with client quality requirements. These can range from ISO9000 general quality requirements to ISO6215 (which is nuclear specific) or ASME codes (which tend to be product specific 'extras' for piping, pressure vessels, etc.).

Clients can have a more direct influence over teams assigned to satisfy specific contracts or projects. Their influence derives from the way the contract is specified to the way in which they ensure that contract compliance is achieved. If the organization has many small clients or major clients who have such influence over specific contracts in this way, the organization tends to operate on a project basis, setting up teams dedicated to specific contracts, and assigning one or more project teams to a 'project quality manager'. From the client's viewpoint, the project quality manager is the guardian of the client's interest, in which case the client pays little attention to any central quality function that may exist. The reason for this is simple: the client is interested in this specific contract or product, and is not particularly concerned about possible future contracts that may not materialize. However, he loses out because of the lack of adequate infrastructure and ethos to support the project, and high levels of client effort arise to ensure its needs are met. In addition, these project quality managers often have no training or experience in quality assurance matters or are assigned for a limited period as part of their general awareness training.

Another reason for a project style approach, with quality managers assigned full or part-time to specific contracts, is because of the nature of the business. A project approach may be adopted where high risks to safety or performance exists, typically in software organizations and the high risk industries such as nuclear and petrochemicals. The latter often have a more balanced attitude between central and project quality management functions.

Where the organization is not perceived to be in a high risk business, the more economic central and departmental quality function approach is usually adopted. This is typical of consumer products and organizations managed on a functional basis. Both the size and the authority of the quality function tend to increase respectively from design to production, from major subcontract management to products with a potential high risk to safety.

Despite all these influences and variations in emphasis, there is remarkably little difference in the total resourcing needs of the quality function for a given level of quality system maturity, no matter what the industry (as the reader will find out in the sections that follow).

Consumer industry estimates for the quality function

Several studies have shown that fairly typical ratios which exist between the three main groups of quality costs in a manufacturing company are:

(a) prevention, 5 per cent;
(b) appraisal, 30 per cent;
(c) failure, 65 per cent.

Further, these costs together constitute 25 to 40 per cent of sales revenue, 75 per cent of which is avoidable waste in all forms.

Other figures indicate that for a mix of mass production industries ranging from footwear to glass manufacturing, quality: cost ratios are likely to be:

(a) prevention, 2.5 per cent;
(b) appraisal, 10 per cent;
(c) failure, 87.5 per cent.

While these figures apply to manufacturing, similar results arise during marketing, design and development, although there is a lack of published data. These cost proportions indicate the size of the quality function. If the assumptions are taken as reasonable, then the quality costs for the first case (manufacturing company) are:

(5 + 30) per cent of from 25 to 40 per cent of sales revenue, which is from 8.75 to 14 per cent of total sales revenue.

Performing a similar calculation for the mass production example gives:

(2.5 + 10) per cent of from 25 to 40 per cent of sales revenue, which is from

3.12 to 5 per cent of total sales revenue.

These are not unexpected results.

Another way to estimate the likely size of a quality function is to look at what might be expected in the industry according to the organization size. This is typically as follows:

1. For a business group of 25, one full-time inspector or quality manager.
2. For a business division of between 50 and 120, one quality manager or chief inspector with one or two inspectors or supporting engineers.
3. For a company of 120 to 500 people, one quality manager with two quality engineers and ten inspectors.

High risk industry estimate for quality and certification functions

Figures from the oil and gas production industry suggest that:

1. The quality function amounts to 4.8 to 9 per cent of effort in project management for clients (typically 5.5 per cent).
2. Quality function involvement in major project management and technical reviews which is not typical of any other industry adds a further 0.6 to 0.7 per cent.
3. Quality functions in this industry often have certification engineers reporting to them to coordinate activities as required by the certification authorities. These government appointed authorities provide independent technical assurance for the integrity of these high risk projects. Unique to high risk industries, this adds a further 0.6 to 5.6 per cent.

The above figures are equally applicable to the nuclear industry, and only apply to client organizations. Similar figures then apply to each supplier to the client, with the exception that suppliers rarely have major project management and technical reviews. These reviews are unique to the high financial risk industries and are geared to establishing whether the whole of the work should cease, continue or change direction. Unfortunately, not enough major clients have these reviews.

It is typical of clients in the high risk industry to employ major contractors to manage or design part or all of the work. These major contractors employ up to four full-time people in a quality function. They spend a large part of their time on subcontract auditing or witnessing subcontract inspection activities. The more enlightened ensure that contract and subcontract project quality plan arrangements are implemented according to declared procedures.

Military industry estimates for the quality function

The military industry tends to insist that a strong central quality function reports to or at managing director level. Consequently it is not unusual to find:

1.   A quality director or central quality manager working for 20 to 30 per cent of the time in a mature organization, or full-time if developing a new quality programme. He/she will be supported by two full-time professional quality engineers responsible for developing and maintaining organization-wide quality documentation and for auditing business groups to ensure compliance with the procedures.
2.   Each business group will typically have a full-time quality manager, supported in a hardware development or production environment by a full-time quality engineer. These managers are responsible for group-wide documentation and for auditing the work within that group (or division).

Where the division or group is organized on a project-by-project basis, which is typical of software organizations, the full-time quality manager is supported by project quality managers amounting to 5-8 per cent of the professional personnel employed on those projects (the higher figure applying when the client takes an active involvement with the project). However, this applies to contractually required projects. It is not untypical of software organizations to have many non-contractual projects which are not subject to quality surveillance. If they are to be the subject of surveillance then the existing 5 per cent is 'stretched' to cover them, reducing the actual proportion of quality personnel to all professional personnel to typically 3 to 4 per cent. If this happens, inadequate assurance and insufficient support arises and the quality function then becomes a burden rather than an asset and all projects suffer.

Quality function sizing: a surprising conclusion

It seems that no matter what the industry, or if the organization style is centrally or project-based, the resulting quality effort spent is always about 5 per cent. Not only is this supported by the figures given in this section, but it is also borne out by major independent studies (see, for example, Rogerson and Moyes, 1983, and Price Waterhouse, 1988).

The work by Rogerson and Moyes gave figures of typically 4 to 9 per cent for suppliers to the high risk industries who were not certified as organizations satisfying ISO9000-type quality system requirements, and 0.8 to 1.6 per cent for well established certified companies. In both groups the design content was minimal and to well established design codes of practice (ASME or equivalent).

The work of Price Waterhouse came to a simple conclusion on this issue, that the cost of a quality function as a percentage of software development effort was estimated to be around 5 per cent.

It is evident that the policy and commitment of senior management determines the actual resources to be allocated to the quality function. With sustained commitment over a number of years, the resourcing requirement reduces as the documented quality system matures. This is evidenced by a shift of focus from contract-centred work to organization-wide audits.

Implementing a formal quality system to ISO9000

The effort needed to implement a formal system to ISO9000 will depend on several factors:

1. The size of the organization, and whether or not it is split across several locations.
2. Whether or not different locations have evolved independently.
3. Status of existing documentation, and whether or not the system is documented as a simple or a complex structure.
4. The range of products and services, and the way in which they are distributed over company locations and customers.
5. The level of automation and mass production used, and the degree to which work is subcontracted or performed in-house.
6. The level of commitment exercised by management, and the extent to which outside consultants are used to assist in upgrading the system.

Because of these variations it is possible only to give general guidance. The figures quoted in Table 5.1 are typical for an organization of about 100 employees implementing ISO9000 for design, production, installation and servicing. These data apply also to service industries, such as hotels and restaurants. Variations of 27, 25 and 22 per cent can be expected for a large organization with several business divisions, a typical business division and a business group, respectively. An example of this variation was one corporation which used 450 and 670

Table 5.1

Total effort needed to meet ISO9001 system requirements. The figures in this table show the total effort needed across an average company or business group (around 100 people) to develop and implement a quality system which can be demonstrated as meeting ISO9001 guidelines.

Item	Effort needed (man days)	Comment
Initial set-up effort		
Quality manual	360	One to two man years needed
Training	120	All staff receive one or two days induction training
Total set-up effort	480	
Subsequent annual effort		
Quality assurance	240	Audit and system maintenance
Quality control	600	Planning and review activity
Total annual effort	840	

Source: Price Waterhouse, 1988

Table 5.2

Ratio of effort according to ISO9001 system level. While every organization should apply ISO9001, some may prefer to limit the initial activity to ISO9002 (production) or ISO9003 (final inspection). This table indicates the resulting variations in effort needed. Note than 1.0 corresponds to the entries in Tables 5.1 and 5.3.

	ISO9001	ISO9002	ISO9003
Business group or small organization (30–60 employees)	0.7	0.57	0.35
Business division or average organization (50–120 employees)	1.0	0.72	0.4
Company or corporation (over 120 employees)	1.3	1.0	0.4

man days in two of its major divisions for the initial setting-up work described in the following section.

Table 5.1 data can be adjusted for the different levels of ISO9000 as shown in Table 5.2.

Initial setting-up work

In summary, the main thrust of ISO9001 is the production of procedures, typically 30 to 60 in number and usually comprising from one to twelve pages of text involving 12 to 14 subject experts (see for example Wood, 1980). The work is shared between these experts, who do most of the writing, and the quality function. In some cases the quality function or outside consultants are expected to do all the writing. The results are put together as a quality manual on procedures and standards (for design and workmanship). These are invariably written from scratch but based on existing documents.

Subsequent annual effort

Auditing to confirm that working practices comply with the documented quality system may take 80 per cent of the annual quality effort. The remaining 20 per cent is shared equally between improving the system and in continuing staff training.

Quality control effort may increase by up to 10 per cent over that which existed before the changes. This typically involves:

1. Up to 2 per cent of design and development effort in methods improvement.
2. Up to 7 per cent of development effort in additional planning, with about half of this for production process control, inspection and testing.

However, none of the suppliers interviewed for the Price Waterhouse 1988 study said that development costs had increased as a result of adjusting their quality systems to satisfy ISO9000, and most were convinced that they were reduced. Indeed, the Price Waterhouse report goes on to demonstrate that net savings can be expected.

ISO9000 quality programme characteristics

ISO9000 quality programmes are characterized by:

1. Contractual pressure rather than organizational desire. The few exceptions are mainly in the high risk industries, and then with the clients rather than the contractors and other suppliers.
2. The effort and commitment is driven from middle management

downwards, with only a few cases starting from top management.
3.　Application is across all disciplines, all at once, after a policy and documentation structure have been formulated, initially starting with guidelines and ending up as standardized procedures.
4.　Short courses are used to get the message across, with the duration of such courses only exceptionally reaching 3 or 5 days.

Other major quality programmes

Other programmes tend to have opposite characteristics to those of ISO9000 and typically:

1.　Top management usually initiate these programmes using outside consultants.
2.　Being driven from the top, the programme tends to be applied progressively as a training programme for management, moving one or two layers at a time down the management chain.
3.　The initial training programme is often longer, being either 3 to 5 days duration or a few hours per week over several months.
4.　They are focused on specific issues, usually attitudes, but lack a sound psychological basis. Others concentrate on statistical control. They are all sponsored by top management and aimed at middle management, with appreciation courses for both.

Consequently the emphasis is not on procedures, but on attitudinal change or the application of specific 'tools'. These naturally require more effort in training.

While the apparent cost is equivalent to a 3–5 day training course for some managers, the actual cost is much higher. These managers have to carry the message through to their colleagues and employees, and create action from training. While it is difficult to estimate the net effect of this, as implementation costs have not been determined or published to date, it is easily seen that they are comparable to the costs of implementing a basic procedural system, hence the subtotals in Table 5.1 are a good starting point.

Of course, wide variation exists between programme types. A total quality management programme aimed at attitudinal change will be of the order of magnitude given in Table 5.1. Training material will be about a third of that of a quality manual, while personnel training is trebled and supervision is added on top. These reduce in subsequent years, mainly to training of new employees, supervision and greater care in achieving better relations or quality of service, etc. These all amount to similar levels of annual effort to that given in Table 5.1.

Programmes aimed at lower and more restricted management groupings, such as quality circles and statistical process control, often misnamed as total quality control, require about one third of the above resources. Because the emphasis is on the lower salary levels this results in programme costs being less than that described earlier.

Certification to ISO9000, or contractor assessment

Third-party certification

Contractor assessment is a review of an organization for compliance with requirements, and is usually undertaken by a client organization. Certification is the same in principle but is undertaken by a third-party certification authority that is generally recognized as being competent for the purpose.

In addition to actually developing the quality system to meet ISO9000 requirements, the certification process adds costs as shown in Table 5.3, with variations by level of ISO9000 given in Table 5.2. The assessment and surveillance activity includes following up any corrective action necessary to satisfy the certification authority, but like all other estimates to date, does not include the cost of amending written procedures, which can be substantial.

The annual surveillance visits by the certification authority typically incur 60–70 per cent of the initial certification assessment effort.

Table 5.3
Estimated costs for third-party certification to ISO9001. The table illustrates the additional effort needed to seek general recognition of quality system adequacy through third-party certification (using, for example, a government recognized certification authority).

Item	Effort required	
	Quality function (Man days)	Certification/ consultancy (Days)
Preparation	5–10	0.5–3.5
Initial assessment	10–20*	11.2–23.2
Annual surveillance	5–10*	6.7–16.2

* These figures include follow-up. *Source*: Price Waterhouse, 1988

Second-party certification

With second-party certification, the cost of the certifying authority is not carried by the assessed party. Also, surveillance costs are reduced because they are either less frequent or non-existent. Typically the effort involved is:

1. Where safety is a major client interest, such as with military and aerospace major procurement agencies, inhouse client effort might be 16–20 man days effort every 18 to 36 months. The factors given in Table 5.2 apply.
2. Where safety is critical, but the client is only concerned with a specific contract and not the whole organization, the initial preparation and assessment effort for non-proprietary products is typically two to four man days, with two or three days per year for surveillance work for the duration of the contract. These figures can be halved for proprietary products.

Other factors to consider

The figures quoted for certification depend on the same factors as those discussed above for implementing a formal quality system to ISO9000 plus:

1. Geographic location, adding travel costs and time incurred by the certification authority.
2. Physical size of the sites, where 'walkabouts' between offices and operator control points can take up a considerable proportion of the visit time.
3. The number of non-compliances found. If these are excessive they can terminate the initial assessment prematurely, requiring a full repeat assessment at a later date. The number of findings can range from a few to many which can significantly affect the report writing time and extent of follow-up to ensure that corrective action has taken place. If few or no problems are found, the initial and annual figures can be reduced by the factor 0.7. This will eventually be the case after about five closely-spaced assessments by different assessment parties on a committed organization.

It should be noted that this section is concerned with certification of the quality system and not of the organization's design capability, technical competence or product or service capability and safety. These come under separate approval arrangements, for which the resources required are about a third to a quarter of those quoted in Table 5.3 (excluding the cost of developing product test schedules for certification purposes).

Quality audits, assessments and reviews

Audits, assessments and reviews are of considerable importance to the quality function and consume a large proportion of its effort. Most organizations tend to carry out a series of audits or assessments either concentrated in a short period or spread out over a year. The results are then combined into a report, which is called a review. The wise organization would have a proper review annually.

Effort needed for an audit or assessment

Audits or assessments typically involve the sampling of activities and do not usually involve any in-depth review of procedures and other documents. In hierarchies, 40 or 50 per cent of the managers at any given level are interviewed, on the assumption that the remainder probably follow similar routines. Subsequent audits or assessments normally concentrate on those not previously interviewed.

Table 5.4 provides a breakdown for estimating the effort needed. A further 20 per cent should be added for supervisory or coordination effort if a team is used to undertake the work.

Effort required for reviews

A typical review requires the same level of effort as third-party or contractor certification. This can be estimated from earlier parts of this chapter or determined from Table 5.4.

Repeat audits, assessments and reviews

These repeat activities depend very much on circumstances. They tend to be programmed:

1. To relate to contract or project milestones.
2. At routine intervals (such as 3 months after work starts and at 6-monthly intervals thereafter, for contract or project work).
3. Annually for internal organizational reviews.
4. At two or three-yearly intervals for key suppliers, or more frequently where confidence is lacking. Sometimes these only occur when there are major changes, such as takeovers and mergers or changes in key management positions (since these can all have major repercussions on quality performance).

The frequency of occurrence, breadth of coverage and depth of investigation depend on the confidence that exists in the organization under examination. Follow-up is crucial. The threat of repeat audits,

Table 5.4
Typical effort needed for audits, assessments and reviews. The table gives a breakdown of non-supervisory effort needed. It is necessary to add 20 per cent to the estimate for travel and supervisory time.

Activity	Man days	Comment
1. Pre-visit document review	0.5–1	Scan for appreciation
	1–3	Evaluate and comment, but take no action
2. Pre-assessment visit	0.5–1	Visit to one or more buildings at a location to determine the scale of the task
3. Planning the assessment	0.2–1	Planning and submission of tentative programme and dates, excluding effort for acquiring and briefing assessors
4. The assessment	0.1–0.3	Initial introductions and clearance of major queries
	0.2–0.5	For each production line (e.g. printed circuit boards, assembly line, stockroom)
	0.2–0.5	For each engineering discipline (e.g. structural, electrical, piping, project management)
	0.2–0.5	For each department (e.g. drawing office, laboratory, trials site)
	0.3–1	For each software team, from study team to software development team
	0.2–0.3	Summary and oral presentation of findings
5. Assessment report	40–60%	of the total assessment time from item 4, including agreement to findings but excluding subsequent changes and typing or retyping.
6. First follow-up	30–60%	of item 4
plus	20–50%	of item 5 depending on the extent of the findings.

assessments or reviews can be an effective way of keeping personnel on their toes, particularly if the results are made known to a management that is keen not to see negative results.

Repeat assessment effort
The repeat assessment effort is typically 40 to 100 per cent of that for the original assessment. It depends on whether the previous findings were good or bad, and on the period which has intervened. Thus the least effort quoted would relate to a repeat assessment made only six months after an assessment which produced good results.

Where the previous results were poor, or where there is little experience of the products or services, a repeat assessment is recommended shortly after the start of work (after three months). In other cases, where previous results were average as measured against other suppliers, and where the products or services are critical six monthly repeat assessments would be warranted every six months.

Good previous results, with assessor confidence in the stability of the assessed organization and its products or services, do not warrant visits more frequently than annually. A 12 to 18-month interval is typical.

If the assessors have confidence in the stability of an assessed organization which had excellent results previously then a two or three-year interval is considered adequate. However, the assessed organization would normally be expected to report changes in key management positions, takeovers and mergers to the assessors, as well as significant changes in organizational structure, production methods and changes to the design of the product or service. The assessor may insist on having his own representative undertake regular visits, even on permanent secondment, to the assessed organization to ensure that standards do not deteriorate during the intervals between assessments.

The hidden extras
The estimates quoted are for trained auditors or assessors working alone. It is advisable to take along trainees to insure impartiality in the findings. Although this can double the effort, the accuracy of the findings will be improved, resulting in less debate.

Some steps are often missed to save time; this can result in incomplete coverage, for example by omitting Steps 1, 2 and 3 of Table 5.4. Hurrying Step 4 creates a superficial result which is invariably perceived as better than reality, as also arises if the emphasis is placed on Step 1 rather than 4. Failure to implement Steps 5 and 6 will invariably result in corrective action not being taken. All these omissions increase the risk that the assessed organization will fail to perform as required.

If no report is issued, the assessed organization could gain a poor impression of the auditors or assessors. This might lead to inadequate response to subsequent requests for improvement action and complacency through a belief that no follow-up action will occur.

Management invariably need reports on the audit and assessment activity and on the number of departments or projects due to be assessed. This reporting, including details of teams not recently visited, can take up considerable effort. This is additional to the effort needed to manage individual audits and assessments.

Investigations should be based on sampling rather than complete coverage. If this is not done, then the effort becomes excessive, as the following figures show:

1.   2.5 man weeks for a typical software team of 3 people.
2.   4 man weeks for an average software development project where the team size ranges from 0.5 to 30 people per project in a commercial organization of 150 to 220 people.
3.   2 man months for the post-implementation audit of a software project.

These are real figures from a software company that went overboard for a short time — until they discovered that sampling was more cost effective and equally illuminating.

Developing global estimates through synthesis

So far the discussion has centred on how big the quality function needs to be. Now the examination turns to the actual effort likely to be needed for individual quality activities.

It is possible to build up a synthetic estimate for the whole organization by aggregating the individual synthesized estimates across all the activities. The great danger with this approach, however, is that it is easy to overlook some activities.

Quality planning
This section relates to quality planning in terms of quality systems for specific contracts and projects. Such work often results in a document

known as a quality plan. This pulls together the overall approach to be adopted for the particular project. It includes key controls such as client and team meetings, and the need for review and hold points. It will give the references of other procedures and standards to be adopted and deviations from them. Special procedures may have to be written for inclusion in the quality plan, for example to accommodate client's requirements. The effort required to produce a quality plan, including associated meetings and the production of new standards and procedures, is indicated in Table 5.5.

Specialist plans

Quality plans are not the only documents which have to be developed. Numerous other plans of comparable complexity may be needed to meet needs such as statutory certification, configuration or document control, integration and commissioning, technical interface, safety and performance assessment programmes. All of these require a similar level of effort to produce as a quality plan. These other plans are usually produced by specialist functions, with a review by the quality function. They would be referred to in the quality plan. The quality function may also be required to witness the activities called up in the plans.

In each case a full-time engineer (not usually from the quality function) is assigned as coordinator for the plan. For example, a weight control engineer would get information from structural and process control engineers and from the engineering drawing office to ensure that structural loading criteria are not exceeded.

Similarly, a full-time certification engineer, who would normally report to the quality function, would be appointed to liaise with statutory authorities regarding the technical certification of major structures such as offshore oil and gas production platforms. The principal activities of this role include document flow control to the certification authority, interpretation of requirements, approval of design to those requirements and witnessing of key fabrication activities. Such an engineer may be the focal point for several statutory agencies for major projects such as local planning, fisheries and environmental control bodies. The list continues, depending on the industry involved. It seems that each specialist function adds about 1 to 2 per cent of the total engineering effort on those projects.

Standards engineering

A notional man week per month per business group of about 30 to 60

Table 5.5

Estimating guidelines for quality activities. The second and third columns in the table show figures based on research findings (Price Waterhouse and Rogerson, respectively). The final column gives recommended estimates based on experience for a typical team of three to six professional staff.

Activity	Per cent of total project		Man days for each project year
	Software[1]	Fabrication[2]	
Quality system development			
Familiarization	—	—	1
Planning	2–4[3]	0.7–12.2[3]	3–10, plus 3 more for client involvement where model plans exist. Otherwise allow 23–60 days to develop from nothing as a single task, the higher estimate applying where multiple client agencies are used to oversee the work
Progress meetings	4–6	0–0.6	12 or over with client involvement, plus 1 day per batch delivery if the client is involved in deliveries
Consultancy	3[4]	—	3.5[5]
Special processes	1–5[6]	1.1–6.2[7]	
Software tests			
Design reviews	2–4	—	3, assuming that 1 in 3 are attended
Code walkthroughs	2–3	—	4, assuming a sample of 2 are attended
Unit and integration testing	—	—	Substantial, not normally witnessed by inspection
System testing	7–10	—	6 for a simple job to 20 for full-time attendance
Commissioning	—	—	Not usually witnessed
Acceptance testing	3–4	—	1–6, otherwise as system testing. Client witness effort

			is typically 70% of active test effort
Purchased software evaluation	10–33% of price	—	1.5–2 days per package
Hardware testing			
Goods inwards check	—	0.06–1.2[8]	2–5, or 2% of value
Inspection and non-destructive tests	—	2.2–31.7[9]	32–149 per item
Monitoring			
Audits	—	0.13–0.6[10]	3–4, assuming 1.5 days every 4–6 months[11]
Document	—	—	2–4 each document
Total for contract	24–39	6.6–30.9	Derive from the above

Notes

1. *Source*: Price Waterhouse (1988). Rework and retest add 14 per cent for highly disciplined teams, 60 per cent or more otherwise.
2. *Source*: Rogerson and Moyes (1983). Figures include reinspection and repeat non-destructive testing.
3. Planning includes documenting the project quality system, data dossier compilation, preproduction and other inhouse meetings.
4. Configuration management, change control and error logging.
5. *Ad hoc* support, review of quality plans and associated papers.
6. Development and application of design tools and methods. The 1–2 per cent quoted in Price Waterhouse (1988) has been increased to 1–5 per cent to reflect wider experience.
7. The production of weld test procedures, with the procedures and the welders examined for separate certification.
8. Visual checks for paperwork only.
9. Assembly and weld inspection and non-destructive testing by X-ray, Magnetic Particle Inspection (MPI), hardness tests, etc.
10. This figure allows only one per contract.
11. This does not include debrief or post-implementation audits for the project or subcontracts.

people is required for standards engineering, this effort increasing to the equivalent of one full-time person for three or more business divisions amounting to, say, 300 people. This effort is used to develop and maintain standards and procedures. A standards engineer is often appointed for this work but, if the organization can support the assignment of specialist personnel to develop these documents, the result will be better than that produced by a generalist acting on information gleaned from specialists. The standards engineer can then concentrate on coordination and distribution, identifying specialists, and editing their work to achieve a consistent format.

Procedures take more time and effort than meets the eye, usually taking from 15 to 75 days of effort to develop fully, and longer in calendar time. Factors such as new or modified standards determine the actual effort required, which typically comprises:

1. Interviews to ascertain practice or intent, typically 8 to 15 man days, with up to 30 man days for complex situations.
2. Transcribing interview results into procedures by writing them up and having the draft checked by those affected. This will typically involve 6 to 10 days' effort, but can be as little as 3 or as much as 15 days' effort.
3. Updating to take account of comments received, typing and distribution to all parts of the organization of the first formal issue of the document takes typically 5 to 9 days, or 15 with multiple reviews prior to their issue.

Equipment calibration

Typically, one full-time mechanical and one full-time electrical calibration engineer will report to the quality function. These may have their own calibration laboratories, which would be temperature and humidity controlled. These engineers are responsible for ensuring that measurement and test equipment in use is periodically calibrated. Some of the calibration work they will undertake themselves, the remainder will be undertaken by specialist subcontractors. Occasionally a standards reference laboratory holding 'intermediate' standards may exist with its full-time engineers, again one for electrical and one for mechanical work. This intermediate laboratory would calibrate the test equipment used by the other laboratories, and have their own measurement standards calibrated by a nationally recognized calibration agency. The alternative is to subcontract the reference laboratory work to a nationally accredited calibration agency (see Chapter 27).

Inspection and testing

Where inspection and testing work is subcontracted, as with most major structural projects, a full-time chief inspector is employed to oversee the work. Whether subcontracted or carried out by directly employed staff, inspection and test personnel typically comprise about

Table 5.6
The effect of certification on quality activity resourcing. This table illustrates the impact on quality resourcing of acquiring certification and the effects of multiple inspection agencies.

Activity	Certified organization, single client inspections	Certified organization, multiple client inspections	Non-certified organization, multiple client inspections
Planning	0.9–4%	2–12.2%	1–2.9%
	23–59 days	30–51 days	36–6.5 days*
Goods-in checks	0.06–0.33%	0.06–0.33%	1.2–1.3%
	2–5 days	2–5 days	2–5 days
Special processes	1.4–3.1%	1.06–4.84%	3.77–6.2*
	9–70 days	5–88 days	4–13 days
Total inspection and non-destructive testing	5.35–6.69%	10.59–18.66%	10.15–24.6%
	112–149 days	153 days	32–37.2 days
Total for contract	6.57–12.1%	17.82–28.8%	26.7–30.9%
	182–205 days	257–278 days	20–79 days per item (many items delivered)

* The smallest figure applies to a simple product, and the higher applies to a complex product of similar complexity to the other columns.
Source: Dervived from data in Rogerson and Moyes, 1983.

10 per cent of the total hardware production effort. The actual figure will depend on product type, the level of automation and whether or not sampling schemes are used (see, for example, tables 5.5 and 5.6).

Purchased components will also require checking. Typical figures for this activity will be found in Table 5.5. The 2 per cent by order value figure refers to the inspection effort per subcontract, and typically involves one man day or more for each subcontract item. An example of a maximum level for this activity would be the 27 man days needed for an electrical generator designed to be driven by an aircraft engine. Although the 2 per cent figure may seem high, this may involve (as appropriate to the item) subcontract order review, preproduction start-up discussions, test witnessing before release from the supplier or inspection on receipt, compilation of documents and checking against documented requirements. The ratio of this kind of inspection effort to the total purchasing effort of buying, expediting and inspection is typically in the range 19 to 25 per cent. It therefore becomes significant when functionality checking and traceability checks are deemed necessary.

Where test witnessing is required on suppliers' premises, 5 man hours should be allowed for simple purchases, rising to 20 man hours for complex products.

Software testing and design evaluation

These activities are invariably undertaken by the design team rather than the quality function. Nevertheless, the quality function will participate to some extent in some of these activities, and so Table 5.5 includes estimates for both design team members (first column) and quality function personnel (last column). In some organizations the quality function may take total responsibility for product acceptance testing of either purchased proprietary products or of the product developed by the organization, in which case the figures in the first column will apply.

System design reviews and software design and code walkthroughs are very effective means of detecting errors. They typically involve three or more people. Software code of 600-900 non-comment source statements will take from one to four hours of review effort per person prior to a half-day review session. These figures double for a review of the source code itself which includes commenting. By comparison the design of those source statements documented, for example in PDL (programme design language), may be reviewed with only one hour's preparation and one hour's discussion.

System design reviews and system test specification reviews typically take from one to three days of preparation effort, and a further day to review the comments generated. This can only be a broad indication as systems vary enormously in size.

Obviously, those responsible for the design should allow at least three times the joint discussion period to implement the corrective actions arising from it, and some effort should be made by the quality function to ensure that corrective action takes place.

Hardware design evaluation

Although unusual nowadays, the quality function may employ technical personnel to evaluate purchased product safety and functionality. This typically involves a review of test specifications, test results and design details against product performance requirements and national safety standards. Assuming the generation and implementation of a test specification is undertaken by the product supplier, the evaluation typically takes five man days for a module of comparable complexity to a digital telephone (if done conscientiously).

Supplier selection and control

The quality function (as opposed to any inspection and test function, particularly for critical products and services) will be involved in tender evaluation, supplier product line approval via quality assessment, supplier product quality plan agreement, supplier design review and progress meeting attendance and quality surveillance activities, often in the form of limited periodic quality assessments. Consequently, all these activities plus tender evaluation involvement can be expected for major subcontract work.

Notwithstanding earlier guidelines for quality assessment activity, an entry for some of this is made under monitoring in Table 5.5 as audits.

Document approval in design

Quite often the quality function is called upon to approve design control procedures as fit for use and as meeting any requirements laid down by quality management standards and contracts. Where this occurs considerable effort can be involved if the fit-for-use criterion is taken seriously, hence the estimates given in Table 5.5.

The impact of quality system certification

The aim of a sound quality system is to prevent problems before they occur. This can only come about by careful planning and control. The process of quality system certification therefore should result in increased planning and prevention measures to ensure that the client gets what was requested. Data from Rogerson and Moyes (1983) are given in Table 5.6 which suggest that this does occur. The analysis in Table 5.6 illustrates the impact of single and multiple agencies overseeing the work on safety critical products of comparable complexity. It suggests that for organizations of similar capability and experience, those with a mature certified quality system:

1. Incur less quality-related costs than for non-certified companies.
2. Multiple agencies overseeing work significantly increase quality function-related costs.

Table 5.7
The effect of certification on inspection and repair estimates.

Activity	Certified organization, single client inspections	Certified organization, multiple client inspections	Non-certified organization, multiple client inspections
Inspection	3.4–0.9%	6.72–9%	0.6–4.15%
Repair inspection	0.46–1.73%	0.12–0.41%	0–4.4%
Non-destructive testing	1.26–4.06%	3.18–8.06%	6–12.2%
Non-destructive testing of repairs	0–0.23%	0.28–1.48%	0–4.8 %

Source: Derived from data in Rogerson and Moyes, 1983.

A finer breakdown on inspection activities alone is given in Table 5.7 as a matter of interest.

Reality : a sad postscript

While this chapter includes realistic guidelines for estimating and resourcing quality tasks, it is very unusual to find quality assurance and quality control estimates being assigned in practice. This is even true when the quality activities have been included in project barcharts or network programmes. Somehow the work gets done. An arbitrary number of people are assigned, and these invariably tailor the work to suit the resources available. Even when the engineering and productive effort is summarized over regular periods, quality activities are treated in the same way as project management and administration, and are often ignored. Yet they constitute a significant overhead expense. Little wonder that there is a tendency to work overtime and cut corners in order to meet imposed timescales.

Further reading and references

Crosby, P. E., *Quality is Free, the Art of Making Quality Certain*, McGraw-Hill, Maidenhead, 1978.

Juran, J. M., *Japanese and Western Quality — a Contrast*, International Conference on Quality Control, Union of Japanese Scientists and Engineers International, Academy of Quality, Tokyo, 1978.

Kitchenham, B., *Metrics in Practice*, contribution to Software Reliability: Models and Measurement, a colloquium held at the Institution of Electrical Engineers, London, March 1985.

Price Waterhouse, *Software Quality Standards: The Costs and Benefits*, a review for the Department of Trade and Industry, London, 1988.

Rogerson, J. H. and Moyes, E. M., *The Reduction of Quality Costs in the Process Plant Industry*, National Economic Development Office, London, 1983.

Wood, K., *Quality Assurance Programmes for Offshore Production Platforms*, Paper EUR202, European Offshore Petroleum Conference, The Society of Petroleum Engineers, London, 1980.

Part Three

QUALITY IN ENGINEERING AND DESIGN

6 Design Objectives

Robin Plummer

Quality management can be summarized in two captions.

Right design
Right execution

These captions capture two principles of quality management, that design must conform to the customers' requirements, and that production must conform to the design. The subject of right execution, or conformance to design, is dealt with elsewhere in this handbook. This chapter deals with conformance of design to the customers' requirements.

Motivation

Why is it so important to get the design objectives clear at the outset?
The cost of correcting a quality defect goes up exponentially with the delay incurred before the defect is corrected. In practical terms, the addition of each extra stage in the life cycle of a product or service before corrective action is taken effectively, can cause a 10-fold increase in the ultimate cost of correction. That can be quite some quality-related cost!

Failing to establish clearly the design objectives, or establishing erroneous design objectives might easily cause a product or service to be unfit for purpose and to fail to sell much after its initial launch. It might cause such expensive corrective action in order to make it fit for purpose, as to render it unviable economically. This could entail its subsequent withdrawal from the market. Failing to establish the design objectives, or erroneously establishing design objectives might cause interactive effects in a system within which the product or service is incorporated. This could render the entire system unfit for purpose and even prompt the demise of a complete technology. This demise might be a fizzling out of a technology as was the case with a major telecommunications software, acknowledged by its makers to have been written on the basis of a misunderstanding of the design objectives. The demise might be a catastrophic failure of some major project because the design objectives produced a component which was unfit for its implied needs. Failure correctly to establish the true design objectives may result in a manufacturing or service specification which is far more stringent than necessary. The inevitable quality-related costs, including additional inspection, rework, disposal, etc., could be avoided simply by relaxing the manufacturing specification to that dictated by realistic design objectives.

Get market intelligence

The first step is to gather market intelligence. Market intelligence can be divided into two broad categories. One category is where a market already exists from which data on design objectives can be drawn. An example of this is the use of the newly discovered aluminium in the fabrication of aircraft in the mid 1930s, with the transition from the Hurricane fighter, built with a tubular steel frame, to the Spitfire, built with a stressed aluminium monococque body. It is true that the Spitfire was in many respects a revolutionary aircraft, with a drag-reducing slimness unheard of before, incorporating engine-cooling water radiators along the leading edges of the mainplanes, among other things, but that is not the point. The point is that the essential parameters of flight were already well known.

The other category is where entirely new ground is to be broken. An example of this is designing stored programme controlled (SPC) switching centres (digital telephone exchanges) where the philosophy of SPC had first to be interpreted before design objectives could even be considered. Another example is the profound electronic potentialities of high temperature superconductors, newly discovered in February 1987.

The former category is the more normal. Experience shows that most of the significant advances in design concept and objectives, occur from small extensions to existing and well proven concepts.

The latter category, of entirely new ground, is the less usual and, naturally, the more difficult to obtain clear objectives about. This is obviously due to the far greater difficulty involved in specifying what the market is ultimately going to want, or how best to realize the potentialities of exciting new discoveries. Analysts have previously stated this problem in terms of coefficients of difficulty of obtaining a precise view of the objectives to be fulfilled. Equations have been formulated and graphs drawn which assist designers in calculating the volume of design effort, and therefore of cost, probably required for a given coefficient of difficulty. This discussion agrees with common sense experience of revolutionary as opposed to evolutionary design.

Market intelligence can be gathered from different sources.

Consider first the case of objectives for evolutionary designs, which make a small advance on existing concepts. New materials, such as aluminium, allow engineers and designers to realize developments in design where an established principle has been in operation for years. In a non-manufacturing case, junk mail has for some time been aimed at specific sectors of the population, for which credit ratings, income and stereotyped tastes are known or predictable. It falls to innovative designers of junk mail merely to make advances on existing design objectives in order to give their junk mail more appeal than that of their competitors. Encyclopaedias are more commonly sold in weekly volumes nowadays, instead of as a job lot. The information being sold is broadly similar to that contained in entire encyclopaedias, but the clientele is still known to feel insecure at the prospect of their precocious offspring missing an unrepeatable opportunity for educational advancement.

In the category of objectives for revolutionary designs, the design effort might be directed at a distillation of market information to try to spot an opening requiring something which has simply never existed before, such as inexpensive computer equipment and audio reproduction systems, which are a well proven technology at a quality, compatibility and price that compete with the international business machine boys. Alternatively, a designer's client may make a request for something which either does not exist or for which the solution is something of pure invention. This case is typified by software solutions in general, and by the information technology revolution in particular. Design for the client often comes in fits and starts. The erratic nature is often due to the client not knowing precisely what he wants, partly because he does not know the full range of options available. The further into the design one gets, the more the client realizes what he could have, and the more the design objectives are capable of being changed. A solution here is to have the maximum of consultation among the interested parties at the earliest stages of the design effort, and to feedback constantly at this crucial time in the life of the product or service. Remember how rapidly the costs of correcting quality defects increase with increased delay before action is taken. For the revolutionary design case, designers and engineers must resort in general to theoretical aspects and climb a steep learning curve very fast. Simultaneously, they must be aware of the problem faced by the client of the enormous diversity of possible design objectives, of which the client may be largely ignorant.

Clarify the express requirements

The design objectives must be ordered top down. This means that design objectives must be ranked in the common sense order in which they must logically be fulfilled. This seemingly trite statement suddenly takes on an instructive importance when you realize that you have forgotten to specify stage payments on a multimillion pound contract, and that the work in progress capital is going to cost you thousand of pounds in interest. Another quality-related cost!

A syndicate exercise, used by the author in his presentations on design objectives, has three syndicate groups. Each group plays the role of a party to the implementation of an advanced information technology project. Half-way through the syndicates' thinking time, the author is habitually asked, 'Can we assume this?' or 'Can we assume that?' The answer is, 'Don't assume anything. Clarify it with the other parties.'

Evaluate the implied requirements

The express requirements of a market or customer are generally more readily determined, and therefore receive more design attention than the implied requirements. A few examples of implied requirements will illustrate some pitfalls to be avoided.

A lady bought a plastic bucket. On the outside of the bucket there was a clear and unequivocal warning not to place boiling water in the bucket, as the bucket was not designed to withstand boiling water temperature. The lady poured boiling water into the bucket which buckled, and the spilling water scalded her legs. She sued the bucket manufacturer. The magistrate threw her case out of court. Even when there is a comprehensive effort to make clear the limitations of a product, people will still abuse the stated limits.

You don't need seat belts, insurance or contraceptives until you actually need them. Design objectives are sometimes approached with a remarkably shuttered attitude. 'No. That can't possibly happen.'

Give a loaded revolver to a child and then tell the child not to shoot itself. Murphy's Law has it that, if it is allowable that an event can occur, then sooner or later it will occur. This is often cited as Sod's Law, that, if it can go wrong, it will!

The design objectives must include requirements that are implied by the use of the product or service, in that the implication can be reasonably foreseen at the time of designing.

At an interview board, the candidates were asked to list the uses to which they could put a common house brick. The listed uses included, of course, an ash tray, a door stop, a weapon, a piece of building material, etc. Attention was clearly being given to prospective employees being able to think laterally.

One major industrial company in Japan employs graduate engineers as trainee designers. Part of their six years of training as designers, is spent, not in design at all, but in retailing. The graduates are sent for two years to company retail outlets to acquire experience of what the public wants to buy, and what they tend to bring back as unfit for purpose. After two years in retailing the graduates spend two years in manufacturing to acquire experience of what manufacturing departments can manufacture and what they can't. Then, after the completion of the other aspects of their training, they finally become designers.

The very important principle is that the express requirements are more readily seen among the design objectives than are the implied requirements.

Clarify the express and implied requirements of related legislation

The *Consumer Protection Act 1987* says that the producer will be liable for damage wholly or partly caused by the product. Defences against this include that the damage could not be reasonably foreseen at the time that the product was designed and produced.

The health and safety legislation is one piece of legislation that most people in industry take more seriously than much other legislation. The acts of Parliament on safety permit operatives to walk off the job rather than subject themselves to dangerous circumstances. (It is worth observing at this point that all companies must have a declared safety policy. It is not only in the personal interests of staff to abide by the policy and to attend to their own personal safety, but also their responsibility in law to do so. How much more quickly would quality management be universally applied, if quality policies were as omnipresent as safety policies, and personnel were responsible for their own quality? In most companies, it would suffice to take the safety policy and change every word relevant to safety to an appropriate word related to quality, for each of those companies to have a comprehensive quality policy.)

The implications of product liability, and health and safety legislation are dealt with in another chapter. Nevertheless they must feature in the design objectives.

Choice of market sector

It is a business management decision to consider in which part of the market are the requirements that the company wishes to satisfy. It is a quality management decision to ensure that the design objectives of a chosen market sector are all comprehensively considered in the design process, insofar as they influence fitness for the customer's purpose.

Consideration of design objectives must include that there may well be an unfulfilled market niche to go for, but one which could involve a volume of work-in-progress investment capital which is unsustainable for the company, or that the returns on investment might be doubtful or speculative or a long time coming. One large research company regularly refuses to accept design commissions on the grounds that preliminary investigation has indicated too uncertain a return on investment.

A particular part of the market may concord with the company's existing corporate image. Other parts may not. Diversification into the money markets by some companies, after the 'Big Bang' liberalization of financial services in November 1987, resulted in some companies catching a cold in an area not traditionally their own. They subsequently returned to their traditional market sectors.

Other design objectives that might influence the choice of market sector include making the choice between long-life, consumer durable or consumer disposable products; whether they should comprise built-in obsolescence or should be state of the art; whether to design for long-life coupled with high reliability as with the nuclear industry, or disposability as with some sealed for life components. Consideration must be given to the fact that certain sectors have market parameters which change or even oscillate with time, sometimes quite dramatically. Design objectives must reflect the potential for market changes. Is the company in the market for a swing into new tooling, e.g. the changes seen in the print industry in recent years. Is the company capable of tracking changes in the degree of advancement of a particular market, e.g. the far tighter tolerances demanded in ships changing from gas turbines to nuclear power. Is the company able to control more stringent processes, e.g. exhaust emission control regulations. Can the company finance fluctuating commodity prices, e.g. strategic metals in time of war, etc. Some companies have developed a capability to adapt with staggering swiftness to market changes and to diverse customer demands. An example is of traditional, light engineering firms, whose set-up times for automatic machine tools run into hours, when a batch of a different product is called for. By using replacement heads for each machine tool, each head being set up for a different product, the set-up time during which the machine is actually out of production is limited to the time it takes to change heads. This has reduced set-up times from hours to, quite literally, tens of seconds. This is a fine example of the just-in-time approach to the management of quality in a rapidly changing environment.

When due weight has been ascribed to each and all of these influences, and a decision reached about which design objectives are sustainable by the company, then the company is in a position to choose its market sector. Of course it might be that the tradition of a company already dictates the market sector. In this case the company must choose whether to stay in its traditional sector or to move to comply with the design objectives of a changing sector. To repeat, that choice is a business management decision. The quality management decision is to ensure that whatever the market sector and whatever the degree of flux or stasis of a company's position, the design objectives have to be fully considered at the outset.

Design parameters

The company management will decide upon a market sector, through a combination of management direction and possessed or acquirable ability to fulfill the market sector's design objectives. Certain design objectives will be left to the designers to decide, but certain will be decided by the market sector. Those design objectives decided by the market sector will include for example, certain aspects of reliability and maintainability, and the extents to which the product is expected to be maintained by the user or by a service organization. Under harsh conditions of use, and where sophisticated support organizations are absent, such as in the arctic or in the desert, it is pointless driving vehicles which can only be tuned electronically, or which have total dependence on one feature such as a sophisticated suspension system. The maintainer needs to be able to keep the vehicle running using a knife and fork and a 5-pence piece for fusewire. The most prevalent cause of keeping bullet-proof cars off the road in some of the more exotic parts of the globe, is failure of the air conditioning system. It renders the car undrivable owing to the heat, and you can't open the windows in a bullet proof car!

The projected lifespan of a product is proportionate, in the minds of some customers, to the cost of the product. A look at the total life cycle cost to the customer of poor design shows, once again, that the lowest life cycle costs are brought about by good design. In countries in the world where progress in design has gone by default, or is stifled as a consequence of a restrictive system, fitness for purpose is very low. Unfortunately, there is always a market for poor quality goods because, in costing less, they are affordable by less affluent people in some nations. The life cycle costs are high, however, because poorly designed products have a short time before replacement is inevitable.

In the case of software, one design objective to be considered is the degree of user-friendliness of the software package. User-friendliness is the extent to which the software package itself guides the user as to the options available in using the package, and to the choices which may be made. The degree of user-friendliness chosen by the designers will depend upon how computer literate are the intended users of the software package. Some computer packages have several levels of user-friendliness which can be switched in or out of use by the user according to his or her knowledge and ability to use the package.

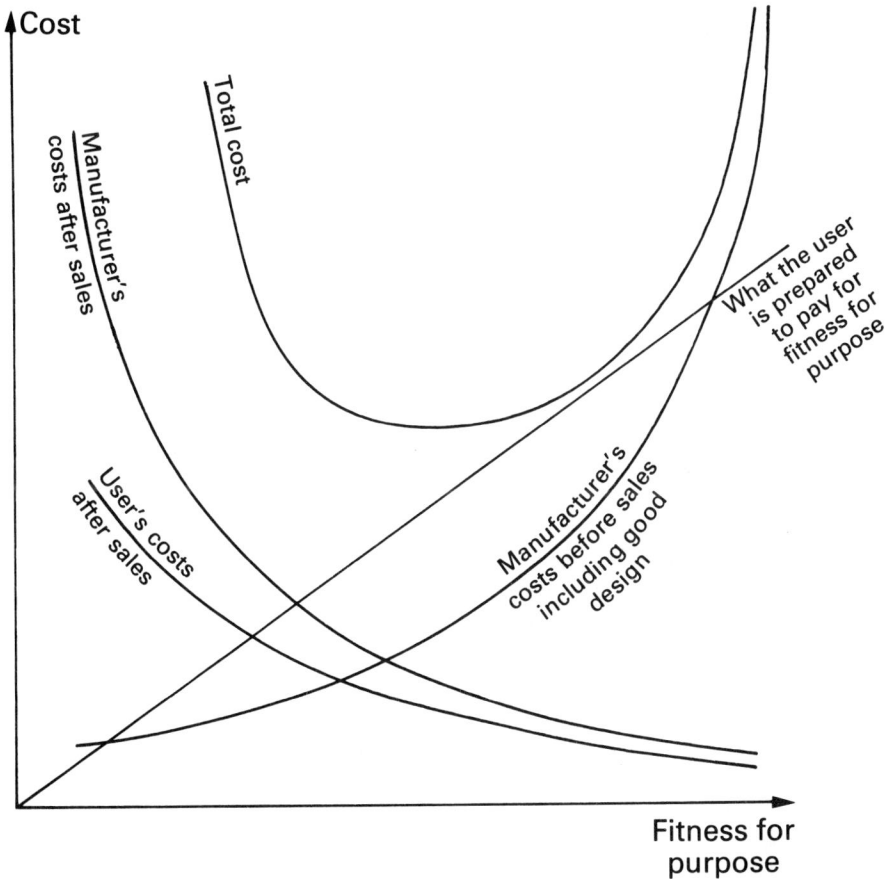

Figure 6.1.   Fitness for purpose in relation to various costs.

The cost-benefit of good design can be indicated by the use of standard curves (see Figure 6.1). Manufacturer's costs before sales, including the cost of design are shown rising with increased fitness for purpose. Both manufacturer's and user's costs after sales are shown falling with increased fitness for purpose. Not surprisingly, the cost-benefit curve shows a nadir which is construed as the minimum cost per fitness for purpose. The indications are however, that users tend to be prepared to pay a total cost which rises in direct proportion to increased fitness for purpose. The cost benefit for increased fitness for purpose is therefore more accurately construed as the optimization of the total cost curve and the straight line representing what the user is prepared to pay. This can clearly be seen to be slightly greater than the minimum cost.

Quality assured design

Quality assured design is covered in detail in another chapter. Essentially, the quality assurance of design is derived by ensuring that all foreseeable design objectives are considered for their influence on fitness for purpose, then using them appropriately as inputs to the design process, and that the output of the design process, the design itself, conforms to the input design objectives.

Failure mode effect and criticality analysis

Failure mode effect and criticality analysis (FMECA) is an analysis performed to evaluate the effect upon the overall design, of a failure in any one of the identifiable failure modes of the design components, and to evaluate how critically that failure will affect the design performance. Each identifiable failure mode has ascribed to it a probability of occurrence, and logical summation of the inclusive probabilities of occurrence of failure modes produces a figure for the reliability of the system as a whole.

Tables of probabilities of occurrence of failure modes have been compiled to assist designers in FMECA. Probabilities for stringent applications, such as military use are cited in documents like US Military Standard 217 at the relevant issue state (affectionately known at the time of writing as MIL STAN 217E). Probabilities for less exacting requirements are quoted in British Telecom's *Handbook of Reliability Data* at the relevant issue state (affectionately known as HRD4). Reference works, compiled by acknowledged authorities in the field of reliability, contain figures for the upper and lower limits of the probability of the occurrence of events and also of the most likely level of probability. The probability has even been calculated of the failure of an operator correctly to operate a manually operated switch.

FMECA can be justly seen as a powerful tool in assessing the extent to which a design meets certain of its design objectives. There is more detailed discussion of this technique in Chapter 11 and further comment in Chapter 20.

Feedback from production

Quality assurance purists will argue that quality assured design should be right first time. So it should be. But part of the quality assurance process of design (as well as with any other stage in the life cycle of a product or service) incorporates the potential for feedback from later stages of the life cycle of the product and ever should it be so. It is worth observing again, however, that the cost of correcting a quality defect goes up exponentially with time in the product or service life cycle, and that right first is unquestionably the most cost effective way of designing. 'Well, we'll rough out a design and if manufacturing can't make then we'll have another go.' Too many companies devote an excessive amount of design effort to correcting design defects whose existence has been reported to them by later stages of the product or service's life cycle. This is a clear example of design effort being included in the category of cost of quality-related failure.

The role of the Design Council

The role of the Design Council is admirably stated in its own publications, and is summarized in some of their own words.

The Design Council exists to promote by all practical means the improvement of design in the products of British industry. It was set up by the Government in 1944 and is incorporated by Royal Charter and registered as a charity.

The Council receives an annual grant-in-aid from the Department of Trade and Industry under conditions that regulate its financial practice and the terms of employment of its staff.

Members are appointed by the Secretary of State for Trade and Industry. They are responsible for approving policy and monitoring its implementation.

Originally known as the Council of Industrial Design, it became the Design Council in 1972 when its role was expanded to embrace engineering design as thoroughly as industrial design.

The Design Council has a number of professional services. Among these, the Design Advisory Service provides continuing help in diagnosing design problems and assisting companies with their solution. The service is available to any company, and membership is free.

The Support for Design scheme, which is operated by the Council's Design Advisory Service on behalf of the Department of Trade and Industry, is the prime means by which the Council seeks to persuade British companies that investment in improved design is one of the keys to commercial success. The scheme provides eligible companies with around two-thirds of the cost of up to fifteen days of design consultancy for an agreed project. The scheme thus enables companies to experience, at minimal cost, the benefits of employing a design consultant.

The Design Advisory Service Information Section has, as its main activity, the identification of appropriate sources of specialist expertise to undertake engineering design or technical consultancy projects, primarily for the Design Advisory Service and the Support for Design scheme. The Section maintains a computer-based record of engineering design expertise.

The Designer Selection Service provides an easy and effective means of finding industrial design consultants to suit the needs and circumstances of different companies and their design projects.

Freelance designers and design consultancies are interviewed regularly and up-to-date information about them is then stored on a computer database supported by a visual record of current work. Details of new design services that meet the Council's standards of expertise and experience are constantly being added and the register contains information about some 1500 delegates.

The Designer Selection Service provides a shortlist of three design consultancies chosen as being capable of meeting each client company's particular brief; the company is then invited to interview these and select the designer that best suits its requirements. The Designer Selection Service covers product, graphics, fashion, textiles and interior design.

The Design Centre Selection is the Council's product approval scheme for consumer and contract goods manufactured in the United

Kingdom. Its chief objectives are to provide a basis for the promotion of well designed British-made products of assured quality, to encourage design improvement in member companies, and to provide examples of good design for education purposes. Products submitted by manufacturers are evaluated by panels of experts against criteria for performance, construction, aesthetics and value for money. In addition, products must meet all the relevant safety standards and pass user and performance tests.

The Council provides a range of marketing services to help manufacturers whose products have been approved for Design Centre Selection to gain commercial advantage both in the United Kingdom and abroad. The Design Centre Shops sell a wide range of approved consumer products to the general public, as well as providing a comprehensive range of design books through the Bookshop. A wide range of merchandise is displayed, covering products areas such as knitwear, glass, small electrical appliances, toys, hardware, stationery, fashion accessories and kitchenware. Orders placed represent a purchasing power of approximately £1 million a year, providing particular help to small manufacturers. Professional buyers from home and overseas are also encouraged to buy approved merchandise. The Council arranges regular displays for groups of manufacturers at trade fairs in Britain and abroad.

The Council organizes a wide range of award schemes and competitions, to recognize design achievement and encourage fresh thinking. Many of these schemes are run in association with other organizations.

The address of the Design Council is:
28 Haymarket,
London,
SW1Y 4SU.

Design objectives

Design objectives must be comprehensively evaluated as early in the life cycle of a product or service as possible. Enormous quality-related costs can be incurred as a consequence of delay in detecting quality defects, and right first time is unquestionably the approach when assessing the design objectives and their influence on fitness for purpose of the product or service.

In making a choice of market sector for which to produce or serve, due regard must be paid to the company's historic ability, capability for change and the capability to research new areas. Express and implied requirements of the market sector must be evaluated in order for the design to conform to requirements, and certain legislation must be adhered to.

Quality assured design should incorporate some form of sensitivity or criticality analysis, and make use of, but not rely upon, feedback from later stages in the life cycle.

The Design Council exists as a thorough and professional body to give guidance and assistance to design projects, and does so with the assistance of government funds in some cases.

7 National and International Engineering Design Standards

Trevor C. Ashton

Effective design standards enable a multitude of everyday spares to be purchased with the confidence that they will be compatible and interchangeable. It is taken for granted that light bulbs and household electric plugs will fit their appropriate mating sockets even though they are bought at different times and places. It isn't necessary to worry whether tyres from different manufacturers will still fit the wheels of your car. Household appliances work on the available electricity supply, bath plugs fit the bath, etc., etc. The list is endless. Likewise it is assumed that, if things were not so, then there would be legitimate cause for complaint. In both these things the consumer places an unconscious reliance on design and quality standards being adopted.

Similar benefits extend to the manufacturer as well as to the consumer. For example, nuts and bolts from various sources can be expected to be to assured levels of performance and quality and within the specified tolerances. Standards of performance, quality, safety and reliability have wide application and influence. The organization for producing them extends from the manufacturer to international limits and has been in existence since the turn of the century. They have produced universally acknowledged specifications of performance, physical attributes, terminology and methods of test to meet the demands for quality and interchangeability.

117

There are no foreseeable limits to the application of standardization as a technique for attaining industrial or economic efficiency. Properly recorded standards are a means of consolidating decisions, whether made by direct mandate or obtained from democratic compromise. In spite of the longevity of the process there is still a need to restate the objectives of standardization to those not previously involved, so this chapter includes a résumé of the history of national and international standards and their aims and principles. This may help the understanding of their contribution to quality and industry.

Aims and principles of standardization

Methods and principles are now formally established, having been produced by the International Organization for Standardization (ISO) or, more accurately, by its standing committee for the study of the principles (code named STACO). These aims are repeated below:

1. Overall economy in terms of human effort, materials, power, etc. in the production and exchange of goods.
2. The protection of consumer interest through adequate and consistent quality of goods and services.
3. Safety, health and the protection of life.
4. Provision of a means of expression and of communication amongst all interested parties.

To achieve these aims seven principles were established in the belief that complete freedom and enterprise, whilst being highly desirable in the development of a high technology world, would require a framework, a degree of order and discipline if they were not to become self confounding.

Principle 1   Standardization is essentially an art of simplification as a result of the conscious effort of society. It calls for the reduction in the number of some things. It not only results in a reduction of complexity but aims at the prevention of unnecessary complexity in the future.

Variety reduction and variety control are examples of this principle in practice. This is frequently to the benefit of the consumer as well as the producer. Markets can be increased to more economic proportions by rationalization. A standardized electricity supply for instance not only provides economic manufacturing quantities for the associated hardware but also provides a means of regulating its safe use.

Principle 2 Standardization is a social as well as an economic activity and should be promoted by the mutual cooperation of all concerned. The establishment of a standard should be based on a general consensus.

Obtaining agreement on a standard should be a democratic process involving all parties with an interest or concern. Although there may be instances where autonomy is necessary to produce a standard within a deadline, it is not recommended. The result may become a stagnant standard. A much more fruitful approach is to invite contributions from as many prospective users as possible, the affected as well as the effectors. Consumer associations should be encouraged to participate in the standards making process. This will generate an interest and produce benefits flowing over into the following.

Principle 3 The mere publication of a standard is of little value unless it can be implemented. Implementation may necessitate sacrifices by the few for the benefit of the many.

There must be some motivation to use standards on a regular basis. This can be achieved in a number of ways. In some countries they are legally enforceable. In industry quality audit programmes are used to police their use. At the grass roots, that is in the office or the factory, it may even be expedient artificially to ease the use of standards and make it more difficult to adopt an alternative non-standard approach. On an individual basis a defaulter may try to prove that using standards incurs some penalty. It is important that, if such penalties are proved to be local, the overall economics are considered and that any benefits or short term gains are compared with the expense of increased variety and a subsequent degradation of the standards policy.

Principle 4 The action to be taken in establishing standards is essentially one of selection followed by fixing.

Recognize, record and rationalize are the three Rs of standards. Recognition involves identification of the various facets of a subject. For example, if the purpose is to control the purchase of bought-out items, the first task is to identify the extent of existing variety by cataloguing. Having all the available data accumulated then permits a selection to be made, considering the pros and cons of retaining the full range and deciding which to discard. The selection must then be confirmed. Publishing an authorized standard is the proper way of doing this and creates a permanent record. If necessary an additional exercise to rationalize the existing range can then be set up.

Principle 5   Standards should be reviewed at regular intervals and revised as necessary. The interval between versions will depend on the particular circumstances.

A formal system must be set up for registering the standards in common use. This requires apportioning responsibility, whether it be a national executive body, a company standards department or a particular office manager. Notification of changes can then be distributed from this source direct to the users. The quality audit departments in an organization will usually monitor their implementation and report on the effectiveness of the maintenance procedures.

Principle 6   When performance or other characteristics of a product are specified, the specification must include a description of the methods and tests to be applied in order to determine whether or not a given article complies with the specification. When sampling is to be adopted the method, and of necessity the size and frequency of the samples should be specified.

Ratings and characteristics can only be reliably compared if the methods of test are constant. Testing one in a hundred will not give the same assessed quality as testing one in fifty or 100 per cent. The BS9000 and CECC systems for components of assessed quality are a prime example of correct interpretation of this principle. Use of one of the many national standards for test methods reduces the possibility of disagreement when goods have to be rejected.

Principle 7   The necessity for legal reinforcement of national standards should deliberately be considered, having regard to the nature of the standard, the level of industrialization and the laws and conditions prevailing in the society for whom the standard has been prepared.

Safety standards in particular are in this category and the principle has been applied in the UK to things such as car seat belts and motorcycle crash helmets. In the UK certain standards are approved by the Secretary of State under the Approval of Safety Standards Regulations 1987. Under this blanket, goods that satisfy the requirements of an approved standard are deemed to satisfy the general safety requirements of the legislation. The British Standards Institution (BSI) have approved test laboratories which support standards and legislation by certification.

Since being published in 1972 all these principles have been confirmed in practice and proved to be a comprehensive guide in present day technology. It would be as well to keep these aims and principles in mind when considering how and where standardization is to be employed in the current pursuit of quality or in helping penetration into foreign markets. It is difficult to imagine that a successful company would wish to be confined to a local market. The investment required to meet competition demands that the widest market available is tapped. This means at least meeting a country's national standards for safety and liability. The adoption of international standards can considerably ease this process and reduce the risk of liability claims in some instances.

International standardization

IEC and ISO

The two major bodies producing world-wide standards are the International Electrotechnical Commission (IEC) and the International Standards Organization (ISO). The first covers electrotechnical matters and the latter mechanical. Both are based in Switzerland and occupy opposite ends of the same building. They retain separate identities and working arrangements, however. Most countries now subscribe to these organizations. The larger and better developed countries presumably participate because influencing or being involved in the standards making process is a prerequisite to the business of becoming a market leader. The smaller or developing countries stand to gain the advantage of cooperating with the acknowledged experts and have some access to their wealth of experience. All avoid reinventing the wheel and have a forum for discussing the latest technology and state of the art. Both IEC and the ISO operate on a committee basis, providing the administration and secretarial support to bring together the essential experts. The results of their efforts are published as IEC or ISO standards.

The IEC was formed in 1906 and has since produced a platform of essential standards on topics such as terminology, methods of test and fundamental units, including the international system of units (SI). Its sister organization, the ISO was founded in 1947 and, while the IEC concentrates on standards in the electrical and electronic fields (including electromedical and nuclear engineering), ISO is concerned with the non-electrical standards. Vital work has been done by ISO on such standards as those produced for ISO metric screw threads. By agreement the two bodies do not compete but, because of the integration of electrical and non-electrical matters in all industries today, they are inclined to cooperate and collaborate on an increasing scale. Both have adopted French and English as the official languages and publications are bilingual.

Certification is the process of confirming conformance by recognized testing methods. International certification is still in its infancy but IEC has developed a system covering electronic components (IECQ) and for safety testing electrical equipment normally used in homes, offices and workshops (IECEE). ISO is developing guidelines for a more general system in cooperation with IEC. Both organizations have also been collaborating on the production of a series of standards on quality management. These have been published by ISO as ISO9000-ISO9004, to be used to assess the quality capability of firms internationally. The standards and other related publications may be purchased from the IEC or ISO in Geneva or from any of the national committees. In the UK this would be the British Standards Institution at Milton Keynes.

European standards

Between worldwide and national there is also a regional activity. The standards organizations of Western Europe have formed the European Committee for Standardization (CEN) which is intended to prevent the drifting apart of the standards of the European Community (EC) and the European Free Trade Area (EFTA). The division is similar to the international arrangement, with CEN covering non-electrical aspects and the European Committee for Electrotechnical Standardization (CENELEC) being responsible for others. European standards are printed or endorsed as national standards as and when they are adopted. They do not have a separate existence as international standards. The European influence extends to military requirements in the form of quality control systems for the North Atlantic Treaty

Organisation (NATO). These are issued as Allied Quality Assurance Publications (AQAP) and are intended to rationalize national defence specifications such as the Ministry of Defence DEF STAN 05-21 *Quality Control Systems for Industry*.

Electrical engineering

As well as those particular bodies who concentrate on worldwide standardization there are about 200 others dealing with various specific aspects of electrical and electronic engineering. They include the likes of the International Atomic Energy Authority (IAEA), The International Telephone and Telegraphic Consultative Committee (CCITT), International Commission for Conformity of Electrical Equipment (CEE) and the International Commission on Illumination (CIE). BSI runs a unique export advisory service sponsored by the Board of Trade for the guidance of British companies seeking to sell their products abroad. Known as Technical Help to Exporters (THE) its main purpose is to identify the foreign technical requirements or regulations which apply to a client's products.

National standards

The British Standards Institution

National involvement in the control of quality began with the first British Standards issued in 1901 by the Engineering Standards Committee, which subsequently was overtaken by the British Engineering Standards Association (BESA) and developed into the British Standards Institution. This was several decades before the Japanese also showed that quality could be improved by introducing a national strategy. The development of their methods into the western world is now history and the combination of organized standards and quality control is an accepted part of the process. National standards bodies are part of an organization stretching upwards into an international scale as well as reaching downwards into the grass roots of industry. Most of them have seen fit to take quality assurance under their wing and devote considerable resources to developing these standards into a system which can be adopted nationally. It has also been shown that the same standards can make a considerable contribution to international harmonization, which is so essential to companies intending to export or import.

A manufacturing company's involvement in national standards making is not normally by the company receiving a direct invitation to serve on national and international committees. The British Standards Institution, as other similar bodies, only invite participation via a representative body such as a recognized trade association, public authority or professional institution. These bodies in turn may organize their own standardization committees and the representatives for the national committees are drawn from them. It is therefore vital that a company having aspirations to be recognized in world markets should consider the advantages of joining and participating at the lower levels to obtain their nomination. A similar pattern is observed from national to international levels, the international committees being appointed from the recognized national bodies. A team and leader of the national contingent are elected by the national committee.

Certification

Conformity with British Standards is not generally mandatory in the UK although this may not be the case in other countries where use of standards is sometimes enforced by legislation. If a BS number is quoted on a product it can be regarded as a claim by the manufacturer that his product has been made and tested to the British Standard. Should any doubt exist, then a customer is entitled to demand proof in the form of the results of tests conducted by an independent test house.

BSI operates two certification schemes which are able to provide assurance that goods are subject to a continuing programme of surveillance:

1. The kitemark (see Figure 7.1). This applies to a wide variety of electrical and non-electrical goods. It can commonly be seen on items such as clinical thermometers and 13amp plugs.
2. The safety mark (see Figure 7.2). Whereas the kitemark scheme indicates that the product is certified for conformity to all requirements (safety, dimensional, performance and so on) the BSI safety mark applies specifically to show that a product complies with a particular safety standard (e.g. electric kettles and other hand-held electrical appliances).

The licences issued under these schemes are subject to annual reassessment and confirm that the manufacturer has satisfactorily met the stringent requirements for good manufacturing practice and

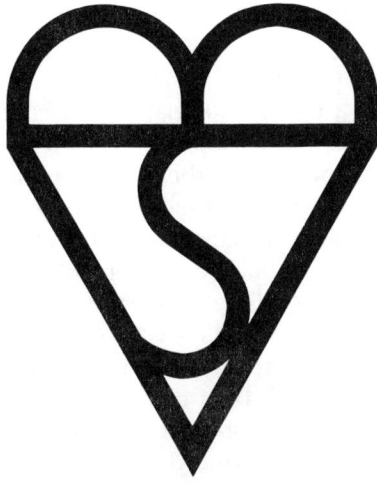

BS 691

Figure 7.1.   The BSI kitemark.

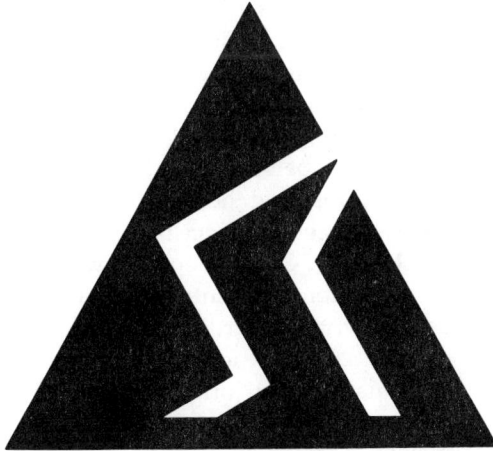

BS 4533

Figure 7.2.   The BSI safety mark.

effective quality control procedures.

Electronic components

Electronics plays a part in the majority of contemporary inventions, whether as a substantial proportion (in items such as television or sound systems) or perhaps as the controls in domestic appliances and everything from toys to missiles. Today's technology therefore involves the use of electronic components in considerable quantities. An assured standard of quality and reliability for components such as resistors, capacitors, switches and even the more complex memory devices and integrated circuits is vital.

This need was recognized first by the Ministry of Defence, who were naturally concerned with their communications, and was eventually taken up by the British Standards Institution. A new scheme of standardization was introduced to incorporate a specification of quality assessment as well as dimensions and performance. This was considered necessary to cater for the large production quantities (which were generally subject to statistical sampling rather than 100 per cent inspection/test) and recognized that the same methods of production could result in varying levels of assessed quality if different sampling plans were adopted.

BSI standards had up till this time been numbered consecutively, having started at number one (c. 1920). BSI had published over 5000 standards when the new system for electronic components was formulated. It was envisaged that the series for electronic components would need to cater for expansion, so that it would be better if a different number series could be allocated which would enable them to be identified easily as belonging to the group. The BS9000 series was allocated for this purpose and the system is now known as 'The BS9000 System'. It has been extended since into Europe under the auspices of the CENELEC Electronic Components Committee (CECC). At the start of 1982 a similar system was introduced by the IEC for electronic component assessment and certification. This is recognized as IECQ. BSI is one of over 20 countries participating. With these schemes gaining in popularity the original BS9000 is gradually being superseded.

All three systems provide similar comprehensive arrangements for the specification, inspection, quality assessment certification and release of electronic components of assessed quality. Further details of the BS9000 system are contained in BS9000 Part 1. The rules of procedure for CECC and IECQ are detailed in CECC00101 – 00113 and

QC001001 and QC001002, respectively.

Company standards

Creating company standards

Properly defined procedures for standards and specifications within a company are a prerequisite to quality control as specified in BS5750 'Quality Systems' or its international equivalent ISO9000 *Quality Management and Quality Assurance Standards — Guidelines for Selection and Use.* Separate parts of BS5750, ISO9000 series, AQAP and DEF STAN 05 series form sets of criteria against which companies may be separately assessed.

In order to conform to these requirements, responsibility must be allocated to produce and maintain documentation and these should be to a reasonably professional standard. There is little reason, with the availability of low cost computers, word processors and copiers, for the documents to be anything less than accurately typed. Standards managers should aim to establish credibility and authority in their specifications by developing a house style and ensuring that the standards carry the necessary authorizing signatures.

Obtaining agreement to produce a standard in cooperatives can have its problems. Autonomous standards originating from the top can be enforced quickly and easily but it is rare for a senior executive to have sufficient facts at his or her disposal to make reliable decisions on technical matters unaided, or even more unlikely that he or she will have the inclination to remain sufficiently involved to ensure that such standards keep up with the state of the art. More commonly, compromises are necessary from a consensus of the views and varying expertise available. This being so, the decisions must be recorded in a manner which materially represents their importance and allows an executive the ultimate power of authority or veto. This kind of credibility can only be achieved by attention to detail and laying down rules in the first instance. After all, these are the foundation. It is equally important to be able to identify the hierarchy of standards and to build up confidence so that they continue to represent the current state of the art.

Product or user standards

Unlike the 1950s and 1960s it is now not unusual for the best brains available in industry and commerce to be seconded to national and international standards committees. For reasons stated earlier, failure to do so can result in very serious loss, if not in immediate business, in market position. A business can leave itself vulnerable to liability claims or fall on its inability to meet the standards or legislation appertaining to the country they are selling into. It is obvious that no company can be represented on all the committees relating not only to its products but also to items or codes of practice they use (e.g. raw materials in the form of aluminium, steel, brass, copper, winding wire or the nuts and bolts, etc.). They may not be able to afford to become too deeply involved with national and international codes of practice covering drawing office practice, electrical diagrams, symbols and so on.

Though the expense of direct involvement and participation in committee work can be justified on the product standards (through the trade association), the cost associated with keeping up to date on the others as users has to be spread much more thinly. The responsibility for these areas is usually assigned to the company standards section or its equivalent. They will monitor the development of national and international 'user' standards on the topics which concern and affect the company or its products. Prominent in these areas are drawing office codes of practice and purchasing specifications. The knowledgeable or experienced standards engineer will establish links with the standards associations and others in the same field to keep in touch with all manner of marginal interests to his company. He will act as custodian of the organization's standards and ensure that as well as creating new standards he keeps the existing ones updated. The section should also provide advice and assistance on their application.

Drawing office standards

Office automation has extended significantly into the drawing office, the pencil and paper gradually being superseded by computers and databases. Introduction of computer-aided drafting systems or computer-aided design (CAD) and computer-aided manufacturing (CAM) has developed further into computer integrated manufacture (CIM). The result of this computerization has been to revolutionize the transfer of manufacturing information by reducing the transcription of written data.

Compensating for the loss of conventional drafting work is the increasing capability of the drawing office to do things which were not previously possible. Computer graphics has evolved to enable a much better standard of in-house artwork for technical publications (not only instruction and maintenance manuals but also sales proposals, publicity and marketing leaflets). The need for standards to control quality in this area is based more on typographical expertise than on conventional drafting skills.

With the tasks in the drawing office becoming more various so is the capability to do them less restricted. No longer is it the sole province of a draftsman to produce artwork sufficiently legible and accurate to be used in production. CAD has put this capability back into the development and engineering sections who had no previous involvement with documentation. This capability carries with it the responsibility to maintain the same standards. These have been evolved over the years to maximize the interchange of drawings throughout different parts of the same company and between the supplier and the customer, and to minimize misinterpretation. Clarity, unambiguity and user convenience therefore have to be considered as diligently as technical accuracy.

Basic standards required in the drawing office and other areas involved with drawing production are:

1. *Drawing office equipment and materials* (covering the materials and equipment such as drawing paper and sizes of drawing sheets). New standards will be needed for CAD plotters and printers. There are also standards for drawing boards, scales, set squares, reference tables and benches (but, as mentioned above, these are losing their significance with the growth of computer methods).
2. *Drawing office practice* dealing with general principles of line thickness, letter height and style, dimensioning, and tolerancing and geometric tolerancing, and also covering drawing practice for engineering diagrams). The most important reference standards on this work are published as BS308 *Engineering drawing practice*, which has been produced to be in line with several ISO standards, and BS5070 *Drawing practice for engineering diagrams.*
3. *Symbols* (including all facets from railway signalling to electronics). It is particularly appropriate to consider these when introducing a computer-aided system to ensure that a library is created which comprehensively covers all user requirements. Failure to create an acceptable symbols library at the outset can result in a rapidly escalating problem of control and communication. Success in this area can conversely save many hours of drafting time.
4. *Miscellaneous* Surface texture, limits and fits, microfilming and use

of the metric system are only a sample of subjects which may come under this category. The use of microfilming for archiving has been gaining popularity as a means of conserving space and improving access to drawings. BS308 caters for the needs of microfilming in general drawing practice. These are supplemented by BS5536 *Specification for preparation of technical drawings for microfilming*.

All the above can be based on available national standards but it will frequently be necessary to support or implement them by producing one's own selective company standards. There will also be other company standards needed in their own right. A drawing office handbook should be issued to all draughtsmen and must be the 'bible' for rationalizing procedures such as coding, drawing sheet sizes and format, parts listing, standard tolerances, drawing practice and change procedures. The designer will also require access to a catalogue of standard parts, electronic components, fasteners and other hardware. If mass or batch production is involved there will also be a number of standard workshop practices. For example, printed circuit manufacture and assembly and wiring will usually be the subject of particular company codes of practice within the national specifications.

The drawing office handbook

Development procedure generally requires a series of identifiable stages by which progress can be judged. This may include a development or 'bread board' stage when the design is fluid. Within the confines of the company standardization policy new components may be tried and discarded until the design objectives are achieved.

A change of state is introduced after this research period so that manufacturing methods can be considered in more detail. This is an opportune time to compare the design with existing company standards in all their aspects. Standards for material, standard hardware, sizes, tolerances, finishes, performance, environmental withstand, quality, health and safety can all be considered in more detail. The object is to reduce subsequent effort in evaluating new methods, materials or processes and hence improve reliability by reducing reliance on the individual for quality and reliability. Standardization is one way of raising the quality of an individual's efforts to that of the highest member of the team. Control of the design process is a function which is essentially the task and responsibility of the design drawing office. It is here that systems are employed for variety control, manufacturing documentation, drawing issue control, specification of bought-out materials and components, and (of vital importance) the procedures for any changes made at a later stage.

The drawing office handbook is a collection of all the essential specifications and codes of practice required by the draughtsman, based on previous experience and knowledge of the current state of the art. It will contain all the standards as mentioned above as well as a number of equally important administrative procedures which are required for the third stage. This is the release of drawings and documentation to production. At and after this stage the design must be considered as 'frozen'. Drawings at this stage are all on recorded issue and any changes must be made in a strictly controlled manner. Typically the handbook will include:

1. *Drawing office practice* Formats and systems, drawing sheet sizes, classification and coding, preferred sizes, change procedure.
2. *Materials and components* Raw materials, hardware, bought-out components, fasteners, name plates, etc.
3. *Tools and equipment* Drill sizes, standard punching and bending tools, machine capacities.
4. *Production processes* Finishes, codes of practice, e.g. printed circuit manufacture.

The drawing office handbook has parallel equivalents in the development engineering handbook, commercial handbook, quality control handbook and others in similar disciplines.

Purchase specifications

If a product contains parts which are bought-in, then their evaluation and specification have to be considered as part of the original selection process. The purchasing department must be given every opportunity to negotiate favourable terms for price and delivery. This is made more difficult (if not impossible) by specifying a trade name from a single source. Such occurrences unhappily are common: for example, Hoover rather than vacuum cleaner, Paxolin rather than phenolic laminated paper and so on. They can be avoided by attention to the purchase specification and the sources of supply at the design stage. This does not imply that it is necessary to produce purchase specifications running into several pages, but rather a well thought-out description to go on the purchase order which takes maximum advantage of national or international standards and certification schemes.

A classification and coding system can be adopted to ensure that components and materials are identified by an inhouse code and not the supplier's. These procedures, together with an inhouse catalogue of bought-out parts and materials, avoid unnecessary changes being made to drawings as a result of supplier type alterations. Any item can also be multisourced and, as a preference, should be.

It is possible that the responsibility for creating the purchase description is allocated to the same person responsible for cataloguing. This is a common task in a company standards section and with the accumulated expertise the specification can not only be checked for accuracy; it can also be vetted for conformance to standards, both inhouse and national.

Classification and coding

Some very sophisticated coding systems have been created to suit drawings and their associated parts and material content. Attempts have also been made to rationalize these where companies have been asssociated by mergers or takeovers. In many respects the benefits of significant coding have been superseded by the computer. Facilities for sorting and selection no longer have to be built in to the original code. Supplementary coding is often a workable alternative. There are other benefits of a well designed code, however, which do not relate to selection. They include identification, filing and control. Control of variety as a regular function can be aided by the discipline of allocating a code and the opportunity it affords to vet new additions routed down this channel.

Coherence between all the codes adopted in a company should also be sought if possible. It can be a help throughout the organization if a code number can be related to a particular range of documents or parts purely by its shape or significance. All coding should be registered at a central point in the company to avoid duplication.

The value of standards

There are some good examples of effective standardization to be observed in the high street. Marks and Spencer, for example, have produced an image based on high standards matched by their goods and service. The benefits are seen in the consistency obtained in their stores at home and abroad. It is obvious that other stores such as Sainsbury adopt a similar approach. Unfortunately, similar examples in industry are not so easy to quote. One in particular comes to mind, that is Rolls-Royce, who are known to have a corporate approach to the use of its logo, letterhead, vehicle livery, etc. Is it a coincidence that those who have succeeded in standardizing their image have also succeeded in producing a reputation for high quality? Mergers and takeovers confuse the image of cooperatives even further. Not all organizations will see the need to set up a specialist standards section. Alternatively the tasks may have to be spread, maybe across the engineering, production and quality control functions. Three main areas have to be controlled within a manufacturing company to enable essential company standardization to be undertaken:

1. Awareness of national and international standards as they affect the company as a *user* as well as the normally recognized *producer* standards.
2. Specification and control of in-house procedures and codes of practice.
3. Specification of components and materials used in the product.

The value of company standards can be summarized as shown in Table 7.1.

Table 7.1
The value of standards, showing methods which may be adopted

Value	Standardization method
1. Availability of information	Handbooks covering organization and quality control. Parts catalogues, specification manuals.
2. Cooperation and coordination	Standards teams, working groups, compatibility of data.
3. Involvement in international and national standardization	Representation on trade association, national and international committees.
4. Dissemination of information	Access to a variety of standards sources.
5. Quality control of bought-out parts and processes	Classification and coding, accurate specification of established processes and preferred codes of practice.
6. Variety control to maximize investment	Constant surveillance and re-evaluation.

Further reading

Douglas-Woodward, C., *The Story of Standards,* The British Standards Institution, London 1972.

Sanders, T.R.B., *The Aims and Principles of Standardization,* The International Organization for Standardization, Switzerland 1972.

Sullivan, Charles D., *Standards and Standardization, Basic Principles and Applications,* Marcel Dekker, New York 1983.

Verman, L.C., *Standardization, a New Discipline,* Archer, USA 1973.

The following publications are published by or are available from the British Standards Institution, Milton Keynes.

BSI Catalogue (Annual)

BSO *A Standard for Standards*

　　　Part 1 — General Principles of Standardization

　　　Part 2 — BSI and its Committee Procedures

　　　Part 3 — Drafting and Presentation of British Standards

BS5750 *Quality Systems*

　　　Part 1 — Specification for design/development, production, installation and servicing

　　　Part 4 — Guide to the use of BS5750: Part 1

BS9000 *Part 1 — General requirements for a system for electronic components of assessed quality. Specification of basic rules and procedures.*

BSI Handbook 22, *Quality Assurance*

PD3542 *The Operation of a Company Standards Department*

PD6470 *The Management of Design for Economic Production*

PD6489 *Guide to the Preparation of a Company Standards Manual*

PD6495 *IFAN — Guide 1, Methods for Determining the Advantages of (Company) Standardization Projects*

PD6515 *IFAN — Guide 2, Company Use of International Standards The International Certification and Approval Schemes*

8 Statutory Provisions and Obligations

David J. Smith*

In recent years the development of health, safety and liability legislation has had a profound impact on the quality and reliability profession. Firstly the *Consumer Protection Act 1987* has focused attention on the reliability, and hence the safety of goods. Secondly, the *Health and Safety at Work Act 1974*, together with the more recent Notification of Installation Handling Hazardous Substances (NIHHS) and Control of Industrial Major Accident Hazards (CIMAH) regulations, (also dealt with in this chapter) have provided a similar impetus in the design of reliable process plant. Before describing the effects of the latter it will be useful to give a brief outline of the Health and Safety Executive and the way in which it operates.

The Health and Safety Executive

The Health and Safety Executive (HSE) was set up by the UK Government under the authority of the *Health and Safety at Work Act 1974*. It is administered through the Department of Employment. The HSE is the executive and operational branch of the Health and Safety

* Copyright of this chapter remains with the author.

Commission (HSC) and it carries out the HSC's policy. The HSE is largely made up of various inspectorates, which operate within the civil service structure.

The HSE headquarters develops policy and provides specialist services; there are 21 area offices, each of which manages direct enforcement activities in its specific geographical area. To deal with any matters affecting whole industries the HSE has set up a number of National Industry Groups (NIGs). A principal inspector in one of the 21 areas is responsible for the HSE participation in each NIG and is the HSE specialist for that industry. General enforcement duties such as hygiene, machine guards, working conditions, etc., are mostly handled by factory inspectors.

The design of plant and its standards of operation, maintenance and repair are monitored by factory inspectors to ensure that existing and proposed installations will be fit for their intended purpose and properly operated. Consideration of any hazards affecting either employees or the public is carried out by specialist inspectors or by specialists from the Major Hazards Advisory Unit.

The plant operator is required to establish, by using formal hazard assessment techniques, the possible ways in which the plant could fail and the nature and extent of any consequences for both the public and employees. If any of these failures is likely to cause death, multiple injury or major damage, the probability of that event must be carefully assessed in order to estimate the magnitude of the risk.

The HSE use these hazard assessments to establish what are known as consultation zones, which are areas surrounding hazardous installations. Planning authorities are required to consult with the HSE when considering applications for development within them.

The HSE is well aware that zero risk (in other words absolute safety) is an unrealistic objective and in fact the law states that industrial activities shall be without risk to health, safety and welfare 'as far as is reasonably practicable'. The test of reasonable practicability ensures that the cost of reducing risk is weighed against the benefits to both public and employees.

The Health and Safety at Work Act 1974

Modern safety legislation is primarily embodied in the *Health and Safety at Work Act*. Although it can hardly be regarded as recent, it is extremely important and imposes responsibilities on everyone. It was drafted as enabling legislation to ensure that the health, safety and welfare of all is not adversely affected by work activities.

Section 1 of the Act sets out the general duties for every employer to ensure, as far as is reasonably practicable, the health, safety and welfare at work of all his employees.

Section 2 goes into detail as to how the employer can discharge these duties.

Section 3 establishes the duty of every employer to conduct his undertaking so as not to affect adversely the health and safety of persons not in his employment.

Section 6 of this Act is important in that it imposes strict liability in respect of articles produced for use at work, although the *Consumer Protection Act* extends this to all areas. It is very wide and embraces designers, manufacturers, suppliers, hirers and employers of industrial plant and equipment. We are now dealing with criminal law: failure to observe the duties laid down in the Act is punishable by fine or imprisonment. Claims for compensation are still dealt with in civil law.

Other sections elaborate on employers' and employees' duties in various respects.

The main duties are to:

- Design and construct products without risk to health or safety.
- Provide adequate information to the user for safe operation.
- Carry out research to discover and eliminate risks.
- Make positive tests to evaluate risks and hazards.
- Carry out tests to ensure that the product is inherently safe.
- Use safe methods of installation. To use safe (proven) substances and materials.

The main concessions are:

- It is a defence that a product has been used without regard to the relevant information supplied by the designer.
- It is a defence that the design was carried out on the basis of a written undertaking by the purchaser to take specified steps sufficient to ensure the safe use of the item.
- One's duty is restricted to matters within one's control.
- One is not required to repeat tests upon which it is reasonable to rely.

Basically everyone concerned in the design and provision of an article is responsible for it. Directors and managers are held responsible for the designs and manufactured articles of their companies and are expected to take steps to assure safety in their products. Employees are also responsible. The 'buck' cannot be passed in either direction.

Industrial hazards

Since the 1960s, developments in the process industries have resulted in large quantities of noxious and flammable substances being stored and transmitted in locations that could, in the event of an incident, affect the public. Society is becoming increasingly aware of these hazards as a result of such major incidents as:

- Flixborough (UK) 1974: 28 deaths due to an explosion involving cyclohexane.
- Beek (The Netherlands) 1975: 14 deaths due to propylene.
- Seveso (Italy) 1976: Unknown number of casualties due to a release of dioxin.
- San Carlos Holiday Camp 1978: About 150 deaths due to a propylene tanker.
- Bhopal (India) 1984: Over 2000 deaths due to a release of methyl isocyanate.
- Chernobyl (USSR) 1986: Unknown number of casualties due to the melt down of a nuclear reactor.
- Piper Alpha (UK) 1988: 167 deaths due to fire on an offshore platform.

Following the Flixborough disaster the HSC (Health and Safety Commission) set up the Advisory Committee on Major Hazards (ACMH) which made various recommendations concerning notification of hazards.

Owing to a general lack of formal controls within the EC, a draft European Directive was issued in 1980. Delays in obtaining agreement resulted in this not being implemented until September 1984. The HSC introduced in January 1983 the Notification of Installation Handling Hazardous Substances (NIHHS) regulations. These require the identification of hazardous installations and assessments of risks and consequences.

The EC regulations (1984) are implemented in the UK as the CIMAH (Control of Industrial Major Accident Hazards) regulations 1984 and are concerned both with people and the environment, covering processes and the storage of dangerous substances. A total of 178 substances are listed, together with quantities which are notifiable. In these cases the regulations call for the preparation of a safety case, which involves a significant hazard and operability study and a probabilistic risk assessment. The purpose of the safety case is to demonstrate either that a particular consequence is relatively minor or that the probability of its occurrence is extremely small. It is also required to describe adequate emergency procedures in the event of an incident. The latest date for the submission of all safety cases was 8 July 1989 except for new installations where a safety case is required three months prior to bringing on site any hazardous materials.

It follows that if the reliability of a particular piece of equipment is pertinent to the safety of a process or storage site, then the failure mode analysis becomes a vital part of the hazard study.

Product liability

Product liability is the liability of a supplier, designer or manufacturer to the customer for injury or loss resulting from a defect in that product. There are reasons why it has recently become the focus of attention. The first is the publication, in July 1985, of a directive by the European Community, and the second is the wave of actions under United States Law resulting in spectacular awards for claims involving death or injury. By 1984, sums awarded resulting from court proceedings often reached $1,000,000. Changes in the United Kingdom became inevitable and the *Consumer Protection Act* reinforces the application of strict liability. It is necessary, therefore, to review the legal position.

The general law

Contract Law
This is largely governed by the *Sale of Goods Act 1979* which requires that goods are of merchantable quality and are reasonably fit for the purpose intended. Privity of Contract exists between the buyer and the seller which means that only the buyer has any remedy for injury or loss and then only against the seller, although the cascade effect of each party suing, in turn, the other would offset this. However, exclusion clauses are void for consumer contracts. This means that conditions excluding the seller from liability would be void in law.

Note that a contract does not have to be in writing and that a sale, in this context, implies the existence of a contract.

Common Law

The relevant area of common law is that relating to the Tort of Negligence, for which damages can be made. Everyone has a duty of care to his neighbour, in law, and failure to exercise reasonable precautions with regard to one's skill, knowledge and the circumstances involved constitutes a breach of that care. A claim for damages for common law negligence is, therefore, open to anyone and not restricted as in Privy of Contract. On the other hand, the onus is with the plaintiff to prove negligence which requires him to prove that:

- The product was defective.
- The defect was the cause of the injury.
- This was foreseeable and that the plaintiff failed in his duty of care.

Statute Law

The main Acts relevant to this area are:

(a) *Sale of Goods Act 1979*
  - Goods must be of Merchantable Quality.
  - Goods must be fit for the purpose.
(b) *Unfair Contract Terms Act 1977*
  - Exclusion of personal injury liability is void.
  - Exclusion of damage liability only if reasonable.
(c) *Consumer Protection Act 1987*
  - Imposes strict liability.
  - Replaces the *Consumer Safety Act 1978*.
(d) *Health and Safety at Work Act 1974* Section 6 (see above)

In summary the situation prior to the *Consumer Protection Act 1987* involved a form of strict liability but:

- Privity of Contract excludes third-parties in contract claims.
- The onus is to prove negligence unless the loss results from a breach of contract.
- Exclusion clauses involving death and personal injury are void.

Strict liability

Concept

The concept of strict liability hinges on the idea that liability exists for no other reason than the mere existence of a defect. No breach of contract or act of negligence is required in order to incur responsibility and a manufacturer will be liable for compensation if his product causes injury.

Defects

A defect, for the purposes of liability, includes:
(a) Manufacturing
   - Presence of impurities or foreign bodies.
   - Fault or failure due to manufacturing or installation.
(b) Design
   - Product not fit for the purpose stated.
   - Inherent safety hazard in the design.
(c) Documentation
   - Lack of necessary warnings.
   - Inadequate or incorrect operating and maintenance instructions, resulting in a hazard.

The Consumer Protection Act 1987

Background

In 1985, after nine years of discussion, the European Community adopted a directive on product liability and member states were required to put this into effect before the end of July 1988. The English and Scottish Law Commissions each produced reports in 1977 and a Royal Commission document (*The Pearson Report*) was published in 1978. All of these reports recommended forms of strict liability.

The Consumer Protection Bill resulted in the *Consumer Protection Act 1987*, which establishes strict liability as already described above.

Provisions of the Act

The Act provides that a producer (and this includes manufacturers, those who import from outside the EEC and retailers of 'own brands') will be liable for damage caused wholly or partly by defective products which include goods, components and materials but exclude unprocessed agricultural produce. Defective is defined as not providing such safety as people are generally entitled to expect, taking into account the manner of marketing, instructions for use, the likely uses and the time at which the product was supplied. Death, personal injury and damage (other than to the product) exceeding £275 are included. The consumer must show that the defect caused the damage but no longer has the onus of proving negligence. Defences include:

- The state of scientific and technical knowledge at the time was such that the producer could not be expected to have discovered the defect. (This is known as the 'development risks' defence.)
- The defect results from the product complying with the law.
- The producer did not supply the product.
- The defect was not present when the product was supplied by the manufacturer.
- The product was not supplied in the course of business.
- The product was in fact a component part in the manufacture of a further product and the defect was not due to this component.

In addition the producer's liability may be reduced by the user's contributory negligence. Further, unlike the privity limitation imposed by contract law, any consumer is covered in addition to the original purchaser.

The Act sets out a general safety requirement for consumer goods and applies it to anyone who supplies goods which are not reasonably safe having regard to the circumstances pertaining. These include published safety standards, the cost of making goods safe and whether or not the goods are new.

Insurance

The effects of product liability on insurance are:

- An increase in the number of claims.
- Higher premiums.
- The creation of separate product liability policies.
- Involvement of insurance companies in defining quality and reliability standards and procedures.
- Contracts requiring the designer to insure the customer against genuine and frivolous consumer claims.

Some critical areas:

- All risks: This only means all risks specified in the policy. It is important to check that one's requirements are met by the policy.
- Comprehensive: Essentially means the same as the above.
- Disclosure: The policyholder is bound to disclose any information relevant to the risk. Failure to do so, whether asked for or not, can invalidate a claim. The test of what should be disclosed is described as 'anything the prudent insurer should know'.
- Exclusions: The *Unfair Contract Terms Act, 1977* does not apply to

insurance, so one should read and negotiate accordingly. For example, defects related to design could be excluded and this would considerably weaken a policy from the product liability standpoint.
● Prompt notification of claims.

Areas of cover
Premiums are usually expressed as a percentage of turnover and cover is divided into three areas:

1. Product liability cover against claims for personal injury or loss.
2. Product guarantee: cover against the expenses of warranty/repair.
3. Product recall: cover against the expenses of recall.

Product recall

Types of recall
A design defect causing a potential hazard to life, health or safety may become evident when a number of products are already in use. It may then become necessary to recall, for replacement or modification, a batch of items, some of which may be spread throughout the chain of distribution. The recall may vary in the degree of urgency depending on whether the hazard is to life, health or merely reputation. A hazard which could reasonably be thought to endanger life, or to create a serious health hazard, should be treated as an emergency recall procedure. Where less critical risks involving minor health and safety hazards are discovered a slightly less urgent approach may suffice. A third category, operated at the vendor's discretion, applies to defects causing little or no personal hazard and where only reputation is at risk.

If it becomes necessary to implement a recall the extent will be determined by the nature of the defect. It might involve every user (in the worst case) or perhaps only a specific batch of items. In some cases the modification may be possible in the field but in others physical return of the item will be required. In any case a full evaluation of the hazard must be made and a report prepared.

Implementing the recall
One person, usually the quality manager, must be responsible for the handling of the recall and he or she must be directly responsible to the managing director or chief executive. The first task is to prepare, if

appropriate, a hazard notice in order to warn those likely to be exposed to the risk. Circulation may involve individual customers (when traceable), the field service staff, distributors or even the news media. It will contain sufficient information to describe the nature of the hazard and the precautions to be taken. Instructions for returning the defective item can be included, preferably with a prepaid return card. Small items can be returned with the card whereas large ones, or products to be modified in the field, will be retained while arrangements are made.

Where products were all dispatched to known customers, a comparison of returns with output records will enable a 100 per cent check to be made on the coverage. Where products have been dispatched in batches to wholesalers or retail outlets the task is not so easy and the quantity of returns can only be compared with a known output, perhaps by area. Individual users cannot then be traced with 100 per cent certainty. Where customers have completed and returned record cards after purchase the effectiveness of the recall is improved.

After the recall exercise has been completed a major investigation into the causes of the defect must be made and the results progressed through the company's quality and reliability programme. Causes could include insufficient:

- test hours;
- test coverage;
- information sought on materials;
- industrial engineering of the product prior to manufacture;
- production testing;
- field/user trails.

The role of quality management

It has to be said that the mere practice of quality and reliability techniques alone does not release one from the obligations of the preceding legislation. Nor does it mitigate one's liability in the event of claims involving death or personal injury. Nevertheless, in view of the high cost and consequences of failure, the cost of quality and reliability efforts is nearly always repaid by a reduction in warranty and other failure-related costs.

Further reading

Smith, David J., *Reliability and Maintainability in Perspective* 3rd edn, Macmillan, London 1988.

9 Quality Control of Design

Robin Plummer

Chapter 6 made clear the importance of evaluating comprehensively the design objectives to determine the extent of their influence on the fitness of the product or service for its intended purpose. Once these objectives have been decided it is important to conduct design in a way which ensures that the result complies with the declared design objectives, and with nothing else. It is also important to be able to show evidence that the design has been thus conducted. This evidence is the visible assurance of quality, or quality assurance.

This chapter deals with monitoring the design activity and discusses the quality control and quality assurance of design.

Definitions

The process or activity of design will be referred to simply as design, and the inputs to the process and outputs from the process will be referred to as design inputs and design outputs.

Quality assurance of design is a concept which is at least as difficult for some people to grasp as that of applying the principles of quality management to the service industry. The concept of quality assurance of design is, in fact, remarkably simple. Essentially, the quality assurance of design is derived by ensuring that all foreseeable design objectives are considered for their influence on fitness for purpose, then using them appropriately as design inputs, and that the design output, the design itself, conforms to the input design objectives.

Quality assurance of design is not an attempt to stifle the flair or initiative of designers. Neither is it an attempt to manipulate the skills of designers into designing something that they would not naturally design. Nor is it an attempt to purloin the creative ideas and original thought of designers, and to plagiarize them under a different guise. All of these concerns are voiced continually by designers in departments with which the author speaks.

Quality assurance of design is derived from, firstly setting a boundary around the design, and then ensuring that only permitted inputs are allowed into the design and that only permitted outputs are allowed out. Subject to this, the designers are allowed to do just about anything they please (but see below) within the boundary as long as the interface requirements across the boundary (i.e. the design inputs and outputs) are complied with.

In practical terms, this is equivalent to shutting a designer in a room with all the facilities and equipment that he needs, handing him a statement of what needs to be designed and broadly how it is to be designed, and then only letting out of the room an output which complies with the original statement. What the designer does while he is in the room, what flair and initiative he uses, whether he designs a moon rocket using a computer or an abacus is entirely up to him.

Design teams

A design team is a group of interested parties to the design, each of which must make a clear statement of the design inputs that it requires to be fulfilled. The group of interested parties should consist, as a minimum, of representatives of:

1. The ultimate users of the product or service to be designed.
2. The manufacturers or developers of the product or service.
3. The project managers who are to implement the overall project.
4. The quality assurance department.
5. Staff who are to oversee the design work.

6. The designers themselves.

Each of these interested parties has different requirements of the design and therefore has different design inputs.

The end user's inputs may include a specification which is as limited as a bare outline of the end product or service that is required. Alternatively, it may be as comprehensive as a full specification of the practical capability of the end product or service, complete with tolerances, choice of materials, choice of contractors to do the design work or to implement the design, costs limits, time limits, penalty clauses, etc.

The manufacturers or developers of the product or service will include in their design input a statement of what is currently or historically capable of being manufactured, or of the known limits to service capability. These known limits may include simple practical hurdles such as the limit to the human resources available for the foreseeable future. The manufacturer's design input may develop, during discussion, to include advice if the design appears to be veering into territory which is unachievable or unknown in manufacturing or service provision. Remember the Japanese company that sends its trainee designers into manufacturing for 2 years during the 6 years of training before ever they become designers. Designers still design products and services which manufacturers or field staff cannot produce or deliver!

From the project managers who are to implement the overall project, (whether solely the design, or more) the design input must include a request for estimates of manning levels, logistics and equipment required, and a statement of what the natural breaks or milestones in the design project are, so that project management meetings can be planned appropriately.

The quality assurance department will provide in its design input a statement of the quality assurance which it will expect to be derived from the design project; a statement of the form that the design architecture will follow; a statement of the design methodologies which must be followed; and a statement of the form that quality assurance audits and reports will take together with mechanisms, authorities and responsibilities for implementing corrective action.

Design overseers must include in their design inputs a statement of the day-to-day supervisory techniques that they expect to employ, and the form of the outputs that they expect to have to check.

The designers themselves will request in their design input a statement of what is required to be designed.

Some of the data and logistics provided by some of the design team members will naturally be expected by others of the team. Some design inputs may come as a surprise to some team members. Some design inputs will actually conflict with other inputs, and resolution or compromise of that conflict will be necessary as a very high priority. Indeed, resolution or compromise of conflict of interest is one of the prime reasons why the design team exists at all.

An interesting conclusion to be drawn is that all the team members have both express and implied requirements of the design, and that it is not any one team member, such as the end user, who has an overriding say in the inputs to the design.

Design interfaces

The majority of quality defects recorded in total quality management systems occur at the interfaces between departments. This is believed to be because managers and staff tend to think in terms of department rather than in terms of process. As a consequence, each department beavers busily away, paying scant regard to who the real customer is, and having only a vague idea of what the customer really wants. In many departments, an attitude is struck, after long years of acceptance that cooperation between departments is an impossibility, that there is no point in even attempting to ask what other departments really want, because nobody is listening. Not surprisingly, when a department comes to interface with other departments in the same process, the product fails (up to 40 per cent of the time in service industries!) to meet the customer's requirements. The customer would have cause for concern if this kind of muddle caused his parachute to fail to open, but possibly a little difficulty in pressing his case.

The same principle is often true of interfaces between design modules which are to be integrated into one overall design. The government of one European country was so corrupt at a time before the 1939-45 war, that orders to purchase new rifles for the army led to a statement being issued which confirmed the purchase, but the money for purchase being pocketed by corrupt officials. When, at a later date, war was imminent, an order was issued to purchase ammunition for the allegedly current rifles, large numbers of infantrymen found themselves in the front line with rifles and bullets which were simply incompatible.

It should come as no surprise, however, that the solution to design interface problems is the same as that for design inputs and outputs, but on a much smaller scale. What has to be done is that each design module has to have functions ascribed to it. Once the functions of all the modules have been chosen, a decision has to be made for each module about which other modules it must interface with. The interface requirements for a given module constitute the inputs and outputs for that module. It is these interface requirements that specify what the module must do. As long as the interface requirements between the modules continue to be complied with, the designer is free to do almost anything he wants (but see later) inside the module in order to achieve the interface requirements.

Design architecture

A design architecture is a hierarchy of steps, of which the most significant in terms of quality is at the top.

The implementation of these steps, conducted from the top downwards, ensures that all the stages of design are completed in the correct order and that each stage is properly completed before proceeding to the next one. Following a design architecture in this fashion results in the realization of, what is known as, stepwise decomposition. Stepwise decomposition can be viewed as being synonymous with the scientific method: i.e. that if each step in a process is conducted correctly, then any subsequent step founded upon it will be traceable back to the origins of the process.

The topmost step in any design architecture is the concept of the product or service to be realized. An example is a means of transport. The first step down is a decomposition of the concept, generally into two or three major divisions, each of which is still very much an idea rather than a realization, but each of which is a stand-alone entity in its own right. Examples are the power unit, the means of power transmission and the rigidity (i.e. structure).

The next step down is a decomposition of each of the two or three major divisions into practical functions that must later be realized. It is probable that some of the functions will need to interface with each other in order for each one to be able to execute its own functions. Examples are the fuel induction system, the system of energy conversion from heat into motion within the power unit, and the control mechanism for timing and regulating the energy conversion process.

The next step down is a decomposition of the functions into blocks of practical functionality, each of which has to interface with other blocks in order for it to be able to execute its own function. Examples are the camshafts and associated equipment which open and close the valves at the correct angles in the engine's cycle.

The next step down decomposes the blocks into modules, each of a size that can be easily managed in terms of project or design management. Each of these modules interfaces with other modules. For example, the cam followers which interact with the camshaft and, either the pushrods or the valves. The advantage of modularity is that as long as the interface requirements continue to be fulfilled, what happens inside the module in order to fulfil the interface requirements is almost irrelevant. The effect of this is that if an ingenious designer discovers a new and more efficient way of realizing the interface requirements, for example, by using less energy or less software processing time, then the module can be replaced in its entirety by an updated module and no liability accrues, as long as the interface requirements continue to be fulfilled.

One remarkable aspect of stepwise decomposition and the modular approach is the surprisingly low level in the decomposition that is reached before the design team needs to commit to, for example, the type of power unit to be used, or the proportion of vehicle functions that are to be done by purely mechanical or by electronic and software means.

There is scope for monitoring progress between each of the steps in the design architecture. This measurement must be undertaken to ensure that the output from each step satisfies the requirements that were the inputs to the step. If the output does not satisfy the input requirements for that particular decomposition, then the design team must return to the inputs to that step, and design again until the output does satisfy the input requirements.

If it should prove that the input requirements themselves were unreasonable or unrealizable, or diverge from the requirements, then the output of the step must be fed back to earlier and earlier stages in the architecture, until the cause of the divergence from requirements becomes clear.

The cause can then of course be corrected. Designers and the design team should not baulk at returning to steps in the decomposition which were long since written off as correct, if evidence arises that an erroneous decomposition was made. Remember, not for the first time, how rapidly the costs of corrective action rise with each advancing step in the decomposition of a design.

The design architecture should exist in a clear and unequivocal written statement, as part of the company's declared quality management system.

In a company which designs variants upon a basic theme, the design architecture will be only slightly project dependent, towards the lower steps of the architecture. Design reviews and audits can then be few since the architecture will have been followed many times and will be familiar to most design team members.

In a company where a wide diversity of products or services is designed, then naturally the design architecture will be project dependent at a much earlier stage in the decomposition. In this case design reviews and audits will need to be greater in number and more searching in order to preempt potential design flaws due to the lesser familiarity with the lower stages of the design architecture.

Design methodology

Design methodology is a statement of the constraints placed upon the design team. The constraints should be as few as possible and should not be regarded as negative or repressive of the designer's natural flair and initiative. On the contrary. The design methodology is there to assist the designers by:

1. Relieving them of certain burdensome and unproductive decisions. Examples are the type of metal to use, what level of personnel to request for authorization, which particular responsible manager to delegate a defect report to, which temporary software datastore to use.
2. Allowing automatic or computerized equipment to take away from the designer distracting tasks. Examples are traceability, such as when part of the software refers to prescribed routines by referring to computer-generated labels, rather than to the line number of the software at which the prescribed routine begins, which changes as the software develops.
3. Guiding the designer in the use of design techniques which are part of an overall strategy within the company. Designers do brilliant work which they steadfastly refuse to document. (Yes, it

still happens!) They subsequently leave the company. How much use are their piles of computer readouts to anyone, if no one has a clue how or why they designed in a particular way, or how to integrate it with other piles of design data. Further, if good designs are implemented but the designers leave, then the maintenance department cannot be expected to know how to work their way through a design technique with which they are totally unfamiliar, in order to maintain it. They might be able to, but the quality-related costs mount, as ever.

A company's design methodology should exist in a clear and unequivocal written statement, as part of the company's declared quality management system. Where the design of any step in the stepwise decomposition fails to comply with the design methodology (quite apart from failing to satisfy the design inputs to that particular step), then a defect report must be issued and the reasons for the failure discovered.

If it proves that the designer simply failed to abide by the design methodology, then the solution to the defect report should record that fact, in case any other designers fail to abide by the methodology. This gives the quality assurance department an opportunity to spot a trend of designers failing to abide by the design methodology, and thereafter seek out any weaknesses in the systematic use of the methodology.

Alternatively, if it proves that design techniques have changed, and that the design methodology has not kept up to date with these changes, then the defect report will give the quality assurance department an opportunity to update the statement of methodology. It might be that a consequence of following the design methodology to the letter results in a design which was not fit for purpose. Put another way, diligent quality assured design can produce avenues of approach which are subsequently found to be futile.

The futile approaches should also be recorded when updating the design methodology, in order to prevent future designers from unwittingly wasting resources by going in the same direction when the same design input arises another time. How many successive and similar designs have each been managed by a different design team, none of whose predecessors wrote down one word of what they did or why, or of the mistakes they made, in order to prevent future design teams from simply reinventing the wheel for each new design? Another quality-related cost!

Design review

Supervision

Supervision of design is basically the task of ensuring that the design architecture and methodology are being followed on a daily basis, and of assisting the designers to keep the customer requirements (i.e. the design inputs) in mind by having someone with whom to share their ideas. Supervisors therefore need familiarity with the architecture and methodology, and must be experienced both in design and, preferably, the design in hand.

In order to ensure compliance by the designers with the architecture and the methodology, supervisors will seek evidence. Common methods of providing evidence which supervisors can check on a daily basis are checklists on which the designers record the execution of activities which must be conducted, and also the results of those activities. In observing the checklists, supervisors must record the number of observations made, and also the number and type of deficiencies found, even if the deficiencies are put right on the spot. This latter information is important in assessing trends of deficiencies and is a source of vital defect information which is very often lost. The layout of computer keyboards is continually under review to take into consideration the occurrences of dangerous keys being struck erroneously owing to their proximity to desired keys. If computer operators never reported these occurrences, believing them to be simply their own lack of dexterity, then no improvement would be possible and hideous errors would continue to be made.

Desk checks

A desk check is a check made on a piece of design by another designer or other suitably qualified person. An independent person is chosen, firstly to make certain that a check will actually be conducted and, secondly, to help to dectect and prevent witting or unwitting bias on the part of the designer who performed the design. For this second reason, the contemporary designer does not have to be engaged upon the same design project, but must be on work which is independent of the piece to be checked. This independence is to assist the impartiality of the desk check. The contemporary designer's purpose is to check that the piece of design complies with its design inputs. Desk checks are one of the milestone events in both the project management and the quality management of the design. The results of desk checks must be recorded. Deficiencies found must be included in the result, even if they are put right on the spot for the same reason as previously stated. The desk check results will form part of the quality assurance evidence of the design, and will be observed by the design supervisor routinely.

Peer group review

Peer group review is self explanatory. It is a system of review conducted by a group of the designer's peers. The group of peers might be some or all of the design team. The purpose of peer group review is to check formally, at milestones in the design process, that the design output complies with the design inputs. In other words, that the designer has designed what he set out to design.

In general terms, a formal meeting is convened at which a stage of design is to be reviewed. Prior to the meeting, and at a sufficient number of days' notice, all the prospective participants at the meeting are provided with a copy of the design inputs, architecture, methodology and a copy of the design output. The peers then take an appropriate length of time to compare, in isolation from one another, the design output with the design inputs. Each then logs anything which in his opinion constitutes a departure from the design requirements. At the peer group review meeting itself, each of the peers has an opportunity to state the places in the design which he considers to be a departure from requirement. Short discussion among the peer group is permitted in order to decide whether or not it is in fact a departure. If a decision can be reached very quickly, then that decision is recorded and the group passes on to the next departure. If a decision cannot be reached quickly as to the validity of the observation, then the observation is recorded for the designer to take away and correct at his leisure, or within a deadline set by the peer group.

The purpose of the peer group review is error detection, not error correction. It is vital that this be borne continually in mind, otherwise the impact and brevity of peer group reviews will be lost and there is a real danger of them becoming just another talking shop.

Documentation change and configuration control (DCCC)

This wordy title, abbreviated to DCCC, roundly describes the activity of keeping under control any and all information about the design which is capable of being modified.

The term document is here defined as a hard or soft copy, the information on which is capable of being modified.

Documentation is here defined as the act of documenting (i.e. the act of subjecting to control) information capable of being modified. This act consists of ascribing some form of identification to each different piece of information.

Change is defined as the process of updating the identification each time the information contained in the document is modified.

Configuration is the term used to refer to one realization of a design, as distinct from the realization of any preceding or succeeding version of the same design, or a different realization of the same design.

Control comprises essentially two things. One thing is ensuring that all separate information or designs, and all the different versions or realizations of the same information or designs are separately identified. The other thing is ensuring that the correct version, and only the correct version, of each piece of information or design is at the correct operating point within the process at all times.

Documentation change is so closely allied to configuration control that it is pointless to treat them separately. Not surprisingly, they are very often managed within the same department in many companies.

When a document or configuration (be it the realization of a product or service) exists, it must have ascribed to it a form of identification. This identification may be as simple as a colour, or it may be as complex as a long alphanumeric identifier. The complexity of the identification number, needless to say, depends upon the complexity of the system or process of which it is a part. The overriding consideration, however, is that the document or configuration must be identified according to the interface requirements that it must fulfil and to the manner in which it fulfils them.

The following example illustrates the principles of DCCC.

A printed circuit board is to be used in the assembly of a large electronic system. The board is given an identification number:

123456

The first configuration of the board is given an identification number often called the issue state:

1

The first modification to the configuration is given an identification letter often called the revision state:

A

The current configuration of the board is thus:

123456   1   A

During development work on the board, at a time before the board is released into production, each consecutive modification by the designers between successive design reviews is given a consecutive revision state. Thus:

123456   1   B

At the design review, the configuration is accepted. The configuration number is incremented and the revision state is dropped. Thus:

123456   2

The board enters production under this number. It is of no consequence that the first time anybody outside the design department sees the board the issue state is not number 1. What is important is that the configuration is controlled. A large number of design reviews may have reesulted in the configuration control number being 12 or 53 before the board sees the light of day. (If this were the case, one would be tempted to question the design procedures and the design department's ability to comply with them!)

Interchangeability
An interchangeable redesign gives a modification which results in a board intended to replace all existing issues for future development. Additionally, the resulting board will replace the existing issue without altering the interface requirements. Lastly, the latest existing issue may, but need not necessarily replace the resulting board. This is the rule of interchangeability. Thus:

123456   3   A

Replacement
A replacement redesign results in wider ranging modifications to the

system. The interface requirements are changed. The newly designed board must now comply with the new set of interface requirements. If the new board cannot satisfy the rule on interchangeability, that is that the latest existing issue state and the new board are to be developed separately, or the new board cannot replace the old one, then a new board number is ascribed. This is the rule on replacement. Thus:

123457   1

Administration

Exactly the same principles apply to the control of documents, quality management documents, specifications, software releases, etc., without exception.

A central office usually manages this control. When new configurations are issued, mechanisms are brought to bear for ensuring that the correct configuration and only the correct configuration of documents or designs remain at the point of operation. These mechanisms depend upon the company demographics, the sensitivity or classification of the information and upon the criticality of the need for withdrawal from the point of operation of succeeded issues. An outline of a change system includes an index in each document of the current issue states of all the documents and configurations contained in the relevant document; a statement associated with the index of what the change to the information was that motivated the documentation change in the first place; a system of change request forms and a hierarchy of granting authorities; a system of 'return receipts' to provide evidence that new configurations have been properly instituted at the point of operation and that superseded configurations have indeed been withdrawn from the point of operation. Careful design of the quality management system will result in the most appropriate system to employ.

There is more on this subject in Chapter 10.

Conclusion

Most of this chapter on quality control and quality assurance of design describes the execution of activities which appear to be quite removed from quality control and assurance. The execution of activities sometimes thought to be 'pure' quality control or quality assurance occupy only a small percentage of this chapter. The conclusion to be drawn, quite correctly, from this is that the 'quality department' cannot shake a magic powder on to the design and make it a 'quality design'. Quality has to be designed in from the very beginning and not rubbed in by magic at the end.

All that the quality management department is doing is to ensure that past acquired knowledge of good ideas is followed and that previously experienced bad ideas are not repeated. The quality department has to ensure that a commonsense top-down approach to design is followed, with sufficient checks in place and adhered to. Results must be collated and acted upon effectively. Finally, of course, there must be evidence that all of this has taken place.

10 Control of Engineering Changes and Design Modifications

Dennis Lock

The concept of an engineering task that proceeds from initial concept to fulfilment without any change *en route* is a Utopian dream unlikely ever to be encountered in real life. Engineering changes can occur at any stage during a design project, and it is well known that modifications can extend right through the production life of manufactured products. Whilst the reason for introducing any particular change might be seen as compelling, it is essential that formal management procedures are followed to consider and implement all proposals if quality is to be safeguarded. This chapter outlines procedures that have been proven in many engineering companies for dealing with requests to change a design or to deviate from the instructions contained in authorized manufacturing drawings. Related procedures for updating documents and for recording build states are also described.

The framework of control

The change committee
A proposed engineering change or other modification may have

influence on commercial, technical or quality matters well beyond the awareness or competence of its originator. For that reason it is prudent, and usual practice, to identify those managers or other suitably qualified individuals whose consideration and approval should be sought whenever a change is requested. These individuals, when brought together, make up a body which is typically known as a change committee.

The composition of a change committee at any particular sitting will depend to some extent on the stage of progress reached in the work and on the nature of the change. Usually the committee comprises an essential core, supplemented by specialists who are coopted as necessary (the purchasing manager, for example). Apart from these occasional specialists, the essential elements of a change committee comprise the people or organizations listed below.

The design authority

It is essential that responsibility for technical design and performance is vested unambiguously in one place, recognizable as the design authority both within and outside the company. The design authority may be personified by the chief engineer, an appointed project manager, or a senior specialist engineer or consultant. This person is responsible for seeing that the technical aspects of any proposed change are considered carefully for its effects on performance, safety and reliability. Where the product concerned is one of several or many being manufactured, the question of interchangeability of the product and of its component parts must also be considered.

The inspecting authority

Within many company organizations the inspecting authority may be the chief inspector or quality assurance manager.

For some government contracts, and for other work where public safety is a special factor (such as in aviation), the inspecting authority might be an external inspectorate. It is common for such an external inspectorate to delegate its authority, under supervision, to the company's own quality manager or chief inspector.

Whatever the arrangement, it is vital that the company's own inspecting authority does not report within the line authority of the design or manufacturing organization. It should, instead, report directly to higher management. This reporting structure, in theory at least, means that the company's own inspecting authority is able to reach its quality decisions independently, and implement them. There must be no question of undue pressure when quality or safety matters appear to be at odds with commercial or production commitments. The role of the inspecting authority must never be compromised.

The commercial authority
Changes typically pose a threat to authorized budgets and to planned progress.

Changes requested by the customer for a project or major product will probably provide the basis for negotiating small contract changes (especially concerning price and delivery). A contracts manager or similarly qualified person should be available to consider such questions, with the background support of planners and cost engineers or estimators.

The manufacturing authority
The manufacturing authority (typically represented by a senior production manager) will need to consider the effects of design changes likely to affect existing stocks, work-in-progress, or production methods and forward scheduling. Some changes could cause existing stocks or work-in-progress to be scrapped. Other changes might call for production techniques that are more difficult and expensive than those previously envisaged, undesirable for other reasons, or even beyond the company's existing capabilities.

Where the product is being manufactured in batches, or as a continuous process, the manufacturing authority's agreement should be obtained regarding the point at which the change can be introduced into the production schedules (known as the point of embodiment). In those cases where the change is meant to remove a hazard, so that immediate (possibly retrospective) action is indicated, the manufacturing authority would obviously not be allowed to dictate the point of embodiment.

Change coordination
A less senior, but none the less essential member of the change management team is the change coordinator. This is a person who can be given responsibility for following every change request through to ensure that the authorized actions and their associated documentation revisions do in fact take place. This coordinator might be a project coordinating engineer, a technical clerk, or some other suitable member of the engineering department.

A register forms the centre of the coordinator's activity. Every new change request, from whatever source, should be described on a standard pro forma that is presented initially to the coordinator for serial numbering and entry in the register. A typical pro forma is shown in Figure 10.1. Thereafter, the coordinator is responsible for placing the change before the committee, and for all follow-up action.

Good practice requires that committee members are given copies of each change request in sufficient time to gather facts concerning the likely effects of the change and discuss these within their own departments. The work of the committee is then made easier and more effective, since all members should come to the meeting fully prepared to discuss each issue.

Change committee meetings may be held on a regular basis, their frequency depending on the number of changes occurring and on the total duration of the project. *Ad hoc* meetings may be justified to consider urgent changes. At all events, the consideration of changes must be coordinated and scheduled to avoid undue delays.

The coordinator will usually be expected to follow the progress of each change request through all stages, ensuring that manufacturing instructions are issued and that all documents are suitably updated. Progressing action might even mean expediting the committee's decision, since delays in considering essential changes can easily cause serious problems in time, cost and quality.

The coordinator must inform the change originator and all other interested parties of the committee's decision. This includes notifying the originator of changes that have been thrown out. The committee's instructions are usually disseminated by distributing copies of the completed change request form. The original forms should be kept in a file to become part of the particular project or product's technical documentation.

Origins and timing of engineering changes and modifications

The originator

On major project contracts, it can reliably be expected that many changes will originate from the client or customer. Changes from this source, although they are likely to be disruptive, are often welcomed by some contractors because they allow renegotiation of fixed prices or price additions. Moreover, this activity usually takes place in a

ENGINEERING CHANGE REQUEST

Project title:

ECR/Mod number:

Project number:

Details of change requested (use continuation sheets if necessary):

Drawings and other documents affected:

Reason for request:

Emergency action requested (if any):

Originator: Date:

Effect on costs: Cost estimate ref:

Customer funded?   If yes, give customer authorization reference:

Effect on project programme:

COMMITTEE INSTRUCTIONS   THIS CHANGE REQUEST IS APPROVED / NOT APPROVED
Special restrictions, point of embodiment, action on stocks and work in progress, units in service, etc:

Authorized (for change committee):   Date:

Figure 10.1.   Engineering change request form.

commercial atmosphere that is favourable to the contractor since he has, by then, a selling monopoly.

Whatever the circumstances, customer-requested changes will always tend to receive sympathetic consideration by the change committee, but they must still receive the same analytical scrutiny for quality and safety as a request from any unfunded source.

It is good practice to incorporate customer-requested changes into the standard coordination system, using the standard pro formas. If it is impracticable to ask the customer to complete such forms, this can be done inhouse on his behalf.

For change requests which arise within the contracting or manufacturing company, it might be thought that only persons above a certain seniority level should be allowed to initiate engineering change requests. This author does not take that view. In some respects the initiation of changes for product improvements (for example) could be viewed as akin to suggestions in a suggestion box, open to allcomers. A change request has no authority, and carries no cost, quality or other commitment until it has been approved and activated by the change committee. It is the change committee which has the real authority, and is able expertly to assess the predicted benefits, penalties and priorities of each request.

Changes before the start of design

Engineering changes are possible even before engineering design has started. It must be assumed, if there is to be any hope of achieving quality design, that a comprehensive engineering specification has been drawn up before any detailed work is allowed to start. This specification may form part of a contract with a customer, or it may be the foundation of an internal engineering investment programme to design a new product for manufacture.

In general, the cost or other commercial aspects of changes requested at this early stage are relatively easy to assess, since there is no detailed design or other work-in-progress to be scrapped or otherwise disrupted.

Predesign changes requested from within the organization should be considered and approved by the same authority which approved the original design specification. As with customer-requested changes, it will be necessary to consider whether there are any time or cost implications. These may be potentially serious, since it may not be possible to reflect any additional costs in the pricing structure.

The integrity of engineering documentation is a vital element of change management. This is no less important at the predesign stage. Although no production drawings exist to be altered, any change in the engineering concept must mean that the design specification is suitably amended and recirculated.

Sometimes design specifications are complicated sets of documents, containing conceptual design sketches, performance data schedules and a variety of other attached papers. It is essential that the method for revising specifications recognizes this complexity so that, at any time, every person involved knows without ambiguity which issue of the specification and every one of its attendant documents is correct. Methods for updating such sets of documents are described later.

Changes originating during engineering design

The kinds of questions to be asked by the change committee before it can approve implementation have already been mentioned. The further into design and (especially) production a project has progressed, then the more potentially expensive or disruptive any change will be. It is easily possible for a keen originator to believe that a proposed change will bring benefits to the product, to the customer and to the company when, in fact, the disruption caused would far outweigh the foreseen benefits. For these reasons, one change committee known to this author applied the following rule to all changes not funded by the customer:

> If it's essential, we do it.
> If it's 'desirable', we don't.

At a certain advanced stage in any engineering design project, a point is usually reached where the introduction of changes can be seen to be particularly disruptive, delaying the issue of badly needed drawings, specifications or other manufacturing instructions. Under these circumstances, some companies impose an embargo on all change requests (unless safety is involved). This state of affairs is known as a design freeze. It typically is extended to include customer changes, the customer being made aware that he will be subject to relatively heavy cost and time penalties if he insists on breaking the freeze conditions.

If the product under development is to be produced in quantities over a period of time, the design freeze may be applied only to the first few units, or to early batches. Changes requested after the design freeze might be considered for authorization at more convenient points of embodiment in units of later manufacture. This is one reason why products released to the outside world for use may differ from each other in varying degrees (see the following section).

Engineering change requests during product manufacture

Once production has been authorized to start, any subsequent change obviously has greater implications to costs and timescale, with risk to stocks and work-in-progress. The screening of unnecessary or undesirable changes will therefore be pursued especially rigorously at this stage.

Where changes are introduced after the first unit has been produced, it is necessary to establish which modifications have, in fact, been incorporated into any particular unit. This is essential for subsequent field repairs, and for aspects of safety and reliability (for example, when particular units have to be identified for retrospective field modification or recall). Under these circumstances it is customary to allocate batch or serial numbers to the units produced, and to record the build and modification state of all units in registers (known as master record indexes or build schedules). These documenting techniques are described later. Note also that different customer specified options (i.e. combinations and permutations of standard designs) also require similar records to be kept.

Class B changes

Change control can be a cumbersome, if necessary business. In some engineering projects there can be a range of minor changes that occur frequently during design development, but which cannot affect reliability, quality or safety, and which do not affect manufacturing. To put such changes through the full rigour of engineering change management might seem unnecessarily tedious, wasting time and raising costs to no quality advantage. It is sometimes possible to identify positively those types of change which fall into this 'Class B' category, and to establish shortcut procedures for dealing with them effectively.

Class B change procedures can be designed to suit the individual situation, but an example from a real project will perhaps be of some guidance. The project in question was for the design, manufacture and supply of automatic test equipment for an aircraft company. The equipment was purpose-built for checking out aircraft systems using software-controlled instrumentation mounted in a towable trailer. The project design specification included a schedule of the aircraft system's performance parameters that the automatic equipment was expected to check, together with their go or no-go limits. Checking out the total aircraft system involved hundreds of such measurements, with about twenty cables connecting the aircraft to the automatic tester.

As the project progressed, there were many changes requested by the customer. (i.e. the aircraft manufacturer) in the values of test limits, or in the cabling connections. At first, a great deal of administrative and engineering effort was spent in considering each of these changes, and every one had to be estimated and priced. But, since each change only affected limits set in the software (programming changes) or simple wiring changes, questions of reliability or safety within the test equipment never arose. Matters came to an administrative bottleneck when commissioning started on the airfield, a process that lasted for a year and involved many hundreds of such changes.

The problem was overcome by identifying each customer request for a programming or wiring change as a Class B change, for which a separate, simplified pricing and control procedure was introduced. A fixed price was agreed for all such changes between the contract parties. This was, in fact based on ½ hour programming and/or wiring time for each change, regardless of the actual work involved. Cost estimating was eliminated.

Changes were recorded on serial numbered forms, arranged in convenient pads. They were originated by the senior commissioning engineer at the airfield, and countersigned by the customer's on-site engineer. The change notes were then passed back to the company's change coordinator for action, as follows:

- A copy of each change note was passed to the engineering design manager, in order that documentation for following units could be updated.
- Another copy was given to the programmers, in order that new software could be developed at once and sent to the field (in the form of an updated program tape)
- One copy was retained in order that emergency wiring changes made by commissioning engineers in the field ('hay-wired' to temporary standards) could eventually be installed by the company's wiremen to normal quality standards.
- Customer invoices were issued at monthly intervals, listing all relevant changes by their serial numbers, all charged at the same agreed set price.

The effective management and quality control of these 'Class B' changes was maintained but, through the streamlined procedure, much waste in time and money was avoided. In fact, if the simpler methods had not been introduced, the engineers on site would probably have ignored the change procedure altogether, so that documents would not show the true build state, future units would not be correctly programmed or wired, and the costs of changes would not have been recovered from the customer. As it was, both the customer and the contracting company benefited from the arrangement.

The message here is that, whilst change control is essential, the full might of change committee procedures may not always be justified. Alternative procedures may be appropriate, provided always that effective cost, documentation and quality control is not put at risk.

Emergency changes

There are often times when a change has to be carried out with urgency on hardware before revised drawings can be issued. In such cases, the committee will attach the necessary instructions to the authorized change note, and that becomes a temporary addition to the manufacturing drawings for all purposes, including inspection. The procedure must ensure that revised drawings are eventually issued, and the coordinator would be expected to follow this up.

There are other occasions when a change has to be carried out even before it can be considered by the committee. Such changes can arise as a result of engineering queries, for example, where production is held up awaiting for the correction of a drawing error. The engineering query procedure can sometimes be used for this purpose (see below). A method often adopted is for the engineer responsible to visit the work station where the problem has arisen, and mark up the manufacturing print of the drawing with the change needed for production to restart. The engineer would sign the marked-up print alongside the correction, thus authorizing the change to be made and allowing the discrepancy from the drawing to be accepted at subsequent inspection stages.

Many quality assurance people do not, quite rightly, look kindly upon the use of marked-up prints. There is always a risk that such changes will not find their way into the drawing system, and they may not have been sufficiently checked or considered technically. It is therefore necessary to use marked-up prints with considerable caution. Short of banning them altogether, they must only be used under strictly controlled circumstances. One way in which emergency changes (including those using marked-up prints) can be handled without bypassing any of the change procedure control points is as follows.

The originator of the change writes out an engineering change note and gets it registered by the change coordinator. After seeking the immediate approval of the chief engineer (or deputy) he passes one copy of the change note to the drawing office for their eventual action on the master drawing or computer file. Another copy is kept by the coordinator, who makes certain that it is seen at the next change committee meeting. The original version of the change note is passed to production control or supervision, where it becomes a part of the issued manufacturing instructions and allows the interrupted manufacturing operation to continue.

Once an emergency change instruction has been issued to a production area, the original engineering change note must accompany the working drawings through all subsequent stages of manufacture and inspection. In the event of the working prints having to be marked up, which may be inevitable if there is insufficient space on the change note form, an identical marked-up print must be sent to the drawing office at the same time. It is better to produce the second copy of the marked-up instructions using a photocopier, if possible, to prevent the introduction of errors by hand copying.

Concessions and related procedures

The flow of manufacturing information is hardly ever a one-way affair from the engineering department to the manufacturing organization. More typically questions begin to arise when the production personnel attempt to achieve the results demanded in the drawings and specifications. There are several ways in which questions or difficulties can manifest themselves within a production department. Sometimes these can lead either to hardware that does not conform strictly to the intentions of the designer, or to a need for the drawings to be changed to make manufacture easier or possible.

Several recognized procedures exist for dealing with such questions in a formal manner, so that quality is not put at risk and proper records are kept. Each procedure has its own type of form, but there is no reason why the administration method should not be identical with that already described for engineering change requests. The change coordinator can also be asked to deal with the progressing of these documents.

The most usually encountered procedures are described below. They are not mutually exclusive, and two or more of them might be operated together in the same organization.

Engineering query notes

There might be a particular feature of a drawing which is difficult to understand, or an operation which is proving impracticable to carry out. Perhaps, for example, a specified material cannot be machined to the surface finish specified, or it may be found that a particular adhesive will not produce a satisfactory bond. These questions, and many others, can arise as soon as the operatives or their supervisors recognize that they have a discrepancy problem, well before the work has reached an inspection stage.

The obvious way in which these difficulties can be overcome is by referring the questions to the engineering department. In many companies this might be done by a simple, personal inquiry. In other companies, a formal query note procedure may be in use. In one company known to this author, a formal written procedure was used because the engineering manager disliked having workmen in dirty (or even clean) overalls within his office boundaries. There are often, however, more valid reasons. This is especially the case in industries where reliability and safety are critical, and where every manufacturing difficulty that could be attributed to engineering design must be properly assessed, be seen to receive suitable expert attention and be adequately documented.

The answer to an engineering query will often consist simply of a more detailed explanation of the instructions that are already conveyed in a drawing or specification. It may be, however, that the drawings are actually inadequate or at fault, in which case they must be revised. In cases where a drawing change is required, production can usually be allowed to proceed without waiting for new drawings to be issued by considering the annotated query note as part of the officially issued manufacturing instructions. The existence of the completed query note alongside the relevant drawings allows the work to be passed through subsequent inspection stages. The query note has then become, in effect, a kind of production permit (Figure 10.2).

ENGINEERING QUERY	Serial number

PART NUMBER .... ISSUE .... WORKS ORDER NUMBER ....

Is work held up? YES/NO

QUERY: to engineering department

Department .... Date .... Raised by .... (FOREMAN)

ANSWER

Signed .... (SENIOR ENGINEER) Date ......

CONCESSION APPROVAL (if appropriate)
The above instructions to deviate from drawings
will not affect reliability/interchangeability/safety   (CHIEF ENGINEER) ......

(CHIEF INSPECTOR) ....

HONEYCOMB PRODUCTS LIMITED, LUTON, BEDFORDSHIRE

Figure 10.2.   Engineering query note.

The drawing change required as the result of an engineering query note can be instituted by the issue of an engineering change request. The change request must refer specifically to the relevant query note by quoting its serial number, and a copy of the annotated query note should accompany the change note on its trip to the change committee. Alternatively, the engineer can use the emergency change procedure described above. Approval of such changes is usually automatic, since their origin lay in the need to improve the drawings or actual design to facilitate production.

Engineering queries are more likely to arise during the production of prototypes or first production batches, when drawing inconsistencies, omissions or errors are most likely to be encountered.

Concessions and production permits

Another form of engineering query is seen in the forms used by manufacturing departments to apply for permission to deviate from the issued instructions (Figure 10.3). Here, there is no criticism or questioning of the design; and, unlike engineering queries, requests for concessions and permits are not necessarily more common in prototype or early design batches. The manufacturing department is simply stating that it cannot on this occasion, for reasons beyond its reasonable control, carry out the instructions as issued. Some degradation of quality may be implied; in other cases, totally acceptable substitution methods may be possible.

The need for a concession request may be recognized by an operative or the relevant supervisor. It is possible that a quality assurance person, such as an inspector, could be involved but that is less likely. The procedure normally used by an inspector would be based on an inspection report form, which can be an alternative route to the granting of a concession (see the next section).

Examples of situations where a concession or production permit might be requested include a temporary shortage of a particular grade of steel, where a different grade with superior or slightly inferior properties might be available as a substitute. Another possibility is that the production department concerned might realize, too late, that a complete stock batch of specially ordered material has been guillotined fractionally undersize. Possibly some chromium-plated brass instrument screws are on a stores shortage list, but alternative screws are available for substitution. There are many possible reasons why small departures from drawing instructions might be thought necessary, even in a well run factory.

PRODUCTION PERMIT / CONCESSION   Application number:

Drawing or
specification number: Rev: Project or job number:

| Batch or serial numbers affected | Is work held up? |
| | Yes | No |

APPLICATION DETAILS We request permission to deviate from the above drawing/specification as follows:

REASON FOR REQUEST:

Department: Requested by: Date:

ENGINEERING ASSESSMENT: DECISION:
Performance/reliability   REFUSED [ ]   GRANTED [ ]

Health and safety

Interchangeability   Design authority - - - - - - - - - - - - Date

For Engineering Department - - - - - - - -   Date - - - - - - - - -   Inspecting authority - - - - - - - - - - Date - - - - - -

Figure 10.3.   Form for production permit or concession.

The procedure for handling production concessions and permits is similar to that described for engineering query notes. Again, expert engineering approval must be obtained, and each concession or permit must be seen as part of the drawings for the relevant unit or batch of units. For some products the approval of the inspecting authority may also be required. Concessions must obviously never be granted where safety would be at risk. They would usually be rejected, also, where the margin of error would render the production non-interchangeable with its fellows.

Since a production concession or permit implies a depature from the designer's intentions, a drawing change will usually not be relevant. The validity of a concession is usually restricted to one unit, or to a limited number of units which are identified by their batch or serial numbers. The manufacturing department would normally be expected to take subsequent steps to get the correct materials, or take whatever other action is necessary, to comply with the drawings for all units following those for which the concession or permit was allowed.

The serial numbers of all concessions or permits relating to each production unit must be recorded, and the concession details filed. This is essential in order to be able to track back over a unit's history should it become necessary to investigate causes of failure in use.

Inspection reports as concessions or production permits

When a manufactured component or assembly fails an inspection stage marginally, or does not meet a specification of performance in every respect during testing, there may be reluctance to scrap it if rectification is not possible.

Where the product embodies a relatively high investment of time and materials, or where its completion is eagerly awaited for an urgent programme, then the production management or the project manager may wish to obtain the inspection release of the product. One way of going about this would be to raise a request for a concession, as just described in the preceding section. But this would be a needless proliferation of paper, and it is easier and more efficient to use the foot of the inspection report form as a concession or permit. The design authority would have to consider the non-conformance and, if granting a concession, would have to certify that reliability and safety were not impaired, and that the product remained interchangeable. Figure 10.4 shows a suitable report form.

Concessions arising as a result of inspection reports relate only to the unit or batch of units undergoing inspection or testing. Recording

```
┌─────────────────────────────────────────────────────────────────────┐
│ INSPECTION REPORT                                                     │
│                                              Report No:               │
│                                                                       │
│ Project number:              Job number;            Date :            │
│ ─────────────────────────────────────────────────────────────────    │
│ JOB INSPECTED/TESTED:       ┆Batch/serial numbers:                    │
│                             ┆                                         │
│ Drawing No:          Rev:   ┆                                         │
│                             ┆                                         │
│ Specification No:    Rev:   ┆                                         │
│ ─────────────────────────────────────────────────────────────────    │
│ DETAILS OF NONCONFORMANCE :                                           │
│                                                                       │
│                                                                       │
│                                                                       │
│                                                                       │
│                                                                       │
│                                                                       │
│                                                                       │
│                                                                       │
│                                            - - - - - - - - - - - - -   │
│                                                          Inspector    │
│ ─────────────────────────────────────────────────────────────────    │
│ REQUEST FOR CONCESSION (if required).                                 │
│       The above nonconformance will not affect reliability, safety    │
│       or interchangeability.                                          │
│ Further comments:                                                     │
│                                                                       │
│                                    ┌──────────────┐                   │
│                                    │ Recommended  │                   │
│                                    ├──────────────┤                   │
│ Requested by: _____    │   Refused    │ - - - - - -       │
│                                    └──────────────┘   Design authority│
│ ─────────────────────────────────────────────────────────────────    │
│ DISPOSAL INSTRUCTIONS                                                 │
│ ─────────────────────────┬──────────────────────┬─────────────────── │
│   Scrap and remake        │ Rectify and reinspect/│ Concession granted │
│                           │ retest                │                    │
│                           │                       │                    │
│                           │                       │                    │
│                           │                       │                    │
│                           │                       │                    │
│ ─────────────────────────┴──────────────────────┴─────────────────── │
│                                                  Inspecting authority  │
└─────────────────────────────────────────────────────────────────────┘
```

Figure 10.4.   Inspection report form (with provision for the granting of a manufacturing concession).

of such concessions is again important, and each concession granted against a rejection inspection report takes its serial reference number from that of the inspection report itself.

Documents and records

Document issues and numbering

All engineers should be familiar with one or more systems used by engineering companies to distinguish different revision states of the same drawing or other document. Some of the basic rules will now be outlined, with comments given where appropriate on some of the pitfalls.

Pre-release and post-issue revisions

Drawings and other documents are often issued at Revision 0, with subsequent issues numbered sequentially as Revision 1, 2, 3 and so on. But there may be several changes to a document before it has been issued for manufacture, perhaps during a phase of a project when technical or commercial discussions are in progress with a customer. A useful procedure is to use different, easily distinguishable systems for such documents to identify those documents that are not authorized for manufacture and those which are.

A well-tried system for achieving this aim is to give all preliminary issues revisions letters, in a simple A, B, C series. The first issue of each document released for manufacture is then coded with numbered revisions, usually starting at Revision 0 (the series may start at Revision 1 if there is a possibility of confusion with the letter O).

The remainder of this chapter will follow usual practice by referring only to revision numbers, even though these may be alphabetical characters in some cases.

Highlighting new or revised information on documents

It is standard practice to add a note on every revised drawing to summarize the changes included at the new issue. The note must be written against the relevant revision number, which must also appear alongside the changed area(s) on the drawing. Often these numbers are written inside inverted triangles, to highlight them and to avoid confusion with other numerical data.

This procedure is equally important on other engineering

documents, such as specifications and schedules. Changes or additions to passages of text must be indicated by placing the revision numbers in the margin alongside each change.

Drawings plotted by computer

At one time the original master of a drawing was easily distinguishable from copies printed and issued for manufacture. The original could be kept in a drawings registry, only being allowed out if it was to be changed (prints being issued by the registry for all other purposes). This procedure imposed some discipline on revision procedures, since the registry clerk would expect the drawing to be returned to file with an updated revision number. It was therefore unlikely that two versions of prints from the same drawing could exist with the same revision number.

With the advent of computer plotters, each new plotted drawing looks like a new master drawing (although several identical plots could be produced). It is therefore particularly important to impose a discipline on engineers using CAD equipment to ensure that every reissue of a drawing does in fact get a new revision number added.

Here is a short case example to illustrate the danger. This author was responsible, as office manager, for fitting out a new engineering office, and the plans for layouts and internal services were produced on a new inhouse CAD system. The engineers responsible were treating this project as a training exercise, to obtain proficiency with the new system. The task started by producing, in the computer file, a skeleton plan of the area with walls, doors and windows shown. This plan was numbered DLL 1. Thereafter, all internal layouts and service diagrams were produced as overlays on this skeleton. But, no one thought to give any of the new derivatives a new drawing number. Plotted drawings were run off as required, simply by calling up the relevant computer files. But every plot looked like a master drawing, and all were number DLL 1. This provided a good training object lesson.

Drawings on microfilm

It is easily possible to get confused between correct drawing issues when microfilm files exist. Sets of duplicate aperture cards can be very useful as satellite files, but trouble comes when revised issues of the microfilm fail to find their way into one or more of the files.

One method for preventing trouble in this area is to ban the issue of prints for any purpose other than engineering reference from any satellite file. It is even possible to fix a stencilled mask in the print paper plane within each local printer so that the words 'for reference only' appear on each print. The complementary side to this system requires that the only microfilm prints allowed for issue to the manufacturing department are those from a master file held in a central registry.

In the days before CAD, where every drawing change had to be made to a hard original, the system was further strengthened by using the master microfilm aperture card as a loan ticket for the original drawing. This meant that whenever an original was out from the registry to be changed, the master microfilm card was not available for the production of manufacturing prints at the earlier revision state.

Interchangeability

It is a golden rule that whenever a change renders a product, or part of a product non-interchangeable with its fellows, then the changed item must be given a new part number (i.e. a new drawing number and not simply a new revision number). The family resemblance between such changed parts can, if desired, still be retained in the new number. This can be achieved by the use of additional digits or suffix numbers.

Reissues of multiple page documents

It often happens that a drawing, schedule or specification comprises many pages, of which only one or two are affected by a particular change. There are several ways of coping administratively with this situation.

The safest way of updating a multiple paged document is to update the issue of every sheet, and reissue the whole document. In some projects, however, the distribution of such documents can run into the tens or twenties, and some documents might comprise hundreds of sheets or pages. The only real reason for contemplating this wasteful approach is seen when some or all of the copies are to be sent to departments which have inept or badly trained clerks, who could not be relied upon to carry out individual page insertions or changes. This state of affairs is sometimes seen in overseas projects, where the client's personnel have not had the opportunity of sufficient clerical training.

A more economical way of dealing with changes to individual sheets is to provide every multipaged document with a schedule of contents. This schedule must list every page and its revision number. An example is given in Figure 10.5.

Now consider such a document when it is first issued for

DOCUMENT INDEX		Sheet number: 1

DOCUMENT INDEX

Document title:

Document number:

Sheet number: 1
Document rev:
Date:

In order to conform correctly to the revision number stated above, this document must comprise the sheets listed in the following table, together with the attachments defined below (if any). Should further revision be necessary, only revised or additional sheets will be issued. All holders of this document are responsible for inserting the fresh sheets in the correct place, and destroying superseded pages.

Sheet	Rev	Sheet	Rev	Sheet	Rev	Sheet	Rev	Sheet	Rev	Sheet	Rev	Sheet	Rev	Sheet	Rev	Sheet	Rev	Sheet	Rev

Attachments   The following attachments form part of this document:

Summary of issues and revisions

Rev	Date	Reason for re-issue or revision (give brief details, modification number, etc)

Project title:	Project number:	Approved by:

Figure 10.5.   A document index sheet.

manufacture at Revision 0. Every page should be at Revision 0, and the schedule sheet(s) should also be at Revision 0. When the first change occurs, only the affected sheets will be reissued, at Revision 1. The schedule sheet (or all of them, if there is more than one) will also be updated to Revision 1. As the work proceeds and more sheets are changed or added, the schedule will be revised at each change and reissued with only those document pages affected. At any time, therefore, the schedule sheet(s) revision number will always be the same as that of the latest revised document page. The document revision state can therefore be given without ambiguity by referring to the revision number of the contents schedule.

This process is also valid for sets of documents, such as design specifications, which are really combinations of several pages of text, performance schedules and drawings. All these attached documents will not only bear different revision numbers but, more fundamentally, they will have different drawing or reference numbers. A master contents schedule serves to couple the whole lot together, giving a positive identity of one collective reference number and one current revision number.

Build records

Build state of one-off products or projects
At the end of any project it is necessary to record the as-built condition. This is a straightforward list of all drawings and other relevant documents, giving in each case the serial number and appropriate revision number. In most projects this is the final version of the drawings list and bill of materials (or drawing and purchase schedules). The process is usually facilitated by the use of a computer.

The existence of such records in company files is essential for the purpose of field service and repair, and for engineering use should the customer or client request modifications or extensions to the project in the future. There are also obvious reliability and safety implications in being able to trace a project back to its correct drawing and specification content.

All companies would recognize the importance of maintaining such records, but there are reasons why changes might be overlooked for inclusion in the final records. These include particularly changes made during arduous commissioning conditions, and other work carried out on remote sites. Engineering change procedures similar to those described earlier in this chapter are indispensable if accurate final as-built records are to be achieved.

Changes made to a product by the user after it has been commissioned and handed over are more difficult to cater for. Prudent companies will include a clause in their terms of business that restrict or invalidate any subsequent obligations of warranty or provision of service if the customer carries out unauthorized changes.

Build state of multiple products

Records showing the content of products manufactured in quantities of two or more will have to recognize that individual units can differ in their build state.

The first prerequisite is that every individual unit should be physically identifiable, and this is usually achieved through the attachment of labels bearing serial numbers. Thus any individual product can be identified positively by giving its part number and serial number.

Except for major capital products, an as-built schedule is not normally feasible or necessary for every single unit. Rather, changes are related to production batches, each batch being relevant to a range of serial numbers. It is then only necessary to record and keep schedules for each batch. Such build schedules are sometimes known as master record indexes. An example of a form for clerical use is shown in Figure 10.6 to illustrate the principle. Computerized listing would be used in practice, and microfiche copies can be made available for spares stockists and service organizations for products which are widely distributed.

Modification labelling

Modification labels are often used to indicate those changes which have actually been incorporated in a particular unit. This procedure is particularly applicable to changes necessary after a unit has been sold, so that the manufacturer's instructions for field modifications or recall work can be seen to have been carried out. Such labels may also carry modifications made during late stages of manufacture or stocking. Modification labelling is of particular importance for subsequent maintenance, repair and field servicing. It may also have operational implications, where the operating instructions specify different procedures according to the modification state of a product.

Traceability records

Much of this part of the chapter has stressed the need to be able to

MASTER RECORD INDEX		Sheet 1 of sheets

MASTER RECORD INDEX — Sheet 1 of sheets, Revision No:, Date issued:

Product/project

Title: Identification number:

For a product, list the batch or serial numbers affected here:

This index lists drawings and related documents which together define the build state of the product/project described above. Note that the revision numbers listed here relate specifically to the correct build state and are not necessarily the latest revisions in all cases

Document number	Sheet	Rev	Document number	Sheet	Rev	Document number	Sheet	Rev

MODIFICATIONS INCORPORATED AT THIS BUILD STATE

Drawn by   Checked by   Approved

Figure 10.6.   A master record index or build schedule form.

track back through the history of a product in order to establish its build standard.

For some critical products, for example, in military weapons, the reliability requirements demand that the physical content of every individual item can be traced back to source. Thus, in the event (for example) of a fatigue fracture of a bolt, the source of the bolt could be found, together with its batch number. Then all other products with similar bolts from the same batch fitted could be traced, and the bolts changed.

Traceability at this detailed level depends on the existence of detailed inspection and manufacturing records. Every bought-out or manufactured component must be issued for incorporation against a specific release note, and the serial numbers of all release notes are recorded when the production assemblies are kitted up by stores. Physical stores discipline is vital, with all released items being held in bond, and with the batch quantities on each release note being checked against the actual stock quantities. Thus, only those items specified on the release notes as being of approved quality should actually be used, and the issue and build records will allow investigators to track the smallest component back through its manufacturing and raw material purchasing stages.

Quality management, usually with external supervision from an offical inspectorate, play the key role in ensuring that the release note system and subsequent stores and manufacturing procedures provide the necessary traceability records.

11 Product Reliability

Peter Foyer and Eric Wallbank

When you buy a product, be it a pair of pliers, a television or an aeroplane, you cannot tell whether it is going to be reliable. By looking at it, measuring it or even using it, you cannot honestly tell a potential lifelong friend from a total rogue. The person who made it may have a little more knowledge than you, and may be able to tell when he has impaired a particular example's reliability by poor processing or something similar. But it is unlikely that testing a particular unit at the end of the production line will reveal unreliability. It is even more difficult for the manufacturer of a component or subassembly to know whether or not he has succeeded in achieving a reliability target.

The designer, who knows, or should know, a product's inner secrets, is in the best position to know whether there are significant risks of unreliability. He should even know how to make each particular example reliable. Yet third-parties make massive incomes out of unreliability: the Automobile Association, Lloyds Inspectors, the Civil Aviation Authority and laboratories worldwide are all good examples. Fortunes are lost: the De Havilland Comet, the Sinclair ZX computer, the Rover SD1 and the Advanced Passenger Train all cost their originators dearly because of massive unreliability. And fortunes are also made: for example, Japanese companies whose products sell on their reputation for reliability.

This chapter is about unreliability — how it arises, and how to set out to minimize it. It is a design job that no-one really likes, causes trouble when it goes wrong and costs a great deal.

Reliability: the crucial 'hygiene factor'

Most products that increase their market share do so by their performance, appearance and 'application friendliness'. It is also important that these are presented in the best possible light by good advertising, public relations and point-of-sale publicity — but the effect of a reputation for unreliability is to make all these efforts valueless and possibly dishonest.

Reliability is fairly easy to define but very difficult and painstaking to achieve: it is not the 99 per cent good in a product which counts, but the 1 per cent mistakes which cause the problem. A reliable product can be identified by four negative characteristics. It does not:

1. Stop carrying out its function.
2. Allow the quality of its results to deteriorate.
3. Endanger or inconvenience its user or other people.
4. Resist attempts to maintain its functioning.

The first of these has been achieved when the product keeps going during its planned lifetime (or time between planned maintenance), and does not stop involuntarily. In practice this is measured by the mean time between failures, the percentage of time it is available for use, and the consequences and nuisance value of failure.

Reliability also means that there is adequate control (through design and other things) over the rate of deterioration during its lifetime. The three most common causes of deterioration are corrosion, fatigue and wear. Equally important in many situations are chemical changes (due to heat or radiation, for example) and loss or poisoning of working fluids. These effects result in loss of performance, deterioration in appearance, and ultimately failure in service.

Thirdly, reliability means safety and convenience in use. Most products are used close enough to people to mean that certain kinds of failure or deterioration will affect those around them — not necessarily the users. The effects vary from risks of electric shock from small appliances to the worldwide effects of the Chernobyl nuclear plant failure.

Last, reliability means ensuring that routine maintenance is simple and relatively cheap. Products for special applications, such as space vehicles, undersea cables and heart pacemakers, are expected and designed to survive without servicing or repair. But most 'normal' products are expected to need servicing (inspection in use) or repair during their lives, in order to give a reasonable lifespan at acceptable cost. We would not expect to replace a car instrument panel simply because one of its display lighting bulbs failed. Equally, we do not now expect to have to reset a lathe when a cutting tool tip wears out. A problem in the past has been that short-life elements of products have not been recognized and improved in either life or serviceability.

Good reliability does not normally attract people to buy a particular product, unless the competition is noticeably unsatisfactory, or the consequences of likely failure are very serious — even death. However, poor reliability has been the end of many attractive, marketable products because performance, availability, safety or cost have been unacceptably or unpredictably low.

Why is reliability not achieved?

Contrary to popular opinion, reliable products do not look different from unreliable ones: they often pass equally smoothly out of the factory and into use. Yet, in use, failures start to occur in one product and not in another. Extreme causes can sometimes be found in product acceptance testing, but this is the exception rather than the rule. The usual cause of unreliability is the failure to take account of any one of three factors during the development of a product:

- Possible results of failure need to be recognized (loss of revenue, danger, excess cost).
- Possible chains of events leading to failure need to be identified.
- The means of prevention need to be decided and implemented.

Often, the results of failure are thought about only in terms of known failure models. For instance, television sets are known to fail because of annoying, but not hazardous, malfunctions in their tuner or picture circuits, and by gradual loss of picture quality. But in the USSR significant numbers of people have been injured by cathode ray tube implosions. This is obviously an extremely dangerous type of failure when it occurs, and the engineers did not appear to have considered the risk adequately, or perhaps had not taken sufficient precautions to prevent the problem occurring.

Similarly, many failures become serious only when more than one event in a chain has occurred. A classic example is vehicle transmissions. Slow loss of oil through a seal is of little consequence — it causes some mess and means that extra oil has to be added at servicing. However, at the next stage of failure, the sequence of events is dramatic:

- the transmission runs out of oil;
- it seizes up;
- the vehicle becomes uncontrollable, and other failures may also occur;
- there may be a serious accident affecting the vehicle, other vehicles and their occupants.

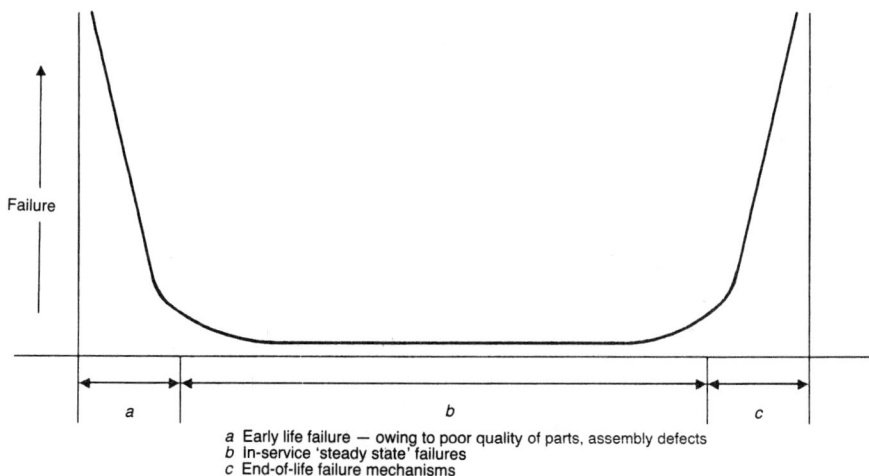

a Early life failure — owing to poor quality of parts, assembly defects
b In-service 'steady state' failures
c End-of-life failure mechanisms

Figure 11.1.   Typical failure pattern.

Finally, even when a failure mode is identified, the means of either preventing it altogether or making the consequences benign are often not pursued and executed. Standard methods include strengthening, providing warning devices for the operator, and building-in automatic shutdown equipment. Most products will exhibit a 'bathtub' pattern of failure: high in early and end-of-life stages, low in-between (Figure 11.1).

However, a final word of warning. Many failures are made more likely, or more significant, by excessive complexity. Adding more potentially unreliable equipment may simply increase the chances of premature failure and operator unawareness in a developing critical situation.

Methodologies for achieving reliability

It cannot be assumed that any product will automatically be as reliable as is necessary. This means that specific actions to achieve reliability must be built-in at each stage of planning, detailing, manufacture and beyond.

Planning and user specifications

In planning a new product, or in updating or even significantly modifying an existing one, reliability should normally feature in three areas of the user specification:

1. The customer's criteria of performance, appearance, market and availability.
2. The interfaces with the customer's world.
3. Economic criteria for total life operating cost.

In the area of customer needs and expectations, the durability specification is normally for the time or usage which should be achieved before an unacceptable level of deterioration has occurred (e.g. 90 per cent of new vehicle maximum speed after 200 000 km; no visible rusting after five years in North Sea conditions).

The interfaces with the customer's world present the most difficult specification area, because it is necessary to specify the acceptable risks to people and other equipment. For instance, recent discussion about water pollution has questioned the safety of even low levels of radioactive material. Equally there is a problem in identifying all the known subjects of risk. People are relatively identifiable. Other risks include corruption (inwards and outwards) of data by electromagnetic or line-borne interference. It is still important to specify as many interface risk subjects as possible. Every interface presents an inward and/or an outward risk. The critical factor is to establish the *real* way that the product will be used or abused.

Total life operating cost will dictate further limitations on unreliability. In this case, the usual criteria are availability of the equipment for use and its repair cost. The total life operating cost calculation usually includes:

- equipment running costs (energy, consumables, supervision);
- capital depreciation and finance cost;
- maintenance and repair costs;
- loss of business through unavailability.

192 Quality in Engineering and Design

Capital costs may be increased by having to have spare equipment in case of failure. Maintenance costs for an unsound product may be higher either because it has to be repaired, or because it has to be prevented from failing. Unavailability could mean that certain revenue opportunities are lost or it might mean that even larger installations become unavailable.

To achieve the target cost and/or income levels for the user, certain levels of reliability and availability — mean time between failures (MTBF) and mean time to repair (MTTR) — will be needed. The specifications for the results of failure which will cause problems, and the acceptable levels of failure, must be an integral part of the broader user specification for the product or system.

Concept stage
In the concept stage, reliability needs to be built-in just like performance, availability and price. This implies both the generation of options deliberately aimed at achieving reliability targets and the use of structured simulation techniques to test options for potential risks.

Product structure
The key to design for reliability is simplicity. The more parts, complexity and unnecessary variety a design has, the more vulnerable it must be to failure. Product structure concepts should aim to obtain all the necessary functions with the minimum number of parts, and with minimum variety of processes and features. This makes it easier to achieve reliability as well as performance and cost targets.

Reliability of elements
At this point, an overall reliability computer model can be built, showing each of the main functions and interfaces. For each function and interface, acceptable levels of out-time (MTBF and MTTR) can be built in from the user specification. Where two functions contribute to one user need, or where total availability is the driving criterion, the user-level need must be broken down into acceptable (lower) levels of failure for each function.

In designing for performance and appearance, adequate margins for deterioration must be built-in, as well as the usual ones for variability. There is usually little data (except perhaps empirical data from past experience) to support these calculations. However, these calculations can usually be separated from failure calculations because they are more concerned with ultimate life, residual value to the user, and market image.

At interfaces, the issues are different:

- Risks of the equipment damaging outside people and equipment.
- Risk of outside influences damaging the equipment.

These do affect the design approach to overall reliability and availability, but only if the risk of occurrence can be defined.

So for the concept we have a static mathematical model which contains estimates of acceptable reliability, life to unacceptable performance, appearance or safety, and risk to third-party people and things. There are several mathematical and logical techniques, mostly empirical, which can help in the process of defining risk:

1. Failure mode and effect analysis (FMEA).
2. Fault tree analysis (FTA).
3. Consequence analysis.
4. Stress calculations (finite element analysis, etc.).
5. Fatigue calculations.
6. Animation, on the screen or by simplified models.
7. Wear models.
8. Corrosion and stress corrosion modelling techniques.
9. Simulation of electrical and mechanical systems.
10. Carefully designed rig testing to establish (at this stage) failure modes rather than lives.
11. Historical and empirical life data.

There are numerous computer tools for carrying out the above, many of which are suitable for running on PCs.

Failure mode and effect analysis

Failure mode and effect analysis is a systematic procedure by which faults at the parts or components level are identified. Then, by using failure rates for the appropriate stress levels, their effect at the system level is determined. Each part is considered, in turn, as having failed in each possible mode. The effect of each of these failures at various system levels is noted, and a failure rate is assigned from available data.

Each system level failure mode will be seen to result from various possible component failures. These can be grouped together to calculate the system failure rate. It is usual to consider only primary failure mode effects on system performance. In some cases secondary

Component	Stress ratio	Failure rate (per machine hour)	Failure rate, mode 1 Loss of output		Failure rate, mode 2 Spurious output	
			Mode	λ	Mode	λ
Resistor R23	0.5	0.001	Open circuit	0.001	Short circuit	Negligible
Transformer TR1	—	0.1	Open circuit	0.003	Not applicable	—
Relay R6						
coil		0.5	Not applicable	—	Open circuit	0.05
contact		0.15	Short circuit	0.015	Open circuit	0.135
Quad op. amp IC8		0.1	50%	0.05	25%	0.025
Totals		5.75		2.55		1.45

Figure 11.2.   A typical failure mode analysis worksheet.

effects and their consequences are also considered. Figure 11.2 shows a typical failure mode analysis worksheet.

The results of the failure mode analysis provide failure rate totals for each block in a system. These are then applied to reliability block diagrams. Calculation of mean time between failures (MTBF) or reliability is then a question of applying the appropriate mathematics (see Smith, 1988).

Consequence analysis

Consequence analysis takes the form of a decision tree in which chains of possible events are developed in terms of consequences. Starting points are the real problem. These can come from:

(a) experience of previous similar designs;
(b) known risk areas arising from analytical techniques (i.e. high-stress points);
(c) input risks from interfaces defined at the user specification;
(d) brainstorming sessions.

Chains of events need to be pursued logically and, again, by brainstorming. The decision trees developing from each initial event need to be mapped and carefully compared afterwards with the trees initiated by other events. The effects of two failures are more difficult to predict, particularly where the numbers of potential risks are large. Similarly, consequences well away from the original failure (in electrical distribution systems for instance) are often very difficult to predict. Failure 11.3 shows a simple, partial consequence model for failure of a vehicle stub axle.

The consequence tree must be pursued exhaustively until all its branches have reached points where all possible consequences have been identified. For each consequence, everyone must be agreed either that it is benign, or that one of the primary risks in the user specification has become the consequence; for example, the risk of injury to a person. (In terms of risk to an operator, the event must be pursued to understand the consequences to the rest of the system if the operator is thereby rendered unable to control it.)

Figure 11.3 shows the consequence tree developed to two of its end-points: a benign one with the vehicle stopped safely and out of action; and a dangerous chain of events where the driver loses control and the vehicle collides with other objects.

Fault tree analysis

Fault tree analysis (FTA) is, as its name implies, another decision tree

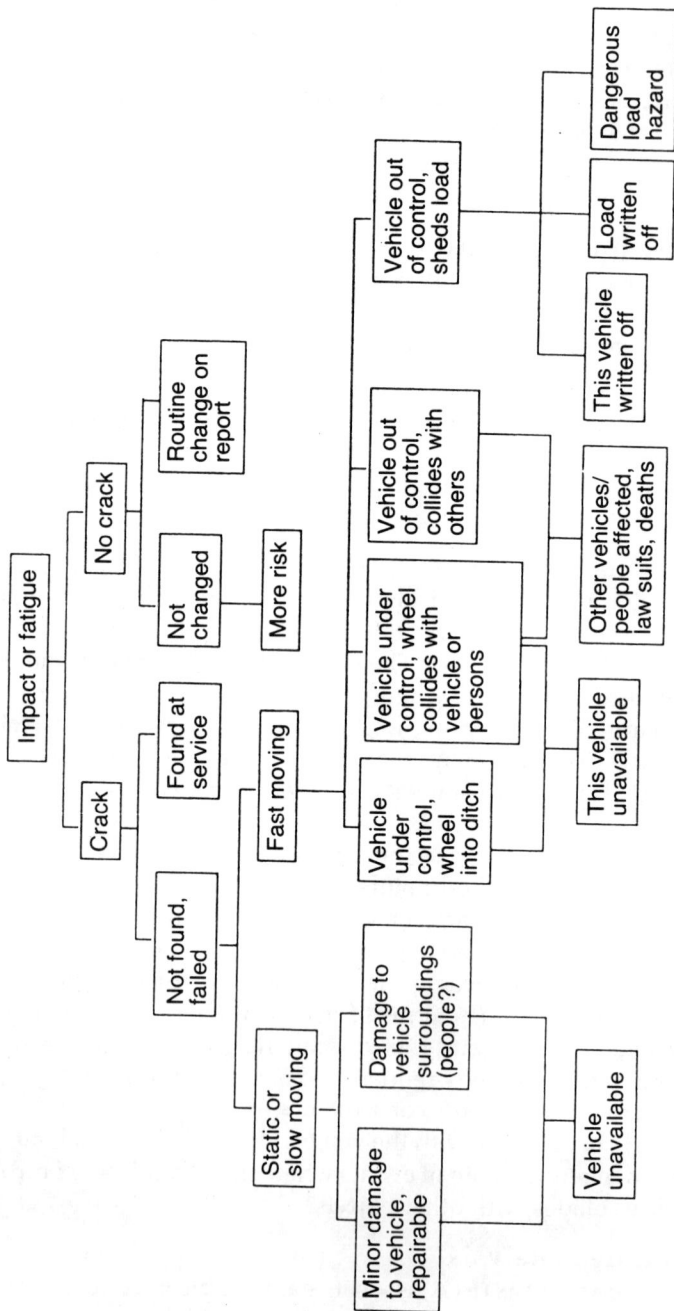

Figure 11.3. Consequence analysis for a road vehicle stub axle.

technique. Unlike the approaches so far described, FTA does not start by looking at the consequences of a single component failure, but considers instead the operation of the whole system. Specific system failure modes are selected (dubbed 'top events') and a separate tree is drawn for each from which possible causal failures lower down in the total system hierarchy can be identified. The fault tree diagram has the advantage that it is not limited to the consideration of a single fault: it can accommodate the possibility of more than one fault or failure occurring in the system at the same time.

The faults or failures taken into account are not confined to physical events such as mechanical or electrical breakdowns, but can include such things as human errors made by the product user or operator.

The method lends itself to a quantified approach. If the probability of any lower event can be assessed, then it is possible to reflect the combination of events in calculations that yield the probability of the specified top event happening. By assessing the probable effects of different lower event combinations on the total system, potentially unreliable or even hazardous situations can be predicted.

Because the number of possible lower event combinations can be great (even for a relatively simple product) computer assistance is necessary for identifying the lower level events, or combinations of these events, which are most likely to result in the top event. The effort is usually worthwhile, and has been adopted as standard practice in industries where the process or plant safety is considered to be critical (such as in the nuclear, oil and gas industries).

Fault tree analysis is also discussed in Chapter 20.

Simulation

Simulation is also a potential tool, until now generally unexploited. However, simulation models are often produced of electronic systems and for parts of manufacturing systems. The techniques differ and neither is really valuable in its present form:

1. Electronic simulation does not normally have a stochastic, event-sequence element to bring accumulating failures to a head.
2. Manufacturing simulation considers only logistical consequences.

However, a combination of the two techniques, particularly if initiated from FMEA analysis (to isolate single failure risks) could be exceptionally powerful, and applicable to several diverse types of systems.

In simulation, a computer model of the system is built. Its form is most closely related to a computer software 'flow diagram' or an electrical circuit diagram. The behaviour of each element of the system, in terms of its response to stimuli and failure modes, needs to be defined mathematically. The links between them also need to be defined — these are often significant elements in themselves.

In a true stochastic testing routine, three kinds of variables are changed under the influence of random number generators:

- Demands on the system.
- Inputs to the system.
- Performance of elements of the system.

The response to demand patterns, in the face of variation in input and performance, can be analysed as overall quality, quantity and perhaps cost of output, and as the isolation of failure modes which can have serious consequences.

FMEA and/or simulation will reveal parts of the system whose design is critical. More exploration of these parts is essential to ensure that:

1. Their operation is fully understood.
2. Their potential modes of failure are all identified.
3. Their roles in the system are fully understood.

After correction, where serious consequences such as risk to life, total failure to operate or complex failure modes are involved, the FMEA and simulation models must be rerun to represent the modified product and ensure that adequate levels of reliability and benign consequences have been achieved.

Design calculations

The classical forms of design calculation to assure performance and reliability usually work well. Computer techniques have allowed detailed analytical methods to replace more generalized or empirical methods. Typical examples include:

1. Finite element analysis (stress, fluid flow, heat transfer, etc.).
2. Reliable performance calculation.
3. Bearing wear models.
4. Gear stress and dynamics.
5. Electrical circuit design techniques.
6. Numerous specialist programmes.

The problem is that these produce results whose consequences to the user are unpredictable. A highly stressed bolt may have serious consequences if it fails, or may simply transfer its load to several more fastenings. A capacitor carrying out a simple smoothing function might incapacitate a whole system if it suffers an insulation breakdown. This is why it is so essential to use calculation methods in conjunction with FMEA and for simulation to give assurance of reliability.

Model and rig testing

Where consequences of failure are potentially catastrophic, the risks of calculation or logic being wrong may be so serious that physical testing is the only safe method. If this is the case, it is done well before a full prototype is available. Critical factors are:

- Realism and accuracy in understanding the real situation.
- Design of the experiment to understand the risks which matter.
- Keeping timing ahead of user risk or business risk (i.e. sale of an unreliable product or use in uncharted life territory).

A rig test may, therefore, need to be run in a demanding manner for the full life of critical parts of the product. FMEA and simulation can once again be used to indicate features where little is known or predictable, but potential consequences are serious. The rig experiment normally needs to be well planned to test subsets of the whole system. This requires that the rig is:

1. An accurate representation of part of the eventual system.
2. Interfaced accurately and in a fully reproducible manner.
3. Tested in a manner which accurately reproduces actual use in all respects.
4. Kept ahead of all expected or known users in terms of experience.
5. Run in a controlled and logged manner, all inputs, outputs and conditions being recorded.
6. Related to full prototype and field experience in a formal manner.

Another problem is that accelerated testing experiments can lead to false conclusions, owing to lack of realism. For example, a model might have undergone testing satisfactorily, but the real product could fail through corrosion, breakdown of lubricants, or long periods of inactivity.

Modifications

Engineering changes and modifications were discussed at length in the preceding chapter, but some comments specific to reliability are relevant here. Product reliability is often adversely affected by modifications and cost-saving exercises. These, by their nature, are often carried out under more pressure of time and with tighter budgets than new design work, and without full understanding of use and of original design. The track record is poor. The worst example in recent times was the Manchester air disaster, in which the key element was apparently sheer confusion about what modifications had been done and a series of half-satisfactory solutions implemented in a hurry.

Modifications to factories, as opposed to the products they make, can also have unnoticed effects. For instance, changes to heat treatment plant, metal forming processes and paint processes can all present unseen risks to product reliability and/or life.

Criteria for decisions about retesting of even military and aerospace products are often vague and inconsistent. In surface transport, the rules are even less well-defined.

A sensible approach would seem to be to revisit the FMEA and simulation exercises, and to understand:

1. Whether new failure modes are likely in the new design.
2. Whether the risk of particular modes occurring is increased, for instance by higher loadings.
3. Whether the mode of use is changed, thus creating either new demands or new inputs (for instance, connection of an electric appliance to the mains instead of battery power).

If any of these factors is adversely affected, new rig tests, prototype trials and reliability tests should be instigated.

Availability calculations

An availability model can be built for many established or completed but evolutionary designs.

With the product broken into functional submodules, the key causes of unavailability and their consequences have been established by FMEA and simulation techniques. Likely mean times when the product will be out of service can be calculated from these results, based on experience of call-out and repair times for similar products and circumstances in the past. These mean out-of-service times are often referred to as mean 'out-times', 'down-times' or time to repair (MTTR). Times for regular inspection, testing and routine repairs can be calculated in a similar manner.

Much more difficult is the calculation of the likely frequency of particular failures. The first step is segregation by means of FMEA of failures into:

1. Potentially lethal or financially or personally crippling failures.
2. Failures which will stop the equipment immediately or before regular inspection/repair opportunity.
3. Failures which can generally wait until the next regular inspection/repair opportunity.

For potentially lethal or crippling failures, every possible route to them must be evaluated, and alternative methods of risk analysis used. For instance, in our earlier example of vehicle transmission seizure, a number of routes based on past similar products can be used:

1. Experience of oil-loss from servicing records of similar vehicles and transmissions.
2. Experience of bearing seizures of similar bearings in similar situations.
3. Statistical results of rig tests aimed at showing the risk of two gears being engaged at once.
4. Experience of internal breakages of similar transmissions in similar circumstances.
5. Fatigue and wear calculations for key items.

For non-lethal failures, the calculations follow similar lines. From FMEA and simulation, potentially stopping failures and their causes can be identified. Their likelihood can be estimated for each unit or sub-assembly, or for critical parts from past experience, or from fatigue or wear calculations. The critical factors are:

1. To ensure that all causes are covered.
2. To ensure that any change in product manufacture or duty is identified and conservatively treated.

For most companies, most of a new product is in some way evolutionary. The amount of calculation from pure theory (or indeed guesswork) should be limited, and backed (as stated previously) by rig testing.

In many cases, unavailability can be reduced by regular inspection and repair, preferably using time not needed for useful operation. This task consists of:

- Inspection against lethal failure (and repair if needed).

- Inspection, repair and routine change against out-time.
- Clearing up non-critical wear and failures.

For lethal failures, the frequency of inspection must be sufficiently often to keep the risks minimal — in the region of one in several hundred million. For stoppage risks, inspection must be often enough for total unavailability to be kept down to an acceptable level. For other problems, experience will be the main guide as to how often it is needed to prevent long-term customer dissatisfaction or product deterioration.

The total unavailability is then:

- The sum of (MTTR [out time] × frequency) for all failures.
- The sum of (inspection/repair time × frequency) for routine repairs (including minor repairs).

The mean time between failures is defined as:

Total up-time divided by number of unscheduled stoppages

The aim is then to minimize:

- Total unavailability (by optimizing routine versus unscheduled stoppages).
- Number of unscheduled stoppages (by similar means but different rules).
- Maintenance costs.
- Total operating cost (by optimizing maintenance costs and revenue from operation).

The prototype phase

In many companies the prototype phase is particularly ineffective in that very expensive products are built and little is learned. Prototypes can only be a 'dress rehearsal' for first production. This means that the functioning, appearance and performance of the product can be tested. Also, the manufacturing processes and tooling can be tried out. For many products, trial marketing, proposals and customer response can also be initiated.

The function of full prototypes as reliability test-beds can only be long term. In the short term, only serious mistakes which should have been isolated by design appraisal techniques (FMEA, fault tree analysis, simulation, stress analysis, etc.) will be found. Recovery is very difficult without creating additional risk, costs are immense, and there is a real possibility that market potential will be lost.

Nevertheless, prototypes have an essential role in long term reliability testing. This is true only if they are properly planned and managed. They are much more expensive than rig tests and simulation, yet management is often ineffective in getting any real reliability data from them.

Principal criteria for prototype evaluation are:

1. Realism, e.g. built using production tooling where possible.
2. Representative testing in the most vulnerable modes.
3. Experience ahead of the most-used customer examples.
4. Proper experimental design.
5. Proper monitoring and recording of results.
6. Feedback to design for both product support and related new products.
7. Comparison with product support data.

Experimental design to achieve representative testing is based on the same criteria as planning for tests on design concepts. The work should concentrate on areas of expected:

- Risk to customer satisfaction.
- Risk to integrity and safety.
- Coincident likely failure and major customer disadvantage.
- Important long term effects (corrosion, fatigue, etc.).
- Or in areas where the effects of user practices are not understood.

For each test activity, the purpose, duration and potential consequences should be defined numerically. The test programme and test-log should also provide indications of key deterioration and failure modes for reporting of all experiences, and for regular checks of condition. In some industries, the Japanese Taguchi techniques have been well established to predict likely failures and to speed up experimental work.

As product support data becomes available, it should be compared to prototype test data to establish:

- Any common patterns emerging.
- Any differences between prototype and customer experience.

This can be particularly useful if prototypes are put into customers' hands at the outset.

From early experience, potential failure and warranty rates can be assessed. Expected total warranty cost levels over 1 per cent of sales value, and 0.001 per cent of product failing in the same manner during the warranty period, are both indicators of problems needing attention. Any failure having potential for lethal or severe commercial consequences needs investigation. Failure rates must be progressively planned out: what is good enough in Year 1 will not be adequate in Year 2, and so on.

When prototypes are to be used to test modifications, two problems need to be faced:

1.   The test model must be representative of the modified product as it will be when sold.
2.   The potential to find possible unreliability defects on unmodified products still in service must not be destroyed.

Basically, it is a matter of understanding from the FMEA analysis whether key items in bad failure modes are likely to continue to receive proper trials in both modes.

To conclude, prototypes used intelligently are good value. Unrepresentative, late prototypes, sloppily tested and monitored, are an expensive waste and give delusions of security. Key points are:

1.   Plan concept testing by subsystem tests and analytical techniques.
2.   Use prototypes to test realistic usage patterns and keep ahead of customers in product experience.
3.   Continuously log and monitor prototype performance and agree action plans on *any* failure.
4.   Apply Taguchi analytical techniques to cut test and failure costs and risks.
5.   Carry out statistical analysis (e.g. Wieball plots) to establish failure rates.

In-service activities

In most companies the balance between after-failure support and failure prevention is wrong. Recovery costs after a failure are always excessive, and can easily lead to loss of business as well as excess cost. Much of the failure prevention activity must concentrate on new design, because this implies no recovery costs and no loss of business. However, there are useful gains to be made from monitoring field experience.

Customer trial prototypes are a method already discussed. Others include:

- Effective warranty schemes encouraging reporting of premature failure or deterioration.
- Monitoring the service records of selected companies (agents, repairers, etc.).
- Sample recoveries of second-hand products.
- Monitoring of replacement purchases.

Many consumer-goods companies operate warranty schemes designed not only to recover from failures, but also to monitor and record accurately all known failures and deterioration, and often to recover failed material. Most machinery companies do not do this, but should.

In the motor vehicle business, repair records of selected dealers and service outlets are a source of valuable information about their own and competitors' products. The practice is to sample all repair and service records for, say, a month, and use statistical techniques to relate them to the whole product population.

Secondhand products are also a good source of data about product durability, wherever there is a noticeable secondhand market. Motor vehicles and 'white goods' are good examples. Again, the practice is feasible for machinery companies, but few known examples of this practice exist.

A practice which is also largely unexploited is monitoring by means of surveys and questionnaires of replacement purchases. Some brand replacements are easy to monitor (by using the goodwill situation of the repeat purchase), although they may be overoptimistic in terms of opinions expressed. Changes in favour of a brand are also feasible by this method. Changes away from a brand are more difficult, but not always impossible to organize. Again, capital and industrial goods manufacturers, despite their close customer contacts, do not use this source as much as they should.

Jaguar Cars has recently adopted the practice of telephoning all owners three months after delivery to establish any reliability or service problems. This has revealed several common quality problems not reported through the service and warranty mechanisms.

Total life economics

For purchases of mature products, particularly for industrial and mundane domestic purposes, cost is an important purchase consideration. Purchasers should, however, be influenced by the total life operating cost of a product, rather than taking the short term and short-sighted view that is restricted only to purchase price. A sales representative's motor car is a familiar example. The initial cost might be £10 000. If the company life of the car is three years, it might cover 100 000 miles, costing another £6000 for fuel over the period. Figure 11.4 illustrates other costs contributing to the total life cost in this example.

£ 20 000?

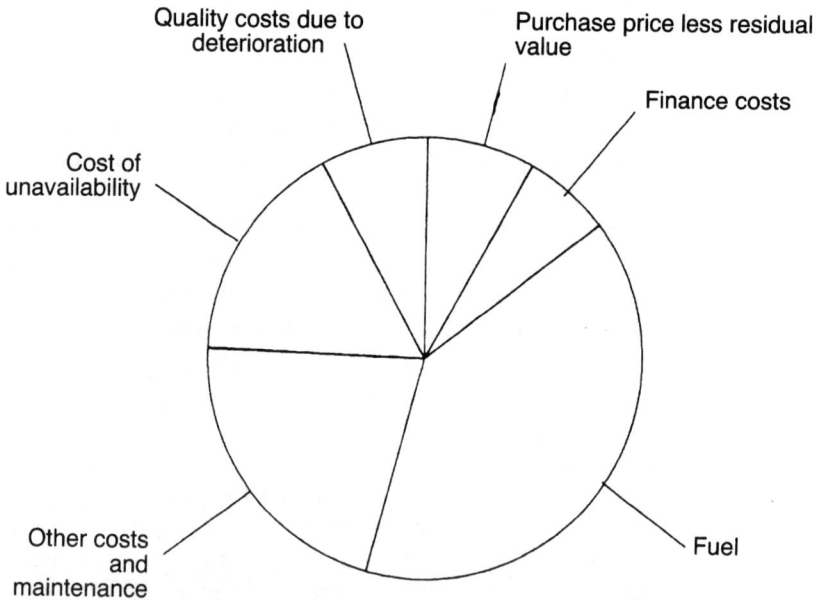

Figure 11.4.   Car cost over three years.

In general, the total life cost of a product sold for industrial use (such as a machine tool) would include the following elements:

1. The initial purchase price, together with any associated financing costs.
2. The obvious operating costs (fuel, power supply, consumables,

repairs, maintenance, labour).
3.   The opportunity cost of having to use alternative solutions when the product is unavailable.
4.   Loss of output or business when the product is unavailable.
5.   Loss of business or extra cost through deterioration in quality.

The main problem is that many of the key factors in total life costing are difficult to quantify, despite their significant size. Yet they may be crucial to purchase decisions.

Purchase and finance costs are set at the outset and unlikely to change significantly during the life of the equipment. Fuel and general maintenance costs have a strong reliability/durability element in them, and calculations concerning deterioration of prime movers and controls will have as their end-effect increases in operating cost. Similarly, inconvenient failures of small items with no other consequence will simply add to operating cost.

Unavailability, whether due to 'planned maintenance' or to unexpected 'casual' failure, can impinge on cost in a number of ways:

*   Increase the number of machines required to carry out a specific task.
*   Reduce the amount of business it is possible to perform.
*   Put the business at risk owing to failure during the performance of a task.
*   Expose the business to being sued for causing damage to customers, employees or others.

In the first two situations, increases in cost to the user can arise either progressively or, very often, have a 'threshold' effect where availability limits the activity levels possible unless major extra investment is undertaken.

There is also a significant element of quality in determining the amount of business which will be performed. If the quality of the product or service offered falls significantly as a result of deterioration or unexpected failure, the volume of business obtained will be restricted by customer willingness to purchase. The amounts of money involved may be very significant and difficult to quantify. There are, however, methods of quantifying loss of business, although not with traditional accounting precision.

It is sensible to build a financial model of the user's perceived costs of a product. This is one of the primary factors in reliability planning for new and improved products. Using spreadsheet techniques, it is

Initial cost	Finance cost	Output value	Operating cost	Quality cost indirect	Quality cost	Capacity and availability costs
Function 1	Life	Direct output	Direct input	Less volume	Wasted output	Capacity
Function 2	Interest		Energy	Lower price	Reworked output	In-use availability
Function 3	Repayment	By-products	Manning			Servicing
Unallocated to function	Depreciation		Consumables		Wasted material	Casual failure
Installation	Residual value		Housing		Low value output	Temporary/permanent duplication
Spares	Insurance		Maintenance		Danger	
Inventory	Work-in-progress		Repair		Pollution/environmentals	First available
Start-up costs					Warranty	

Figure 11.5.   Total life cost model.

possible to provide for multiple options, in both the initial price of a product and reliability factors. Key blocks in the model are:

1. An itemized breakdown of initial cost, preferably recognizing the product's main functions separately.
2. Optional financing routes for the user, including differences influenced by product expected life.
3. Operating costs, particularly concerned with fuel and manning.
4. Operating quality costs, concerned with quality of output and service, waste of material, knock-on quality costs.
5. Operating capacity costs, concerned with ultimate capacity (having regard to customer need) and availability.
6. Value of business which is likely to be performed, recognizing both capacity and quality restrictions.

The work model should have a time-base at least 50 per cent longer than the nominal product life (see Figure 11.5).

Some conclusions

Reliability engineering is a difficult task, if only because all feedback of results occurs too late and constitutes a business risk. Key tasks are not well done at present, and expose customers in many situations to unnecessary inconvenience, business risk and even personal risk. There are six important steps:

1. Write reliability risks and target achievement levels into the initial user specification.
2. Test concepts by FMEA, FTA, simulation, calculation and rig test before building prototypes.
3. Use prototypes to be ahead of user experience.
4. Take advantage of all possible field experience.
5. Treat modifications as seriously as new design.
6. Remember, communication at the design stage is the essence of good reliability — all other methods are too late.

References and further reading

British Standard (BS) 5760, *Reliability of Constructed or Manufactured*

Products, Systems, Equipments and Components, British Standards Institution, Milton Keynes.

Gunter, B., 'A Perspective on the Taguchi Methods', *Quality Progress,* (monthly journal), American Society of Quality Control, June 1987.

O'Connor, Patrick D. T., *Practical Reliability Engineering* 2nd edn, John Wiley, Chichester 1985.

Quality and Reliability Engineering International, a journal published by John Wiley, Chichester.

Smith, D. J., *Reliability and Maintainability in Perspective* 3rd edn, Macmillan, London 1988.

Part Four
SOFTWARE QUALITY

12   The Traditional Approach to Software Quality

David J. Smith*

Historically, quality assurance and quality control have developed through the need to identify, eliminate and indeed prevent hardware failures. Towards the end of the 1960s there was an awareness of the problem of software-related failures. It became clear that, with tolerably reliable hardware, those failures arising purely from aspects of the software could dominate the total number. Furthermore, compared with hardware failures they are extremely difficult to diagnose and impossible to predict, due to the limited visibility which exists in computer software. There was, even at that time, a general feeling that they related to the structure of the design process which generated the software.

Software failures

Failures arise from three basic causes including the design itself. These are often described by means of the bathtub curve first shown in Figure

11.1. Figure 12.1 shows three distributions as follows:

(a)   early failures related to manufacturing imperfections, in other words, populations of inherent failures due to microscopic flaws;
(b)   so-called random failures, assumed to be due to fluctuations in stress;
(c)   wearout failures due to mechanisms of physical change.

Owing to the digital nature of software it can show neither of the last two characteristics since it has no physical entity. There remains then, only that inherent population of defects which arise from one's inability to foresee the total logic of a software package.

Unlike hardware failures there is no physical change which causes a unit to cease functioning. Software failures are errors which, owing to the complexity of code, seldom become evident immediately. Figure 12.2 illustrates the concept of *fault/error/failure*.

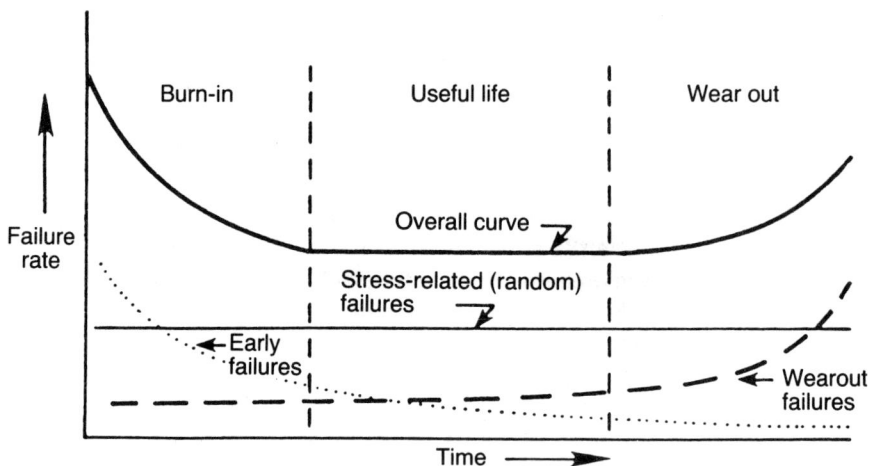

Figure 12.1.   The bathtub curve.

Faults may occur in both hardware and software. Software faults — often known as 'bugs' — will arise as a result of code being used for the first time or because of corruption due to outside influence. The presence of a fault in a program does not necessarily result in either error or failure. A long time may elapse before that portion of the code is used under circumstances which lead to failure.

A *fault* (bug) may lead to an incorrect state. A data value or an instruction is thus incorrect and remains so until the particular part of the code is executed.

An *error* may propagate to become a *failure* if the system does not contain some error recovery logic capable of dealing with and minimizing its effect.

A *failure*, be it hardware or software-related, is the termination of the ability of an item to perform its specified function.

There is evidence that most errors (over 60 per cent) are committed during the requirements and design phases. The remaining 40 per cent occur during coding. That is not to say that coding is not a part of the design but it is only the final activity in a much larger process. The more complex the system, the more faults will be likely to stem from ambiguities and omissions in the specification stages. Major sources of faults are given below.

The requirements specification

(a) incorrect requirements due to:
    — model not a good fit to the physical situation;
    — incorrect document cross-references;
(b) inconsistent or incompatible requirements;
    — two references giving conflicting information;
(c) requirement unclear or illogical;
(d) requirement omitted, e.g. handling of invalid inputs.

The design

(a) unstructured-approach to the design breakdown (i.e. detail is considered first);
(b) use of non-standard language;
(c) lack of change control;
(d) specification was misunderstood.

Coding

(a) semantic errors involving incorrect use of statements;
(b) logical errors in translating the design into code;
(c) detailed syntax errors which may have escaped detection by the compiler;
(d) use of an incorrect condition at a branch;
(e) poor data validation (e.g. no default condition after a data input);
(f) variables not initialized, or used incorrectly;
(g) insufficient arithmetical accuracy;
(h) insufficient range checks (e.g. divide by zero);

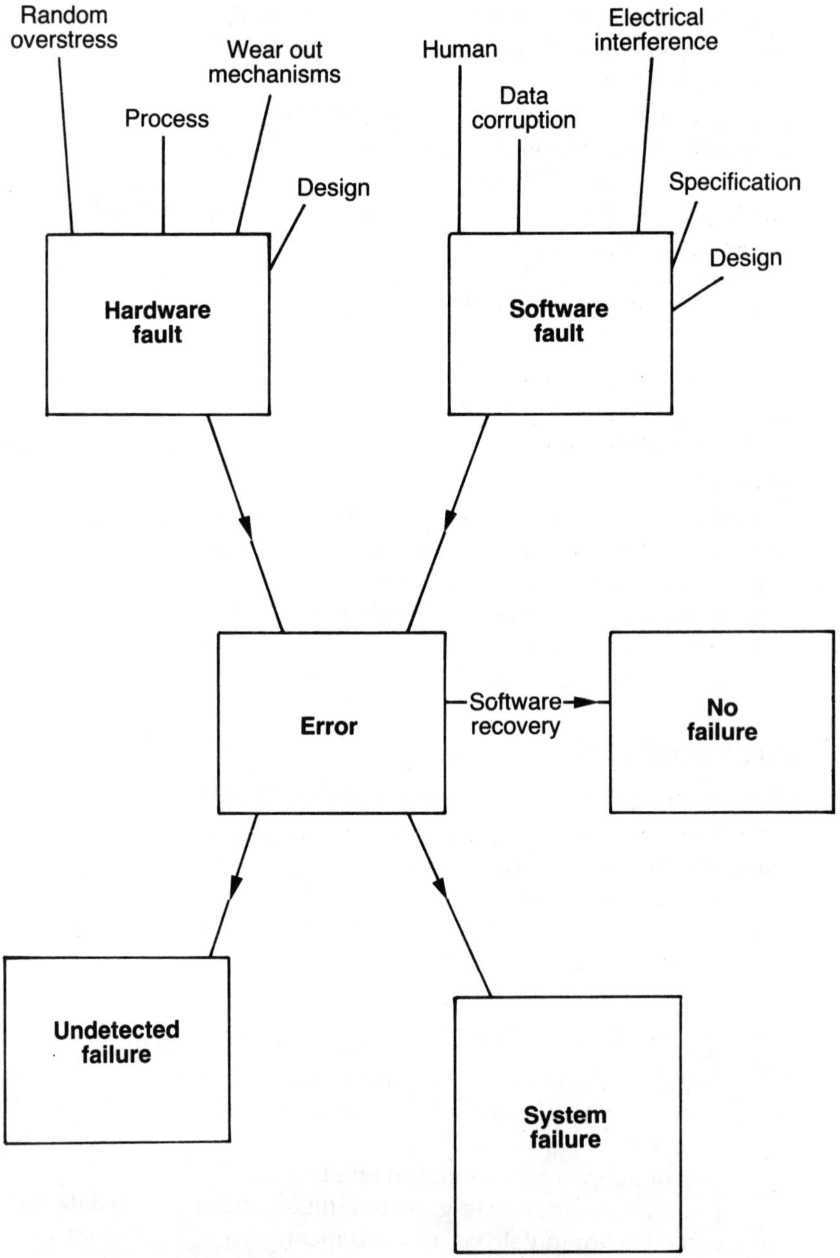

Figure 12.2.   Fault/error/failure.

(i) type mismatch (e.g. string used as variable);

(j) residual errors in compilers.

The need for a qualitative approach

Software failures are not time-related since they are revealed as a result of exercising new paths in the software in conjunction with combinations of real time inputs to the system. At present, attempts to model distributions of failures are hampered by lack of adequate field data to validate them. Thus, owing to the lack of precision, there is little benefit in terms of achieved reliability to be gained from software failure rate modelling.

Software quality is enhanced by preventing and/or removing faults during the design process. This is achieved by means of discipline and reviews and therefore one should concentrate on these qualitative activities.

Reliability is a quantitative parameter used to explore the rate of failure. Quality is on the other hand a wider description and need not always have to involve a statistical measurement or demonstration. The term software quality is preferable in this context whereas software reliability refers to the various modelling activities.

Growth of standards and guidelines

Owing to the proliferation of programmable systems, and to their rapidly widening application over the last 10 years into safety-related equipment, many standards and guidelines have been produced. Even if an exhaustive list were given here it would be out of date before publication. The most important are listed below.

The safe use of programmable electronic systems **(Health and Safety Executive) 1987.**

In 1981 the HSE issued a booklet *Microprocessors in Industry,* which broadly addressed the problem of microprocessors in plant applications. This led to the drafting of (and subsequent public comment on) a document which was published in 1987.

It has been recognized that, due to the wide spectrum of programmable electronic system (PES) applications, further second-tier documents, covering guidance on the development of specific applications, should follow. This should ultimately lead to simpler guidance and a more consistent approach to specific applications.

The guidelines are aimed at giving generic guidance on optimizing the integrity of programmable equipment wherever it is used to provide a safety system. If the safety features are adequately satisfied by non-programmable equipment then the document does not apply, although the principles, in fact, apply equally well to any software or hardware system. The document is in two volumes comprising an overview and the main document. The assessment strategy addresses three characteristics:

(a) the configuration;

(b) the hardware reliability;

(c) the system integrity, which includes the quality of design and implementation of the hardware and software.

Guidelines for the documentation of software in industrial computer systems, The Institution of Electrical Engineers, 1985

This document was prepared by the Institution of Electrical Engineers (IEE) Computing Standards Subcommittee and published in 1985. It is a fairly thorough treatment of the major documents required for software requirements and design documentation.

A Group of EEA (Electronic Engineering Association) guides

The EEA has published several concise guides to various areas of software quality.

EWICS TC7 (European Workshop on Industrial Computer Systems)

This group was funded by the EC, to produce guidelines on various aspects of systems integrity, safety, assessment and metrics.

IEEE Software Engineering Standards (USA)

This set of standards is being developed by the IEEE (Institute of Electrical and Electronics Engineers (U.S.)) to enhance communications between software engineers and to provide guidance on the types, formats and contents of software design documents as well as on the activities in the development cycle. They are intended to be 'how to' standards which explain the activities in detail rather than giving broad advice. The IEEE software engineering standards are submitted to ANSI (the American National Standards Institute) for review as national standards.

The STARTS Guide

This is a DTI (Department of Trade and Industry) initiative which has resulted in a guide, now in its second edition. Its emphasis is on software tools and methods which aid the management and control of software development. Five main areas are:

- Project management
- Configuration management
- Project support environments
- Requirements definition and design
- Verification, validation and test

As interest in software quality grows it is certain that the list of guidelines will continue to expand. There is much common ground between the documents since each organization wishes to be seen to address the topic. The outline of methods in this and the following chapter broadly describes the guidance given in the various documents, many of which are supported by extensive checklists. Two such checklists are provided at the end of this chapter. The use of checklists has both advantages and disadvantages:

(a) they provide an *aide-mémoire* so that essential features are not overlooked;
(b) they should not be used slavishly but as a menu from which to select the pertinent areas for the task in hand and should therefore be used only by experienced auditors;
(c) they constrain lateral thinking by giving the impression of being exhaustive.

Traditional methods

The traditional software quality methods can be grouped under the five headings shown in Figure 12.3.

Documentation controls

The documentation will vary, according to the size of the product, from a complex hierarchy of specifications, as illustrated in Figure 12.4, to a few pages consisting of:

- a functional description;
- design texts and diagrams;
- a program listing (lines of source code).

```
┌─────────────────────────────────────────────┐
│                                               │
│  Documentation controls  ⎫                    │
│                          ⎬  Prevention        │
│  Programming standards   ⎭                    │
│                                               │
│  Fault tolerant design                        │
│                                               │
│                                               │
│  Design review           ⎫                    │
│                          ⎬  Correction        │
│  Test                    ⎭                    │
│                                               │
└─────────────────────────────────────────────┘
```

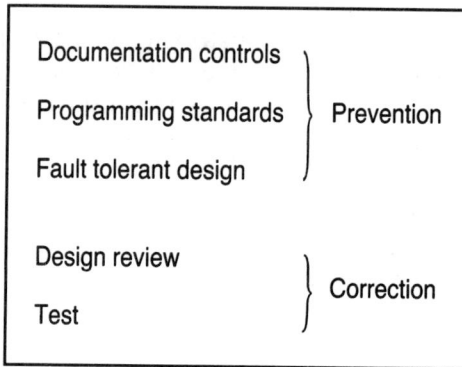

Figure 12.3.   Traditional software quality methods.

In more complex systems the structured hierarchy (Figure 12.4) is essential. It represents a top-down approach whereby the requirement is decomposed from the user requirements specification through the various levels of design specification to the source code listings.

It is now widely accepted that the so-called top-down approach provides the best result. Briefly the approach takes the whole system and decomposes it functionally into major subsystems. Each subsystem can then be decomposed in a similar manner until there are codeable modules. The major advantage of the top-down approach is that it treats the system as a whole and not as piecemeal components as in a 'bottom-up' design. The format, numbering and control of this document hierarchy is essential in order to trace and audit requirements — in other words to implement the remainder of what constitutes software quality. It is this author's experience that lack of a visible documentation structure reflecting the system described above, nearly always coincides with design problems and delays, and vastly higher failure rates during test and commissioning.

Programming standards

The brain is not well adapted to retaining random information hence standardized rules and concepts substantially reduce the probability of error.

A standard approach to creating files, polling output devices, handling interrupt routines, etc constrains the programmer to proven methods. A further step in that direction is the use of standard subroutines to perform common functions within the system. Reinventing the wheel is both a waste of time and an unnecessary

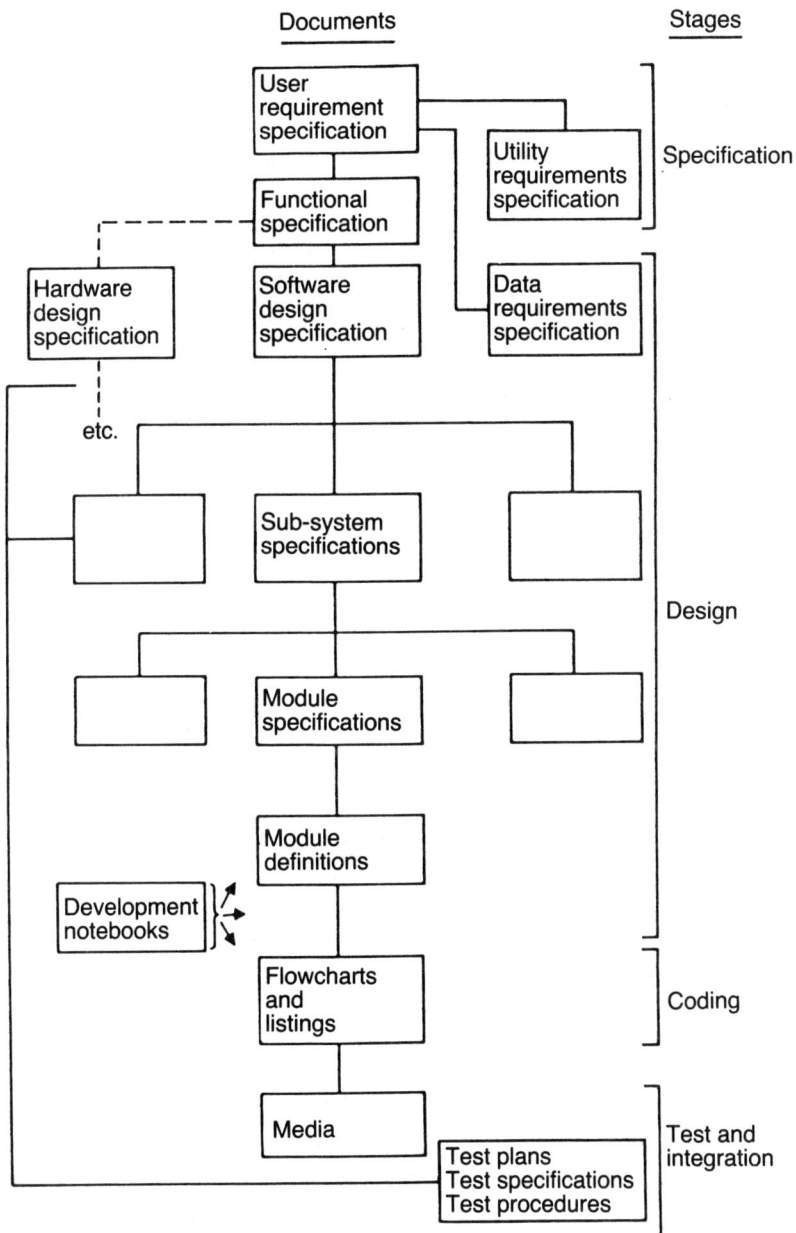

Figure 12.4.   Documentation hierarchy.

source of error. Examples are:

- extended memory addressing (EMA) buffer management;
- EMA table access;
- system error routine
- commonly-used data structures.

The undisciplined use of GOTO statements in high level language is dangerous and leads to difficulties in perceiving the functions when reading source code. This is known as spaghetti code. Modern block structured languages often contain no GOTO statements. Modules should have only one entry point and it is desirable that they have only one clearly defined exit.

To avoid data corruption the use of globals should be minimized so that modules can only access data local to their subsystem. Where global data is required, then standard subroutines must be used for access. A good guide to module size might be 30-60 lines of code plus 20 lines of comment, but the ultimate criterion is total perceivability in order to grasp the function.

Fault-tolerant design

A frequent misconception is that the elimination of faults is the sole factor in achieving quality software. This is too simplistic an assumption. In practice all software is likely to contain residual faults, albeit at very low levels even after extensive quality assurance. Compare, therefore, two safety systems one of which has a few unknown residual faults and the other of which has twice as many. Assume that the code having the greater number of faults has been carefully structured in such a way as to restrict the propagation of errors. Assume, also, that there are a number of error check routines in the code which enable the program to reinitialize at known acceptable values when an error is detected.

If, in addition to these features, the safety system and its software are designed in such a way that individual failures do not cause total loss of function then they will at least continue to offer a degraded level of protection. An example would be a fire protection system which measures more than one parameter (i.e. UV light, smoke, rate of temperature rise). The interpretation of each type of input and the generation of executive action could be dealt with by separate pieces of hardware and software. This fault-tolerant type of design offers a far higher level of integrity than a system with less faults and far worse consequences in the event of failure.

Configuration and diversity

Redundancy is often used as a means of improving system reliability. Peripheral signals are fed to two (or more) channels or processors and outputs are voted. However, any software fault, with simple hardware redundancy, will be a common cause failure since the identical code will exist in each equipment. Recent studies have shown that the number of common cause failures due to software in real time redundant systems is greater than for other equipment. One defence involves *software diversity*, a form of redundancy involving the design and coding of separate software for each of the replicated channels. Sometimes called 'N version programming', this is not only expensive but is also not a total defence since specification-related faults will propagate through each of the N designs.

Fault-tolerant designs

A number of software features can be included which improve the integrity of systems under fault conditions. These include:

(a)   fault identification, by the use of:
- watchdog timers,
- cyclic memory checks,
- relay runner techniques,
- built-in tests,
- range and variable checks;

(b)   error correction, by means of:
- parity,
- checksums,
- reinitialization at known states,
- recovery blocks,
- exception handling.

Graceful degradation and recovery

The overall design philosophy should take account of the need to operate in degraded modes. Functions should be partitioned so that single failures cause only degraded performance rather than loss of the total safety function. This can only be achieved if taken into account by the requirements, where functional diversity can be specified, levels of function can be defined and operating requirements grouped into categories.

The software design should attempt to minimize the routes of communication between groups of modules so that errors are discouraged from propagating. Thus errors are more likely to be confined to single functions. The system may then be able to provide service, albeit at a degraded level, by means of other functions. This is of particular importance in controlling hazardous processes.

Design review

Two common misconceptions about design reviews are:

- that they are schedule progress meetings,
- that they enable one to appraise the designer.

These are both dangerous misunderstandings and will result in the reviews not being effective. Their purpose is to verify the design, at specific milestones, against the requirements — not to establish reasons for delay. The features of a design review should therefore be geared to:

(a)   making the design visible;
(b)   providing a means of tracing the requirement through the specifications and design;
(c)   measuring the functions against the requirement;
(d)   identifying faults.

In other words, the design review must provide a feedback loop verifying each stage in order to judge the adequacy and completeness of the design and thus provide confidence to proceed to the next level of design.

Procedures should identify:

1.   Which design stages will be subject to review.
2.   The participants and the persons with overall responsibility.
3.   Details of records to be kept and rules for the control of follow-up action.
4.   Rules for review of follow-up actions.
5.   Checklists for guidance — see the end of this chapter for a sample.
6.   Preparations to be made in advance of each design review (documentation, etc.)

There are two levels of review. At the module level the less formal review may involve only members of the design team and might be implemented as a continuing project activity. A log will be kept, either by way of the notebook or by adding notes to the module definition papers. Persons involved in this type of review include peers of the designer and other members of the team.

At a more formal level, planned design reviews at specific

milestones will involve persons from outside as well as inside the design team. These will be scheduled as major project activities at defined points in the development cycle.

Testing

Traditionally much of the focus in software quality has been on testing. Although this is an important area, the major part of the quality effort should have been expended on the earlier design activities. Nevertheless, there needs to be a hierarchy of test documents and a structured approach to testing from coded modules upwards to system test. Its purpose is to reveal the hidden population of defects which are created during the specification, design and coding stages of development.

Progressing through the structured plan of test gradually builds confidence. First, modules are proved by applying inputs and measuring the data outputs against the specification. Later, modules are integrated and required to respond to a greater range of inputs. Finally, the product performance is demonstrated in a range of functional tests.

This is no small aspect of the development life cycle since it is not easily possible to foresee the types of failure which will occur and, therefore, it is difficult to construct a range (or structure) of tests which will seek them out. As much as a half of the programmer's time may be consumed by debugging and error correction, as a result of which any effective improvements in test methodology, or any automated tools which reduce the time consumed by testing, will have a major effect on design time and life cycle cost.

Software is usually embedded into a system where it becomes an integral part of the function and configuration of the product. A large number of software systems are now real time control systems and are required to interface with a large number of external stimuli. Failures are therefore more critical than in simple batch processing applications. Most of these embedded programs are large and contain many modules. Similar combinations of input conditions can produce different outputs for very small changes in timing or environmental conditions. It is thus impossible to ensure that every eventuality has been tested.

Integrity of safety-related systems

Applications of programmable equipment now include equipment carrying out safety functions. Examples are fire and gas detection apparatus, shut-down and control systems in process plant, medical electronics, aircraft controls, machine tool control, nuclear plant and weapon systems. The consequences of failure under these circumstances are often severe and thus attract particular attention.

Using software in potentially hazardous situations leads to two main difficulties:

(a)   due to the complexity of software failure modes the possibility of hazardous failure is greater;

(b)   since the use of software makes failures difficult to predict it is difficult to perceive whether or not the integrity of a system is adequate.

There are three basic design approaches which should be considered when incorporating software elements into a safety system:

1.   *The software directly controls the safety function.* Figure 12.5a shows a contact providing an input to a programmable electronic system (PES) which, in turn, provides an output. The PES output energizes a relay coil whose contacts cause some safety action. It is possible to imagine the PES causing an unwanted operation, or even failing to operate when required. Owing to the uncertainty associated with software failures, this solution is seldom favoured.

2.   *The system retains hard-wired control.* Figure 12.5b shows an arrangement in which the PES carries out functions, but where the safety relay circuit is operated directly from the input signal. Currently this system is usually adopted.

3.   *Diverse software is provided.* Diverse software is employed so that the electronic systems are duplicated, triplicated or multiplied even further, and with each PES separately designed and programmed. Some measure of protection against software failure is thus obtained, and the outputs from the diverse systems can be compared and voted. This arrangement is illustrated in Figure 12.5c.

Typical checklists

Checklist A: Documentation and control

1.   Is there an adequate structure of documentation?
2.   Are all the documents available?
3.   Do specifications define what must not happen as well as what must?

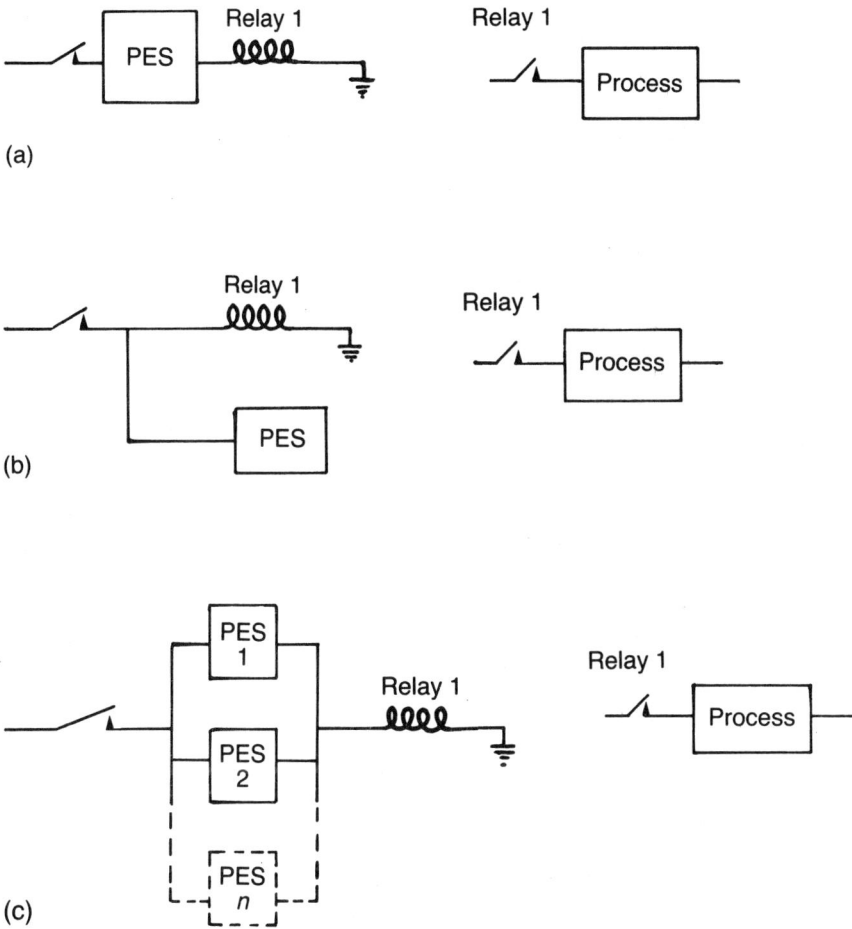

Figure 12.5. Safety system configurations.

4. Is the format of the documents consistent?
5. Is change control in operation?
6. Are development notebooks in use? (If so, audit a sample for completeness.)
7. Are the requirements of the higher level specifications accurately reflected down through the other documents to module level?
8. Are there a significant number of parameters left 'To be determined'?

9. Is 'automatic coding' (use of coding on flowcharts) in use?
10. Do actual documents and firmware (PROMs) correspond to the build state records? (Do sample checks).
11. Are maintenance manuals:
    - adequately detailed and illustrated?
    - prepared during the design?
    - objectively tested?

Checklist B: Programming standards

1. Is there a document defining program standards?
2. Is it project specific?
3. Is each of the following covered?
   - block length,
   - module size,
   - use of globals,
   - use of GOTO statements,
   - operator error security (error traps),
   - authorized use security,
   - data organization and structures,
   - memory organization and backup,
   - error correction code,
   - fault diagnosis,
   - layout,
   - comment (REM statements)
4. Is there a library of common program modules?
5. Is there conscious justification of the choice of high level or assembler languages?

Further reading

Smith, David J. and Wood, Kenneth B., *Engineering Quality Software*, Elsevier, Barking, Essex 1987.

13 Software Quality through Formal Methods

David J. Smith*

This chapter continues the subject of software quality which was introduced in the previous chapter. In this chapter the methods described are more formal, in the sense that the approach is more sharply defined and disciplined, with automated procedures used where these are available.

The software design cycle

The concept of a software design cycle is illustrated in Figure 13.1. This is a convenient model which serves two purposes. Firstly, it displays the process of software conception in a graphical and logical form. Secondly, it provides a framework around which the quality assurance activities can be built in a disciplined manner.

The important feature of Figure 13.1 is the existence of the loops, which represent a review or test at each stage of the design. Faults discovered earlier in the design cycle as a result of these reviews and tests will cost less to remedy and will be less likely to propagate into

*Copyright of this chapter remains with the author.

229

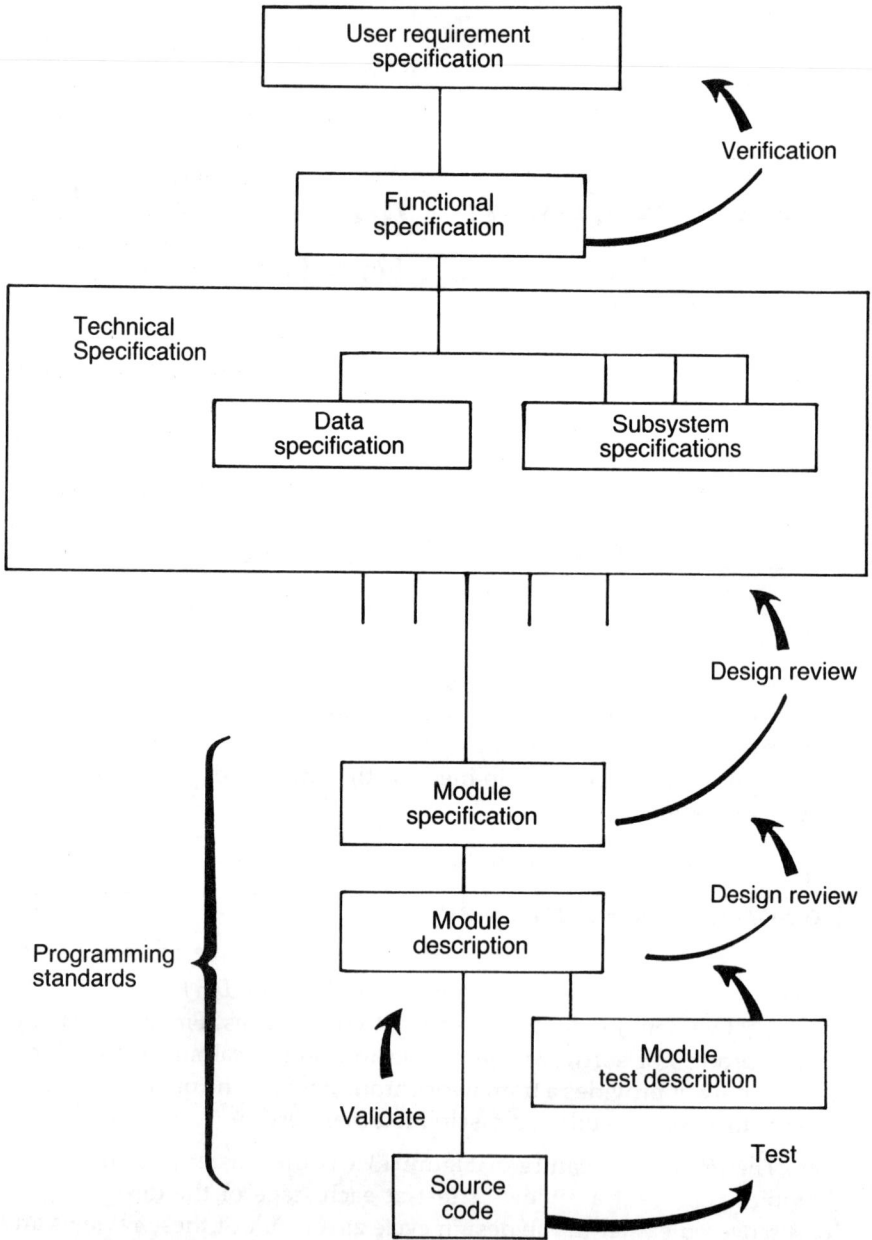

Figure 13.1.   Software design cycle.

field use.

In the software life cycle it is important to distinguish between the two words *specification* and *design*.

The specification (the top part of Figure 13.1) is a description of requirements, usually written by the user. It is vital that such a requirements specification is an accurate statement of what is needed. An incorrect or ambiguous statement at this stage will simply be reflected into the design. The error or deficiency may not become evident until much later, when testing reveals that the product is not that which was wanted.

The process of designing is the breaking down of the requirements specification into a logical hierarchy of successive descriptions, resulting eventually in a program code. The middle part of Figure 13.1 deals with this activity. The design itself is the set of documents and code listings which are produced.

Figure 13.2 represents the proportions of effort and (therefore) costs spent on the design cycle. The approach to the design cycle has been very much that illustrated by the upper half of the figure. Expenditure on design has given way quickly to expenditure on coding: all too

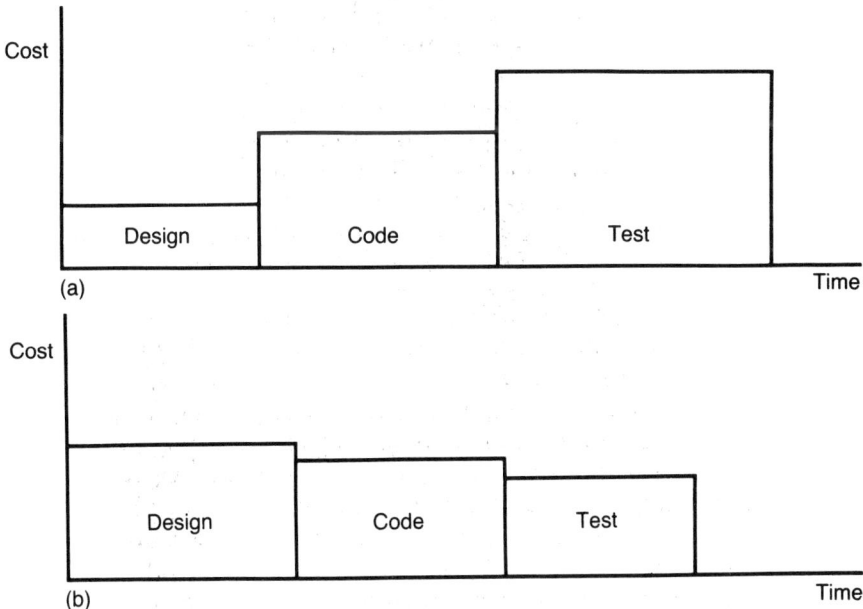

Figure 13.2. Distribution of time and costs in software production. (a) Common approach. (b) Enlightened approach.

frequently these activities are started together. The result is that the cost of testing is often excessive.

The lower part of Figure 13.2 shows the aim of enlightened software engineering. More is spent on design, as a result of which coding and testing costs are less. The overall expenditure is reduced. It is no secret that schedules and quality are also improved. The aim of software quality is to encourage this process.

Limitations of traditional methods

In order to discuss the limitations of quality methods currently used it is necessary to understand the 'three quality problems'. Figure 13.3 presents the design cycle in another way, so as to emphasize the difficulties.

Firstly, whereas much of the design and coding is carried out using formal computer languages, the user requirements are expressed in 'free language'. This provides the environment for faults of ambiguity and omission which in turn lead to errors and failures. These are the hardest to identify during design review and test since most attempts at validation only establish 'correctness' against the requirements as they are stated.

Secondly, the requirement to validate the correctness of code against the preceeding requirements of the hierarchy of specifications has traditionally been tackled informally. Open-ended design review techniques, such as code inspection and structured walkthrough, succeed in finding some of the faults but cannot provide assurance that *all* problems have been identified.

Thirdly, testing of software is, by the very nature of programmed instructions with their branching statements, only a small sample of the total possibilities. Even relatively simple software systems have permutations of inputs and outputs, and of program execution which number in millions. Even automated test methods provide only a sample view of the system. Furthermore, it is seldom remembered that the mere extension of test time only increases confidence in the *hardware* reliability. It proves no more regarding the software quality unless additional combinations of input/output and execution are involved.

In general these problems are only reduced by the application of more formal and automated methods. That is not to say that traditional software quality methods are not valuable, but simply that they should be enhanced by the use of the newer formal techniques as these are developed and become available. Other drawbacks to the existing

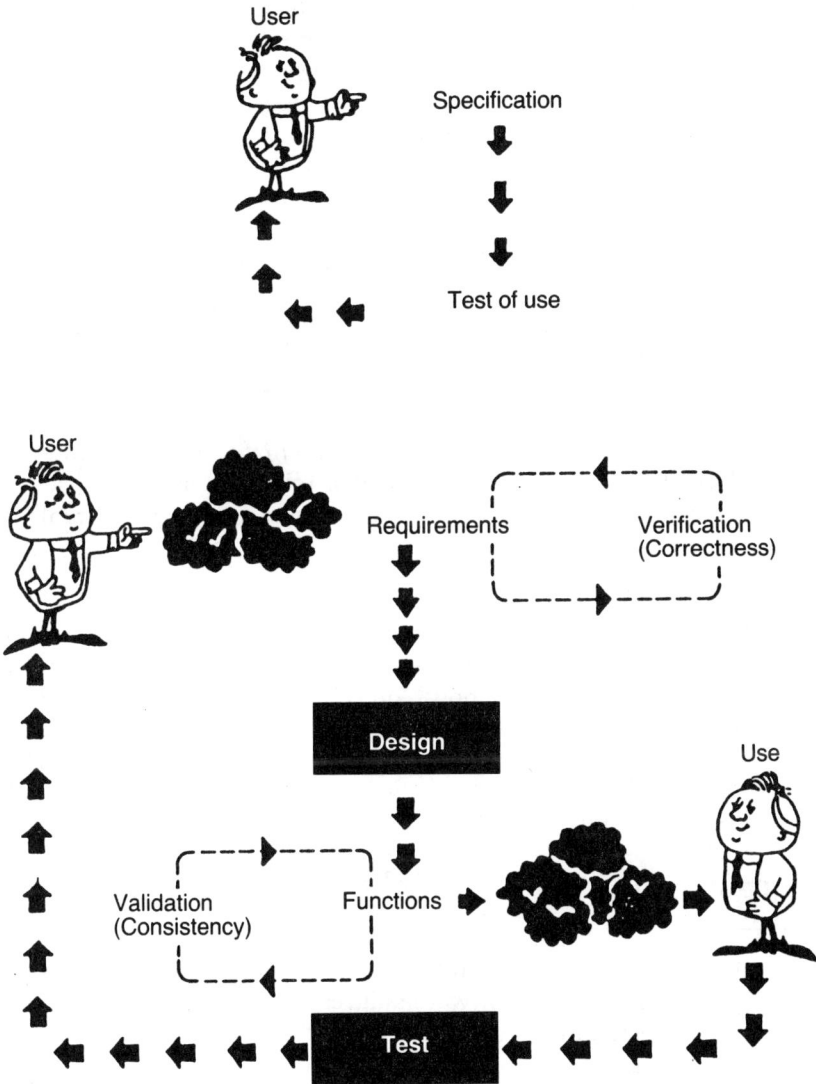

Figure 13.3.   The three quality problems.

open-ended informal methods are outlined below.

Addressing relevant parameters
In most cases, assessments address those aspects of software design

which are covered by traditional quality assurance. Inevitably the questions which are posed in each of these areas tend to be of a generic nature and, as a consequence, do not permit conclusive answers. Indeed, both positive and negative responses can be justified from a single question as, for example:

Have documentation and coding standards been adequately addressed?

From one point of view the answer can be 'Yes' in that some reasonable level of guidelines has been provided. An equally justifiable 'No' can be suggested in that the coding and design standards cannot guarantee the absence of faults. This open-ended qualitative checklist approach implies a lack of precision, making software quality impossible to assure.

Such controls and reviews eliminate many software-related faults. Nevertheless they are applied at a relatively superficial level with respect to those factors, in the design and code, which actually create errors.

False confidence
Despite the above shortcomings, there is a tendency to assume that because a safety system has been assessed then the mere fact of assessment has somehow 'qualified' the software. It does not recognize that inherent faults will almost certainly exist and that the assessment process did not admit the precision necessary to reveal them.

Formal requirements methods

It has already been stated that the original requirements specification is a major source of software failures. Clearly, if the programmer has been directed to solve the wrong problem, or if the requirements are incomplete, ambiguous or not understood, then even error-free design will still result in system failures as perceived in use. The potential for creating faults in the requirements specification arises largely from the fact that they are written in freely expressed English (or other) language. On the one hand this permits a comprehensive description but, on the other, it provides a vehicle for ambiguity and lack of clarity.

Formal requirements languages are fairly new, dating from the middle 1970s, and in most cases are still under development along with the software tools which accompany them. They constrain the writer to the use of mathematically precise methods and expressions and, as a result protect against ambiguity. Because they involve mathematical rules it is possible to verify a requirements specification by formal analysis methods. These 'proofs' are highly theoretical and are mostly carried out manually. In the future this process will certainly become automated and indeed some tools already exist.

The fact is that system requirements are highly complex, interactive and often ill-defined. There is no avoiding this problem and it must be faced that inadequacies in requirements definition lead to faulty design. Hence a requirements specification must embrace the following descriptions which together comprise the total requirement:

(a) why the system is needed, in technical, economic, maintenance and operating terms;

(b) what functions the system needs to fulfil. This does not include how the functions are actually to be performed, since that is part of the design;

(c) conditions which place limitations on the design.

The difficulty inherent in specification is the language. If plain English is used to express the specification then it is necessary to embrace not only the problem to be defined but the imprecisions and ambiguities of the language. Pitfalls include:

- Dangling ELSE, e.g. 'A must equal B or C.' No mention of what happens if it does not.
- Ambiguity of reference, e.g. 'add X to Y. This must be positive.' What? X, Y or their sum?
- Ambiguous words, e.g. usually, quickly.
- Ambiguous logic.

There are several 'requirements languages' and 'design methodologies' under development. These are referred to by abbreviations. They include, VDM, Z, OBJ.

One of the characteristics of these methodologies is that, in the past, they have been 'pencil and paper' techniques. More recently several of the techniques have begun to appear in automated form which allow the designer to manipulate diagrams on a workstation. These systems usually have, at their core, a database or data dictionary which allows the designer to keep track of the various entities which he has created. The automation of design methodologies is a major step forward since it removes much of the drudgery in creating the diagrammatic requirements of each. Figure 13.4 illustrates this idea.

At the outset, specification techniques have been based on computer systems since it was recognized that the high level of checking which is necessary in specifications can only be performed in that way.

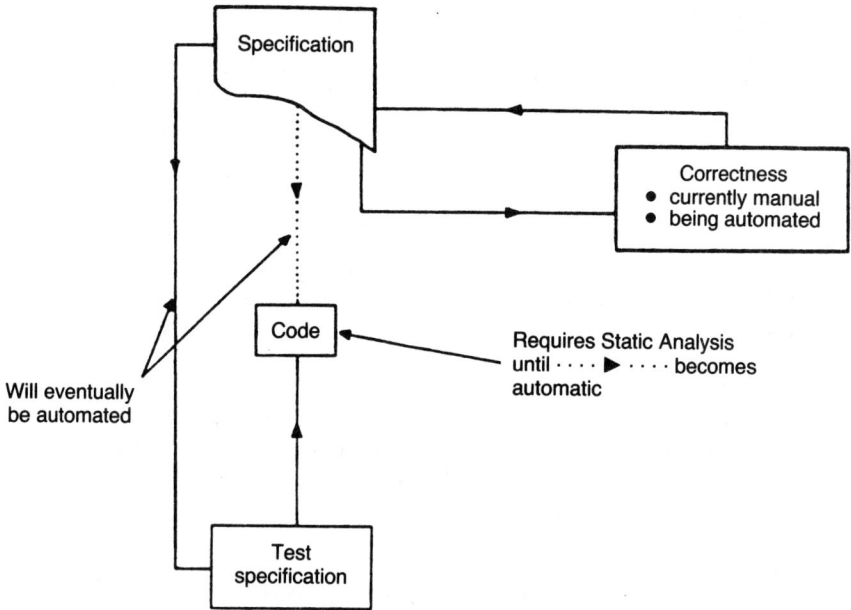

Figure 13.4.   Automated design.

The main tasks confronting the software industry today are specification techniques and the 'wrapping up' of the whole life cycle into a largely automated system so that self-checking for consistency, completeness and so on can be left to the computer. A number of projects are running which will achieve this goal in the near future. Figure 13.4 illustrates this view of the design cycle. A great deal of work is also in progress on a variety of analysis systems which provide some degree of proof of correctness.

The use of requirements languages will not dominate software engineering overnight. The capital cost of introducing them is high and thus they will gradually find applications — perhaps in safety-related equipment — where there is an incentive for high integrity software.

Static analysis

Static analysis involves tests which do not actually execute the program but examine the logic and paths within it. To some extent a compiler performs a static test by checking for syntax errors and undeclared variables.

Static analysers examine the code algebraically without the use of actual input and output data values to a far greater depth than does a compiler.

They are actually suites of routines, each of which carries out specific checks. The software is not executed but mathematical techniques are used to reveal the structure and functional relationships within the code. The high level language (e.g. FORTRAN, CORAL, PASCAL, etc.) has to be translated into a suitable form for analysis by the suite and an intermediate language is thus employed. This needs to be developed for each high level language.

Control flow analysers
These identify all possible starts and ends, unreachable code and 'black holes'. They give an initial feel for the quality of the program. If this is not good then there is very little likelihood that subsequent analysis will result in a good program.

Data use analysers
These identify all the inputs and outputs, and check that data is not being incorrectly handled (e.g. read before it has been written).

Information flow analysers
Outputs are analysed to describe which inputs they depend on (e.g. output Z depends on inputs A, B and F).

Partial program generators
These extract subprograms which cater for particular variables of interest. This helps to reduce complexity. These subprograms can then be submitted to the semantic analyser.

Semantic analysers
These provide the functional relationships between variables, for example, P is derived from $A^*CsqH-(D+T)$ [ie $A \times C^2 \times H - (D + T)$]. They identify what the program is doing for each path and thus provide a means of assessing whether the program meets the specification.

Compliance analysers

These take the outputs from the semantic analyser and compare them with an embedded specification. For example, if X must be in the range 7 to 45 the analyser tests to see if the condition is met in the program.

At present the available static analysis suites are:

- MALPAS; available from Rex Thompson and Partners, Farnham, Surrey.
- SPADE; available from Program Development Ltd, Southampton.
- LDRA; available from Liverpool University.

Currently intermediate languages are available for several of the commonly-used programming languages.

The implementation of static analysis is relatively inexpensive being in the order of a few tens of thousands of pounds. This is cost effective in all but the smallest real-time software development; revealing but a few faults earlier on will save the cost of the exercise.

Another benefit of static analysis is that it forces the use of more formal methods in order to provide the structure and thoroughness of design which it requires. Poor design and inadequate or ambiguous requirements are soon revealed by the analysis.

Dynamic test tools

It was mentioned, earlier in this chapter, that testing in real-time software systems is usually limited to a small sample of the total possible states.

Dynamic tests rely on executing the program with either simulated or real inputs. These include all forms of functional program testing such as:

- Stress tests which impose a range of abnormal and illegal input conditions so as to stress the capabilities of the software. The rate and volume of input data, processing time, utilization of data and memory are all tested beyond the design capability. The length and depth of the test will depend on the complexity of the application.
- Environmental tests, including electromagnetic interference are important for software systems since these are prone to data corruption resulting from both mains and airborne interference.

The important fact to remember is that, whereas hardware testing is enhanced by the passage of time, software testing requires that different paths are exercised.

The test process lends itself to automation and much effort is being invested in the development of automated test-beds and animators. The current description is test environments and these involve automation of test stimuli as well as interpreting and displaying the results of the tests. Examples include:

- Drivers. These provide a means of stimulating inputs.
- Test beds. These provide simulations and also a means of displaying data, variables and the code as it is executed through the test.
- Emulators. Provide an 'environment' which simulates responses as well as inputs.
- Analysers. Test alternate paths, execute software at extreme values and seed incorrect values.

Metrics

A controversial area which has attracted some interest in recent years involves the search for repeatable models whereby the failure rate of code is assessed from such parameters as:

- The number of lines of code.
- The number of branching statements.
- The coding time.
- The number of changes.
- The number of pages of documents.

These are known as quality metrics and the problem lies in the repeatability of any models which might be established for relating the variables. If this area is to progress, only the continued collection and analysis of field failure data will enable such regression models to be established.

Accreditation

In September 1986 the DTI (Department of Trade and Industry) sponsored ACARD (Advisory Council for Applied Research and Development) committee published a report entitled *Software — Vital key to UK Competitiveness.* This stressed the need for accreditation of:

- methods,
- tools,
- applications,
- products,
- software engineers.

The traditional methods described in the preceeding chapter and the formal techniques described in this one address all but the last and perhaps most important item in that list.

If the trend to perfect better software quality tools is to succeed then industry must demand formal education and training structures in order to breed a generation of software engineers who can embrace these disciplines and methods.

Further reading

Smith, David J. and Wood, Kenneth B. *Engineering Quality Software,* Elsevier, Barking, Essex 1987.

Part Five

STATISTICAL METHODS FOR QUALITY CONTROL IN MANUFACTURING

14 An Introduction to Statistics for Quality Applications

David Newton

The subject of statistics is concerned with the analysis and interpretation of data in situations of uncertainty and variability. Such variability is inescapable in most industrial situations, so statistical thinking should permeate all analyses of industrial data. This is particularly the case in the control of manufacturing processes. The following four chapters are concerned with statistical methods in quality assurance. This chapter gives an introduction to statistical analysis. Chapter 15 shows how the ideas contained in this chapter are applied to the assessment of process variability and its comparison with what is required of the process — referred to as 'process capability analysis'. Chapters 16 and 17 then build on these principles to establish methods for continuing control of production processes.

Data

Numerical data in statistical analysis can take two forms:

1. Continuous data.
2. Discrete data.

Continuous data are observations of continuous variables. A

continuous variable is a measurement that has no restriction on the values that can be observed apart from the physical constraints of the process that is generating them. For example, the dimensions of any machined component have ranges of values within which manufacture is possible, but within such a range there is no constraint on the values that can be achieved. The only limit to the number of decimal places to which a dimension is quoted is the resolution of the measuring equipment.

In contrast, discrete data can consist only of non-negative integers. These consist of counts of the number of times something happened (known as 'frequency') rather than measurements. In the quality assurance context, the count is usually of the number of items in a sample that are in some way defective. When such counts are being used in a quality control procedure, the procedure is described as 'by attributes' (as in 'control charting by attributes' and 'acceptance sampling by attributes'), the attribute in question being the defectiveness (or otherwise) of the item.

Examples of data are shown in Figures 14.1 and 14.2. Figure 14.1 shows an example of a continuous variable, and Figure 14.2 a discrete variable. As they stand, these tables give little information about the patterns of variability, and ways must be found of describing the data in a more helpful way. There are two ways of doing this — using pictures and using numbers.

5.14	4.81	5.02	5.56	5.31
4.73	5.19	5.00	4.81	5.07
5.74	5.10	5.25	5.44	4.88
5.32	5.16	4.78	5.38	5.22

Figure 14.1. Table of breaking loads (kg) of 20 test specimens of aluminium wire.

2	4	2	0	1	2	0	3	3	0	1	2
0	1	1	0	0	1	2	1	3	1	2	3
5	1	2	1	0	2	0	4	2	1	5	2
2	1	1	3	7	1	2	1	2	0	1	0
3	0	3	1	0	2	1	4	4	1	0	2

Figure 14.2. Number of breakdowns in machining centre in 60 successive weeks of operation.

Describing data using pictures
Slightly different approaches are needed for continuous and discrete data.

Continuous data
The data are represented pictorially using a 'histogram'. This is obtained by dividing the observed extent of the variable into a number of convenient 'class intervals' of equal width, and counting the number of data items (the frequency) that occurs in each interval. For Figure 14.1, we have:

Class Interval	Frequency
4.6 a.u. 4.8	2
4.8 a.u. 5.0	3
5.0 a.u. 5.2	7
5.2 a.u. 5.4	5
5.4 a.u. 5.6	2
5.6 a.u. 5.8	1

The abbreviation 'a.u.' stands for 'and under', simply to resolve arbitrarily the issue of which class interval includes values (such as 5.20) that occur exactly on a boundary. These values can then be shown pictorially in a histogram as shown in Figure 14.3, where the

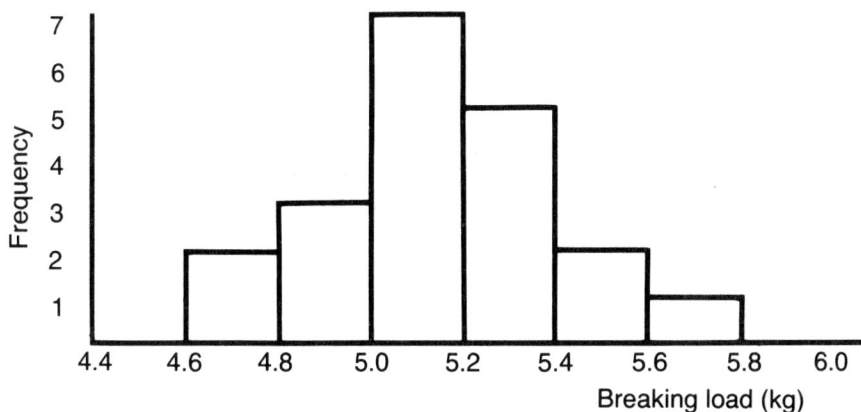

Figure 14.3.   Histogram of the data which was shown in Figure 14.1.

frequencies are represented by heights of blocks drawn across each class interval. Figure 14.3 shows the way in which most of the data are in the interval 5.0 to 5.2, with the frequencies reducing fairly symmetrically on either side. The choice of class interval is fairly arbitrary — either too wide or too narrow an interval width will reduce the information to be obtained from the picture. Trial and error is the usual way to the best choice, though there is a rule known as 'Sturges' Rule', which helps in choosing a sensible number of class intervals:

$$k = 1 + 3.3\log(n)$$

where the number of class intervals used should be a convenient number close to k for a sample size of n data items. For the data in Figure 14.1, Sturges' rule gives

$$k = 1 + 3.3\log(20) = 5.29$$

showing that the choice of six intervals was reasonable.

There are variations on the histogram that are sometimes useful. A common modification is to rescale the vertical axis by dividing the frequencies by n, the sample size, to give relative frequencies. In the example in Figure 14.1, this would replace 1, 2, 3, 4, 5, 6 and 7 by 0.05, 0.10, 0.14, 0.20, 0.25, 0.30 and 0.35, respectively. This permits comparison of two samples, or (as described later), comparison of a sample with a theoretical model without the comparison being confused by differences in sample size. Another variation is to use a

Class interval	Frequency	Cumulative frequency	Cumulative relative frequency
4.6 a.u. 4.8	2	2	0.10
4.8 a.u. 5.0	3	5	0.25
5.0 a.u. 5.2	7	12	0.60
5.2 a.u. 5.4	5	17	0.85
5.4 a.u. 5.6	2	19	0.95
5.6 a.u. 5.8	1	20	1.00

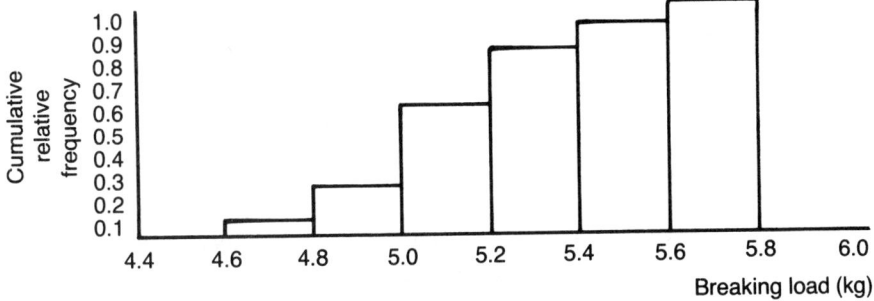

Figure 14.4.   Cumulative frequency diagram for the data in Figure 14.2.

cumulative frequency diagram (sometimes called an 'Ogive') in which the cumulative frequency less than the top of each class interval is plotted, as in the table on page 246 and in Figure 14.4.

Discrete data
As discrete data can only take integer values, it is not necessary to use class intervals. A frequency diagram is usually similar to that shown in Figure 14.5, which shows the data in Figure 14.2 (as summarized overleaf):

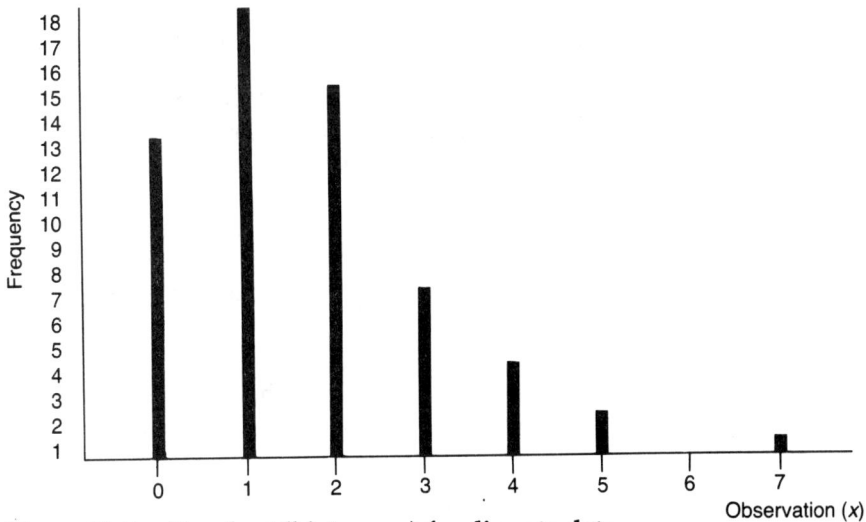

Figure 14.5.   Bar chart (histogram) for discrete data.

Observation (x)	0	1	2	3	4	5	6	7
Frequency (f)	13	18	15	7	4	2	0	1

Describing data with numbers

While pictures are a very succinct way of summarizing and presenting data, they do have the drawback that they cannot be stored and manipulated algebraically. To do these we need numbers, but numbers which summarize the data rather than the data points themselves. Such numbers are known as 'summary measures', different measures being used to quantify different aspects of the data. The most useful summary measures are 'measures of location' and 'measures of dispersion'.

Measures of location

Measures of location describe where the 'middle' of the data is located. There are three measurements generally in use: the mode, the median and the arithmetic mean.

Mode

The mode is usually defined as the most frequently occurring value in a sample. This makes sense in the case of discrete data. By inspection of the table accompanying Figure 14.5, it can be seen that the mode for this data is one breakdown, which occurs with a frequency of 18, the highest value in the sample. For the continuous variable in Figure 14.1, however, we cannot define a mode because all the 20 values are different, each having a frequency of one. What we have to do instead is use the mid-point of the class interval with the highest frequency, giving a value of 5.1. Although the mode is useful for discrete data, and can be obtained simply by inspection, it is less satisfactory for continuous data. It has further drawbacks. It is not necessarily unique (there can be ties for the highest frequency), and it can be misleading for data which is markedly non-symmetrical (referred to as 'skewed').

Median

The median is the central observation when the data are arranged in ascending order. For example, writing the data of Figure 14.1 in ascending order gives:

4.73, 4.78, 4.81, 4.88, 4.95, 5.00, 5.02, 5.07, 5.10, 5.14, 5.16, 5.19, 5.22, 5.25, 5.31, 5.32, 5.38, 5.44, 5.56, 5.74

As there are 20 values, there is not a central value (true for any sample of an even number of items), so we have to adopt the convention of using the mid-point of the 10th and 11th values, 5.14 and 5.16, respectively, giving a median of 5.15.

For the discrete data in Figure 13.2, the ordered data set is:

0 0 0 0 0 0 0 0 0 0 0 0 0 1 1 1 1 1 1 1 1 1 1 1 1 1 1 1 1 1 1 2 2 2 2 2 2 2 2 2 2
2 2 2 2 2 3 3 3 3 3 3 3 3 4 4 4 4 5 5 7

As there are 60 items, the median is the mid-point of the 30th and 31st. As these are both 1, the median is 1.

The median, like the mode, is obtained simply by inspection of the data without any calculations. Although it will always give a unique value, it is still misleading for skewed data. It finds application in control charting, where its simplicity as a measure of location for a small, odd-numbered sample size is attractive.

Mean
The most widely used measure of central tendency is the arithmetic mean (usually referred to simply as the mean) — the sum of all the observations in the sample divided by the number of observations.

For the continuous data in Figure 14.1, the mean is:

$(5.14 + 4.81 + 5.02 + \ldots + 5.38 + 5.22) \div 20$
$= 102.88 \div 20$
$= 5.144$

For a general notation for the mean of a sample, the observations in each sample are denoted by a subscripted letter. For example, the data in Figure 14.1 can be denoted by x_1, x_2, x_3, etc., up to x_{20}. Which particular value of x is given a particular subscript value is unimportant, so long as all 20 are uniquely identified.

The mean, in the general case of a sample of n observations, is given by:

$$\frac{1}{n} (x_1 + x_2 + x_3 + x_4 + \ldots + x_{(n-1)} + x_n)$$

for which the conventional notation is:

$$\bar{x} = \frac{1}{n} \Sigma_{i=1}^{n} x_i$$

The symbol Σ (Greek upper case sigma) stands for 'summation' — all the values following are added together. The terms '$i=1$' and 'n', respectively, above and below the Σ indicate the starting and finishing points for the summation — it starts at x_1 and finishes at x_n. When the range of summation is obvious, these limits are often omitted.

When the same numerical value occurs several times in the data, as in discrete data as in Figure 14.2, rather than giving each reappearance of the same number a different subscript, it is usual to re-express the formula for the mean as:

$$\bar{x} = \frac{1}{n} \Sigma_{i=1}^{k} f_i x_i$$

where the subscript i now represents each of the k different numerical values in the sample, and f_i the frequency with which that value occurs. For example, from the data in Figure 14.3, $\Sigma f_i x_i$ *is calculated as:*

$$(13 \times 0) + (18 \times 1) + (14 \times 2) + (7 \times 3) + (4 \times 4) + (2 \times 5) + (0 \times 6) + (1 \times 7) = 100$$

and the total number of observations (i.e. the sample size, n) is:

$$13 + 18 + 14 + 7 + 4 + 2 + 0 + 1 = 59,$$

so the mean $\bar{x}$ is $100/59 = 1.695$.

For continuous data which are presented in class intervals without access to the original data, the same procedure can be used, with x_i being the mid-point of the ith class interval, and f_i the observed frequency in that interval. This method should *not* be used when the original ungrouped data are available — this would introduce unnecessary errors due to the assumption that all the observations in an interval are at the mid-point. If their actual location in the interval is known, this information should be used.

Measures of dispersion

Measures of dispersion measure the spread of the data about the mean. Consider the sample of 20 observations shown in Figure 14.6.

5.14	5.03	5.12	5.21	5.18
5.10	5.19	5.08	5.12	5.09
5.22	5.10	5.15	5.19	5.05
5.27	5.10	5.13	5.21	5.20

Figure 14.6.

These are seen to have an initial similarity to those in Figure 14.1. Calculation confirms that they have exactly the same sample mean of 5.144. Further inspection, however, shows that there is a very important difference in that the data are clustered much more closely round the mean. This can be confirmed by drawing a histogram of the data. The purpose of a measure of dispersion is to provide a single number for each sample that quantifies the 'spread'.

Range

An obvious measure to use is that of the range within the sample — the difference between the largest and the smallest value. In figure 14.1, the range is 5.74−4.73 = 1.01, whereas in Figure 14.6 the value is 5.27−5.03 = 0.24. The range does have its uses. As shown above, it does provide a usable measure with minimal calculation. It does, however, have severe drawbacks. The most important one is sheer inefficiency — whatever the size of the sample, it only makes use of two observations. The value obtained will also tend to increase as the sample size increases, because extreme observations become more likely. For these reasons, it should be used with care and only in tightly defined situations. As will be seen in Chapter 16, it is widely used in control charting where sample sizes are usually small and it is important to obtain a rapid measure with the minimum of calculation.

Variance and standard deviation

For a single observation, the quantity $(x_i - \bar{x})$ measures its deviation from the mean. At first sight, adding together all such values might form a basis for a measure of spread including all the observations, but this summation would always come to exactly zero, as the positive and negative values would cancel each other out. This problem can be circumvented by using the absolute values (i.e. ignoring the signs). To eliminate the effect of sample size, the summation is divided by the sample size, to give a measure known as the 'mean absolute deviation' (MAD):

$$\text{MAD} = \frac{1}{n} \sum_{i=1}^{n} |x_i - \bar{x}|$$

Whilst this measure does work (and finds some applications in work study), problems are presented by the discontinuity at $\bar{x}$ of the absolute value. Instead, we make the measure always positive by squaring it. The average is then the 'mean square deviation' (MSD):

$$\text{MSD} = \frac{1}{n} \sum_{i=1}^{n} (x_i - \bar{x})^2$$

For reasons that will be explained later (under the heading of 'estimation'), one further modification is necessary. Instead of using the sample size as a divisor, we use $(n-1)$ (known as the 'degrees of freedom'). This results in a measure known as the sample variance, denoted s^2, i.e.

$$s^2 = \frac{1}{n-1} \sum_{i=1}^{n} (x_i - \bar{x})^2$$

The sample variance is the definitive measure of dispersion. The fact that it is dimensioned in the square of the original unit of measurement of the data can cause confusion, for which reason it is usual to refer to its square root, known as the standard deviation (s), i.e.

$$s = \sqrt{\frac{1}{(n-1)} \sum_{i=1}^{n} (x_i - \bar{x})^2}$$

By squaring out the term in brackets, an alternative form of the expression for variance emerges that is slightly easier for calculation, and does not require the use of x:

$$s^2 = \frac{1}{n-1} [\sum (x_i)^2 - \frac{(\sum x_i)^2}{n}]$$

As an example, consider again the data of Figure 14.1.

$\sum (x_i)^2$ is $(5.14)^2 + (4.81)^2 + (5.02)^2 + \ldots + (5.38)^2 + (5.22)^2$
$\qquad = 26.4196 + 23.1361 + 25.2004 + \ldots + 28.9444 + 27.2484$
$\qquad = 530.6254$

$\sum x_i$ was previously calculated as 102.88, and n is 20, so the variance is given by:

$$s^2 = \frac{1}{19} [530.6254 - \frac{(102.88)^2}{20}]$$

$$= \frac{1}{19} (530.6254 - 529.1472)$$

$$= 1.4782/19 = 0.0778$$

and the standard deviation, $s = \sqrt{0.0778} = 0.279$.
For the data in Figure 14.3

$\sum (x_i)^2$ is $(5.14)^2 + (5.03)^2 + (5.12)^2 + \ldots + (5.21)^2 + (5.20)^2$
$\qquad = 529.2898$

$\sum x_i$ is again 102.88 and $n=20$, so the variance is

$$= \frac{1}{19} (529.2898 - 529.1472)$$

$$= 0.1426/19 = 0.0075$$

and the standard deviation, $s = \sqrt{0.0075} = 0.0866$.

In both the above variance calculations the quantity in brackets is a very small difference between two large numbers. Any small error in calculation of either of the numbers gives a possibly very large error in the final result. For this reason, it is important to maintain accuracy in calculation. Rounding during the calculation must be avoided, and all significant figures must be carried. It is, of course, acceptable to round the final result.

Variance calculations with grouped data

As for the mean, when observations x_i occur with frequency f_i, it is easier to use a modified expression for variance, namely:

$$s^2 = \frac{1}{n=1} [\Sigma(f_i x_i^2) - \frac{(\Sigma f_i x_i)^2}{n}]$$

Applying this to the data in Figure 14.3, we have already obtained the result that $\Sigma f_i x_i = 100$. $\Sigma(f_i x_i^2)$ *is calculated as:*

$$(13 \times 0^2) + (18 \times 1^2) + (14 \times 2^2) + (7 \times 3^2) + (4 \times 4^2) + (2 \times 5^2) + (0 \times 6^2) + (1 \times 7^2)$$
$$= 0 + 18 + 56 + 63 + 64 + 50 + 0 + 49 = 300$$

i.e. $s^2 = \frac{1}{58}[300 - \frac{100^2}{59}] = 2.25$

and standard deviation $s = \sqrt{2.25} = 1.5$

Populations and estimation

Information contained in samples is rarely of much interest in its own right. Its value is in estimating the corresponding measures in the 'population' from which the sample was drawn. This terminology comes from the use of statistics in demography — if we wanted to know, for example, the average height of the adult male UK population, practical constraints would prevent us measuring the 20 million or so subjects in this category, so we would obtain an estimate by measuring a small sample. The same principle would apply for the variance of the height, or for any other summary statistic for any other measurement. In many industrial situations, the population cannot even be viewed as having a finite number of members. If we are sampling items from some manufacturing process, and measuring a particular dimension, the mean and variance obtained from the sample are estimates of the mean and variance of the process at that time. The population is conceptually all the components that could be produced from the process when it is operating under the conditions applying when the sample was taken.

It is obviously important that the sample results provide 'good' estimates of the corresponding population values (known as population 'parameters'). There are several criteria of 'goodness', but one of the more important ones is that of lack of bias. Repeated sample estimates from a single population will themselves be subject to variation, but are 'unbiased' if the average of an infinite number of such estimates is exactly equal to the corresponding population parameter. As population parameters are generally unknown, there is no way of testing any particular estimated value for bias — we have instead to rely on theoretical justification beyond the scope of this book. This will confirm that:

Sample mean ($\bar{x}$) is an unbiased estimator for population mean (μ).
Sample variance (s^2) is an unbiased estimator for population variance (σ^2).

Note, in the case of variance, that the mean square deviation,

$$\text{MSD} = \frac{1}{n} \Sigma_{i=1}^{n}(x_i - \bar{x})^2$$

gives a biased estimator of population variance — it underestimates by a factor $(n-1/n)$. To unbias the estimate, it is multiplied by $(n/n-1)$, giving the result for s^2. (It should be noted that there are a few texts which quote the value with n in the denominator for s^2, and therefore require multiplication by $(n/(n-1)$ to give an unbiased estimate of σ^2).

Use of calculators
Most calculators on the market described as either 'statistical' or 'scientific' have built-in functions for the calculation of sample means and standard deviations, and their use can in most circumstances by-pass the stages of calculation described above. There are, however, two points of caution. The first is that very few machines include a facility for dealing with grouped data, so it is necessary either to enter each observation individually, or use the method shown above. The second is that of a lack of consistency in what emerges when the 'standard deviation' button is pressed. Some use n as the denominator, others use $n-1$. It doesn't matter so long as it is known which, an issue that can be reslved by checking a sample calculation. One popular make of calculator gives the choice of either — denoted σ_n or σ_{n-1},

respectively. (Strictly, the keys should be labelled s rather than σ, as even electronic calculators cannot produce population parameters from sample data.)

Other summary measures
The measures of location (mean, median, mode) and dispersion

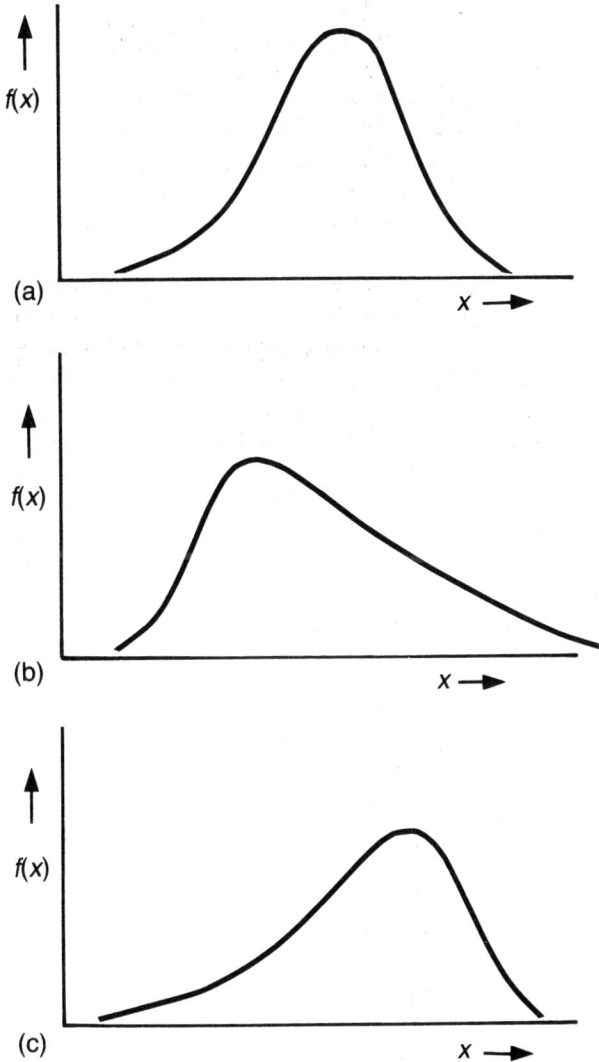

Figure 14.7.   Skewness (a) Symmetrical (coefficient = 0). (b) Positively skewed (coefficient > 0). (c) Negatively skewed (cofficient < 0).

(variance, standard deviation, sample range) described above are usually sufficient to describe the data. Occasionally, other measures can be invoked to give further information on the shape of the distribution of data. For consistency in terminology, define:

$$m_1 = \bar{x}$$

$$m_2 = \frac{1}{n-1} \sum_{i=1}^{n} (x_i - \bar{x})^2 \quad (=s^2)$$

$$m_3 = \frac{1}{n-1} \sum_{i=1}^{n} (x_i - \bar{x})^3$$

$$m_4 = \frac{1}{n-1} \sum_{i=1}^{n} (x_i - \bar{x})^4$$

From these statistics (where m_1, m_2, m_3, and m_4 are, respectively, the first, second, third and fourth moments of the sample data) two further summary measures can be produced:

Coefficient of skewness $= m_3^2/m_2^3$
Coefficient of kurtosis $= (m_4/m_2^2)-3$

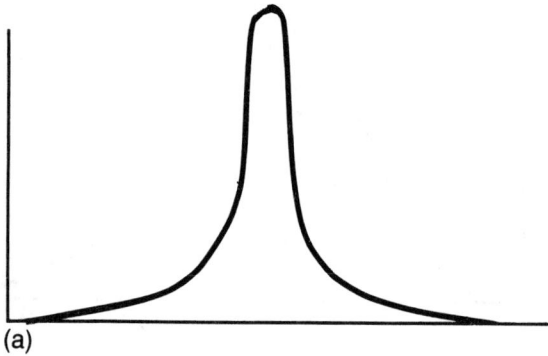

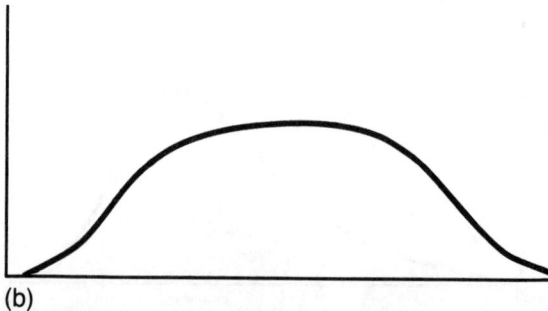

(a)

(b)

Figure 14.8.   Kurtosis. (a) Leptokurtic (coefficient > 0). (b) Platykurtic (coefficient < 0).

The coefficient of skewness measures the symmetry of the data, and the coefficient of kurtosis measures whether the shape of the distribution is flat (platykurtic) or 'peaky' (leptokurtic). Such information can sometimes be of use during process capability analysis, as described in the next chapter. The behaviour of these coefficients is illustrated in Figures 14.7 and 14.8.

Probability

Probability theory is a very large area of study. This section is restricted to a very brief outline of some of the aspects necessary for the remainder of this chapter, and the following three chapters.

Consider some event A. The probability of this event occurring is denoted $P(A)$. The value of this probability must be somewhere between 0 and 1 inclusive.

$P(A)=0$ means that A cannot occur (it is impossible)
$P(A)=1$ means that A must occur (it is certain)

More generally, if we consider the total extent of possible outcomes to a 'trial' (which is simply an opportunity for an event to occur), $P(A)$ is the proportion of these outcomes that consist of event A as the number of trials tends to infinity. This probability can be quantified in various ways:

1. *Experimentally*   If n trials were undertaken, and event A occurred in x of them, then the *estimate* of $P(A)$ is x/n.
2. *A priori*   There are some situations where the answer is obvious from prior knowledge of the physical process generating the events. For example, it can be said before the event that the probability of an unbiased tossed coin coming up 'heads' is 1/2; the probability of a randomly selected playing card being the ace of spades is 1/52, etc, without any need to undertake experiments. (There are many situations where it is easy to be tempted into *a priori* judgements which cannot be justified. This often happens in industry. It is also prevalent in gambling, where the profitability of that particular industry depends almost exclusively on the customer's insistence on making incorrect *a priori* assessments.)
3. *By modelling*   In situations where experimentation is impractical and there is no immediately obvious *a priori* value, some theoretical model of the situation can often be developed in the

guise of a 'probability distribution', as described later.

Compound probabilities

The event A has so far been considered as a 'simple event' which is not readily decomposed into further events. A 'compound event' is an event consisting of two or more simple events. For simplicity, this discussion will be limited to compound events that consist of two simple events only — denoted A and B.

Multiplication rule

For the two simple events A and B, the probability of both A *and* B occurring is denoted $P(AB)$ (or $P(A \cap B)$), where the $\cap$ implies the 'intersection' of the two events.

$$P(AB) = P(A) \times P(B|A)$$

$P(B|A)$ is the probability of event B given that event A has already occurred. For example, consider an almost-finished packet of mixed peanuts and raisins, which now contains seven peanuts and five raisins. If A is obtaining a peanut when one item is selected at random from the bag (i.e. assuming that we can neither see nor feel what is being selected), and B is obtaining a raisin, then obviously $P(A)$ is 7/12 and $P(B|A)$ is 5/11, giving $P(AB) = 35/132 = 0.265$.

Note that if the peanut and the raisin had been considered in the reverse order, the same result would have been obtained, i.e. $P(A) \times P(B|A) = P(B) \times P(A|B)$ (known as Bayes' formula). In many situations, $P(A|B) = P(A)$ and $P(B|A) = P(B)$, in which case A and B are said to be *independent*. This means that the occurrence of A has no influence on the probability of B, and vice versa. This would be the case in the above example if, after obtaining our first sample peanut or raisin, instead of eating it, it was returned to the bag before the second sample was taken. In this case

$$P(AB) = P(A) \times P(B) = 7/12 \times 5/12 = 35/144 = 0.243$$

Such independence is usually assumed in quality control applications — the value of a sample observation from a manufacturing process is usually assumed to have no influence on the value of a subsequent sample.

Addition rule

For two simple events A and B, the probability of A *or* B occurring is denoted $P(A + B)$ (or $P(A \cup B)$, where the $\cup$ implies the 'union' of the two events).

$$P(A + B) = P(A) + P(B) - P(AB)$$

$P(AB)$ is the probability of both A and B, as described above.

For example, further complicate the bag of peanuts and raisins by adding 15 cashew nuts, so there are now 27 items in the bag. The probability that our selection is either a peanut or a raisin is obtained from:

Probability of a peanut, $P(A) = 7/27$
Probability of a raisin, $P(B)$ $= 5/27$
Probability of our selection being simultaneously a peanut and a raisin, $P(AB) = 0$ (obviously, by definition);
so $P(A + B) = 7/27 + 5/27 - 0 = 12/27$

The fact that $P(AB)$ is zero defines the two events as being *mutually exclusive*. If this is so (as in the above example), then we have the simple result:

$$P(A + B) = P(A) = P(B)$$

This also is usually assumed to be the case in the later exploration of techniques in quality control, but it is wise to always be alive to the possibility of both the assumptions of independence and mutual exclusivity not being valid.

Probability distributions

Probability distributions are theoretical models of the behaviour of random variables. Descriptions of the behaviour of variables usually consist of a combination of an assumed probability distribution, and estimates of the parameters of the distribution from sample data. As with the analysis of sample data, it is convenient to treat separately the applications to discrete and to continuous data.

Continuous probability distributions

Consider a continuous random variable, X, with probability distribution as shown in Figure 14.9. The shape is determined by the function $f(X)$. This function is always such that the total area under the curve is unity, i.e.

$$\int_{-\infty}^{\infty} f(X)dX + 1$$

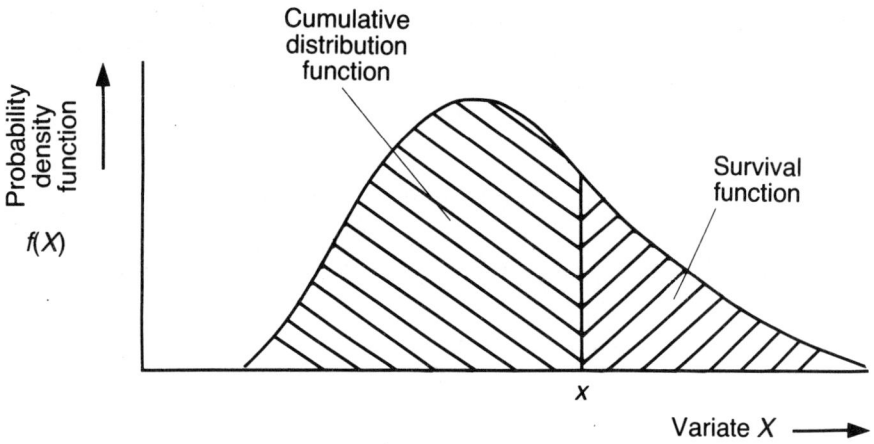

Figure 14.9.   Continuous probability distribution.

and is known as the *probability density function* (PDF). The area under the curve between any two defined values of X represents the probability of the variable being between these values. More specifically,

$$\int_{-\infty}^{x} f(X)dX = F(x) - \text{the cumulative density function (CDF)}$$

and

$$\int_{x}^{\infty} (X)dX = R(x) - \text{the survival or reliability function}$$

where, of course, $F(x) + R(x) = 1$ for all values of x.

The mean of a continuous probability distribution, μ, is given by:

$$\mu = \int_{-\infty}^{\infty} X f(X)dX$$

and the variance by:

$$\sigma = \int_{-\infty}^{\infty} X^2 f(X)dX$$

Specific models for continuous probability distributions

There is an endless list of possibilities for the function $f(X)$, giving an equally endless list of possible shapes for probability distributions. The only constraint is that the total enclosed area is unity. There are, however, relatively few that find practical application, usually through a combination of realistic underlying assumptions, mathematical simplicity and observed correspondence to the actual behaviour of real variables. Of the many possible models, just four of the more widely used ones will be introduced: the normal, log–normal, exponential and Weibull. The normal distribution will be explained in detail, followed by brief descriptions of the others.

Normal distribution

The normal distribution is arguably the most useful and widely used model in statistical analysis. It is certainly the one on which most of the standard techniques of statistical testing depend. Its origin is usually attributed to the French mathematician Demoivre in 1733, though others such as Gauss and Laplace also lay claim. Its mathematical form is:

$$f(X) = \frac{1}{\sigma\sqrt{(2)\pi}}\ e^{\dfrac{-(X-\mu)^2}{(2\sigma^2)}}$$

where μ is the mean and s^2 is the variance, and its shape is the well-known symmetrical bell-shaped curve as shown in Figure 14.10.

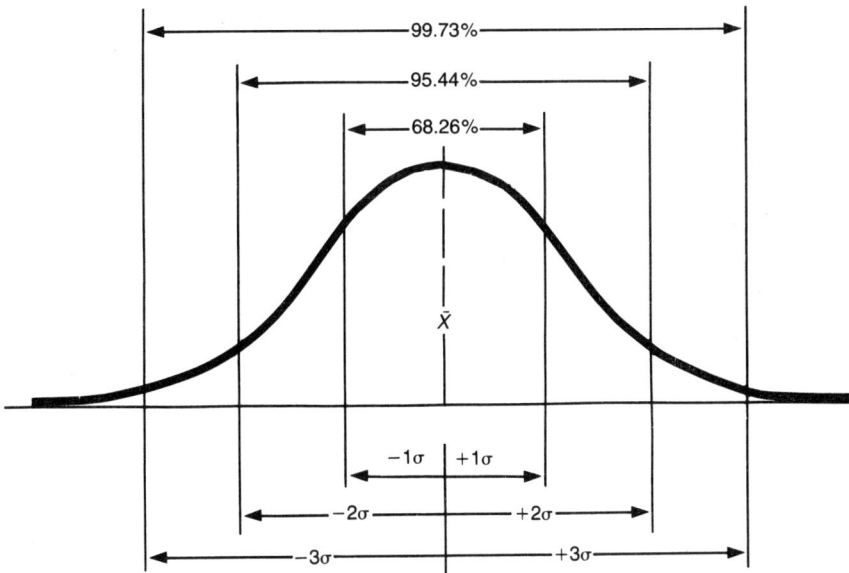

Figure 14.10.   Normal distribution.

The derivation assumes that X is diverted from its target by a large number of small factors whose effects are additive and whose average value is zero (i.e. the negative and positive ones cancel each other out). This has an immediate similarity to manufacturing processes where such factors can be imagined as affecting, for example, a machined dimension. It is important to recognize that no physical dimension of property will ever be exactly normally distributed, as this would imply finite probabilities for all values between $\pm\infty$. What can be done is to accept it as an adequate model for many such dimensions and properties, where its use is helpful and does not give rise to unacceptable inaccuracies, as is often the case in statistical process control as described in the next three chapters. Another consequence of its widespread use is a school of thought that there is, by definition, something wrong with a manufacturing process that does not give rise to normally distributed properties. This is, of course, nonsense — there is nothing automatically wrong in a situation simply because a particular bit of theory does not fit. In such cases it is usually the theory that is wrong, and we need to find a more suitable distribution.

Calculating normal probabilities

To avoid the need to evaluate areas under normal curves by integration, it is usual to use tables of such values. As there are infinite possible values of both μ and σ, it is clearly impossible to tabulate all possible normal distributions. Instead, tables are provided for only one pair of values, namely $\mu=0$ and $\sigma=1$. This is known as the 'standardized normal distribution', which has the form:

$$f(u) = \frac{1}{\sqrt{2\pi}} \, e^{\left(-\frac{u^2}{2}\right)}$$

and is shown in Figure 14.11.

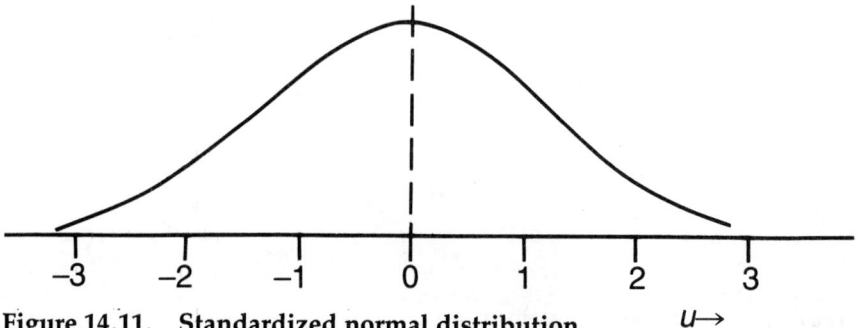

Figure 14.11.   Standardized normal distribution.

The function tabulated is $1 - \Phi(u)$ where $\Phi(u)$ is the cumulative distribution function of a standardized Normal variable u.

Thus $1 - \Phi(u) = \dfrac{1}{\sqrt{2\pi}} \displaystyle\int_{\mu}^{\infty} e^{-u^2/2}\, du$ is the probability that a standardized Normal variable selected at random will be greater than a value of

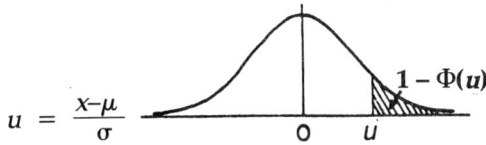

$$u = \frac{x-\mu}{\sigma}$$

$\dfrac{(x-\mu)}{\sigma}$	0.00	0.01	0.02	0.03	0.04	0.05	0.06	0.07	0.08	0.09
0.0	0.5000	0.4960	0.4920	0.4880	0.4840	0.4801	0.4761	0.4721	0.4681	0.4641
0.1	0.4602	0.4562	0.4522	0.4483	0.4443	0.4404	0.4364	0.4325	0.4286	0.4247
0.2	0.4207	0.4168	0.4129	0.4090	0.4052	0.4013	0.3974	0.3936	0.3897	0.3859
0.3	0.3821	0.3783	0.3745	0.3707	0.3669	0.3632	0.3594	0.3557	0.3520	0.3843
0.4	0.3446	0.3409	0.3372	0.3336	0.3300	0.3264	0.3228	0.3192	0.3156	0.3121
0.5	0.3085	0.3050	0.3015	0.2981	0.2946	0.2912	0.2877	0.2843	0.2810	0.2776
0.6	0.2743	0.2709	0.2676	0.2643	0.2611	0.2578	0.2546	0.2514	0.2483	0.2451
0.7	0.2420	0.2389	0.2358	0.2327	0.2296	0.2266	0.2236	0.2206	0.2177	0.2148
0.8	0.2119	0.2090	0.2061	0.2033	0.2005	0.1977	0.1949	0.1922	0.1894	0.1867
0.9	0.1841	0.1814	0.1788	0.1762	0.1736	0.1711	0.1685	0.1660	0.1635	0.1611
1.0	0.1587	0.1562	0.1539	0.1515	0.1492	0.1469	0.1446	0.1423	0.1401	0.1379
1.1	0.1357	0.1335	0.1314	0.1292	0.1271	0.1251	0.1230	0.1210	0.1190	0.1170
1.2	0.1151	0.1131	0.1112	0.1093	0.1075	0.1056	0.1038	0.1020	0.1003	0.0985
1.3	0.0968	0.0951	0.0934	0.0918	0.0901	0.0885	0.0869	0.0853	0.0838	0.0823
1.4	0.0808	0.0793	0.0778	0.0764	0.0749	0.0735	0.0721	0.0708	0.0694	0.0681
1.5	0.0668	0.0655	0.0643	0.0630	0.0618	0.0606	0.0594	0.0582	0.0571	0.0559
1.6	0.0548	0.0537	0.0526	0.0516	0.0505	0.0495	0.0485	0.0475	0.0465	0.0455
1.7	0.0446	0.0436	0.0422	0.0418	0.0409	0.0401	0.0392	0.0384	0.0375	0.0367
1.8	0.0359	0.0351	0.0344	0.0336	0.0329	0.0322	0.0314	0.0307	0.0301	0.0294
1.9	0.0287	0.0281	0.0274	0.0268	0.0262	0.0256	0.0250	0.0244	0.0239	0.0233
2.0	0.02275	0.02222	0.02169	0.02118	0.02068	0.02018	0.01970	0.01923	0.01876	0.01831
2.1	0.01786	0.01743	0.01700	0.01659	0.01618	0.01578	0.01539	0.01500	0.01463	0.01426
2.2	0.01390	0.01355	0.01321	0.01287	0.01255	0.01222	0.01191	0.01160	0.01130	0.01101
2.3	0.01072	0.01044	0.01017	0.00990	0.00964	0.00939	0.00914	0.00889	0.00866	0.00842
2.4	0.00820	0.00798	0.00776	0.00755	0.00734	0.00714	0.00695	0.00676	0.00657	0.00639
2.5	0.00621	0.00604	0.00587	0.00570	0.00554	0.00539	0.00523	0.00508	0.00494	0.00480
2.6	0.00466	0.00453	0.00440	0.00427	0.00415	0.00402	0.00391	0.00379	0.00368	0.00357
2.7	0.00347	0.00336	0.00326	0.00317	0.00307	0.00298	0.00289	0.00280	0.00272	0.00264
2.8	0.00256	0.00248	0.00240	0.00233	0.00226	0.00219	0.00212	0.00205	0.00199	0.00193
2.9	0.00187	0.00181	0.00175	0.00169	0.00164	0.00159	0.00154	0.00149	0.00144	0.00139
3.0	0.00135	3.1	0.00097	3.2	0.00069	3.3		0.00048	3.4	0.00034
3.5	0.00023									
3.6	0.00016									
3.7	0.00011									
3.8	0.00007									
3.9	0.00005									
4.0	0.00003									

Table 14.1. Normal distribution table.

(Murdoch, J. and Barnes, J. A., Statistical Tables for Science, Engineering, Management and Business Studies, Macmillan, 1986.)

The variate is known as a 'standardized normal deviate', with the conventional symbol u. To convert an x from any normal distribution into a u, so that tables of the standardized normal distribution may be used, the conversion is:

$$u = \frac{(x-\mu)}{\sigma}$$

(i.e. u is the distance of x above the mean expressed as a number of standard deviations).

A table of the normal distribution is given in Table 14.1. Its use is best illustrated by example. Suppose a dimension of a component is specified as 5.00 ± 0.10mm. If it is known that this dimension is normally distributed with a mean of 5.02mm and standard deviation 0.05mm, what proportion of the components will have that dimension outside the specified limits? The situation is shown in Figure 14.12. The shaded areas represent the probabilities of dimensions being outside the two limits.

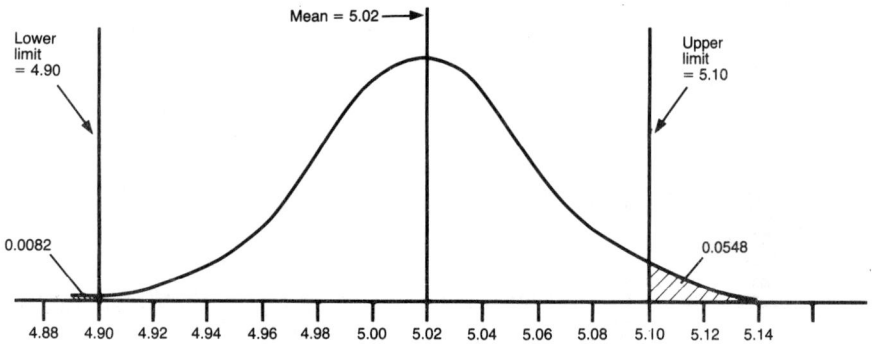

Figure 14.12.   Normal distribution example.

For the lower limit, $x = 4.90$ and

$$u = \frac{(x-\mu)}{\sigma} = \frac{(4.90 - 5.02)}{0.05} = -2.4$$

The minus sign simply tells us that we are dealing with the lower tail of the distribution. Reference to Table 14.1 gives a tail area of 0.0082, which is the probability of obtaining a component below the bottom limit. Similarly, for the upper limit at $x = 5.10$,

$$u = \frac{(x-\mu)}{\sigma} = \frac{(5.10 - 5.02)}{0.05} = 1.6$$

for which the tail probability is 0.0548.

The total proportion outside these limits is the sum of these two areas, i.e. $0.0082 + 0.0548 = 0.063$.

Sampling from the normal distribution

If a large number of sample observations was taken from a normal distribution of mean μ and standard deviation σ, a histogram of the observed values could be drawn. As the number of observations becomes very large, so the width of the class intervals can be reduced, as shown in Figure 14.13.

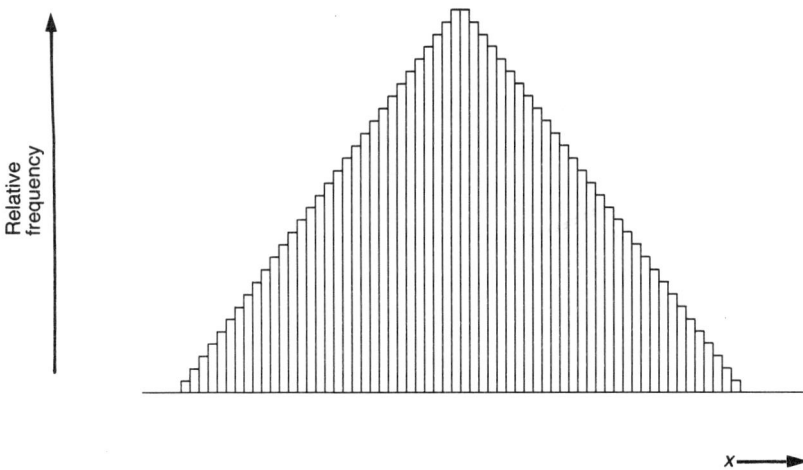

Figure 14.13. Frequency distribution — histogram for a very large sample.

Taking this idea to its conclusion, as the number of observations tends to infinity, so the class interval width tends to zero and the histogram's envelope becomes a smooth curve. If the histogram is of relative frequencies, this curve is the probability distribution. At the same time, the calculated estimates of mean and variance, $\bar{x}$ and s^2, from this infinite sample would become equal to μ and σ^2. (This, of course, assumes that the 'unbiased' form for s^2 is being used, with $(n - 1)$ in the denominator.)

This fact, that sample observations from an infinite sample assume the probability distribution of the sampled variable, whilst being fundamental may not seem of much interest. The interest lies in the extension of this idea to samples that do not consist of individual observations, but instead consist of n observations (n = sample size).

In such cases, we can examine the behaviour of statistics (such as the sample means) calculated from the samples. The probability distributions of such statistics are known as *sampling distributions*.

Sampling distribution of sample means
Consider the situation where a sample of n independent observations is drawn from a normal distribution. The sample mean, $\bar{x}$, will be an unbiased estimator of the true mean μ, but will not be equal to μ. We could continue to take an infinite number of such samples. Each sample would have its own individual x. The probability distribution of these x values (i.e. the sampling distribution of x) will have a mean equal to the population mean μ (as did the distribution of individual observations), but will have a smaller variance than σ^2, the variance of the distribution from which the samples are being drawn. This is, of course, to be expected, as each sample mean must be closer to μ than the outer extreme single observation in the sample.

Specifically, the variance of the distribution of the averages of samples of size n drawn from a normal distribution of mean μ and variance σ^2 will be a normal distribution with the same mean, μ, but with variance σ^2/n. (i.e. with standard deviation $\sigma/\sqrt{n}$), as shown in

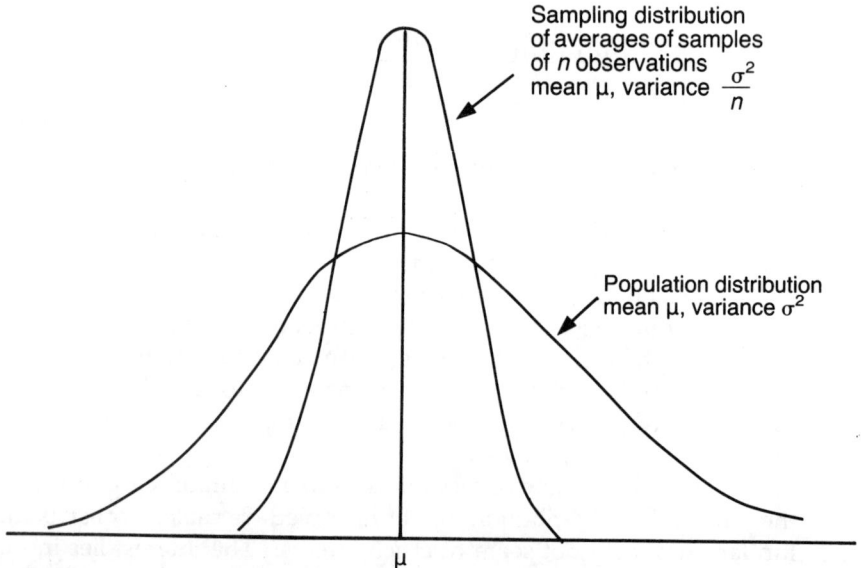

Sampling distribution
of averages of samples
of n observations
mean μ, variance $\dfrac{\sigma^2}{n}$

Population distribution
mean μ, variance σ^2

μ

Figure 14.14. Sampling distribution of sample averages.

Figure 14.14. The standard deviation of sample averages $(\sigma/\sqrt{n})$ is known as the *standard error*.

As an example, consider a packaged product where it is a requirement that the average nett weight of a randomly selected sample of 50 packages must not be less than 250g. If the standard deviation of the filling process is 2.0g, where should the mean contents be set to ensure that there is a probability of 0.95 that the requirement is met when such a sample is taken? The situation is shown diagrammatically in Figure 14.15.

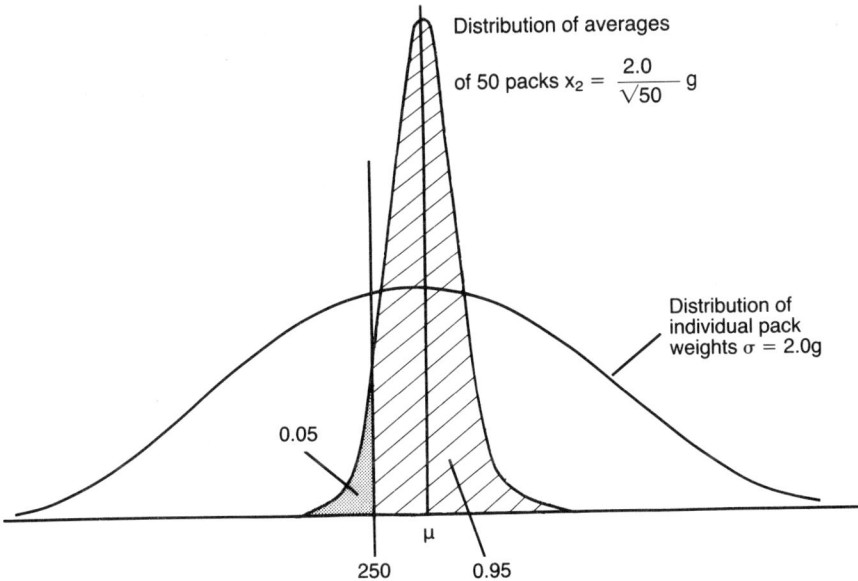

Distribution of averages

of 50 packs $x_2 = \dfrac{2.0}{\sqrt{50}}$ g

Distribution of individual pack weights $\sigma = 2.0$g

0.05

μ

250   0.95

Figure 14.15.   Sampling distribution of averages of 50 packs

The standardized normal deviate is now

$$u_{0.05} = \frac{(\bar{x} - \mu)}{(\sigma/\sqrt{n})}$$

$$= 1.645 \text{ (from Table 14.1)}$$

giving $\mu = 1.645 \times (2.0/\sqrt{50}) + 250$
$= 250.47$g.

Note that for *individual* packages, the standard deviation is 2.0, and the proportion below the declared weight will be obtained using:

$$\frac{u}{} = \frac{(x - \mu)}{\sigma} = \frac{(250 - 250.47)}{2.0} = -0.235$$

from which reference to Table 14.1 tells us that the corresponding value of α is 0.4071 (averaging the results of u values of 0.23 and 0.24). This tells us that even though the risk of an average of 50 samples being below 250 g is only 0.05, approximately 40 per cent of individual packages will be under this value — an interesting comment on the effect of the current practice of declaring contents by average rather than the previous use of minimum contents declaration.

The log–normal distribution

This distribution occurs when the variable X is such that log (X) follows a normal distribution. This distribution is positively skewed, as shown in Figure 14.16. This distribution is often used to model variables that have a target value of zero, but where in practice there will always be small positive values — such things as impurities in chemicals, and distortion measurements such as squareness, eccentricity, parallelism, etc.

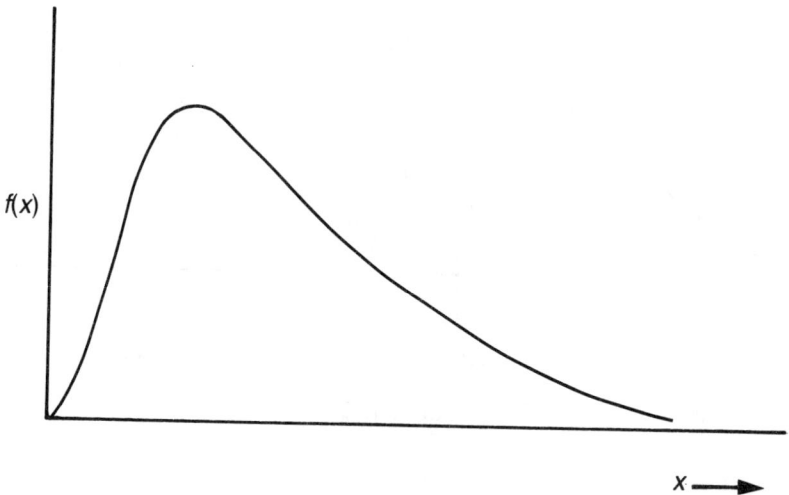

Figure 14.16.   Log–normal distribution.

Analysis of log–normal variates is undertaken by transforming them into normal variates. For example, consider the ovality measurement of a turned cylinder which is log–normally distributed with a mean of 20 μm and a variance of 16 μm^2. What proportion will have ovality greater than the specification maximum of 35μm?

The logarithm of the ovality will be normally distributed with mean log(20) (=1.3), and standard deviation log($\sqrt{16}$) (=0.6). We want to know the proportion of this distribution greater than log(35) (=1.54). In the usual normal distribution terminology

$$u_\alpha = \frac{(x - \mu)}{\sigma} = \frac{(1.54 - 1.30)}{0.6} = 0.40$$

Table 14.1 gives the corresponding α value as 0.345: i.e. about 35 per cent of the cylinders would be expected to have eccentricities above the specification limit.

The exponential distribution

This distribution is used to describe the extent of sample space between successive occurrences of events that occur in a completely random manner, but at a constant underlying rate. Such events are said to be generated by a 'homogeneous Poisson process' (HPP). In manufacturing, common examples are such things as blemishes in painted surfaces, insulation defects in coated conductors, assembly defects, etc. The exponential distribution would describe, respectively, the distribution of the area painted between the occurrence of each blemish; the length of conductor between each defect and the number of assemblies (or assembly operations) between each defect. Another popular application in quality assurance is in the field of reliability and life testing, where the distribution is used to describe the times between successive failures of randomly failing equipment.

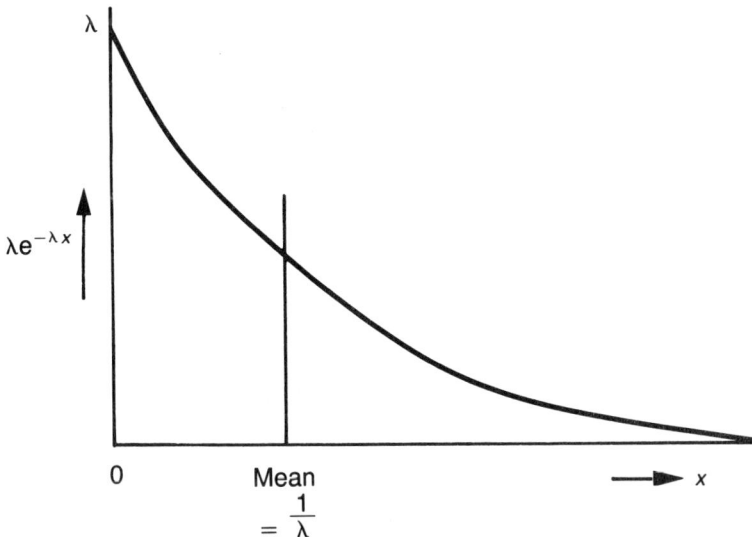

Figure 14.17.   Exponential distribution.

The distribution itself is extremely simple. It has only one parameter, λ, which is the rate (events per unit of sample space) at which events occur. The density function is an exponential curve.

$$f(x) = \lambda e^{-\lambda x}$$

as shown in Figure 14.17. The term e is the exponential constant, 2.7183.

The mean is at $1/\lambda$, and this is also equal to the standard deviation. By inspection, the mode is always at 0. To evaluate probabilities under the exponential distribution, tables are unnecessary as the area under the curve between zero and x (the distribution function, $F(x)$) is simply $1-e^{-\lambda x}$. Consider an equipment that fails on average at a rate of one failure per 427 hours of operation. What is the probability that it will last for 500 hours without failure?

The rate of failures, λ, is $1/427 = 0.00234$ failures per hour. The probability of there being a failure in the interval $0 - 500$ hours is $e^{-(500\times0.00234)} = e^{-1.17} = 0.31$. The probability of there *not* being a failure is therefore

$$1-0.31 = 0.69$$

Note that for any probability calculated under the exponential distribution, the value of the sample space at which $x=0$ is completely arbitrary. The time represented by $x=0$ in the above example, for instance, need not necessarily be the time of the previous failure. The underlying basic principle is that events are totally random, and therefore uninfluenced by the point in the sample at which they occur.

The sample estimate of λ is obtained from the mean of sample data. For example, if a randomly chosen 200 metre length of wire contained three insulation defects, the estimate of λ is simply $3/200 = 0.015$ defects per metre. To test the assumption of the exponential distribution, a simple way is to calculate the estimate of the standard deviation of the x values. If this is close to $1/\lambda$, the assumption is likely to be valid. In any estimation involving sequenced data, it is important that the sample is randomly selected. In particular, any sample that is terminated by an event (such as a sample that is terminated by a defect in the wire, or at the time of an equipment failure) is *not* random, and will overestimate the rate.

The Weibull distribution

This is a simple extension of the exponential distribution, whose distribution function is given by:

$$F(x) = 1 - e^{-(\lambda x)^\beta}$$

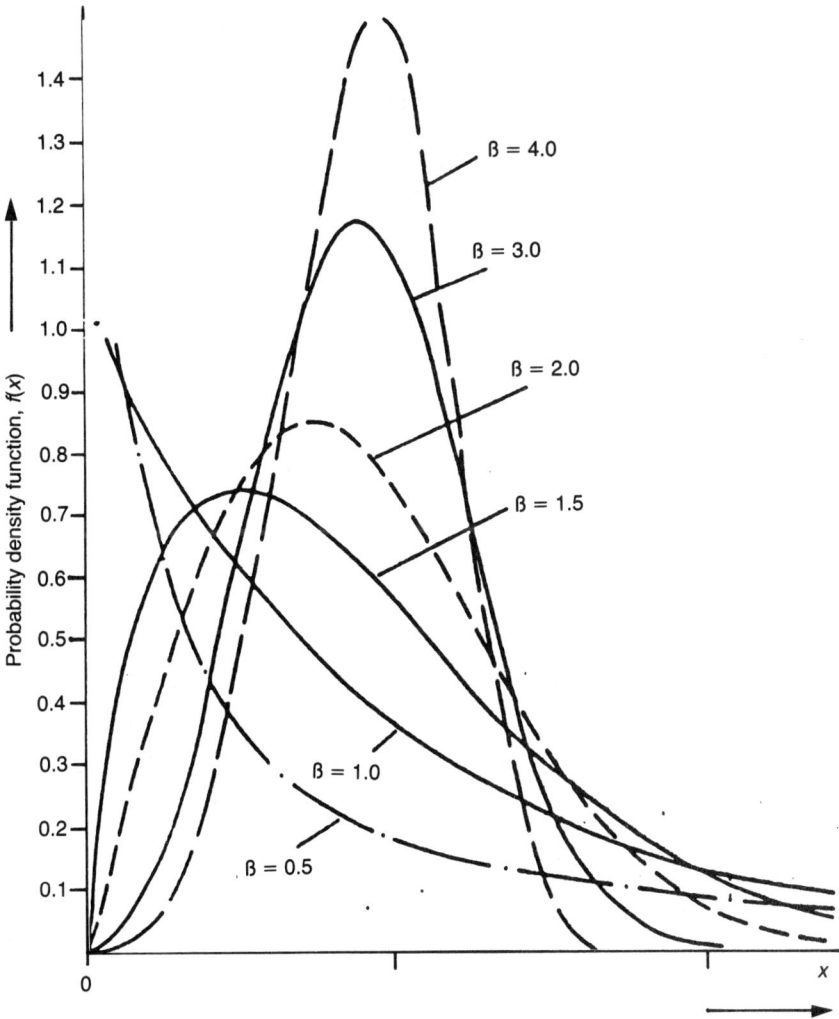

Figure 14.18.   **The Weibull probability density function, $f(x)$, for different values of the shape parameter β.**

or, more usually by using the symbol η for $1/\lambda$, i.e.

$$F(x) = 1 - e^{\left(-\frac{x}{\eta}\right)^{\beta}}$$

η is known as the 'characteristic life' — it is a measure of location, but is only equal to the mean when ß=1. More generally, it is the value of the variate at which the area under the distribution (i.e. the distribution function) is equal to $1-e^{-1} = 0.632$.

ß is known as the 'shape parameter' — as can be seen from Figure 14.18, changing its value changes the shape of the distribution. If ß=1, it is an exponential distribution (as is apparent from the above formulae). For ß=3.44 it forms a close approximation to the normal distribution. For values in between these two it approximates to a log–normal. It can therefore be seen that it has potential as a very flexible distribution that is none the less mathematically fairly simple, with only two parameters. In practice, it is widely used in failure data analysis, but only rarely elsewhere. This is largely due to difficulties in estimating ß and η from sample data. Algebraic methods need iterative solution of equations (usually using computer algorithms). The distribution does, however, lend itself to graphical parameter estimation using probability plotting, as described below.

Probability plotting

Probability plotting is a simple graphical technique that is used for assessing the fit of sample data to continuous probability distributions. It also provides informal estimates of the parameters of the distributions.

The procedure cosists simply of drawing a curve representing the distribution function as estimated from the data. This is compared with the distribution function of the assumed model. To obviate the difficulty of comparing curves, special graph paper is available with transformed probability scales that give a straight line plot for data conforming exactly with the distribution for each particular type of paper.

As an example, consider the data that were introduced in Figure 14.1. To produce the distribution function, it is first of all necessary to write the data down in ascending order of magnitude. In the table below, the data in Figure 14.1 are rearranged in this way, with $x_{(1)}$

being the ith ordered observation (i.e. $x_{(1)}$ is the first, $x_{(2)}$ is the second, and so on).

i	1	2	3	4	5	6	7	8	9	10
$x_{(i)}$	4.73	4.78	4.81	4.88	4.95	5.00	5.02	5.07	5.10	5.14

i	11	12	13	14	15	16	17	18	19	20
$x_{(i)}$	5.16	5.19	5.22	5.25	5.31	5.32	5.38	5.44	5.56	5.74

The sample estimate of the distribution function at any randomly chosen value of x (i.e. the proportion of the population less than that of x) is given by i/n. Care must be taken, however, in treating sample data as the $x_{(1)}$ values are not random samples — they are fixed at the observed data points. A modified, and less biased, estimate of the distribution function is obtained by a modified statistic. Many have been proposed — a suitable one in most circumstances is 'mean rank', $i/(n+1)$. In the example, as the sample size, n, is 20, the mean ranks are the order number, i, divided by 21. A further consideration is the fact that most commercially produced probability plotting graph paper expresses the distribution function estimate as a percentage rather than a proportion, so it is necessary to additionally multiply the estimate by 100 if this is the case. The table below calculates the distribution function values on this basis.

Normal probability plots

Plotting paper is available for most of the more widely used distribution models. For illustration, the above data are plotted on one of the commercially available normal probability plotting papers ('Chartwell' ref. 5571) in Figure 14.19. From the plot the following comments can be made:

1. The fact that it gives a reasonable straight line confirms that the normal distribution is a reasonable fit to the data. A near-perfect fit should never be expected. Remember that all the sample points are all subject to sampling variation. Too good a fit should, in fact, raise suspicions that the data are not truly random, but may have been 'adjusted' to fit the required answer. Note that, in fitting the line to the data points, the fit should emphasize the points towards the centre. Because of the highly non-linear probability scale,

i	$x_{(i)}$	$(i/21)\times100$
1	4.73	4.76
2	4.78	9.52
3	4.81	14.28
4	4.88	19.04
5	4.95	23.80
6	5.00	28.57
7	5.02	33.33
8	5.07	38.09
9	5.10	42.86
10	5.14	47.62
11	5.16	52.38
12	5.19	57.14
13	5.22	61.90
14	5.25	66.67
15	5.31	71.43
16	5.32	76.19
17	5.38	80.95
18	5.44	85.71
19	5.56	90.48
20	5.74	95.24

   apparent outliers at the ends of the line (as in Figure 14.16) are not
   as much in error as they initially appear.
2. The mean and the median for a symmetrical distribution (such as
   the normal) are coincident. The mean can therefore be estimated
   by reading the value of x corresponding to 50 per cent probability.
   This is shown in Figure 14.16, giving a value of 5.145.
3. The slope of the plot estimates the standard deviation — the
   steeper the plot, the greater the value. To obtain a value from the
   non-linear scales, the usual method is to identify the 5 and 95 per
   cent points from the plot. From our knowledge of the normal
   distribution, these points are 3.29 standard deviations apart, so
   the distance between the 5 and 95 per cent points, divided by 3.29,
   estimates the standard deviation. Specifically, in this example:

The 5 per cent point is at $x = 4.69$
The 95 per cent point is at $x = 5.60$

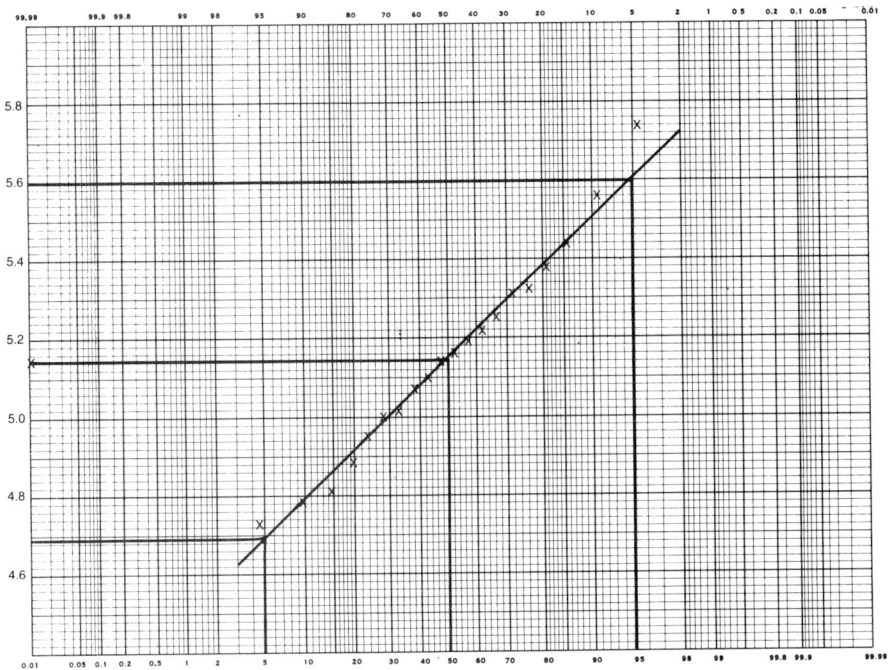

Figure 14.19. Normal probability plot (data from Figure 14.1).

so the estimate of the standard deviation is:

$$\frac{(5.60 - 4.69)}{3.29} = 0.277$$

It can be seen that the results agree closely with those obtained previously by calculation.

Probability plotting with grouped data

When data are grouped into class intervals, the approach to probability plotting has to be slightly modified. The variate values are plotted at the *top* of each class interval against the cumulative proportion at that point. The procedure is illustrated below, again using the data from Figure 14.1.

Note that when using class intervals, the cumulative percentages are plotted direct without using $i/(n+1)$. This is because the points are now plotted at predetermined variate values rather than predetermined cumulative percentages. It does give the drawback, however, that the last point cannot be plotted. The reader can verify that the plot gives similar results to those in Figure 14.16, but there is less certainty about

Top of interval	Cumulative relative frequency (per cent)
4.8	10
5.0	25
5.2	60
5.4	85
5.6	95
5.8	100

the fit of the line as there are now only 5 points instead of the previous 20. This repeats the point made in discussion of mean and various estimates in general that analysis using grouped data should *not* be used if the individual 'raw' data are available. The plotting procedure for grouped data should only be used in the cases of discrete data, or of continuous data that are available only already categorized into groups.

Probability plotting for non-normal distributions

For log–normal data, either the logarithms of the data can be plotted on normal probability paper, or, alternatively, plotting paper is available with a logarithmic variate scale. Probability plotting is a particularly well-used method of parameter estimation for the Weibull and exponential distributions (the exponential being simply a special case of the Weibull with the shape parameter ß equal to one). These distributions are mainly used in modelling the distribution of lives to failure, both in engineering reliability and human mortality studies. Special plotting paper is again available (for example, Chartwell 6572). A comprehensive description of its use is given in Davidson (1988). A general overview of probability plotting for a wide range of distributions is given by King (1971).

Discrete probability distributions

For a discrete random variable X, the probability that X takes a particular discrete value x is denoted $P(x)$. This is called the 'probability function', which can be represented graphically as shown in Figure 14.20. Note the similarity to the discrete frequency distribution in Figure 14.5.

There are two discrete probability distribution models that find widespread use in quality assurance: the binomial distribution and the Poisson distribution.

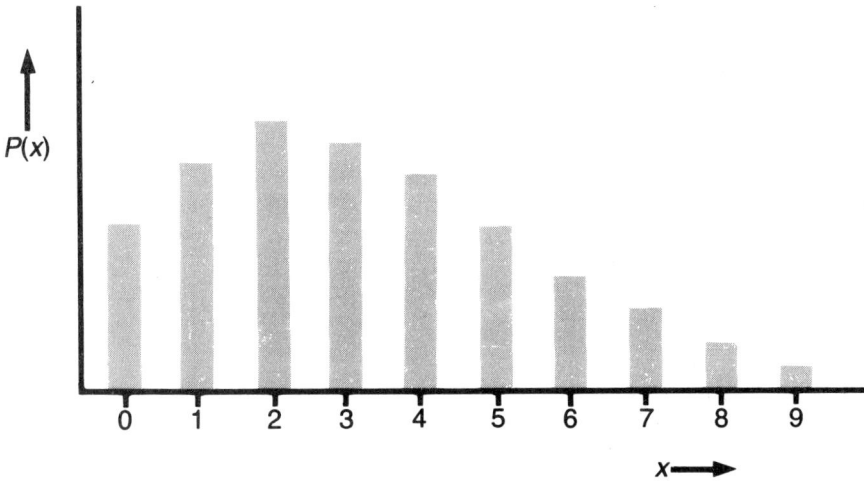

Figure 14.20.   Discrete probability distribution.

The binomial distribution

The binomial distribution (literally 'two names') is concerned with trials that have two possible outcomes, usually referred to as 'success' and 'failure'. This terminology, whilst being perfectly sensible for general application, becomes the source of some confusion in quality assurance applications where a 'success' is usually the occurrence of a defective item. For the purposes of this chapter's aim of describing applied statistics in a quality assurance context, this confusion will be avoided by making the two classifications 'defective' and 'good'. (There are further dangers in the use of the word 'defective' that are discussed in Chapter 16.)

Suppose a process generates a small, random proportion of defective items, p. If we were to take a random sample of n items from the process, consider the possibility of getting x defective items followed by $(n-x)$ good items, i.e.:

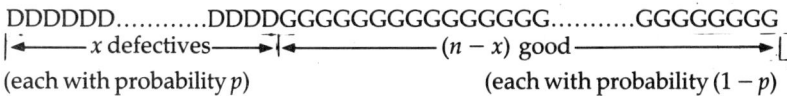

DDDDDD...........DDDDGGGGGGGGGGGGGGGG...........GGGGGGGG
|◄——— x defectives——►|◄——————— $(n-x)$ good —————————►|
(each with probability p)   (each with probability $(1-p)$)

The product rule of probabilities tells us that the probability of obtaining x consecutive defective items, each with probability p, is

$$p \times p \times p \times p \times p \ldots \times p \ (x \text{ times}) = p^x$$

and similarly, the probability of obtaining $(n-x)$ good items, each with probability $(1-p)$, is

$$(1-p) \times (1-p) \times (1-p) \times (1-p) \ldots \times (1-p) \; ((n-x) \text{ times})$$
$$= (1-p)^{(n-x)}.$$

The probability of both these occurring is, again using the product rule.

$$p^{x}(1-p)^{(n-x)}$$

The particular sequence we have considered (x defective, followed by $(n-x)$ good) is, however, only one of a large number of possible combinations. It can be shown that the number of combinations of x defectives and $(n-x)$ good (denoted $_{n}C_{x}$) is:

$$\frac{n!}{x! \, (n-x)!}$$

where the '!' denotes 'factorial', the factorial of a number being that number successfully multiplied by the previous number minus one until the multiplier reduces to one (for example, $5! = 5 \times 4 \times 3 \times 2 \times 1 = 120$).

As there is not usually any interest in the precise order in which defectives occur in a sample, but are concerned only with the total number, these results can be combined (now using the addition rule) to give the general result that the probability of x defectives in a sample of n that is drawn from a population that is proportion p defective is given by $P(x)$ where:

$$P(x) = \frac{n!}{(x! \, (n-x))!} \; p^{x} \, (1-p)^{(n-x)}$$

This is the *binomial probability formula*. The mean (i.e. expected) number of defectives is np, and the variance of the number of defectives is $np(1-p)$.

As an example, consider the case of a sample of 20 items drawn from a population that is 8 per cent (0.08) defective. The probability of 0 defectives is:

$$P(0) = \frac{20!}{(0! \, 20!)} \; 0.08^{0} \, 0.92^{20} = 0.92^{20} = 0.1887$$

(Note that $0! = 1$.) Similarly:

$$P(1) = \frac{20!}{(1! \, 19!)} \; 0.08^{1} \, 0.92^{19} = 0.3282$$

$$P(2) = \frac{20!}{(2! \ 18!)} \ 0.08^2 \ 0.92^{18} = 0.2711$$

$$P(3) = \frac{20!}{(3! \ 17!)} \ 0.08^3 \ 0.92^{17} = 0.1414$$

and so on up to $P(20)$. (Note that if all the terms are evaluated, their sum will be exactly 1.

These probabilities form a binomial probability distribution. The complete picture for this particular distribution is shown in Figure 14.21. This distribution has mean $= np = 20 \times 0.08 = 1.6$ and variance $= np(1-p) = 20 \times 0.08 \times 0.92 = 1.472$ (standard deviation $= 1.213$).

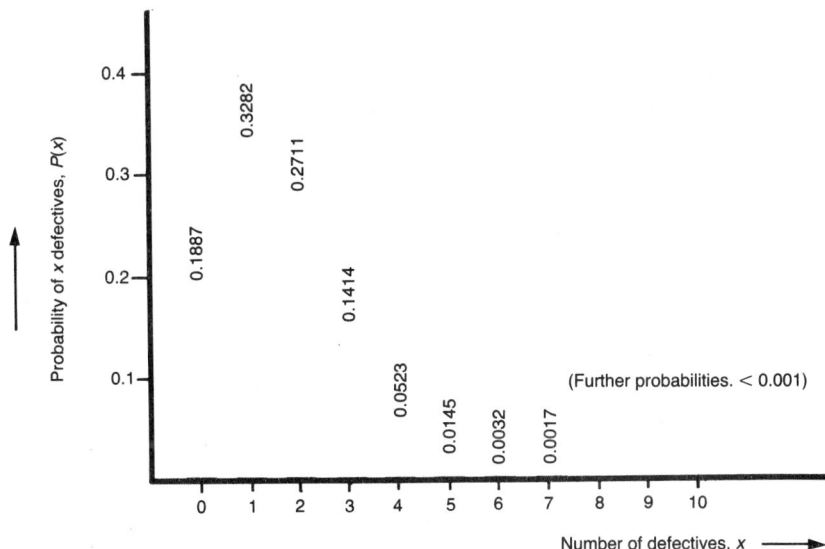

Figure 14.21. **Binomial distribution with $n = 20$, $p = 0.08$.**

A particular distribution is identified by its two parameters, n and p. A selection of distributions for other values of n and p is shown in Figure 14.22.

From Figure 14.22 an overall appreciation of the different shapes of the distribution can be obtained. Note in particular the exact symmetry of the distribution when $p=0.5$, and the closeness to symmetry when $(n \times p)$ (which is the mean, i.e. the expected number of defectives) becomes large. This is of particular relevance in the consideration of attributes control charts in Chapter 17.

A note on calculation of binomial probabilities
In most practical applications, rather than wanting to know the

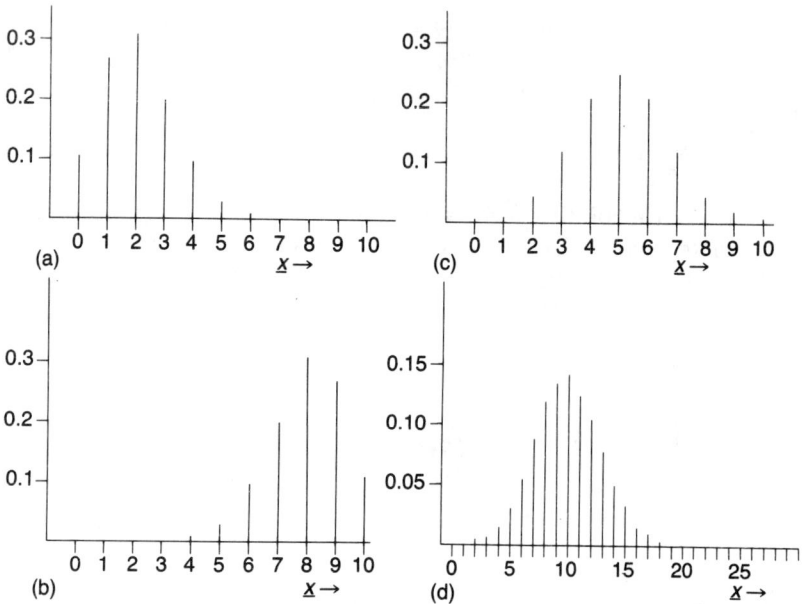

Figure 14.22.   **Binomial distributions. (a) $n = 10$, $p = 0.2$; (b) $n = 10$, $p = 0.8$; (c) $n = 10$, $p = 0.5$; (d) $n = 50$, $p = 0.2$.**

probability of exactly x defectives, it is usual to want to know the probability of 'c or fewer' or 'r or more' ('c' and 'r' simply being conventional symbols for the integer in question).

To calculate the probability of c or fewer simply add all the binomial probabilities from zero up to c. For example, in the case already explored of $n=20$ and $p=0.08$, the probability of two or fewer defectives is

$P(0) + P(1) + P(2) = 0.1887 + 0.3282 + 0.2711 = 0.7880$

The evaluation of successive binomial probabilities can be simplified by using the recursion relationship:

$$P(x) = P(x-1) \times \frac{(n-x+1)}{x} \times \frac{p}{(1-p)}$$

Reverting again to the example of $n=20$ and $p=0.08$, it is simple to calculate $P(0) = 0.92^{20} = 0.1887$. From this:

$$P(1) = 0.1887 \times \frac{20}{1} \times \frac{0.08}{0.92} = 0.3283$$

$$P(2) = 0.3282 \times \frac{19}{2} \times \frac{0.08}{0.92} = 0.2711$$

and so on, as far as is required.

An even simpler alternative, of course, is simply to obtain the values from a set of tables. The difficulty with the binomial is that it is not possible to standardize the variates, so a table containing even a restricted set of values of n and p is going to be a massive document. A very restricted set of tabulations for the probability of r or more defectives is given in Murdoch and Barnes (1986, Table 2), but this is only for n values of 2, 5, 10, 20 and 100. If tables are to be used, it is more usual to use the Poisson distribution (see below) as an approximation.

Poisson distribution

The Poisson distribution is used to described homogeneous Poisson processes (HPPs) as already introduced under the heading of the exponential distribution. Whereas the exponential is a continuous distribution describing the amount of sample space between events, the Poisson is a discrete distribution describing the number of events in a given sample space. The equation for the distribution (the Poisson probability function) is:

$$P(x) = \frac{e^{-m} m^x}{m!}$$

where $P(x)$ is the probability of x events occurring in an HPP when m events are expected. The term m is the only parameter of the Poisson distribution, and is equal to both the mean and the variance of the distribution. Referring to the section dealing with the exponential distribution, m is equal to λx, where λ is the rate per unit sample space at which events occur and x is the extent of the sample space.

For example, if a painting process produces blemishes at an average rate of one per 3.7 m², the expected number of blemishes on a panel of area 2.5 m² is 3.7/2.5 = 1.48. Using this for m:

Probability of 0 blemishes on a panel, $P(0) = e^{-1.48} = 0.228$

Probability of one blemish, $P(1) = \frac{e^{-1.48} 1.48^1}{1} = 0.337$

Similarly,

$$P(2) = \frac{e^{-1.48} 1.48^2}{2!} = 0.249$$

$$P(3) = \frac{e^{-1.48} 1.48^3}{3!} = 0.123$$

and so on. There is a very simple recursion formula for Poisson probabilities:

$$P(x) = P(x-1) \times \frac{m}{x}$$

so, in the above example, from $P(0) = 0.228$ it follows that:

$$P(1) = 0.288 \times \frac{1.48}{1} = 0.337$$

$$P(2) = 0.337 \times \frac{1.48}{2} = 0.249$$

etc.

The Poisson as an approximation to the binomial

The only situation modelled exactly by the Poisson is that of the HPP. While this does have applications in quality assurance (as, for example, in the use of '*c*' charts which will be described in Chapter 16), it is more usually applied as an approximation to the binomial. This opens the field of application to other types of attributes control chart, and also to acceptance sampling by attributes (as, for example, in British Standard BS6001 and its international equivalent, ISO2859).

The approximation is applied by putting the Poisson mean (m) equal to the binomial mean (np). Referring to the example used to illustrate the binomial distribution with $n=20$ and $p=0.08$, the mean $np = 20 \times 0.08 = 1.6$. Using 1.6 as the Poisson 'm', this gives:

$$P(0) = e^{-1.6} \qquad\quad = 0.202$$
$$P(1) = 0.202 \times 1.6 \quad = 0.323$$
$$P(2) = 0.323 \times 1.6/2 = 0.258$$
$$P(3) = 0.258 \times 1.6/3 = 0.138$$
etc.

Comparison with the binomial figures shows that, whilst there is some disparity, the agreement is probably close enough for practical purposes. Provided that np is suitably small (usually taken as being less than 0.1), this approximation is usually made use of as it greatly simplifies the calculations. It also facilitates the use of tabulated probabilities (as, for example, in Table 2 of Murdoch and Barnes (1986)) as there is now only one parameter to enter in the tables, and it will deal with any value of sample size.

The smaller the value of p, the better the approximation, with the limiting value of 0.1 merely being an arbitrary value. In quality assurance applications, it is to be hoped that real proportions defective never get this high, so the use of the Poisson in such applications is generally justified. A distinction should always be made, however, between the exact application (in an HPP) and the approximation to the binomial.

The normal distribution as an approximation to binomial and Poisson distributions

Inspection of Figure 14.22 shows that for large values of the binomial mean, the distribution becomes fairly symmetrical with a shape similar to that of the normal distribution. The Poisson behaves in a similar way. This opens the possibility of using the normal as an approximation to the binomial and Poisson with large means. This sometimes can simplify calculations of cumulative probabilities, but it is a procedure that must be used with care as it uses a continuous approximation to a discrete situation. It is best illustrated by example.

Suppose it is required to calculate the probability of there being between 15 and 25 (inclusive) defective items in a sample of 75 with a proportion defective 0.3. Calculation using the binomial is perfectly possible, but would necessitate the calculation of 10 separate terms, with some rather large numbers involved (the doubting reader is invited to try it!). The Poisson is no use as an approximation as p is far too large.

The use of the normal as an approximation involves equating the normal and (in this case) binomial means and variances. For this binomial:

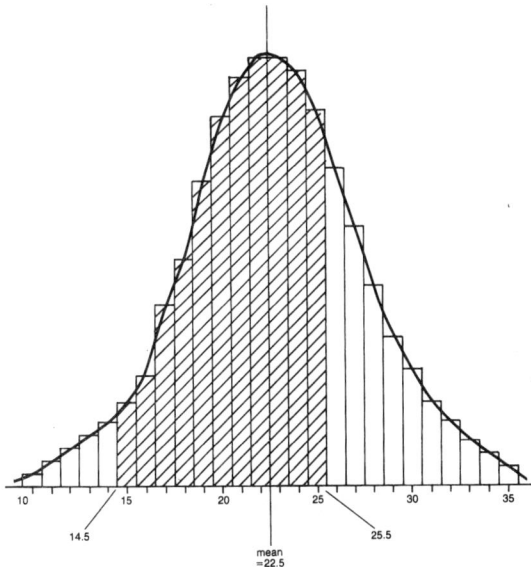

Figure 14.23. Example: normal approximation to the binomial. The required area is shaded.

The mean is $np = 75 \times 0.3 = 22.5$
The variance is $np(1 - p) = 75 \times 0.3 \times 0.7 = 15.75$
The standard deviation is $\sqrt{15.75} = 3.97$
The approximating normal therefore has $\mu = 22.5$ and $\sigma = 3.97$. The distributions are as shown in Figure 14.23.

The required part of the binomial is shown superimposed on the approximating normal. Note that the 'cut-off' points for the required tails are at 14.5 and 25.5. The problem as to whether to add or subtract this 0.5 continuity correction is a frequent source of difficulty. Rather than try to provide a necessarily complex set of rules, the simple solution is always to draw a sketch of the situation (as in Figure 14.23) when the solution becomes obvious. For the lower tail,

$$u_\alpha = \frac{14.5 - 22.5}{3.97} = -2.015$$

for which the tail area (which is the probability of *less than* 15 defectives) is 0.022, and, for the upper tail,

$$u_\alpha = \frac{25.5 - 22.5}{3.97} = -0.755$$

for which the tail area (the probability of more than 25 defectives) is 0.225. The probability of obtaining between 15 and 25 (inclusive) is therefore $1-(0.022+0.225) = 0.753$.

In dealing with attributes control charts (in Chapter 16) it will be seen that this approximation is often used implicitly even where the criteria for it being an adequate approximation are far from being met. The justification for this is that it is more important to have simple procedures than accurate probabilities — an issue that is discussed more fully in that chapter.

Further reading

This chapter has been limited to fundamental ideas with particular relevance to quality assurance. The subject of statistics goes far beyond this introduction. There are many hundreds of books on applied statistics, very few of which are unworthy of recommendation, so suggestions for further reading are to some extent personal preferences. On this basis, Chatfield (1983) is a very readable text, which has a particular leaning towards industrial applications and quality assurance. Miller and Freund (1977) is a rather more comprehensive text along the same lines. Beyond these, the best text is the one that the reader finds most 'user-friendly'.

It is not possible to undertake statistical analysis without recourse to statistical tables. Murdoch and Barnes (1986) is, in common with most 'compact' tables, mainly a compilation of standard tables that have mostly been published elsewhere. But they are particularly clearly presented, and contain in one volume many of the more usual tables and several that are of specific application to quality control.

Chatfield, C. *Statistics for Technology* 3rd edn., Science Paperbacks, Chapman & Hall, London 1983.

Davidson, J. (ed.) *The Reliability of Mechanical Systems*, Mechanical Engineering Publications, London 1988.

King, J., *Probability Charts for Decision Making*, Industrial Press, New York, 1971.

Miller, I. and Freund, J. E. *Probability and Statistics for Engineers*, Prentice Hall, New York, 1977.

Murdoch, J. and Barnes, J. A. *Statistical Tables for Science, Engineering, Management and Business Studies*, Macmillan, London, 1986.

15 Process Capability

David Newton

No two manufactured items are ever exactly alike. All the dimensions and other measurable properties will vary under the influence of a large number of factors — conventionally known as 'noise' factors. Examples of these could be:

1. 'Internal noise' factors that are inherent in the process itself, such as:
   - heating of machinery through use;
   - wear of bearings and sliding surfaces;
   - variations in properties of lubricants with time;
   - variations within raw materials;
   etc.
2. 'External noise' due to factors external to the process, such as:
   - environmental changes (temperature, humidity and so on);
   - different operators;
   - different sources of raw materials;
   - fluctuations in power supplies;
   etc.

The objective of statistical process control (SPC) is to understand and quantify this variation as a means of assessing its acceptability and, subsequently, to compare the current state of the process with this assessed variation in order to detect the onset of any deterioration on the process. This constitutes a continuous control of the process, but which is conventionally considered as two separate but closely related aspects. The first of these is the assessment of variation, which is considered in this chapter. The second is the subsequent routine monitoring of the process using control charting methods, which is described in Chapters 16 and 17.

Note that in reading this chapter the section on 'random variation of the mean' can be omitted without affecting the understanding of the rest of the chapter, or of the following two chapters. This section does, however, describe an important aspect that should be understood, perhaps at a later stage of reading.

Assignable and unassignable causes

The variation due to 'noise' factors (as described above) is commonly said to be due to 'unassignable causes' of variation. The presumption in process capability analysis is that these factors will always be present. The individual effect of a particular variable will generally be very small. There will, however, be a very large number of individual noise variables. Some of these we may be able to identify, but there will often be very many individually very small ones that are not known in any way. Their overall effect is assumed to be additive, and this will give rise to a total level of variation that can be substantial — even to the extent that it renders the process quite incapable of manufacturing within the limits imposed upon it. Process capability studies have the objective of measuring the variation due to unassignable causes.

If the process has a stable mean value and its variation is due only to unassignable causes, it is said to be 'in control'. Being in control only implies stability. It does not imply acceptability. A process whose inherent variability due to unassignable causes is too large with respect to its specified limits can be perfectly in control and yet be producing large quantities of defective product.

The objective of a control chart is to compare samples from the current process with the results of the process capability analysis, so as to detect any departure from the in-control state. Any such departure is said to be due to an assignable cause. This may be an increase in the variability, a change in the mean level, or both. The implication here is that once the change is detected, the cause can be assigned and corrective action taken to remove the cause.

In some terminology, particularly in the automotive industry, unassignable causes are referred to as 'common causes' and assignable causes as 'special causes'.

Capability analysis

Capability analysis is the analysis undertaken to quantify the variation due to unassignable causes. The assumption usually made is that, for an 'in control' process, the mean level of a measured variable from the process has a mean that is absolutely stable. All the variation in the process is then measured by the variance about that stable mean value. This assumption permits a simple approach to the analysis, but can occasionally give rise to an over-optimistic view of the capability — an aspect which is explored later in this chapter in the section on 'random variation of the mean'.

Measuring the variation

To evaluate the variation of a process, samples need to be taken of the measurement in question. It is, as always, a case of 'the bigger the sample the better', but conventionally a minimum sample of 50 observations is required. Rather than take a single block of observations from the process, it is preferable to adopt the same procedure that will be used later for control charting. In this, a series of small samples of typically 4, 5 or 6 observations are taken. The samples in each small subgroup are taken consecutively, with an interval (typically of around 50 items) between each successive group. The reasoning behind this is that estimates of the variance obtained within each group will give an estimate of the short term variation about the mean uninfluenced by any variation in the mean itself. If the mean was absolutely stable, there would of course be exactly the same information about the variance in, for example, a single sample of 50 as in ten samples of 5. The larger sample would, however, give a misleadingly large value for the variation if there had been any instability of the mean while the sample was being taken. The approach of taking a series of small 'snapshot' samples circumvents this problem, and also establishes the same procedure that will be used subsequently for control charting.

Every small subgroup that is taken will produce a small-sample estimate of the process mean, μ (as an $\bar{x}$ value), and of the process standard deviation, σ (as either a value of sample standard deviation s, or of sample range R). The calculation of these estimates is described in Chapter 14.

Example

Consider, as an example, a machining process which has a particular critical ground diameter with a nominal value of 15.00 mm. To assess the capability, samples of five items are taken at intervals during an assessment running of the process. The results of the first seven samples are shown in Table 15.1.

Table 15.1.
Measurement of process variation based on seven samples.
(s.d. = standard deviation).

Sample No.	Measurements (mm)					Average $\bar{x}$	Range R	s.d. σ
	1	2	3	4	5			
1	15.028	15.024	15.049	15.017	15.055	15.034	0.038	0.016
2	15.030	15.034	15.027	15.030	15.054	15.035	0.024	0.011
3	15.034	15.051	15.058	15.075	15.041	15.052	0.041	0.016
4	15.038	15.033	15.042	15.023	15.035	15.034	0.019	0.007
5	15.020	15.053	15.010	15.045	15.041	15.034	0.033	0.018
6	15.040	15.037	15.038	15.038	15.041	15.039	0.004	0.002
7	15.034	15.032	15.026	15.042	15.033	15.033	0.016	0.006

By this stage in the study it has become obvious that, whatever else may be happening, the process mean is too high as reflected by the $\bar{x}$ values being consistently well above the nominal value. The average of all these $\bar{x}$ values is 15.037, so the process was reset downwards in an attempt to correct the offset of 0.037 mm, and the analysis was then continued with the results shown in Table 15.2.

Throughout the analysis so far, the variability as revealed by the sample ranges and standard deviations does not appear to show any trends or step changes (plotting a graph will help to confirm this), so an estimate of the inherent process standard deviation can be calculated. This can be from either the s values or from the R values. (There is, of course, no need to calculate both estimates — one is sufficient as they are both expected to give the same answer.) From the s values:

Table 15.2.
Measurement of process variation after adjustment
(s.d. = standard deviation).

Sample	Measurements (mm)					Average	Range	S.D.
No.	1	2	3	4	5	$\bar{x}$	R	σ
8	15.028	15.024	15.005	15.025	15.008	15.018	0.023	0.011
9	14.992	15.023	15.008	14.996	15.004	15.004	0.031	0.012
10	15.007	15.016	15.037	15.025	15.008	15.019	0.030	0.018
11	15.007	14.986	15.006	15.003	15.012	15.012	0.031	0.012
12	15.027	15.022	14.995	15.026	15.009	15.016	0.031	0.014
13	15.016	15.025	15.031	15.005	15.014	15.018	0.026	0.010

The estimate of the process standard deviation, σ, is obtained from the square root of the average of the values of s^2 values.

$$\sigma = 1/13\sqrt{(0.016^2+0.011^2+0.016^2+0.007^2+ \ldots +0.012^2+0.014^2+0.010^2)}$$
$$= 0.0129$$

From the R values:

Under the assumption of the normal distribution, ranges can be converted into estimates of standard deviation by dividing by a conversion factor, d_n. The same conversion can be applied to $\bar{R}$, the average of the observed ranges. The value of the factor d_n varies with the sample size, as shown below:

Sample size (n)	2	3	4	5	6	7	8
Conversion factor d_n	1.128	1.693	2.059	2.326	2.534	2.704	2.847

In the example, this gives

$$\bar{R} = \frac{(0.038+0.034+0.041+ \cdots +0.031+0.031+0.026)}{13}$$

$= 0.0275$, and hence:
$\sigma = 0.0275/d_5 = 0.0275/2.326 = 0.0118$

Note that the standard deviations obtained by the two methods differ slightly. This is to be expected as the use of d_n factors introduces another stage of estimation with its own associated variability. It is therefore always slightly preferable to calculate the estimate using the first method, namely, directly from the sample standard deviations.

Machine and process capability

As it is usually not possible to synthesize the effects of all the external noise factors during process capability analysis, the approach that is often adopted is to control these factors as tightly as possible. For example, only one operator would be used, only one batch of raw material processed, etc., and as far as possible the process would be run with all environmental conditions held constant. This would result in a measure of variability that applies only under these somewhat idealized conditions. This is sometimes referred to as 'machine capability' rather than process capability. The more representative process capability variation will consist of the machine capability variation plus the extra element due the external noise factors.

Relation to specification tolerances

Despite the growing acceptance of concepts such as the Taguchi quadratic loss function, and the related broader acceptance of continuing process improvement by reduction of variability, most products still have their measurable characteristics defined by conventional specification tolerances. One of the primary functions of process capability studies is to compare the process variation with these tolerances.

In the above example, the process standard deviation was estimated as 0.0129 mm (using the larger of the estimates). Assume that the specification limits for this dimension are 15.00 mm ± 0.05 mm. If a

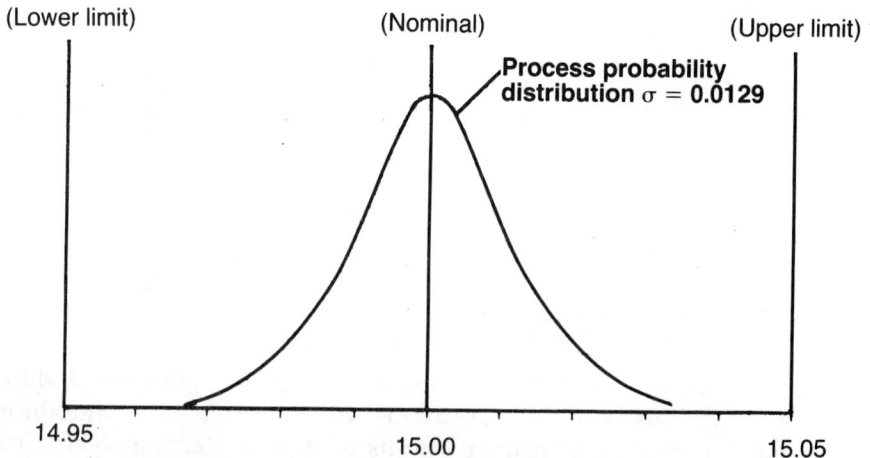

Figure 15.1. Relationship of process and specification tolerance (assuming that the process can be centred on 15.00).

normal distribution is assumed, and it is also assumed that, given further samples, it will be possible to centre the process on its nominal value of 15.00 mm, the relation of the process to its specification limits will be as shown in Figure 15.1.

The process is just contained within the specification limits, so, provided that no assignable causes appear to change the mean or increase the variation, the process is capable of working to these limits. It would be judged to be a 'medium precision' process — capable of working within limits, but needing to be controlled closely to ensure that any changes from this situation are speedily detected. This, and other situations, are categorized in broad terms as shown in Figure 15.2.

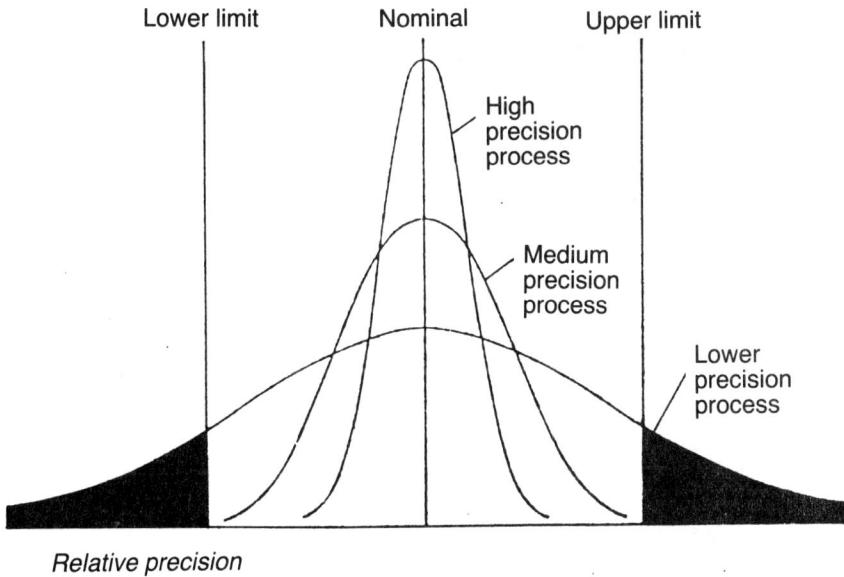

Relative precision

Figure 15.2. Relative precision.

A high precision process is one in which the variation is very small compared with the specification limits. Although the view can be taken that it would be unnecessary to apply control charting to such a process except to guard against it moving dangerously close to the specification limits, the modern way of thinking for such a process is that SPC should be applied in the usual way in the quest for process consistency as a valuable target in its own right, irrespective of the specification limits.

Conversely, a low precision process is one in which the variation is so large that it is inherently incapable of working within the specification limits. The best that SPC can then offer is to control the mean at a value that minimizes the consequences of being outside limits. If the overall proportion outside both limits needs to be minimized, the mean would be set centrally. If, as is often the case, the rejects in one tail are more costly than those in the other, the mean would be controlled at a value closer to the less expensive tail. In any of these cases, there would be the necessity for 100 per cent inspection of the product. To improve the precision of such a process, either the variation has to be reduced, or the specification tolerances increased. The latter approach is the obvious one to adopt first. Tolerancing is often both conservative and arbitrary, and can frequently be opened for further discussion in the light of high costs of working within them. Approaches such as probabilistic tolerancing in assembly build-up can help considerably. The conventional approach of a design office in assembly tolerancing is to make the assembly tolerance the sum of the component tolerances, i.e.

$$T_{ASSY} = T_1 + T_2 + T_3 + \ldots, \text{etc.}$$

whereas the probabilistic approach considers the low probability of randomly chosen components being on the same extreme of tolerance. A detailed description of probabilistic tolerancing is beyond the scope of this chapter, but a good starting point is an approach based on the additivity of variances, with each T being considered as a constant proportion of its individual specification limit. This gives:

$$T_{ASSY} = \sqrt{(T_1^2 + T_2^2 + T_3^2 + \ldots \text{etc.})}$$

which will permit larger values for the individual component tolerances T_1, T_2, T_3, etc.

Quantifying process capability

This introduces the idea of the 'natural tolerance' of a process — the total extent of the measurement over which it can be expected to vary. This is usually taken to be six standard deviations. This comes from the assumption of a normal distribution where (the mean) ± (three standard deviations) contains 99.73 per cent of the measurements, which is near enough to all of them for practical purposes. In practice, real processes will always depart from the assumption of normality, often to a considerable extent, but the concept of 6σ as the natural tolerance still gives a useful basis for capability assessment.

The basic measure of capability is the 'process capability index', C_P. This is given by:

$$C_P = \frac{\text{Upper limit} - \text{Lower limit}}{6\sigma} \; (= \frac{\text{Specification tolerance}}{\text{Natural tolerance}})$$

For a process to be considered capable, C_P should always be greater than 1. If the analysis has been strictly one of machine capability, an arbitrary 'safety factor' of at least one-third should be added to the acceptable minimum value of the index, so that C_P in this case should be no lower than 1.33. The capability index when referred to machine capability is sometimes given the symbol C_M.

In the example, C_P is $0.10/6\times0.0129 = 1.29$. This is barely adequate (and is particularly marginal if it is strictly a C_M rather than a C_P). In this case, it is possibly sufficiently close to 1.33 to permit production, but only if the process is closely monitored using control charts and further efforts are made to reduce the variation. The process is in the lower end of the medium precision category, but the philosophy of 'never-ending improvement' requires that efforts continue to increase the value of the capability index. One of the comments occasionally heard concerning comparisons between western and eastern attitudes to quality is that the West talks in terms of acceptable C_P values of 'one point something' whereas the eastern approach is to try to achieve values of three or more.

Setting accuracy

The discussion so far has been concerned only with the precision (i.e. the variation) of the process. In many processes, the mean level is capable of adjustment to any required value within the specification limits. It is still useful to quantify any error in setting the mean, and this will be particularly true in any case when the setting is not amenable to adjustment — as, for instance, in the case of a component produced in a press tool.

The setting index is denoted C_{Pk} and is given by the lower of:

$$\frac{\text{Upper specification limit} - \bar{x}}{3\sigma} \quad \text{or} \quad \frac{\bar{x} - \text{lower specification limit}}{3\sigma}$$

This again has the requirement of exceeding 1 (if σ refers to overall process capability), or of exceeding 1.33 (if σ refers only to machine capability, in which case the index is sometimes known as C_{Mk}).

The term $\bar{x}$ is the overall average from the process capability study (i.e. the average of the $\bar{x}$ values over a period during which they were stable). In the example, for the first seven samples the lower value of C_P is $(15.05 - 15.037)/3 \times 0.0129 = 0.34$ which is plainly inadequate. This fact was recognized informally and the process was reset. For the remaining samples, the new overall mean was 15.016, giving a revised C_{Pk} value of 0.88. This tells us that further adjustment is still required. After further resetting of the process in this example, further samples should be taken until there is a clear demonstration that the process is stable. As a general rule, at least 20 subgroups (or a total of at least 200 individual samples) are necessary before the capability can be viewed as fully assessed. This process merges into routine production control charting, as described in the next two chapters. It is not usually possible (or necessary) to draw a clear distinction between the end of process capability analysis and the beginning of production charting. Further, the quest for process improvement should be continued throughout the life of the process.

Note that if the process is set exactly on nominal, C_{Pk} becomes equal to C_P, so that for a process that is only marginally acceptable (as in this case), the only acceptable setting for the process mean is exactly on the nominal value. For processes of higher capability, a threshold region of acceptable settings will appear on either side of the nominal, which gives scope for setting processes liable to drift away from the limit at an initial value on the opposite side of nominal which they are drifting.

Relative precision index
This is an alternative series of indices that are used in British Standards. Instead of relating the index to the process standard deviation (as with C_P), the relative precision index (RPI) is the ratio

$$\frac{\text{Upper specification limit} - \text{lower specification limit}}{\bar{R}}$$

where $\bar{R}$ is the average of the ranges of the samples. This has the problem that the index will depend on the sample size. A table of minimum values of the index is given in British Standard BS 2564, and is reproduced in Table 15.3.

In the example, the RPI is $0.10/0.0275 = 3.64$, which is greater than the minimum for a sample of five and so assesses the process as capable for manufacture.

Dangers in capability indices

All the indices described in the previous two sections give a simple assessment of the capability of the process. Inherent in this simplicity, however, is a danger of misleading results if any of the assumptions built in to the indices are not valid. They are liable to mislead if the process distribution is markedly non-normal, and are effectively meaningless if the mean value is not stable. These aspects are considered in the next two sections.

Testing for normality

Once sufficient data have been gathered from a stable process — around 50 or more individual observations — it is possible to investigate the form of the probability distribution describing the data. A convenient way of doing this is by way of a probability plot on normal probability paper, as described in Chapter 14 and illustrated in Figure 14.19. Such a plot gives informal estimates of the mean and standard deviation of the process which should confirm the values obtained direct from the data. It will also test the data for normality and for outliers.

Any marked non-linearity in the plot suggests a departure from the assumption of normality, as shown in Figure 15.3. The skewed distribution, as in Figure 15.3a is a common occurrence. It is to be expected in the case of measurements with target value of zero, but with actual values that will always be non-negative — such things as percentages of impurities and dimensions such as surface finishes, eccentricity, ovality, parallelism, etc. Leptokurtic and platykurtic forms can also give non-linearities as in Figures 15.3b and c. Apparent

Table 15.3.
Minimum values of relative precision index.

Sample size n	Minimum value of index
2	5.321
3	3.544
4	2.914
5	2.580
6	2.363
7	2.210
8	2.108

skewness and departures from normality in terms of kurtosis can be confirmed by calculation of the appropriate coefficients, as described in Chapter 14 (see also Figures 14.7 and 14.8).

It is important to appreciate that there is nothing necessarily amiss with a process that is non-normal. There is no particular reason why the normal distribution should apply to manufacturing processes — it is simply a convenient mathematical form that is usually an adequate approximation. Its convenience comes from its properties being widely understood and extensively tabulated. In the case of a positively skewed distribution, the distribution of the logarithms of the measurements will usually be adequately close to normal, and these can be used to assess the capability. The example on page 244 of Chapter 14 illustrates how this is done. Alternatively, the data can be plotted on log-normal probability plotting paper.

Apart from this adaptation of the procedure for estimating process capability for skewed distributions, there is little that needs to be done in the case of non-normal distributions. The central limit theorem will, except in instances of extreme skew, make the sample averages adequately close to a normal for the usual control charting rules to apply on the averages chart. The ranges chart rules will give risks different from those under the assumption of normality, but experience shows this to be of little importance. For extremely skewed distributions, there might be a case for operating the control chart on the logarithms of the measurements.

Random variation of the mean

The standard approach to process capability so far described has made the assumption that the process mean is completely stable. It frequently happens that this is not the case, and instead the mean itself is subject to small random variations (as in Figure 15.4) which are still due to unassignable causes.

The presence of such additional variation will have implications regarding both process capability (where the previous, simple analysis will give over optimistic results) and in control charting. Define:

σ_0 = the standard deviation of the process about the mean (i.e. what we have previously referred to simply as σ).

σ_1 = the standard deviation of the process mean about the overall process average.

σ_t = the effective total standard deviation of the process.

Distributions

Normal probability plots

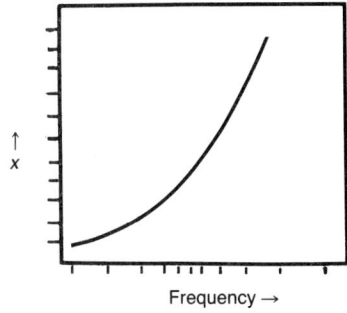

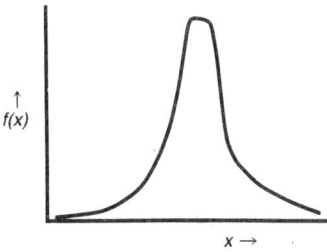

(a) Skewed

(b) 'Peaked' (leptokurtic)

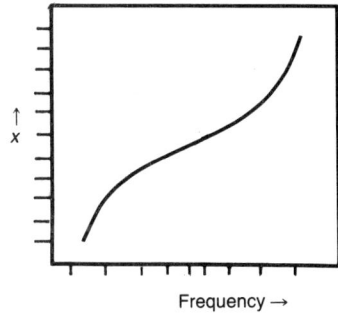

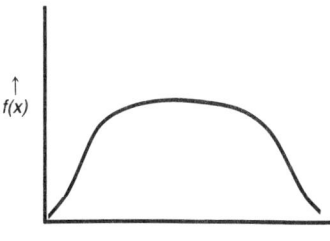

(c) 'Flat' (platykurtic)

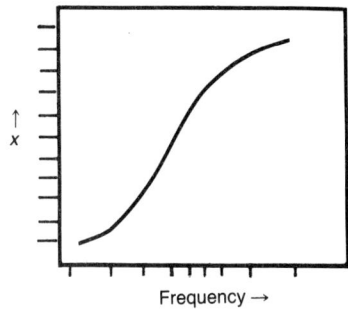

Figure 15.3. Effects of non-normality on probability plots. (a) Skewed;
(b) 'peaked' (leptocurtic); (c) 'flat' (platykurtic).

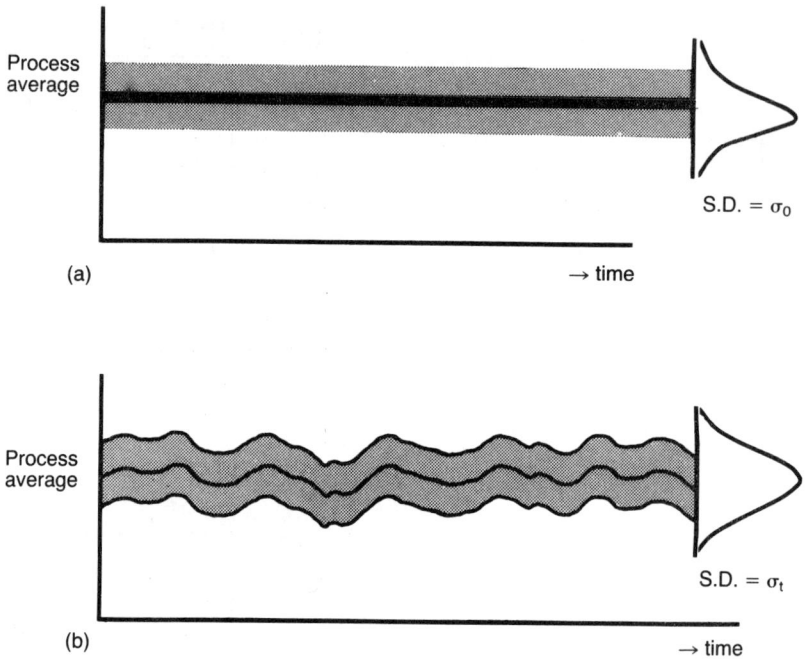

Figure 15.4.   Random variation of the mean. (a) Stable process average; (b) Average subject to random variation.

These are related by:

$$\sigma_t^2 = \sigma_0^2 + \sigma_1^2$$

To see if this extra variability exists, the variation of the sample means that was observed is compared with the value it should have taken if σ_1 were zero. The standard deviation of a series of observed $\bar{x}$ values over a period of apparent stability in the capability data is calculated in the usual way. This is the calculated standard error, denoted σ_e. Under the assumption of constant mean, the expected value of this standard error is $\sigma_0/\sqrt{n}$ (where n is the subgroup sample size). The variance of the mean is obtained from the difference between the two variances, i.e.

$$\sigma_1^2 = \sigma_e^2 - \sigma_0^2/n$$

As an illustration, consider samples 8 to 13 in the example.

σ_0^2 is the average of the observed variances, i.e.
$\sigma_0^2 = 1/6(0.011^2+0.012^2+0.018^2+0.012^2+0.014^2+0.010^2)$
$= 0.000155$
($\sigma_0 = \sqrt{0.000172} = 0.0124$, which, as a check, is close to the value of 0.0129 obtained earlier from the entire data set.)
σ_e is the standard deviation of the $\bar{x}$ values, i.e. of 15.018, 15.004, 15.019, 15.012, 15.016 and 15.018, which gives $\sigma_e = 0.0057$.

The expected standard deviation under the assumption of constant mean is $0.0124/\sqrt{5} = 0.0055$.

As the two values (σ_e and $\sigma_0/\sqrt{n}$) are almost the same (i.e. the difference between them, representing σ_1, is effectively negligible), in this particular process the assumption of a stable mean is justified.

Table 15.4.
Process capability data for 26 samples.

Sample no.	Average $\bar{x}$	Range R	Sample no.	Average $\bar{x}$	Range R
1	249.99	1.4	14	250.01	2.4
2	250.32	1.1	15	250.38	1.2
3	250.54	1.0	16	250.00	1.2
4	250.30	0.7	17	249.92	0.9
5	249.87	0.9	18	249.86	0.5
6	249.98	1.4	19	250.22	1.6
7	250.01	0.6	20	249.80	0.8
8	249.47	2.0	21	250.66	1.7
9	249.78	1.5	22	249.62	1.0
10	250.59	2.2	23	250.25	1.3
11	250.15	0.9	24	249.16	1.6
12	249.69	1.0	25	250.19	1.5
13	249.84	1.8	26	251.03	1.1

From this, all the various indices are validated from this aspect, and there is no need to modify the assessment of process capability.

To illustrate a situation when this is not the case, and to show the effect on capability analysis, consider another set of process capability data as shown in Table 15.4. The data consist of averages and ranges of samples of 5 drawn from a container filling process. The specification is 250±2 ml.

The overall average is 250.07 ml. The average of the ranges $\bar{R}$, is

1.281, giving an estimate of the standard deviation σ of $\bar{R}/d_5 =$ 1.281/2.326 = 0.55 ml.

Using, initially, the simple approach assuming a stable mean, this gives capability indices:

$C_P = 4/(6 \times 0.55) = 1.21$
$C_{Pk} = (252.00 - 250.07)/(3 \times 0.55) = 0.79$.

These indices show both that the process is highly marginal as regards capability. (C_P falling short of the required value of 1.33) and requires more accurate centring.

To investigate the stability of the mean,

$\sigma_e = 0.397$ (by direct calculation from the $\bar{x}$ values)
$\sigma_0 = 0.55$ (i.e. σ as used above), giving $\sigma_0/\sqrt{5} = 0.246$.

The value of σ_e is now much bigger than its 'expected' value, showing that there is instability in the mean. This could be due to an assignable cause, but a sample-by-sample plot of $\bar{x}$ shows no evidence of this, so the effect is a purely random one due to unassignable causes. The standard deviation of the sample average, σ_1, is evaluated by

$\sigma_1^2 = \sigma_e^2 - \sigma_0^2/n$, i.e. $\sigma_1^2 = 0.397^2 - 0.55^2/5 = 0.0971$
$\sigma_1 = \sqrt{0.0971} = 0.312$.

The overall process standard deviation σ_t will be comprised of both these within sample and between-sample elements.

$\sigma_t^2 = \sigma_0^2 + \sigma_1^2 = 0.55^2 + 0.312^2 = 0.3996$
$\sigma_t = \sqrt{0.3996} = 0.632$

This total effect should be used in evaluating the capability. Revised values are:

$C_P = 4/(6 \times 0.632) = 1.05$
$C_{Pk} = (252.00 - 250.07)/(3 \times 0.632) = 0.69$

both of which show a situation considerably worse than the previous analysis.

This example demonstrates that, if there is random variation in the mean (and there very often is in real production processes), the conventional simple approach to process capability can give over optimistic answers. Whenever a capability study appears to demonstrate marginal acceptability, an analysis similar to the example just described should be undertaken to ensure that the situation is not, in reality, one of unacceptability. These considerations will also have a bearing on limits for control charts for averages, as discussed in the next chapter.

16 Control Charts: 1. Shewhart Charts

David Newton

Chapter 15 described how the variation inherent in a process is measured and how it is compared with specified limits in order to quantify process capability. In so doing, the idea was introduced of a time-based chart on which was plotted sample averages of the process characteristic in question. Control charting is simply an extension of this procedure into the routine production operation of the manufacturing process. The purpose of the chart now becomes that of detecting change from the inherent, 'in control' situation defined in the process capability analysis. Objective decision criteria are introduced for decisions as to whether or not such a change has occurred. The need for control of the variation of the process as well as its mean level is explained. The definitive control chart for measured variables is the '$\bar{x}$, R' chart which combines these two requirements with data from the same sample being plotted on both charts simultaneously. Similar approaches can be applied to attributes control, where the process characteristic is a count of non-conforming items or of defects. Control charts of this type are sometimes referred to as 'Shewhart' charts (Shewhart, 1931).

To interfere or to ignore?

When a process is 'in control' it is behaving in a completely random (i.e. unpredictable) manner influenced only by its 'common causes' of chance variation. The objective of any control chart is to signal any departure from this situation due to 'special' (or sometimes called 'assignable') causes, whether they affect the mean level or the variability of the process. The objectives are accordingly two-fold:

- To take action when a change occurs.
- To refrain from action in the absence of a change.

It is easy to lose sight of the importance of the second aspect. Human nature is to 'fiddle' with a process when any apparent change occurs. It is easily demonstrated that if the variation is purely random, any such fiddling is bound to make the process deteriorate. The Table 16.1 shows fifteen consecutive samples from a stable, 'in control' process with a mean of exactly 250. Column 1 shows the averages of samples of five observations. Column 2 shows the error of these from the mean. Column 3 shows the adjusted values of Column 1 if the process had been corrected by adjusting it to compensate for the error in the previous sample.

Table 16.1.
Data for 15 samples taken from a stable, 'in control' process.

Sample average (1)	Error (2)	Average after correction (3)
251.23	+1.23	251.23
250.94	−0.39	249.71
248.26	−1.35	248.65
250.99	+2.34	252.34
249.81	−2.53	247.47
251.87	+4.40	254.40
249.98	−4.42	245.58
249.35	+3.77	253.77
248.85	−4.92	245.08
250.10	+5.02	255.02

The increased variation is immediately apparent, and is shown even more clearly in Figure 16.1 where the two sets of data are charted. Even if the process had not been 'corrected' on every sample, or if the corrections had been less than the total error, the variation would still have increased.

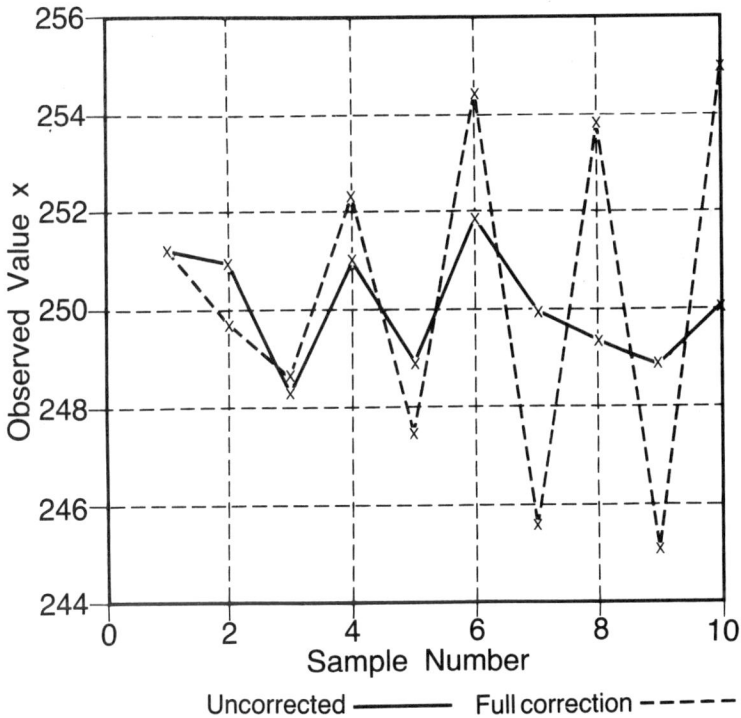

Figure 16.1.   The effect of correcting the mean.

Whilst it is, of course, important to take some form of action if a process really changes due to a special cause, any attempt to correct or adjust a process where no special causes are present will *always* make matters worse than if the process were left alone.

The control chart for sample averages

This is an extension of the process capability analysis into the production process. It relates to measurements of a single process characteristic. Samples are taken from the process at regular intervals. Each sample is of n items. The value of n, the sample size, is usually between 1 and 8. 5 is a popular value – it is sufficiently large to take advantage of the central limit theorem in any assumption of normality, and any further increase in size is subject to diminishing returns in that the information contained in the sample increases only in proportion to the square root of the sample size.

The choice of the time interval between successive samplings from the process is largely an economic one, based on the maximum time it would be considered tolerable for the process to remain in an undetected 'out-of-control' state. The intervals between samplings should be approximately equal. It is, however, worthwhile bearing in mind the risks of being too predictable, particularly in the case of processes influenced by operators who might be inclined to make a special effort when a sampling is due.

Figure 16.2 shows a simple averages control chart for averages of samples of size five. The target value is 50.00 and process capability analysis has produced an estimate of 0.73 for σ. There is no obvious pattern to the plots except that there appears to be a downward movement of the averages towards the end, and, in particular, the most recent value, 48.87, seems particularly low. Bearing in mind what has been said about the dangers of trying to correct an in-control process, however, we need to be fairly certain that this apparent move downwards is a real change in the process before any move to reset it.

This can be assessed by reference to the probability distribution of the averages under the 'in control' assumption. This will have a mean equal to the target value of 50.00. From what was learned in Chapter 15, the standard deviation of averages of samples of size n (the 'standard error') will be the inherent standard deviation σ divided by the square root of the sample size (i.e. $\sigma / \sqrt{5}$). We also learned that, as a result of the central limit theorem, these averages will be approximately normally distributed, so we can use normal distribution tables to assess probabilities.

In this example, the standard error is $0.73/\sqrt{5} = 0.326$, so the last plotted point is $(50.00-48.87)/0.326 = 3.47$ standard errors away from the target value. Reference to tables of the normal distribution (see, for example, Table 14.1 in Chapter 14) shows that the probability of obtaining an average this far away from the target under the assumed distribution is very small (approximately 0.00025, or one chance in 4000), so we are justified in assuming that our observed value comes

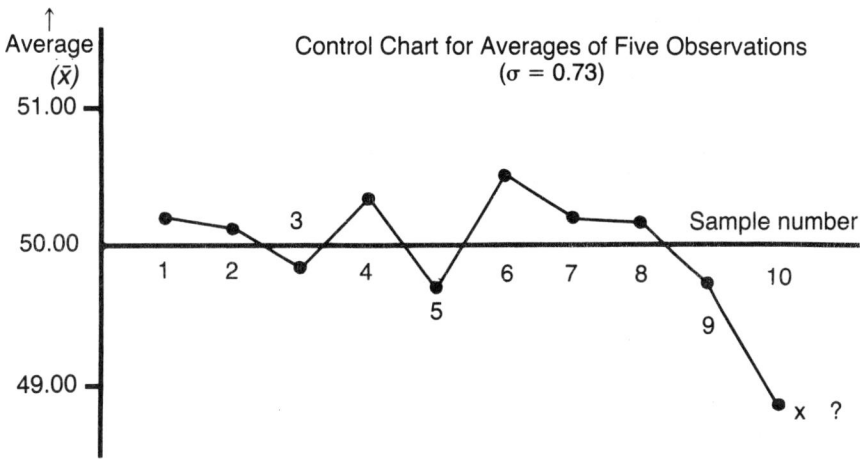

Figure 16.2. **Averages control chart – has the process average changed?**

from some other distribution. The obvious conclusion is that it came from one with a mean of less than 50.00, so it now makes sense to readjust the process upwards, taking several additional samples until it is demonstrated that the mean is back on, or near to, the target value.

Control lines

Rather than assess the probabilities of each point as it is plotted, it is more usual to set decision criteria in advance by drawing control lines on the chart equispaced either side of the mean, at a distance such that a plotted point on or outside the lines makes it fairly certain that a change has occurred. The conventional position for these lines is three standard errors either side of the target, i.e. $T \pm 3\sigma / \sqrt{n}$. (Note that it is acceptable, or even preferable to use $T \pm 3\sigma_e$ if a value of σ_e has been obtained direct from the process capability study, as was discussed in Chapter 15.)

The probability of getting a point on or outside a line (assuming normality) is approximately 1 in 1000 (0.00135 to be more exact), so if we interpret such a point as meaning a change in the process, there is approximately a 0.999 probability that we are correct in doing so.

Other positions for control lines are of course possible — the use of 3 as the multiplier has evolved as a value that works satisfactorily in most circumstances. British Standards use a value of 3.09, for which the number of standard errors away from the mean corresponds to a normal distribution probability of exactly one thousandth. The difference this makes in practice can be ignored. Values of less than 3 are quite common in circumstances where it is critical to detect changes in mean level. If such values are adopted, there is a concomitant increase in the risk of a spurious action decision where no change has in fact occurred. The value of this risk (known, in general, as the 'Type I' or 'α' risk) can be read from normal distribution tables. For example, if we use $\pm$ 2.5 instead of $\pm$ 3, the Type I risk increases from 0.00135 to 0.0062.

Refinements to decision criteria

Warning lines

Sometimes, an additional pair of lines is positioned inside the control lines, with the rule that two consecutive points outside the same line constitute an action decision. This increases the sensitivity of the chart. Conventionally, these are positioned at $\pm$ 2 standard errors either side of the target, which is approximately at the 1 in 40 probability point. (British Standards use $\pm$ 1.96 to give an exact one fortieth probability under the assumption of normality.) If warning lines are in use, once one point is obtained outside a line it is a signal also that the next sample should be taken sooner than usual, so that the suspicion of change can be confirmed or allayed as soon as possible.

A control chart with both control and warning lines is shown in Figure 16.3.

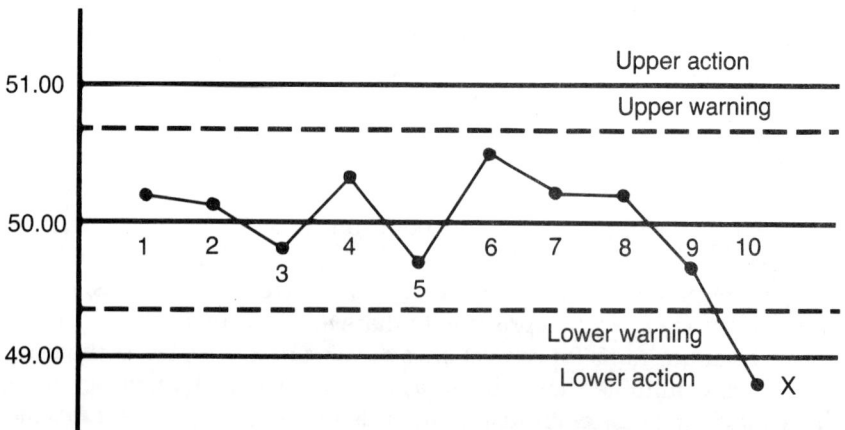

Figure 16.3.   Averages chart with action and warning lines. The data are the same as in Figure 16.2.

Runs of observations
If a chart shows either a run of several plotted averages the same side
of the target (as in Figure 16.4a), or a run of several averages where
each one is consistently greater than or less than its predecessor (as in
Figure 16.4b), this can again be taken as a criterion for action.
Conventionally, a run of eight such observations is needed — the
chance of either of these happening purely by chance is no greater than
$0.5^8 = 0.004$.

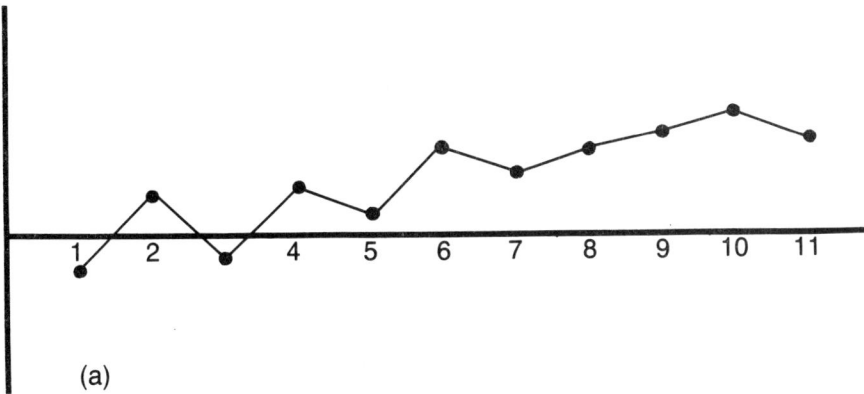

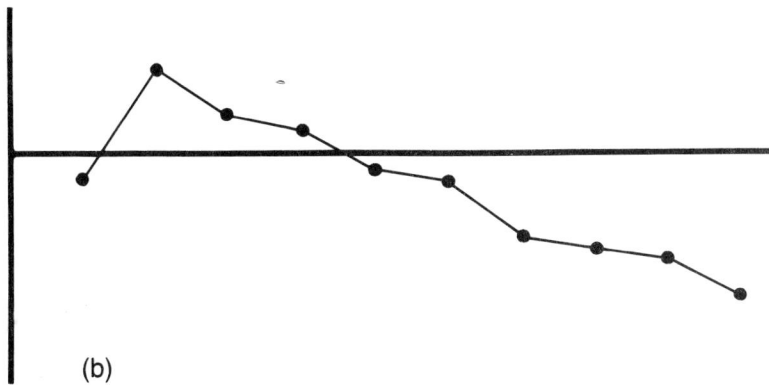

(a)

(b)

**Figure 16.4.   Examples of runs of consecutive points. (a) Run of points
above target (samples 3-11); (b) run of consistently reducing points.**

Other criteria
Plotting a control chart reveals aspects of the process that might not
necessarily be encompassed by any of these decision criteria. For this

reason, the plot should always be studied for evidence of any patterns which could indicate problems that might be anticipated for a particular process. This must, however, be done with great care bearing in mind what has been said about the dangers of interfering with a stable process.

Control of variation: the ranges chart

In processes controlled by a measured variable, there are possible out-of-control situations other than a movement in the average away from the target. Specifically, it is essential to detect any increase in variation above the inherent value demonstrated by the process capability analysis. Such an increase can often happen without any change in the process average. To detect such increases, it is necessary to plot some statistic that measures the variation of the process as reflected by the sample. The statistic most widely used is the sample range (R), which is simply the difference between the largest and smallest observations in the sample. (The sample will be the same one that was used to provide $\bar{x}$, the sample average.)

Control lines for ranges charts

The probability distribution for sample ranges is not normal, even for normally distributed measurements, unless the sample size is much bigger than those in conventional use in control charting. Further, the distribution is asymmetrical, which precludes the use of simple '±' rules as for the averages chart. Factors for these lines have been calculated, and are available in many sources. The values in Table 16.2 have been reproduced from British Standard BS5700: 1984 and are used as follows:

> For an inherent process standard deviation σ:
> The action line is at σ multiplied by $D_{0.001}$
> The warning line, if used, is at σ multiplied by $D_{0.025}$

The option is also given for calculating these limits from process variation expressed as an expected average range, μ_R (which was estimated by the observed average range, $\bar{R}$). In this case:

> The action line is at μ_R multiplied by $D'_{0.001}$
> The warning line, if used, is at μ_R multiplied by $D'_{0.025}$

Table 16.2

Table of control line factors for charts for sample range. (Taken from BS5700 by permission of the British Standards Institution.)

Sample size (n)	Factors for standard deviation, σ		Factors for average range, μ_R			Conversion factor d_n ($\sigma = \mu_R \div d_n$)
	Control $D_{0.001}$	Warning $D_{0.025}$	Control $D'_{0.001}$	Warning $D'_{0.025}$	Control (US) D_4	
2	4.65	3.17	4.12	2.81	3.27	1.128
3	5.05	3.68	2.98	2.17	2.57	1.693
4	5.30	3.98	2.57	1.93	2.28	2.059
5	5.45	4.20	2.34	1.81	2.11	2.326
6	5.60	4.36	2.21	1.72	2.00	2.534
7	5.70	4.49	2.11	1.66	1.92	2.704
8	5.80	4.61	2.04	1.62	1.86	2.847

An 'American' factor for sample range, D_4, is also given. This is an empirical factor due originally to Shewhart which is commonly used in the United States. It gives risk values between those of BS type control and warning lines. It is based on $\mu_R + (3 \times$ the standard deviation of μ_R).

In the example previously used for calculating the averages chart limits, with $\sigma = 0.326$,

For sample size five, $D_{0 \cdot 001} = 5.45$
$$D_{0 \cdot 025} = 4.20$$

giving an action line at $0.326 \times 5.45 = 1.777$ and a warning line, if required, at $0.326 \times 4.20 = 1.369$

The standard deviations chart

Control charting was developed in the days before electronic calculators. It was essential that calculations in the use of such charts were kept to a minimum to permit easy application on the shopfloor. For this reason, range was used as the measure of variation instead of the theoretically much sounder use of standard deviation. Range has the related drawbacks of inefficiency (in that it only uses two pieces of information from the n available in the sample) and a dependency upon the assumption of normality in the derivation of the control lines.

The use of standard deviation is nowadays much more acceptable as the complexities of its calculation can be avoided by the use of a calculator — the result is just as easy to obtain as the range. Despite this, the traditional use of range predominates, largely as a result of its use in various national and company standards. Table 16.3 gives control chart factors for standard deviation — in the same simple empirical '± 3σ' theme that applies to American limits, it is simply σ + (3 × the standard deviation of σ). The control limit is at $B_4 \times \sigma$.

Table 16.3.
Table of control limit factors for charts for standard deviation

Sample size	2	3	4	5	6	7	8
B_4	3.27	2.57	2.27	2.09	1.97	1.88	1.81

Lower limits for charts for ranges and standard deviations

It is unlikely that any manufacturing process will, without outside intervention, become more precise through a reduction in its variability. For this reason, there is no usual need for lower limits for range or standard deviation charts although it is straightforward enough to derive factors for such limits. They are, for example, given in BS2564 for D and D^1 factors, the suffixes for control and warning limits being 0.999 and 0.975, respectively (referring, as with the upper line, to the probabilities of obtaining a point above the line when 'in control'). The 'American' equivalent factor for the lower control line is given in Grant & Leavenworth as D_3. The corresponding factor for standard deviation charts is given in the same reference as B_3.

There is one reason for the application of lower limits that is, perhaps, worth consideration. This is the possible apparent reduction of variability due to errors in measuring equipment — an example once encountered was a cylindrical grinding process whose remarkable consistency was found to be due not to the process at all, but to the fact that the pointer on the air gauge dial was firmly stuck to the glass.

Outliers and the ranges chart

The designed intention of the range chart is to detect any change (usually an increase) in the variation inherent in the process. It also serves a very important additional function of signalling any individual sample observations that are a long way from the target value. Such values would often not have sufficient effect on the average to give an 'action' signal on the $\bar{x}$ chart (due to the centralizing effect of the others in the sample), but a single 'rogue' value would be more likely to give an upper 'action' signal on a ranges (or standard deviations) chart. Such values can occur due to a single faulty component in the sample, or simply due to an error in recording the data. This function of the ranges chart alone is sufficient justification for such a chart always to be used in conjunction with an averages chart, as described below.

The average and range ($\bar{x}$, R) chart

The definitive control chart for measured variables is one which controls mean level and variability simultaneously. The most widely used version of this is the chart for average and range. In such a chart, the average and the range are both calculated from the same sample.

An example of production data from which such a chart might be constructed is given in Table 16.4. The process is the press-forming of a spring clip, where the process is monitored by the free length dimension which has specification limits of 20.00 mm ± 1.5 mm. An earlier process capability study showed that when in control, the process gave a mean very close to the nominal, and a standard deviation of 0.50 mm. This standard deviation converts into an expected range for samples of five of $0.50 \times d_5$, i.e. $0.50 \times 2.326 = 1.16$.

The $\bar{x}$, R chart in action

Figure 16.5 shows the data in Table 16.4 plotted on a typical charting form as used in industry. This particular example is reproduced by kind permission of the Ford Motor Company.

Choice of sample size

The sample has to be sufficiently large to give adequate precision to estimates of mean and range, and also for the central limit theorem to make reasonable the assumption of normality implicit in the averages chart limits. Conversely, we need a sample small enough to provide an instant 'snapshot' of the process. Experience has shown that the best compromise is reached with sample sizes in the range four to eight, with five being a particularly popular value. There are times when the nature of the process constrains the choice — for example, a sample size of six would be sensible for a six spindle automatic lathe. (Although more rigorous control would be provided by plotting a separate chart for each spindle, to do so would probably

Table 16.4.
Example data for $\bar{x}$, R chart.

Sample number	Measured values					Average $\bar{x}$	Range R
	1	2	3	4	5		
1	19.3	19.4	20.7	20.0	20.6	20.00	1.4
2	20.3	19.8	19.7	20.8	20.3	20.18	1.1
3	19.5	21.4	20.5	19.7	20.5	20.32	1.9
4	20.3	19.9	19.9	20.6	20.2	20.18	0.7
5	20.3	20.3	19.9	20.4	19.5	19.94	0.9
6	19.5	20.6	19.3	20.7	19.5	20.02	1.4
7	20.3	19.7	20.0	20.2	19.7	19.98	0.6
8	20.1	19.5	18.5	20.5	19.3	19.58	2.0
9	19.8	19.2	19.1	20.6	20.6	19.86	1.5
10	20.9	19.5	19.8	21.7	20.6	20.50	2.2
11	19.7	20.1	20.1	19.9	20.6	20.08	0.9
12	20.0	19.2	20.2	19.7	19.2	19.66	1.0
13	19.0	20.8	19.8	19.3	20.7	19.92	1.8
14	21.2	19.7	20.0	20.0	18.8	19.94	2.4
15	20.3	21.0	20.3	20.3	19.8	20.36	1.2
16	20.3	19.9	20.5	19.6	20.5	19.98	0.9
17	19.6	20.0	20.1	19.9	19.9	19.90	0.5
18	19.8	20.2	21.1	21.2	19.6	20.38	1.6
19	19.5	19.7	19.8	19.4	20.2	19.72	0.8
20	20.7	21.4	20.3	20.6	19.7	20.54	1.7
21	19.4	19.4	19.6	20.1	19.1	19.52	1.0
22	20.3	19.6	20.3	20.2	20.9	20.26	1.3
23	19.2	18.9	20.0	18.4	19.3	19.16	1.6
24	20.2	19.6	20.3	20.0	20.8	20.24	1.2
25	21.0	19.6	19.8	20.2	19.5	20.02	1.5

result in too much effort devoted to plotting charts and insufficient to running the machine. A compromise has to be achieved between effectiveness of the control procedure and the effort necessary to achieve it.) In contrast, there are processes where the sample size has to be one: for example, where the measurement cannot be referred to discrete sample items, but may be a single reading of a meter, or a sample drawn from a bulk tank of liquid. In such cases the averages chart becomes one for individual observations, which is statistically very inefficient, and a ranges chart cannot be plotted. In these circumstances, the use of cumulative sum methods as described in BS5703 is an attractive alternative.

Choice of the interval between samples

This choice is largely based on the economics of the process. The interval should not exceed that within which the maximum tolerable amount of unacceptable product would be produced, on the pessimistic assumption that the process went out of control immediately after the previous sampling. Implicit in this approach is the requirement that all product between one sampling and the next is suspect until the state of the process is defined by that next sample. Should that sample show the process to be out of control, this intervening product must be identified and recoverable for any inspection, rectification or scrapping that subsequent investigation deems necessary.

Plotting the data

Reference to Figure 16.5 shows that this chart requires all the observations in the sample to be individually recorded. This is a valuable discipline in that it helps to ensure that all the samples are taken and measured correctly, and allows a check to see if any out-of-control points are a result of mistakes in calculations. Another noteworthy aspect is the recording on the chart of *everything* that occurs that might have some bearing on the behaviour of the process. The majority of such comments may eventually turn out to be of no relevance, but the occasional one may be of vital importance in the investigation of a major problem. If they are always noted, there is no need to rely on uncertain memories in unravelling the history of a process.

It can also be seen that provision is made for building-up a histogram of the data as it arises. This can be of assistance in revealing any problems reflected in any obvious non-normality in the data, and in informally relating the process to specification limits.

Comments on Figure 16.5

The only out-of-control point on the chart was at sample 23 when the sample average was so far below the control line that it was off the chart. The appropriate investigative action and the subsequent correction of the process were noted on the chart.

Although the ranges chart gave no action decisions, one point came

(Actual Form is A3 size)

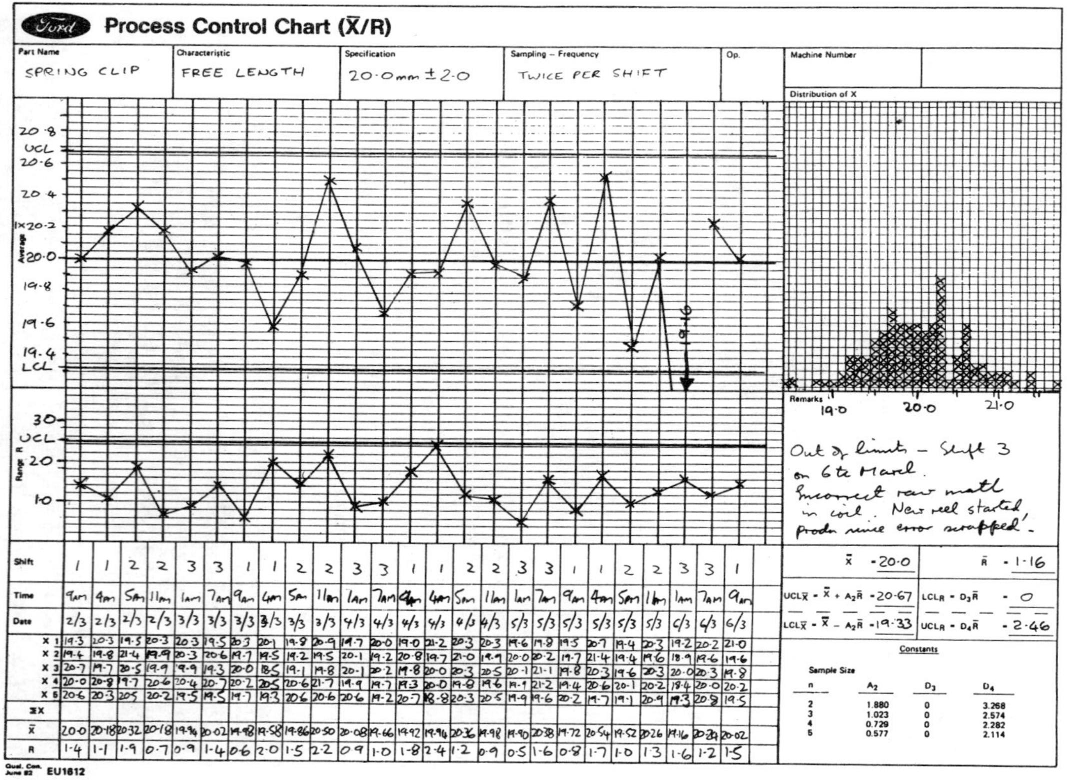

Figure 16.5. A typical charting form as used in industry, containing data from Table 16.4. (The form is reproduced by permission of the Ford Motor Company. The data used are for illustration only and have no connection with Ford.)

318

extremely close to the control line, which merits a reassessment of the process variation. The average of the observed sample ranges was calculated, the result being 1.32 mm, i.e. the standard deviation is estimated to be 1.32/2.326 = 0.57 mm. This is rather larger than the process capability figure of 0.50, and has reduced the effective C_p value from 1.33 (which was barely adequate) to 1.17 (which is unacceptable), so some action is necessary to improve the process precision even though the chart did not give an action decision on any individual point.

The histogram does not show anything particularly useful in this instance, except for the strange absence of values of 20.4, and the contrasting high frequency of 20.3. Together, these may merit an examination of the measuring process.

The chart used action lines only. These were calculated using the constants given in the bottom right of figure 16.5. The averages chart limits are effectively straightforward $\pm 3\sigma/\sqrt{n}$ values. The range chart limit is the D_4 value as in Table 16.2.

Who does the plotting?

The obvious person to plot the chart is whoever is responsible for the operation of the process. This ensures that what is plotted has the best chance of being accurate, and that all production conditions are recorded. Even more important, it ensures that the operator has the information to control the process immediately available. For operator control to be effective, very careful training is necessary in the principles of control charting. To invest in this is a far preferable alternative to having the charts run by a s .all coterie of 'experts' with the operator taking the role of a bemused spectator.

What about specification limits?

There has been no mention of specification limits in the description of control charting. This is deliberate — the chart is concerned only with the consistency of the process. The process capability study established the relation between the inherent capability of the process and the specified limits. Having done so, the function of the control chart is to detect any changes from this pattern and requires corrective action whatever the notional precision of the process. The climate should be one where at worst this consistency should be the goal, but an even better objective in a long-running process is to aim to improve the process by making 'assignable' some of the hitherto 'unassignable' causes of variation, and progressively eliminating them. This idea of 'never-ending process improvement' is in sharp contrast to the more relaxed view that the arbitrary presence of a wide tolerance is something that is to be exploited.

Retrospective process capability

The objective of the chart is to assess the current behaviour of the process using the information from the process capability analysis as a basis for comparison. This will, *inter alia*, tell us when the variation has increased. For any long-term process, the aim should be to improve the process through a reduction in variation. This can usually only be achieved by a relentless elimination of causes of variation that we originally judged to be 'unassignable'. Such improvements will generally be individually fairly small, such that they would not be detected by, for example, a lower limit on a ranges chart. They will, however, be revealed by revaluating process capability over several recent samplings from the process over which the control chart shows it to be stable and 'in control'. A survey over a number of such samples over a stable process gives more information than individual samples on their own, and such a periodic retrospective analysis should be an integral feature of control charting.

The process capability is usually recalculated after approximately 20-30 samples (i.e. typically after the completion of each sheet as in Figure 16.5). The average of the sample ranges is multiplied by the appropriate value of d_n (see Table 16.2) to give an estimate of the current value of the inherent standard deviation, σ. If this is substantially lower than the previous value (conventionally, reduced by 10 per cent or more), the reduced value should be used for recalculating the limits for both the $\bar{x}$ and R charts. Figure 16.5 also provides a grid on which the individual observations can be entered as a histogram as the results are obtained. This gives a developing picture of the overall variation, and highlights any departure from the distribution pattern (normal, log-normal, etc.) that was revealed in the original capability analysis. If the new value is higher, the previous value should still be used, and efforts made to identify and eliminate the assignable cause of the deterioration of the process.

Control charts for attributes

This form of charting can be applied to two distinct situations:
1. Discrete items that can be classified as *acceptable* or as *non-*

conforming. They can arise as either what can be termed genuine attributes (where the item is placed into one or the other category without any measurement being involved), or through limit gauging on a measured variable. Control charts for this application can be either:

- control charts for number non-conforming (*np* charts) or
- control charts for proportion non-conforming (*p* charts).

2. Processes that generate non-conformities where the sample is not defined by a number of discrete items, but by a sample 'space' within which the non-conformities occur. Examples might be assembly non-conformities in a television set, or blemishes in a painted panel. The situation is characterized by it being impossible to define the number of non-conformities that did not occur — it is impossible to state the number of blemishes that were not present on the painted panel. Control charts for this application can be either:

- control charts for non-conformities (*c* charts) or
- control charts for non-conformities per unit (*u* charts).

Terminology

The use of the terms 'non-conforming' and 'non-conformities' may seem rather laboured in contrast with simpler terminology such as 'defective' and 'defects'. The problem with the use of this latter terminology is that the ever-increasing emphasis on product liability gives rise to a risk that such terminology could imply safety shortcomings. While such an implication is very rarely valid, it has become accepted practice to use the more cumbersome terminology to avoid any possible problems.

Control charts for non-conforming units (defectives)

Such charts are based on the premise that there is a small proportion (*p*) of non-conforming items being produced when the process is 'in control'. The chart's purpose is to signal any change in this proportion. It needs to be established at the outset that the procedures of attributes charting imply that a small finite value of *p* is therefore acceptable, so they are not applicable to situations where the 'in control' *p* is truly zero. It is perhaps too easy to use this as an excuse for not using attributes control, as there are many circumstances where non-zero proportions non-conforming arise in intermediate stages of manufacture. An example occurs in the manufacture of electronics. Individual circuit boards are manufactured in large quantities, and 100 per cent functional inspection at the board stage would be timeconsuming and expensive. When the final assemblies are produced, they are all subjected to a rigorous testing programme that is certain to detect any malfunction due to a faulty board. Provided that the level of faulty boards is kept low, the cost of removing and replacing them at final test can often be tolerated. In such a case the attributes chart would be used to control the proportion of non-conforming boards to a suitably low level. The only difference between an *np* chart and a *p* chart is that the former assumes a sample of fixed size, and the latter allows the sample size to vary to a limited extent.

Control charts for number non-conforming ('*n p*' charts)

Samples of size *n* are taken at internals from the process. The non-conforming items in the sample are identified and counted, and this number is plotted on the control chart, as shown in Figure 16.6. (The charting form used is again reproduced by kind permission of the Ford Motor Company.) It will be seen that the same basic form can be used for all four types of chart: it can be used for '*p*', '*c*' and '*u*' charts in addition to '*np*' charting.

The number of non-conforming units in the sample will be described by a binomial distribution of parameters *n* (the sample size) and *p* (the proportion non-conforming), as described in Chapter 14. It would therefore be reasonable to expect that the control lines would be based on this distribution. For reasons of simplicity, this is not the case and simplifying approximations are used. There is, however, a complication in that there are two widely used, but quite different, methods of obtaining control limits. Both will be described, but before doing so it is necessary to consider the choice of sample size.

Choice of sample size

The amount of information in a sample for an attributes chart is a function of the number of non-conforming items in the sample. The sample size should therefore be selected to give an expected number of non-conforming units (which is the product $n \times p$) that is reasonably large. The British Standard on Attributes Charting, BS5701, recommends that this number should be between 1 and 4. It can be seen that this will yield sample sizes that are considerably larger than those used in variables charting. For example, if a process has an 'in control' proportion non-conforming of 0.025 (2½ per cent), a sample of 40 would be needed to give an expected number non-conforming of 1, a sample of 80 would give an expected value of 2, etc.

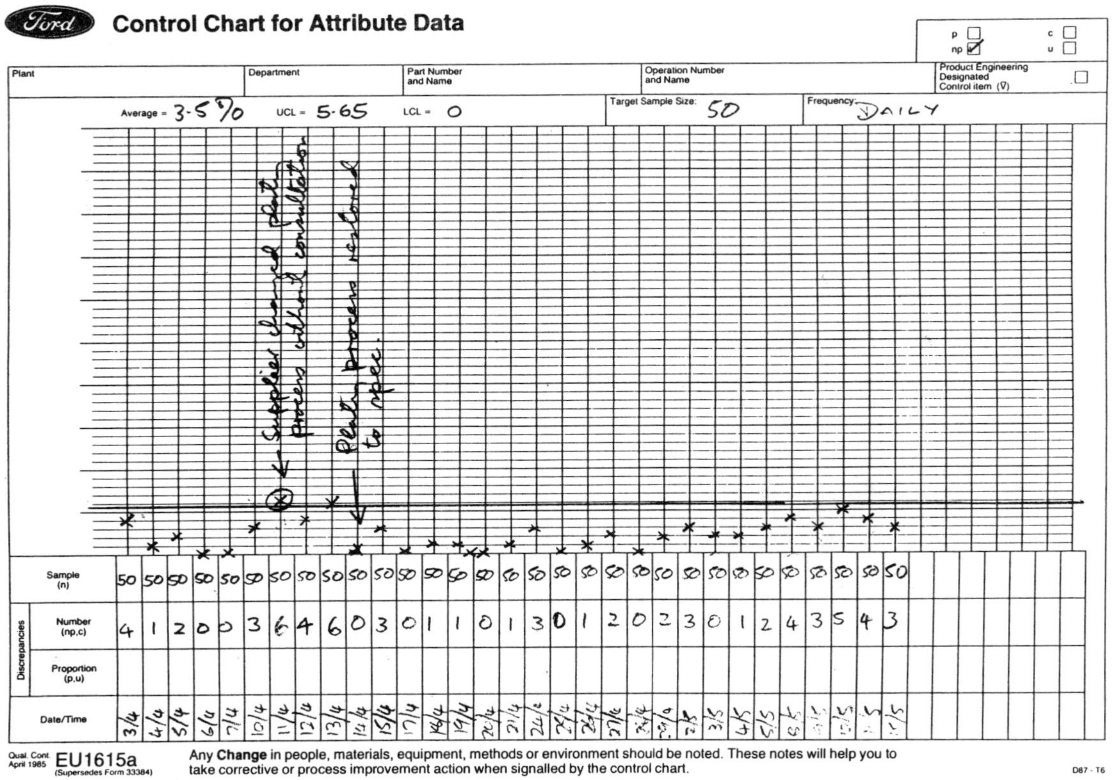

Figure 16.6. Attributes chart (*np* chart for numbers nonconforming). (Chart reproduced by permission of the Ford Motor Company. The data are for example and have no connection with Ford.)

Control limits ('American' method)
This method uses the 'mean ± 3σ' heuristic familiar from variables charting. The fact that the normal distribution is nowhere near to applying to binomial situations with small expected values is simply viewed as irrelevant. No claim is made that the limits are related to any particular probability values.

The mean of the binomial distribution is np and its standard deviation is $\sqrt{[np(1-p)]}$. Accordingly, the control limits are set at

$$np \pm 3\sqrt{[np(1-p)]}$$

For small values of np, this will yield negative values for the lower limit. In such circumstances, the lower limit is taken as zero, and it is not possible to signal an improvement in the process (i.e. a reduction in p).

As an example, consider the case of $p=0.035$ with a sample size of 50. The expected number non-conforming is $np = 0.035\times50 = 1.75$. The control limits are therefore

$$1.75 \pm 3\sqrt{(1.75\times0.965)}$$

i.e. 1.75 ± 3.90

i.e. at 5.65 and zero (as the lower limit is negative). If these limits are superimposed on Figure 16.6, it can be seen that an action decision was in fact given at sample number 7.

Control limits (British Standard BS5701)

These are based on the Poisson distribution used as an approximation to the binomial — an approximation which is valid provided p is less than about 0.1, which should apply in any organization that is still in business! The control lines are at approximately the 1/200 probability point. They are chosen from the value of m, putting $m=np$, the expected number of units non-conforming in the sample, and are given in Table 16.5, which is an extract from BS5701. The lines are not drawn at integer values, but at 0.3 below, so that points cannot occur on the line. A further, optional refinement in BS5701 is the provision of warning lines. These are always exactly one below the control line, and are associated with a 'critical gap'. Action is taken if the gap between any two points outside the warning line is less than this critical gap.

In using Table 16.5, should the value of m not coincide with one in the table, the next higher value should be used. The limits under

Table 16.5.
Table of control limits for attribute charts. (Extract from Table 1 BS5701,
by permission of the British Standards Institution.)

m	Control line	Warning line	Critical gap	
0.10	1.7	0.7	1	
0.33	2.7	1.7	2	Group 1
0.67	3.7	2.7	2	
1.08	4.7	3.7	3	
1.53	5.7	4.7	3	
2.04	6.7	5.7	4	Group 2
2.57	7.7	6.7	4	
3.13	8.7	7.7	4	
3.72	9.7	8.7	4	

Group 1 are 'non-preferred' and should only be used where it is essential that very small sample sizes are used such that the expected number non-conforming per sample does not reach the recommended values. Group 2 limits are recommended for general use.

Repeating the previous example with $m = np = 1.75$, Table 16.5 gives the control line at 6.7, the warning line at 5.7 and a critical gap of 4 (using tabulated $m = 2.04$). This would fail to give the action decision at sample number 7, but would give one at sample number 9 as this second warning line is within the critical gap.

Number non-conforming charts for measured variables

A control chart for number non-conforming can be used to control a measured variable by considering any measurement outside specification limits as making the item non-conforming. In general, this is much less efficient than using a chart for variables, and will require much larger sample sizes. It does have a compensating advantage in that limit gauging is usually quicker and cheaper than measurement.

A further problem is contained in the fact that a process of adequate precision will not, when in control, produce any non-conforming ideas, so there is no value of p on which to base the chart. This problem can be circumvented by the use of *compressed limits*. These are gauging limits that are set inside the specification limits so that a significant proportion of the output will be outside the limits and deemed 'non-conforming' for the purposes of charting (but still acceptable with respect to the 'true' limits). BS5701 recommends that the compressed limits are chosen so as to produce about 10–15 per cent outside the limits when 'in control', adjusting the sample size to give an expected 1–4 per sample outside limits. Use of such limits is explained in detail in Newton (1986).

'PRE Control'

'PRE control' is a method of using attributes control (using limit gauges) for measurable dimensions. It has achieved some popularity as an extremely simple control procedure, and was promulgated specifically as a method suitable for operator control. It is described in detail in Juran (1974). Its only advantage over other methods is its simplicity — its sensitivity to process changes is inferior to other methods. It has also the fundamental drawback of being based on specification limits rather than process performance. Nonetheless, it has had some successful applications in industry, where it has been the first step in introducing SPC prior to the introduction of more efficient methods.

PRE control acts as integrated process capability and process control loop. The basis is the division of the specification limits into four bands of equal width as shown in Figure 16.7.

The central two bands are referred to as the 'green' region and the outer two bands as the 'yellow' region. Anything outside the specification limits constitutes the 'red' region. The intention is that limit gauges are appropriately coloured. It is sometimes the case that measuring equipment is used, but the measurement scales are replaced by appropriately coloured bands.

The procedure is as follows:

Set-up: The process is operated and adjusted, with every resulting component being gauged. When five consecutive items are in the green region, the process is judged satisfactory, and sampling control is introduced.

Sampling: Every twenty-fifth item produced is sampled. If the result is in the green region, production continues. If it is in the yellow region, another sample is taken immediately. If this second sample is in the same yellow band as the first, the process is investigated and adjusted (with the suspicion being that the process average has moved in the direction of the yellow band in question, although it would also be

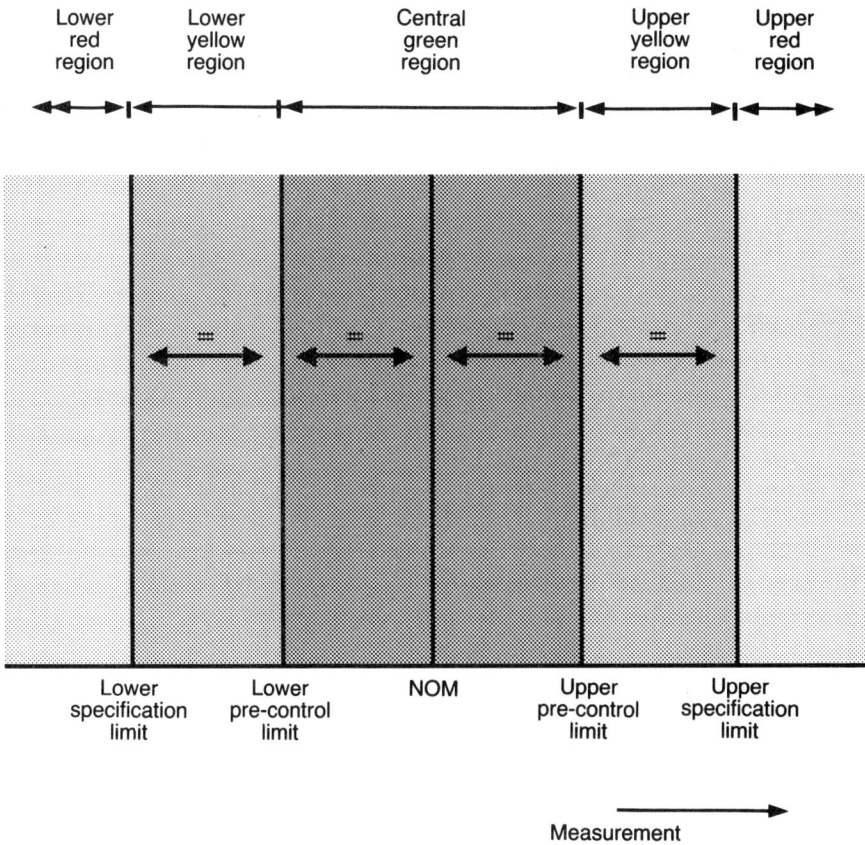

| Lower red region | Lower yellow region | Central green region | Upper yellow region | Upper red region |

| Lower specification limit | Lower pre-control limit | NOM | Upper pre-control limit | Upper specification limit |

Measurement

Figure 16.7.   PRE control.

possible for the explanation to be an increase in variability). If the second sample is in the opposite yellow band, the obvious conclusion is that the variation has increased, and appropriate corrective action is necessary. Should the second sample be in the green region, no action is taken and sampling continues. Should a sample appear in the red region, corrective action is of course required immediately.

Whenever corrective action has been necessary, the process reverts to the 'set'up' procedure.

Control charts for proportion non-conforming ('p' charts)

These charts are similar to charts for number non-conforming except that they allow for variations in sample size. (For fixed sample sizes, they are effectively the same as number non-conforming.) The plotted value is x/n, where x is the observed number non-conforming in a sample of n items.

As the standard deviation of x/n is $\sqrt{[np(1-p)/n} = \sqrt{[p(1-p)/n]}$ the control limits are $p \pm 3\sqrt{[p(1-p)/n]}$.

It is seen that the control limits will therefore have to be adjusted for different sample sizes, which would at first sight negate the point of having such a chart. Conventionally, however, this is not deemed necessary unless the sample size varies more than 25 per cent from the value for which the limits were calculated. Unless circumstances dictate variations in sample size, it is recommended that number non-conforming charts are used in preference to this type of chart.

Control charts for non-conformities

These charts are used for the second situation outlined on pp. 320-321, that of non-conformities arising in a sample that is described by a 'sample space' (such as a length, an area, elapsed time, etc.) The in-control situation is defined by 'c', the expected number of non-conformities per sample. Charts for this situation can be 'c' charts, for non-conformities per sample or, less frequently used, 'u' charts for non-conformities per unit.

Charts for number of non-conformities per sampe ('c' charts)

The plotted value is simply the number of non-conformities per sample. Control limits are based on the Poisson distribution (in this case without any approximation involved). The control limits can be either 'American':

$$c \pm 3\sqrt{c}$$

or based on BS5701, where c is equated to 'm' in Table 16.5.

As an example, consider a painting process which, when in control, generates minor appearance blemishes at the mean rate of one per 3.5m^2. A sample area of 5m^2 is inspected every production shift to control against any deterioration of the process. The value of c is therefore $5\sqrt{3.5} = 1.43$ blemishes per sample. Using the 'American' limits, the control lines would be at

$1.43 \pm 3\sqrt{1.43}$,   i.e. 1.43 ± 3.59

i.e. an upper limit only, at 5.02.

Using Table 16.5, the upper limit would be at 5.7. In both cases, the answer is effectively the same: we would need to observe six blemishes in the sample to give an action decision.

The '*c*' charts can also be used for controlling the level of non-conformities in discrete complex assemblies such as televisions, car engines, etc. The sample consists of a fixed number of such assemblies ('units'), which can be anything from one upwards. The plotted value is the total number of non-conformities across these units. For a target value of *c*, the control limits are calculated in the same way as described above.

Control charts for non-conformities per unit ('*u*' charts)

In using a '*c*' chart in the way described in the previous paragraph, it could be that the number of units sampled varied from one sampling to the next. This might occur, for example, if the time and resources available to perform the inspection were not constant. In such a case, the chart limits would have to be recalculated for each sample, making the chart confusing and difficult to read. A way out of this difficulty is to divide the observed number of non-conformities, *c*, by the number of units sampled, *n*. Then *c/n* is denoted by '*u*'.

A control chart plotting non-conformities per unit would have limits of

$$u \pm 3\sqrt{(u/n)}$$

where *u* is the 'in control' value of non-conformities per unit.

The limits are affected by the number of units sampled, but conventionally, it is not considered necessary to recalculate them unless this varies by more than 25 per cent.

Software for statistical process control (SPC)

The industrial practice of control charting often, and increasingly, makes use of computers. This can be at various levels of sophistication. At one extreme there is the on-line gathering and recording of data from measurement transducers networked to a powerful central computer. At the other extreme there is the use of simple applications software on a stand-alone microcomputer, with keyboard entry of the data. Systems on the market fall into two broad categories:

1. Integrated measurement and analysis systems, usually developed and marketed by suppliers of metrology equipment.

2. Applications software for microcomputers, which can usually accept direct input from measuring equipment via a suitable interface.

The use of computers in control charting is effective in eliminating some of the more tedious aspects of calculating suitable statistics and plotting them on graphs. They also facilitate storage of data, which is becoming ever more important in demonstrating that effective quality procedures have been used in manufacture. It is important, however, that the system used does not let its impressive technology obscure the simplicity and immediacy of charting. If control charting is being introduced into an organization, it is usual to do so initially on a manual basis, so that learning to use the method is not complicated by simultaneously having to learn to use the software.

Journals provide a useful source of information on applications and on new developments. In the UK, *Quality Assurance*, *Quality Today* and the *Quality and Reliability International* often contain articles on SPC. The equivalent American journal is *Quality Progress*. For the statistically brave, such journals as the *Journal of Quality Technology* and *Technometrics* nearly always contain papers on SPC methods and applications.

The extent of software available is considerable, and ever-expanding. The maxim of 'try before you buy' applies here as for all other software. A good source of guidance is the annual software review in *Quality Progress*.

Further reading

The references given below relate to Chapters 15 and 16. The 'classic' in the field of SPC is Grant and Leavenworth (1972). This is a massive text (of around 700 pages) that first appeared in 1946, and has been progressively updated since. It contains reference to just about every technique known on the subject, although treatment of some of the more modern aspects is occasionally a little sketchy. Considerable use is made of illustrative examples. The style is anecdotal, and 100 per cent American, but it forms a very useful reference book. Oakland's book (1986) is a recent British text which has comprehensive coverage, is more up-to-date and describes both UK and American conventions. For a briefer description, the Open University text by Newton (1986) is available. The British Standards on the subject are also worthy of consideration. BS2564 (for variables) and BS5701 (for attributes) are 'how to do it' standards with minimal explanatory text. BS5700 is, in contrast, a guide to the methods involved and their statistical origins. Also, the original British Standard on the subject, BS600, is another 'classic' that is still available and well worth consulting.

Books

Gitlow, H., Gitlow, S., Oppenheim, A. and Oppenheim, R., 1989. *Tools and Methods for the Improvement of Quality*, Irwin, Boston MA.

Grant, E. L. and Leavenworth, R. S., 1972. *Statistical Quality Control*, 4th edn. (international student edition, paperback), McGraw-Hill Kogakusha, Tokyo,

Juran, J. (ed.), 1974. *Quality Control Handbook*, McGraw-Hill, New York.

Newton, D. W., 1986. *Statistical Quality Control of Production*, The Open University Press, Milton Keynes.

Oakland, J. S., 1986. *Statistical Process Control*, Heinemann, London.

Shewhart, W. A., 1931. *Economic Control of Manufactured Product*, Van Nostrand, New York.

Journals

Quality Assurance Published monthly by the Institute of Quality Assurance, London.

Quality Today Published monthly by Whitehall Press Ltd, Maidstone.

Quality and Reliability Engineering International Published quarterly by J. Wiley, Chichester, UK.

Quality Progress Published monthly.

Journal of Quality Technology Published quarterly.

Technometrics Published quarterly.

All by the American Society for Quality Control, Milwaukee, Wisconsin.

British Standards

BS600 (1935) *Application of Statistical Methods to Industrial Standardisation and Quality Control*.

BS2564 (1955) *Control Chart Technique when Manufacturing to a Specification*.

BS5700 (1984) *Introductory Guide to Control Charting and Cusums*.

BS5701 (1980) *Guide to Number-Defective Charts for Quality Control*.

Note: Extracts from British Standards used in this chapter are reproduced with the permission of BSI. Complete copies of the documents can be obtained by post from BSI Sales, Linford Wood, Milton Keynes, Bucks, MK14 6LE.

17   Control Charts: 2. Cusum Charts

David Newton

In this chapter a type of control chart is described which has the same objectives as the conventional (or 'Shewhart') charts described so far, but uses a completely different method of plotting. A conventional chart shows the current state of the process by the vertical position of a plotted point. A cumulative sum ('cusum') chart uses instead the slope of the plot to show the current level. The procedure is applicable to any of the variables and attributes situations described in Chapter 16.

Basic cusum procedure

For the charted quantity, the reference value (T) is first defined. This will usually be the nominal, or target, value for that quantity. If the ith measurement of the quantity is denoted x_i, the target value is first subtracted, giving (x_i-T). The cusum is then calculated by adding this value to the sum of all the previous values, i.e.

Cusum $= \Sigma_i(x_i-T)$

As an example, consider the following 10 observations from a process, which has a target value of 10:

11, 8, 5, 20, 12, 10, 11, 9, 15, 13

The cusums are calculated as shown in Table 17.1.

Table 17.1.
The cusums of 10 process observations.

Observation number (i)	x_i	$(x_i - T)$	Cusum $\Sigma(x_i - T)$
1	11	1	1
2	8	-2	-1
3	5	-5	-6
4	20	10	4
5	12	2	6
6	10	0	6
7	11	1	7
8	9	-1	6
9	15	5	11
10	13	3	14

The cusum is simply the cumulative deviation from a target value. Whilst the concept is sometimes viewed as a rather sophisticated one in SPC, it is encountered in everyday life without any problems of understanding. For example, Bissell (1984) instances the fact that scoring in golf is by cusum — rather than count the total number of strokes, it is easier to consider the cumulative score above or below 'par'. This is, in fact, a rather sophisticated cusum where the reference value ('par') changes from one sample (hole) to the next.

Cusum charts for variables

Just as in conventional Shewhart charting, charts can be produced for sample average, for sample ranges and for single observations.

Cusum charts for sample averages
Table 17.2 shows a sequence of 30 averages of samples of size 4 from a process with target value 150.0. The table also shows the cusum values. These are plotted in Figure 17.1, which demonstrates the essential features of a cusum chart.

The most important aspect to understand is that the average of the process measurement is shown by the *slope* of the plot. Referring to

Table 17.2.
Cusum tabulation for sample averages.

Sample no. (i)	Average $\bar{x}_i$	Corrected Ave. ($\bar{x}_i - 150$)	Cusum $\Sigma_i(\bar{x}_i - 150)$
1	140.0	−10.0	−10.0
2	156.7	6.7	−3.3
3	146.7	−3.3	−6.6
4	146.6	−3.4	−10.0
5	156.7	6.7	−3.3
6	153.3	3.3	0.0
7	147.3	−2.7	−2.7
8	140.0	−10.0	−12.7
9	146.3	−3.7	−16.4
10	149.2	−0.8	−17.2
11	152.3	2.3	−14.9
12	140.0	−10.0	−24.9
13	148.9	−1.1	−26.0
14	155.6	5.6	−20.4
15	145.6	−4.4	−24.8
16	148.8	−1.2	−26.0
17	138.9	−11.1	−37.1
18	142.1	−7.9	−45.0
19	145.5	−4.5	−49.5
20	155.3	5.3	−44.2
21	155.2	5.2	−39.0
22	155.0	5.0	−34.0
23	158.9	8.9	−25.1
24	146.1	−3.9	−29.0
25	148.7	−1.3	−30.3
26	151.5	1.5	−28.8
27	152.4	2.4	−26.4
28	161.5	11.5	−14.9
29	155.6	5.6	−9.3
30	150.8	0.8	−8.5

Figure 17.1, it can be seen that the plot has three distinct sections:

- From sample 1 to 8 the slope is slightly upwards, showing that the average is slightly above the reference value of 50.

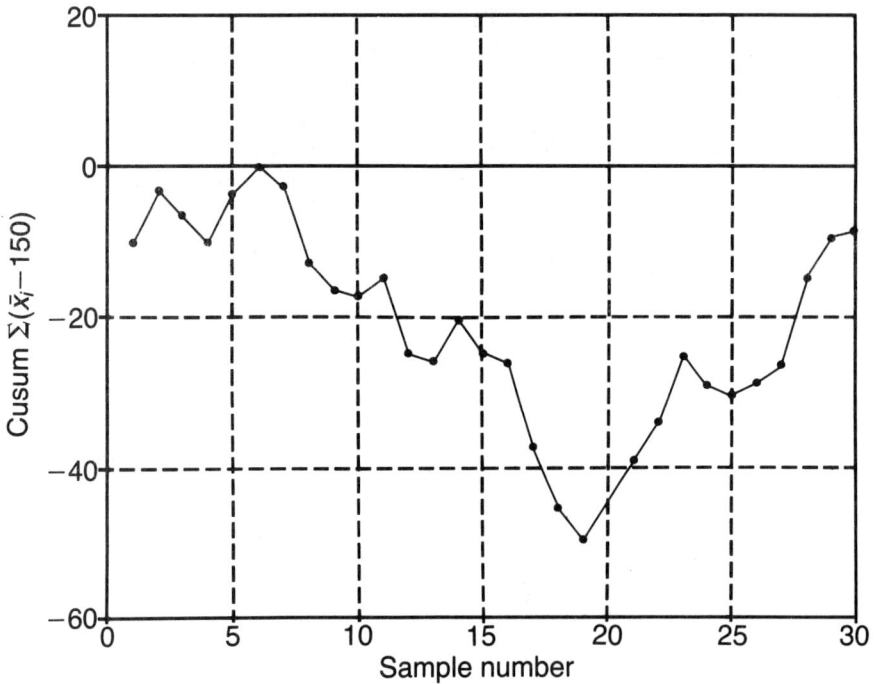

Figure 17.1.   Cumulative sum chart (using data in Table 17.2).

- From sample 9 to sample 19 the slope is strongly downwards, showing an average below 50.
- From sample 20 onwards, the slope is steeply upwards, showing a mean well above 50.

These observations can be quantified by measuring the slope. Over any sequence of consecutive points, the process average between the $(j+1)$th and $(j+r)$th points is given by:

$$\frac{(S_{(j+r)} - S_j)}{r} + T$$

where S is the cusum at a point indexed by the subscript. For example, the mean between sample 2 and sample 8 is

$$\frac{S_7 - S_1}{6} + 150 = \frac{(-2.7)-(-10.0)}{6} + 150 = 151.21$$

Similarly, between points 8 and 19 the mean is

$$\frac{S_{19} - S_7}{12} + 150 = \frac{(-49.5)-(-2.7)}{12} + 150 = 146.10$$

and between points 20 and 30 is:

$$\frac{S_{30} - S_{19}}{11} + 150 = \frac{(-8.5)-(-49.5)}{11} + 15J = 153.72$$

The clarity of the indications of the different mean values, and the points at which changes occurred is one of the main attractions of cusum plotting. This clarity is such that it is often deemed unnecessary to use any control limits for this type of charts — the location and magnitude of any changes are obvious from the plot. This should be contrasted with the conventional 'Shewhart' chart of the same data where these aspects are much less obvious — see Figure 17.2.

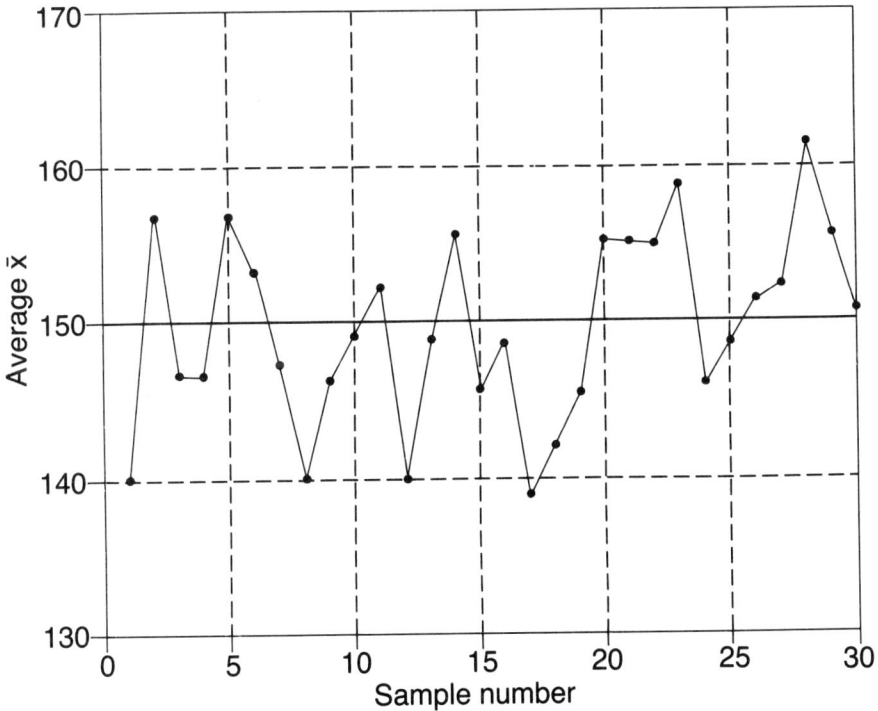

Figure 17.2.   A Shewhart chart (using the same data as Figure 17.1).

Choice of scale

The impression of mean level and the magnitude of any changes as shown in a cusum chart will be influenced by the choice of scale, as illustrated in Figure 17.3.

Compression of the vertical scale, as in Figure 17.3a suppresses the effect of short term 'ripples' on the chart, but gives the impression of small changes in mean value. Conversely, for the same data, expansion of the scale as in Figure 17.3b exaggerates the changes in mean. Both charts are of the same data as in Figure 17.1.

The choice of scale is an arbitrary one which is related only to the visual impact and interpretation of the chart. The recommendation in British Standard BS5703 is that the scale ratio a is equal to two standard deviations of the plotted variable, rounded to the nearest convenient scale. The term a is defined as the distance on the vertical scale equal

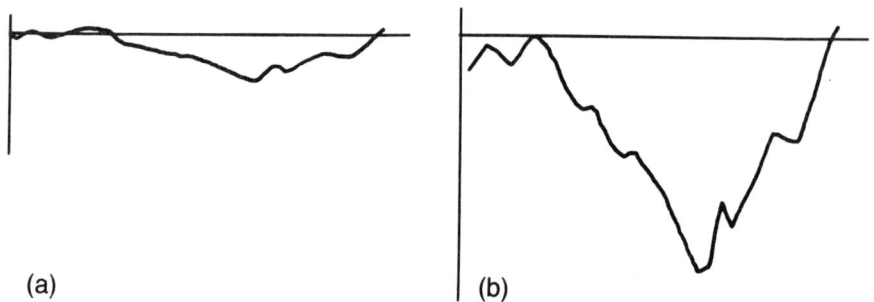

(a)   (b)

Figure 17.3.   Effect of scale ratio on cusum plots for similar data. (a) Compressed vertical scale (*a* large); (b) expanded vertical scale (*a* small).

to the horizontal distance between successive plots (the 'horizontal plotting interval'). For example, if the x_i values had a standard deviation of 4.3 units, and the horizontal scale was 1 cm per horizontal plotting interval, the recommended vertical scale would be 1 cm = 8.6 units. This would be rounded to the nearest convenient usable scale of 1 cm = 10 units. As another example, consider the data in Table 17.2, and assume that the standard deviation σ of the process was 4.22 units. The cusum plot is of averages of samples of 4, so the expected standard deviation of these averages (the expected standard error) is σ divided by the square root of the sample size, i.e. $4.22/\sqrt{4} = 2.11$. The value of a is therefore $2.11 \times 2 = 4.22$ — which, for simplicity of scaling, has been rounded up to 5 in Figure 17.1 (exemplifying the fact that the a values are merely a guide that can be adapted to suit particular circumstances).

Decision criteria for cusum charts for averages
Although the cusum chart gives a much clearer indication of changes than a conventional control chart, there is still a need for objective

decision criteria analogous to control lines. Control lines cannot be used in the conventional way, as it is the slope of the chart that needs to be monitored rather than the vertical position of plotted points. Various decision criteria have been suggested as the subject of cusums has developed. These have culminated in a standardized procedure in BS5703 known as the 'decision mask'. The mask is in the form of a template that is superimposed on the chart as each point is plotted. Various masks are available in the standard, but they all have the general shape shown in Figure 17.4.

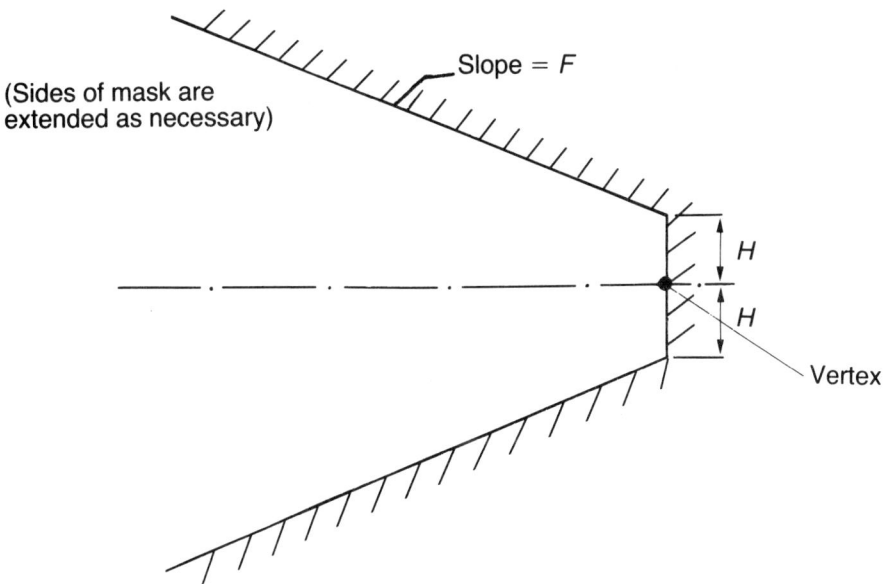

Figure 17.4. General form of decision mask.

The most widely used mask is known as the '5–10–10' mask, where *H* in Figure 17.4 is set at five standard deviations of the plotted variable, and the slope of the sides of the mask is set at 0.5 standard deviations per plotting interval. Thus, at a position ten plotting intervals to the left of the 'vertex' of the mask, the sides of the mask are $[5 + (0.5 \times 10)] = 10$ standard deviations either side of the central line. In use, the vertex of the mask is placed on the last plotted point, with the central line horizontal. If any of the previous plot intersects the sides of the mask, this gives an 'action' decision. Otherwise, no change is deemed to have occurred, and the process mean is assumed to be still 'under control'. This is illustrated in Figure 17.5. The mask can take any convenient form — they are usually either cut from card, or engraved on 'Perspex' or similar material.

The '5–10–10' mask is widely used because it behaves in a similar way to a conventional chart with action and warning lines when the process is 'in control'. It is, however, much more sensitive to small

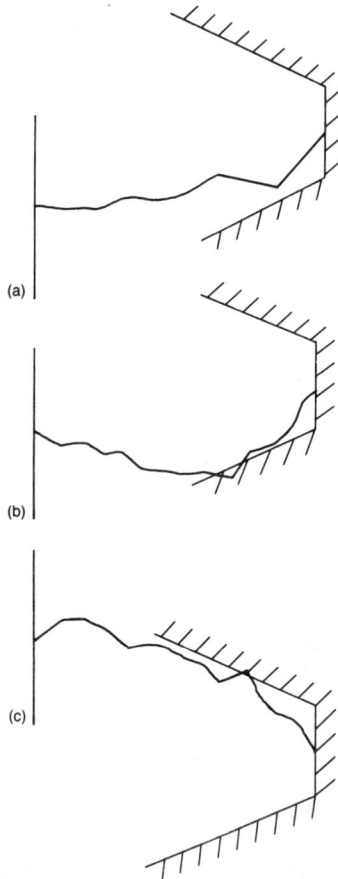

Figure 17.5.   Use of decision mask. (a) No decision; (b) upward change; (c) downward change.

changes in process mean than conventional charts. It is also possible to 'tune' the mask to make it more or less sensitive to changes of particular magnitudes by altering the slope and intercept of the mask away from the '5–10–10' convention. This is explained in detail in Part 3 of BS5703.

Cusum charts for range

It is no less important to simultaneously control average and range when using cusums as when using conventional charts. The sample range could, of course, still be monitored with a conventional chart whilst using a cusum chart for the averages, but it is more usual to use cusums for both. The cusum range procedure is based on μ^R, the expected average range whose value is estimated as described in Chapter 15.

The cusum is now of $\Sigma(R_i - \mu_R)$, where R_i are the observed sample ranges. The mask used for such a chart is usually only 'single sided' as shown in Figure 17.6. It consists of the lower half only of the masks as it is only necessary to detect increases in process variation, as reflected in an upward movement in the chart.

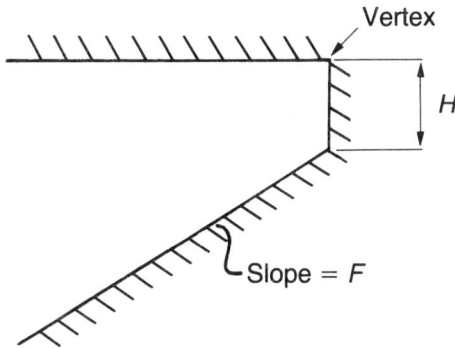

Figure 17.6.   Half mask for cusum ranges chart.

The intercept of the mask, H, is given by $h \times \mu_R$ and the slope, F, by $f \times \mu_R$, where h and f are constants whose value depends on sample size and desired risk behaviour of the chart. For a 'middle of the road' scheme whose behaviour when the process variation is 'in control' is again similar to a conventional ranges chart with action and warning lines, values of h and f are shown in Table 17.3, which is an extract from Table 10 of BS5703 Part 3. The a values are the recommended scale ratios.

As an example of a cusum range chart, consider the process whose average values are shown in Figure 17.1. The process standard deviation was 4.22, so μ_R is estimated by $\sigma \times d_4$. The value of d_4 is obtained from Table 16.2, and equals 2.059, so the expected sample range is $4.22 \times 2.059 = 8.69$. A tabulation of observed sample ranges for the first twelve samples is given in Table 17.4. These data are plotted in Figure 17.7. The plotting scale ratio is obtained from Table 17.3 as $a \times \mu_R = 0.85 \times 8.69 = 7.39$, which is rounded up to 10.

Table 17.3.
Mask parameters for cusum range charts. (Taken from Table 10 of BS5703, Part 3, by permission of the British Standards Institution.)

Sample size n	h	f	a
2	2.50	0.85	1.50
3	1.75	0.55	1.00
4	1.25	0.50	0.85
5	1.00	0.45	0.75
6	0.85	0.45	0.65

Table 17.4.
Cusum range chart data.

Sample number i	Range R_i	Range$-\mu_R$ $(R_i-8.69)$	Cusum $\Sigma(R_i-8.69)$
1	7.06	−1.63	−1.63
2	5.37	−3.32	−4.95
3	12.15	3.46	−1.49
4	9.10	0.41	−1.08
5	8.24	−0.45	−1.53
6	11.67	2.98	1.45
7	9.56	0.87	2.32
8	11.04	2.35	4.67
9	15.82	7.13	11.80
10	13.16	4.47	16.27
11	19.94	11.25	27.52
12	15.27	6.58	34.10

The mask parameters are:

$H = 8.69 \times 1.25 = 10.86$, and $F = 8.69 \times 0.5 = 0.35$.

The reader may wish to produce this mask, and confirm that it gives an action decision at sample number 11. It is also of interest to note that the conventional action and warning lines would be at 22.33 and

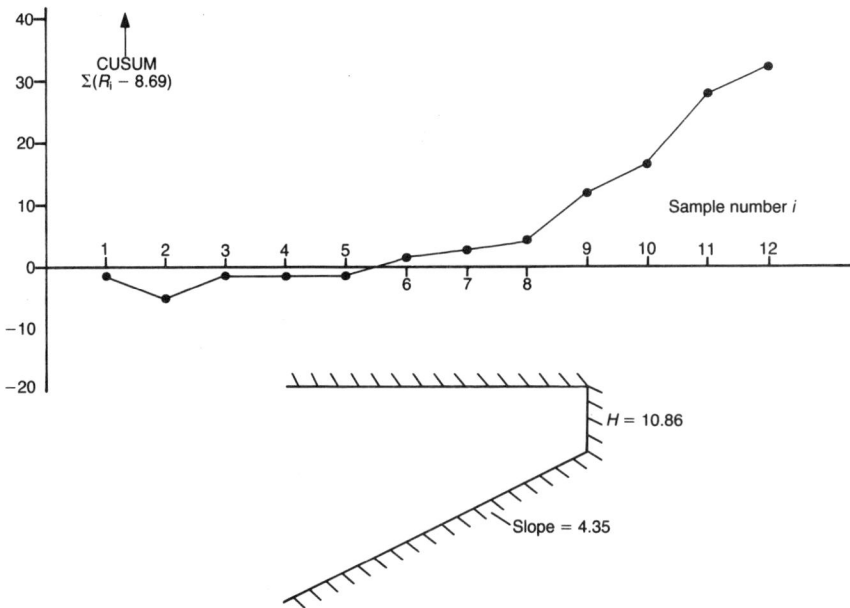

Figure 17.7.   A cusum range chart (using data in Table 17.4).

16.77, respectively (calculated using the constants in Table 16.4), which would not have given any 'action' decision.

Cusums for single observations

When the observations (x_i) are individual observations rather than sample averages, the procedure for the averages chart is the same, except that these sample observations are used directly in calculating the cusum. It is, of course, not possible to produce a ranges chart for single observations. One way of circumventing this difficulty is to plot a ranges cusum chart for ranges of samples of 2, each sample range being the difference between the current sample and the previous one. Although this is theoretically unsound (as the ranges would also be affected by any change in mean), it is better than doing nothing to control variation, and seems to work adequately in practice.

Cusum charts for attributes

Cusum charts can be applied to any of the attribute charting situations described in Chapter 16. The reference value for the cusum is always m, the expected number of non-conforming items (defectives) or non-

Table 17.5.
Data of Figure 16.6 expressed as cusums.

Sample no.	Non-conforming items (x)	($x - 1.75$)	Cusum $\Sigma(x - 1.75)$
1	4	2.25	2.25
2	1	−0.75	1.50
3	2	0.25	1.75
4	0	−1.75	0.00
5	0	−1.75	−1.75
6	3	1.25	−0.50
7	6	4.75	5.25
8	4	2.25	7.50
9	6	4.75	12.25
*10	4	2.25	* 2.25
11	3	1.25	3.50
12	0	−1.75	1.75
13	1	−0.75	1.00
14	1	−0.75	0.25
15	0	−1.75	−1.50
16	1	−0.75	−2.25
17	3	1.25	−1.00
18	0	−1.75	−2.75
19	1	−0.75	−3.50
20	2	0.75	−2.75
21	0	−1.75	−4.50
22	2	0.25	−4.25
23	3	1.25	−3.00
24	0	−1.75	−4.75
25	1	−0.75	−5.50
26	2	0.25	−5.25
27	4	2.25	−3.00
28	4	2.25	−0.75
29	5	3.35	2.50
30	4	2.25	4.75
31	3	1.25	6.00

* Cusum restarted after corrective action.

conformities (defects) per sample. The sample size criteria are also the same as for conventional charting in that the sample should produce an expected 1 to 4 non-conforming items (or non-conformities) per sample when the process is stable and 'in control'. However, the increased sensitivity of the cusum method permits smaller samples to be used if necessary, and mask parameters are tabulated for values of m as low as 0.1 per sample.

As an example, consider the 'np' chart in Table 16.5. The target proportion non-conforming is 0.035 and the sample size is 50, giving an expected number of non-conforming items per sample of $50 \times 0.035 = 1.75$. This is the value used for 'm' in Table 17.5, where the data of Figure 16.6 are re-expressed as cusums. These data are plotted on a cusum chart in Figure 17.8. The recommended scale ratio for an

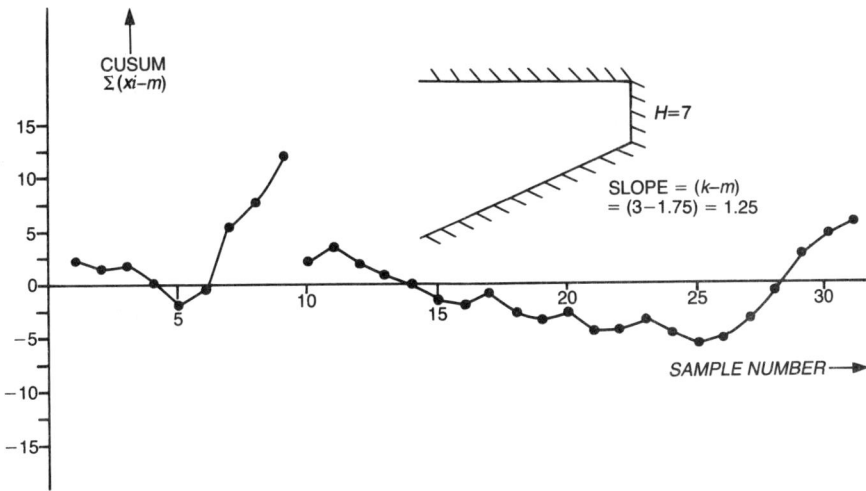

Figure 17.8.   Cusum chart for number non-conforming (data from Figure 16.6).

attributes plot is simply $2\sqrt{m}$ — in this case, it is $2\sqrt{1.75} = 2.65$. The actual value used in Figure 17.8 is 2.5. Note the way that the cusum is restarted at sample 10, after the identified problem has been dealt with. This is a useful convention, highlighting the fact that there is a discontinuity in the process.

Comparison with Figure 16.6 emphasizes the clarity with which the cusum reveals changes. The large increase in the number of non-conforming items around samples 7 to 9 is obvious from both charts. There is an improvement between samples 10 and 25, and a deterioration from sample 26 onwards, which are much more clearly shown on the cusum.

Mask parameters for attribute cusums

As in the case of variables, there is a wide choice of mask parameters available to suit differing circumstances. The values tabulated in Table 17.6 are taken from BS5703 Part 4, and are chosen to give similar properties to conventional charts for an 'in control' process.

Table 17.6.
Table of mask parameters for cusums for attributes.

m	0.1	0.2	0.4	0.5	0.8	1.0	2.0	4.0	5.0	8.0	10.0
H	1.5	3.5	2.5	3.0	5.0	5.0	7.0	8.0	9.0	9.0	11.0
K	0.75	0.5	1.5	1.5	1.5	2.0	3.0	6.0	7.0	11.0	13.0

The intercept of the mask is H, and the slope is $(K-m)$. In this example, the parameters are chosen for $m=2$, being the nearest value to the 'true' m of 1.75. (If the use of BS5703 mask procedures is intended, it is preferable to choose a sample size that gives an m value coinciding with one in Table 17.6.) The mask is shown in Figure 17.8. Superimposition of the mask on the plot will demonstrate that the change at Sample 7, which was detected by the conventional chart, is also detected. The mask also gives an 'action' decision at Sample 30 showing an increase in the level of non-conforming items. Although this increase is visible on Table 16.5, it does not give an action decision using either of the variants of conventional control lines.

Summary and recommendations for further reading

Cusums have two major advantages over conventional control charts:

- They give a much clearer pictorial representation of the behaviour of the process.
- Objective decision criteria (such as the BS mask) are much more sensitive to small changes than control lines on conventional charts.

To offset these advantages, it is sometimes argued that they are more complicated to use. Whilst this may be marginally true, the real source of objection is more likely to be rooted in their unfamiliarity compared with the 50-year tradition of more conventional methods.

There is only one major reference work on cusums to be

recommended, namely the four parts of British Standard BS5703. This has distilled, simplified and developed the work of various earlier authors, and is comprehensive in its coverage of all aspects of cusums. It also includes computer program listings for the charting and decision procedures to permit the user to automate the cusum. The development of the standard is largely due to Dr A. F. Bissell, who has also written an outline guide to the subject, referenced below.

References

Bissell, A.F., *Cusum Techniques for Quality Control*. The Institute of Statisticians, London 1984.

BS5703, 1980, 1981, 1982. *Guide to Data Analysis and Quality Control using Cusums*. Parts 1–4. British Standards Institution, Milton Keynes.

Part Six

PARTICIPATIVE QUALITY IMPROVEMENT

18 Common and Special Problems

John Edge

There is a widely held belief that an organization would have few, if any, problems if only workers would do their jobs correctly. In fact, the potential to eliminate mistakes and errors lies mostly in improving the systems through which work is done, not in changing the workers. Drs J.M. Juran and W.E. Deming have maintained since the early 1950s that at least 85 per cent of an organization's failures are the fault of management-controlled systems. Workers can control fewer than 15 per cent of the problems.

This observation has evolved into the rule of thumb that at least 85 per cent of problems can only be corrected by changing the systems (which are very largely determined by management) and that less than 15 per cent are under a worker's control — and the split may lean even more towards the system. For example, a production line worker cannot do a top quality job when working with faulty tools or parts. Even when it does appear that an individual is doing something wrong, often the trouble lies in how that worker was trained, which is a system problem.

Once people recognize that systems create the majority of problems, they will stop blaming individual workers. They will instead ask which system aspects need improvement, and will be more likely to seek them out and search for the true source of the problems.

Management-controllable variation

Most European and US managers do business through a management approach that is called management by results. Management by results is only interested in numerical targets. It pays little or no attention to processes and systems.

Management by results has its own logic and structure. As shown in Figure 18.1, it emphasizes a chain of command and a hierarchy of objectives, controls and accountabilities. Traditional organizational charts, therefore, portray a chain of financial accountability where objectives are translated into sales targets. The performance of all employees is guided and judged according to these numerical goals, which are the heart and driving force of traditional management practices.

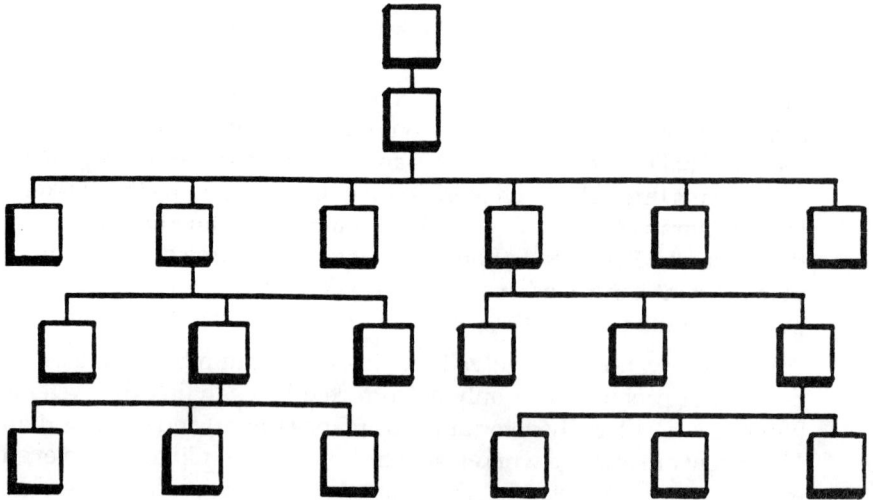

Figure 18.1.   Organization for management by results.

The shortcomings of management by results are rooted in the numerical goals. Management by results pays little, if any, attention to processes and systems; these, however, express the real capabilities of the organization as a whole. Sales targets are nothing but arbitrary numerical goals. Eventually, workers, supervisors and managers get caught up in games; looking 'good' overshadows a concern for the organization's long term success. Too often, they lose sight of the broader purpose of the work they do.

The consequences can be catastrophic. In this system of numerical objectives and sales targets, efforts are measurable in the short term. The near horizon gets attention; immediately countable results get priority, even though the company's survival may depend on unmeasurable activities which need to be undertaken to reach long term goals.

Top managers impose goals on lower managers, who impose goals on their workers. The workers struggle to meet their goals, forced to ignore how much they distort efforts in other parts of the company. Everyone struggles to survive distortions inherited from these other times or places. The cycle becomes self-reinforcing. Employees are too busy meeting sales targets to worry about what is shipped to customers, or what is happening in the rest of the system.

Systems of numerical controls cause internal company conflict. The controls that direct one unit's short term gain more often than not contradicts the controls given to another unit. For example, when salespeople are exhorted to boost business, they make promises production cannot keep. Engineers rush goods into production too quickly. Purchasing buys materials that the warehouse cannot store and people on the line cannot use. Planners and policymakers develop programmes that service personnel are not equipped to provide.

Frequently, imposed measurable goals are unattainable; they lie beyond a system's real capability. But since people or departments could lose status if they failed to reach the goals, they have to make it look as though they are conforming. They are forced by the system to fudge figures, alter records, or just 'play the game!' — to work around the system instead of improving it. This charade fosters guarded communication and minor, sometimes major, dishonesty.

When managers and workers do not understand the system's capabilities, a numerical goal is nothing more than guesswork; simple guesswork. The guess will either overestimate the capabilities or underestimate them. Either way, it does little to help the workers, the organization or the customers.

Rather than looking outward at the world in which the customer operates, management by results encourages a company to look inwards. Accomplishment comes from meeting a numerical goal, rather than delight in providing a product or service that works and satisfies the customers. Internal politics becomes more important than the company's long term future.

Conflict becomes rife. Management policies are subject to great variation. The company, as a system, is soon out of control. Being out of control, its performance is unpredictable. For example: management policy variations and caprice become the norm; the growth of employees is neglected; divisive competition between different parts of the company are encouraged and even rewarded; simple matters become complex; personnel become cynical hearing management 'pep' talks and slogans; suppliers are not assessed and inadequate raw materials are bought and judged only on their price tag. Carelessness and variation permeates everything. To quote Deming (1975):

> To call to the attention of a worker a careless act, in a climate of general carelessness, is a waste of time and can only generate hard feelings, because the condition of general carelessness belongs to everybody and is the fault of management, not of any one worker, nor of all workers.

Deming has described variation as common or special causes (Deming, 1982). Common-cause variation is 85 per cent management-controllable and is typically due to a large number of small sources of variation. The sum of these small causes may result in a high level of variation or a large number of defects or mistakes. It is the sum of the common causes that determines the inherent variation of the system or process and thus determines its limits and its capabilities as it is currently operated.

One approach to reduction of variation is management standardization: getting everyone to use the same procedures, materials, equipment and so forth. This alone has enormous potential to make the outputs of the system and process more uniform.

A second approach is to study the system or process as it now operates, look for potential sources of variation, and gather data. You can then structure data collection to see if these factors do affect your output. This approach requires knowledge of data collection and simple statistical techniques.

If standardization or the use of statistical techniques is limited to one department or one aspect of a development, both common and special causes can impact on the results, since many causes are outside the control of the department's workers and often its management. Standardization falls into disuse. The department (and company) soon become out of the range and control of even simple statistical techniques.

Thus an improvement in one part of the company can be destroyed by variation in another part. Improvement of the company is not possible unless there is a steady company-wide management improvement, viewing the company as an integrated system. For statistical data collection to be meaningfully interpreted, and to give useful information, data must be collected on an integrated company-wide basis.

Only management can bring about this steady company-wide improvement; only management can make an unstable system stable and an unpredictable system predictable.

Worker-controllable variation

Although the emphasis of this chapter is on the management-controllable 85 per cent of variation, we will briefly examine the special causes of variation. Special causes are not part of the system or process all the time and arise because of specific circumstances.

Every operator, machine or process has inherent variability. The extent of this variability determines capability. Hence there is a need for management to:

1. Establish the process capability of proposed work methods to determine their suitability for the defined input and output.
2. Establish the capability of existing plant and where necessary bring it up to specified requirements.
3. Control and monitor capability continually to detect and eliminate potential causes of variation.

Different types of product and process will clearly be influenced by different factors and hence require different emphasis in the controls applied. There are also different categories of dominance capability.

The modern high technology manufacturing environment is information dominant and depends on programmed information. Its capability depends on data. This can be entered manually or automatically and is produced automatically. Data then has to be interpreted to give information. With wrong or variable data, information loses much of its value and manufacturing processes becomes less capable. Information dominance is not discussed more fully here, since the following chapters are concerned with programmable automation in a manufacturing environment, and its management. For a full discussion see Rede Group (1988).

Most of the traditional craft industries relied heavily upon *operator dominance*, i.e, the skill and experience of the craftsman. Variability in the output could only be controlled by ensuring operator capability through acquisition of the relevant skills and provision of the correct tools. The skill element would often cover such areas as the appropriate selection of materials, the best sequence of operations and maintenance of the tools. Examples of operator dominance include: soldering, brazing, arc welding and forging. Managements, however, must provide adequate definitions of skill requirements for personnel, ensure proper training and formally define workmanship standards. If these are lacking there will be variation, and the fault will lie with management.

Set-up dominance capability arises where once the appropriate tooling has been selected and adjusted to its optimum operating condition it should continue to produce consistently acceptable products, i.e, there is little or no process drift and any changes will be the result of unforeseen calamity such as tool breakages. Examples include plastic moulding, metal casting and heat treatments. It is essential with this type of process that all critical features and sources of variation are thoroughly understood by the manufacturer and its management. Such information will usually be obtained only from carefully planned management capability studies and thorough application of the findings.

For the operator to do his job, managements must have done their jobs too. Comprehensive instructions for setting up, stopping and operating must be specified; the most appropriate equipment (jigs and fixtures) must be available; evidence of the manufacturer's capability studies must be obtained.

Whereas set-up dominant processes are inherently capable and remain so, *machine dominated* processes are inherently capable at the time of set-up, but subsequently drift under the effect of known influences, often at a known rate of change. Examples include tool wear, temperature changes, chemical dilution and ageing of catalysts. These are not random variations, but steady drifts which can be predicted. Management requirements, if the operator is to do his job, are as for set-up dominance but with regular monitoring of the machine processes.

As information is collected over a period of time and the operating characteristics become better known, management must ensure that information is fed back to production planning and maintenance groups. This will allow quantities and routine maintenance to be matched to the inherent needs of the process.

Finally, we have *component or raw material dominance* capability. There are two types of operation where no matter how much control the company management and workers exercise over their own operations, the benefits can be totally offset by substandard supplies. These operations are those using natural raw materials and those principally engaged in the assembly of bought-out components and subassemblies. Examples include chemical processes using raw ores, food processing and electronic assembly. Here the management must ensure that suppliers are assessed and audited and that materials are inspected and tested on receipt.

Managing organizations and people: when quality participation does not work

We have been told by Juran and Deming, since the early 1950s that only managements can change the system. Some companies have tried and succeeded; some have tried and failed. What lessons have we in Europe and America learnt in these years? According to a report in late 1988, we have not learnt a lot (The Yankee Group Europe, 1988). Studies looked at organizational and cultural change. Again and again The Yankee Group Europe found that the most difficult aspects in the implementation of advanced manufacturing technology was changing the organization and 'people'.

The problems and issues found were not tied to any one manufacturing methodology. They are the common problems and issues of the contemporary manufacturing industry. Each of the companies profiled had to make choices of how and what parts of the methodologies to implement. None of these methodologies was a solution in itself; they were tools. Thus the report concentrated on the factors leading to the successful implementation of these tools, in other words, the human factors. The key discipline was not one of technology but changing the organization and attitudes so that the technology could be managed.

Problems during implementation

Many attempts have been made to change organizations and attitudes by introducing participative quality — sometimes by quality circles and sometimes by a team approach. Let's look at some of the things which can go wrong in their implementation.

Quality circles (QCs) and other team and company-wide programmes have to some extent replaced suggestion schemes, which have always been popular. However, investigations have shown that the purposes to which the QCs and similar programmes have been put are often doomed to failure (Lawler and Mohrman, 1985).

Before proceeding, consider what is meant by a QC and company-wide participative quality.

A quality circle is a group of employees that meets regularly to solve problems affecting its work area. Generally, six to twelve volunteers from the same work area make up the circle. The members receive training in problem solving, statistical quality control and group dynamics. Quality circles generally recommend solutions on quality and productivity problems which management may then implement.

A facilitator, usually a specially trained member of management, helps train circle members and ensures that things run smoothly. Typical objectives of QC programmes include quality improvement, productivity enhancement and employee involvement. Circles generally meet several hours a month in company time. Members may get recognition but rarely receive financial rewards.

Company-wide participative quality is just that — everybody in the company, irrespective of their position is involved, from the chief executive officer to the receptionists, without exception. Common goals and objectives are established so that everyone has the same purpose and pulls in the same direction. The main theme of the common goals and objectives is to provide products and services that will delight the customer.

The company-wide approach provides the framework within which this can be done. On a company-wide basis, to help isolate variation, data is collected, using simple statistical techniques. The causes of the variation are then tackled by teams or task forces. Data, however, must be collected.

Like any planned and thought-through organizational change effort, participative programmes go through a series of phases in their evolution. Each phase contains its own key activities, as well as threats to its existence. The phases are now discussed.

Phase 1: Start-up
During the start-up phase, few serious threats to the programmes arise. The worst are an insufficient number of volunteers, inadequate training, inability of volunteers to learn the dynamics of group

activities, and, finally, lack of funding for meetings, facilitator time and training.

As many consulting firms offer good training packages for programme participants, their costs are not high and since many people like to participate in problem-solving groups, most organizations are able to deal effectively with the threats during the start-up phase.

As decades of research have pointed out, people want to contribute to the company they work for and want to participate in decision-making; and the management has put the money up-front and said 'get on with it'.

Phase 2: Initial problem solving

Once people are trained and officially sanctioned, they turn to problem solving. It is at this point that they identify the problems they are going to work on and begin to come up with solutions. As in the start-up phase, few serious threats to the continued existence of the programmes occur at this stage. Some programmes get in trouble because they are unable to agree on which problem to tackle.

This is particularly likely when representatives from different areas make up the group and no tractable issue affects everyone. Nevertheless, most programmes do identify common concerns and begin to solve problems. These are best solved one at a time for real progress to be made.

Once it starts, a group may find it has inadequate knowledge to deal with the problems. Management can overcome this barrier by providing additional training or by adding expertise to the programme, sometimes in the form of people who have technical resources at their disposal. In most programmes, therefore, they do solve problems and experience success.

Phase 3: Approval of initial suggestions

In many companies the programmes will form a parallel structure to the company organization and the group must report its solutions back to decision-makers in the line organization. This report-back activity is very important. The reports must be relevant and thorough. The presentation of solutions must be done in a professional and knowledgeable way, if attention is to be paid. The line organization must respond quickly, knowledgeably, and in most cases, positively. It is during this phase that the typical programme first encounters serious threats to its continuation.

Usually the people who have to accept and act on the ideas the programme generates are middle-level managers, many of whom will want no role in the programme and have little experience either of soliciting or responding to ideas from subordinates. They may be uncomfortable listening to ideas that they should have thought of themselves or that will change their own work activities. They will often feel threatened. Also, they may be too busy.

In any event, not surprisingly, these middle managers often resist the new ideas; they either formally reject them or take a long time to respond. As a result of the time and resources invested in the programme and because middle managers know that the programme will lose its momentum if they don't accept the ideas, middle managers feel a great deal of pressure to accept early suggestions. There are known situations in which top management has ordered middle management to accept all initial suggestions.

Such situations heighten bad feelings about the programme. Middle managers then receive subsequent ideas far less positively. After the programmes make their suggestions, the managers to whom they are presented sometimes do literally nothing. Often, a clear rejection is better than what happens to suggestions in these two cases.

If in a high percentage of cases managers react negatively, or not at all, to suggestions, the programmes usually end. The people in the programme become discouraged and stop meeting. The programme's participants get discouraged and feel that the programme is a sham, a waste of time and a management trick.

If middle management is not committed to change, then it is invariably the result of senior management not being committed. It is not sufficient for management to put the money up-front and say 'get on with it'. Management itself must equally get on with it.

Few companies and commentators are willing to talk about failed QC programmes. An excellent account however is to be found in Guthrie (1987). It details Ford (UK)'s attempt in its 'After Japan' programme. Here management did not get on with it — they did not change but they expected the workers to produce more with less.

Where upper and middle managements accept the ideas and appreciate their need for change the programmes will move to the next phase.

Phase 4: Implementation of solutions
In most organizations, approval does not mean implementation. Indeed, time after time situations are found where managers accepted

many of the initial ideas with great fanfare but didn't implement them. The result is a serious loss of credibility to both the programme and management.

Implementing ideas often involves the cooperation of many people and, of course, requires money and manpower. As was noted earlier, in many cases the people who are in charge of putting the programme's ideas into action are not involved in the initial activities and therefore have little investment in them. In addition, only those individuals who develop the ideas, not those who implement them, receive recognition and rewards. Time is also a factor.

Manufacturing, engineering and maintenance employees, and middle managers are often faced with a choice between continuing their normal activities and picking up ideas that the programmes have suggested. Unless they are willing to put their regular duties aside, these organizations will never implement the ideas.

Just as with approval, if the ideas are never converted into action, programmes usually lose their momentum and die. Official approval of their ideas may please participants but isn't enough to motivate them to come up with new ideas. People need to see their ideas in action and to receive feedback on how they are working.

Since it is so hard to effect change in organizations, a significant percentage of programmes end at this point. In some cases, however, some of the ideas from the programmes are implemented and produce large savings. In these situations, the programmes move on to the next phase.

Phase 5: Expansion of problem solving

During this phase the programme is often expanded to include organizationally-related or new groups, and old programmes are either phased out or redirected to address additional problems. In general, if the programme gets this far, management has committed a considerable amount of resources to it, and it has become a part of the organization. Threats to continuation do, however, appear during this phase. Simply reaching this phase provides no guarantee that the programme will continue.

Problems that confront a programme at this point are many and varied. Some of them are a product of the initial success of the programme while others are related to the fact that the programmes require a parallel organizational structure.

The initial success of the programme spurs formerly disinterested people to want to get into a programme. Non-participants become jealous of programme members and wonder why they cannot have the luxury of meeting and solving problems during work hours. They also resent the recognition and status successful programme members receive.

To a degree, managers can meet this issue by expanding the number of programmes to include more people, but almost always an insider–outsider culture arises, even though the approach is intended to be moving towards company-wide participation.

Success of the first programmes may also raise group members' aspirations. These increased hopes can take several forms. They may, for example, lead people to desire greater upward career mobility as well as additional training. Also, members often become uncomfortable with the split between the way they are treated in programme meetings and how they are treated in the day-to-day operations of the organization. As their desire for influence rises they may ask for more participation in managing the daily work of the organization.

Having initially picked off the easiest problems to solve, some programmes run out of problems. They then find themselves in a situation where, with a limited mandate and training, they can do little more. At this point, the programme may simply go out of existence or take on other areas — even those beyond its mandate.

The initial success may also lead participants to ask for financial rewards. They are particularly likely to do this when management talks about the great savings they have produced for the organization. In the European and American culture, people who have contributed to company gains perceive they they have the right to share in them. Management can deal with this issue through various financial sharing plans, but to do so requires changing the basic structure of the programme.

Expanding the programme may boost its price tag. The need for training time rises, as does the need for time to coordinate, facilitate and meet. All this costs a great deal, and ultimately many managers question whether the savings justify the expense.

Unfortunately, when executives try to document the savings from the early programme's ideas, they often turn out to be smaller than originally estimated. It is found that management based the initial expansion of the programme on optimistic estimates of just how much it was going to save and, indeed, may have rewarded people for projected, rather than actual, savings.

Disappointment over the actual savings from early ideas and the significant expense of running the programme often combine to provide the single most serious threat to its continued existence.

Given the many forces and pressures that develop during this phase, it is not surprising that the typical programme either begins to decline or becomes a different kind of programme at this point.

Phase 6: Decline

Few programmes turn into other kinds of programmes; more commonly, decline sets in. During this period, people meet less often, they become less productive, and the resources committed to the programme dwindle. The main reason they continue at all is because of the social satisfaction and pleasure the members experience rather than the problem-solving effectiveness. As managers begin to recognize this, they cut back further on resources.

As a result, the programme shrinks. The people who all along have resisted the programme recognized that it is less powerful than it once was, and they openly reject and resist the ideas it generates. The combination of overt resistance from middle managers and staff, budget cuts, and participants' waning enthusiasm usually precipitates the decline of the programme.

Other problems

A number of other factors can also weigh against the success of programmes.

First, the programmes are accessible: for a fixed price, managers can buy a standardized package complete with training and support materials and instructions on how to proceed. The turnkey approach appeals to many managers because it is similar to the way they buy other things, such as machines and training programmes. Unfortunately, managers do not appreciate that they are the crux of the programme. They, too, must change.

Second, since programmes do not have to involve everyone at the same time, management can easily control the number of people involved as well as the size and cost (mainly for start-up and training) of the programme. With little risk, it can test the waters with a small number of programmes and expand that number if they work.

Third, because programmes have limited decision-making power, managers don't have to give up any control or prerogatives. Also, because they are run parallel to the organization's structure, which frequently does not change to reflect the new approach, top management can easily eliminate them if they become troublesome.

Fourth, participative programmes are, as everyone knows, a fad.

Some companies have tried programmes on a trial basis simply because they symbolize modern participative management. In a number of cases senior management of the company have seen a television programme or read a magazine article praising programmes and decided to give them a try. Senior management then ordered the personnel department to start a few to see how they worked. In these cases, programmes were simply something the top told the middle to do to the bottom.

Fifth, the right facilitator has to be involved, especially in QCs. The facilitator is often somebody who can be 'spared' not the best person — who can't be spared. Few have done the job before and the organization lacks the know-how. Often facilitators and their superiors lack an understanding of what the job entails. There are no guidelines and no quality steering support. It can get very lonely (Jowett *et al.*, 1987).

In summary, programmes encounter many threats to their continued existence. Because of these threats, it is not likely that managers will institutionalize and sustain programmes over a long time. Ironically, participative programmes contain in their initial design many of the elements that lead to their elimination and destruction.

Although the QC and team approach have many problems to overcome, this does not mean that managements should avoid them. Companies can capitalize on them in three limited participative ways.

Team and circle suggestion programmes

Team and circle members of programmes can effectively collect the ideas of the individuals closest to the work. If management has no interest in shifting its style towards participation or in creating an elaborate parallel structure, it can create teams and circles with limited mandates, capture the ideas they produce, and then stop them.

This approach recognizes the strengths and limitations of the team and circle process and capitalizes on them. It relies on the initial enthusiasm and knowledge of workers who get an opportunity to meet and make suggestions. It recognizes that programmes are difficult to maintain and therefore plans for their being phased out.

The chief benefits of this approach are the good ideas that result in company savings. The approach also improves communication, particularly upward, and raises the consciousness of employees concerning issues of quality and productivity. In addition, managers note that as a result of exposure to the programmes supervisors develop more skills and have an opportunity to identify workers with a lot of potential.

The danger of this approach is that workers may feel that they have been manipulated: they see their ideas saving the company money, but they find no change in their daily work lives or in their opportunity to get involved on a continuing basis.

Also when employees become aware of the difficulty of getting ideas approved and implemented, as well as of the cumbersome organizational decision-making and resource-allocation processes, they may become cynical about their organization and its management.

Special project teams and circles

Companies can also use teams and circles effectively to deal with temporary or critical organizational issues. For instance, in introducing new technologies, retooling for new product lines or helping to solve major quality problems, management can use both to work out the problems as well as to help workers accept the change. This approach implies a limited degree of movement towards participative management.

When managers use this tactic, they should let the problem at hand define the team's or circle's lifetime. For example, they should be disbanded when the new technology problems have been solved or when quality has been brought within acceptable bounds.

Since the team's and the circle's activities can make an appreciable difference in a chosen problem area and management is concerned enough to be responsive to good ideas, workers are enthusiastic about this approach.

Some companies have used team and circle programmes for many years and have gone through successive cycles of start-up and decline. A start-up typically occurs when a company is introducing a new product or new technology and wants employee input. At those points, managers spontaneously rediscover quality teams and circles, and start the activity again. Experience makes the start-up and development of the teams and circles much quicker and easier.

This approach to teams and circles represents a significant but limited development in the direction of employee participation. Employees benefit from influencing change, which affects their work lives, and from contributing to quality improvements, which fosters pride of workmanship.

On the other hand, their daily work lives and job content do not shift much toward increased responsibility. Also team and circle activity is limited to management-defined problems. There are numerous examples where participants in such special purpose teams and circles think that the company benefits but they don't.

Transitional mechanism

Management can use teams and circles as an interim or transitional device in moving towards a more participative management system and culture. What often happens is that a company embarks on a programme, discovers its limitations and then sets out on a course of action to further develop the participative culture of the organization.

Teams and circles can evolve into other forms of employee participation and expand organizational commitment. Employees often want to work on issues that extend beyond their work area. Many of the issues that participants identify in their brainstorming sessions (see Chapter 20) involve questions of intergroup relations and of organization-wide policies and practices.

Members become frustrated when they are unable to initiate needed changes in these work areas, particularly when they see a close relationship between the problems they identify and organizational performance. The team and circle activity may lead members to want to transcend their status as a parallel suggestion system to become an integral part of the decision-making system.

Managements can move from the team and circle approach by expanding the participative activities into task forces composed of people from different work areas and at different organizational levels. They can then be mandated to work on organization-wide problems.

It can also transfer decision-making authority to the task forces by providing them with the information, expertise and resources needed to make and implement decisions.

In either case, however, if they remain dependent on others to approve and implement their ideas, neither approach will be stable, and their futures must be doubtful.

The need for statistical control techniques

For a company-wide participative programme to work, data must be collected from everyone on their performance. Common techniques need to be used for ease of comparison. With the collection and analysis of data, variation can be tackled. The techniques depend on simple statistics. A range of values is agreed for performance characteristics. The tolerances of the ranges are gradually tightened; so begins the process of never-ending incremental company-wide quality improvement.

In the United Kingdom there have been research studies funded by the Government on quality control practice and the implementation of statistical control (Followell and Oakland, 1985). The findings of these were not very encouraging, the main conclusions being that a significant lack of understanding of the techniques existed, with poor management commitment and insufficient attention to training. Unfortunately, some years later this failure of appreciation at management level is still widespread, with many organizations having little understanding of the requirements.

There is a general lack of appreciation of the need to collect data across the whole of the company; there is a failure to understand the necessity to plan for the introduction of statistical techniques. The purpose of statistical process control (SPC) is to reduce variation in process input and output by establishing whether a process is under statistical control; then getting it under control by eliminating 'special' causes of variation and by management striving to reduce 'common' causes of variation. In many organizations the sole reason for using SPC is to satisfy the demands of a major customer. Such organizations are missing the point of SPC, plus the opportunity to launch a quality improvement programme and develop a company-wide approach to quality.

The only approach to SPC that can be recommended is that advocated by the managing director who will address delegates to the company's SPC course by saying 'Forget Ford and General Motors: we need SPC for our own corporate well-being!' Whilst this approach is not unique, there is little evidence of a universal commitment of such a positive nature (Shaw and Dale, 1987).

SPC is a very important quality improvement technique. Some organizations see it as an end in itself, rather than as a means to an end, i.e., that of total quality management. The benefits of any quality technique, and SPC is no exception, will be transient in nature unless they are underpinned by a total company-wide approach to quality.

SPC can only be successful over the longer-term when operated within a framework of total quality management. The use of statistical methods is an integral part of the Deming philosophy. (Deming, 1982). His 14 points for management have much wider implications than purely SPC. (These points are detailed in the next section.) They point the way forward, just as do the teachings of other internationally famous quality experts, such as Crosby and Juran, to total quality management (Crosby, 1984; Juran, 1987).

The application of statistical methods to most processes whether manufacturing or administration is relatively straightforward. A much more difficult exercise is the implementation of Deming's 14 points — in short, creating a quality management culture within an organization. That is the cornerstone of success.

If the organization already has a participative approach, SPC should support it. In their haste to introduce SPC, companies have been known to ask quality circles to eliminate, as an activity, potential causes of process variation, but without the authority.

The implementation of SPC will almost certainly require fundamental changes to the customs and practices of the organization. Changing behaviour patterns within an organization is very difficult.

The need to make changes has to be communicated by management and accepted by management. A directive from the top of the organization making clear the policy, with the opportunity for each employee to establish how the process will affect him, is required. These are often lacking.

Lack of commitment from within the necessary support functions for the change process has been identified as a frequent reason for the failure of SPC implementation. Often the change process has to be forced on organizations by their major customers, who are demanding that suppliers demonstrate that their processes are in statistical control and capable of continuous improvement. (Lascelles and Dale, 1986)

There is often much concern amongst senior and middle managers that the implementation of SPC could be a costly exercise; a common question is 'How much will SPC cost and what are the potential savings?' There is no definitive answer — the response to their question is another question, 'How much is it costing you in not using SPC?' Few of them have much idea of what quality-related costs their respective organizations are incurring. Plunkett claimed that such costs can be between 5 – 25 per cent of an organization's sales turnover. If senior managers need to be convinced of the benefits of SPC, displaying quality non-conformances in cost terms is a good way of getting their attention. (Plunkett *et al.*, 1985).

If SPC is to be successful, senior managers must take the lead and provide the necessary visible commitment and resources. They should all attend quality awareness courses; many do not. The senior managers must see the need to increase their own knowledge of SPC and quality management understanding, before requesting training programmes for their employees.

These courses should provide the ideal forum for the most senior management to outline the organization's policy on SPC, total quality management and what is required from the rest of the senior management team. The next problem, however, is that of transferring the knowledge gained whilst on the courses to the delegate's own organization. On returning to his or her own factory culture a delegate often has to educate, motivate and change the attitude of others. This is a potent reason why there is a gap between the amount of SPC training which has been conducted in the United Kingdom and actual SPC implementations.

Another major barrier to change is the form of organization existing within a business. Traditional organization structures, (as described before), based on a series of departments each with their own goals, specialisms and command structures, have a natural tendency to focus on their own priorities, such that overall business and company-wide objectives are neglected.

The formal command structures present within each department create a complex communications network which makes it more difficult to keep people informed. Only the most senior managements can impose the need for such organizational change.

There is a need, therefore, to create simpler, flatter structures with added 'flexibility' and which secure involvement from the total workforce. The process must be management-led with the objective of unlocking the latent skills of all. The result of this is to create shorter links to customers and suppliers, such that changing circumstances can be quickly perceived and actioned.

In quality-conscious organizations everybody has a part to play in company-wide quality improvement programmes. Everyone is in one sense both a customer and a supplier. SPC should be, but often is not, used in the non-manufacturing departments to bring about improved performance. It may be that conventional SPC control charts are not used. That does not matter as long as some 'quality' performance indicator can be established and concerted efforts are made by each person to improve his or her 'service', and reduce variation.

It is only when senior managers recognize this, that the organization will start to move down the road of total quality management. At the opposite end of the spectrum some senior managers are found verbally supporting the introduction of SPC before neatly side-stepping the issue; quality education and training is seen as something for others.

Some managements will say that they do not need SPC since they have not had non-conforming materials/parts in years and see no need for it. When asked whether they have defective work, rejects, scrap, etc., the answer is invariably 'Yes'. They need SPC and, more importantly, have failed to understand the philosophy of never-ending improvement.

Job-grading issues can be created with the introduction of SPC, if, for instance, it is perceived that it requires a higher-graded person to put a point on a chart. Only management effort can involve everyone at all levels and resolve such problems, before they arise.

Companies often start by using higher-graded people to do the charts, but there is no doubt that the biggest benefits only come by having the operator who controls the process and understands the principles of what he is doing, completing the chart.

Any major change of operating practice is likely to create concerns from the trades unions. The unions should be involved very early in any discussions regarding the introduction of SPC. How these issues arise and are dealt with will depend on the relationships existing in each particular plant. If mutual trust exists, and the union takes the view that the interests of its members are best served by improving profitability, then it can be an aid in the change process. On the other hand there may be suspicion of management motives and attempts to block the introduction or use the introduction as a bargaining ploy in wage negotiations. In either case, the only plan is to have thorough discussions and take the senior union people through the training process. We should never forget that SPC can only work on a company-wide basis.

Many companies have introduced diagram and control charts with tremendous vigour, thinking that SPC is just concerned with producing diagrams and charts for as many processes as possible. The logic behind SPC is to study a process and ask 'How can it be improved?' and 'How can SPC help?' Its introduction has to be planned. It just does not happen.

In situations where little analysis and subsequent action is taken, on the data provided by the charts, SPC will lose credibility and will have to be withdrawn. Operators who have been spending time completing charts need to see the benefits of their efforts, otherwise they will treat it as a waste of effort.

Collecting data, using control charts, is not introducing SPC. This stage is reached only when the data collected from the processes are acted on at all levels in the organizational hierarchy. Many companies have developed control charts to collect information about the process and, once this has been collected, do not know how to use it in order to improve the process. No matter how great the enthusiasm for SPC, it is wasted without management follow-up action.

Companies often fail to make use of the data they already have on their files prior to introducing SPC. From the analysis of such data they can acquire some indication of the variability of their processes.

Companies must appoint SPC coordinators. The role is a vital one. Companies need to think deeply about who they want in this position. It is not good enough to select someone just because he or she has some 'surplus' time. It is not uncommon for people to be told that they have the responsibility for introducing SPC, after attending an SPC course. On their return, they then have to start making plans for introducing SPC. These unfortunate individuals get caught in the middle. On one side management expecting/demanding the introduction of SPC, and on the other a bemused/bewildered workforce reluctant to be exposed to the technique.

In some organizations the expertise and knowledge about SPC is limited to a small group of people. These people then guard the data jealously since they have little involvement in the manufacturing and production processes. Here data is being collected only; there is no attempt to integrate and interpret the data on a company-wide scale. Clearly SPC planning is weak and management have failed to appreciate the company-wide approach.

Unwillingly managements often create an elitism or what the rest of the employees regard as such, due to their lack of education and training. Whilst it is important that an organization and/or department has an SPC expert, the prerequisites of a healthy programme is that everybody in the organization has:

1. A training in basic statistical methods.
2. An understanding of the philosophy underlying their use.
3. Applications of the methods.

Managements fail to devote attention to the role of the manufacturing and quality departments in the introduction and implementation of SPC. The manufacturing department needs to take day-to-day responsibility for SPC with operators charting the data. The role of the quality department is that of adviser/coordinator.

The quality department, however, may be too set in its 'traditional ways' to carry out this role effectively; this is a danger which needs to be recognized by management. If there are any 'traditional ways' these are due to the company culture, the management style, and a misunderstanding of the new quality department's role. Only management can change the culture.

Management should be sensitive to any worries which operators might have about SPC. They are often concerned that recording data and carrying out a few simple calculations will expose their limitations on literacy and numeracy. The involvement of manufacturing departments in SPC has been interpreted by some managements as a signal to reduce the number of traditional quality inspection staff, or even eliminate them altogether.

The introduction of SPC should not be taken as an automatic sign to reduce the number of traditional quality staff. The requirement is for a reshaping of their responsibilities and activities. The sharing of the responsibility for SPC between manufacturing and quality departments should bring potential enemies together. Only management commitment can cement the relationship.

Some managements of companies do not think through or even decide what data SPC format they should use. They make no distinction between variable and attribute data formats. The analysis of variation data becomes meaningless; the actioning and processing of controlled change not possible. Price's rules of quality control are not implementable (Price, 1984). These rules are:

1. No measurement or inspection without recording.
2. No recording without analysis.
3. No analysis without action.

Managements cannot always decide what characteristics they should measure.

The answer is whatever characteristic determines the quality of the product or process. For example, product design may take a different view of the importance of a particular characteristic from manufacturing. There is a need for all those with expertise in the design and manufacturing of the product or process to agree amongst themselves on what these characteristics are.

Management may have to agree a study of the process. The study should be used to focus on those characteristics or operations, which, from experience and knowledge, have given the greatest problems. If nobody possesses this knowledge, it is then necessary to become more intimate with the process and find out where variation is occurring.

Similarly managements do not think through how frequently processes should be investigated and data gathered. It is not understood by managements that frequency of investigation is a balance. It should always be remembered that one of the objectives of SPC is to prevent non-conforming products being made and to obtain fast feedback on how the process is performing.

Taking a sample, however, along with the subsequent measurement and recording activities, causes some minor disruption to the process. The balance is between this interruption and the quick feedback of information about process performance. The greater the frequency of sampling, the greater the disruption to manufacturing but greater knowledge is gained about the process's performance.

The lower the frequency of inspection the less is known about the process's performance. There is no easy solution: operators, setters, engineers and managers must use their experience of the process to determine the frequency of sampling. In some processes little variation may occur within, say, an hour but in others great variation may enable the adequate identification of variations.

Managements fail to appreciate that SPC is a dynamic technique and the thinking behind its application needs to be kept flexible. If knowledge of the process and its output dictates that the frequency of sampling needs to be changed, then change it!

Again, it is not appreciated by managements that SPC is applicable to all manufacturing and all administrative activities since it is concerned with the ability to predict the performance of a process. It matters not whether a manufacturing system is producing items in thousands or hundreds or one-offs. If a record is made of how a process has performed, with sufficient data it is possible to predict how it will perform when it is next run. The quantity, order or component is irrelevant. If it does behave differently management efforts should be directed to finding out the cause of variation and striving to reduce it.

We have examined some of the difficulties which are encountered when an attempt is made to involve personnel more fully in their company. The very great majority of these difficulties arise from the attitude of management and the system for which they are responsible.

The next chapter will detail what the quality experts have been telling us for over 30 years, since what they have been telling us is still not widely appreciated let alone implemented.

Further reading

Crosby, P., *Quality Without Tears*, McGraw-Hill Book Co., New York 1984.

Deming, W.E., 'On Some Statistical Aids Towards Economic Production', *Interfaces*, 1975, Vol. 5, No. 4, August, pp.

Deming, W.E., *Quality Productivity and Competitive Position*, MIT Press, Massachusetts 1982.

Followell, R.F. and Oakland, J.S., 'Research into Methods of Implementing Statistical Process Control', *Quality Assurance* June 1985, Vol. 11, No. 2, pp. 27–32.

Guthrie, G., ' "After Japan" and Beyond: A Study of the Experience of Quality Circles in Ford Motor Company', *Quality Assurance*, 1987, Vol. 13, No. 2, June, pp. 37–40.

Jowett, T., Mansfield, B. and Hill, P., 'The Loneliness of the Quality Circle Facilitator, *Quality Assurance News*, 1987, Vol. 13, issue 8, August, pp. 262–3.

Juran, J.M., Gryna, F.M. and Bingham, R.S., (eds) *Quality Control Handbook*, 4th ed., McGraw-Hill Book Co., New York 1987.

Lascelles, D.M. and Dale, B.G., 'How Change Agents Can Effect Quality Improvement', *Proceedings on Second National Conference on Production Research*, 1986, September, Vol. 2, pp. 132–45.

Lawler, E.E. and Mohrman, S.A., 'Quality Circles After the Fad', *Harvard Business Review*, 1985, Vol. 63, issue 1, January-February, pp. 65–71.

Plunkett, J.J., Dale, B.G. and Tyrell, R.W., *Quality Costs*, Department of Trade and Industry, London 1985.

Price, F., *Right First Time*, Gower Press, Aldershot 1984.

Rede Group, *Lead Assessor Course*, Swindon, United Kingdom 1988.

Shaw, P. and Dale, B.G., 'Some Problems in Applying Statistical Process Control', *Quality Assurance*, 1987, Vol. 13, No. 1, March, pp. 14–17.

The Yankee Group Europe, *Advanced Manufacturing Philosophies*, Watford, United Kingdom 1988.

19 Quality Improvement: Lessons for Management

John Edge

The previous chapter identified and described some of the serious and chronic management problems of variation and organization which can affect any participative quality improvement programme. This chapter explores the backgrounds of those programmes which have been successful in terms of the management approach to quality. The thinking which has inspired that management approach is also considered.

Identifying those quality concepts which the Japanese and many Western high technology companies have developed and applied to manufacturing industry is an important step. The implementation of these, as discussed in the previous chapter, is fraught with difficulties. However, the generic nature of 'quality' means that it is applicable whether the product be from the heavy iron and steel industry or the recent high technology ones. This suggests that the variable element is not quality itself, but the management commitment, the programme implementation and the assumptions on which it is based.

The Approach to quality in the late 1980s

Managers have to learn from their own commercial and quality experiences as well as from those of other people. This must be fundamental. Equally fundamental, if managers are to learn, they must be prepared to question many of the assumptions on which commercial and quality decisions are based.

Every organization needs to exercise financial prudence in its dealings. It needs to know where the money has gone, for what purposes it was used, and whether or not it was used wisely. It also must know where money will need to be allocated in the future, how much will be needed, and the risks associated with the allocation. Money, however, is merely a measure of how good a company's product is, how much the product is desired in the marketplace and how much it fulfills the expectations of the buyer and the community.

If the product is not right for the market, financial prudence counts for little. Product quality prudence, therefore, must come first or there will be little money to count and no need for an analysis of where it went. The question to be asked, therefore, is: 'Why do companies have financial systems, but not quality systems?' since quality prudence is as crucial as financial prudence.

Managements must understand that they have to operate within a broader community and within the political and social constraints of the community. Products must conform, therefore, to the aspirations of that society. Those which do not, and their producers, will not last long. Quality prudence is being forced on companies by product liability legislation, consumer and environmentalist pressure, and international competition. It is easy for an industry and company to get a bad name for its lack of quality: for example Bhopal, Flixborough, Seveso and the wiring and component manufacture of Boeing airliners. Worldwide communications spread the news of a bad product quickly. We must learn from our own experiences and from those of others.

The above is a summary of what is sometimes called macroquality economics, since it is company-wide and the company is part of a national and international social organization. However, the macroscopic view is the sum total of all the identifiable individual activities and functions which go into the making of the company's products; thus we also have microquality economics.

Every material item and its processing, management and worker activity and function, in a company, has a direct or indirect effect on the quality of the company's products. The quality of a product, however, starts before a contract is even signed; the company has to ensure that it has the capability, resources and experience to embark on a contract to supply a product for a particular customer. Also before the contract is signed, the company knows that in many cases it must be able to offer, on-demand, post-delivery services to the customer.

Contracts and products pass through various phases in their life cycle, ranging from initial study or conception to eventual disposal. All the materials, processing activities and other functions which affect quality directly or indirectly, and which comprises the life cycle, need to be formalized and integrated into company-wide, top–down life cycle management policies. These management policies must embrace all the various systems which make up the company in society.

These integrated company policies lead to a more substantial description of quality than 'fitness for purpose'. Instead, quality can be described as the integration of various management systems which provide assurance that the contractual, legal and product obligations of the company to the customer and to the community are fulfilled on all occasions. This description implicitly incorporates safety, reliability and maintainability, as well as conformance to requirements.

The approach is a systems one, with the many subsystems integrated into a totality. For a comprehensive study of this reasoning and approach see Deming (1982).

Commercial and quality assumptions

Much has been written about why Japanese manufacturers continue to outperform their European and US competitors in cost, quality, and on-time delivery. Most experts point to practices like just-in-time production total quality control, and the aggressive use of flexible manufacturing technologies.

One area that has received less attention, but contributes mightily to Japanese competitiveness, is how many companies' management accounting systems reinforce a commitment to process and product innovation and quality improvement from top to bottom, at all levels of management and workers.

Studies of management accounting systems at Japanese companies in major industries, including automobiles, computers, consumer electronics and semiconductors, suggest similar and related accounting practices. These practices differentiate important aspects of Japanese management accounting from established practices in Europe and the US (Hiromoto, 1988; Kaplan, 1984). Like their European and US counterparts, Japanese companies must value inventory for tax purposes and financial statements. But the Japanese don't let these accounting procedures determine how they measure and control organizational activities.

Japanese companies tend to use their management control systems to support and reinforce their manufacturing strategies. A more direct link therefore exists between management accounting practices and corporate goals. These accounting systems are used more to motivate all levels and types of employees to act in accordance with long term manufacturing strategies than to provide senior management with precise data on costs, variances and profits. Accounting therefore plays more of an *influencing* role than an *informing* role.

Accounting in Japan also reflects and reinforces an overriding commitment to market-driven management. When estimating costs on new products, for example, many companies make it a point not to rely completely on prevailing engineering and manufacturing standards. Instead, they establish target costs derived from estimates of a competitive market price. These target costs are usually well below currently achievable costs, which are based on standard technologies and processes. Managers then set benchmarks to measure incremental progress toward meeting the target cost objectives.

Companies also de-emphasize standard cost systems for monitoring factory performance. In general, Japanese management accounting does not stress optimizing within existing constraints. Rather, it encourages employees to make continual improvements by tightening those constraints.

These accounting practices point to a central principle that seems to guide management accounting in Japan — that accounting policies should be subservient to corporate strategy, not independent of it.

Japanese manufacturing strategy places high premiums on quality and timely delivery in addition to low cost production. Thus companies make extensive use, certainly more than many of their European and US competitors, of non financial measures to evaluate factory performance. The reason is straightforward: if a management accounting system measures only costs (as in management by results) employees tend to focus on costs exclusively, to the crucial neglect of the intangibles.

For companies to maintain competitive advantage, employees must be continually innovative and reduce variation. This requires motivation, an intangible. A product designer must be motivated to play a significant role in cost reduction. Shop floor workers and managers must constantly strive to improve efficiency beyond what 'best practice' currently dictates.

The Japanese have demonstrated that management accounting can play a significant role in integrating the innovative efforts of employees with the company's long term commercial strategies and goals.

Foreign-based competitors continue their assault on European and US markets, exploiting their low wages or superior commitment and technological sophistication. Consumers are requiring ever-higher levels of quality and diversity, which has forced manufacturers to upgrade tolerances and designs, eliminate defects, and accelerate the rate of new product introduction. Meanwhile, just-in-time production systems are putting pressure on both manufacturers and suppliers to surpass their old standards of delivery and service. Staggering challenges face European and US manufacturing companies.

Within the framework of a commercial strategy, manufacturing managers have new resources with which to respond to these challenges — a set of technologies that are collectively referred to as programmable automation. These include computer-aided design (CAD), computer-aided manufacturing (CAM), computer-aided engineering (CAE), flexible manufacturing systems (FMS), robotics and computer integrated manufacturing (CIM). These advances promise to improve everything: cost, quality, flexibility, delivery, speed, design — everything.

Many traditional Taylor-like command and control managed companies (discussed in the next chapter) must question long-held beliefs and practices. They are having difficulty reaping the advantages of programmable automation. For years they have acquired new equipment much in the way a family buys a new car. Drive out the old, drive in the new, enjoy the faster, smoother, more economical ride — and go on with the same attitudes and organization as before. With the new technology, however, 'as before' can mean disaster. Executives are discovering that acquiring an FMS or any of the other advanced manufacturing systems is more like replacing that old car with a helicopter (Hayes and Jaikumar, 1988).

If you fail to understand and prepare for the revolutionary capabilities of these systems, they will become as much an inconvenience as a benefit — and a lot more expensive. You have to plan and organize for the new manufacturing technologies.

The new manufacturing technologies can shock a commercial organization — as a helicopter would disrupt one's home life — because they require a quantum jump in a manufacturing organization's precision and integration.

Automated machine tools can produce parts to more exacting specifications than can the most skilled human machinist, but to do so they need explicit, unambiguous instructions in the form of computer programs.

The new hardware provides added freedom, but it also makes possible more ways to succeed or fail. It therefore requires new skills on the part of managers — an integrative imagination, a passion for detail. To prevent processing contamination, for example, it is no longer possible to rely on people who have a 'feel' for their machines, or just to note on a drawing that operators should 'remove iron filings from the part'. When using the new automated machine tools, everything must be stated with mathematical precision: where is the blower that removes the filings, and what is the orientation of the part during operation of the blower?

Moreover, the tightness of the procedures that govern automated machine operations magnifies the harmful effects that faulty upstream processes have on downstream processes. Without machine operators physically handling parts, there is no one to realign them in a fixture, tweak cutting tools, or compensate for small machining or operational errors, and nobody to inspect parts for holes, cracks or other material defects.

To replicate a machinist's talent for recognizing errors, engineers and managers of an automated system need either access to an elaborate database incorporating, say, an expert system detailing the implicit rules of the skilled machinist, or a scientific understanding of the technology itself.

Process engineering must provide sensors to detect errors and programmed controllers to interpret signals from these sensors to initiate corrective actions or shut down the machine. Indeed, production-control data will increasingly become useless to human operators in real-time as batches of materials move down the line. It is the computer that analyses the microstructure of processing from one microsecond to the next and then takes action against a badly made part.

In the new manufacturing era, therefore, the manager's job is mainly taken up with making the pieces fit together (both the equipment hardware and the programmed software). To maximize the capabilities of the new technologies, managers must learn to think more like computer analysts and programmers — people who break down production into a sequence of microsteps.

A manager who doesn't understand one part of a factory process as well as the other parts will find it impossible to make the necessary trade-offs — between cost and smoothness, say, or between speed and robustness. Managers need to develop procedures in advance, even before starting up a plant, to take into consideration all possible consequences from design to assembly. It will no longer be possible for '. . . decisions and policies (to be) made by people twice and thrice removed from the manufacturing arena' (Schonberger, 1986).

Clearly, the new manufacturing hardware will work best in an organization geared for the tight integration of design, engineering and plant control. Schonberger provides many examples of how less makes more, across all aspects of a plant. Hall (1987) makes similar and related points about the need of management to integrate and not fragment '. . . contributions by various functional staffs'.

These new organizations have flat structures. They are often self-managing within a framework of general corporate objectives. The organization, however, comprises many 'units' charged with specific research and development, engineering and manufacturing tasks. The units are highly motivated and their personnel educated and often specialists. Many high technology manufacturing companies now have this approach. Production lead times have been cut dramatically (Takeuchi and Nonaka, 1986).

The managers who preside over advanced manufacturing tasks must think more like cross-disciplinary generalists, people with a deep understanding of machine design, software engineering and manufacturing processes. They can no longer be professional bureaucrats; Schonberger (1986) said of these people 'venturing out into the plant was, well venturing'.

These new managers must learn to direct highly educated people working in small, tightly knit groups. They must encourage corporate learning, harmonize the efforts of specialists and be able to respond efficiently and quickly to changing market demands. This race for corporate manufacturing and technological survival has been well presented in a number of publications (see IEEE, 1987; and Lorenz, 1987 for example).

Quality management

Now consider the quality thinkers who have changed our thinking on the subject of quality and quality management by having learned from the mistakes of others and by having challenged commercial, management and worker assumptions.

To explain the Japanese quality miracle Ishikawa gave six features of quality work (Ishikawa, 1978, 1985). These are:

1. A company-wide quality control programme.
2. Top management are subject to quality audits.
3. Industrial education and training.
4. Quality circle (QC) activities.
5. Nationwide quality control promotion activities.
6. Application of statistical techniques.

A company-wide quality control programme

Every department and all levels and types of personnel, within the company, are engaged in systematic work, guided by written quality policies. These quality policies are endorsed by upper management and their successful implementation is driven by management.

The consequence of this approach is that all personnel are committed to producing a quality product or providing a quality service, since management is itself consciously seeking to achieve this objective by known and agreed means.

In Europe and the US quality control often relates to the day-to-day activities of personel implementing quality, with quality assurance being the management function of auditing and reviewing those activities. In Japan quality control embraces both these notions and is more akin to total quality management.

Top management are subject to quality audits

A quality executive team visits each company department to identify, isolate and help solve any obstacles to the production of quality products or services. Normally audits are done by the quality experts, but periodically a quality executive team is required to calibrate the department management and its products or services. Conversations are directed at the users of the product or service, company quality experts, department production and manufacturing management and shop floor workers.

Industrial education and training

Education and training in quality must be given to everybody in all departments at each level since company-wide quality requires participation by everyone involved.

The initial training has to take place within the quality department so that the quality personnel 'train ourselves before we are fit to train others'. Only then do quality personnel start to train personnel in other departments.

These training programmes are intensive and are attended by all managers and workers. This is a necessary step, but not sufficient, to make personnel quality managers or quality workers. Training has to be complemented by continuing education which brings awareness and discipline; from these the quality conscious evolves.

The training is given by the quality personnel involved in the day-to-day activities of the department. They are aware of its problems and their evaluation. Personnel from the department bring uniformity to the educational process and provide a common pool of experience, from which all can draw.

Quality circle (QC) activities

A quality circle is 'A small group which meets voluntarily to perform quality control within the workshop to which they belong' (JUSE, 1980). The QC had traditionally been applied to the manufacturing process but was expanded to include management and engineering quality. The QC provides a forum to discuss the department's problems; its full benefits are only seen in a company-wide quality approach. QCs are discussed in some detail in the next chapter.

Nationwide quality control promotion activities

November is Quality Month in Japan; the Deming Prize is awarded that month. The Deming Prize is used to advertise a company's products since it ensures such a high degree of customer confidence that the customer can be sure of a quality product. This type of quality awareness reinforces quality ideas across the whole of society.

Application of statistical techniques

Statistical techniques for quality control include: Pareto analysis, cause and effect analysis, process analysis, histograms and various Shewhart type control charts.

These statistical techniques enabled the Japanese to quantify quality and give it a high degree of 'scientific' objectivity. Deming was largely responsible for their introduction and his guidance laid the foundation for the quality revolution. They are discussed in the next chapter.

Another thinker who realized the link between management and quality was Juran (1981a and 1981b). He has highlighted three target quality areas to challenge assumptions and to change thinking. These are:

1. Upper management leadership of each company's approach to product quality.

2. Massive quality oriented training programmes.
3. Structured annual improvements in quality.

Upper management leadership of each company's approach to product quality

This point has been made by many observers. An example of Japanese upper management commitment to quality was made by Sandholm to the International Quality Control Conference held in Tokyo in 1978. Almost half of the Japanese participants at the conference were from upper management — presidents, general managers, division heads and directors.

At conferences held in Europe or the United States, almost all participants are from the quality profession — quality assurance engineers, reliability engineers, quality managers, etc. There are few upper managers (Sandholm, 1983).

Deming (1975) also observed that in Japan top people in the companies take hold of the problems of production and quality. All the reports quoted by Deming showing successful implementations of quality principles were written by men with the rank of company president, managing director or chairman of the board.

As Deming has stressed:

> All of the top management came, not only to listen, but to work. They had already seen evidence from their own engineers that what you've got is this chain reaction. As you improve the quality, costs go down. You can lower the price. You capture the market with quality and price. Americans do not understand it. Americans think that as you improve quality, you increase your cost (Gottlieb, 1975).

The need for upper management leadership, emphasizes Juran, stems from the need to create major changes, two of which include annual improvements in quality and a massive quality-oriented training programme, discussed below. The recommended step for Western upper management is to perform a comprehensive company-wide quality audit to understand what needs to be done.

An organizational weakness in the West is the large company central quality department with the numerous functions of quality planning, engineering, coordination, auditing, inspection and test. In Japan, most of these quality-oriented functions are carried out by line personnel, who have the necessary training.

The Japanese do have quality departments, but they are small in terms of personnel and they perform a limited array of functions: broad planning, consulting services and audits. Upper management quality audits calibrate the effectiveness of the organization and only upper management has the authority to institute the necessary changes.

The commitment of all upper manufacturing management is necessary to instigate the needed quality changes. Then to delegate the responsibility for implementation to the manufacturing departments. This helps foster close links and collaboration.

Massive quality-oriented training programmes

Selective training in quality in the West has been largely confined to members of the specialized quality departments, which constitute only about 5 per cent of the managerial and specialist personnel of companies. In contrast, the Japanese have trained close to 100 per cent of their managers and specialists in quality and made it a quantifiable science.

This massive quality-oriented training programme carries the education and training philosophy of Ishikawa to its logical conclusion. Juran points out that common quality training must include an understanding of:

(a) The universal sequence of events for improving quality and reducing quality-related costs (creation of beneficial change);
(b) The universal feedback loop for control (prevention of adverse change);
(c) Fundamentals of data collection and analysis.

Structured annual improvements in quality

In the early 1950s, the Japanese faced a grim reality. They had an inability to sell products. Since their major limitation was quality, not price, they directed their revolution at improving quality. They learned how to improve quality, became proficient at it, and are now reaping the rewards. Their managers are equally at home in meeting current targets and planning improvements for the future.

The story of the Japanese electronics industry with transistor radios, for example, illustrates the dedication to annual improvements in quality that exists in Japan.

As mentioned earlier in this chapter, with regard to programmable automation, computer-based manufacturing systems require a radically new approach by management. Too many systems will never meet their requirements, either to internal or external customers.

Manufacturing management must plan for and make a total commitment, like Japan's, to quality improvement from within. The programmable systems require a structured strategy and implementation if they are to be successful. Structured annual improvement programmes by companies should provide the overall framework for this. To accomplish these annual quality improvements Juran (1981b) advises that a team:

(a)   study the symptoms of the defects and failures;
(b)   develop a theory on the causes of these symptoms;
(c)   test the theory until the cause(s) is known;
(d)   stimulate remedial action by the appropriate department(s).

Well-established manufacturing quality techniques have been able to identify and categorize defects in products, although this is less easy when dealing with programmable systems. As techniques for defect identification mature, the steps required for annual quality improvements can be applied to computer-based manufacturing. These are discussed in the next chapter.

Defects can be separated into those which are worker-controllable and those which are management-controllable. The latter category includes defects that cannot possibly be avoided by workers. Whether a certain defect should be regarded as a worker-controllable defect or a management-controllable defect depends on the extent to which the following conditions are met:

(a)   the workers know what to do;
(b)   the workers know the result of their own work;
(c)   the workers have the means of controlling the result.

If all three conditions are met and the work is still defective, the worker is responsible. However, if one or more of the conditions have not been met, this is a management-controllable defect (Juran, 1966).

On the responsibility for defects Deming (1975b) has made the following point:

> To call to the attention of a worker a careless act, in a climate of general carelessness, is a waste of time and can only generate hard feelings, because the condition of general carelessness belongs to everybody and is the fault of management, not of any one worker, nor of all workers.

Many managers assume they have solved all the problems once they have brought worker-controllable defects under control. In fact, they are, as Deming also reminds us, just ready to tackle the most important problems of variation, namely, the management-controllable causes (Deming, 1967).

During programmable manufacturing processes many worker-controllable defects can be controlled by the workers. However, there is a wide class of defects in such systems that arise because the worker does not know what to do. This condition occurs because of the inevitable intertwining of hardware, software, specification and implementation.

Limitations of available implementation technology may force a specification change. The hardware hosting the computer software may require software workarounds because of technological limitations. Implementation choices may suggest enhancements to the original specification. That is, as more is accomplished, more is learned, making it reasonable to take a different approach than was originally specified.

To learn more and take a better approach, problems need to be identified and isolated. There has to be analysis and synthesis with every problem, yet everything has to work as an integrated system, and be understood in that framework.

That the workers know the result of their own work in programmable automation and software is very immediate and sometimes humbling for the worker who has made a 'silly mistake'. The worker receives the results, whether correct or incorrect, immediately from the computer exactly as commanded. On the other hand there are the subtle defects that are not found for years. This is a worker-controllable defect, but one where the workers do not know the result of their work. Quality programmable automation must continually search to resolve this type of defect.

In programmable automation the worker has the means of influencing the result. Assuming a reasonable task assignment, the worker is directly involved in the production of the resulting product and is often the first to see that result. Consider, for example, a situation in which the worker loses that influence because the FMS is unavailable. It is usually not worker-controllable that the FMS is or is not available.

To summarize this discussion of the annual quality improvements suggested by Juran. It is clear that, in the automated environment, the workers must first know the conditions before setting up the programme for improvement. In this area, to know where one stands from a quality viewpoint is essential.

To achieve high technology management quality, a four-point attack is needed, as advocated by Sandholm at Westinghouse Defense Center in May 1983. The points are:

High Technology Corporation
Statement of Quality Policy

As a supplier of products and services to users, it is the policy of the High Technology Corporation management to ensure that these products and services are of the highest quality, commensurate with the users' requirements, needs and expectations.

To assure these services, therefore, it is the stated quality policy of the High Technology Corporation, that the implementation of this Policy will be in conformance with the requirements of the International Standards Organization (ISO) 9000 series; this series is concerned with quality management systems.

The implementation of the ISO quality management system requirements, will limit quality problems arising, by the careful planning and execution of all activities; associated with each activity, will be the detailed identification of responsibilities and authorities.

The final responsibility for ensuring that the High Technology Corporation quality management system exists and is implemented, rests with its Executive Manager. In turn, this responsibility must be borne on a day-to-day basis by all managers, who must instruct the personnel reporting to them of their own quality responsibilities. Each individual, therefore, must be made responsible for his or her own work and must be actively encouraged by management to seek ways of improving quality.

It is recognized that the most cost effective way of achieving the necessary quality of any product, or service is by doing the task 'right first time.' Right first time management depends on personnel with suitable qualifications, responsibilities and authorities, supported by the appropriate methods, techniques, tools, standards and procedures, being in place.

The overall success of any business enterprise depends on the business, as a system, working in a coordinated manner, to known objectives and the whole enterprise being suitably monitored by those with corporate quality responsibility for its overall efficient operations.

Executive Manager
15 January 1989

Figure 19.1.   Statement of quality policy.

1. Quality policy.
2. Quality objectives.
3. Quality system.
4. Quality organization (Sandholm, 1983b).

The quality policy

This is a statement that expresses the need for corporate-wide quality. It is supported by a statement of commitment to quality by the corporation. It provides the direction for all employees to implement the quality policy. As with all policies, it emanates from the highest executive in the corporation. An example of a quality policy statement for a European high technology company is shown in Figure 19.1.

The ISO9000 Quality Management Series is derived from the British Standard BS5750 Quality Management System Series. By 1992 ISO9000 will have become *the* European quality management system with the removal of trade barriers and the harmonization of standards (ISO, 1987).

High technology companies like IBM and Digital Equipment Corporation (DEC) take management commitment very seriously. DEC held their Second European Quality Symposium in 1986. Falotti the European President of DEC said:

> We as managers are responsible for too many compromises. We compromise every day and we think it is not important but people see that management is compromising and, therefore, it is all right to compromise. Extend this chain all along and the result is a poor quality company. (Falotti, 1986).

Quality objectives

These are statements of measurable improvements usually achievable on an annual basis. The implication is that there is a quality baseline established so that the quality improvements may be measured. The presumption is that each professional manager and worker knows the quality of the items being manufactured.

In practice it depends on maturity, degree of professionalism and many intangibles about people. With that awareness in mind, quality objectives should be set with the manufacturing managers to improve in a quantifiable way the quality of the manufacturing process and items produced. For example, records of the number of errors, their circumstances and severity during the enhancement of a programmable system.

The quality system

This is the means used to achieve the quality objectives. Traditionally, this is the heavy tome of standards and procedures for quality personnel to follow step-by-step — not very effective, but usually necessary to meet contractual and specification requirements. To have really all pervasive quality awareness throughout the organization would be more effective, with every manager and worker striving to achieve the company-wide quality objectives.

For developments using programmable automation a quality system should include standards and procedures, methods, tools and techniques decided by, and committed to, by senior management. Examples of these include, but are not limited to: programmable quality assurance (PQA) procedures, design methods and aids, programming and coding standards, testing strategies and diagnostic guides. All these documents need to be produced and integrated within the framework of the management requirements for the product and the company. The PQA procedures and guidelines need to be particularized for each programmable product; this is usually accomplished by means of a PQA project plan for each product.

The quality assurance organization

This should be small and efficient in keeping with the previous statements. Such a quality assurance organization can then act as a monitoring mechanism to focus the total organizational effort towards quality improvement.

Crosby in his book *Quality is Free* (1979) sought to measure the management attitude to quality by the five categories shown in Table 19.1, the quality management maturity grid:

Stage 1

Measurement category of uncertainty, clearly highlights that managements who lack an understanding of quality, and have the wrong attitude to it, will never have the quality organization to handle problems, cost quality, improve it and have a quality posture or policy.

In this stage of management uncertainty there are a number of deeply rooted facts that everyone knows. Namely:

(a)   quality means goodness, it cannot be defined;
(b)   because it cannot be defined, quality cannot be measured;
(c)   the trouble with quality is that European and American workers don't give a damn;
(d)   quality is fine, but we can't afford it.

Table 19.1.

Quality management maturity grid (from Crosby; *Quality is Free*, 1979).

Measurement categories	Stage 1: uncertainty	Stage 2: awakening	Stage 3: enlightenment	Stage 4: wisdom	Stage 5: certainty
Management understanding and attitude	No comprehension of quality as a management tool. Tend to blame quality departments for 'quality problems'.	Recognizing that quality management may be of value but not willing to provide money or time to make it all happen.	While going through quality improvement programme learn more about quality management; becoming supportive and helpful.	Participating. Understand absolutes of quality management. Recognize their personal role in continuing emphasis.	Consider quality management an essential part of company system.
Quality organization status	Quality is hidden in manufacturing or engineering departments. Inspection probably not part of organization. Emphasis on appraisal or sorting.	A stronger quality leader is appointed but main emphasis is still on appraisal and moving the product. Still part of manufacturing or other.	Quality department reports to top management, all appraisal is incorporated and manager has role in management of company.	Quality manager is an officer of company; effective status reporting and preventive action. Involved with consumer affairs and special assignments.	Quality manager on board of directors. Prevention is main concern. Quality is a thought leader.
Problem handling	Problems are fought as they occur; no resolution; inadequate definition; lots of yelling and accusations.	Teams are set up to attack major problems. Long-range solutions are not solicited.	Corrective action communication established. Problems are faced openly and resolved in an orderly way.	Problems are identified early in their development. All functions are open to suggestion and improvement.	Except in the most unusual cases, problems are prevented.
Cost of quality as per cent of sales	Reported: unknown Actual: 20%	Reported: 3% Actual: 18%	Reported: 8% Actual: 12%	Reported: 6.5% Actual: 8%	Reported: 2.5% Actual: 2.5%
Quality improvement actions	No organized activities. No understanding of such activities.	Trying obvious 'motivational' short-range efforts.	Implementation of the 14-step programme with thorough understanding and establishment of each step.	Continuing the 14-step programme and starting 'Make Certain' programme.	Quality improvement is a normal and continued activity.
Summation of company quality posture	'We don't know why we have problems with quality.'	'Is it absolutely necessary to always have problems with quality?'	'Through management commitment and quality improvement we are identifying and resolving our problems.'	'Defect prevention is a routine part of our operation.'	'We know why we do not have problems with quality.'

With this management understanding and attitude, these facts are self-evident truths. Management education is needed to dispel these erroneous facts.

When education is completed, there is usually a lip service to quality: people will say 'yes' from their minds while they feel 'no' in the pits of their stomachs; they will pay lip service to quality without really realizing it. They will say they want quality but will continue to judge performance solely by schedule and budget.

There seems to be an implied assumption that the three goals of quality, cost and schedule are conflicting and therefore mutually exclusive. It is not true. Significant improvements in both cost and schedule can be achieved as a result of focusing on quality (Craig, 1983). Fundamental to Deming's teachings is that the only way to increase productivity and reduce costs is to increase quality (Deming, 1982).

Any company's policy must be to supply exactly what the customer wants. It sounds too elementary to be important. This is Crosby's first absolute, conformance to requirements. (Crosby 1984). Too often managements emphasize making the shipment, whether it is right or close to being right.

Costs will be incurred from the massive educational, organizational and procedural effort that will be required. Each manager and worker will have to learn what it really takes to achieve quality in manufacturing. To effectively increase quality, the quality personnel will have to get involved with the management of the company to ensure that relearning takes place for all managers and workers, in all aspects of engineering and manufacturing.

Stage 2

Measurement category awakening, quality personnel are sought out in times of crisis. Difficulties with customers and internal manufacturing and engineering departments will lead to quality personnel being asked to act as a buffer and even being asked to carry out investigations into the reasons for the difficulties.

The value of audits begins to be appreciated. Checklists start to be generated and used, against which all customer and product conformance to requirements conditions can be compared and even measured. For the first time in the company, management can begin to sense the real quality perspective.

Stage 3

Measurement category enlightenment, is reached when it is

understood that quality contributes in a meaningful way, for the benefit of both management and workers.

Quality goals and objectives must be established first as a matter of corporate policy and then enforced through management involvement, company organization, procedural policy and universal commitment. In essence, the quality role becomes a management role in which quality principles and objectives are upheld at the start of each new contract by management and workers. Manufacturing and engineering practices must be driven by these quality objectives.

With the organizational changes, the need for planning to a common purpose becomes clear — the old interdepartmental fights and accusations become things of the past. Each department has its own job to do and gets on with it, within the framework of the overall planned company environment, which is increasingly driven by upper management. Quality requirements begin to be considered before manufacturing and even research and development. That quality must be built in — not added which it can't be — becomes widely appreciated.

Quality planning and quality plans are considered. Audits are complemented by reviews at various points in the manufacturing and engineering processes. Control points begin to be used against which quality can be compared, data collected, measurements and accurate predictions made. The scene is being set for a company-wide participative quality programme.

Stage 4

Measurement category wisdom, is reached when everyone knows that a real conscious effort has to be made by everyone to build in quality. Quality is a stated management objective, which is known to the total workforce. Quality matters appear as the first item on agendas; quality requirements are firmly established before the first manufacturing and engineering activity has taken place; all subcontractors will come within the quality objectives.

Very significant gains are seen as a result of the quality improvement. Productivity increases, the order book grows. Satisfied customers tell potential customers about the quality of the product or service.

Quality is also good marketing. For example, American industry, particularly the car industry, has undergone an inquisition on the subject of poor quality. A study by the Ford Motor Company revealed that if the customer is happy with a product he is going to tell, on

average, 8 other people that he is really happy. The interesting thing
is, if he is not happy, he is going to tell 22 (Falotti, 1986).

Stage 5

Measurement category certainty arrives when quality becomes the
'ideas centre' of the company. Quality is everyone's total commitment.

W. E. Deming introduced the Japanese to statistical techniques in
1948. Together with Juran, they transformed the Japanese perspective
on quality. Deming, in particular, introduced them to data analysis
and simple analytical and statistical techniques. He also introduced the
Plan–Do–Check–Analyse approach. This is shown in Figure 19.2, and
is known to the Japanese as the Deming Circle. This approach urged

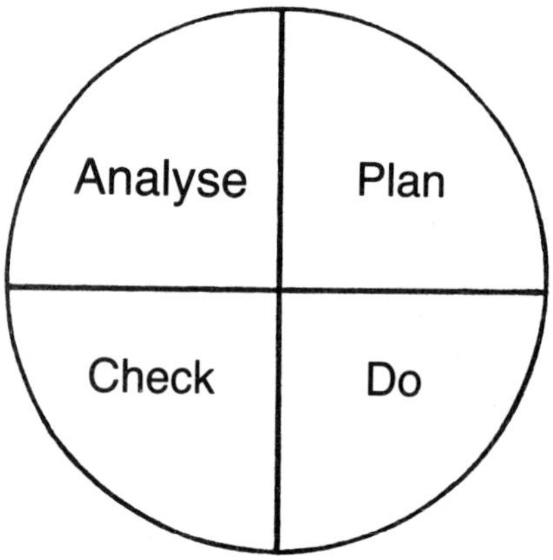

Figure 19.2.   The Deming circle.

that everyone learned a common method of describing and attacking
problems. This commonality is an absolute requirement if personnel
from different parts of the same company are to work together on
company-wide quality improvement. Thus when the executive audit
team or the company executive himself visits any of the company's
operations, there is a well established framework, the Deming Circle,
within which all parties can discuss problems and suggest
improvements.

This is in stark contrast to management by exception, described by
Tribus, where when things go wrong, the management have to try to
work out where it went wrong, why it went wrong and what they have
to do to correct it (Tribus, 1984). By subjecting each department,

activity and process to this common framework attention is focused on the problem area.

By the late 1960s, the data analysis and statistical techniques Deming introduced were upsetting the economy of the world. They demonstrated what could be achieved by the serious study and adoption of statistical techniques and the implementation of statistical logic in industry. It must, however, be at all levels of the company, from the chief executive downwards, be company-wide and within the framework of known policies and objectives.

Although statistical methods have wide applications, Deming (1967) argues that there is only one statistical theory. There is not a separate and distinct theory for process control, acceptance sampling, reliability, estimation, experimental design, material testing and engineering — there is only one statistical theory. That statistical theory, incorporating the statistical control of quality, is directed at the economic satisfaction of demand; it includes all aspects of the life cycle of the product (or service) from initial conception to operations and disposal, when all the data collected becomes part of a corporate database (Deming, 1975).

As Deming (1980) also points out, by doing 100 per cent testing, using automatic testing equipment, you cannot put quality into a process or product. Quality is either there to satisfy the economic demand of customers or it is not.

When applied comprehensively throughout a company, data analysis and statistical techniques can make a dramatic impact. A structured company-wide approach is needed incorporating all aspects of the company's functioning. It is pointless delegating the responsibility for the introduction of the techniques to the quality department. There must be company-wide organization, planning, communications and training.

To succeed this structured approach must be driven by all levels of management; the whole company must be committed. This means the management itself must understand the subject, be able to explain it to all workers and know how to introduce the techniques into the company.

Its introduction starts with an emphasis on what the customer wants, then how it is to be specified, then the company's ability to produce and control the product or service and its continuing quality.

To Deming the most important part of the production line is the customer. However, the 1986/87 European ISO Quality Vocabulary

International Standards Organization 1987 standard defines quality as:

> the totality of features and characteristics of a product or service that bear
> on its ability to satisfy stated or implied needs.

This definition hardly touches Deming's customer-driven approach,
which requires that quality be company-wide with the appropriate
management–worker–customer common policies and objectives.
Although the above definition of quality is not satisfactory, a draft
British Standard, BS4891 is being prepared to address company-wide
quality. To quote Deming (1986):

> It will not suffice to have customers that are merely satisfied. An unhappy
> customer will switch. Unfortunately, a satisfied customer may also switch,
> on the theory that he could not lose much, and might gain. Profit in
> business comes from repeat customers, customers that boast about your
> products and service, and that bring friends with them.

Deming also speaks frequently on the need for staying ahead of the
customer. The customer does not know what he will need one, three,
five years from now. If you, as the supplier, wait till then to find out,
you will hardly be ready to serve him. Only if the quality approach is
company-wide can sales and marketing report meaningfully what
customers want, or think they want; only then can research and
development have prototyped potential products to satisfy stated or
implied customer needs; only then can management have done the
appropriate planning for the introduction of programmable automation, retooling, new suppliers and retraining.

There is a systems approach underlying all of Deming's thinking.
This is noticed as early as July 1950. Thus there was a:

> chain reaction . . . [which] . . . was on the blackboard of every meeting with
> top management in Japan from July 1950 onward (Deming, 1986).

This chain reaction is summed up in Figure 19.3.

A central thesis of Deming is that productivity improvement must
begin with attention to quality (Deming, 1982, 1986). The reasoning,
supported by the empirical data from Japan's economic growth, is as
follows:

1. As a starting point you need stability (lack of variation) of products
    and personnel.

Costs decrease because of
less rework, fewer
Improve ⟶ mistakes, fewer delays, ⟶ Productivity
quality snags; better use of improves
machine-time and
materials

Capture the
market with better ⟶ Stay in ⟶ Provide jobs
quality and lower business and more jobs
price

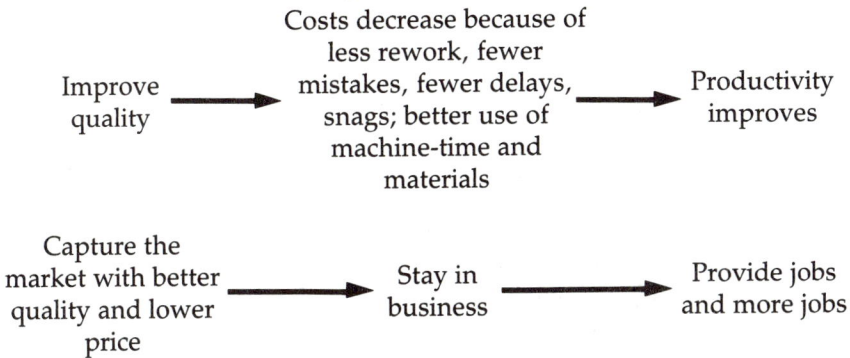

Figure 19.3.   The chain reaction.

2. Stability gives management and workers increasing control over
   the manufacturing environment.
3. With control you can start to keep consistently collected records,
   for comparison and contrast, using various statistical techniques.
4. With such records you can begin to isolate and measure areas of
   malfunction.
5. Measurement enables you to identify 'leverage points' so that
   improvements can be applied to these malfunctioning areas.
6. Leverage point improvement then increases quality.
7. Only with increased quality can you get an improvement in
   productivity.
8. Only with increased productivity can you improve your price
   competitiveness in the commercial world.

What European and American companies have to do is well known.
The information, techniques, methods and policies are available in the
public domain, from many sources and countries, mostly Japan and
the US. We have to learn not only from our own mistakes, but from
others in related situations. Deming has developed 14 points for the
transformation of industrial quality. These are listed in Figure 19.4.

The Deming philosophy can be summarized as an equilateral
triangle, Figure 19.5. It is also known as the Joiner triangle and is
described in Chapter 20 (Joiner, 1988). This representation shows
quality as the apex, achieved by the coalescence of two forces: total
teamwork and the 'scientific approach'. The scientific approach
requires understanding of the nature of variation, particularly its
division into controlled and uncontrolled variation due to

1. Create constancy of purpose toward improvement of product and service, with the aim to become competitive and to stay in business, and to provide jobs.
2. Adopt the new philosophy. We are in a new economic age. Western management must awaken to the challenge, must learn their responsibilities, and take on leadership for change.
3. Cease dependence on inspection to achieve quality. Eliminate the need for inspection on a mass basis by building quality into the product in the first place.
4. End the practice of awarding business on the basis of price tag. Instead, minimize total cost. Move toward a single supplier for any one item, on a long-term relationship of loyalty and trust.
5. Improve constantly and forever the system of production and service, to improve quality and productivity, and thus constantly decrease costs.
6. Institute training on the job.
7. Institute leadership. The aim of leadership should be to help people and machines and gadgets to do a better job. Leadership of management is in need of overhaul, as well as leadership of production workers.
8. Drive out fear, so that everyone may work effectively for the company.
9. Break down barriers between departments. People in research, design, sales and production must work as a team, to foresee problems of production and in use that may be encountered with the product or service.
10. Eliminate slogans, exhortations and targets for the work force asking for zero defects and new levels of productivity. Such exhortations only create adversarial relationships, as the bulk of the causes of low quality and low productivity belong to the system and thus lie beyond the power of the work force.
11. (a) Eliminate work standards (quotas) on the factory floor. Substitute leadership. (b) Eliminate management by objective. Eliminate management by numbers, numerical goals. Substitute leadership.
12. (a) Remove barriers that rob the hourly worker of his right to pride of workmanship. The responsibility of supervisors must be changed from sheer numbers to quality. (b) Remove barriers that rob people in management and in engineering of their right to pride of workmanship. This means, *inter alia*, abolishment of the annual or merit rating and of management by objective.
13. Institute a vigorous program of education and self-improvement.
14. Put everybody in the company to work to accomplish the transformation. The transformation is everybody's job.

Figure 19.4. Deming's 14 points for the transformation of industrial quality.

management-controllable common and worker-controllable special causes.

It is only by management and workers correctly diagnosing the most important sources of variation, and then reducing or even eliminating them, that quality (reliability, consistency, predictability, dependability) can be improved. The scientific approach calls for decision-making and policy-making on the basis of solid information, both numerical and non-numerical and not by 'gut feel', opinion or mere short term considerations.

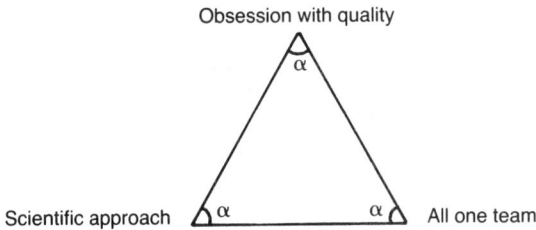

Figure 19.5.   The Deming philosophy.

It includes the use of data collection and analysis and statistical techniques — but also knowledge and understanding of their limitations and awareness of the crucial importance of phenomena which cannot be quantified. These phenomena are Deming's seven 'deadly diseases' of Western management (Deming, 1986). They are listed in Figure 19.6.

Deming frequently quotes Dr Lloyd Nelson, Director of Statistical Methods for the Nashua Corporation:

> The most important figures needed for management of any organization are unknown and unknowable.

Those who find this statement surprising have not begun to understand Deming's teachings. All our calculations, business policies and decisions have to begin with assumptions and incomplete data. Some assumptions, however, are more soundly based than others since there are variation records and data to support our decision. They are statistically under control. This encourages constancy of purpose and long term planning.

Figures which are usually unknown are the costs of quality, reworks, warranty claims, concessions. Figures which are unknowable concern people — being able to take a pride in their work, being motivated and loyal, doing the job well and keeping the customer delighted.

1. Lack of constancy of purpose to plan product and service that will have a market and keep the company in business, and provide jobs.

2. Emphasis on short term profits: short term thinking (just the opposite from constancy of purpose to stay in business), fed by fear of unfriendly takeover, and by push from bankers and owners for dividends.

3. Personal review system, or evaluation of performance, merit rating, annual review, or annual appraisal, by whatever name, for people in management, the effects of which are devastating. Management by objective, on a go, no-go basis, without a method for accomplishment of the objective, is the same thing by another name. Even management by fear would be better.

4. Mobility of management: job hopping.

5. Use of visible figures only for management, with little or no consideration of figures that are unknown or unknowable.

6. Excessive medical costs.

7. Excessive costs of liability, fuelled by lawyers that work on contingency fees.

Figure 19.6.   Deming's seven deadly diseases of Western management.

The Taylor command and control management style (see Chapter 20) renders genuine teamwork almost impossible, as does management by results, annual performance appraisals and the use of arbitrary numerical goals and targets — all of which foster competition and conflict between company personnel and sometimes between whole departments, as opposed to their working together for the true benefit of the company.

Several well-intentioned quality improvement notions can constitute similarly serious obstacles if not all embracing within the company as a system: examples are cost of quality and Crosby's zero defects (Crosby, 1984). Concepts which are essentially beneficial can do more harm than good if used in an unsuitable environment: these include quality circles and just-in-time (JIT) systems.

JIT depends on zero defects; the production line must be continuous and not stop–start. That can only happen, however, when the total management approach is that of an integrated system, with known policies and procedures, operating within statistical control limits.

The true comprehension of Deming's message is when he talks of the need for the total transformation of Western style managements

— and he means it! To conclude this chapter, here is a final quotation, a stark warning from Deming's book *Out of the Crisis* (1986). This is a short section entitled simply 'Survival of the Fittest':

> Who will survive? Companies that adopt constancy of purpose for quality, productivity, and service, and go about it with intelligence and perseverance, have a chance to survive. They must, of course, offer products and services that have a market. Charles Darwin's law of survival of the fittest, and that the unfit do not survive, holds in free enterprise as well as in natural selection. It is a cruel law, unrelenting.
>
> Actually, the problem will solve itself. The only survivors will be companies with constancy of purpose for quality, productivity, and service.

In this chapter we have outlined what quality has come to mean in the late 1980s and the thinking of the experts behind it. New company-wide quality policies, procedures and techniques, to integrate management, workers and customers, have come to the fore and are still in rapid evolution. The next chapter will look at some of the day-to-day activities, methods and techniques used to implement this rapid quality evolution.

Further reading

Craig, W., 'Management Commitment to Quality: Hewlett-Packard Company', *Quality Progress*, 1983, Vol XVI, issue 8, August pp. 22–24.

Crosby, P.B., *Quality is Free*, Mentor, New American Library, New York, 1979.

Crosby, P.B., *Quality Without Tears*, McGraw-Hill Book Co., New York, 1984.

Deming, W.E., 'What Happened in Japan', *Industrial Quality Control*, 1967, Vol. 24, No. 2, August, p. 91.

Deming, W.E., 'My View of Quality Control in Japan', *Reports of Statistical Application Research*, 1975a, Vol. 22, No. 2, p. 77.

Deming, W.E., 'On Some Statistical Aids Towards Economic Production', *Interfaces*, 1975b, Vol. 5, No. 4, August, p. 8.

Deming, W.E., 'It Does Work', *Quality*, 1980, Vol. 19, issue 8, August, p. 31, (pp. Q26–Q31).

Deming, W.E., *Quality, Productivity and Competitive Position*, MIT Press, Massachusetts 1982.

Deming, W.E., *Out of the Crisis*, MIT Press, Massachusetts, 1986.

Falotti, P.C., Opening Address on Quality, Second European Quality Symposium, Digital Equipment Corporation (DEC), 1986, February.

Gottlieb, D., 'The Outlook Interview: W. Edwards Deming, US Guru to Japanese Industry, talks to Daniel Gottlieb, *The Washington Post*, 1975, 15 January.

Hall, R.W., *Attaining Manufacturing Excellence*, Dow Jones – Irwin, Chicago, 1987.

Hayes, R.H. and Jaikumar, R., 'Manufacturing's Crisis: New Technologies, Obsolete Organizations'. *Harvard Business Review*, 1988, Vol. 66, issue 5, September–October, pp. 77–85.

Hiromoto, T., 'Another Hidden Edge — Japanese Management Accounting', *Harvard Business Review*, 1988, Vol. 66, issue 4, July–August, pp. 22–6.

Institute of Electrical and Electronics Engineers, *IEEE Spectrum*, 1987, May. A special edition devoted to designing successful systems in the 1990s.

International Standards Organization (ISO), *Quality Systems BS 5750/ ISO9000, parts 0, 1, 2 and 3*, British Standards Institution, Milton Keynes, United Kingdom, 1987.

International Standards Organization, *Quality Vocabulary*, BS 4778, Part 1, International Terms ISO 8402-1986. British Standards Institution, Milton Keynes, United Kingdom, 1987.

Ishikawa, K., 'Quality Control in Japan,' *13th International Association of Quality*, 1978, Kyoto, Japan.

Ishikawa, K., *What is Total Quality Control? The Japanese Way*, Prentice Hall, Englewood Cliffs, New Jersey, 1985.

Japanese Union of Scientists and Engineers, (JUSE) 'General Principles of the QC Circles', *QC Circle Koryo*, 1980, Tokyo.

Joiner Associates Inc. *The Team Handbook: How to Use Teams to Improve Quality*, Joiner Associates Inc., Madison, Wisconsin, 1988. An excellent account of how to use the Deming philosophy in anger.

Juran, J.M., 'Quality Problems, Remedies and Nostrums', *Industrial Quality Control*, 1966, Vol. 22, No. 12, pp. 647–53.

Juran, J.M., 'Product Quality — A Prescription for the West: (Part 1) Training and Improvement Programs', *Management Review*, 1981a, July.

Juran, J.M., 'Product Quality — A Prescription for the West: (Part 2) Upper Management Leadership and Employee Relations, *Management Review*, 1981b, July.

Kaplan, R., 'Yesterday's Accounting Undermines Production',

Harvard Business Review, 1984, Vol. 62, issue 4, July–August, pp. 95–101.

Lorenz, C., 'Management: Seizing the Initiative in a Struggle for Survival — the Product Race', *The Financial Times*, 1987, 17 June, then a series of 6 weekly articles starting on 19 June.

Sandholm, L., 'Japanese Quality Circles — A Remedy for the West's Quality Problems?' *Quality Progress*, 1983, February, pp. 20–3.

Sandholm, L., 'Quality Overview', *Quality Department Lecture Series*, Westinghouse Defense and Electronics Center, 1983b, May.

Schonberger, R.J., *World Class Manufacturing: The Lessons of Simplicity Applied*, The Free Press, Macmillan Inc., New York, 1986.

Takeuchi, H. and Nonaka, I., 'The New Product Development Game', *Harvard Business Review*, 1986, Vol. 64, issue 1, January–February, pp. 137–46.

Tribus, M., 'Prize-winning Japanese Firms' Quality Management Programs Pass Inspection', *Management Review*, February, 1984.

20 Quality Improvement Activities and Techniques

John Edge

As both Deming and Drucker have pointed out, the only long term aim of any company is to survive. Those companies most likely to survive will have learnt from the experts and challenged assumptions. They will have a total commitment to quality.

With overcapacity, global competition and new standards of manufacturing efficiency, companies need a new start — with a blank piece of paper. To compete successfully in their global market four conditions now need to be satisfied: quality and cost are necessary but not sufficient conditions; variety of products and time of production are the extra dimensions.

These requirements of quality, cost, flexibility and responsiveness are incompatible in the traditional manufacturing environment: in the new they are not. What then must the manufacturing organization do to survive? By making the shop floor the centre of attention, and tapping the potential of the workforce, their full creativity is engaged; and survival is enhanced.

This is the new manufacturing, explicitly encouraging people to contribute, whereas the old minimized their role. The new requires the right mix and balance of a people based organization, supported by appropriate programmable automation.

Involving people: quality and project improvement teams

Quality is not free. Quality experts estimate the cost at between 5 and 25 per cent of revenues in a typical company. The exorbitant cost of quality shows up in many ways — too many inspectors, excessive product engineering and redesign, product returns, price concessions, high service costs, inventory waste, supplier returns, manufacturing slowdowns, loss of market share. The list goes on.

If 25 per cent of revenue is literally given away each year, because of costs related directly to quality, it is no wonder the issue has captured the attention of managements throughout the world.

The traditional ways of 'controlling' quality simply are no longer sufficient, since they call for control at levels that are currently profit-draining and unacceptable, in a rapidly changing world.

The Juran approach urges companies to 'break the chain of the past' and reach improved quality levels, on a continuous basis (Juran, 1964, 1980, 1987).

Juran describes the management 'breakthrough' as the 'organized creation of beneficial change'. It is this organized, step-by-step approach to creating the management breakthrough that is the hallmark of the Juran quality improvement process. Juran teaches that quality improvement is not a one-off process. To attack these quality problems successfully, organizations must develop the attitude of creating annual improvements year after year after year. It is an attitude that refuses to accept today's quality levels as good enough.

The quality improvement effort must go on forever, and become formalized into the company's planning and operational practices, just like the corporate budget, the product development schedule and the annual marketing plan.

Every worthwhile corporate effort must begin with a quantified objective. Juran suggests that a reasonable company objective is to cut the costs of poor quality in half over a period of five years. This means cutting in two the field failure rates, the internal waste and all other similar costs of poor quality.

The prime objective of the Juran quality improvement process is to help the company's management team develop the habit of annual quality improvements and the annual reduction in quality-related costs. A further objective is that of training the management team in the special quality-oriented concepts, tools, techniques and skills that are essential to the habit of continual quality improvement.

To attain these objectives, the Juran process calls for the establishment of quality improvement project teams, starting at the top of the company with a senior management level quality team. In addition, because most quality problems are interdepartmental, the team approach helps all participants perfect the habit of tackling problems on a team basis, placing the emphasis on the solution, and not on politics or blame.

A company cannot make annual quality improvements unless the members of the senior management team themselves make annual improvement. The Juran process, therefore, starts at the top of the company.

The programme proposes that all members of the senior management team, without exception, accept the concept of annual quality improvements as a way of life for the future. In most companies, this concept is a radical departure from past practice. New management priorities, therefore, need to be established and new habits learned.

This radical departure, from the usual lack of senior management involvement, proposed by the Juran programme is that each member of the senior management personally engages in the quality improvement process. This has the effect of raising the quality improvement projects to a level of priority paralleling that of the company balancing its books.

In fact, Juran proposes that the first quality improvement project be undertaken by a team consisting of the senior managers of the company. Their project will be more strategic and far-reaching than the projects at the day-to-day operational management levels. But this first hands-on senior management involvement is integral to the Juran quality improvement process. It sends very strong signals throughout the company that senior management is committed.

Project teams are the nerve centre. Typically, a quality steering council is created, comprising key members of the senior management team and other key team participants. The steering council determines the broad policy for the quality improvement programmes, determines how the appropriate training will be implemented throughout all levels of the company and drives the management project teams to begin the improvement process.

The teams can use Juran's quality improvement guides in the selection of potentially rewarding projects, and in the implementation of the breakthrough process. A typical project team meets weekly, for about three months, and should arrive at a quality improvement solution. Once a team is finished, it is dismissed and a new one formed to define and tackle another quality improvement project. This process is repeated. In large companies, it is not uncommon to have dozens of quality improvement team projects going on simultaneously.

In this new company environment, virtually everyone works on quality improvement during the course of a year. An entire organization is working together to improve the quality of every aspect of the organization — manufacturing, marketing, finance, engineering, customer service.

Through the savings that result from the quality improvement projects, the results are tangible. However, the intangible results are equally as powerful. People work together towards a distinctly more common and positive goal. Management at all levels develop a far more effective method of working together as a team. As all managers strive for improved quality and increased efficiency, the effective management span of control increases knowing that all levels of management have the same objectives.

Involving people: quality circles

Participative quality programmes must take into account the role of people, their aspirations, skills and responsibilities, and encourage their creative involvement. This runs counter to the traditional manufacturing approach.

The traditional approach is often called 'Taylorism' after F. W. Taylor (1856-1915), the American engineer who, through workshop management, pioneered scientific management. The only real model available to Taylor was the command and control one, from the army, with responsibilities and authorities handed down and never up the chain of command. This model required that personnel tasks be broken down into their smallest elements; wherever possible, little skill was required to handle these small tasks. No decisions had to be made and tasks were reduced to a series of operations or steps, which were the same, again and again for each series of operations. Once the steps have been learned personnel involvement ends; there is no involvement other than routine machine-like repetition.

Management priorities are usually very different from those of the worker reduced to 'a cog in a wheel' or a 'payroll number'. Management does the planning of all the tasks to be performed in the context of the overall commercial enterprise. The workers then do the operations required by the planning activities. Next managers check to see that the steps have been performed correctly. Finally, any discrepancies between the planning–doing–checking activities are corrected by management problem solving. Management control, supported by appropriate specialists (e.g. work study) make all the decisions and solve all the problems. The worker has no decision-making or problem-solving role. These distinctions became part of the organization of companies in general and manufacturing more specifically.

This organizational approach was introduced into Japan in the aftermath of the Second World War. By the early 1950s the Japanese economy was in a mess, with serious labour alienation. The Japanese had experienced the negative effects of Taylorism (i.e. low motivation and job interest, absenteeism) and not its positive effects (i.e. cheap and plentiful products) as had Europe and America. The Japanese identified Taylorism with their weakened economy, falling exports and labour unrest. They were the first nation to appreciate the need to break the organizational mould.

A new approach was required: a management approach was sought that combined all the benefits of Taylorism with all the benefits of a motivated and proud craft worker. These advantages and disadvantages have been succinctly stated by Hutchins (1986) and are shown in Figure 20.1.

The new management approach must combine the benefits of both and avoid their disadvantages. This is achieved by bringing the concept of craftmanship to a group of workers, rather than individuals. Rather than an individual being responsible and having job control, the group as a team combine skills. The team acts like the craftsman, being responsible for its work and controlling its own performance.

In essence this is what quality circles are about — people-based organizations. If managed properly, from them there should be a ripple effect through the whole organization. Under Taylorism the supervisor himself becomes semi-skilled; with the craftsmanship approach the supervisor becomes the head of the team, since he is the most skilled.

The supervisor is the crucial link between management and the craft team. Initially the supervisors need to be educated and trained, and the training should be continuous — it is not a one-off exercise. Good supervisors, like good managers, never cease to learn new methods and techniques, from one another, from members of the craft team and

(a)   Advantages and disadvantages of Taylorism.

Advantages	Disadvantages
• High productivity at low cost • Interchangeability of items • Low skill workers • Lower wage costs/unit • Accurate forecasting • Predictable results • Sophisticated, highly trained problem solvers • High wages	• Control by others • Low worker morale caused by frustration, boredom, low self-confidence of the worker • Poor quality, absenteeism, lack of job pride, alienation • Poor company image reflected by workers who interface with customer • No opportunity for self-development • Supervisory problems • Loyalty of specialist to specialism rather than to the employer

(b)   Advantages and disadvantages of craftsmanship.

Advantages	Disadvantages
• Self-control • Pride in work • Self-confidence/self-assurance • Loyalty to the work • Sense of responsibility • Motivated and involved • Good quality workmanship • Self-improving • High level of job interest • 'Unique' product	• High cost of labour • Low output per individual • Low interchangeability of items • 'Unique' product • Scheduling difficulties • Monitoring problems leading to poor control • Low wages

Figure 20.1.   Advantages and disadvantages of Taylorism and craftmanship (Hutchins, 1986).

management.

Under the Taylor system the supervisor was often replaced by a specialist from outside the organization, or a buffer middle management was introduced, or control was induced by payment-by-results schemes. A communications gap developed between workers and management and was only bridged when the trained craft supervisor became the link again between management and the craft team. With this bridge, communications up and down the company organization became possible. The creative talents of those on the shop floor could reach upper management, via the highly skilled supervisor; corporate policies and objectives likewise were conveyed to the craft team.

There is thus a constant cross-fertilization of ideas. Education and training never cease: job self-improvement and knowledge grow for everyone in the craft team — if they do not, morale will remain low. Management, therefore, must ensure that the idea of self-responsibility and self-accountability reach to every member of every team. This is reinforced by the team's supervisor, through his own education and training, being able to train his own group. Only he can train them, not an outside specialist. It must be further reinforced by management making clear statements of policies and objectives, by making information and data available to the craft teams. '. . . in other words management must treat the groups (craft teams) in the same way as it treats managers at other levels' (Hutchins, 1986).

A comparison of suggestion schemes and quality circles

Any serious quality commitment is forever. All programmes run out of steam. One key to the success of Toyota, Japan's most quality conscious company, has been its suggestion scheme. From very small beginnings, 5000 suggestions in 1960, the scheme in the mid 1980s was bringing in over 1 900 000 suggestions. Of these 95 per cent were implemented, with each worker making over 32 suggestions. That is people participation! (Cusumano, 1985)

Many companies run suggestion schemes. In the US, companies often run Scanlon-type gain or profit sharing schemes (Lawler and Mohrman, 1985). Here the department as a whole rather than the company gains any bonuses based on improved performance. There are often hierarchies of committees, so that problems which can't be solved are passed to higher management. Those which can be solved are often implemented only in the department concerned, since this is the extent of the Scanlon-type group authority.

Suggestion schemes and quality circles are not in conflict. The former do not require special training from participants. They are cheap to run. Suggestions are often evaluated by a committee and either an individual or group rewarded. It is important, however, that there is feedback on suggestions.

Quality circles need company time — often with suggestion schemes an idea is simply written down and dropped into a box. Circles will also require training, as will the circle's facilitator; that again means expenditure to the company. Circles are limited to solving one problem at a time, whereas schemes are usually department based. Nevertheless the two approaches do work. Loyalty to a circle or department profit scheme each requires that management has confidence and trust in both.

Presentations and publicity

Presentations to management of a team's or circle's solutions are a very good mechanism for fostering commitment and cooperation between management and workers.

When the work activity is completed, with data collected and analysed, and solutions confirmed, the workers should be encouraged to present their work findings to their management and to others, especially where they have tackled a specific problem relevant to others.

Managements should never try to undermine the presentations; these are the climax of the work effort. Presentations are used to:

1. Allow management to judge for itself the advantages of allowing workers to use their initiative expertise and knowledge in problem solving.
2. Enable management to recognize the achievements of the workers and to give them recognition.
3. Encourage the participation message to gain wider acceptance throughout the company by regular meetings and discussions, by which ideas can be exchanged.
4. Free workers to solve problems and then to allow them to implement their solutions. When this happens there is management–worker commitment and cooperation.

It is important that adequate training be given to those making the presentations, so that it can be done professionally. Presenters need, therefore, to be able to use the terminology which management understands, i.e. impact on schedules, cost implications and improvements, and quality implications and improvements.

Managers are not under any obligation to accept any aspects of the workers' activities even though the workers should be able to give alternatives in the language of management. However, as they will be aware of the problems being tackled, it is unlikely that the results will be totally unacceptable in an environment of management–worker commitment and cooperation.

Publicity is a powerful way of influencing people's attitudes. It can be used to establish the need for change. IBM have used publicity as part of their quality communication message (Ogilvie, 1987). Posters and newspapers highlighted the necessity for teamwork and customer satisfaction. Others equated the skills of the craftsman with inhouse manufacturing skills, with the theme 'Quality is in our hands'.

The factory as a people-driven system

As General Motors management has found, no world class manufacturing company can attribute its success to advanced technology alone (Caulkins, 1989). To succeed, any company must manage its information flows and information content, layout and format. Information is a resource just like a machine tool or a valve. To survive, companies must be able to manage their information resources and use those resources to their competitive advantage (Matsudaira, 1987).

Information, however, is only of value to people, whether management or worker, whether it is produced automatically or manually. People are the essence of the situation. They must have ready access to reliable and accurate information and have the organizational scope to act on it. Their total involvement, therefore, at all stages of manufacturing is demanded if the factory is to use the information it produces competitively. This information must embrace: manpower, machines, methods and materials (Ishikawa's '4 Ms' — see later) and the company environment. This is the factory as an integrated system. This approach is found in Deming's work as early as 1950.

The notion of information as a resource, like quality, must be company-wide to be of maximum value. Once management have gone through the frugal manufacturing phase, (see KISS — Keep it simple silly — later) simplified, reorganized and accurately defined their commercial objectives, introduced company-wide information resourcing and quality, then and only then should programmable automation be considered, from the perspective of the factory as a system.

There are fundamentally two approaches to manufacturing: one-at-a-time or mass production. Both are consistent approaches that can produce a high quality product. The difference resides in the fact that mass production offers speed and lower costs. In addition workers can easily be trained and put into production. On the other hand, the one-at-a-time approach is slower and usually has higher costs. It requires workers to be intimate with all aspects of the product.

Either way, those involved in programmable automation have to be totally integrated into the factory as a system. They too are involved in an engineering, manufacturing and commercial enterprise. The computer experts have to be trained to think like engineers and architects, rather than analysts and programmers. Only a company-wide approach to resourcing and quality, driven by management, can make this happen.

There are many similarities between the requirements of those involved in manufacturing systems and those of computer-based information systems. Figure 20.2 shows a typical manufacturing company. To establish a manufacturing environment, three elements are required: assembly lines, materials management and production control. These three elements form the 'critical checks and balances' needed to make a product (see Figure 20.3).

The manufacturing assembly line consists of a series of workstations where parts of a product are assembled in an organized manner. This is analogous to a methodology with defined phases of work, which is common in many approaches to computerization. See, for example, Computer Sciences Corporation, Digital Systems Development Methodology (1989) and M. Bryce Associates' PRIDE Development Methodology (1988).

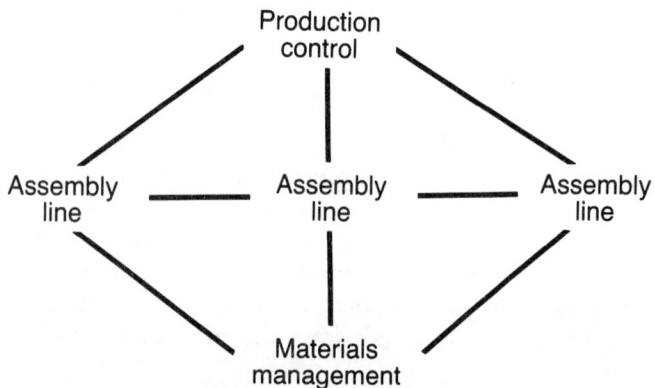

Figure 20.2.   Typical manufacturing company.

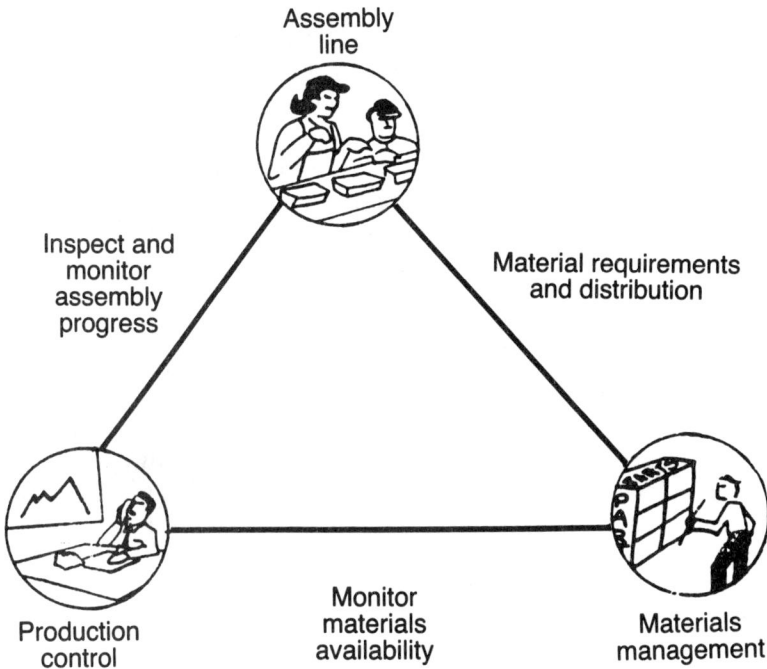

Figure 20.3. **Checks and balances in manufacturing a product.**

Production control is responsible for monitoring and inspecting the progress of the assembly lines and the availability of materials. Corrective action is initiated if any problems arise. This is the project management; by the method it is integrated into the manufacturing processes.

Materials management is responsible for supplying the assembly lines with the necessary parts. When developing or modifying the product they are also consulted in order to make available the required materials. This is analogous to data and information management, where both are controlled and reused.

A manufacturing organization of this type is 'held' together by the information derived from its computer-controlled processes, into a system. Only people can act on information. Management needs therefore to impose responsibilities and accountabilities across the organization to make the system work economically. Only management using a people-based method, with known common procedures, objectives and company-wide policies can bring about the integration of information, and the 4Ms within the total company environment, including suppliers, distributors and customers.

A people-based method cannot be imposed top–down, since management often lack the detailed technical knowledge and the cooperation of the shop floor is required. It can only be achieved, not by a once and for all upheaval, but by a constant process of continuous improvement, with teams gathering data and measurements being made, involving every aspect of the organization and all levels and types of management and workers.

Keep it simple silly (KISS)

It used to be said that the best way for companies to get value for money from programmable automation was for management to undertake all the necessary reorganization and then forget about the computers. Two of the computer manufacturers, IBM and Hewlett-Packard have realized this; IBM now integrate people's skills and improve staff motivation. Computers on the shop floor have not improved manufacturing economics (Caulkins, 1989).

Companies are moving towards real-time manufacturing. A Japanese shoe manufacturer has installed laser measuring equipment in shoe shops, which transfer information back to the factory so that it can then automatically make up the made-to-measure shoes overnight. Their secret lies not in programmable automation but in a simple truth. Computers in manufacturing are only really useful to manufacturers which are efficient already. For companies which do the simple things well, computers can further speed the manufacturing cycle. For those that have been persuaded by simplistic slogans to automate themselves out of inefficiency, they can be disastrous.

John Deere and Caterpillar, two large and powerful US companies tried to move direct to programmable automation — and only started recovering when they radically scaled down their automation attempts in favour of simpler manufacturing solutions (The Yankee Group, 1988). Raleigh, the United Kingdom cycle manufacturer computerized its manufacturing resource planning system to control inventory and speed throughout. The system was so complex that an untrained shopfloor took elaborate pains to circumvent it and the company verged on bankruptcy.

Managers welcome the advent of cheaper programmable automation in factories in the belief that it will help them manage ever increasing complexity. In fact, much of the complexity which firms think they need programmable automation to handle, is not God-given, but self-inflicted. Their products are too complicated and contain too many parts produced by too many suppliers. They are manufactured on systems yielding varying results. Instead of trying to compute the problems away, a better solution is to reduce the part count by designing for manufacture, cultivating long term relationships with the very best of the supplier base and reorganizing the factory into cells or flow lines.

The tragedy of the computerized approach to factory problems is that it treats conditions as immutable, whereas in many cases they are not. Rather than reducing waste, a computerized approach adds to it by burdening an already inefficient system with the cost of computerization.

The idea of waste is the key to the new manufacturing. It involves distinguishing between value-adding and non-value-adding elements, and progressively eliminating the latter. The aim is continuous self-improvement in order to do constantly more with less: better quality with fewer quality controllers, more accounting with fewer accountants, more throughput using less time, less capital, less factory space and less unnecessary programmable automation. This is not as impossible as it sounds. As the Japanese quickly discovered, simplicity, like complexity, is a self-reinforcing spiral — only benevolent rather than vicious.

After the Second World War, Japan had nothing: no raw materials, no capital equipment and, most crucially of all, no industrial workforce. Instead of attacking industrial problems in the Western manner, by throwing money at them, they were forced to use brains: to adapt conventional cheap machinery to individual purposes, to use systems so simple that they could be understood by an uneducated and unskilled workforce, and above all to eschew waste. (See Schonberger, 1986, and Hall, 1987).

Take a simple example. At Toyota engineers cut the time taken to exchange dies on presses from hours to minutes, eventually aiming at one-touch exchanges of dies. Set-up times became minimal, allowing smaller batch sizes. The smaller the batches, the fewer parts needed to be stored, which meant that less time was needed in tracking them and the parts spent less time waiting. When the batch size was finally reduced to one, so that work was passed directly from one workstation to the next, there was no buffer inventory at all.

There were, in consequence, no fork-lift trucks, progress chasers or stores, and a smaller factory. There was also no complicated tracking system to tell people what to do next — just a card or a token to signal when the next part was due. The second result was that Toyota did not need complex and expensive computer-controlled machining centres to achieve flexibility. It could use specially modified conventional machines which were cheaper and more robust.

Consider General Motors, the greatest automation spender of all. Its most modern plants are being outperformed by its ageing unautomated Californian plant — which is a joint venture with Toyota!! (Caulkins, 1989)

In the United Kingdom, Lucas Diesel at Sudbury, found that they did not need expensive capital investment or advanced technology to turn the company round. They needed rigorous but simple management thinking and reorganization (Jones, 1988). Sudbury's key decision was to simplify. Internally, it broke the organization down into three mini-factories, each building a coherent family (in production terms) of parts. Changes in management and personnel mirrored those of the factory layout. Managers now ran each product line as a separate business, and within those, each cell had its own performance responsibilities. The seven management layers came down to three. At the same time, job specifications at the manufacturing level were completely rewritten to support the transformation of the workforce from the human robots of the past, to participative problem solvers, moving flexibly both within cells and across them.

Frugal manufacturing is the new manufacturing management starting method. This approach quickly identifies areas which can be simplified. Before the introduction of top–down or islands of manufacturing programmable automation, it is essential that product design and factory organization assumptions be questioned, and new methods and people-based aproaches thought through. When this is done and implemented successfully, management can consider the introduction of programmable automation.

There are three rival methods of speeding the raw material and product flow towards the completed product. There are two complex computer-based approaches, manufacturing resources planning and optimized production technology. Then there is just-in-time (JIT).

JIT is starkly simple conceptually. Its origins are also Japanese — with an unskilled workforce the most simple methods were necessary. JIT removes buffer stocks between workstations. JIT exposes obstacles to smoother and smoother manufacturing flows. Every workstation is turned into a supplier and a customer. There is instant feedback on quality and quantity; otherwise the production line stops. Quality and productivity are knitted together in a process of self-improvement.

JIT is a potent force in reorganization. It demands simplifications of physical layout and considerably simplified management structures to match. Traditional machine shops and tortuous product routes, are being replaced by workstation factories — workstations within workstations, reinforcing personnel and departmental integration.

For an excellent account of the KISS approach, and other factors affecting quality, see Peters (1988).

People-driven product development

International competition means that companies must be able to perform well in terms of product flexibility and response times in addition to quality and cost. The thinking behind quality circles and the team approach is vital for product flexibility and response times. Several studies have indicated the benefits of the participative approach. Takeuchi and Nonaka examined new product development approaches of Fuji-Xerox, Canon, Honda, NEC, Epson, Brother, The 3M Company, Xerox and Hewlett-Packard (see Takeuchi, 1986).

Companies are realizing increasingly that the old sequential approach to developing new products will not get the job done in a competitive and evolving world. Instead, companies in Japan and the US are using a holistic method, as in a ball game where the ball gets passed as the team moves up the field as a unit. This approach has been found to have six characteristics.

1. *Built-in instability* Upper management offers the development team a wide measure of freedom but establishes extremely challenging goals; for example at Fuji-Xerox, to produce a radically different copier, at half the cost of its most expensive copiers, which would perform equally as well, but within 2 years.
2. *Self-organizing teams* There should be limited involvement by top management. The team sets its own direction and is virtually autonomous. The teams were found to be steadily increasing their own performance and pushing R&D and technology to the limits. Teams consisted of members from varying specializations and backgrounds, including R&D, engineering, manufacturing and sales. This resulted in the cross-fertilization of ideas, especially with all the team working in the same room.
3. *Overlapping development phases* The self-organizing teams created rhythms, of the group as a whole and its individual members. This drove the team and its members forward, as a unit. Outside

suppliers were invited to be part of the team and information flows were kept open at all times. This unified approach smoothed out the bottlenecks of the separated phase method. Continuity was maintained; the overlapping enhanced the sharing of responsibilities and cooperation; involvement and commitment grew with concentrated problem solving efforts. The division of labour, part of managements' practices in the phased method, was removed: there was a continuous continuity of purpose.

4. *Multilearning* Since all the team members were in close touch every day, they could easily disseminate new ideas and respond to changing requirements in the marketplace. The members' skills grew and they became versatile problem solvers. The desire to learn spread throughout the teams and helped create company-wide corporate learning. Multilearning became part of the company's human resource management programmes, and served as the basis for organizational transition.

5. *Subtle control* Although the teams were largely free from top management involvement and had freedom of direction and creativity, they were expected to exercise self-control. They had common values and objectives; there were peer responsibilities and accountabilities; evaluation and rewards were made on a group basis; mistakes were anticipated and tolerated.

6. *Transfer of learning* The desire to accumulate knowledge is only one aspect of learning. Team members also had very strong desires to transfer that learning to others outside of the team. Thus new product development teams were kept abreast of the latest ideas, techniques and methods. By a process of osmosis, knowledge was transmitted across the whole company, with teams learning from one another. These new ideas, techniques and methods often become company policy. Old organizational structures and attitudes were broken down, as the company environment became more responsive to change and the need for market flexibility.

The six pieces fit together like a jigsaw puzzle, forming a fast and flexible process for new product development. Just as important, the new approach can act as a change agent: it is a vehicle for introducing creative, market-driven ideas and processes into an old, rigid organization.

Changes in the environment — intensified competition, a splintered mass market, shortened product life cycles and advanced technology and automation — are forcing managements to reconsider the traditional ways of creating products. A product that arrives a few months late can easily lose very many months payback. To achieve speed and flexibility, companies must manage the product development process differently. Three kinds of change should be considered.

1. *Management style* Companies need to adopt a management style that can promote the process. Executives must recognize at the outset that product development proceeds in a linear and static manner. It involves an iterative and dynamic process of trial and error. To manage such a process, companies must maintain a highly adaptive style. Because projects do not proceed in a totally rational and consistent manner, adaptability is particularly important. Management must exercise subtle forms of control throughout the development process, so that seemingly contradictory goals do not create confusion. Subtle control is consistent with the self-organizing character of the project teams.

2. *Learning approach* A different kind of learning is needed. Under the traditional approach, new product development was entrusted to a group of specialists. An élite group of technical experts did most of the learning. Knowledge was accumulated on an individual basis within a narrow area of focus — the process known as learning in depth.

   By contrast, under the new approach (in its extreme form) non-experts undertake product development. They are encouraged to acquire the necessary knowledge and skills on the job. Unlike the experts, who cannot tolerate mistakes, the non-experts are willing to change the status quo. To do so, they must accumulate knowledge from across all areas of management, different levels of the organization, functional specializations and even organizational boundaries. Such learning in breadth is the necessary condition for shared divisions of labour to function effectively.

3. *A new perspective* Management should assign a different perspective to product development. Most companies have treated it primarily as a generator of future revenue. But in some companies new product development also acts as a catalyst for changing the organization.

   The personal computer project, for example, is said to have changed the way in which IBM thinks. Projects coming out of Hewlett-Packard's personal computer group have changed its engineering-drive culture.

No company finds it easy to mobilize itself for change, especially in non-crisis situations. But the self-transcendent nature of the project teams and the hectic pace at which the team members work can help to trigger a sense of crisis or urgency throughout the organization. A development project of strategic importance to the company, therefore, can create a wartime working environment even during times of peace.

Changes affecting the entire organization are also difficult to carry out within highly structured companies, especially seniority-based companies. But unconventional moves, which may be difficult to pull off during times of peace, can be legitimized during times of war. Thus management can uproot a competent manager or assign a very young engineer to the project without encountering much resistance.

The big issue in all of this is people, and the speed at which they can take up a change of attitudes, technology, organization and systems. With their built-in tendency towards teamwork and flexibility, this is precisely where the Japanese have built their main competitive advantage against the individualistic West. It is the very heart of the product race.

A number of studies have graphically detailed the new attitudes. (See, for example, Lorenz, 1987, and IEEE 1987.)

In describing the Deming method, Walton (1986) quotes the case of product development at Ford in the US. Until the advent of the Taurus model all product development had been sequential:

> Designers designed a car on paper, then gave it to the engineers, who figured out how to make it. Their plans were passed along to the manufacturing and purchasing people who, respectively, set up the lines and selected the suppliers on competitive bids. The next step in the process was the production plant. Then came marketing, the legal and dealer service departments, and then finally the customers. In each stage, if a major glitch developed, the car was bumped back to the design phase for changes. The farther along in the sequence, however, the more difficult it was to make changes. In manufacturing, for example, 'We wouldn't see the plans until maybe a year before production started', (Taurus project leader Lew Veraldi said). 'We would go back to engineering and say can you do it this way? They'd say, 'Go peddle your papers. It's already tooled. I can't afford it.'

That's all changed, Walton reports, again quoting project leader Veraldi:

> With Taurus . . . we brought all disciplines together, and did the whole

process simultaneously as well as sequentially. The manufacturing people worked right with the design people, engineering people, sales and purchasing, legal, service and marketing.

In sales and marketing we had dealers come in and tell us what they wanted in a car to make it more user-friendly, to make it adapt to a customer, based on problems they saw on the floor in selling.

We had insurance companies tell us how to design a car so when accidents occur it would minimize the customer's expense in fixing it after a collision . . . Team Taurus included Ford's legal and safety advisers, who advised on forthcoming trends in the laws so we could design for them rather than patching later on.'

Manufacturing was brought into the act early. Veraldi observes:

'We went to all the stamping plants, assembly plants and put layouts on the walls. We asked them how to make it easier to build. We talked to hourly people. Team Taurus collected thousands of suggestions and incorporated most of them. It's amazing,' he said, 'the dedication and commitment you can get from people . . . We will never go back to the old ways because we know so much about what they can bring to the party.'

Probably the most profound difference was in Ford's relations with suppliers. Again quoting Veraldi:

'The common way of doing business is to choose the lowest bidder on advertised specifications. For Taurus, the company identified its highest quality suppliers and sought their advice in the beginning stages. In return for their contributions, Ford pledged to make them, as far as possible, the sole supplier.'

To quote Schonberger (1986) on the meaning of participation:

'Do it, judge it, measure it, fix it, manage it on the factory floor. Don't wait to find out about it by reading a report later.'

The application of the Deming method, leads to new views on the structure of organizations. The traditional organization, for management by results, was shown in Figure 18.1. The new view of organizations is shown in Figure 20.4.

Brainstorming

Brainstorming can be the source of fruitful ideas within an organization, especially where the management encourages participation. The collective thinking power of people, in an environment

Suppliers   Customers

Feedback

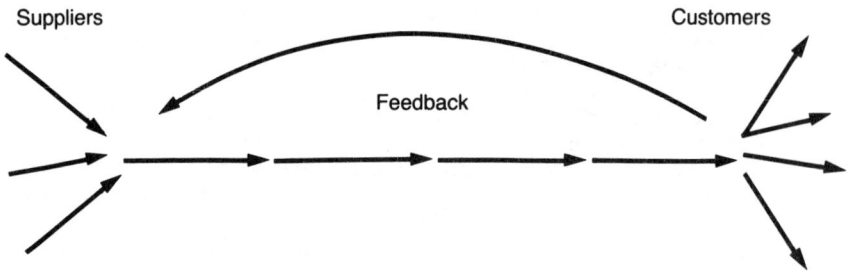

Figure 20.4.   The new view of organizations.

which welcomes a free flow of suggestions can produce some startling combinations of ideas leading to problem identification, analysis and solution.

Identification and analysis are crucial; some problems when identified, analysed and evaluated have only one solution or an obvious solution from a number. In some cases solutions will have to be decided by higher management, or other parts of the organization may have to be involved and their agreement sought.

In a participative environment, no special training is needed for brainstorming activities. With the cooperation and support of management, most people will begin to think creatively and then laterally. Within a group or team working towards common policies and objectives, the knowledge of a common shared purpose helps reduce conflict, often found in a committee-type approach to problems; it fosters commonality and cohesion of purpose. Teams and groups create their own rhythms. Brainstorming sessions provide their own momentum and continuity, but only if given the right environment.

Sessions start with a blank sheet of paper on a flip chart or wall-mounted whiteboards. All participants can see what is written. Each team member can highlight problems in his or her work area. The team can comprise managers, workers and specialists. There is no constraint or censure on problem identification. Nothing identified as a problem should be thought silly or ridiculous. At this early stage, there is no discussion of the problems identified.

Several hundred problems might be identified at a session. These can cover wide ranging aspects of the team's work. Probably some problems will be company-wide or interdepartmental. Only when it is agreed that the problems identified are representative will an evaluation begin.

Problem evaluation leads to problems being classified into the following categories:

1. Problems which can be controlled by the brainstorming team.
2. Problems over which the team only has partial control.
3. Problems over which the team has no control.

The last two classes might not be clear in all cases: these problems should be put into another class, awaiting investigation. Problems in the last category, over which the team has no control, would have to be referred.

Those problems which are controllable will be further evaluated and will have priorities attached to them. It is usual to tackle the easiest problems first, but higher priority would be given to a complex problem if it was having a severe impact on the work of the team. Thought needs to be given to this approach, since failure to correct a complex problem (which would take time) could lead to friction within the team. Some less time consuming smaller problem evaluations and solutions should be considered; or the one-by-one evaluation and solution to problems which impinge on the complex one, could be tackled. With the smaller beginnings, the team builds up confidence in itself and starts to set its own pace or rhythm.

With complex problems, the team will often have to have further brainstorming sessions to identify problems in more detail. Essentially this will involve listing all the possible causes of the problem. It will often mean that data has to be collected.

Data collection

Collection of adequate data is vital, if there is to be any comprehensive study into the causes of problems, errors and defects (whether these originate with management or workers). The data must be complete, consistent and testable. Those who collect the data must avoid drawing hasty conclusions and, in addition, must only base opinions on the available evidence — not on the collector's personal predilections. Limitations of data collection techniques and of the collectors must always be borne in mind.

It is important that the proper training be given to anyone involved in data collection and that they are made aware of all limiting factors. This is especially true in the high technology industries where programmable software systems are embedded in electronic hardware and firmware systems and these are often then embedded in larger electromechanical systems. In these circumstances, common in

Item No.	Item	Comments
3A.1	Is there a formal design programme incorporating administrative and supervisory procedures, for example design reviews, aimed at: (i) ensuring that all the requirements of the hardware specification are met? Y N NA (ii) eliminating errors in design? (iii) ensuring that safety targets are met? (iv) ensuring that aspects relevant to construction, installation operation, maintenance and modification are considered?	
3A.2	Does the design programme incorporate procedures for the consideration of new information or changes to the requirements as the design proceeds? Y N NA	
3A.3	Is there an effective system for ensuring coordination between different sections or organisations involved in the project (eg design sub-contractors, manufacturers)? Y N NA	
3A.4	Is there liaison between the designers and the operational administration in order to ensure that: (i) the principles of operation, maintenance and test assumed in the design are correct? Y N NA (ii) adequate facilities are provided for operational requirements?	
3A.5	(i) Where it is possible to use proven designs of hardware, have they been used? Y N NA (ii) If a proven design is used, has it been critically examined for suitability to the new environment? (iii) Has previous experience of failure as well as successful operation been sought and examined?	
3A.6	Are all equipments and components operated within their rated performance for the specified operating and environmental conditions? Y N NA	

3A.7	Are all inputs and outputs protected from damage from voltage spikes which may be induced on input cables?	Y N NA ☐☐☐
3A.8	Are all outputs which switch inductive loads protected from damage from switching spikes?	Y N NA ☐☐☐
3A.9	Has a philosophy been adopted in the design of the system hardware so that a large proportion of failures tend to put the plant into a safe state?	Y N NA ☐☐☐
	For example is the system designed to put the plant into a safe state in the event of:	
	(i) loss of power supply?	Y N NA ☐☐☐
	(ii) cabling faults (open or short circuit or earth faults)?	☐☐☐
	(iii) loss of instrument air?	☐☐☐
	(iv) loss of hydraulic supply?	☐☐☐
3A.10	What measures have been adopted to detect those failures which do not automatically result in a safe plant state?	
	For example, has a dynamic rather than a static mode of operation been adopted so that failures resulting in a system state can be detected. eg by watchdog timer?	Y N NA ☐☐☐
3A.11	Are the positions and functions of switches and controls clearly indicated?	Y N NA ☐☐☐
3A.12	(i) Does the design use only those features which are fully specified by the manufacturer?	Y N NA ☐☐☐
	(ii) Are all components used under the conditions for which their performance is specified?	☐☐☐

Project/Product: Checklist No:
Date: Copies to:
Completed by: Signature:
Reviewed by: Signature:

Figure 20.5.   Hardware design checklist. This is checklist number 3A from the Health and Safety Executive.

manufacturing industries, data collection must be on a plant or company-wide basis.

In industries which are increasingly dominated by programmable automation, traditional *checksheet* means of data collection are inappropriate. The processing is hidden from the operator, who communicates with the production line via a display unit. One useful approach in these circumstances is to use *checklists*. These focus attention on specific processing and product requirements, characteristics and parameters. They concentrate the mind on areas which are known from previous experience to be likely causes of concern. They can equally address management and technical areas. An example, from the Health and Safety Executive (see HSE, 1987) is shown in Figure 20.5.

The checklists should be easy to use, unambiguous, consistent and objective using well-defined terminology to minimize personal bias. They should also allow for comments to be recorded. This means that the circumstances under which the data were collected, can be reproduced.

Decisions have to be made about what data has to be collected, where it has to be collected, when it has to be collected, as well as why it has to be collected, how and by whom (Kipling, 1902). In addition, decisions have to be made about the various types of data. (i.e. variable and countable). Also to be decided are the techniques to be used, for example sampling, inspection, various kinds of charts and graphs, drawings for locating problem areas, checksheets (for collecting and totalling data about items on a matrix), checklists and the uses of control data.

Much of this lies within the domain of statistics, and the reader is referred to the many textbooks on introductions to statistics, and to Chapters 14 to 17 in this handbook. Elementary statistics has wide power, even when probability theory and standard deviation are excluded. The use of statistical techniques can be introduced with very great benefit and, with suitable training, the applications and their resulting benefits will increase rapidly.

Pareto analysis
Once data have been collected, the difficult question is how to deal with it. It is necessary to concentrate on the vital few rather than the trivial many. This approach to quality management is advocated by Juran (1964, 1987). Juran noted that a vital few data elements accounted for most of the total effect in any situation and, conversely, that the

bulk of the data elements accounted for very little of the total effect. This phenomenon is generally known as the Pareto principle, after the Italian economist Vilfredo Pareto (1848-1923) who came to the same conclusion with specific application to the distribution of wealth. The principle has since been widely applied in many other areas, of which stock control has long been a notable example. The principle is often referred to as the 80/20 rule, meaning that 80 per cent of an effect is caused by only 20 per cent of the contributing items. In stock control, for example, this means that 20 per cent of the items held will probably account for 80 per cent of total inventory value, leaving the other 80 per cent of items to account for the remaining 20 per cent of value. The Pareto principle (or 80/20 rule) is often represented by the graph shown in Figure 20.6.

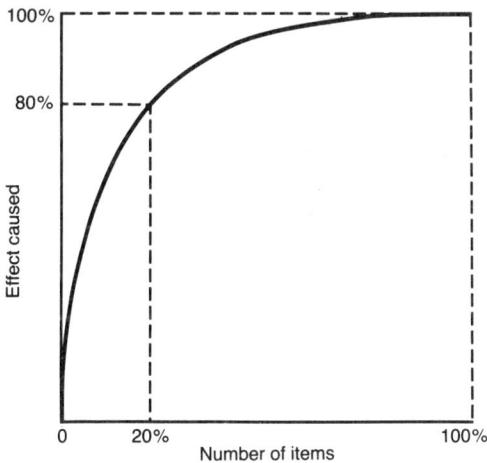

Figure 20.6.   Graphical representation of the Pareto principle. The graph illustrates the statement of this principle (also known as the 80/20 rule), namely that 80 per cent of a total effect is likely to be caused by only 20 per cent of the contributing items.

Juran's examples are specially relevant to quality in traditional engineering and manufacturing processes, where data is collected against well-established and known-cause classifications and error/ defect identifications. Instances are in hardware reliability, maintainability, accuracy, timing, availability and longevity; in sheet metal fabrication drill presses, spot and arc welding, machine shops, operators, jigs and fixtures.

For programmable automation, Juran's techniques have to be extended and adapted. The principle and its applications still provide an integrated and methodical approach. The application of the Pareto principle to the newer technologies is not yet well documented, but is covered in some detail in Schulmeyer (1987).

An example given is the principle's application to the different functions performed in several computer/software-based organizations. Analysis revealed that about 80 per cent of the personnel functions were concerned with the 'trivial many', accounting for about 20 per cent of the hours expended. The converse was that although 80 per cent of the hours expended addressed the 'vital few', this was done by only 20 per cent of the personnel functions. Further, this vital few was entirely crisis management. Application of the Pareto principle highlighted the weaknesses in the organizations' infrastructures, with inadequate planning, monitoring, scheduling, reviewing, decision-making, documentation, training and task preparation. Schulmeyer gives several other examples of the Pareto principle as applied to computer-based systems.

Error and defect identification

Error and defect identification is an area which has been well documented for the long established engineering and manufacturing processes (Juran, 1987). This is fertile ground for applying the Pareto principle and for analysing the results.

It is not an easy task to identify error classes in an environment where programmable automation is paramount. The total system requires the integration of man and machines, combining hardware, software, training, facilities, documentation and manufacturing applications.

Errors and defects manifest themselves in many different ways. An attempt must be made to identify all error and defect classes. In a high technology manufacturing environment error classes might be identified according to the need to satisfy the following system requirements:

- Functional capability of system
- Performance
- Workload capacity/bandwidth
- Reliability/availability/maintainability
- Man–machine interface
- Environment
- Safety

- Security
- System interfaces
- Communications
- Expansion/flexibility
- Documentation

The identification of error classes in this example and subsequent ones, means that they can be used in practice like checklists (described earlier).

An initial attempt must be made to identify errors and defects according to some list of system requirements, like the one above. The errors and defects found against each system requirement would be converted to a percentage; the highest percentage of system requirement error classes would then be analysed to the next level of detail. The next level, for example, of system interface requirements might have the following error classes:

1. Electrical characteristics, including resistance, impedance, capacitance, termination resistance, signal characteristics, pulse rate, pulse width, logic and noise levels, rise and fall times, data format and signal tolerance.
2. Physical characteristics, including cable type, length, location, terminations, line amplifiers and grounding characteristics.
3. Protocols between system components.
4. Message block formats, parameter formats, common data formats and content.
5. Signalling and response restrictions and any sequence or timing constraints.
6. Verification and response protocols.
7. User–system interface requirements.

If there were to be a high percentage of protocol or message block errors, a further level of error classes would be generated. Eventually the level of detail would be such that the error classes of hardware design or software programming being addressed become very specific.

An example, where percentages of errors were found for the above list of system interface requirements, is shown in Figure 20.7. Figure 20.7a shows the frequency of occurrence for each of the various error classes. In Figure 20.7b the chart has been rearranged, with the bars drawn in descending order of occurrence. This arrangement is more meaningful, directing attention to the vital error classes in accordance with the Pareto principle. This, in turn, allows concentration on the causes of the errors.

Inspections

The Pareto principle has been applied to assembly line inspection by Juran (1987). Like the assembly line, the products of programmable automation also have a series of processes or operational steps through which the product passes. This inspection approach to production was discussed earlier in this chapter in the section headed 'The factory as

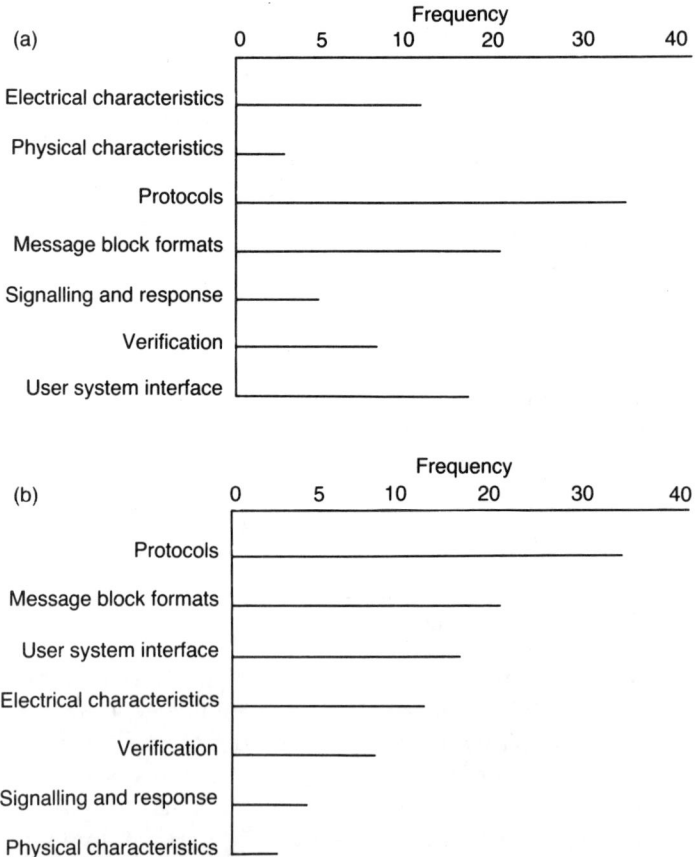

Figure 20.7.   **Error classification of system interfaces. In (b) the bars have been rearranged to highlight the Pareto principle's insight into distinguishing between the 'vital few' and the 'trivial many'.**

a people-driven system'. Trained staff monitor and inspect workstations to establish variability during all production stages. This is far more valuable than having inspectors at the end of the production processes. Early defects and errors are not hidden by later processes. Processes are classified using the Pareto principle, and these classifications are used as aids to management in planning the distribution of inspection effort among workstations.

Manufacturing which depends on automation has an identifiable series of processes. Each step in the series has its own entrance and exit criteria, which must be satisfied if the process is to produce a quality product. At every step in production the product must be available for inspection or test. Over a period data will have been collected against the entrance and exit criteria and the inspections or tests measured against that criteria.

Fagan's work is crucial here (Fagan, 1976). For design inspections the participants have to understand the design intent as well as its logic. The participants are first made familiar with the principle's vital few error classes. This concentrates minds. Then they concentrate on the error classes. Extensive use is made of checklists and checksheets. Inspections provide detailed feedback when the early steps of the production process are examined. Timely action is thus possible. From error identification, the logical extension is to seek the cause of the error.

Cause and effect analysis
Error identification has taken place using the Pareto principle. The next step is to isolate the causes of the errors.

An early quality circle innovation was the use of Ishikawa 'fishbone' diagrams to show the relationships between error cause and error effect (Ishikawa, 1976). Fishbone diagrams are used to highlight important factors and control points, with arrows pointing to the effect. The most important internal company factors are the 4Ms and their relationship to the broader environment. The 4Ms are shown schematically in Figure 20.8.

A basic requirement for all quality planning is that the 4Ms and environment are clearly defined. Thus:

1. *Manpower* Early in quality planning, the requirements of the organization, skills, training, etc, for any new product should be evaluated against those existing. All supplier's planning systems should have inbuilt mechanisms to ensure that previous

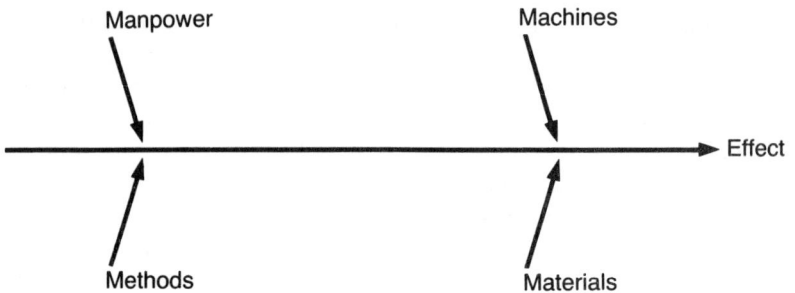

Figure 20.8.   Ishikawa 4Ms fishbone diagram.

experiences and the results of audits and system reviews have
been taken into account. This should include methods of
identifying the strengths and weaknesses of the organization,
communication and implementing actions to improve personal
effectiveness.

2. *Methods* Quality planning should embrace all methods and
    systems used across the broad spectrum of the company's
    activities, especially those which are concerned with systems and
    methods which have a direct bearing on the quality of any new
    products. However, the company's overall systems for planning
    should cover other aspects which should be integrated into the
    new product plan to include the marketing, financial, commercial
    and technology functions. The strengths and weaknesses of the
    planning system will be indicated by the results of previous audits
    and system reviews which have been carried out and which
    should be evaluated against the specific requirements for the new
    products.

3. *Machines* Machines are often the principal constraints on the
    product which can be manufactured, the approach to design and
    the methods of inspection and test. Whereas personnel can be
    retrained, redeployed or new people recruited, the existing plant
    and machinery which is in place usually has a fixed capability and
    limited scope for change or development.

4. *Materials* Changes of materials from which the products are
    made generally require very specific and careful planning to avoid
    potential improvements becoming quality problems. Designers
    are often the first to initiate a change of material, based on
    information provided by the material manufacturers, published
    papers and other information sources and whilst some evaluation

data may be available in this form, it is essential that the planning ensures that the material is fully evaluated in the context of the particular product application.

5. *Environment:* The 4Ms apply internally to the company, but the company has to operate within a broader situation. We must include suppliers. The suppliers should therefore have systems which ensure that the plant and machinery capability is fully understood including the tolerances which can be achieved, the sizes which can be accommodated, the layout, the flow routes and capacities.

   Likewise distributors should have the capability to successfully store and distribute the product. Also within the environment, sometimes specific company aspects must be considered, e.g. general facilities. Anything which can impinge on the quality of the product (e.g. poor air-conditioning) must be considered and planned into the manufacture of the product.

When the error has been identified, brainstorming sessions are held, as described previously. Possible causes are listed, using the 4Ms fishbone diagram as a framework. It is sometimes possible to classify a possible cause under more than one 4Ms heading. For example, the method could be right, but the man could be using it wrongly or the opposite. Such points need to be fully evaluated.

These brainstorming sessions, therefore, often span two meetings. Not all the ideas can be fully explored at one meeting. Those involved need to think over possible causes, make observations and talk to others. The latter enables those outside the session to make a contribution. Often a diagram is displayed in the work area to encourage comments and suggestions from others.

All comments and suggestions have to be evaluated. Now the aim is to identify specific error causes, from the many possible ones. All the possible causes are evaluated; the ones most likely to be the causes are highlighted with a circle. The causes circled are then given a priority rating. An example of a worked Ishikawa diagram is shown in Figure 20.9.

The most likely causes are overwork, poor design and lack of technical support. These possible causes will have to be investigated and evidence gathered. Data will be collected to give objective quantifiable evidence. If poor design is found to be the major cause, improvements to design methods will be suggested with, for example, new techniques. If improving the poor design does not improve

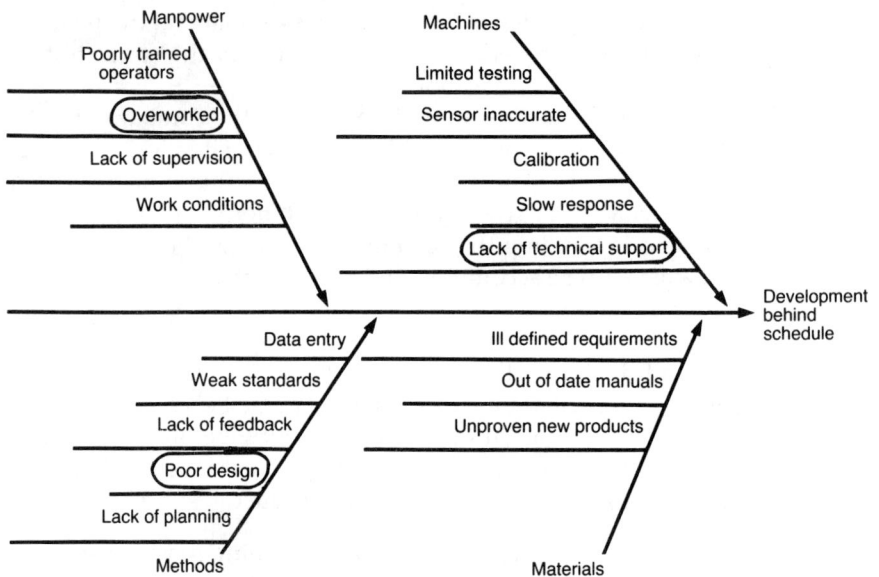

Figure 20.9.   A worked Ishikawa diagram.

development, the second item on the priority list will be evaluated.

The evaluation process itself may use one or many different data collection methods and techniques to find a satisfactory solution. Hence training in their application is necessary, as described under the heading 'Data collection'. The uses of the 4Ms fishbone diagram have been well described by Tribus (1984).

Process analysis

Some causes will require a very deep analysis into their origins. Thus if lack of technical support is considered to be of high priority then it should be noted in the effect box and the 4Ms completed. A further brainstorming session could be conducted, or process analysis might be used.

Process analysis is particularly helpful if a problem can arise at one or more steps in a process. The description of the effect is written in a box on the right and the antecedent processes are described in boxes. An example is shown in Figure 20.10.

A further brainstorming session would be held and all possible causes feeding into the process boxes would be listed using the 4Ms. For logistics, the worked process analysis/cause analysis diagram is shown in Figure 20.11.

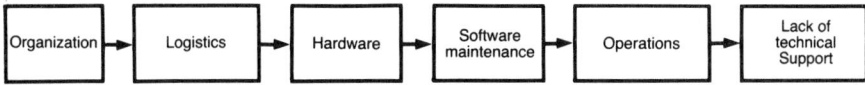

Figure 20.10. Process analysis.

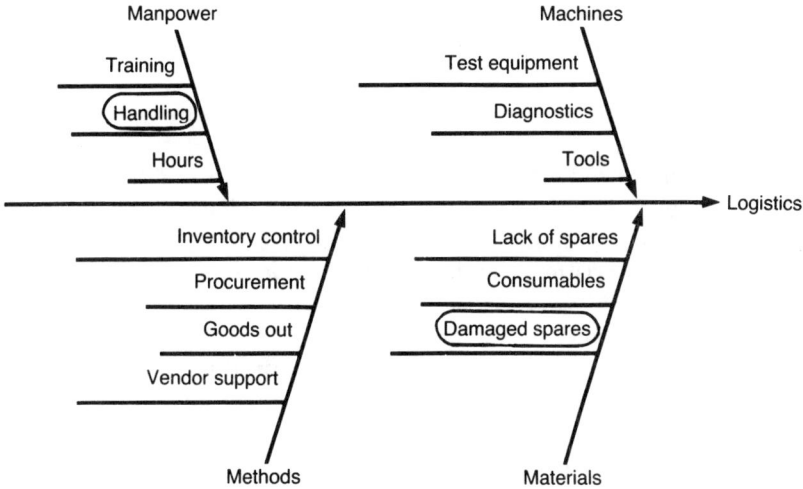

Figure 20.11. A worked process/cause analysis diagram.

The need for self-motivation and cooperation in the implementation of a cause and effect corrective action programme, to eliminate human error, is well argued in Towe (1987).

Stratification and is/is not analysis

Once errors have been identified, stratification and is/is not analysis are both ways to split or 'stratify' data in ways that expose underlying error patterns. Discovering such error patterns helps localize a problem, making it easier to identify the cause of the problem. This analysis both precedes data collection (so that the investigators will know what kind of differences to look for) and follows it (so that the investigators can discover which factors actually affected the results).

To stratify data, the investigators first examine the process to see what characteristics could lead to biases in data — these are not necessarily factors that actually do cause differences, only ones that could. For example, might western districts differ appreciably from eastern districts? Could differerent shifts account for differences in results? Are the mistakes made by new employees much different from those made by more experienced workers? Does output on Monday differ substantially from that for the rest of the week?

Investigators (either as individuals or a team) make a list of the characteristics they think could cause systematic differences in the results. The information is incorporated into checklists, checksheets or data collection forms. For example recording day of the week and time will indicate whether the results depend on a day, a time or both. When all data have been collected, a search for patterns related to time or sequence must be made. Then a check has to be made for systematic differences between days of the week, shifts, operators and so on.

One structured form of stratification is the 'is/is not' matrix based on ideas developed by Kepner and Tregoe (1981). This helps sort observed characteristics so that investigators can speculate on possible causes for the patterns which have been identified.

Failure modes and effects analysis

Companies starting new developments, products or strategies can minimize the probability of failure by analysing the identifiable error classes and possible causes in very great detail. The purpose of failure modes and effects analysis (FMEA) is to identify modes of failures that can occur in a system and evaluate the consequential effects of these failures.

This technique was described in Chapter 11, and an example of an FMEA worksheet was given in Figure 11.2.

Fault tree analysis

Whereas FMEA is a bottom-up approach to identifying error classes companies can go through a similar exercise, but top–down, using fault tree analysis (FTA). Here the failure of several undesirable top level events or errors are considered. FTA focuses attention on single undesirable events to be eliminated. The undesirable events may be the failure of a system, occurrences that pose danger to human lives, or loss of expensive equipment.

FMEA performs a bottom-up approach analysis of a system starting from the failure of lower level items to its effects on sub-system, system and objectives. In contrast to this approach, the FTA performs a top–down approach analysis of an undesirable top event such as failure of an objective or system. It starts from the top to lower and lower levels of subevents that are the immediate cause(s) of the event above it.

The fault tree (FT) goes down until it finally reaches the various primary events (primals). A separate FT is developed for each top undesired event and the FT is unique to that event.

Although two fault trees may have several common items or primals, the analysis made for one FT cannot be applied to the other. To develop an FT, one has to understand in detail how the system functions normally and how it could malfunction under abnormal conditions.

The FT depicts the logical relationship (logical 'AND' and 'OR' of the top event through various intermediate events, called gates, to basic events, called primals. By a boolean manipulation of the logical relationship, all minimal combinations for the top event are derived. This represents a minimum combination of basic events that, if they all occur with a time overlap, will cause the top event to occur.

FT analysis can provide the following information:

1. A graphic representation of the FT, the primals, the gates, the top event and the logical connections.
2. A listing of all combinations starting with single points of failure through low orders of failure to higher orders up to the extent desired. (It is usually wasteful to develop combinations of higher order because their probability of occurrence is extremely low.)
3. Frequency and probability of occurrence of top and intermediate events.
4. The relative importance of primary events in triggering the top event. Note that even though a particular primal may not be a single point of failure, because it does not occur alone in any situation its occurrence in many combinations will make it an appropriate target for further investigation with a view to eliminate it.

During the system design and development phases, it is highly desirable (almost mandatory) to perform an availability, reliability and maintainability (ARM) analysis to ensure that the system requirements are met and the subsystems are allocated realistic ARM values capable of being achieved with the state-of-the-art components within the cost constraints.

FMEA and/or FTA are required when a system's success is to be achieved with a very high degree of probability. Every foreseeable cause(s) of system failure should be eliminated by performing FMEA and FTA. FTA especially focuses attention in a quantitative manner (in a probabilistic way) on various basic events leading to a top undesirable event. Under these circumstances the cost and effort of performing these analyses would be justified.

Statistical techniques

Statistical techniques are applicable to the whole range of engineering, manufacturing and administrative processes and activities and not just the parts of industry concerned with precision-made products. Statistical process control (SPC) is a generic way of collecting and presenting data about variation in the conditions of the characteristics of an activity or process; the information being most usefully presented in a diagram or chart to both help determine characteristic performance and guide any decision-making and preventative actions. SPC, therefore, is an all embracing term which encompasses techniques for assessing the acceptability of any process, product or activity. A comparison of SPC with traditional quality control is shown in Figure 20.12.

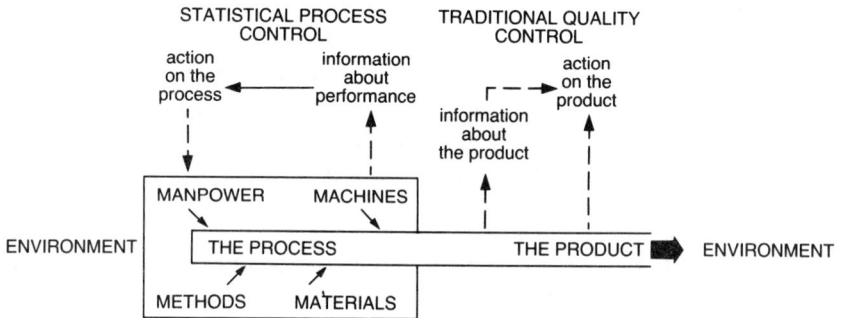

Figure 20.12.   SPC and traditional quality control.

A number of standards on statistical techniques are available from the British Standards Institution and its equivalent organizations in other countries. Chapters 14 to 17 of this handbook deal with statistical principles and associated charting methods in some detail. The remainder of this chapter concentrates on the introduction and management of these techniques on a company-wide basis.

Company-wide application of statistical techniques

Measurement is a vital element in the company-wide approach. It can also be very straightforward:

Data recording comes first. The tools are cheap and simple: pencils and chalk. Give those simple tools for recording data to each operator. Then make it a natural part of the operator's job to record disturbances and measurements on charts and blackboards. The person who records data is inclined to analyze, and the analyzer is inclined to think of solutions. (Schonberger, 1986).

Company-wide management commitment to SPC is crucial. The overwhelming requirement for success is to have total management commitment from the top of the organization, to lead and drive its introduction, and continue to monitor its progress against a time-phased plan.

As a means of defining what has to be done and who should do it, the provision by management of basic procedures covering the points outlined below will be of considerable value. Prior to issue, management must ensure that these have been agreed by all the users at an SPC implementation review meeting. The objective of this is to gain both further understanding of what is required, and commitment from each area affected so that they understand their responsibilities and agree to carry them out:

1. *Classification of characteristic requirements* This is necessary to identify safety, functional, processing or other characteristic requirements according to their importance. After this selection process, the features are considered relative to the manufacturing capability method to be applied. Finally the features to which SPC will be applied, are agreed.

2. *Determination of process capability* Because this can suffer from various interpretations, care has to be taken to ensure that everyone within the organization uses the same definition and approach, and knows why. These procedures, therefore, need to detail the approach to machines and processes, how assessments are to be made, what records kept, when and by whom.

3. *Application of SPC* This needs to cover how diagrams and charts are operated, issued, collected, stored and actioned, along with details of the types of diagrams to be used and how control data ranges are to be calculated.

4. *Quality information equipment capability* This should define the limits of accuracy required of the measuring equipment used and how this is verified.

Although the statistics most commonly required are of a simplified type, there is nevertheless a need for management to have a statistical 'expert' readily available who can help with difficulties and assist in planning or carrying out statistical training. The provision of 'experts' with statistical knowledge throughout the various parts of the organization will also add strength to the implementation. Some managements provide 'self help' training materials to employees.

A fundamental aspect of SPC is that the characteristics of the items chosen for control must be capable of being measured to a sufficient degree of accuracy, for the particular items and processes involved. Approximated limit gauges of the go/no-go type are not satisfactory. Where a single feature only is being controlled a micrometer type instrument can be used. Where several features are involved in one process an electronic recording system is better to save time and increase accuracy in making the checks. These electronic systems enable data to be captured from many parts of the plant and company; they can be linked to a mini-computer.

With SPC implementation a vital first need of management is to ensure that good communications channels exist both up and down throughout the organization. These should be used on a regular basis, with information being passed on company and process performance, what new directions are being or should be pursued, so that everyone in the organization is aware of the progress of the SPC implementation, why it is being done and how it will affect them. This last aspect is most important in emphasizing the priority management is giving to the programme, and needs continual reiteration to produce the cultural change which is absolutely necessary to get the best results.

There will be many doubters but the need is for management to produce a change of attitude and move from the concept of solving problems by traditional quality control product inspection and sorting, to integrated process improvement using statistical thinking.

Training in SPC must apply to everyone, from the managing director to the typists; all must attend a 'core' programme, irrespective of background and knowledge. Although the core programme should be applied to all employees, additional courses should be designed for particular groups of employees; others should be tailored for specific individuals. To help gain commitment to both the training and cultural change, the programmes should be run first for the most senior management and operational managers. They should then lead some of the courses, act as trainers for other sessions, and go on regular refresher courses, to reinforce their commitment.

It is essential for all levels of management to be able to deal with problems identified, wherever these are, so that the idea of continuous improvement is never-ending and does not falter.

Thomas (1987) describes an example of SPC implementation where a three-stage approach proved successful.

Since the right conditions and environment must be established, stage 1 is the analysis of the current situation. This must be investigated to decide accurately what needs to be created, changed, developed and obtained. Establishing the right conditions means a management commitment, starting with a quality policy statement (an example is shown in Figure 19.1).

Stage 2 can proceed when prevailing conditions are known. Work can begin on making the necessary adjustments and satisfying any requirements. Objectives and actions can now be agreed. Company-wide policies and procedures must be documented, also company-wide motivation programmes, starting with the company's most senior management. The right skills, knowledge and expert help should be made available. Information must flow freely both up and down (and not just down); management must listen to workers. Data on existing problems must be collected, and process and product performance characteristics and requirements agreed.

SPC can be implemented with the appropriate diagrams/charts as stage 3. All processes and activities have some degree of variation. It is this variation which affects performance. As Thomas reminds us variation can be the result of what Deming calls common causes (i.e. small but predictable management-controllable variations which are always present) and special causes (i.e, irregular variations due to the operator, machine or process).

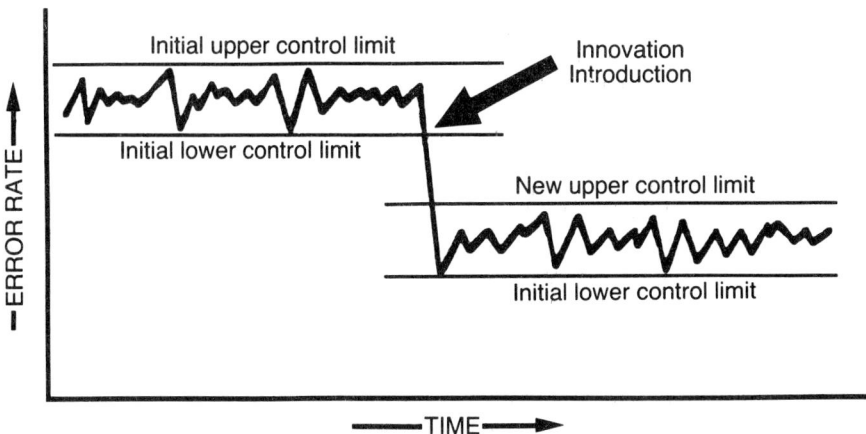

Figure 20.13. Innovation improves process performance.

Once a process is within the range of statistical control limits, performance improvements are readily apparent. Figure 20.13 illustrates the effect of successful innovation on a process's performance, plotted on a control diagram.

Participative quality: summary and conclusion

The main architects of the various approaches to participative quality have been Deming, Juran, Ishikawa and Crosby. Since the early 1980s a new voice on the approach to total quality philosophy has been heard. This is Taguchi. His views are controversial. They are, however, starting to make an impact. They provide an overall conceptual quality framework, using statistical techniques but encompassing both the company and the society in which the company operates. There are essentially seven basic elements in his philosophy. One of these, and the subject of much discussion, is the notion of the total loss generated by a product to society, where that product fails to meet the customer's requirements.

Taguchi's approach and methods are fully explained in a series of articles in *Quality Assurance* (1987). The articles contain comprehensive reading lists.

The main thrust of these three chapters on participative quality (Chapters 18, 19 and 20) has been derived from the work of Deming. Figure 20.14 is an adaptation of the Joiner triangle, which embodies the Deming philosophy (Joiner, 1988).

QUALITY

- Develop an obsession with quality:
  of products and services
  of processes and activities
  of performance
  of work motivation

- Quality is determined by the customers' needs and expectations:
  external customers
  internal customers

- Quality is achieved by improved processes and activities not by inspection

- Continual, never-ending improvement

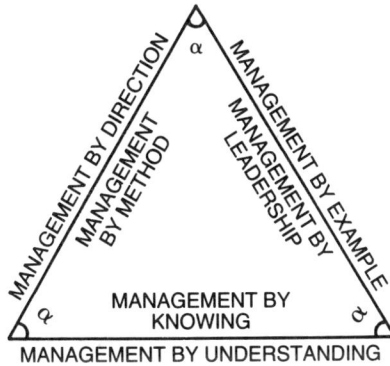

SCIENTIFIC APPROACH

- Focusing on processes
- Identifying problems
- Isolating root causes
- Evaluating solutions
- Monitoring progress
- Eliminating variation

ALL IN ONE TEAM

- Everyone seeking improvements
- Everone gaining from improvement
- Everyone trained for quality
- Everyone trained for their job
- Everyone working as a team

Figure 20.14. The Joiner triangle embodies the Deming philosophy

Further reading

British Standards Institution Control Chart Technique, 1955, British Standards Institution, Milton Keynes.

Bryce, M. and Associates Inc. *PRIDE Development Method* 1988 M. Bryce & Associates Inc., Palm Harbor, Florida.

Caulkins, S. 'The New Manufacturing: Minimal IT for Maximum Profit,' *The Economist*, 1989.

Computer Sciences Corporation, *Digital Systems Development Methodology*, Version 3, Computer Sciences Corporation, El Segunda, California and Slough 1989.

Cusumano, M.A., *The Japanese Automobile Industry*, Harvard University Press, 1985.

Deming, W.E., *Quality Productivity and Competitive Position*, MIT Press, Massachussetts 1982.

Fagan, M.E., 'Design and Code Inspections to Reduce Errors in Program Development,' *IBM Systems Journal*, 1976, Vol. 15, No. 3, pp. 182–211.

Hall, R.W., *Attaining Manufacturing Excellence*, Dow Jones-Irwin, Chicago 1987.

Harrington, H.J., *Excellence: The IBM Way*, IBM Technical Reports 1986.

Health and Safety Executive, *Programmable Electronic Systems in Safety Related Applications Part 2, General Technical Guidelines*, Her Majesty's Stationery Office, London 1987.

Hutchins, D., *Quality Circles Handbook*, Pitman Publishing, London 1986.

Institute of Electrical and Electronics Engineers, *IEEE Spectrum*, May 1987. A special edition devoted to designing successful systems in the 1990s.

Institute of Quality Assurance, *Quality Assurance*, 1987, Vol. 13, No. 3, September, (pp. 65-99).

Ishikawa, K., *Guide to Quality Control*, Asian Productivity Organization, Tokyo 1976. Details the tools taught to Japanese foreman for use in quality circles.

Joiner Associates Inc., *The Team Handbook: How to Use Teams to Improve Quality*, Joiner Associates Inc., Madison Wisconsin 1988. An excellent account of how to use the Deming philosophy in anger.

Jones, B., Foy, P., Drury, J, and Young, S., 'Britain's Best Factories', *Management Today* 1988, September, pp. 59–80.

Juran, J.M., *Managerial Breakthrough*, McGraw-Hill Book Co., New York 1964.

Juran, J.M. and Gryna, F.M., *Quality Planning and Analysis*, McGraw-Hill Book Co., New York 1980.

Juran, J.M., Gryna, F.M. and Bingham, R.S. (eds) *Quality Control Handbook*, 4th ed., McGraw-Hill Book Co., New York 1987.

Kepner, C.H. and Tregoe, B.B., *The New Rational Manager*, Princetown Research Press, Princetown, New Jersey 1981.

Kipling, R., *The Elephant's Child*, Just So Stories, 1902; Kipling's Six Honest Men: what, where, when, why, how, who.

Lawler, E.E. and Mohrman, S.A., 'Quality Circles After the Fad', *Harvard Business Review*, 1985, Vol. 63, issue 1, Cambridge, Massachusetts, January–February, pp. 65–71.

Lorenz, C., 'Management: Seizing the Initiative in a Struggle for Survival — The Product Race', *The Financial Times*, London 1987, 17 June and then a series of 5 weekly articles starting on 19th June.

Matsudaira, K., 'Japanese System Factories', *Management Visions*, 1987, Vol. 3, No. 3, December, pp. 1–2.

Ogilvie, J., 'Quality Improvement at Work', *Quality Assurance*, 1987, Vol. 13, No. 4, December, pp. 112–16.

Peters, T., *Thriving on Chaos*, Macmillan, London 1988.

Preston, G., 'Management Aspects of Statistical Process Control Implementation', *Quality Assurance*, 1987, Vol. 13, No. 1, March, pp. 5–9.

Schonberger, R.J., *World Class Manufacturing: The Lessons of Simplicity Applied*, The Free Press, Macmillan Inc., New York 1986.

Schulmeyer, G.G. and McManus, J.I. (eds), *Handbook of Software Quality Assurance*, Van Nostrand Reinhold, New York, 1987, Ch. 10.

Takeuchi, H. and Nonaka, I., 'The New Product Development Game', *Harvard Business Review*, 1986, Vol. 64, issue 1, January–February, pp. 137–46.

Thomas, M.A., 'The Implementation and Benefits of Statistical Process Control', *Quality Assurance*, 1987, Vol. 13, No. 1, March, pp. 10–13.

Towe, N.J., 'Quality or Productivity?' *Quality Assurance*, 1987, Vol. 13, No. 2, June, pp. 46–50.

Tribus, M., 'Prize-winning Japanese Firms Quality Management Programs Pass Inspection', *Management Review*, 1984, February.

Walton, M., *The Deming Management Method*, Dodd, Mead & Company Inc., New York 1986.

The Yankee Group Europe, *Advanced Manufacturing Philosophies*, Watford, Herts, 1988.

Part Seven

QUALITY PLANNING FOR MANUFACTURE

21 Just-in-time and Supplier Development

D. M. Lascelles and B. G. Dale

Just-in-Time (JIT) production has been hailed by some commentators as one of the miracles of the Japanese economic revolution. The concept of JIT is elegant in its simplicity: the production of parts in the exact quantity required just in time for use. This concept embraces not only the final user but also all preceding stages in the supply chain, both internal and external. It is an idealized philosophy of zero inventory in which the elimination of waste is the central goal. The reduction of stocks in the manufacturing system means that a company can respond more readily to the demands of the marketplace.

The attraction of JIT is obvious in terms of its positive effect on business, but it is a high risk strategy because stocks are kept to a minimum and planning is short term. Key requirements, include short set-up times so that it is economical to manufacture very small batches, simple material flows, effective material handling, damage-free material, no equipment breakdowns, no product non-conformances and effective production scheduling. The ideal is make one piece just in time for the next processing operation. There is a low level of contingency in the system and failure of any part of the system can be catastrophic.

451

Product quality is a key issue with JIT. This has implications for the way in which the business and supplier base is managed. Suppliers need to be educated by the customer on what is required of them. The need for a continuous process of supplier development becomes critical, otherwise a company might as well forget about JIT purchasing. Supplier development revolves around the establishment of a long-term business partnership between a company and its supplier community to the competitive advantage of both parties.

This chapter opens by reviewing the concept of JIT and examines the importance of Total Quality Management (TQM) and supplier development for the effective use of JIT. Then, drawing on the findings of a number of research projects on the subject of TQM and supplier development, the chapter examines the important issues of supplier development, outlines how such a programme might be initiated and describes its main features.

The JIT concept

JIT is concerned with the reduction and eventual elimination of waste. Hay (1984) defines waste as anything other than the minimum resources required to add value to the product. Taiichi Ohno, who is generally recognized as the 'father of JIT' due to his pioneering work at Toyota in the 1950s and 1960s, classified the waste incurred in the production process into: overproduction, waiting time at workcentres, transportation, manufacturing processes, holding unnecessary inventories, unnecessary motion and producing defective goods.

Ohno believes that overproduction leads to waste in other areas. To eliminate the problem, he devised the concept of just-in-time production; that is, bringing the exact number of required units to each successive stage of production at the required time. Putting this concept into practice necessitated a radical change in production from 'push' to 'pull'. In other words, abandoning the traditional 'push' system that is based on a forecast generated at the outset from which a production plan is developed to meet the forecast demand (the plan then drives manufacturing through the issue of work orders), and replacing it with a 'pull' system in which nothing is produced until it is needed, effectively allowing customer demand for finished goods to pull components and material through the system. The result was a significant decline in inventory levels. Even after Ohno initiated the concept on a trial basis in machining and assembly work in 1952, it took almost 10 years before it was adopted in all Toyota's plants.

Once the JIT concept became established at Toyota, Ohno began extending it to subcontractors and suppliers. The Toyota JIT production system is now legendary. A critical lesson comes from the Toyota experience: a company must successfully implement JIT inhouse before it attempts to extend the process to its suppliers. It is worth noting that in a number of Japanese companies products are built and shipped the same day.

By its very nature, JIT is a high risk strategy; stocks which have traditionally acted as the 'safety net' to buffer failure and hide problems are minimized and planning is short term. The prime concern of JIT is to avoid interruptions to production. A company will create for itself a number of problems by adopting JIT unless the quality of parts flowing through the system is satisfactory. In the absence of 'safety' stock, the production line will very quickly stop every time a non-conforming part is found. The effect ripples back through the previous processes and eventually the entire production system grinds to a halt. The key issue is finding the optimum level of stocks for cost effective production. Plant breakdowns will have the same effect. In addition, delays will be caused by a production scheduling system that is unresponsive to an environment with a planning horizon that is measured in hours rather than weeks. Therefore, the implementation of JIT demands a risk minimization strategy featuring Kanban, simple material flows, Total Productivity Maintenance (TPM) and TQM.

The term 'Kanban' is often seen as being synonymous with JIT. Kanban, meaning signboard or label, is used as a communication and production control tool in the JIT system. A Kanban signifying the delivery of a given quantity is attached to each container of parts as they are fed into the production system. When the parts have been used the same label (i.e. Kanban) is returned to its origin where it becomes an order for more parts. For a detailed description of 'pure' Kanban systems the reader is referred to Schonberger (1982).

Not all Kanban systems use Kanban cards; some feature traffic light type signals. There are also similar pull type production control systems in existence which use 'Kanban squares'; these are controlled inventory locations between manufacturing areas and processes. Between each process, inventory is held in a fixed size container or fixed area square within sight of the area producing the items held and the area consuming them. A process is not allowed to start work on an item until there is a space within the Kanban square to put the finished item after the process has been completed. In effect, the 'single bin' stock control principle has been applied to a dynamic interprocess inventory situation. This approach has been used extensively by Hewlett-Packard. However, all Kanban systems have several common characteristics: they are pull type production control systems, they are dynamic, they are visual, the signals are easy to understand and they facilitate rapid communication.

In JIT manufacture it is essential that the layout of production processes and equipment facilitates continuous and unidirectional material flow. A parallel objective is to eliminate or at least minimize operations which do not add value to the material or cause delays (e.g. inspections, transportations and storage). Therefore, material flows are a key consideration in the planning of JIT manufacture. This may require some replanning of manufacturing operations, changing the process sequence or some redesign of the product to ensure manufacturability and optimize production line efficiency. In some cases this may involve rationalizing manufacturing operations so that all products follow the same standard process sequence, in others changing the shape of flow lines. Another option may be the implementation of manufacturing cells (i.e. group technology) to produce families of components (categorized by their component geometry, material, process sequence and equipment). Group technology cells reduce the need for repeatedly transporting workpieces between departments, although attention must be given to work movements and layout within the cells to ensure their efficient operation. Decisions have to be made regarding manufacturing technology and automation, whether to invest in flexible or dedicated production lines. Some flexibility is also required from the labour force in terms of job rotation and in the tasks they perform. Extra production capacity may be needed to provide cover for breakdowns and, on occasions, to smooth out loading on machine groups.

TPM is now practiced by a large number of Japanese manufacturing companies. TPM is defined by the Japan Institute of Plant Maintenance as: . . . aiming to maximise the effectiveness of production equipment with a total system of preventive maintenance throughout its entire life. Involving everyone in all departments and at all levels, it motivates people for plant maintenance through small group and voluntary activities.

Preventive maintenance is usually associated with regular equipment inspection to diagnose impending failure, and servicing in order to reduce wear so as to prevent or delay breakdowns. TPM goes beyond this. In Japan, TPM is seen as a company-wide activity in which everyone is imbued with a collective responsibility — just like TQM.

TQM is a way of managing the business to achieve a total quality organization. Any organization is a network of administrative and technical processes each of which has a supplier and a customer and where every employee is committed to continuous improvement of their part of the operation. It involves teamwork and extends to external suppliers and customers. This concept requires a fundamental change in the way in which people approach their work. It means respecting the work of all people in the company by ensuring that the output of one's work (whether it be a physical component or a piece of paper containing information) is correct before it is passed on to the next person.

TQM is an essential prerequisite for JIT. In reality, JIT has no real hope of success unless a company has embraced the TQM ethic.

The customer–supplier relationship

The simplicity of the JIT concept belies the extreme difficulty which companies experience when attempting its implementation. JIT involves cultural changes at every level within the organization and among its suppliers, and even its customers. JIT is a total concept like TQM and, therefore, organizations must adopt the complete package, not just the elements they like. The supplier must be viewed as part of the manufacturing chain, and so the JIT philosophy of producing small quantities of conforming product must be acceptable to them. They must not think that they are being forced to hold stocks for their customers.

Two surveys of JIT purchasing practices in the United States (Hutchins, 1986; Ansari and Modarress, 1986) revealed that companies were finding the implementation of JIT more difficult than they originally expected. Companies discovered that JIT is a regime which requires more than merely reducing the number of suppliers, renegotiating supplier contracts and tinkering with plant layout; changes in behaviour and attitudes are required too. Hutchins (1986) cites several examples of unsuccessful JIT programmes. The most frequent cause of failure was the way in which companies were perceived as treating JIT as a means of getting suppliers to hold inventories on their behalf. In many cases, relationships deteriorated as suppliers complained about new inventory practices that served only to benefit the purchaser. Ansari and Modarress (1986) identified poor supplier support, followed by inadequate understanding and commitment by top management in the purchasing company as the most significant problems associated with the implementation of JIT. To minimize these problems they recommended three steps: the education and training of suppliers; the development of long term relationships with suppliers; and encouragement of senior managers to visit companies with successful JIT programmes. Hutchins concluded that JIT suppliers need a lot of 'hand holding' from their customers, but in dealing with suppliers the old adversarial ways die hard.

The traditional relationship between the purchasing organization and its supplier community is an adversarial one, with the customer and suppliers having differing objectives. The focus tends to be on negative issues and is characterized by uncertainty. Suppliers are kept at arm's length and are provided with only the bare minimum of data on such issues as the schedule, financial information, future work programme, product changes and their own performance ratings. In general, suppliers are regarded with a certain amount of suspicion by the purchasing organization. On the other hand, the purchasing organization is seen by suppliers as not being concerned about their future business prospects and being very much price-driven in contractual negotiation; quality is a secondary consideration. If a purchasing organization starts to place some emphasis on quality, the typical reaction from suppliers is 'you can have quality but it will cost you'. Some people have likened the relationship (if one can call it that) to a game of cat and mouse.

In the traditional relationship, if the purchasing organization has not provided feedback data on performance, the suppliers tend to believe that their performance is acceptable to the purchaser. Most suppliers are not encouraged to ask the purchaser how their product is performing in practice. Lack of feedback on quality performance is a frequent complaint amongst suppliers. Suppliers, however, react to differing demands and prior experience of their customers. An example of this is the grading of their output to different levels according to individual customer requirements: 'this will not be accepted by Company X, but Company Y will take it'.

To protect themselves in this uneasy relationship with suppliers, the purchasing organization will employ a multiple sourcing strategy, resulting in a large supplier base. Writers on the subject of single versus multiple sourcing cite a number of reasons to support the practice of multiple sourcing, the main ones being that it:

- Provides some security in the event of strikes or catastrophies.
- Gives some flexibility to cater for changes in demand for the supplies.
- Reduces stock.
- Protects against a monopoly situation.
- Facilitates competition.
- Minimizes risk.
- Has price-related reasons (one supplier can be 'played off' against another).

A number of the reasons given can be classified as defensive.

Another characteristic of the traditional relationship is that the customer organization does not have clearly defined responsibilities and accountability for the total quality performance of the supplier base. It is not uncommon to find that a number of people and departments are requesting and providing information to suppliers but no single area is taking overall responsibility. The points of contact are frequently ill-defined resulting in uncoordinated data flow. In particular, the allocation of responsibilities between the purchasing department and quality department are not clear; purchasing personnel often view assistance from the quality department as interference. This results in weaknesses in the communication system and procedures used by the purchasing organization in dealing with suppliers.

Clearly, JIT requires a radically new form of customer–supplier relationship. The Philips Group (1985) coined the phrase 'co-makership' to describe it. Co-makership means working together towards a common goal. It is based on the principle that both parties can gain more benefit through cooperation than by separately pursuing their own self-interests. Co-makership means establishing a long term business partnership with each supplier based on common aims and aspirations, mutual trust and cooperation, a desire by both parties to improve the product continuously, and to understand responsibilities clearly.

The Ford Motor Company is one major organization which has set out to build partnerships with its suppliers in which a joint approach is stressed: 'It is Ford and her suppliers who make cars'. The following points illustrate how the Ford Motor Company endeavours to cooperate with its supplier base:

- Change from supplier quality assurance to supplier quality assistance with the introduction of a new combined function of supplier quality engineering.
- Participation of suppliers in process improvement teams.
- Liaison with suppliers on their use of process FMEA and providing assistance.
- Provision of training in SPC and other techniques to suppliers (this has been used by more than 6000 employees from 1200 suppliers).
- Launch of the interactive video disc programme as a continuing training aid.
- Introduction to the Q1 award.
- Reduction of number of suppliers from 2100 in 1980 to 1200 in 1988 to intensify cooperation and improve quality.
- Fifty per cent of the bills of materials are now covered by long term contracts of 3 to 5 years' duration.
- Extension of early involvement and source nomination for new programmes, improved communication between prototype and production buyers and suppliers: 99 per cent of early components from final production vendors.
- Introduction of just-in-time and supplier communications programme.

To develop a co-makership type of relationship, considerable changes in behaviour and attitude are required in both the customer and supplier. Customers have to be prepared to develop plans and procedures for working with suppliers, and to commit resources to this. On the other hand, suppliers have to accept full responsibility for the quality of their shipped product, and not rely on the customer's receiving inspection to verify that the product is to specification. As a prerequisite of the new relationship, both parties have to reach an agreement on how they will work together (i.e. establish the ground rules).

Barriers to supplier development

As part of a research programme to investigate the effects a major customer might have on supplier awareness and attitudes towards quality management and the methods and systems employed, the authors (Lascelles and Dale, 1988) have carried out a postal questionnaire survey of the supplier communities of three automotive companies (over 300 suppliers in total). In addition to the questionnaire survey, representatives from a number of the suppliers were interviewed, and time was spent in the purchasing companies observing how they operated and interacted with suppliers.

The findings of this research reveal that certain aspects of the customer–supplier relationship can act as a barrier to supplier development. They include poor communication and feedback, supplier complacency, misguided supplier improvement objectives, the credibility of the customer as viewed by their suppliers and misconceptions regarding purchasing power.

Poor communication and feedback

In general, communication and feedback in the supply chain is not good. Moreover, suppliers and customers often do not realize how poor they are at communicating with each other. It was found that whilst the majority of suppliers surveyed perceived as realistic the quality performance requirements of the three collaborating automotive companies, a substantial number of them felt that communications and feedback between customer and supplier could be improved. Furthermore, it was found that not all dissatisfied suppliers communicate their dissatisfaction to the customer; a typical outcome of what was seen to be an adversarial relationship.

Non-conformance of purchased items is often due to the customer's inability to communicate clearly their requirements. Ishikawa (1985) claims that at least 70 per cent of the blame for non-conforming purchased items lies with the customer. It is up to the buyer to ensure the existence of a clear specification which defines the exact requirements, but this in itself is not enough to assure conformance. The supplier must be given the opportunity to understand the function of the part and discuss design details, particularly with regard to the manufacturability of purchased or subcontracted items, before requirements are finalized.

Some purchasing managers and supplier quality assurance engineers seem to think that the quality performance of their suppliers can be achieved almost by remote control and are disappointed and often surprised when non-conforming items are received. During the course of the study, the authors came across several people who genuinely believed they engaged in joint quality planning with suppliers, whereas in fact the communication process was all one-way (from customer to supplier) and feedback from suppliers was discouraged (either because it was *ad hoc* and ignored, or it was never sought in the first place). For example, in one case the supplier was asked if they remembered the non-conforming product they had shipped in some months ago. They were then told that the same problem had recurred and were instructed to visit the company with a drill to rectify the non-conformance.

Supplier complacency

Many suppliers appear complacent about customer satisfaction with the quality of their product or service and do not proactively seek out such information. Respondents to the authors' survey were asked if they had any positive way of measuring how well their product satisfied their customers' requirements. Two hundred and six respondent suppliers claimed they recorded measures of customer satisfaction: however, all but two reported only reactive measures.

Examples of reactive measures include internal failure data (e.g. scrap reports, non-conformity analysis), external failure data (e.g. customer rejections, warranty claims), customer assessment rating and audit reports, verbal feedback from meetings with customers, and requirements outlined in the customers' vendor improvement programme. It is clear that many suppliers see customer satisfaction in very simple terms; if the customer does not return our product then quality and reliability must be satisfactory. This is a short term view which will ultimately result in lost business opportunities. Suppliers should wherever possible utilize proactive measures of customer satisfaction. These include: benchmarking, workshops, customer interviews, evaluating competitors' products, reliability analysis, value analysis and life cycle costing and advanced quality planning carried out in conjunction with customers.

Misguided supplier improvement objectives

Companies are often not sure what they want from a process of supplier improvement. Comments made by respondents indicate that some of their customers (who may be a first- or second-line supplier to a major automotive company) do not understand the fundamentals of total quality management. Many have formal vendor audit programmes but no clear supplier development objectives. There also appears to be a dilution of the quality message as requirements are passed down the supply chain. For example, when faced with demands from customers for improved quality, suppliers are reacting by implementing specific quality techniques and in turn are insisting that their own suppliers use the same techniques. Very few customers are actively involved with their suppliers in helping them to solve quality problems, and there appears to be blind faith in the power of statistical process control (SPC) to do the trick. It is clear that many companies assume that introducing SPC is the same as beginning a process of total quality management. Similarly, these companies are under the equally mistaken impression that the imposition of a particular quality technique on their suppliers as a condition of purchase is the same as supplier development. But the implementation of techniques without behaviour and attitude change means that any benefits gained will only be short-lived.

Lack of customer credibility

A purchasing organization's lack of credibility in the eyes of its suppliers is another barrier to supplier development; suppliers need to be convinced that a customer is serious about quality improvement and that this is demonstrated by the customer's behaviour and attitudes. Poor purchasing and supplies management practices such as a competitive pricing policy, frequent switches from one supplier to another, unpredictable and inflated production schedules, last minute changes to schedules, poor engineering design/production/ supplier liaison, overstringent specifications and inflexibility, in general all lead to a credibility gap in the customer–supplier relationship. It is not uncommon for a customer to preach the gospel of quality to its suppliers and then act quite differently by relegating quality to secondary importance behind, for example, price or meeting the production schedule. Similarly, there is little value in holding quality improvement conferences and seminars for suppliers if the purchasing organization continues to adopt an adversarial approach to its suppliers, or is seen to accord a low priority to quality unless there is a serious non-conformance. In the words of one supplier quality assurance engineer: 'No one cares about vendor performance until the production line stops'.

Failure to respond to supplier requests for information or feedback on specification requirements, component functionality, and to provide a design FMEA, etc., is a further way in which a purchaser's credibility can be seriously undermined.

Purchasing power: a misconception

Purchasing power is a major influence in the relationship between a customer and its supplier community. Lack of power is a commonly cited reason for lack of success in improving supplier quality performance. There is little doubt that a purchaser's influence on its suppliers varies with its purchasing power, and that the greater this power the more effective its supplier quality assurance activities will be.

However, companies with considerable purchasing power may well cause the supplier to improve the quality of supplied items but this may not necessarily mean that TQM becomes embedded in the supplier's organizational culture. There is a tendency for some vendors to treat powerful customers as sacred cows leading to 'stratified quality assurance'. The authors' research findings indicate that a number of companies do grade the quality of their products at different levels according to past experience of individual customer expectations: 'Company A won't accept this non-conformity but Company B will'. This often stems from the traditional misconceptions that quality is an optional product attribute or extra for which the customer must pay. Such a philosophy ignores the benefits of a continuous quality improvement process (e.g. positive workforce attitudes, less waste, reduced handling costs, etc.) which will accrue to the supplier.

Starting supplier development

Before involving suppliers in an improvement process it is necessary for the purchasing organization to give attention to issues such as: the objectives of supplier development, developing a strategy to accomplish these objectives, and deciding which vendors to involve. But perhaps the first task is to carry out a critical review of the key aspects of the purchasing organization's own operation which affect supplier performance. These include purchase specifications, communications, training and organizational roles. The delivery of non-conforming product from a supplier can often be attributed to an ambiguous purchasing specification. Purchasing specifications are working documents used by both customer and supplier, and must be treated as such. A good specification will define precisely the characteristics of the material to be supplied. It is also important to recognize that the supplier is knowledgeable in his own field of operation, and should be given every opportunity to provide a design input to the preparation of the specification. This is a prerequisite in obtaining a supplier's continued commitment to his product after delivery to the customer. The authors' survey findings indicate that suppliers are more likely to accept responsibility for warranty costs if they are involved in the design of the product or formally agree the customer's specification and drawing.

At an early stage in the formulation of a supplier development strategy, the most effective mechanism for communication and feedback has to be established. Typically purchasing, quality, design and production personnel all talk to suppliers, but with no single functional area accepting total responsibility for the price, delivery and quality of bought-out items. The need for clear accountability is an important factor in ensuring that channels of communication between customers and suppliers are effective. Both parties must nominate a representative (or 'account executive') through whom all communications are directed. Such representatives should also be given sufficient authority to ensure that all necessary actions are carried out.

Professional supplier development programmes need to be supported by well-trained personnel capable of helping suppliers achieve the objectives laid down. It is essential that purchasing staff can undertand the capabilities of their suppliers' manufacturing processes and systrems and have a good working knowledge of the philosophy and techniques of total quality management. The survey findings indicate that out of the sample of 300 companies, only 70 gave quality-related skills training to their purchasing staff. Embarking on a supplier development programme with insufficient regard to the needs of the purchasing organization's skills base is likely to result in frustration and possibly eventual failure of the programme.

The increasing complexity of the task of obtaining conforming supplies at the right time and at the right price suggests that the conventional form and organization of the purchasing management function may no longer be adequate. Traditional staff structures based on tight functional groups (e.g. purchasing, materials planning, supplier quality assurance, engineering, etc.) has resulted in compartmentalized attitudes to suppliers which hinders a co-makership approach to supplier development. Several companies have carried out some restructuring of their purchasing, quality and engineering departments to ensure that they have the right skills in dealing with suppliers, and that functional accountability and logistics are adequate for the process of supplier development.

Supplier development objectives
To assist their suppliers, some major organizations have documented the fundamental requirements for the control of quality and the achievement of quality improvement. It is a requirement of the purchase order agreement that suppliers must ensure that their product complies with these requirements. For example, Ford *Q-101, Quality System Standard* (1987) and Nissan Motor Manufacturing (UK), Quality Standard (1985).

Priorities for action

For a company with many suppliers and bought-out items, it may take several years to develop an effective supplier development programme. Before starting it is therefore essential to prioritize action in some way. One approach adopted by many companies is to concentrate on new products and new vendors. Another approach involves the use of Pareto analysis to focus priorities by ranking bought-out components and materials according to some appropriate parameter (e.g. gross annual spend). It is commonly found that some 20 per cent of the bought-out items account for 80 per cent of the total purchasing spend.

Reducing the supplier base

One outcome of the trend to co-makership is that an increasing number of major purchasing organizations are awarding contracts based on the life of a part. Strategic sourcing (i.e. single or dual sourcing) is considered by many writers and practitioners to be a complementary policy to co-makership. This has, in recent years, led to reductions in the size of organizations' supplier bases. In a survey of 158 suppliers in the motor industry by Dale *et al.* (1989) only 57 had no plans to reduce their number of suppliers; the majority of suppliers had achieved at least a 10 per cent reduction. Organizations are thinking carefully about the number of suppliers they need and how to maintain it at an optimum level. The reduction in the supplier base results in benefits such as: less variation in the characteristics of the supplied product, increases the amount of time supplier quality assurance and purchasing personnel can devote to vendors, improved and simplified communications, less paperwork, less transportation, less handling and inspection activity, less accounts to maintain and reduced costs for both parties. Nor should it be forgotten that there are competitive advantages for the supplier in being recognized as a preferred source of supply to a major purchaser. For example, obtaining the Ford Q1 award.

It is easier to develop a long term relationship if the suppliers are in close proximity to the customer. Consequently, a number of customers are now reversing their international sourcing strategies to develop shorter supply lines. Closeness is also a vital element in the use of Just-in-time purchasing strategy.

It is worth mentioning also that it is the policy of some purchasing organizations to take up to a certain proportion only of a supplier's output — the captive supplier issue; this sometimes results in dual sourcing even though the policy is to single source. In other cases, the opposite is true.

The supplier development programme

Having selected suitable suppliers for inclusion in the development programme, the next step is to get them involved and obtain their commitment. This entails making a serious attempt to communicate to suppliers what is required and, based on a set of common objectives, to reach an understanding with them.

Initially, the most practical way of setting about this task is to hold presentations to outline to suppliers the new approach, the quality system standard to be used, how suppliers' performance will be assessed and how the assessment will be communicated to them. Presentations to suppliers can be held either on the customer's premises or at individual supplier's sites. The authors have come across several examples of how major purchasing organizations communicate their supplier development programme requirements to vendors. When the Ford Motor Company relaunched Q-101 in the UK they wrote to the chief executives of the entire supplier base to secure top management commitment. The letter was followed up by presentations made by teams from buying and quality using a specially produced video: 'Ford Cares About Quality'. At Nissan Motor Manufacturing (UK), potential new suppliers attend a meeting where the senior management outline the Nissan philosophy and quality requirements. The attendees are encouraged to discuss frankly with Nissan's management any areas of concern. IBM, Havant, take considerable care and time in ensuring that their suppliers know how their particular material, component or subassembly fits into IBM's final product. They hold what is termed a 'road show' where IBM representatives visit suppliers with examples of their product. The supplier's personnel are encouraged to examine the product and ask questions.

From their research work, the authors have found that the best results are achieved when the chief executives of both the customer and the supplier are involved in face-to-face discussions.

Once a supplier's senior management have agreed to participate in the development programme, it is necessary for the purchasing organization to visit the supplier's factory and carry out a formal vendor approval survey. The objective of the survey is to assess the supplier's suitability as a business partner. The survey is a multidisciplinary task which in a number of cases involves the customer's purchasing, SQA (supplier quality assurance) and engineering personnel. The survey should cover areas such as control, plant, quality systems, attitude, response, tooling, planning and handling. Some form of checklist is generally used to structure the survey.

As part of its assessment a major purchasing organization should assess the supplier's commitment to advanced quality planning, this is a joint exercise involving both customer and supplier, and focuses on the methods by which quality is designed and manufactured into the product. Advanced quality planning commences with a joint review of the specification and classification of product characteristics. Failure mode and effects analysis (FMEA) and quality function deployment would also be carried out. The supplier then prepares a control plan to summarize the quality planning for significant product characteristics. This would include a description of the manufacturing operation and process flows, equipment used, control characteristics, control plans, specification limits, the use of SPC, inspection details and corrective action methods. The supplier would provide initial samples for evaluation, this would be supported by data on machine and process capability on the key characteristics identified by both parties, plus test results. Following successful evaluation of initial samples, the supplier is now in a position to start a trial production run followed by volume routine production.

Once the customer has assessed the adequacy of the supplier's policies, systems, procedures and manufacturing methods, and the supplier is able to demonstrate the quality of his shipped product, the goods inward inspection of supplies can be reduced considerably; in some cases down to the ideal situation of direct line supply. At this point, 'preferred' or 'certified supplier' status can be conferred on the supplier in recognition of the achievement.

This assessment exercise is not necessarily confined to new suppliers; an increasing number of major purchasing organizations will at regular intervals review the adequacy of the quality assurance systems of all their suppliers. This is to assure the purchasing organization that conformance to the assessment awarded to the supplier's quality assurance system is being maintained; most enlightened customers are looking for improvement. The frequency with which reassessments are carried out is dependent on such factors as: the supplier's current quality performance; the classification awarded to the supplier; the type of item being supplied; the volume of parts being supplied; the occurrence of a major change (e.g. change of management, change of facilities) at the supplier; and at the request of suppliers. A programme of continuing assessment will help suppliers and the purchaser to achieve quality improvements by providing a common database.

Supplier development does not end there; it is a continuous process aimed at building-up an effective business relationship — a relationship which demands a greater and quicker exchange of information between both parties. A number of major purchasing organizations are encouraging electronic data interchanges with their key vendors. The data exchange relates not only to quality but also covers technical requirements and specifications, schedules, manufacturing programmes, lead times, inventory management and invoicing. Suppliers are obliged to communicate any changes to materials, processes or methods that may affect the dimensional, functional, compositional or appearance characteristics of the product. Customers are obliged to provide sufficient information and assistance to aid development of their suppliers' approach to TQM (including training where necessary). In some cases, this extends to joint problem-solving activities, with customer and supplier striving to improve the product and reduce its cost. Over the longer term it is the total cost of doing business with a supplier which is important and not the price per piece. The end results of the long term relationship, joint problem-solving activities, and the increased level of supplier participation in the early stages of product design and development will bring about cost reductions to the mutual benefit of customer and supplier.

References and further reading

Ansari, A. and Modarress, B., 'JIT Purchasing: problems and solutions', *Journal of Purchasing Materials Management*, 1986, Vol. 22, No. 2, pp. 11–15.

Dale, B. G., Owen, M. and Shaw, P., *SPC in the Motor Industry: What is the State-of-the-Art?* Manchester School of Management, UMIST Occasional Paper Series, Occasional Paper 8906, 1989.

Deming, W.E., *Quality, Productivity and Competitive Position*, MIT, Cambridge 1982.

Ford Motor Company, *Q-101, Quality System Standard*, Ford Motor Company, Brentwood 1987.

Hay, E.J., Will the Real Just-in-Time Purchasing Please Stand Up', in

Readings in Zero Inventories, American Production and Inventory Control Society, 1984.

Hay, E.J., *The Just-in-Time Breakthrough*, John Wiley & Sons, New York, 1988.

Hutchins, D., 'Having a Hard Time with Just-in-Time,' *Fortune*, 1986, 9 June, pp. 56–8.

Hutchins, D., *Just-in-Time*, Gower, Aldershot 1988.

Imai, M., *Kaizen: The key to Japan's Competitive Success*, Random House, New York, 1986.

Ishikawa, K., *What is Total Quality Control?: The Japanese Way*, Prentice-Hall, Englewood Cliffs 1985.

Lascelles, D.M. and Dale, B.G., *Supplier Quality Management: Attitudes, techniques and systems, (UMIST Occasional Paper Number 8805)*, Manchester School of Management, Manchester 1988.

Mass, R. A., *World Class Quality*, ASQC Quality Press, Milwaukee 1988.

Nissan, N.M.U.K., *Nissan Quality Standard*, Nissan Motor Manufacturing (UK), Washington New Town 1985.

Sloan, D. and Weiss, S., *Supplier Improvement Process Handbook*, American Society for Quality Control, Milwaukee 1987.

Schonberger, R.J., *Japanese Manufacturing Techniques*, Free Press, New York 1982.

Voss, C.A., *Just-In-Time Manufacturing*, IFS Publications, New York 1987.

Acknowledgement

Part of this chapter is based on Lascelles, D.M. and Dale, B.G., Chapter 18, Product Quality Improvement Through Supplier Development, in Dale, B.G. and Plunkett, J.J. (eds), *Managing Quality*, Philip Allan, Oxford 1989.

22   Essential Quality Procedures

David J. Smith* and John Edge

The various quality activities described throughout this book are applied and implemented by means of a hierarchy of procedures and work instructions. This chapter outlines a typical framework of procedures, such as might be found in a medium-sized manufacturing company. It could well be used as a pattern for developing a quality system within a company. The system described is based on the layout of British Standard BS5750, Part 1 (1987) and will therefore harmonize with the ISO9000 series of requirements.

The need for procedures

Unlike computers, the human being is neither well suited to the exact repetition of methods nor to the application of consistent standards when dealing with measurement or other criteria. It is therefore necessary to provide written standards and procedures if a quality system is to work effectively.

Written procedures are a snapshot of the actual activities taking place in a company at a particular point in time. They should therefore evolve and be subjected to review and change to meet the changing needs of the business. Proper documentation control, including the use of issue numbers, is as necessary for quality procedural documents as it is for all the other drawings and specifications used by the company.

Quality manuals and procedures are not just for show. They are for day-to-day use, and must therefore be concise and readable. Well-used copies should be much in evidence. A single pristine set in each manager's office indicates that little of the system is being implemented.

Hierarchy of procedures

A typical, and effective, approach is to develop a hierarchy of procedures so that the general principles and rules are described in a top level document (quality manual) which refers to subsequent levels of procedures and work instructions that provide the detail.

The arrangement shown in Figure 22.1 is a typical quality document

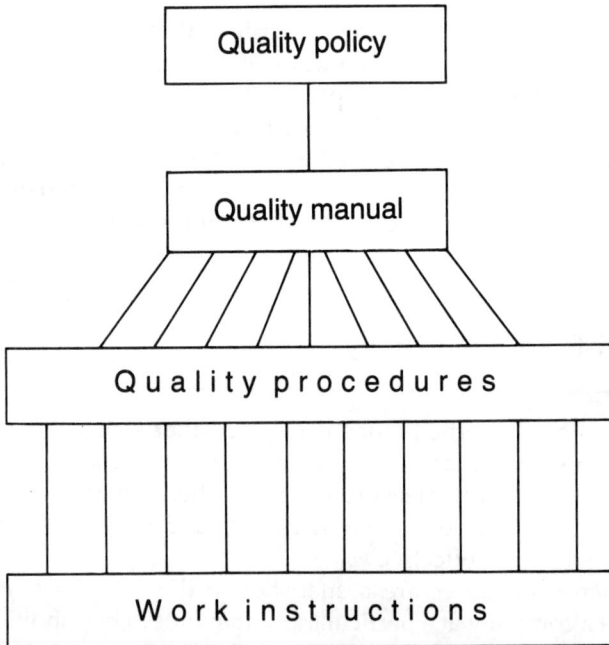

Figure 22.1. Hierarchy of quality procedures.

system, and might be suitable for a small or medium-sized engineering manufacturing company.

Quality manual

A quality manual describes the general quality policy and the organization of the company, together with the responsibilities for quality. It then outlines the specific areas for control and defines by reference the lower level documents needed to carry out quality control and assurance.

The format and content of a typical quality manual are best demonstrated by example, and a complete document is reproduced as Appendix 1 to this chapter. The company represented is, of course, imaginary.

Where certain quality requirements can be described adequately by a few simple statements, then the quality manual may provide sufficient procedure in itself. In the example given in Appendix 1, this is the case for management review and for internal audit, both of which are covered within the quality manual and require no procedures at the lower level.

The section numbering in the example has been chosen so that the numbering of Section 4 coincides with the requirements of BS5750, Part 1 (1987).

Quality procedures

Listed in the quality manual, quality procedures provide detailed instructions. The type of information given includes the routing of forms (such as defect sheets, purchase orders, manufacturing concession notes, engineering change notes and so on), information to be recorded, responsibilities for each action, etc.

A typical quality procedure is given as Appendix 2 to this chapter. This example deals with goods inwards and inspection.

Work instructions

Work instructions deal with a lower level of activities than the quality procedures. Whereas procedures describe who does what, work instructions give specific information about the standards to be achieved. These documents, as with the procedures, are listed in the quality manual. An example of a work instruction is given as Appendix 3 to this chapter.

Appendix 1

Example of a typical quality manual

Quality Manual

Foreword

The prosperity of Gowertronics Ltd can only be assured by the continued satisfaction of its customers. Product quality and reliability are hence essential elements of this objective.

The company has some years of experience in design and manufacture, assembly and operation of its products. The level of success achieved to date can only be maintained by a continuing programme of quality and reliability improvement.

Whilst quality procedures can be specified, their effectiveness depends upon the attitudes of personnel at all levels within the organizational structure. The aim, therefore, is to foster quality awareness by all the means at our disposal.

Declaration
This Quality Manual is devoted to describing the activities within Gowertronics Ltd, the aim of which is to provide products and services to satisfy the standards and requirements of our customers. The objective of the company quality assurance system is to deliver the agreed product through a policy of set procedures operated throughout the entire organization.

The provisions of this quality manual have been reviewed by me and I certify that it will be used as a working document, enforced by the engineering and quality assurance manager who shall have the necessary authority for ensuring that the requirements are implemented and maintained.

Signed ....

MANAGING DIRECTOR

Appendix 1

Quality Manual

Contents

0. Introduction
1. Scope Applicable
2. Applicable References
3. Definitions
4. Quality system requirements
   - 4.1.   Management Responsibility
   - 4.2.   Quality System
   - 4.3.   Contract Review
   - 4.4.   Design Control
   - 4.5.   Document Control
   - 4.6.   Purchasing
   - 4.7.   Purchaser Supplied Product
   - 4.8.   Product Identification and Traceability
   - 4.9.   Process Control
   - 4.10.   Inspection and Testing
   - 4.11.   Inspection, Measuring and Test Equipment
   - 4.12.   Inspection and Test Status
   - 4.13.   Control of Non-Conforming Product
   - 4.14.   Corrective Action
   - 4.15.   Handling, Storage, Packing and Delivery
   - 4.16.   Quality Records
   - 4.17.   Internal Quality Audits
   - 4.18.   Training
   - 4.19.   Servicing
   - 4.20.   Statistical Techniques
5. List of Quality Procedures
6. List of work instructions

Chart 1.   Company Organization

Appendix 1

0. Introduction

The Gowertronics quality assurance procedures and work instructions have been compiled to ensure that products are designed and manufactured to the requirements of BS5750: Part 1: 1987 (ISO9001: 1987).

The responsibility for ensuring compliance with contract requirements and standards has been delegated to the quality assurance manager by the managing director.

Section 4 of this manual is numbered using the identical paragraph numbers to the requirements in BS5750: Part 1: 1987.

0.1. Distribution and updating of the manual

The engineering and quality manager or his appointed deputy is responsible for distributing and updating the manual. The engineering and quality manager alone is responsible for the administration and the raising and incorporation of all amendments. Each holder of the Quality Manual is responsible for maintaining and keeping his/her copy up to date when revisions are issued.

All copies of the manual shall be returned to the engineering and quality manager when a registered holder resigns, or for any other reason has no further need of it.

The engineering and quality manager may distribute 'uncontrolled copies' of the Quality Manual to external companies. These copies will not be updated. He will periodically review and revise the quality system.

1. Scope applicable

This Quality Manual describes and designates the management responsibilities and procedures in design, planning, procurement, manufacture, inspection, test and quality that will be applied by Gowertronics Ltd to meet the requirements of BS5750: Part 1: 1987 (ISO9001: 1987).

The contents of this manual are mandatory and must not be altered or omitted without the written authority of the engineering and quality manager.

2. Applicable References

1. BS5750: Part 1: 1987 (ISO9001: 1987) Quality Systems — Specifications for Design/Development, Production, Installation and Servicing.
2. BS4778: 1987 (ISO8402: 1986) Quality Vocabulary — International Terms.

Appendix 1

3. Gowertronics Ltd quality procedures and work instructions referred to in several sections of this document and listed in Section 5 and Section 6, respectively.
4. BS6000 Guide to the use of BS6001.
   BS6001 Sampling Procedures and Tables for Inspection by Attribute.
5. BS6200 series: Soldering and Board Assembly.

3. Definitions

For the purposes of this manual the definitions given in BS4778: Part 1: 1987 (ISO8402: 1986) shall apply.

4. Quality system requirements

4.1. Management responsibility

4.1.1. Company Quality Policy

The objective of management policy is to ensure that products and services supplied by the company are fit for their intended purpose, ensuring safety and reliability in operation. This policy is implemented and understood at all levels within the organization through well-defined company procedures and work instructions which operate and maintain a quality system in compliance with BS5750: Part 1: 1987 (ISO9001: 1987).

4.1.2. Organization

4.1.2.1. Responsibility and Authority
Gowertronics Ltd is based at the address shown on the front sheet. It is a completely independent company under the direction of Mr A. N. Other.

Gowertronics Ltd is a compact progressive company, staffed by a blend of experienced personnel skilled in the design and manufacture of components and equipments.

The managing director has complete authority over all matters pertaining to quality. Through the engineering and quality manager he has the responsibility for ensuring that procedures, work instructions, job sheets and documentation used by any personnel of Gowertronics Ltd are coordinated so that the products and services supplied are in full compliance with contract requirements.

The organization of the company is shown in Chart 1. Job descriptions are held by the engineering and quality manager.

Appendix 1

4.1.2.2.   Verification Resources and Personnel
The requirements for inhouse verification of design, procurement, manufacture, testing, installation and servicing of all Gowertronics Ltd products are identified in the procedures and work instructions.

For a list of project procedures and work instructions see Sections 5 and 6, respectively.

Inspections, internal audits and design reviews are carried out by personnel independent of those responsible for the work being performed.

4.1.2.3.   Management Representative
The engineering and quality manager is the appointed representative of the company for all matters pertaining to product quality. He has invested in him the authority and responsibility for ensuring that the company quality policy is maintained.

4.1.3.   Management Review
The managing director shall review the quality system by assessing the results of internal quality audits and by arranging third party audits.

There is no separate procedure for this item but the managing director will maintain a file of planned and past reviews together with details of results and corrective action.

4.2.   Quality system

4.2.1.
The elements of the company quality system are:

(a)   applicable national standards;
(b)   formalized company procedures:
(c)   company work instructions.

The effectiveness of the quality system is the responsibility of the engineering and quality manager acting on behalf of the managing director for the:

(a)   coordination and monitoring of the quality system;
(b)   resolution of any non-conformance in the system;
(c)   implementation of effective actions to be taken by appropriate personnel to ensure compliance with specific requirements;
(d)   updating of quality control procedures, work instructions, job sheets, processes and testing techniques as necessary;
(e)   identification and preparation of quality records;
(f)   internal quality audits.

Appendix 1

4.3. Contract review

4.3.1.

A contract is defined as an agreement, verbal or written, to perform a service or provide a product, at some future time, for a financial consideration.

It is the responsibility of the sales manager to initiate reviews of any activities which bear on the ability of the company to meet the requirements of each order. He will involve the engineering and quality manager in the review of each contract involving non-standard parts.

Sales and contract control is covered by:

> *QP 012 — Sales and Contract Control.*

4.4. Design control

4.4.1. General

Compliance is achieved by verifying that the design criteria comply with specific requirements so that data and methods are valid for the range of application and that completed designs satisfy design criteria. The implementation of company procedures is the mechanism by which control of design is achieved.

4.4.2. Design and Development Planning

Each product design and development is the subject of a design sheet agreed prior to the contract commencing.

This will be done for both Gowertronics Ltd's products and any subcontracted products.

4.4.2.1. *Assignment of Responsibilities*

Design and verification activities are the responsibility of the engineering and quality department to ensure that adequate resources are provided so as to permit effective execution of the development.

4.4.2.2. *Organization and Technical interface*

Technical interfaces will be at manager level.

4.4.3. Design Input

Design requirements are clearly identified by discussions with the client. These are documented and agreed by means of the design sheet. Incomplete or conflicting requirements of the contract are to be resolved, where possible, before proceeding with the task.

4.4.4. Design Output

Procedures are implemented to review the design for correctness to

Appendix 1

specification and performance. Also that specific requirements for quality have been met when measured against any appropriate regulatory codes, procedures and standards.

4.4.5. Design Verification

Original design data is independently verified for compliance with specific criteria and any project work is documented and maintained in a project file.

The extent of design verification is dependent upon the features, complexity and requirements of the item under consideration. The design methodology, wherever possible, uses authenticated methods to minimize the probability of errors and uncertainties, by utilizing established practices and standards, and maintaining extra care in any extrapolation beyond previous experience.

The verification of the design of new equipment is established by prototype testing and detailed analysis of the performance of first-off production units. Service life performance may be sought from the use of accelerated life test programmes if deemed necessary by the engineering and quality manager. Design reviews are carried out at predetermined stages in order to conduct a formal examination of all aspects of design and development; also to verify that technical and quality control requirements are being met and that necessary corrective actions are being taken where necessary.

Design is controlled by:

QP 001 Calibration of Measuring Equipment
QP 003 Configuration and Change Control
QP 005 Hardware Design and Review
QP 012 Contract and Sales Control
WI 001 Engineering Drawing

4.5. Document Control

4.5.1. Documentation Approval and Change Control

The routines established cover all documents related to the performance and quality of work in progress such as procedures, work instructions, job sheets, drawings, certificates and general office administration. The control of such documents is a task which is the responsibility of all, in order to authenticate the work undertaken.

The preparation, issue and change of documents are controlled to ensure that correct documents are being employed. Such documents, including changes thereto, are reviewed for adequacy and approval for release by authorized personnel.

Appendix 1

The approval of documents that form part of the final documentation will be a continuous process throughout any given contract. Proposed changes within the content of particular contracts initiated by either the company or its clients are agreed by the sales and engineering and quality managers. A formal written transmittal, between both parties, on the nature of the change proposal and the action to be taken, is then sent.

Pertinent number issues of appropriate documents are then brought under internal change control. The internal control of drawing issues is through a document register. Details of job sheets, component items and their drawing issues, are contained therein.

Document control is controlled by:

QP 003 Configuration and Change Control
WI 002 Archiving

4.6. Purchasing

4.6.1. General
The purchase of material, components and services is the responsibility of the administration manager who shall endorse purchase orders raised by stores. Where necessary a quotation will first be requested.

4.6.2. Assessment of Subcontractor
All sources of supply must be evaluated and approved by the engineering and quality manager prior to the placement of the order. The type and extent of the evaluation shall depend on the nature of the goods or services to be provided and the degree of previous experience with the supplier.

Where possible suppliers shall be BS5750 registered.

To enable the engineering and quality manager to carry out an onsite supplier evaluation, a checklist is available. Suitable suppliers will be placed on an approved suppliers list. The engineering and quality assurance manager shall be responsible for ensuring that the records of suppliers' performance are kept and that regular assessments are made. A history of all rejected goods will be maintained in respect of individual suppliers and this will be used to monitor their performance. Suppliers regularly appearing on the rejected section of component preparation and conformity sheets are first advised that they must improve their quality. If no improvement is noted their names will be removed from the Approved Suppliers List.

4.6.3. Purchasing Data
All purchase orders will contain adequate data to enable the supplier to provide

Appendix 1

the correct quantity and quality of material or services.

All purchase orders will be reviewed and signed by the managing director.

4.6.4.
Facilities are provided at Gowertronics Ltd for customers to witness products at any stage of manufacture.

Purchased goods are controlled by:

> *QP 002 Purchasing and Supplier Assessment*
> *QP 006 Goods Inwards and Inspection*
> *WI 004 Statistical Analysis*

4.7. Purchaser supplied product

4.7.1.
In some instances the customer may supply free issue material which will be treated as a purchased item and will follow the appropriate procedures, including inspection, storage and maintenance. If any such material is lost, damaged or otherwise unsuitable it shall be recorded and reported to the purchaser.

This is controlled by:

> *QP 002 Purchasing and Supplier Assessment*
> *QP 006 Goods Inwards and Inspection*
> *WI 004 Statistical Analysis*

4.8. Product identification and traceability

4.8.1.
All material which has passed the goods inwards inspection is transferred to the appropriate store, segregated and individually identified, where possible.

All packages containing products are marked with appropriate product identification labels, when in the manufacturing areas. Cartons or boxes are marked with similar labels for identification. Large items of equipment also have labels attached for identification.

This is controlled by:

> *QP 004 Job Control*
> *QP 009 Control of Production*
> *QP 010 Stores*
> *QP 011 Equipment Production*
> *WI 003 Product Identification and Traceability*

Appendix 1

4.9. Process control

4.9.1. General

Manufacturing, assembly and testing operations are performed under controlled conditions. These conditions include drawings and work instructions, job sheets and test procedures used during and on completion of assembly. Testing and inspection procedures, which define the method and sequences of all manufacturing operations and quality criteria, are provided.

4.9.2. Special Processes

From the job sheets data are collected for reporting the long term performance of products installed as operational systems. Appropriate records are maintained for analysis by design and manufacturing.

4.10. Inspection and testing

4.10.1. Receiving Inspection and Testing

All goods which arrive at Gowertronics Ltd are received at goods inwards. The goods will be placed on the appropriate shelf in the goods inwards area to await inspection.

Bulk manufactured parts and electrical components coming into the goods inwards area are inspected in accordance with the appropriate quality sampling procedures in BS6001.

All finished items, subassemblies and assemblies are inspected and 100 per cent tested in accordance with appropriate drawings, specifications and work instructions, and are identified as follows:

Green Spot   Goods which have passed inspection.

Yellow Spot Goods offered for concession since they do not meet requirements. These goods are kept on closed-off or locked shelves until the concession is resolved.

Red Spot   Non-conforming goods. These goods are normally returned to the supplier with a letter but may be rectified by agreement between the supplier and Gowertronics Ltd. During this period they are kept on closed-off or locked shelves. Non-conforming goods include those where items are less than on the purchase order.

4.10.2. In-Process Inspection and Testing

During the course of product assembly, inspections and tests are carried out in accordance with applicable documented procedures, drawings and job sheets, clients' specifications, etc. The results of inspections and tests are recorded on job sheets attached to each batch of manufactured items to cover various stages

Appendix 1

in their assembly. Non-conforming items are identified, noted on the job sheets, and reported to the engineering and quality manager for segregation and appropriate action. Within each batch all items are individually identified on the job sheets.

4.10.3. Final Inspecting and Testing
All assemblies are tested functionally prior to despatch. Such tests can be witnessed by the client. Test processes and acceptance criteria are marked on the job sheets. These are agreed with the client before any testing is carried out. On satisfactory completion of testing, where necessary, acceptance certificates are signed by the client and by Gowertronics Ltd.

4.10.4. Inspection and Test Records
Material certificates, manufacturing data, drawings, test results, etc., are all collated as a contract progresses and are maintained in the job control file. At the end of the contract the file will be archived.

Inspection and Testing are controlled by:

> *QP 001 Calibration of Measuring Equipment*
> *QP 004 Job Control*
> *QP 006 Goods Inwards and Inspection*
> *QP 007 Nonconformance, Corrective Action and Records*
> *QP 008 Inline and Final Inspection and Test*
> *WI 004 Statistical Analysis*

4.11.   Inspection, measuring and test equipment

4.11.1. General
All inspection and test equipment used to verify compliance is subjected to regular calibration checks where applicable.

Each instrument is allocated a unique reference number and is checked against master references which are traceable to National Standards. Where equipment cannot be calibrated inhouse, an approved testing house, which is a member of the British Calibration Service, is utilized.

A label is fixed to each instrument stating the date on which it was last calibrated. Records of calibration results are maintained in the calibration register held by the engineering and quality manager.

This is controlled by:

> *QP 001 Calibration of Measuring Equipment*

Appendix 1

4.12. Inspection and test status

4.12.1. Goods Inwards Stage
The status of items at the goods receiving and inspection stage is referenced in Section 4.10.

4.12.2. During Assembly
The inspection status of items during assembly is recorded in the job control file, one of which is attached to each batch of manufactured items as work progresses to final assembly. Each item within a batch may be uniquely identifiable as appropriate.

4.12.3. Release of Conforming Products
Completed items are not released until final inspection and testing has been carried out, sometimes in the presence of the client. The job file will record details of inspection and tests. In the case of customer-witnessed inspection the signature of the customer on the acceptance certificate (or release note) shall constitute acceptance that the product conforms with its specification.

This is covered by:

QP 004 Job Control

4.13. Control of non-conforming product

Those actions pertaining to the control of non-conforming products are located at goods inwards inspection, where appropriate closed-off or locked shelves exist.

Additionally, items which fail within this non-conforming category during assembly and testing of the manufactured product, are similarly segregated and actioned by the engineering and quality manager.

In the latter case, the job files shall be completed, indicating which units of a batch failed and at which point of assembly.

This is covered by:

QP 007 Nonconformance, Corrective Action and Records

4.14. Corrective action

4.14.1. General
At various stages of a contract, e.g. design, purchasing and manufacture, it is sometimes necessary to initiate corrective actions to ensure compliance with standards, procedures and specifications. The corrective actions are

Appendix 1

documented in the procedures and work instructions and cover the investigation and analysis of faults, fault reporting, repairs to items returned from site.

QP 007 Nonconformance, Corrective Action and Records

4.15. Handling, storage, packaging and delivery

4.15.1. General
Items and completed assemblies are moved around the workshop manually.

4.15.2. Handling
Staff are instructed in the safe handling of items so as to prevent deterioration.

4.15.3. Storage
Secure storage areas are provided for all work-in-progress, where the areas are protected to prevent deterioration of stock.

4.15.4. Packaging
Items in stores are kept on shelves marked with the appropriate labels. These identification labels should be transferred to the cartons or boxes in which the items are packed.

4.15.5. Delivery
Preservation of completed assemblies for despatch and delivery is sometimes stipulated by clients in the contract specification. Packing and crating of completed items is in accordance with contract specifications. In some cases specialist carriers are used to convey items to clients.

This is covered by:

WI 005 Packaging and Despatch

4.16. Quality records

4.16.1. General
Records are maintained which verify the effective operation of the quality system. These records include drawings, specifications, procedures, job files, certificates, reports, corrective actions, inspection results, calibration results and test reports. The records for each contract are collated in a project file, a copy of which is maintained in the Gowertronics Ltd archive for a minimum of 3 years, or longer if the contract stipulates. During the retention period clients shall have access to the project files in the archives.

Most of the quality system documents are applicable.

Appendix 1

4.17. Internal quality audits

4.17.1.
Internal quality audits are carried out to verify that quality activities comply with the planned arrangements and also to determine the effectiveness of the quality system.

Audits are carried out on a regular and planned basis. The results and corrective actions are notified to the managing director. There shall be a re-audit within a specified period to terminate the corrective action.

There is no separate procedure for this item but the engineering and quality manager will maintain a file of planned and past audits together with details of results and corrective action.

4.18. Training

4.18.1. Recruiting and Training Programme
Manpower resources and facilities in the company are periodically and systematically reviewed against past, present, planned and forecast levels of business activity by product type, volume and mix to determine and regulate the forward programmes of recruitment and training from which future manpower resources will be met.

The managing director is responsible for specifying the minimum entry requirements, appraisal of applicants, and selection and induction of the new entrant. He is also responsible for identifying and satisfying the training needs of all existing personnel in his area of operation.

Training programmes which comply with the requirements of appropriate external bodies, such as the Engineering Industry Training Board, can be used to satisfy training requirements.

WI 009 Induction Training

4.19. Servicing

4.19.1.
Contracts could include a requirement for servicing and maintenance whereby the quality of the product is retained.

The duties called for within a service contract would be performed by suitably qualified personnel having the required skills and experience.

Appendix 1

4.20. Statistical techniques

4.20.1.
Procedures will be established to verify the acceptability of a product and any processes.

These procedures will establish statistical techniques, quality measures and their implementation. The data used in the quality measures will be collated, collected against a product specification in terms of its conformance to its specification and may include:

(a) reliability;
(b) accuracy;
(c) precision.

This data can only be collected when sufficient records are available. Trend analysis will then be carried out.

The relevant document is:

WI 004 Statistical Analysis

5. List of quality procedures

Procedure No.	Title
QP 001	Calibration of Measuring Equipment
QP 002	Purchasing and Supplier Assessment
QP 003	Configuration and Change Control
QP 004	Job Control
QP 005	Hardware Design and Review
QP 006	Goods Inwards and Inspection
QP 007	Nonconformance, Corrective Action and Records
QP 008	Inline and Final Inspection and Test
QP 009	Control of Production
QP 010	Stores
QP 011	Equipment Production
QP 012	Sales and Contract Control

6. List of work instructions

WI 001	Engineering Drawing
WI 002	Archiving

Appendix 1

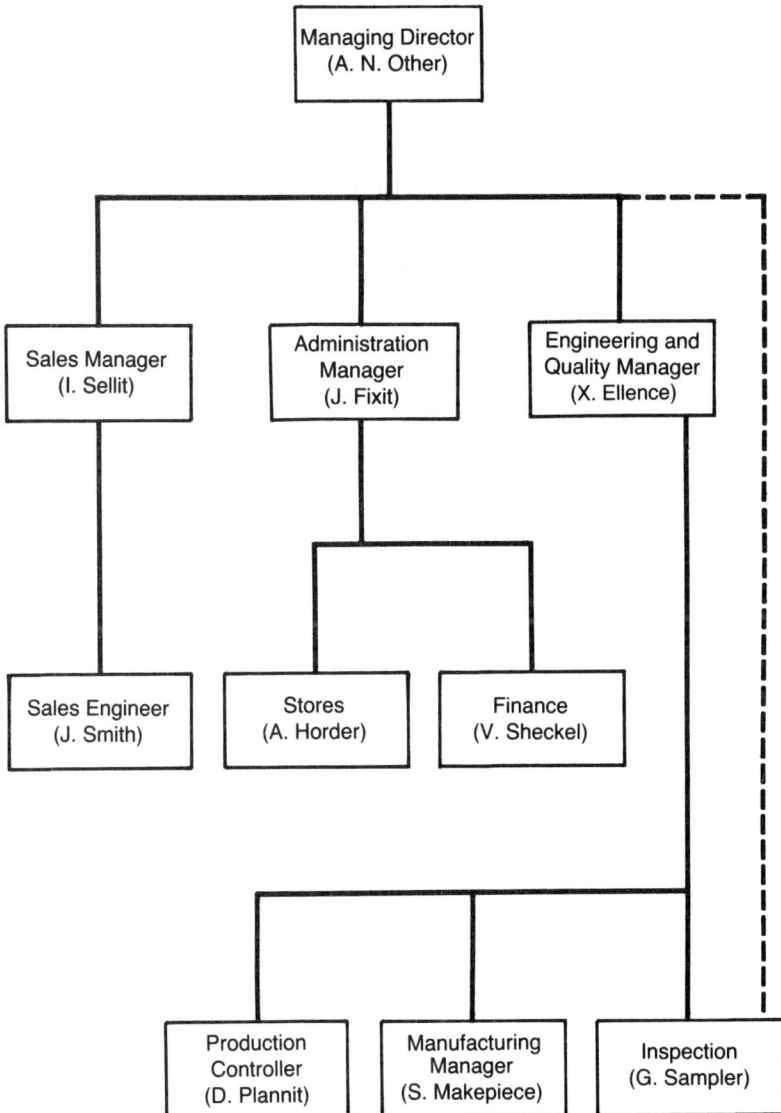

Chart 1.   Company organization

Appendix 1

WI 003	Product Indentification and Traceability
WI 004	Statistical Analysis
WI 005	Packaging and Despatch
WI 006	General Housekeeping
WI 007	Component Manufacturing Workshop
WI 008	Equipment Production
WI 009	Induction Training
WI 501	Widget Test Procedure

Appendix 2

Example of a quality procedure

Gowertronics Ltd

Quality Procedure QP xxx

Goods inwards and inspection

Compiled By ....

Checked By ....

Approved By ....

Date ....

Appendix 2

1. Until such time that the amount of goods received into the Company is large enough to merit the employment of a Goods Receiving Clerk and a Goods Receiving Inspector the two functions will be combined.

2. Goods arriving at the Company will normally be delivered to the Goods Receiving area and will be handled in the following manner.

   (a) The person delivering the goods will present a Delivery Note to be signed. Before doing so the recipient will ensure that the package is not damaged, if damage is observed the Delivery Note will be signed with the rider 'Goods received with packing damaged'.

   (b) The parcel/package will then be opened and the Advice Note withdrawn and quantity and type verified. The purchase order will be taken from file and checked against the Advice Note. If correct a Goods Inwards Note will be made out filling in the purchase order no., type no., quantity and date. If the quantity is found to be incorrect or wrong type is received, a Reject Note will be raised and the Supplier notified. In the case of wrong type or overshipment the goods will be returned to the Supplier after discussion with Administration.

   (c) The operator will then withdraw the record card from file and inspect goods in accordance with Procedure QAPxxx. If the goods are satisfactory the details will be entered on a record card, the Goods Inq. Note signed and goods passed into Stores with the Yellow copy. Copy of GI Note is attached to the order which is then filed. Reject material will be processed as described in the previous paragraph. If a Certificate of Conformity is received with the goods a copy will be made and attached to the purchase order, the original travelling with the goods.

   (d) If for any reason goods cannot be passed into Stores, they will be held in an area clearly marked 'Quarantined Material' with details of shipment until such time as further action is taken.

   (e) The disposition of Goods Inwards Notes is as follows:

   White copy filed with order in Goods Receiving Department.

   Green copy to Administration (Purchasing) Department.

   Red copy to Administration (Accounts) Department.

   Yellow copy to Stores with goods.

   (f) The disposition of Reject Notes is as follows:

   One copy to supplier by post.

Appendix 2

One copy with goods to Supplier.

One copy filed in Goods Inwards Department.

One copy to Administration.

(g) *Concession Notes*

There are instances where goods or materials will be received with minor faults and may be used without detriment to the performance of finished product. In such cases the Goods Inwards Operator will raise a Concession Note stating order number, Supplier, description of goods, drawing number and nature of fault and concession required. The form will then be signed by the Quality and Engineering Manager giving approval. The goods will then be passed into Stores, the Concession Note number written on Goods In Note. A copy of the Concession Note will be sent to the Supplier intimating that further deterioration will result in rejection.

Appendix 3

A typical work instruction document

Gowertronics Ltd

Work Instruction WI zzz

General housekeeping

Compiled By ....

Checked By ....

Approved By ....

Date ....

Appendix 3

General housekeeping

1. Maintaining a suitable working environment is an integral part of the job description for all personnel.

    The following will apply:

    ● Floors will be checked each morning and cleaned as necessary.

    ● Shelving will be cleaned once per month by vacuum cleaner.

    ● Partaking of food and drink will be away from the vicinity of equipment and components.

    ● Partly or fully assembled equipment will be covered when not being worked on.

    ● Smoking is not permitted in any certain parts of the factory or offices as indicated.

    ● Benches are the responsibility of individuals who will keep their workplaces clean and tidy.

    ● Personnel will be instructed in the principles of good housekeeping.

2. It is the engineering and quality manager's responsibility to ensure that these activities are carried out.

23 Quality Audits and Reviews

Gordon Staples

An audit is the means by which management of a company determines whether the people in the organization are carrying out their duties in the way that management intends them to. A review is the means by which management determines whether the organization is being effective in meeting corporate goals (increased customer satisfaction, growing market share, rising profit) and whether the audits carried out are doing their part in monitoring the organization's effectiveness towards those goals.

Reasons for audits

Any business which is going to undertake quality audits needs to make the requirement for audits a clear mandate from the top. It would be expected that the belief in and the authority for audits would be enshrined in the quality policy of the business. In this case, the management want audits to be carried out so that they can control operations.

Of course there are other reasons for carrying out audits. All quality standards contain a requirement, explicit in some, implicit in others, that companies do audits. However, if done for this reason only, audits are unlikely to be particularly searching or useful. Unfortunately, there are still many companies in which audits are carried out to show that procedures are still slavishly followed, regardless of whether these procedures are contributing to the health of the business. The company may even proudly proclaim that it does audits, and the auditors within it may be extremely busy working the prescribed programme of audits and maintaining lots of file space full of audit reports.

To consider the best way to set up an audit system therefore, it is as well to be clear about why the audit system is wanted and what the company will have or potentially have, when series of audits have been completed. In order to determine that, it is necessary to consider what the systems are there for; also whether there is a way to think about the systems such that the needs of the business are addressed and the audit can be related directly to those needs.

Needs of a business

Whilst profit undoubtedly figures very highly when considering what businesses need, it can be appreciated fairly quickly that sustained profit and particularly increases in profit, can only come from an established base of satisfied customers.

So the organization's main goal is to create and increase this base of happy customers. But there is another step which must be taken. Is the 'customer' always the 'user' of the product? The answer often is a negative one and therefore any business in the marketplace has to determine exactly how its product is going to be used and what the expectations of the user are from that product. Anything a business can do in order to make its products actually *fitter for use* than those of the competitors will give that business a market edge, provided it can bring those quality characteristics within the perception of the marketplace.

The needs of a business thus must be very closely aligned with the needs of the user/customer.

Having established its needs the business has to decide how it is going to achieve them through its functional divisions and departments. Their duty is to work within that stated policy and provide their own policy hence their output to the requirements developed in line with the policy. Departments within an organization are required to work to timescale, budgets, output targets, capital allocations, etc. Each department then has to work to conform with the requirements so that the customer/user is supplied with a service which is progressively being thought of as excellent. The word 'service' is deliberately used since every perception which a customer or user has of a product, including the way it was supplied, is going to influence the opinion held about it. *All* businesses are in the service business.

Now, within the business, each of these functional departments is working away to meet the requirements laid down for it, but few departments work in total isolation from the rest of the company. Each is dependent on others for information. In processing areas one department is dependent on another for the timely receipt of the product in a state *fit for their use*. So it is also for those departments who merely exchange information. These days it is possible to move and distribute large amounts of data around a company and it can be painful to identify and extract the little piece of useful information which the package contains.

Therefore, it becomes clear that each department (and ultimately each person in an organization) is at one time or another playing one of three roles. These roles may be considered in any order.

The first role is that of customer/user. Other departments supply information or product (often both) so that the user can process it and pass it on to the next user. The departments supplying the input are suppliers. Any customer is entitled to get what is fit for his use, provided of course he has told his supplier precisely and unambiguously exactly what is wanted, when it's wanted, etc.

In passing the product on to the next user the department concerned is acting in a second role — as a supplier. In order to be a good supplier, he should find out what his customer's needs are and define in conjunction with this customer how quality will be determined. In the ideal situation which is being expounded here, it requires no great intellect to realize that the internal customers and suppliers in a company need to work very closely together in order to cut down the barriers which can exist and which prevent the even flow of fit-for-use product or information. Only by working in that way will a satisfactory compromise, as it may have to be, be worked out. Anything which restricts the efficient flow is waste and should be removed. It is termed the 'cost of non-conformance'.

There is also the third role, perhaps the most important. The role is one of processor — of doing the function the department or person is employed to do. The function can be done correctly provided the input for it is correct and fit for conversion to the output. The process of conversion of course must be fit for purpose too. Any process is subject to variation. In order to keep a process under control it is necessary to recognize the variables which are going to prevent the output from being achieved. These variables are unwanted inputs.

So now this picture is complete. Every department, no, every individual is at one time or another a supplier, a customer and a processor. If every one of those supplier–customer links is improved one little iota, should not the organization be more effective measured in terms of cost and time? Might it not satisfy the external customer quicker, more often and engender that confidence which customers like so much — perhaps with an edge over the competition?

That's what quality is about, that's where audits and reviews should be aimed. If audits and reviews do not instigate more benefit than they cost then their effectiveness has to be questioned.

The base for setting up a programme for audits therefore is established. It is a strategic position. The implementation consists of planning, of doing, of reporting, of follow-up and of getting corrective action taken and providing feedback.

Types of audits

Before launching into an audit programme it is necessary to distinguish between the different types of audits. For example, a customer may audit a supplier against the contract requirements to examine how closely this supplier is working to the agreed contract conditions. This audit may include requirements invested in a quality standard system such as ISO9000.

A company may audit a potential supplier against requirements proposed to operate were a contract to be placed. These requirements can be prescribed in suppliers' internal documents and these may again include the requirements invested in a quality systems standard.

Audits can obviously take place before, during or after contracts, and all are external audits. In the cases outlined above they are commonly called 'second-party'. In the history of quality assurance these originally outnumbered other types of audit and they are still commonplace.

A company may carry out audits internally to determine for management purposes how closely the various departments are working to the procedures prescribed for each department. It would be intended to provide the results of these results to management who would use the information and other management information to determine by review whether the policy is being complied with.

Such audits are internal audits and are commonly called 'first-party'. Some organizations subcontract the audit to outside organizations and an external party comes into the company and audits them against their own procedures, perhaps because the organization placing the subcontract is limited in expertise and or resources.

Provided the audit is carried out within the expressed policy and requirements of the company placing the subcontract and is not designed by the subcontractor to lead towards further work, perhaps consultancy, then the audit may be still considered as a proper internal audit within the 'intent' of the quality systems of the company.

As far as the subcontract company is concerned of course, an audit carried out in such a way is a second-party audit.

There is, of course, a third type of audit within the scope of this discussion. The National Quality Campaign and subsequently 'Management Into the Nineties' in the UK, encouraged by the government, gave rise to accredited certification bodies who can show that they are organized and competent to do this work through assessment by the NACCB (National Accreditation Council for Certifying Bodies).

These companies will assess organizations against a quality systems standard and provide a certificate which records their perception that the organization at the time of the assessment has management systems which comply with the standards. A fee is charged for this service and the certificate can be withdrawn if continued compliance with this standard is not established.

This third-party method is considered to provide users of that organization's products with confidence and therefore reduce the need for second-party audits. The organization's certified compliance with the standard is also believed to give that organization a market edge.

Third-party certification is growing in the UK and parts of Europe. Time will tell whether it has been of any value to the organization in increasing market share, reducing costs of doing business, raising customers' expectations, improving employees' quality of worklife and increasing profit.

This chapter will concentrate on first and second-party audits of management systems. The word 'audit' is often associated with finance, safety, costs, product and other subjects. While many of the principles are the same, great professional expertise of long-standing has developed many of those other audits into specialized procedures, and they are therefore not covered here.

It is by no means typical for an organization to decide to carry out audits on itself before proceeding to carry them out on suppliers. However, without wishing to argue with the major purchasers in the land, it will be stated here that an organization should look inside itself first. How can it decide what is best outside unless it is first clear inside about what it wants?

Internal audits

Many organizations write down their business mission, then their quality policy, then their business objectives in the long and short term, then more detailed procedures for the troops to achieve those objectives. The former may be thought of as strategy, the latter as tactics. Such a hierarchy of documents is often pictured as a triangle (as shown in Figure 23.1).

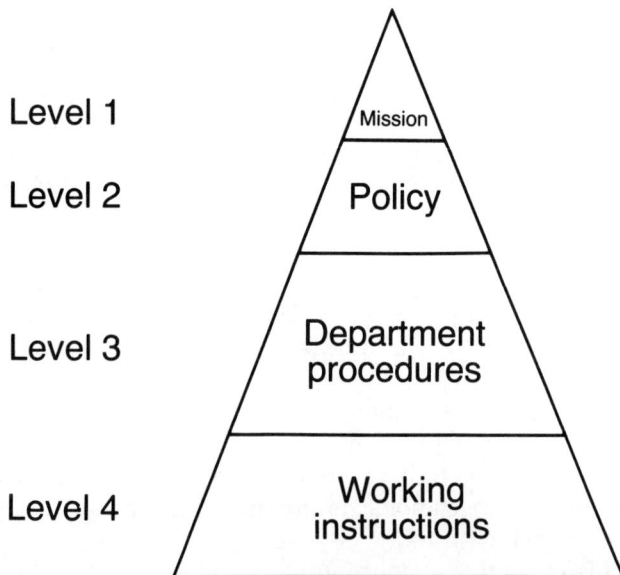

Level 1 — Mission

Level 2 — Policy

Level 3 — Department procedures

Level 4 — Working instructions

Figure 23.1.   Document hierarchy.

If the management of an organization sees the need for internal audits in order to check that each step in the hierarchy is operating properly, then it is clear that the need for internal audits should be enshrined in the quality policy (along with the need for relevant corrective actions). Having established this belief from the top of the company the question must then be asked, 'Who is going to do the audit?'

Definitions of audit nearly always stress the element of independence. Some companies have therefore provided a separate department in the organization to carry out audits. This department exists to audit everyone else. Typically, the quality department gets the job. Some companies which originally organized their audits in this way have been suspicious that the department is not really being as effective as it should be in this respect. Certainly the correct forms are being filled in at the appropriate times against programmes and schedules of audits but the same order and type of deficiencies continue to arise. The fault may, of course, lie with the procedures which are being audited. The audit may be doing no more than ensuring that the status quo is being maintained. In these circumstances it may not be inappropriate to translate 'the status quo' as 'the mess we are in'.

Those companies which originally set up their independent departments began to ask

> 'Why do we have to have these people? They add to our costs without adding value to our product or service and we are only duplicating activities that management throughout the company should be doing in any case'.

So these companies began to train their managers, supervisors and specialists in the art of audit. Thus at the very senior level managers were required to ensure that departments got together and established their customer – supplier links. Questions took the form 'What are the products and services being traded?' and 'What are the features and characteristics by which one department can measure the performance of another?' Having established the answers a means of measurement had to be provided for both parties, in quantifiable units (the units may differ in each case). Then, within each department a similar arrangement was set up among sections and people.

It follows from this development that the three basic questions of auditing can be asked at each stage:

1. Is there a way of doing things?

2.   Has it been put into practice?
3.   Is it effective?

Thus, procedures must be documented to the extent necessary to establish the best way of doing things. Then there is the need to show that this is being done, using records. Finally, there must be a measure of whether the effort was worthwhile, via a satisfied 'customer' (who will also keep a record).

An auditing schedule can be established, not very different from traditional schedules in format but perhaps with an emphasis placed on what the company is in business for. Schedules are illustrated in Figures 23.2 and 23.3.

The operating forces (managers, supervisors and specialists) would decide what the relationships are, what measurements are necessary, how forward communications and feedback will be determined, the timescales for action and when problems are likely to arise.

Senior management must be determined that these activities are extended throughout the organization. They would therefore initiate reports, perhaps collated and summarized by the quality department. This department has not totally disappeared, but it now provides a service in training for auditing, assistance in problem-solving and enables managers to collect relevant data. Thus the quality assurance department has become quality assistance, which is a more useful role. The extent of assurance necessary is left in the hands of the experts, the people employed to do the job, with less need for the 'QA paper chase'.

Based on the triple role model explained earlier, it would first of all be necessary for series of individuals from each pair of interacting departments to have met and for them to have determined the major products and services passed between them, i.e. in what specific ways are they customers (users) and suppliers of each other? They would also have to say what constitutes adequate quality of service, what gives difficulty to the other party and what improvement opportunities are available. There would need to be measurements made in units agreed by both parties and a means of recording performance. The two parties in each case will need to review these on a regular basis as the 'products' change.

The basis for the relationship and its functioning would need to be formally defined and agreed much as a standard procedure might be. In this condition, it can be easily audited.

The audits early in the development of this process would be searching for existence of a growing number of the formal

Customer department	Supplier's departments ———→			
Research and development	Marketing	Finance	Administration	Purchasing
Relationship established				
Products defined				
Quality criteria agreed				
Performance measured				
Review of system				

Figure 23.2. **Internal audit schedule. Suggested content for examining customer–supplier links.**

Function / department	Month of audit	Report issued	Corrective actions agreed	First follow-up	Second follow-up	Close out
Administration	1	✓	✓			
date :						
Mechanical	2	✓	✓			
date :						
Electrical	3					
date :						
Textile	4					
date :						
Physical	5					
date :						
Chemistry	6					
date :						
Metallurgy	9					
date :						

Figure 23.3. **Internal audit schedule. Traditional style, department by department.**

relationships between departments, and subsequent development of waste removal and efficiency improvements.

There are some different possibilities for who carries out the audits. A concept of 'internal second party' might operate, whereby each user audits his suppliers. A concept of internal third-party might operate whereby one party audits sets of other users/suppliers. One could maintain an independent department doing the audits — itself audited by the Chief Executive or nominee. There is no ideal answer to this. It would seem that a combination of these options is likely to prove most effective.

The natural development of this process must lead to whatever the objectives of the organization are. Areas of improvement may be a reduction in staff turnover, in absenteeism and lateness, a cost reduction, an increase in business, a reduction in external complaints/returns/warranty, etc.

There is something blocking the development process somewhere if some of these things do not happen. The management review of operations naturally is interested in reviewing the effectiveness of the user/supplier process, driven by the ultimate user. Like any management tool requiring careful and prolonged attention, it may be sacrificed on the altar of short term gains.

External audits

There may be a variety of reasons for carrying out external audits:

- Because it is a requirement of QA standards that such audits be carried out.
- To provide an input to the rating of established suppliers or of selecting and approving potential suppliers.
- To bring about a greater understanding by the supplier of the user's needs and thereby instigate progressive improvement in the relationship between supplier and purchaser (user).

Whilst any audit (internal or external) should have the third of these reasons as an objective, the second may be at least partially relevant. If for only the first reason, the audit will be costly for all and of little real use.

There is as yet no agreed national or international standard for carrying out audits, though there are impressive and useful books by L. Marvin Johnson and others. These books record the substantial unanimity there is about the way in which audits should be carried out. It is strongly recommended that auditors should follow conventional procedures to audit vendors.

The word 'vendor' as used here means any supplier or subcontractor, potential or established. Conformance to the expectations of companies being audited (auditees) makes those audits more acceptable to them. Johnson wrote his books before many companies (apart from certain in the defence-related industries) were carrying out audits on vendors. The methods now accepted are very close to those originally described. Those audits demanded a certain way of preparation, conduct and reporting of audits. It was of interest in the prevailing adversarial relationship between customer and supplier to have an internal audit system so that the internal system would find deficiencies before the external system did.

In laying down here the recommendations for an external audit of its vendors, the company is interested in a specific service from each vendor. It has to find out by audit how each vendor determines what his customer wants and how the vendor ensures consistent supply of that service to this customer.

The various quality system standards were produced in order to provide a list of features which, if companies developed to the extent necessary for their services could be used for the assessment of one company by another. The idea behind the standards and the intent of each clause within them are excellent but, like any tool, can be quite dangerous in the wrong hands.

Preparation for an external audit

The whole auditing activity must be planned in a formal and systematic manner and it is necessary to formulate a forward programme of vendor audits. This programme should be documented so that it can be shown to and discussed with interested parties inside and outside the company (e.g. user departments and/or visiting auditors). There are a number of factors to be considered along with those already considered earlier in this chapter:

- The requirements of current and pending contracts. It may be desirable to carry out audits early during a major contract to assure effective QA during the design/development and early procurement phases.
- The time which has elapsed since a particular vendor was last audited.

- The number and nature of the findings of previous audits.
- The resources available for auditing.

The programme must be reasonably flexible to allow for contingencies. For example, it may be desirable to arrange an immediate audit on a vendor whose products are failing to meet standards. The purchasing department may wish to open a new source of supply for some product and it may be decided that an evaluation of the vendor is needed prior to contract award.

The first step taken in the audit preparation is the selection of the audit team leader. His/hers will be the responsibility for planning, performance and reporting of the audit.

The team leader therefore needs to be fully briefed about the objectives of the audit. What decisions can be made and what actions can be taken when the audit has been carried out? Audits may be carried out to assess a vendor's ability to supply a given product, to manage a given project, to complete a given project within a timescale, etc. Unless the team leader knows this, the audit will be unsuccessful.

Similarly, the team leader must be advised of the scope. Are all products, all parts of the vendor to be audited or just some?

Once objectives and scope are clear, then some decisions can be made about the man days necessary to complete the audit. These decisions must be made at this early stage.

The company to be audited should be given ample warning of the intention to carry out an audit and the proposed date(s). Who does this is immaterial. It often falls to the procurement function but it is reasonable and not untypical for the audit team leader to make this initial contact.

In order to plan properly, the auditors need a considerable amount of information about the company — its activities, organization, policies and procedures. The usual source of such information is the quality manual. Different companies have very different ideas about what is a quality manual and about what should be in it. The manual may include all documented procedures or it may be only the part dealing with policy.

Companies are often unwilling to release a copy of procedures which may be confidential and useful to competitors. They may, however, allow the auditor to see procedures whilst he is in the company.

Companies may have no quality manual which they can pass over to the auditor. What is important to the auditor is that he gains sufficient information before the audit about the way the company controls its operations. Depending on cost and the resources available there are many ways open.

The auditor can make a detailed preparation if the company has a document or set of documents which describe the company operations in sufficient detail for him to understand the management controls used in the various areas of interest. The company may call this a quality manual, but it may have been written for the company's own benefit and not for external auditors. The auditor may have some work to do in order to find the information he wants. This is not a criticism of the manual, unless a requirement within the scope of the audit is violated.

Where difficulty in procuring the information is experienced or there appears to be no such information available the auditor has two choices.

Firstly he can visit the company on a preliminary basis and discuss with them the information necessary. This has added benefit as the relevant personnel meet one another, thereby removing some of the formality present at the start of any new relationship. This is, however, impossible where great distances are involved and therefore great time or costs, to be able to make a preliminary visit.

The second choice, therefore, is to make preparations without the more detailed information requested.

There may be other choices according to the auditor's own company policies. These may require the vendor to prepare such a document. The audit either waits or is cancelled along with the business between the two companies.

Assuming that documented information has been supplied by the vendor, the auditor must prepare his own checklist or *aide-mémoire* for carrying out the audit.

The initial information gathering being complete, a decision is now necessary about how many auditors, for how long, will be necessary to achieve the objectives of the audit within the required scope. Many audits are undertaken by one person alone and internal audits are often done this way quite satisfactorily. External audits may also be done this way, especially if the audited company is small and the auditor is comfortable in the technology involved.

However, if it were considered that eight man days were required as audit effort, it might be preferable to have four people for two days or two for four days rather than one person for eight days. Audits can be disruptive and the less time spent in actually being disruptive the better.

Audits carried out by one person can be successful, but audits carried out by two auditors working together as a team can be more than twice as successful. An audit team where the members corroborate notes and statements where necessary, and provide each other with support and help is a joy to behold. The second person in any audit team is often able to view the situation more objectively than the leader when the situation becomes 'heated' or where the line of questioning is yielding little of value. The second person may also act as timekeeper to help to keep the audit on schedule.

The second team member may be someone who has technical knowledge or direct experience of working in the industry being audited. Some major auditing organizations in the UK for example, make audit teams up of experienced systems team leaders and assessor(s) from mechanical, electrical, chemical, and other disciplines as necessary. This is considered to keep the auditors in a more pragmatic frame of mind regarding the industry being audited, and the organization's objectives from the audit.

Programme for the audit

Now that the auditors have decided how much time is needed at the auditee company, it is necessary to lay down a programme for the visit. It is reasonable to do this. The auditors can not see everything in the company during the audit. They take a 'snapshot' of activities in selected parts of the company in order to arrive at a conclusion about the organization's degree of compliance with a set of criteria. They will therefore take a sample of departments throughout the company and allocate some time to each.

The programme needs to be agreed with the auditee before the audit. The auditee may be able to make suggestions about the route proposed in order to save time (or the auditors' legs) during the audit.

There is another more important reason for agreeing the programme with the auditee before the audit. Few companies are willing to allow auditors (or any other visitors for that matter) to wander around their facilities unaccompanied. It is discourteous to the auditors and may in fact be hazardous to them. The auditee will be requested to supply a guide who is responsible for taking the auditors from point A to point B and so on. The auditee will also need to have someone of requisite authority, a management representative, available in each department, to explain to the auditors about how the department works and to answer the auditors' questions. The guide and the management representative may be the same person for parts of the audit.

Audit programme

Company: XXXX Limited

Dates: ....

Auditors: **Team leader:**

Auditor:

Day one

09.30 – 10.00	Opening meeting
10.00 – 10.30	Quality manual
10.30 – 12.30	Contracts department
13.30 – 15.30	Design department
15.30 – 17.00	Purchasing department

Day two

09.00 – 09.30	Review meeting
09.30 – 11.30	Storage: Stockyard
	Covered stores
11.30 – 12.30	Instrument shop
13.30 – 15.00	Test house
15.00 – 17.00	Fabrication shop

Day three

09.00 – 09.30	Review meeting
09.30 – 11.30	Assembly shop
11.30 – 12.30	Drawing office and standards
13.30 – 14.30	Quality office
14.30 – 15.15	Paint shop
15.15 – 16.00	Preparation, closing meeting
16.00 – 17.00 (proposed)	Closing meeting

Figure 23.4. Typical external audit programme.

Figure 23.4 is a typical programme for an audit covering three days with two auditors. The example is a manufacturing company with some design activities. In preparing this programme the auditors will also have decided their strategy for the audit. There are various options.

Some auditors favour starting at the point in a company where enquiries and orders are received, then following the process through various departments finishing with the despatch area, taking in specialized areas along the way. This may be termed 'top-down' or 'downstream audit'. The auditors follow a specific order through the system, examining other examples, documents and stages as they go. They follow the process route and take examples of other orders at each stage and thus gain their 'snapshots'. This has certain advantages, particularly if making comparisons amongst a number of vendors with the same kind of service. However, it can be superficial unless the auditors use other techniques as well.

Another approach is to go in entirely the other direction. Take a completed product or its records and go back 'upstream' and check the systems that got it there. This can be very searching but if only one order or product is being examined, it may 'bias' the audit conclusion.

The answer of course should be that there is no 'right' way. The audit has an objective and the combination of techniques has to be one that will achieve that objective.

Checklists

The auditor must remember that the quality system is made up of many parts. There is that part which is written down in manuals and procedures, the people who are expected to follow those procedures, plus the machinery, equipment and materials used in the process. The auditor must always ask whether there is a system, whether this is put into practice and whether it is effective by taking into account the people, the procedures, the machines, the equipment and the materials. Otherwise the audit may not be considering properly all the factors that it should.

Having established the overall audit programme, the auditors need to establish therefore the detailed samples within each chosen area. This will entail the preparation of checklists or *aide-mémoires*. The word 'checklist' has an unfortunate connotation and smacks of ticks and crosses or 'yes' and 'no' answers. The checklists are not meant to be that at all. The checklists will in fact define the sample. This sample cannot be statistically valid (though some auditors would like to make it so) but it should be as representative as the auditor can make it.

The style and format of a checklist are at the auditor's discretion. An inexperienced auditor may frame full questions on a checklist, whilst a more experienced auditor may use keywords instead. A good guide to the preparation of checklists is to think in terms of 'what to look at' and 'what to look for'. Thus it may be decided to look at documents, records, products, equipment. Respectively these may be examined for approval, completeness, status and condition. This is a very simple example. It may be decided to look at the internal audit system and to look for statement of its authority, comprehensive coverage of the system, training of auditors, timely action on findings, procedures and understanding of them by auditors, etc. The objectives of the audit must be clear in the auditor's mind when these checklists are being prepared therefore.

To return to the preparation of a representative sample it is reasonable that, if the audit is to examine a given department, it should include a look at what the department spends most of its time doing. Thus a drawing office may be mainly preparing drawings and parts lists, a merchandiser in a retail organization may be mainly assessing products and placing orders, and a laboratory may be mainly making up standard formulations. If the purpose of the audit is to establish the degree of compliance with established criteria then the representative sample should reflect the major activities of each relevant department.

All departments have 'their job'. There are also special or different activities they may undertake. Thus drawing offices may also carry out troubleshooting, provide technical advice, prepare sales literature and take technical customer enquiries. Merchandisers may influence outlet pricing, methods of display and safety policy. Laboratories may do special studies and experiments, and provide specialist advice, etc.

Yet another aspect must be considered by the auditor. What happens when a department's systems fail? How does the department attempt to put things right and prevent the error from occurring again? Perhaps audits in some organizations should look at this aspect and no other!

There is therefore considerable choice open to the would-be auditor. His selection of subjects is up to him. The leader of an audit team may insist that certain samples are taken but another team of auditors may make a different choice. Neither is necessarily wrong. It would be impossible to define the sample (though some believe they can).

Few auditors are given total freedom in their choice. The audit has a purpose and is initiated by management; therefore there are management priorities and concerns which have to be addressed. This collection of requirements can often be quite large. Auditors look at it and consider that the time allowed for the audit must therefore be used very carefully. One of the essential features of planning the audit very carefully before the audit itself is to ensure that no time during the audit shall be wasted. It must be spent auditing and not planning what is next.

Some auditors believe that they can do a good audit by arriving at the auditee with a blank piece of paper and then 'following their nose'! No one has been shown to have done an effective audit in this way and all such auditors have done the profession a great disservice. Such audits are generally biased and provide good material for the individual auditor's particular 'hobby horse'. It is likely the audit will reach a conclusion based on very scant information, or which is unrelated to the audit objective.

The audit team leader, with his team members (or subteams) therefore draws up a total sample for the audit.

There is a school of thought which says that checklists should be sent to the auditee before the audit. This may have the advantage of saving time during the audit as certain information can be made available in advance. However, other schools of thought would be opposed to this. It does rather depend on what the checklist contains. In principle, it should not matter that the checklists are sent if they are understood by the auditee and if this contributes to the achievement of audit objectives.

This point is related to another. Some auditors prefer not to advise the auditee that an audit is going to be carried out. In this way, it is argued, the 'tidyings up' are not carried out and the audit will find a more typical condition. However, at least once in a while the place does get tidied up so the audit instigates some improvement. The sort of management system error that can be easily tidied up is generally not major and therefore does not deserve any lengthy attention from the auditor.

Now that the programme has been agreed with the auditee and checklists have been prepared by the audit team, it is the end of the planning stage and the start of the audit stage.

Opening meeting

Good audit practice would recommend that the team leader telephones his contact at the auditee the day before the audit is to start and check that all arrangements are in hand. It is disconcerting to find that nobody is expecting the audit team when they arrive after a long and expensive journey.

The same good practice would recommend that the team arrives promptly — neither early nor late. Either is embarrassing for both parties and unprofessional.

The opening meeting or pre-audit conference is typically held in a conference room of the auditee. The audit team leader should come prepared with an 'agenda' and ensure that certain points are covered quickly and efficiently. It should be remembered that this meeting may be the first time the two parties — auditee and auditor — have met. The way it is carried out can set the style or 'tone' of the audit. The meeting is the place to set the rules for conduct of the audit. Matters to be addressed include: introduction of personnel; purpose and scope of the audit; reviewing the audit programme; and administration arrangements.

Introduction of personnel
The audit team leader should introduce himself and his team, explaining how the people are organized (whether there is more than one team, for example). It may be the case that the auditee representatives are not particularly senior. Whilst the audit team leader may have expected to find some senior management representative available he need not be concerned if he has done all his preparations beforehand. The auditors cannot insist on meeting someone senior.

If a large number of people appear at the opening meeting, it is easier for the audit team leader to pass around a sheet of paper and ask for names and titles to be entered. Legend has it that the number of people at an opening meeting is indirectly proportional to the number of deficiencies the auditors will find.

Restatement of purpose and scope
Just in case there is any doubt in the auditees' minds about why the audit is being carried out and the extent to which the company is going to be examined, the audit team leader needs to restate these. As the nominated leader of the team he may also tell the auditee about his organization and the way they are organized to carry out such audits. The restatement of purpose and scope may also include a statement about the authority for conducting it.

Review of the audit programme
The programme will have been discussed and agreed. Confirmation

that auditee 'management representatives' are aware and available is necessary as is an assurance from the audit team leader that he will keep to his programme.

Administration arrangements

Introductions are necessary for those auditee's staff nominated to act as guides for the audit team or teams. Part of the audit preparation will have included a room or suitable space for the auditors to use during the audit. Lunch arrangements need to be confirmed. Typically these take the form of a working lunch or something fairly simple. Audit legend contains all the usual stories of huge three or four-hour banquets laid on for the auditors usually at some distance from the company. These are no longer practical and should be avoided.

If it is a large site, it may be necessary to arrange for transport.

If there are areas of the company where restrictions may be placed on the auditors these should be discussed and agreed. These can be various:

1. *Clean or hazardous areas*   If it is necessary for the auditors to visit these areas the team leader should ask that any essential protective clothing is made available in advance, in order that time shall not be wasted.

2. *Sensitive union/staff relationships*   Personnel in companies can be rather concerned where there have been redundancies or rumours of, or where there have been bitter exchanges between staff, management and unions, to see strangers walking around on an official basis and taking notes. Once these people realize who the audit team is and what they are doing, there is little difficulty. It seems amazing to find how many companies do not tell all their staff that some visitors from or representing their customer are going to be in the company for a time.

3. *No go areas — secrecy*   Where the *Official Secrets Act* operates in companies there are obvious restrictions placed. Appropriate clearances must be raised and received prior to the audit. However, purely from a commercial point of view, it may be that the company has an area where it is carrying out work that it knows would be of value to its competitors and therefore it may place a restriction on auditors' access. Unless it is specifically a part of the audit scope to examine such areas, the auditors must accept the limitation.

4. *Audit is a representative sample*   The audit team leader should make

it clear that the programme is a sample of the company's operations; also that what will be examined within that is also a sample and subject therefore to the limitations of sampling. Both acceptable and non-conforming aspects will be seen and missed.

5. *Confidentiality* The fact that the audit is taking place is confidential between the auditee and the auditors' company. Similarly, everything the auditors see and discuss during the audit is confidential between the parties. Auditors with professional auditing qualifications are bound by their own code of ethics but it is the duty of all auditors to be discreet and professional about the information they may become privy to. The team leader should therefore make a statement about confidentiality.

6. *Response to auditee's questions* Other questions of a general nature might arise. Such questions may be concerned with the method of reporting to be used by the auditors. This should be explained, especially if there are documents which will have to be signed during the audit. When all these matters have been cleared, the team leader should bring the meeting to a close by thanking the management, and by confirming the date and time of the closing meeting (to which he looks forward).

The audit investigation

At any given time during the audit there may be many people involved. This is not conducive to easy control by the team leader. Those involved could include:

- The team leader.
- The leader's colleague or second person.
- The nominated guide.
- The management representative from the area being audited.
- Other staff.
- Observers accompanying the audit party (possibly trainee auditors).
- Interpreter, where there are foreign language difficulties.

It is in the auditor's interest to limit the size of the group. But with patience, and by keeping in mind the audit objectives, the team leader can carry out the audit even with a large following.

In keeping control of the audit, the audit team leader is looking for three things:

1. *Compliance with the standard* Examination of documents before the

audit will have led the leader and the team to consider the extent to which the apparently prescribed system conforms with the appropriate standard (ISO9001, for example). The prescribed system defined by the company therefore becomes the ruling document for the audit.

2. *Implementation of the prescribed system*   Examination of what people are doing will reveal the extent to which they are operating as laid down in their own documents.

3. *Effectiveness*   Each procedure, both the written and the practice, is there for a reason. Each procedure must produce some result, and there must be a means of showing what has been achieved.

Information will come to the auditors in many ways. For this information to be of use, it must be objective evidence. Objective evidence is fact that is established in a manner that would be acceptable in, for example, a court of law. It therefore includes what is seen by the auditors and what is said to them.

It is essential to have a 'management representative' at each department visited by the auditor to act as the department's 'expert witness'. Statements made by this person are 'admissible evidence', provided that they relate to the areas within his responsibility. Anything that this expert says about matters outside the range of his responsibility is hearsay evidence, and not admissible. The auditor therefore needs to be able to differentiate between evidence which is admissible and inadmissible, and keep the audit on course whilst also considering things he may hear for subsequent investigation later in the audit.

The investigation involves talking to people about the working of the quality system and verifying its operation by examination of documents, materials, equipment, etc. The auditor must develop skills in both these types of activity.

The biggest problem facing the audit team leader is the management of the audit in terms of keeping to programme, looking at and examining enough evidence in each area and slowly building up his informed judgement about the degree of compliance seen. Any auditor therefore will be well advised to have his own way of working within any area and then adapt the various techniques as each situation demands.

On entering an area and being introduced to the management representative by the guide, the auditor should run over his audit plan for that area with the guide and management representative and take their advice as to the most logical sequence to follow. The amount of time the auditor has to spend talking to the management in each area about their system will vary according to how much information was originally made available to the auditor. Where there was very little, then more time may need to be spent on the audit to determine some of the basic controls.

The items on the checklist can then be worked through in a systematic manner. If the auditors find no evidence of non-compliance they can and should proceed quickly. Having covered the 'sample' they should move on. Auditors should never continue the investigation 'until [we] find something wrong'.

As the investigation proceeds the auditors need to make notes of what they see and hear. Only the most experienced auditors make sufficient notes of all the relevant things seen and heard, and that is yet another reason why audits carried out by different people can yield such different results.

Perhaps the biggest challenge for the auditor is the fact that finding out information depends on his communication skills with people. Within a very short time of meeting someone the auditor needs to have developed a degree of rapport but remain sufficiently objective to gain the facts essential to the investigation. If these facts are indicative of a lack of management control in the area, it does not take much imagination to realize that if not done correctly, the implied criticism can produce a very unfavourable reaction from the auditee.

The auditor's main method of gaining information is by asking questions in a series of interviews. Though it is not always fully appreciated, the best interviewers are those who say least and have an ability to listen and hear what is said. By applying the right sort of technique, the auditor generates the kind of environment in which good communication can take place.

In all circumstances, the auditor needs to be polite, have respect for everyone he or she questions and needs to show an interest in the person being questioned. Being polite covers many activities and some auditors will never make it, for it means not openly disagreeing or arguing, it also means not contradicting people, it means allowing them to have their say, it means giving the auditee the benefit of the doubt. Showing respect demands that the auditor is not obsequious in his approach to senior people nor superior to more junior people but maintains the discussions around the point and strives for facts.

Showing interest in the people being addressed means maintaining a degree of eye contact, showing by small verbal acknowledgements, 'I see', 'ah, yes' and so on that the communication is being received.

Facial expression is important as are head movements (as long as these are normal).

Questioning techniques

An apt quotation is that by Rudyard Kipling which though in danger of being overquoted is nevertheless the basis of all successful questioning. 'I keep six honest serving men, they taught me all I knew, their names are how and why and what and when and where and who'. Elsewhere, particularly in quality circle teaching, they are called 'five Ws and an 'H'.' Though a clumsy description, the idea is the same. Questions beginning with these words will elicit more than 'yes' and 'no' answers, and are therefore called open ended questions. It takes longer to answer such a question than it does to ask; the auditor gets some thinking time. The auditor can control the tone of discussion to advantage with the use of these questions.

There are of course different types of open-ended questions. For example, there are questions which provide a topic before the question is asked. 'Talking of calibration control, how do you. . .?' Topics needing expansion demand questions that create a high level of empathy between the auditor and auditee, showing obvious interest by the auditor. 'How important is it for you to have this document. . .?' and 'Why do you feel. . .?' or 'What other areas are you thinking of. . .?'

Questions which ask for the auditee's opinion are often neglected but, apart from the danger of straying from fact, the opinion question can be useful for gaining someone's attention or for gaining new approaches to problem solving. They can also encourage auditees who consider they are the 'local expert' to say more, or to encourage junior people to talk.

Investigation questions are most useful when the auditor is not sure if the auditee has fully understood what has been said, but does not want to make this obvious. 'To what extent do you feel documented methods would fit into the way you work at the moment. . .?' and 'How do you actually approach this test. . .?' The auditee can feel at ease and the point gets clarified.

Non-verbal questions may seem to be a contradiction in terms, but the raising of eyebrows whilst maintaining eye contact can, with proper timing, encourage the auditee to give yet more information.

Repetitive questions are used to gain time and to establish confirmation of a situation. It keeps the conversation going. For example, 'I don't think procedures are necessary', and asking 'You don't think procedures are necessary?' the auditee is obliged to some degree to continue. This question should be used like the 'dumb question'. No question should be considered too stupid for the auditor to ask if fact is going to be the result. However, repetitive or dumb questions should be used sparingly. If over used, repetitive questions indicate that the auditor is unable to communicate. Dumb questions imply something about the auditor's competence.

Hypothetical questions should also be used with care. It is reasonable to ask people what they would do if an instruction is not received for example, or if things go wrong, but there is usually enough material in actual current practice rather than overdoing hypotheses. It can be a good way to find out what people's priorities are, and can also give an insight into the sort of contingency planning which has gone into the department's operations.

Closed questions are ones which can be answered 'yes' or 'no'. They are assumptive and can be powerful. They also save time. However, they should only be used when the yes or no answer can be quite definitely given because of what has gone on before. To ask such questions without the auditee having had an opportunity to explain is equivalent to his sitting in the witness box being grilled by an opposing advocate.

Leading questions are common in bad audits but very sparse in good ones. The auditor should not lead the auditee to an answer before attempts have been made to reach a conclusion by all other methods.

A number of organizations find that an understanding of the foregoing is particularly useful before undergoing external audit by a second or third-party. Whilst making no recommendation here of such a practice, it is true to say that if an auditee answers precisely and only the question the auditor asks, the auditor has to work very hard. Some auditors have been heard to complain at such a tactic. Who is at fault?

After each and every contact the auditor has with people, he should thank them for their time, give recognition for good management control if that has been apparent and get on with the rest of the audit.

Recording non-compliances

Much could be written about definitions in quality assurance and nowhere is this truer than when discussing deficiencies, discrepancies, non-compliances, non-conformities, findings, etc. These words are used almost interchangeably to describe a condition which is found during an audit and is adverse to quality (i.e. it violates a specified requirement). Specified requirements are the following in order of precedence:

1. Contract requirements agreed between contractor and vendor.
2. Quality assurance manual and procedures.
3. Ruling standard, i.e. ISO9001.

The auditor is examining all the evidence with these requirements in mind. As the audit proceeds, situations will arise which appear to conflict with one or all of these.

These situations are not meant to be kept secret by the auditor. As soon as he is concerned that what is said or seen is in conflict with requirements, he should voice his thoughts to the management representative. In this way both their understandings of the situation can be improved. By establishing what the exact situation is and determining what the facts are around the issue the auditor may have a deficiency and the management has an opportunity to improve. Some time must be allowed to determine all the facts and decide the extent of the problem. If an isolated case, the auditor may note it but not as a deficiency. If more serious, then he is obliged to dig further and ensure he has all the information.

A golden rule for auditors is to write the relevant information down as soon as possible, along with all the necessary references, i.e. document numbers, product identity, place (department), etc.

Some organizations are required to have a signature from the management representative that he or she understands the written statement. This can be done but there are certain disadvantages:

- *The time taken*   it can actually take quite a long time to write these statements out in a form good enough that the management representative can understand clearly and put his signature to.
- *Subsequent information*   it is quite often the case that other information may arise on another part of the audit which can alter or even remove the finding. The auditor may be better advised to take this broad view.
- *'Parking ticket'*   the auditor must be careful not to 'play the numbers game' or initiate this within the auditee company. Issuing these documents at the time in each department can be effective, but can also degrade the audit, with the receipt of documents perceived in a similar way to motorists 'getting tickets'.

In order that there are no surprises to the company at the conclusion of the audit, the auditor must ensure that the management in a given area is clear about any deficiencies which are going to be reported in that area at the time and before he leaves it. Providing a record can at least accomplish that.

The wording of a deficiency document is crucial. It needs to contain an exact observation of the facts, state where, what and who (avoiding names of people and certainly those of very junior staff). The statement needs to make it clear why it is a non-compliance with specified requirements.

The reasons for using specified requirements are twofold. Firstly, these provide both parties with a set of agreed criteria. Secondly, the deficiencies stated can depersonalize the findings, because it is a management system which is being criticized. The auditor must avoid 'pointing the finger' himself, though it may often be clear where the responsibility lies.

There are four criteria to be used in assessing deficiency statements.

1. Is the statement factual? If it contains words like 'think', 'opinion', 'dislike', 'feel', 'seems', etc., then there may be a shortage of fact.
2. Is the statement complete? If it does not contain enough information, so that anyone with the need to do so could go back and find it again after the audit, then it is not complete.
3. Is the statement helpful? In stating the exact deficiency and the requirement which it violates and the evidence, the statement should point to what has to be done to put it right.
4. Is the statement brief? This is the last point and is the least important, but writing out very long statements and presenting these at the conclusion of the audit is time consuming. The auditor needs to practise conciseness, though not at the expense of objectivity and completeness.

It is also a good idea to use the company's or the industry's terminology. It will be more easily understood and shows the auditee that the auditor has taken sufficient effort to 'talk in his language'.

Here are some examples of deficiency statements:

(a) Contract 5730/6 requires prior client approval of all changes to Quality Plan 5730/QA/016.
Procedures HP29 issue 3 to 4 HP38 issue 1 to 2, and HP86 issue 3 to 4 have been changed without this approval. (Deficiency is a violation of a contract requirement.)
(b) Engineering Instruction 10/009 states that panels will be painted within 1 hour of shot blasting. Panel 968/a in Paint Bay 3 on (date) was blasted at 11.15 and painted at 15.45 hours — 4.5 hours

between blasting and painting.
(Deficiency is a violation of an internal procedure requirement.)

(c)   There is no procedure to ensure that copies of modified drawings are removed from the Shop Central Drawing Store.

Outdated copies of drawing numbers 10835/B, 10952/D, 102/A, 1409/C were found in the 'Current Drawing' file in the Store. Drawing Office Master Register and relevant drawings show that 10835 is now issue 'D', 10952 issue 'E', 102 issue 'D' and 1409 issue
'F'. The changes had been in effect for two months. Drawing Office Manager stated that the Technical Clerk should periodically check the Store drawings. (Deficiency is a violation of a quality management standard – Document Control.)

These statements are not all brief but they are factual, complete and to a degree, helpful.

This last point leads to another. To what degree can or should the auditor make suggestions about corrective action? Different assessment and auditing organizations have very different policies on this.

The responsibility within a company for the way it runs its business is that of all company's management at all levels. The auditor's job is not to run that company but to collect factual information so that an informed decision can be reached about the compliance of the management systems with the specified requirements. An auditor therefore is not in a position to make suggestions and should avoid it, particularly as an external auditor. It is not his duty to make suggestions and he may even be quoted afterwards, particularly if the company spent money on his suggestion and it did not work!

As an internal auditor, the situation is different. If invited to participate in decision-making which is going to assist in improvements, he should throw his checklist away and roll his sleeves up and help.

So the external auditor must be careful about any constructive comments he may reasonably be expected to make. The deficiency statement should say it all but there are some aspects not yet addressed. There can be many deficiency statements raised during an audit over two or three days, varying from complete lack of a necessary management system to isolated occurrences due to minor lapses.

There needs to be some means of differentiating between those which are considered serious and those which are not. The auditor is not always able to make this decision but he needs to be able to answer two questions about each deficiency:

1. What could go wrong if this deficiency remains uncorrected? and
2. What is the likelihood of such a thing going wrong?

A comparative exercise can then be carried out which will allow the findings to be put in some kind of perspective.

Certain organizations use numerical values or class findings as major or minor. These systems provide some guidance. What is important is that the auditor realizes when something is important or serious and also when something is not.

The auditor has some freedom about the way that is used for assembling all the information. If there is a common theme in the findings, e.g. they all are a failing of the same management system and the same department, then they possibly can be put together. However, this is not recommended if they are all serious and require extensive corrective action. It is then better to have them separated so that they can be discretely identified and corrected.

As the audit proceeds, the audit team leader should make a practice of bringing the overall management representatives up to date, at lunch times and at the end of each day with the progress, any deficiencies raised, any difficulties (minor) alterations to the programme, etc. Keeping the company well advised is professional and conventional and has become an expectation of auditees.

During the course of the audit, the audit team needs to review its progress and make any changes necessary. Whilst the extensive planning undertaken was designed to prevent wholesale alteration of the programme, the audit team leader is entitled to change it with proper consultation. This can arise through the finding of deficiencies. As an audit progresses, a number of 'leads' appear which an auditor can follow or ignore. Sometimes it is the correct action to follow these leads, sometimes it is not, and this may not be apparent until some considerable time has elapsed. Making the right decision comes from considerable experience. The auditor who sticks absolutely rigidly to his checklist can be as bad as the one who does no preparation at all.

Once the management realize that the auditor is not just looking for failure, they will assist in most helpful ways and become as interested as the auditor in examining the management systems. In fact, one school of thought says that the management representative should be a full member of the audit team.

Distractions during the audit

Audits present a vast amount of information to the auditors — some of it useful, some of it not. Some of the distractions which occur may not be accidental. Such things include film shows about the company, new technology areas, unusual or brand new equipment, detours to see all these things. Unless the audit is going to benefit, the team leader must be firm and politely resist such distractions.

Other time-wasters are the situation where the auditor asks for a piece of information and the auditee disappears for a lengthy time to fetch it. He is better accompanied by the auditor; it will take far less time, or he can send someone else while the audit continues.

Auditee reactions

It is necessary for the auditor to develop considerable skills in questioning, note-taking, time-management, 'thinking on his feet' and doing all this whilst maintaining the momentum and pace of the audit. This can only be done with practice and a considerable amount of patience and diplomacy. Not everyone the auditor meets is pleased to see him.

A list of some of the reactions is as follows:

1. *Authority*   Auditees who are very senior or who have previously not been audited, feel threatened and sometimes react by suggesting they are above the audit. Whilst this is usually through ignorance, the auditor must avoid showing he realizes this and must be very patient and explaining perhaps many times during an audit, what he is there to do.
2. *Antagonism*   This usually arises from ignorance or lack of knowledge and tests the auditor's patience, politeness, objectivity, impartiality, etc., to their utmost.
3. *Information volunteered*   Sometimes people give the auditor information he did not request. The auditor must listen very carefully and if the information is relevant then a determination of the facts must follow then or later.
4. *Internal conflicts*   Audits put stress on people and auditees may get into arguments and differences of opinion whilst the audit is in progress. These can be highly entertaining and may even tell the auditor something about the management style of the company, but the auditor must politely insist that the audit continues and that they discuss it another time.
5. *Deception*   The auditor may find that the auditee has deliberately lied or prepared false documentary information. This is most

serious and the auditor must avoid making accusations. It is crucial that facts do establish this absolutely and without any doubt.

Quality system effectiveness

The audit investigation is to result in an assessment of the effectiveness of the auditee's quality system. The auditee management should be interested too, regardless of the auditor. The auditor may look at many management systems during an audit but there are those of a broad nature that give a broad measure of the Company's approach to quality:

1. *Failures — internal* What is the extent of avoidable mistakes, problems and non-conformance? Is there a report of scrap, rework, modification? What are they doing about these?
2. *Failures — external* Complaints, warranty recalls, replacements. Are these measured and the causes determined and corrected?
3. *Frequency/trends* Are the problems increasing or decreasing?
4. *Internal audits* Do management at all levels take an interest in these and take responsive corrective action?
5. *Management attitude* Do they take part in the system management and improvement? Are they aware of the kinds of problems which exist at the lower levels of the organization?

No single finding is going to answer all these questions but it is known from bitter experience in the West that nothing worthwhile gets done and stays done unless senior management in a company wants it. Management gets the systems and people it deserves.

As the investigative part of the audit concludes, the audit team should be gathering the information so that an adequate summary can be prepared. Whilst pieces of this are put together overnight, the team should meet to plan the closing meeting and present the findings in a balanced and objective way.

Audit team meeting

At some point about an hour before the closing meeting, the audit team leader should ensure he gathers the audit team together for preparation of the presentation to be made to the auditee management at the closing meeting.

Auditors sometimes feel they should 'try and get some more auditing in quickly'. The law of diminishing returns operates unfortunately and rushing the audit will yield little of extra value.

The audit team leader is responsible for control of this meeting. His priorities must be to ensure his team members complete their deficiency statements. Those 'findings' which have not been discussed and agreed with management are discarded. The leader needs to be sure he can understand the findings and may suggest alterations. He will also decide with his members who will present all the findings and he needs to be able to read and understand them all.

An agenda should be prepared for the closing meeting. An example is given in Figure 23.5.

The other major duty of the team leader at this time is to prepare a summary report. A key purpose of this report is to make clear to the audited company the informed judgement of the auditors. This report must be presented before the auditors leave.

The audit team leader can do worse than answer the three original questions in his summary:

1. Is there a system?
2. Has it been put into practice?
3. Is it doing what it's meant to be doing?

The deficiencies raised will give certain pointers to the kind of weaknesses there are in the management systems examined in the audit. Conversely, lack of deficiencies may indicate a stronger system in a given area. The findings are, of course, tempered by the limitations of any audit — subject as it is to sampling errors.

Lastly in this meeting, the team leader should delegate to his second man the duty of collecting the names and position of everyone who attends the closing meeting.

The closing meeting

Promptly at the pre-agreed time, the audit team should assemble at the chosen venue for the closing meeting (also called 'wash up', 'post-audit conference', 'exit meeting' and so on). Typically they are welcomed by a member of the company management who looks forward to hearing the findings and conclusions of the audit.

The audit team leader is now in the chair and is responsible for conducting the meeting. This point is an added strain on the team leader. He has led the audit, perhaps over a number of days, met many people, been in some stressful situations, possibly has had to reschedule some audit activities and has generally had to keep the audit running on time. Auditors therefore need stamina if, at the end of all this, they are to be able to make a good final presentation.

Good planning will again assist the team leader, and the agenda items can be taken in turn. Most companies do not mind being given copies of the agenda, but it is then necessary to know in advance who will be attending, or at least the numbers.

Item	Duty
Item	**Duty**
1. Introduction and thanks	Team leader
2. Restatement of objectives	Team leader
3. Restatement of audit scope	Team leader
4. Report introduction	Team leader
5. Report limitations	Team leader
6. Principal fittings	
Items 1 to 8	Team leader
Items 9 to 12	Second auditor
7. Summary	Team leader
8. Clarifications	Team leader, assisted by second auditor as necessary

Figure 23.5. An agenda for a closing meeting.

The agenda may take the form shown in Figure 23.5, upon which the following item descriptions are based.

1. The team leader should start by thanking the company for their courtesy, for giving access to the team, and for the facilities and help provided. The guides and company representatives for the audited areas should be thanked. The remainder of the agenda can then be followed.
2. It is good practice to remind the company what the objectives of the audit were. The audit may have covered many areas, and it

can clear up any possible misunderstandings if the original objectives are restated.

3. For similar reasons, the scope should be restated. The specified scope may necessarily have limited the audit to certain areas/products/plants.

4. The system of reporting should be stated. Some companies give auditees full reports, others less, but certainly the auditee should be given copies of the deficiencies found and a statement of conclusion.

5. Any audit cannot examine everything. Therefore the report will carry a statement which the team leader should make at this time, thus; 'The audit was a representative sample of activities only. The possibility therefore exists that there are similar deficiencies in areas not audited.'

6. It is strongly recommended here that the findings are read out one after another. This may seem strange to some but the findings are statements of fact. When people (and auditors) try to orally present the deficiencies, the presentation often become unnecessarily wordy and other odd words creep in. These should be avoided. Auditee management may want to intercede during this presentation to discuss deficiencies. The team leader should politely request that they hear all the findings first then they will be given an opportunity to clarify any after.

   Many inexperienced auditors are almost apologetic about the deficiencies; reading them out in the words in which they are written will help to alleviate this problem. They can be read in a clear firm voice.

   Opinions differ in the profession but it is recommended here that if copies of deficiencies have not already been given out, they are given out now.

7. The overall summary of the audit findings is then presented. At this stage it is a rough draft. The 'sense' of it should not change though the content may and the prose and spelling, etc., will be changed for the final report. A typical summary might be as follows:

This audit evaluated the quality management systems of the noted company for the possible supply of .... products.

The company has only recently adopted ISO9001 as a policy and has undergone no previous audits by external parties.

The quality system seen in this audit is not yet fully documented and is still undergoing some development. Aspects of inspection status and product non-conformance control are not yet fully covered.

A total of twelve deficiencies were found, eight of which were concerned with non-compliance to operating procedures mainly in areas of goods inwards and final test. One major finding in design was the lack of follow-up action on design review.

Corrective action from internal audits and management reviews was well documented and verification of improvements noted as a prominent feature.

Auditors rarely, if ever, actually make the decision of whether to purchase, so it is often difficult if not impossible to tell the company whether they can supply or not at this stage. The team leader can usually state that a response from the company within say 2-3 weeks from receipt of the report about proposed corrective action will be likely to impress the customer.

The team leader should not expect the company to suggest corrective action at the closing meeting. Proper effective corrective action needs careful thought and analysis of the deficiency to get at the cause. Decisions like that can not properly be made at the closing meeting.

Of course closing meetings do not go always to plan, what can go awry?

It is reasonable to expect that somebody fairly senior from the company will represent them at the closing meeting. The team leader cannot insist who attends, but if he considers the representative as not being senior enough, he should ask whether there is somebody available and attempt to persuade him or her to attend. He should point out that there are deficiencies which could affect future business. . .

However, if nobody senior is forthcoming, then the closing meeting should be held with whomever is present. If that person is presented as being the representative of the company, then anything he says in that capacity is admissible as reflecting company policy. Naturally, the audit report reflects this.

Sometimes a deficiency is raised and evidence is then produced that it is no longer a deficiency. If the auditor was originally wrong and is sure he should gracefully withdraw it. If the deficiency has been corrected since it was found, the deficiency stays in the report but if the auditor is satisfied it can be closed out there and then.

Often the senior representative was not present during any of the audit. Therefore he is dependent upon the findings statements. There should be no discussion of facts — these have been discussed and

agreed with the various management representatives during the audit
— the people responsible for operating the quality system.

If the audit team has done a thorough job then the closing meeting
becomes what it is meant to be — a formality in which to present the
collective factual findings of the audit to the company management.
Once that is done, the audit team leader should restate his team's
thanks, appreciate that the company management's time is valuable
and depart.

If the audit team can depart from the company and both parties still
fully respect one another, regardless of the findings, the team has been
successful.

Audit reports and records

External audit reports

Someone back at base is interested in the findings of the audit, so a
full and proper report must be prepared. The team leader has to know
who is interested.

The content outlined in the previous sections is probably the
minimum which is produced. However, the recipients at home office
of the report do not usually want a lengthy treatise, so the summary
as prepared during the audit but polished up a little, plus the findings
are all that is necessary.

One aspect of the report which must be available perhaps as a
record, is the defined sample. Therefore, the auditor's checklists
should be part of audit records.

There are many formats for reports. Common features might
include:

- Audit number
- Date
- Team: Leader: _____
          Members: _____
- Contacts: Opening meeting _____
            Closing meeting _____
- Purpose of audit _____
- Scope
- Ruling standard
- Reference documents

- Summary (in 'polished' form)
- Deficiencies (exactly as worded for audit)
- Prepared by
- Approved by

Depending upon company policy, there may be space on the report for recommendations. The list above does not include these for the reasons stated — they are likely to be of only limited value.

After preparation and approval, the report should be submitted within the timescale agreed together with an expected date for response and corrective actions proposed.

Internal audit reports

Internal audit reports are initiated to activate correction action. There is less need generally for summaries though a short one is often prepared for senior management. Usually all that needs to be prepared is a corrective action request (CAR), which contains spaces for the deficiency, for the auditee to propose corrective action, for the auditor to agree it and also space to provide evidence that the auditor has followed up and closed out the corrective action.

The report format might include:

- Audit number
- Date
- Auditor
- Auditee manager
- Department/Section/Function
- Finding
- Proposed corrective action
- Follow up date and close out
- Prepared ....
- Approved ....

Audit records

The reports (and summaries) provide evidence of the audit. Checklists are retained to show the audit sample and also to use for future audits. It is not necessary to look at exactly the same things on successive audits. Examining old checklists can provide for a different approach.

The last items which should be discussed are the auditors' notes. All auditors make many notes, often rather untidily, but these are evidence. As such they should be retained. Retention times are difficult to specify but a decision must be made. There are already precedents set in different countries of the world where the auditor has been ordered to attend a legal gathering and to produce his notes made at the time.

Many auditors now write all their notes into easily retained form (e.g. a large diary) for this very reason.

Follow-up activities

External audits

The audit is not complete until the deficiencies have been followed up and closed out. The only exception to this is where the audit was part of a vendor selection process. If it is decided that there will be no business, then there is little point in carrying out follow-up.

Even so, it is remarkable how many major organizations go to the trouble of carrying out audits and do not have an active follow-up system.

As a result of issuing the report, the auditor expects from the auditee a response with a commitment of corrective action to be taken by a given time. The time is agreed between the two parties and, for major deficiencies, may be weeks or months.

The action proposed is best evaluated by the the team leader and/or team member who raised the deficiency; to evaluate it correctly the auditor needs the ability to understand the likely root cause. In fact, this is very difficult unless the auditor has many more facts. In all but the most trivial of deficiencies, the root cause may need considerable data analysis to determine. However, if it is felt that the proposals would, in fact, remove the deficiency then the proposals can be endorsed.

Verification of the corrective action is then necessary. Again in trivial matters certain of this evidence can be provided by correspondence, copies of documents, etc. In other cases a further visit by the team leader, team member or suitably trained local representative can carry out verification. This latter person is highly dependent on the completeness of the finding statement. It is a convention that such verification is limited to the audit findings only.

If action has not been effective then there must be some form of escalation. The ultimate escalation in the external case is removal of business.

Internal audit findings

The actions outlined in the foregoing are applicable to the external audit (which they basically describe) and in principle to the internal audit. However, internal audits to examine a department's compliance with its own procedures do not generally require the formality of a detailed programme for an audit, or the setting up of opening and closing meetings. But courtesy obviously demands that the responsible manager is advised of the audit and of its results at the time. He should be encouraged also to take part in it.

Escalation resulting from deficiencies in internal audits is often viewed as a difficult subject. It need not be if the escalation system provides for the deficiency to be brought to the attention of successively higher levels of management until the situation is corrected. The quality policy statement of the company should make this clear. It must not be the auditor who requires this escalation but the management system owned by the chief executive and the board.

If the principles outlined in earlier sections of this chapter have been followed so that each department, section and person is viewed as supplier, processor and customer, the abrasive situations historically associated with the auditor/auditee relationship will not exist. Any deficiencies in the system are opportunities for improvement. If corrected, they will make the company better able to supply the customer.

Conclusion

The stage is set. Now the review of the company's operations can look at departmental improvements, interdepartmental improvements, increases in understanding of the corporate goals, and measured achievements in reducing the avoidable costs in the business.

Clearly, the audit systems outlined have a great part to play. It is a serious business but it needs imagination, honesty and single-mindedness from the top to the 'bottom' of the company. If this chapter assists in developing true control of quality, then let the audits commence.

Part Eight

QUALITY FUNCTIONS IN MANUFACTURING

24 Quality of Bought-out Materials

R. Plummer

Ensuring the quality of bought-out goods can be viewed in the light of a closed control loop, in which feedback signals are used to correct unwanted distortions and errors. This chapter discusses tools and techniques which are widely used to ensure the quality of purchased goods, comparing their use with this control loop analogy. The relevant tools and techniques include, but are not limited to, the following stages:

1. Auditing and assessing.
2. Purchase specifications.
3. Purchase orders.
4. Goods inwards procedures.
5. Stores procedures.
6. Vendor rating.
7. Inspection.

Although there is clearly a chronological order to these stages, this is by no means rigid. Expedience usually dictates the order in which some of the stages occur in the control loop. Indeed some stages, such as purchase order procedures, can actually feed information forward to prepare later stages of the loop in advance.

Auditing and assessing, techniques, theory and practice

The purchaser needs to acquire a satisfactory degree of assurance that goods bought in from a particular supplier are of a suitable quality (i.e. to acquire quality assurance). To do this, it is necessary for the purchaser to send to the supplying company a formal representative (known as the purchaser's representative) to perform an assessment or an audit. The purchaser's representative must have the full authority of the purchasing company that he represents.

In principle and in practice an assessment is a formal and thorough examination of the supplier's entire quality management system in order to see whether or not it complies with a declared quality management standard (such as BS5750, AQAP, DefStan, etc.). This examination is usually for the purposes of registering the company's quality management system as complying with the declared standard.

The standard may be declared unilaterally by the supplier as the one to which he wishes to work. The standard may alternatively be declared unilaterally by the purchaser as a contractual requirement. Finally, of course, the declared standard may be the subject of agreement between the two, although it is generally fairly clearly indicated by the field of endeavour and by the nature of the activities conducted by the supplier.

Similarly an audit is a formal and thorough examination of a part of the supplier's quality management system in order to see whether or not that part complies with the declared quality management standard. There are two places where this type of examination is appropriate. The first place is where an assessment of a large supplier would be too lengthy to be conducted in one visit. Here, a series of examinations is conducted at intervals over say 6 months or a year until every area of assessable activity has been covered. The second place is where it is necessary (for contractual or any other reasons) to examine only one part of a supplier's quality management system, such as the manufacture of a particular product or the conduct of a particular process.

It is stressed that even when an audit is intended to cover only a part of a company or a part of its quality management system, then that part should still be audited in the light of the whole quality management standard (or part thereof) which has been declared as relevant. It should not be audited only in the light of those paragraphs of the standard which bear the same name as the part of the quality management system to be audited.

The purchaser's representative may be a member of the purchasing company. Alternatively, the purchaser may have no employee competent in the skills of auditing or assessing, in which case he may engage the services of an assessor to carry out the audit or assessment on his behalf. Preferably this should be a lead assessor who is registered under the registration scheme for lead assessors of quality management systems which is operated by the Institute of Quality Assurance.

Proper auditing or assessing of a supplier will result in a statement of those areas of the supplier's activity which fail to comply with the declared quality management standard. These failures are called non-compliances and a carefully worded contract should see to it that observed non-compliances will be corrected.

The skill and importance of auditing and assessing do constitute a whole field of endeavour in themselves and it is possible to do no more than the most cursory examination of the subject in a chapter such as this.

Purchase specifications

The purchaser has now decided which of several prospective suppliers should be invited to tender to supply the bought-in goods. The purchaser must clearly specify to the prospective suppliers precisely what it is that he wishes to buy. If the purchaser does not know exactly what he wants then he should consult suppliers to find out what is capable of being supplied.

The contents and scope of the purchase specification will obviously depend on the nature of the goods to be purchased. For raw materials it may be sufficient to specify the goods by means of a quoted British Standard. Where the items to be supplied are to be specially manufactured, the specification may contain some or all of the following:

1. Drawings and other documents which define the construction of the goods.
2. National or international standards.
3. Regulatory documents that apply to the use of the goods (these may depend on the country in which the goods are to be used and

would include such subjects as electrical regulations and health and safety legislation).

4. Performance parameters, with centre values and tolerances.
5. Quality of workmanship.
6. Commercial requirements, especially quality, delivery and price.
7. A list of supporting documents to be provided by the supplier, which might include:

   - recommended list of spares;
   - installation instructions;
   - operating and maintenance instructions;
   - test certificates.

8. Approval arrangements for supplier's own drawings.
9. Arrangements for visits to supplier's premises for expediting or inspection.

Purchase orders

When a supplier has been chosen who is capable of meeting the specification and the time has come to order the goods, a purchase order must be issued. The purchase order can be used to convey a great deal of information about the transaction, and to communicate this to a number of departments within the purchaser's organization. An illustration will assist.

Imagine a purchase order which has an original plus several copies. The original is compiled by a member of staff, who might be a manager, member of the purchasing department or other person (known in all cases as the originator). After being signed by the appropriate authorized person, the original is sent to the supplier to order the goods and acts as a promissory note.

To continue this typical illustration, the copies would be distributed as follows:

- The first copy goes to the finance department to notify them that funds need to be made available and that an authentic request for payment is to be expected.
- The second copy, the confirmation of receipt, is retained by the originator until the goods arrive in a satisfactory condition.
- The third copy is retained by the originator as a permanent record.

- The fourth and fifth copies go to stores to notify them that goods are coming.

The way the system works is that when the supplier has received the original order, he delivers the goods and forwards an invoice to the customer's accounts department, quoting the purchase order number.

When the originator who ordered the goods has received them and is satisfied with their condition, he signs the second copy and forwards it to the finance department.

Equally if he is dissatisfied with the goods then the second copy can be filled in and forwarded to an incident or defect report centre as a ready-made incident report with all relevant information already and correctly in place.

It is not until the finance department has received both the invoice from the supplier and the confirmation of satisfactory receipt from the originator that payment is released.

The fourth and fifth copies are used by the storekeeper to check the number and quality of the incoming goods when they arrive. One copy is kept by the storekeeper as a permanent record and the other is sent to notify the originator that his goods have indeed arrived.

· The quality assurance of the whole transaction is derived from the use of duplicate copies remaining at or travelling between clearly defined points within the company.

The number of copies generated in practice will depend on the organizational requirements, in other words the number of departments or individuals who need to be informed. The copies can be produced using carbon sets, 'no carbon required' sets, in a computer system or by using a pack of photographically generated foils.

When the photographic method is used, a master foil is prepared which contains every piece of information relevant to the purchase order. Different parts of this information are printed on to different foils in the pack by use of a photographic process. This process masks, appropriately, areas of those foils which do not need to have all the information. This is simply because not every department to which a foil will be sent requires all the information. It might also be to preserve commercial secrecy.

The foils are then sent to their designated departments.

When the procedures of each department are concluded for that order, each department returns its foil or a copy of its foil to a central point, such as the finance department, and payment is made.

Goods inwards

When goods arrive they need to be checked against the purchase specification. These checks may, however, be performed with differing degrees of thoroughness. The appropriate degrees of thoroughness should be developed by the purchasing company over a period of time.

The degrees of thoroughness depend as a minimum upon:

1. Knowledge of the suppliers via a schedule of quality assurance audits previously conducted and kept up to date.

2. Experience of the historic, received level of conforming parts from particular suppliers. This is known as the average outgoing quality level or AOQL (see below).

3. How seriously a failure of the bought-in part would affect the performance of the product into which it is to be incorporated. (This information can be found by carrying out a failure mode effect and criticality analysis [FMECA] on the product design.)

The degree of thoroughness of the checks performed means in practice the percentage of goods ordered which has to be examined before one can say with a certain amount of confidence that the number of defective parts is satisfactorily low. The approach to this, called statistical sampling, is more rigorously dealt with in other chapters of this handbook and in other standard texts.

On occasions, defects are found in individual items, or in whole batches of items which fail statistical sampling checks. On these occasions, the rejected goods must immediately be handled in such a way as to prevent as far as is reasonably possible their use. This also applies to incoming stock whose identity is unknown or is uncertain.

Reasonable steps to prevent their use include, but are not limited to, quarantine areas of floor, clearly marked by posts or bright paint, or by their physical separation from healthy stock. Steps may also include quarantine by locking in a cage the non-conforming or doubtful goods.

If it is necessary to incorporate doubtful incoming goods into the production cycle, then it is paramount that those doubtful goods retain full traceability until such time as doubt has been removed. If doubt cannot be removed or suspicions are confirmed, then clearly the full traceability enables the defective parts to be withdrawn at will.

Stores procedures

Following on almost without perceptible break from goods inwards is the store and its procedures. It is of no consequence from the point of view of quality assurance whether the stores are manually operated by storekeepers with paper controls, or whether they are fully automated and driven entirely by computer received orders and operated by robots. Of prime concern are logging in and out, traceability, and handling and storage in such a fashion as to prevent the deterioration of the stock.

Logging in and out may be done by any chosen medium. Software, needless to say, needs to be backed up both by hard and soft copy at regular intervals.

A stock number for every different item of stock is required. The exception to this rule is for items of stock whose differences are identified by revision states or issue numbers but which to all intents and purposes are interchangeable according to the company's rules on interchangeability.

A data sheet is required whose records of individual stock items can be incremented and decremented with the flow and ebb of stock at the time that such flow and ebb occur.

Traceability is the business of ensuring that the location of every item of stock is known at all times. (How naive! . . . 'I know it's here somewhere.' You've heard that before.) Traceability can be achieved by attaching identity (stock number and serial number) and test status information to the stock item, placing it on a shelf or in a bin declared for that particular item and then recording in the datastore (ledger or computer store) the same identity and test status, and the location of the stock item. Of course this data is the minimum and can be cross referred to any other data about the stock item that the company sees fit.

Handling and storage require thought. Butter and wood require different specifications of environment for storage than do steel or advanced technology electronic circuit boards.

In order to detect deterioration, the condition of stock should be checked periodically. Data systems should cater for information on shelf life and be capable of indicating when shelf life is in danger of expiry. Environmental controls need to be established and monitored.

Advanced, computerized stock control has the ability to receive orders via the public switched telephone network from customers' computers communicating with the store computer. The store computer then consults a data table to find where each ordered item is stored. The moment that a robot (which need only be a fully automated stacker truck) is free, it is instructed by the computer to go to the cell or location in the storage warehouse where the bin containing the required stock item resides. Of course the robot then follows the computer's instructions to take the bin to an output bay. There the bin is placed on a bed of conveyors which respond to computer instructions. The stock item is eventually removed by a human. Thereafter it is boxed and despatched.

Guaranteed turnaround times of 24hrs from the receipt of the order to the arrival of stock at customers' premises anywhere in the world have been claimed by one manufacturer of advanced technology goods.

Vendor rating

Vendor rating forms a significant but fractional part of the whole field of vendor relations.

Vendor relations consist of the total liaison between the purchaser and the vendor. This liaison includes, at its most comprehensive, the process of the vendor qualifying for contracts, audits of the vendor's quality management system, planning with the vendor in economic technological and quality improvement terms, constant two way communication, the provision by the vendor of proof that he can conform with the specification, and vendor rating.

Vendor relations need the most comprehensive attention when the goods being bought are rare or unique, are not readily interchangeable with other goods, or when their failure would seriously affect the performance of the end product into which they are to be incorporated.

The vendor qualification process will include the acquisition by the purchaser of proof that the vendor can conduct his business in a professional manner and that his product is of a satisfactory quality. Both these matters should be the subject of thorough investigation by a purchaser if more than trivial quantities are to be purchased. Such investigations should be conducted by competent, project-related purchasers' staff.

Vendor quality assurance audits provide a more far reaching view of the vendor's quality management capability. Quality assurance audits, described above, can give a good indication of the quality of all the influences affecting the goods expected but are not to be taken as isolated proof of quality capability.

Planning in economic, technological and quality improvement terms are clearly part and parcel of a more intimate and longer term relationship with the vendor. The purchasing company has to consider, however, the potential for too close a liaison with its vendors blurring the loyalties of the liaising parties.

Constant two-way communication can take the form of periodic meetings. It can also take the form of periodic reports to the vendor stating the nature and number of defects found by the purchaser, or of periodic or lot-related statements by the vendor to the purchaser of the vendor's own quality control measurements.

Proof of conformance to the specification could be achieved by type testing by the vendor or the purchaser, or by a combination of both.

Vendor rating, finally, invokes several of the aspects of vendor relations already listed. But first, a look at a bit of sampling theory.

Acceptable quality level is defined (BS4778: 1971) as the maximum per cent defective (or the maximum number of defects per 100 units) that, for purposes of acceptance sampling, can be considered satisfactory as a process average.

The sampling plan to be used by a vendor must first be the subject of agreement between the vendor and the purchaser. This is a requirement of BS5750. The plan will indicate the probability of acceptance of a lot which contains no more than a clearly specified number of defectives or defects. The sampling plan will also indicate the probability of rejection for a lot which contains more than a different (but equally clearly specified) number of defectives or defects. In a well-designed sampling plan, the probability of rejection for a sample containing an unacceptably high number of defectives or defects is very high.

Lots which are passed by the vendor are delivered to the purchaser. Lots which are failed by the vendor can now be 100 per cent tested by the vendor and the defectives replaced, then delivered to the purchaser. The total per cent defectives after this replacement process has been completed is called the average outgoing quality (AOQ).

The first half-dozen or so lots received by the purchaser should now be sample tested according to the same sampling plan as that used by the vendor. If the purchaser's sample tests authenticate the vendor's own data then the purchaser can reasonably rely upon the vendor's data, performing only the occasional audit of that data to ensure that the vendor's data continue to be reliable.

A purchaser should now keep historic records of the AOQ of each of his vendors for each type of goods and should endeavour to acquire this information about vendors that he does not routinely use. This gives the purchaser a choice of vendors about whom he now knows a satisfactory amount of information.

The same exercise can be repeated for price reduction information, delivery lead times, etc., so that a whole dossier of information about current or likely vendors can be compiled and kept up to date, as a practical piece of commercial intelligence.

Inspection was covered to some extent in the last section, on vendor relations, and the subject is dealt with more generally in Chapter 26.

It has been indicated that inspection can be reduced to the bare minimum of auditing vendors' own inspection data, once a trusting vendor relationship has been developed. But where the commonality of parts is low, or the sensitivity of a built-out commodity to bought-in parts is high, then goods inwards inspection must clearly be conducted in proportion to the assessed risk.

25 Quality of bought-out Services

R. Plummer

The myth must first be dispelled that quality management cannot be brought to bear on service industries. It can. Of course there is, to some minds, an understandable gulf of comprehension as to how quality management can be equally applicable both to manufacturing and to services. Even seasoned industrial managers can at times find themselves unable to make a rapid transition from the application of the principles of quality management in manufacturing, to their application in service industries.

The purpose of this chapter is to discuss how the principles apply equally well to service industries as to manufacturing, and to explain tools and techniques which apply those principles in the face of the very real and different problems found in service industries.

The tools and techniques include but are not limited to the following:

1. An understanding of the problem.
2. Analysis of the 'building blocks' of a service.
3. Statistical process control as a tool in continuous quality improvement.
4. Incident reporting as a tool of continuous quality improvement.

5. Specifying the objectives to be achieved by the service.
6. Auditing and assessing.

These will be discussed one at a time.

An understanding of the problem

In order to describe how the purchaser is to get the best quality of bought-out services, it might prove advantageous to examine the problems that the supplier of those services has to overcome to be able to institute his own quality management system.

The first obvious difference between manufacturing and service is that the intangible service cannot be passed through a gauge to measure whether or not it conforms to a specification. This is the principal apparent stumbling block, which leads immediately to the notion of how a service should be specified:

1. Can it be specified?
2. In what terms?
3. What constitutes a result?
4. What criteria represent pass or fail (i.e. conformance or non-conformance to specification)?
5. How are those criteria to be measured, and with what?

Suppose a supplier of services performs fewer than, say, 10 contracts per year, to provide his services. What volume of data about the supplier's capability is there to analyse in order to form a view of the quality of the bought-out service?

Some might suggest that to engage a service company which subsequently concludes its contract satisfactorily on the contract completion date is to have chosen a quality service company. But how can it be assured that the contracted lead time to completion was as short as it could have been? Or that the best service solution was found? Or that colateral damage was not done by the field service agent in the execution of his service visit? These are all perfectly reasonable questions for the purchaser of bought-out services to ask. The answers are, at best, elusive.

However, to dwell too closely on the search for a way to measure the quality of the service itself might be misleading. Instead, attention could be focused on the activities within the service company which, taken together, add up to the provision of the service.

If each of the building blocks which contribute to the service is tuned to maximum efficiency (or, in quality management terms, tuned to display minimum quality costs), then it can be concluded that the service itself is displaying minimum quality costs, and is therefore defined as a quality service.

Slowly, then the problem to be addressed is one which is being broken down into those parts which are the building blocks of the service, rather than one of the 'service' itself.

The building blocks

As ever, the simple control loop can be brought to bear (as mentioned in Chapter 24). Within service industries, the control loop must be applied to each of the building blocks. A specified output must be declared, which is sampled. The sample is compared with the specified requirement. If deviation is found, then a correction is fed back until conformance returns to the specified requirement.

It falls to management to identify the individual processes or building blocks which go to make up the service. Each building block is generally, and not surprisingly, a natural aggregation of similar activities, or an aggregation of the sum of the different activities required to produce a small, contributing part of the service.

This is not always the case, however. It is entirely possible for the different activities which produce a small part of a service to be distributed throughout a company (perhaps because of the way in which parts of the company are located geographically, for example). Management should be careful to identify situations where such distribution exists.

Identification of building blocks is eased by using the notion that every process within the service has both a supplier and a customer. It is impossible to overstate how useful this notion is as an analytical tool.

Once the interfaces have been found between successive suppliers and customers, which each contribute a part to the service being provided by the company, then the building blocks become clear.

An example of a building block will help. Consider the processing of travel expense claims. A procedure for processing claims has been laid down in a particular company for a number of years. Some staff who know the procedure well will process the claim and the claim form far quicker than staff of lesser experience or lesser ability. There will therefore be a spread in the time taken to process travel claims. There will also be a mean time to process travel claims.

The mean time to process and the spread of lead times to process must now be measured. A pattern will emerge which will take the form of a Gaussian (also called 'normal') distribution. The distribution might be slightly skewed but this is not that important.

Examination of those factors which cause certain staff habitually to process claims more quickly than others should be undertaken. An examination should also be conducted of those factors which cause other staff habitually to be slower. Whatever it is that the faster staff are doing to process the claims more quickly may well be of considerable interest to the slower staff.

Consider next that the lessons of the faster staff are capable of being applied to the slower staff (remembering of course that some people are of nature less able than others) and that the lessons are then successfully applied. The spread of lead times to process claims will be narrowed. And since it is the slower ones who are now faster, then the mean time to process travel claims will be shorter.

Going one step further, if the procedures for processing the travel claims are, themselves, found to be capable of improvement, and are then successfully modified, this will result in a direct shortening of the mean time taken to process the claims.

One major service company found that by following existing procedures each claim form had to be turned over or back by the clerk 14 times. By redesigning the form only three turns were needed, which reduced the mean time taken and the number of errors.

Once the processing of travel claims has settled down into its new procedure, the mean time to process and the spread of lead times to process must be measured on a continuing basis in order to ensure that the gains in efficiency are being held. The simple expedient of logging the date, time in and time out of every claim form provides the control data necessary for management.

Finally, once a mean time and a spread of lead times has become clear in the steady state condition, then management may set the maintenance of the mean time and of the spread of lead times as a target to be achieved or even improved upon for that department for the year.

Clearly the practices just described are an example of statistical process control (SPC).

Statistical process control

The great virtue of statistical process control is that it is applicable to all the building blocks of a service in a manner exactly similar to the travel claims example just given. Consider some other possible applications.

Can improvement be made in the time taken and the accuracy of work achieved in replying to a tender offer, by the use of tables of standard costings which are more up to date?

Can a reduction be made in the number of redrafts or plans and drawings, by first logging the number and type of observations made and the number and type of deficiencies found, even though the deficiencies may have been corrected as trivial, and on the spot? (The results of logging will be collated to detect any avoidable patterns of errors.)

Can a reduction be made in the lead time to compile a service contract instruction by holding on file standard paragraphs or clauses which have previously been audited by peer group review? (The results of successive peer group reviews have naturally been collected and collated to spot avoidable patterns of problems!)

Are there standing instructions, rigorously enforced to ensure that cash or cheques are not left unpaid into accounts which might otherwise be charging interest? (This case is far less likely to warrant a quality improvement project owing to how dearly some managers — especially accountants — hold their money to their hearts. It is, nevertheless, an aspect of quality management.)

So it is clear that the 'unmeasurable service' is only apparently a stumbling block to the institution of quality management in a service industry.

One word of caution here (among many that could be offered) is that safeguards must be taken to ensure that what is being measured is in fact what management previously set out to measure. It is altogether too easy for those with vested interests to contrive to distort data in order to protect themselves or even to gain additional benefits. A case in point is the reliance placed on the accurate booking of times to jobs by semi-autonomous groups of workers. It is within the bounds of human nature that service jobs completed ahead of time may not be correctly reported where this would mean surrendering hours for which the workers might be paid.

Accordingly, at all times it must be remembered that management is all about people. The acquisition of accurately reported data, arising from a programme of education, could well be a quality improvement project in itself.

More detailed descriptions of statistical process control were given in earlier chapers, but the feature which should by now be very apparent in process analysis was once summarized by an American analyst who only ever said three things:

1. Plot the data.
2. Plot the data.
3. Plot the data!

Incident reporting

Another data collection technique, complementary to that just described, is incident reporting. This is also known as departure, defect or fault reporting.

Incident reporting has the tremendous advantage that data can be accumulated on problems which are widely separated in time and in space and which, therefore, may not be recognized as being costly. It is only when the data are accumulated centrally that the size of the problem becomes apparent.

In principle and in practice, incident reporting works as follows.

A set of codes (called failure mode analysis codes) is devised in the light of experienced knowledge of what is likely to go wrong in that particular industry or service, or of what has historically been known to go wrong. Each code describes a symptom by which one or a number of incidents is observed.

Originators (staff members, managers, members of the workforce, customers, field service agents, etc.) notify a central point by some agreed medium, that incidents have occurred which depart from agreed or expected practice.

The incident reporting central point logs the incident reports on a database. The database operators next apply the most logical code number according to the observed symptoms.

Where a failure mode analysis code does not exist to describe a particular incident, the list of codes is simply extended by the allocation of a new code which relates to the newly discovered set of symptoms.

While this logging, plotting and analysing is in progress, operational requirements dictate that the problem itself must be cured, where at all possible, in order to keep things moving. This cure is sought by a designated responsible manager. Those incidents which do not have an immediate cure must wait on the database for a trend of similar incidents to form.

Periodically, a summary is taken from the database which shows the distribution of incidents by type, by place of origin, by the type of operation reporting them, and so on. Analysis of the code numbers (a form of failure mode analysis) will result in a plot of the incidents. This plot will display how the incidents are distributed, showing which incidents occur most and which represent the greatest loss cost. It is then the responsibility of designated managers to apply solutions in order of priority, tackling the costliest problems first.

The beauty of incident reporting is that it is capable of application as universally as SPC. Quality cost reductions can be achieved using either or both techniques. These reductions can be recorded and associated with the fields of endeavour to which they relate.

How then is the purchaser of bought-out services to make use of the knowledge of the supplier's problems and solutions and quantified improvements? A return to the viewpoint of the purchaser of bought-out services is now in order.

Specifying the objectives to be achieved by the service

The service to be achieved must be specified in writing. The purchaser of a bought-out service should also specify that the provider should operate an approved quality management system. This quality management system must state that the service company operates a system of continuous quality improvement. It should then go on to describe how the system of continuous quality improvement works, and how its workings can be validated.

It falls to the representatives of the purchasing company to examine the records of the supplier of the service, in order that a view can be formed. This view should encompass whether or not the quality management system is under control, whether or not real progress is being made in the exercise of quality cost reduction, and whether or not the quantified quality-related costs are consistent with those achieved in other service companies in the same industry.

This last point is to assist the formulation of a view as to whether or not the quoted quality cost reductions have an authentic ring about them. It should not be used as a rule of thumb that, just because a company has quality-related costs similar to those of other companies in the same industry, that company must be of the same quality. The supplier of bought-out services should be able to demonstrate its *continued* commitment to quality cost reduction.

Unfortunately, here a problem is encountered in that new ground is being broken at the time of writing. Many companies in Great Britain have had much valuable work done over the past 5 to 10 years to achieve quality cost reductions in their manufacturing departments and could state the savings made in many cases. Many of those same companies could now benefit from repeating the whole exercise in the service departments within their own companies. This is a recognized concomitant of the statements in the earliest lines of this chapter about managers failing to grasp the applicability of quality management techniques to service. In many companies manufacturing has been singled out as the only area for which quality management techniques are applicable, but this is only part of where the problems lie.

Accordingly, there is little data with which to make comparisons of achieved quality cost reductions among service companies in the same industry. At the time of writing, this situation seems set to undergo significant change.

Auditing and assessing

Auditors and assessors find it somewhat more difficult to audit the quality management systems of service companies than those of manufacturers. This is for the same reasons of making the philosophical leap that were described earlier in this chapter. Nevertheless, with one eye on quality management and the other on what constitutes a quality service company (i.e. a company of low loss cost) the skilled auditor will have no problem in isolating non-compliances against the quality management specification.

Quality management of services such as maintenance contracts

The mark of a good maintenance organization is not how quickly it can restore a failed system but how rarely the system fails. (Detractors will say that good design has a lot to do with it. And so it has!)

Given competing service organizations, vying to maintain equipment with similar foibles, then the quality assurance auditor is well positioned to determine which service company is likely to provide the better service (i.e. the service of lowest loss cost).

Consider the example that some instructions for maintaining a particular piece of plant state that components should be examined at every service and should be replaced as necessary.

How much is the buying-in company paying for examination of components that would continue to function satisfactorily, undisturbed for years?

How much, now, is the decision left to the field service agent as to whether or not to change a part? What consistency or levelling is in operation when different field service agents take different views of what can and cannot be returned to service? Ask any one who has kept a motor vehicle running in the desert, for months at a time, how far it is possible to return worn parts to service. Then try and persuade your friendly neighbourhood car enthusiast of the same.

The quality assurance auditor will be looking for, among other things, instructions which state clearly the repetition frequency for inspecting components. This frequency should be the result of hard research and the quality service company should be able to justify its quoted frequencies by citing that research.

The auditor will also seek instructions which remove, as far as possible, the need for the field service agent to make judgements at all. Such instructions will take the form of descriptions of what is returnable to service as well as descriptions of what is not returnable. The contrast is thus clear and the service agent need now only make a comparison. The comparative instructions can take the form of a paradigm or sample, such as the full colour photographs of spark plugs to be found in some car maintenance manuals.

The direction of the last paragraphs is heading towards removal of unnecessary effort and the removal of variability in the decisions made by operatives. This is SPC again.

The quality assurance auditor must include as items for special attention during the audit, procedures for minimizing waste and variability. (Remember always that an audit must be conducted in the light of the whole of the relevant quality management specification.)

This then assists the purchasing company in accruing information about a service company in order to form a view, prior to buying in services.

Consultancy

The buying-in company must seek a pedigree of any intended consultant. A history of the consultant's work will assist the formation of a view:

1. Does the consultant have a record of delivering efficacious solutions?
2. Does his record indicate whether or not he has had to make more than one attempt at devising a solution which worked, after his own early failures?

A software consultancy might be approached by a company intending to buy-in software or a custom-built application system. The buying-in company should satisfy itself that the software consultant has paid regard to at least the following:

1. On established software, the consultant should possess up-to-date records of service failures and their top–down solutions.
2. On custom software the consultant should be able to demonstrate in his quality management system, software and documentation hierarchies, design methodologies and evidence that these are being adhered to.

Failure on the part of the buying-in company to attract such evidence should cause alarm bells to start ringing.

Product and design support

A product supplier might have its own after-sales product support system or department. Consider that a service failure occurs in the bought-out product which results from design defects. These design defects might well be put right by the design teams associated with that particular product. This procedure of corrective action should of course be found in the supplying company's declared quality management documentation.

Consider however, that the supplying company abides by a procedure, also to be found in the quality management documentation, that newly configured designs are provided to the buying-in company only at intervals, unrelated to product development and arbitrarily specified by the supplying company. These intervals could be, for example, associated with the next routine service. That service could be months away.

Consider, worse, that the supplying company only provides the configuration update when the buying-in company demands it. That could be only after a breakdown has occurred, caused by the very design defect that the configuration update was contrived to prevent!

An examination of the supplying company's configuration update procedures will soon reveal how quickly configuration updates can be expected to be provided to the buying-in company, and a view can be formed of the extent of the risk associated with any delay.

If the delay (and the associated potential quality-related cost) is considered unacceptable, then the buying-in company must make it a condition of contract that the supplying company shall deliver configuration updates with the minimum period of delay, thereby minimizing the quality related (i.e. loss) cost. What actually constitutes the minimum period of delay is a matter for negotiated agreement between the parties.

Conclusion

Summarizing the principles which have been outlined in this chapter:

1. Mean times to completion must be reduced.
2. The spread of lead times taken to complete work must be narrowed.
3. The mean and variability of all processes which constitute the service must be reduced.
4. The customer's representative must assure himself that these principles are enshrined in the service supplier's quality management documentation.
5. The customer's representative must find evidence that these principles are being complied with and that quantifiable improvements are achieved and maintained.

If these principles are not followed, the buyer should find another supplier of services in which they are.

26 Inspection

R. Plummer

Inspection has traditionally been a part of the quality management process. Necessary though it is, inspection has unfortunately been used by many managers as a prop of quality systems, rather than a tool, in the belief that quality can be somehow 'inspected in' to the product. When a percentage of a company's non-conforming product is found to be reaching external customers, a traditional management reaction is to increase the level of inspection in order to reduce the amount of non-conforming product reaching the customer. Inevitably, of course, this increased inspection detects an increased volume of non-conforming product. The pressure is thereafter put on for ever more inspection. Sooner or later, the processes which are producing the non-conforming product start to creak at the seams with the level of rework, and produce even higher levels of non-conforming product. This result is not the purpose for which inspection is intended.

Quality management seeks, among other things, to remove to the greatest possible extent the need for inspection, and therefore inspection itself. Inspection is essentially wasteful. Inspection by sampling the product or service gives only an indication (albeit an accurate indication) of the number of defectives or defects in a batch, lot or process. One hundred per cent inspection is well known to fail to find as many as 15 per cent to 20 per cent of the defects or defectives in the inspected lot, even when the same lot has been 100 per cent inspected 3 times. It is for these reasons that quality management seeks to eliminate the causes of imperfection and thus the imperfections themselves. In trying to achieve this, there has for some years been a move towards self inspection of the product or service, to exercise quality control at the point of operation.

The fact remains that inspection does need to be carried out for a number of reasons. This chapter deals with those reasons and with how to run efficient inspection activities to satisfy those reasons.

Definition of inspection

In general terms, inspection means determining the quality of some characteristic of a product or service in comparison with an agreed standard. The form which inspection takes can be divided into two broad categories. These are inspection with and inspection without measuring equipment. Both of these broad categories are used to determine about products or services, information which can be used for quite different reasons.

Reasons for inspection

The reasons for inspection fall into some clear categories which are typified by the following.

Can we make it all right?   Here inspection of the product or service is conducted to see if it is even possible to make it to specification. Clearly this form of inspection will take place during pilot runs or during process capability analysis.

Are we making it all right?   When processes are running it is necessary to make periodic checks that the process continues to be capable and that it is producing an output within specification. The periodicity of this type of inspection will depend on a number of things. These will include the length of time over which the process is known to remain stable, the number and type of changes in the inputs to the process and the time between these changes. These inspection observations are usually recorded on Shewhart charts (see Chapter 16) which contain control lines that indicate when a process is producing outside control limits and warn when corrective action is necessary.

Have we made it all right?   Sample inspection is used to distinguish good batches or lots from bad. It can be used at any time in the process such as:

- Acceptance sampling by a production inspector.
- Goods inwards inspection.
- Interdepartmental inspection (remember that in total quality management, failure incidents tend to be interdepartmental breakdowns) and final inspection prior to despatch of the goods or service to the customer.

Which bits did we make wrong?   In this case, inspection is used to sort the bad from the good. One hundred per cent inspection may be used when a bad batch has been detected and the defectives are being sought to be replaced.

Product audit   Inspection may be carried out by inhouse inspectors or purchasers' auditors so that a view can be formed of the quality of the product.

Planning inspection

For inspection to be as efficient and as effective as possible, it is necessary to plan the inspection activities as an integral part of the process to which they relate. An extremely powerful tool in the analysis of processes is flow charting. The resulting flow chart can be analysed, and the number of occurrences of each type of activity, including inspection, can be counted. Once the process has been fully charted and reduced to optimum, the inspection activities should be rigorously planned. Where the process in question is effectively unique, such as with project management of large capital projects, the flow chart is in practice the project management plan. Every project management plan should have incorporated in it, or coexisting with it, a quality plan of which an inspection plan should be an integral part. Identifiable milestones, at natural breaks in the project should have inspection activities integrated into them.

In designing and charting processes, sight should be kept of the potential for self-inspection. Examples of self-inspection are where the process itself subjects the product to more stress than the customers' express or implied requirements will ever do. The aspect of the product which has been thus stressed will clearly not need to be included in later inspection.

Care should be taken to ensure that the inspection activities avoid where possible the potential for human error. Potential human error can be reduced in several ways. Two examples follow.

In the first example, where inspection requires human senses to be used as the tools of the inspection, periodic audits of the inspected product may be necessary to allow a view to be formed of the inspectors' ability. Clearly, this potential for human error can be reduced by replacing the use of human senses with the use of sensing equipment. Advances in data processing capability contribute greatly on this front.

In the second example, sometimes there is potential for a process to be conducted in such a way that a product could be assembled (or connections made in the non-manufacturing case) in more ways than the correct one. In this case careful design should be brought to bear to ensure that only the correct assembly or connection can be made. A simple example of this is the way that motor car brake disc pads are keyed, so that only the correct pads can be fitted, and then only the correct way round. Thus the product is self-inspecting just by being made or assembled. Unfortunately, the reverse of this coin is true. Proper quality assured design should ensure that problems are not designed into a product or service which later demand inspection to filter them out.

Having planned the system of inspection as an integral part of the process, a set of clear specifications must be provided to the inspectors, stating in clear and precise terms what the standards are with which the quality of the products' or services' characteristics must be compared. The inspection specification must say what it means, and mean what it says, in language that is both comprehensible and meaningful to the inspectors. Remember that the inspectors may not have the knowledge or ability to understand the implications of the specification and therefore need to have an unequivocal statement of what they must do. Useful tools to assist sensory inspection are photographs and paradigms. These are especially useful if the set of photographs or paradigms includes samples of what constitutes acceptable product and unacceptable product.

A pitfall to avoid in inspection specifications is in believing that writing an inspection specification more stringent than the ultimate customer specification will result in fewer defects reaching the customer. This increases the cost of inspection, adds other quality-related costs such as additional disposal and rework facilities, and can introduce an unwarranted stress on the inspectors. This stress arises if, after their best efforts to filter out defectives as viewed by the inspection specification, they see those so-called defectives returned to the process at a later date as acceptable to the engineering department.

One reaction in British industry to the release from processes of increased numbers of defectives is to increase the level of inspection of the output. Firstly, this is contrary to the principles of quality management which seeks to eliminate causes and not just their effects. Secondly, a wasteful by-product of these inspection purges is that they tend to hang on long after the reasons for them have disappeared. As with the rest of the quality management system, inspection activities must be reviewed to ensure that they continue to be effective and to ensure their preparedness for forthcoming change.

Planned inspection should include inspection of all the activities within a company. Is packaging being performed correctly? Is the handling of product during loading and transportation compliant with specification? As with all aspects of quality management, the conceptual leap between production activities and non-production activities must be made, otherwise significant and costly omissions will be made.

To engender the cooperation of people whose work is to be inspected, or who will inspect their own work, it is useful to carry these people along the path of inspection with you. To this end if is beneficial to involve the operators and inspectors in the planning process. No-one knows more about any 3 square metres of floor space than the person who has to work in them. So get them on board! This is generally to be done at the flow charting stage, and at a stroke it is possible to refute the allegation of using a police force.

The extent to which inspection should be performed *with* as opposed to *without* measuring equipment should be carefully considered in planning the inspection system. In general terms, the more clearly defined and repetitive the inspection operation, the better suited it is to instrument or machine inspection. The more complex, imprecise or subjective the inspection decison, the better suited it is to human inspection. Where possible, design of the process should remove attributes or variables that need to be inspected, or should downgrade the complexity of the inspection decisions needed so that inspection effort is, in the one case, reduced, and, in the other case, consigned to machines which are less fallible than humans.

Having specified in a comprehensive, meaningful and unambiguous way what the inspectors must do, the entire inspection activity must be enshrined in an inspection manual or a set of operating procedures as part of the quality management documentation. Needless to say, this will be properly laid out with indexes, authorities, responsibilities, cross references, etc., and will be periodically reviewed. Review of the inspection procedures brings the usual benefits in quality assurance terms. It has the additional benefit, purely in terms of inspection, that it enables planners to avoid too many special or custom-made inspection activities. Where a set of good inspection techniques exists they should be built upon rather than reinventing the wheel at each new process to be inspected.

Finally, of course, the results of inspections must be recorded. This is pivotal to quality management. If you don't know what has been going wrong then you don't know what to put right. If the capability of the process is such that it almost never produces outside specification then the discovery of an off-specification piece will not only permit corrective action to be taken, but also produce some wonderment at this rare occurrence. The accumulated knowledge assists in revising existing inspection plans and in evolving new ones, in lengthening or shortening inspection periodicities or in increasing or reducing inspection samples. Inspection planners should take pains to devise inspection records which are simple to use, unambiguous and comprehensible. A fine example of an inspection record is the Shewhart chart (see Chapter 16) which was devised and has been used since before the days of the pocket calculator. The ability of the operator to use an inspection record of some sophistication should not be underestimated, however. Ask your workforce how much they would win on a four horse accumulator with doubles and trebles, and you will soon see the extent of their ability to grasp concepts!

Fitness for purpose

Fitness for purpose is one of the widely accepted definitions of quality. Inspection has to view fitness for purpose in at least two terms. One term is conformance to specification and the other is fitness for use by the customer. Examples have been cited, in other works on quality management, of scratches on the focal plane of optical equipment rendering it unfit for purpose. In this case the optical equipment is both outside specification and unfit for purpose. Do the same scratches on more expensive equipment render that equipment unfit for purpose, if the scratches do not impair the functioning of the product and are out of sight of the customer? Questions such as these have to be addressed and criteria set for inspectors to work to. Otherwise subjective decisions on fitness for purpose might introduce costly rejection of fit product, and increased qu   ʳ costs such as disposal, rework, etc.

How much to inspect

The amount of inspection of a productc or service depends on many things which include:

- How much is known about the process.
- The extent to which a sample of a lot or batch is representative of the lot or batch as a whole.
- What will be the effect on the finished product or service of defects in its component parts.

If a process is known to run stably and in control or if the product is known to be of quality simply by the fact of its being manufactured (i.e. self inspection) then clearly inspection is not required. If the process is known to run stably and in control over a certain length of time then the frequency of inspection should be correspondingly low. If the homogeneity of the product is such that one can be very confident that a small sample is highly representative of the product, then the number of samples and consequent inspection effort are correspondingly small. If a new process is being run and no knowledge of the performance of such a process exists, then much more frequent inspection with larger samples is called for until sufficient data have been acquired about the process that the inspection effort can be reduced. If a process is producing a product or service which critically affects a finished product into which it is to be incorporated, or if the process capability is too poor to meet the customers' requirements, then the most stringent inspection must be applied.

Purists will argue that it is the purpose of total quality management to eliminate the causes which demand inspection, and so it is. However, the use of uninterruptible power supplies as a backup power supply to computer or telecommunications equipment is seen by some as the last resort, and their reputations or even careers may depend upon the quality of the backup. Under these circumstances it is difficult to persuade them that final, prehandover inspection of the most stringent form might be unnecessary.

Invoices which have not been checked, even by the invoice writer, may well find themselves being reworked when an overcharged company returns them. Similarly, an erroneous invoice which undercharges will very soon find itself hanging in a frame and decorating somebody's office for a few weeks before the short payment is made. Another quality related cost! One hundred per cent inspection, even if it is only self-inspection, may be called for here.

Seriousness classification

A method of reducing inspection effort is the use of seriousness classifications. Product defects are classified on the extent to which they affect fitness for purpose.

The extent of this effect can be determined from a failure mode effect and criticality analysis (FMECA). The results of an FMECA will show, for example, that if the upper tolerance limit of a process is exceeded then it would be critical to fitness for use and would result in catastrophic failure. Exceeding the lower tolerance limit would, on the other hand, be of minor importance. By understanding the importance of this contrast, it is possible to reduce the level of inspection, and the complexity and number of sampling plans, to say nothing of reduced rework, scrap and other quality-related costs associated with the disposal of what was once thought unfit product.

Three seriousness classifications are generally used to make this distinction. They are called critical, major and minor. In broad terms, these classifications are defined as follows.

Critical defects are those certain to cause failure in either the product itself or the assembly (or process) of which the product is a part, and the customer will have a product unfit for use at some unspecified future time within the normal useful life.

Major defects are those where there is a high probability of failure and which will require major effort on the customer's part to maintain continued fitness for purpose.

Minor defects are often divided into two subcategories. In the first subcategory, defects are unlikely to cause failure but will probably cause noticeable substandard performance and will require effort on the part of the customer to maintain continued fitness for purpose. Defects in the second subcategory do not affect operation or fitness for purpose but are noticeable to the customer.

Once these classifications of defect have been made, the effect of the classification on process tolerances can be assessed. It should be clear by now that with the second type of minor defect, process tolerances may be slackened or even ignored, provided that the defects cause no interactive effect (i.e. with any other part of the system into which they are integrate). Subject to this condition, inspection can be dispensed with. In the case of the first type of minor defect, process tolerances may be eased by carefully monitored amounts provided that no interactive effects occur, and inspection continued to the new tolerances. For major and critical defects, there is no difference to either process tolerances or inspection. Thus a significant reduction in inspection effort can be achieved by this method.

Inspection stamps

As each stage of the process is concluded, and inspected at a planned and integrated inspection milestone, a record of the inspection or test status must be updated to comply with quality system standards. One of the most commonly used methods of recording is to stamp the product (be it hardware or software). Room on the product for stamping should be designed in at the inspection planning stage. Self-inspection operates here, in that successive operations in the process are not allowed to continue until a positive vetting has found a satisfactory stamp mark from the previous operation. In the absence of such a mark, a defect or incident report should be issued stating that the inspection status of the product is unknown.

In the move towards self-inspection, teams of workers have been given their own inspection stamps. The purpose is to bring quality control to the point of operation, to remove the feeling of a police force present, to provide to the team of workers an increased sense of pride in their workmanship, involvement in the decision-making process, responsibility for the quality of the finished product and more involvement in the notion of meeting the customer's requirements. The inspection stamp is entrusted to the team leader, who may delegate responsibility for its use appropriately. Periodic inspection of the work of each team is required by an inspection supervisor or auditor to ensure that a sample of the work is indeed within specification. The interval between these inspections will, of course, vary in accordance with the degree of conformance found in the samples. If an unacceptably high level of non-conforming work is found, then the inspection stamp may be removed from the team leader, and inspection will revert to the more traditional methods until an acceptable level of conformance has been regained.

Errors in inspection

It is possible for the true capability of a process to be masked by variabilities introduced by different process operators, because of the way that each operator prefers to operate the process. Similarly it is possible for different inspectors to introduce variability into the inspected product, which exceeds the process's intrinsic capability. The variability may be due to different inspectors being too lenient or too stringent, or lacking sufficient discrimination between good and bad. Precise and meaningful inspection specifications, coupled with sufficient training are required here, along with an appropriate level of inspection supervision or auditing.

Reference was made earlier to the fact that 100 per cent inspection of the same lot, even as many as three times, can fail to find up to 15 per cent of defects and defectives. Experiments requiring participants to count the number of occurrences of a given letter in a piece of prose, invariably gave results whose spread is about 20 per cent of the true number of occurrences. Experience gives no clear indication that the percentage of missed occurrences reduces as the length of time available for inspection increases.

Time for inspection is not unlimited, of course, and there is in any case a natural human tendency to inject some pace into inspection. Consequently potential improvement in percentage defects found with increased inspection time tends to be lost as a consequence of trying to be quick. (It is worth observing that participants in these experiments, when counting the occurrences of a given letter in prose of a language not their own, tend to produce results much closer to the true number of occurrences. This fact might be a useful pointer to discovering the reasons why inspectors make errors of such wide diversity).

Some methods for reducing inspector errors have been mentioned already but are worth summarizing. They include error-proof methods of assembly, use of instruments or inspecting machinery, the use of paradigms to obviate judgement by inspectors, and the use of control loop theory to improve human sensory capability. This interesting method relies upon the fact that the inspection control loop, consisting of, for example, the eye, the brain, the shaking hand and a measuring tool held in that hand, can reduce the shake of the hand by interposing a magnifying glass between the measured object and the eye. (This is effectively increasing the feedback path gain of the control loop.) The remarkable result to be achieved is a factor of reduction in hand shake, equal to the power of the magnifying glass, up to certain limits. This long winded way of saying something which agrees with one's own experience has an applicability beyond simple optical aids.

A pitfall to avoid that can stress inspectors and increase quality-related costs was mentioned earlier. That pitfall was overspecifying the inspection. Unfortunately, it is well known that managers have knowingly used the inspection process to try (and succeed) in passing off non-conforming product, or have been sufficiently disinterested in the views on quality related matters of the process operators, that the stressed operators have become disinterested in quality. Poor management attitudes can induce a bad approach to quality in the workforce. This can result in inspection errors ceasing to be inadvertent or technique-based, and becoming conscious and witting. Examples of this are where defectives are held back waiting for an unusually good batch to be produced, with which the defectives can then be mixed and still meet the sample plan pass level.

There are occasions when 'management by terror' causes the workforce conveniently to neglect to declare defectives, which are later 'lost'. Nobody is going to volunteer to face a firing squad.

Misunderstanding of management requirements can lead to inspection returns being falsified to appear to meet requirements, only to have the books 'balanced' at a later date, when quality levels are better.

Finally, inspectors naturally tend to round off results when reading instruments. A quality-related cost arises if the inspection specification is diluted by rounding errors. This problem is typified by motor vehicle speedometers which are graduated in increments of one mile per hour. How many drivers in Britain, who never take their cars abroad, need graduation marks on their speedometers other than 30 mph, and 70 mph? When racing a motor vehicle on a circuit, the driver does not even need a speedometer. It is important to him however to have an engine speed counter, oil temperature gauge, turbocharger pressure, etc. The principle here is to design and use instruments which are fit for the purpose, so that conscious rounding errors, even by conscientious operators, are minimized or avoided altogether.

Cost of inspection

The cost of inspection appears as both prevention, appraisal and failure cost. Under the heading of prevention costs would come inspection activities performed, for example, during the pilot stage of a new process. Here inspection is being conducted to assist evolution of the process, so that the process will have minimum quality costs when it is in full operation. Appraisal costs include the cost of inspection incurred during normal operational running of a process. In this case, the inspection is conducted to appraise the process to acquire data about whether or not it is continuing to produce within the specification limits.

The recurrent theme of this chapter has been to use quality management to reduce the need for inspection as a means purely of detecting non-conforming product. Where inspection is used purely in this category, then it is classed as a cost of failure. It is into this category that inspection activities fall when there has been, for example, an increase of inspection activity owing to increased levels of internal or external product failure. It is up to the quality management system to remove the causes of failure and therefore the need for this category of inspection.

The cost of all metrology facilities and equipment, all the time of inspectors and laboratory staff must be included. However, correct apportionment of these costs to the appropriate category of quality-related cost soon reveals how much inspection effort is being wasted in inspecting solely to separate the good from the bad. Quality improvement projects should then be instituted to remove the need for the inspection costs which are classed as failure costs.

27 Metrology

Jim Bell, National Physical Laboratory*

This chapter is concerned with the role of measurement in assuring quality and with the national measurement system available in the UK for achieving and verifying quality. The considerable extent of the UK measurement industry will be indicated, both in terms of its scale and in terms of the range of facilities provided. It will also be shown that, just as measurement plays a vital part in assuring quality, so equally the principles of quality assurance can themselves be applied to the conduct of the measurement process. Emphasis will be placed on the fact that measurement technology cannot be static, but must develop apace with (indeed ahead of) the changing needs of industry. And it will be shown that, increasingly, the development of measurement technology has to be a cooperative enterprise, both nationally between government and industry, and internationally between laboratories and authorities in different countries.

Some definitions

There exists a variety of definitions of the term 'measurement', to be found in national and international vocabularies, and in technical glossaries throughout the world. While the various definitions differ in detail, they all convey the basic idea that *measurement is the process*

*This chapter is Crown Copyright.

571

of assigning a value to a given physical quantity, such as the length of a rod, the temperature of a furnace, and the electrical resistance of a heating element.

Like measurement, the term 'quality' is also the subject of a variety of definitions. Again, fortunately, most definitions convey the same general idea, in this case the notion that *quality is the capability of a product (or a service) to meet someone's legitimate expectation.* The expectation may be that of a consumer, or of a manufacturer, or it may be that of a retailer who passes a product from manufacturer to consumer. Equally it may be the expectation of a regulatory body that is concerned, say, with the electrical safety of a class of domestic or industrial products.

An expectation can be a mainly qualitative one, for example a connoisseur's expectation of a wine's body and bouquet; or it may be a quantitative expectation, such as that of an excise inspector concerned with the alcohol content of that same wine. Where an expectation is quantitative, it can be formalized in a written *technical specification,* such as a British Standard (BS) specification, an international standard specification, or more locally as a manufacturer's or a purchaser's own inhouse specification. This chapter is concerned with the application of measurement to achieving quality, in the sense of specified quantitative expectations.

The role of measurement in achieving quality

The most obvious and familiar way in which measurement is involved in product quality is through the testing of products against a relevant specification, after completion of manufacture. The tests may be carried out on every product or on selected samples of the product; they may be conducted by the manufacturer or a purchasing body, or by a representative of consumer or legislative interests. Further, similar tests may be performed during a product's life on the shelf or in service, to monitor its continuing compliance with specification.

While testing of the completed product may be the most obvious intervention of measurement into product quality, the role of measurement can begin much earlier in a product's life. In many cases tests are carried out *during* manufacture, on the partially assembled product or on key components, to ensure that the manufacturing process is going as planned and to enable any necessary process adjustments to be made. In modern steel production, for example, *on-*

line analysis of samples to check chemical composition is virtually universal practice: in this and other large scale processes, the penalty of postponing deficiency detection until after a production run has been completed can be catastrophic.

Measurement will often also play a part in other less direct ways, during production. An example is provided by the close monitoring and control of environmental conditions that is necessary in the manufacture of certain sophisticated electronic products or components.

For many or most types of product, the measurement process will have made significant impact even before manufacture commences. One example arises in the testing of models or prototypes, in order to predict performance of planned products, or to demonstrate their compliance with legal requirements such as those arising from environmental or weights and measures legislation.

More generally, the development and installation of manufacturing equipment (whether it be for traditional metal cutting processes or for high-tech integrated circuit deposition) will have entailed detailed prior measurement activities or considerations; this is necessary in order to ensure that the equipment concerned operates within the tolerances necessary to yield an end product that meets the intended design or performance characteristics. It is not practicable to establish a manufacturing facility of any appreciable technical sophistication, without planning one's measurement requirements well in advance and taking account of the technical (and economic) constraints arising from measurement considerations.

So far, the emphasis has been on the application of measurement to achieving product quality, leading to industrial competitiveness, consumer protection and related benefits. However, measurement has a vital part to play in enhancing quality in the more global sense of *quality of life*. In the medical field, measurement contributes to diagnosis and treatment through tissue analysis, radiography and tomography, automatic monitoring of patients in intensive care. Also our everyday environment is made safer and more pleasant, through the monitoring of air, rivers and reservoirs for unacceptable levels of pollutant. Measurement is important in safeguarding us from dangerous levels of radiation in and around the workplace, or at home. Crime is detected, solved and ultimately discouraged or prevented, by measurements carried out in the course of forensic investigation. Measurement is used to combat counterfeiting and fraud. In the form of blood alcohol analysis and vehicle speed monitoring, it helps to make our roads safer. In the field of national security, advanced measurement is indispensable, in the detection and guidance systems intended to safeguard the integrity of our frontiers.

Some of the principal direct users of measurement services are listed in Figure 27.1. The full number of those using and depending on measurement, in its various forms, is legion. Most aspects of daily life are touched by measurement in one way or another. Materials for the clothing we wear are tested for shrink resistance, colour fastness, durability. Petrol is accurately metered when we purchase it from our local filling station. The food we eat, the beverages we drink, even the air we breathe, are subject to testing. We live from day to day in a 'sea of measurement' of which the majority of individuals are, for the most part, not consciously aware.

The range and scale of measurement activity in a modern industrialized society is vast. In this country, it has been estimated, the total cost of measurement in 1988 was £20 000 million. That represented about 5 per cent of our total UK gross domestic product. part, not consciously aware.

Although most of the cost fell on industry and other independent organizations, in human terms it corresponded to over £300 for each man, woman and child in the population. Our total national spending on measurement-related activity is of the same order as that on health, and is comparable to the cost of our armed forces.

The role of Government

For those who rely on the results of measurement in the achievement of quality, it is vital not simply to have access to an adequate range of testing and other services, but also that the measurements are performed competently and with an appropriate accuracy. Government recognizes the need for organizations and individuals throughout the UK to be able to place confidence in the results of measurement, and accepts it as a Government responsibility to promote the conditions for reliable measurement at all levels.

Government policy on measurement is implemented mainly through the Department of Trade and Industry, and most notably through the Department's National Physical Laboratory (NPL), which is the UK's national measurement standards laboratory. NPL's work is of vital strategic importance to the country's present and future measurement needs. The Laboratory serves the future by developing the new and more accurate and more economic measurements

Government departments
    Regulations, defence, forensic, etc.

Procurement bodies
    Compliance with specifications

Manufacturers
    Quality control

Health Services
    Analytical services, safety of equipment

Consumers
    Safety tests, compliance with specifications

Certification bodies
    Correctness of test data for certification of products

Contracting bodies
    Compliance with specifications

Figure 27.1. Some organizations requiring measurement.

standards, and measurement methods that will be demanded by the turn of the century and beyond, by new and evolving technologies. We will touch, later, on NPL's advanced *nanotechnology* programme in this field. First, however, we consider NPL's response to the country's present measurement needs.

There are two principal ways in which the Government, through NPL, strategically influences current metrology in the UK. The first is through the work of NPL measurement divisions, which maintain the UK national standards of measurement and disseminate these by calibration to industry, commerce, health, defence and other fields, thereby providing the basis for national *measurement traceability*. The second way is through the activities of NPL's National Measurement Accreditation Service, NAMAS, which assesses and accredits laboratories, thereby providing the basis for national *measurement assurance*.

Measurement traceability and measurement assurance

It may be helpful, at this stage, to digress briefly in order to explain the distinction between the notions of *measurement traceability* and *measurement assurance* mentioned earlier.

If asked what is the principal factor influencing the accuracy of a

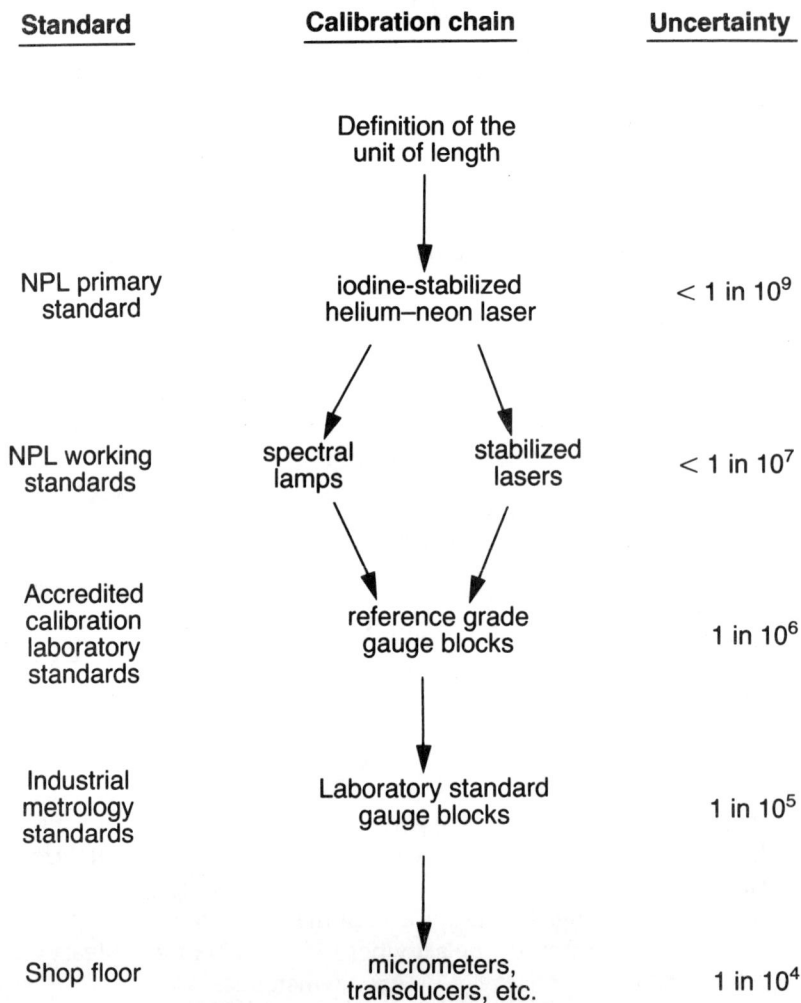

Standard	Calibration chain	Uncertainty
	Definition of the unit of length	
NPL primary standard	iodine-stabilized helium–neon laser	< 1 in 10^9
NPL working standards	spectral lamps stabilized lasers	< 1 in 10^7
Accredited calibration laboratory standards	reference grade gauge blocks	1 in 10^6
Industrial metrology standards	Laboratory standard gauge blocks	1 in 10^5
Shop floor	micrometers, transducers, etc.	1 in 10^4

Figure 27.2.   Traceability chain for length measurements.

measurement, most metrologists are likely to answer, quite correctly, that the accuracy of the measuring equipment is the most significant determining factor.

The way to establish the accuracy of an item of measuring equipment is to test that equipment, in the appropriate way, using a more accurate measuring instrument: or, phrased in specialist metrology terms, to calibrate the equipment against a measurement standard. (Calibration is, quite simply, the testing of metrological characteristics of measuring equipment.)

The accuracy of the measurement standard concerned may in turn be established, in a similar way, by calibration of the standard against a higher, more accurate standard, and so on, through an unbroken chain of calibrations, stretching back to the national measurement standards held at NPL. This ability to relate the properties of an item of measuring equipment through an unbroken chain of calibrations, back to a national measurement standard, is known as *measurement traceability*. A simple example of a traceability chain, for length measurement, is shown in Figure 27.2.

The national measurement standards held at NPL form the anchor for traceability chains serving different levels and sectors throughout the UK (see Figure 27.3). Traceability of measurement is essential, if accuracy of measurement is to be meaningfully assigned, and if

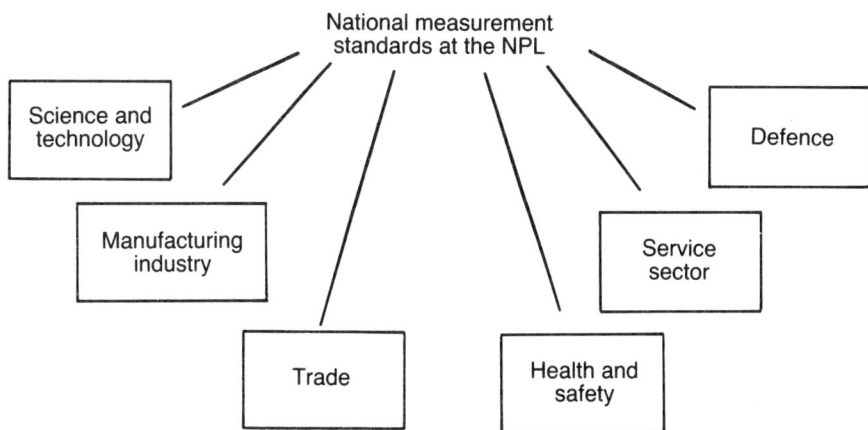

Figure 27.3.   How National Physical Laboratory measurements serve the UK.

measurements made on different instruments or at different times and locations are to be validly combined or intercompared.

While traceability of measurement is essential to the accuracy of measurements, a number of other important considerations can significantly influence the credibility of a measurement result. For example, it is possible for a laboratory to possess accurate equipment, properly calibrated, but for the laboratory's measurements to be carried out with the equipment (or the object to be measured) at the wrong temperature. Or the item to be measured may be incorrectly prepared (inadequate surface finish, for example), or may be confused with another similar item, say through inadequate labelling. An incorrect or out-of-date measurement procedure may be used. Measurement staff may be insufficiently skilled, supervised or briefed in their tasks. Staff may be subject to organizational or operational pressures that impair their judgement. Even where a measurement has been carried out satisfactorily, its usefulness may be undermined due to the result being reported or recorded in an ambiguous or misleading way. A list of major factors influencing the credibility of a

---

Nature of equipment
Measurement traceability
Calibration schedule
Maintenance
Protection of equipment
Environmental control
Staff expertise
Supervision
Sample preparation
Sample protection
Sample identification
Measurement method
Allocation of responsibilities
Reporting results
Measurement records
Organizational pressures
Control of subcontracted work
Documentation
Audit and review

Figure 27.4.   Factors affecting credibility.

laboratory's measurements is given in Figure 27.4.

Only when there exists authenticated measurement traceability and when a laboratory has proper control over all other aspects influencing credibility, can there be proper measurement assurance, giving overall confidence in a laboratory's capability to produce correct measurement results.

It is the purpose of NAMAS to provide measurement assurance within the UK, by assessing laboratories and awarding accreditation (that is, formal recognition of competence) to those demonstrating measurement traceability and proper control over all relevant aspects of laboratory responsibility and activity.

In order to help locate laboratory accreditation more clearly, within the overall context of quality assurance in general, let us return briefly to consider the manufacturing process. Manufacture can be considered to be the application of a sequence of operations, or services, to basic raw materials. To ensure acceptable quality in the finished product, it is necessary to achieve a corresponding level of quality in each of the services constituting the manufacturing process. (Looked at in this way, the notion of quality assurance for services could be considered as more fundamental than that of product quality assurance.) Measurement is just one of the services involved in manufacture, if a very important one, and the laboratory accreditation activities of NAMAS consist largely in the application of accepted quality assurance principles to the measurement service.

The operation of NAMAS

Laboratories that wish to join NAMAS, and that believe they can meet the necessary requirements, submit a formal application to the NAMAS Executive Unit at NPL. Applicant laboratories are visited in due course by skilled NAMAS assessors, and are examined against written criteria covering the responsibilities and activities mentioned above. Laboratories meeting the criteria are awarded accreditation; they are listed, together with the tests or calibrations for which they hold accreditation, in the NAMAS *Directory of Accredited Laboratories;* accredited laboratories are permitted to display the NAMAS logo on relevant test reports or calibration certificates, and on their company notepaper.

Continued accreditation by NAMAS is conditional upon laboratories continuing to comply with NAMAS criteria; NAMAS assessors visit laboratories periodically following accreditation, to ensure that these criteria continue to be met.

NAMAS is a voluntary scheme operated by Government. Laboratories and their clients therefore need to be thoroughly convinced of the merits of accreditation, before sufficient pressures or incentives arise to persuade laboratories to join the scheme. Figure 27.5 lists some of the principal advantages that NAMAS accreditation may be considered to confer. They are all benefits that relate directly to an accredited laboratory's increased confidence in the accuracy and validity of its calibration or test results. That laboratories and their clients perceive these to be real practical benefits is evidenced by the fact that by April 1989, almost 900 laboratories had sought and obtained NAMAS accreditation for various types of testing and calibration, while around 200 further applications for NAMAS membership were being processed. At least as significant as the current totals, is the steady growth in the membership of the scheme. NAMAS accreditations seem likely to be counted, within a few decades, in thousands of laboratories rather than hundreds.

- Confidence in test results
- Confidence in management system
- Confidence in quality system
- Improvement in testing capability
- Reduction in multiple assessments
- Wide acceptance of NAMAS certificates in UK
- International acceptance of NAMAS certificates

Figure 27.5.   Benefits of accreditation.

NAMAS membership comprises independent testing and calibration laboratories, as well as laboratories that form part of larger organizations including Government Departments, public corporations, research and educational establishments, and manufacturing companies.

The fields of calibration and testing served by NAMAS accredited laboratories are shown in Figure 27.6. Accredited measurements range from classical electrical and dimensional calibration, with an accuracy of 1 part in 10^6, to testing thermal insulation and strength of concrete, with rather less exacting accuracy demands of a few per cent. The scheme covers fields as widely diverse as electrical safety testing, chemical analysis and computer software validation.

Calibration	*Testing*
Electrical d.c. and l.f.	Acoustic testing
Electrical r.f. and microwave	Ballistic testing
Mechanical and force	Biological testing
Fluids, flow, pressure, viscometry	Chemical testing
Optical	Corrosion testing
Thermal	Dimensional testing
Radiological	Electrical testing
Thermal conductivity	EMC testing
Chemical analysis and reference	Environmental testing
materials	Fibre counting
Hardness	Fibre testing
Acoustics	Geological testing
Concrete cube testing machine	Mechanical testing
verification	Metallurgical testing
	Microbiological testing
	Non-destructive testing
	Physical testing
	Safety testing
	Computer software testing

Figure 27.6.   NAMAS fields of calibration and testing.

NAMAS enjoys a considerable measure of support throughout all sections of industry and Government, being recognized by manufacturing, certification and regulatory bodies, and by major procurement organizations in both public and private sectors. Like the list of accredited laboratories, the list of supporting organizations continues to increase with time, as the advantages of using accredited laboratories become more widely appreciated and as the technical scope of the scheme grows.

Securing the acceptance of NAMAS accredited test reports and calibration certificates abroad, as well as at home, is regarded as very important. Overseas recognition of UK measurements was a major consideration in the setting up of NAMAS. NAMAS accredited reports are, in fact, widely accepted in many overseas countries on account of the high reputation enjoyed by the scheme. It is the policy of NAMAS to reinforce and extend this acceptance, wherever possible, by negotiating formal mutual recognition agreements (in the form of Memoranda of Understanding, or MoUs) with corresponding schemes overseas. NAMAS has such agreements with accreditation bodies in a number of other countries, including Australia, Federal Republic of Germany, France, Hong Kong, Italy, the Netherlands, New Zealand, Sweden and Switzerland.

It is hoped that the UK's accreditation agreements with its EEC partners will provide a precedent for further MoUs between countries of the Community, leading eventually to a comprehensive basis for the free passage of competently calibrated and tested instruments and products throughout the EEC. The past year has seen intensive discussions within the European Commission on these issues, and NAMAS has played an active part in ensuring that the UK interest is fully represented in such negotiations.

In general terms, the international standing and influence of the UK in the accreditation sphere is extremely high. NAMAS criteria and procedures have been widely adopted abroad, with a number of countries employing direct translations of NAMAS documents in their own national accreditation schemes.

Future measurement needs

Measurement does not remain static, nor can national metrology institutes afford to do so. As the apex of the UK national measurement system, NPL must foresee the future measurement needs of our industry, and must respond by evolving more advanced measurement standards and by developing or promoting the new and more economical measurement techniques that will be required to keep UK industry competitive. It is not sufficient to await the development of an industrial need *before* initiating research on a measurement problem: to do so would be a recipe for industrial obsolescence. NPL metrologists are therefore continuously investigating the possibility of new methods in the various disciplines of physical measurement.

One of the new areas selected for strategic measurement work at NPL is that of *nanotechnology*, the technology of manufacture where dimensions or tolerances in the range 0.1 nm to 100 nm play a critical role (1 nm = 10^{-9}m). It is a technology assuming increasing importance across different sectors of industry, as the ability develops to measure, control and machine with a precision down to atomic dimensions.

Two current NPL projects illustrate work on nanotechnology, one is aimed at *stabilizing against external mechanical or thermal disturbance* for precision machine tools and related equipment, and the other is concerned with *determining the roughness of supersmooth optical surfaces.*

Precision machine tools need to be stiff to minimize the consequences of unintentional forces and vibrations. In any framework, stiffness is enhanced by closing loops, i.e. eliminating cantilevers. Stiffness is further enhanced by directly connecting all apices and intersections to all others – a principle often called triangulation. On a three-dimensional framework, the simplest (and intrinsically stiffest) shape incorporating these features is the tetrahedron.

A prototype machine tool that exploits the inherent stiffness and geometrical symmetry of the tetrahedron, and has thus been named the *Tetraform*, has been designed at NPL. The prototype Tetraform is shown in Figure 27.7.

An equilateral tetrahedron has four axes of symmetry. On the Tetraform only one is used directly, both the basic structure and other components of the machining system being symmetrically disposed about this axis. This axial symmetry can be used to make the Tetraform insensitive to thermal as well as mechanical fluctuations. All components are made of the same material, steel, with similar cross-sections and thus have almost equal thermal response rates. The thermal compensation means that the position of the cutting tool relative to the workpiece (the two interacting on, or close to, the machine axis and geometrical centre) is almost unaffected by temperature changes.

The Tetraform is not intended to be a multiple-motion machine, but rather to have a set of interchangeable components (motions, workpiece carriers, etc.) to produce a range of motion combinations, and thus workpiece geometries. This reduces the error-compounding problems of complex machine tools. The prototype, fitted with a horizontal linear motion and an air-bearing vertical axis rotary motion, will produce flat workpieces up to 100 mm diameter by grinding or turning/fly cutting. Accessories for machining internal and external cylinders, and aspheric optical components are being developed.

The other area of work mentioned, that of determining the roughness of supersmooth optical surfaces, responds to present and future needs across several sectors of industry: current applications include laser gyro mirrors and focusing X-ray optical mirrors; any scattering of light due to surface roughness must be virtually eliminated. To assess surface roughness and check on quality control during manufacture, NPL has developed a novel optical instrument which scans across the surface of an instrument and measures the height of a pinpointed spot with respect to the average height of the surrounding area. The sensitivity of the system corresponds to roughness values of subatomic dimensions integrated over the 1μm

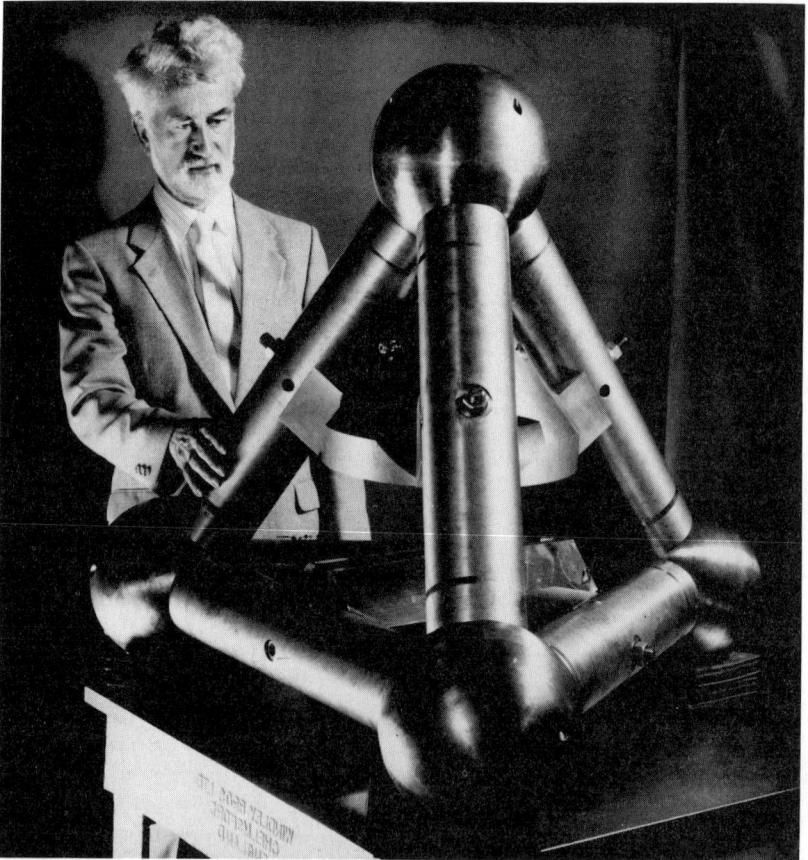

Figure 27.7. The prototype Tetraform. The Tetraform, which was developed at the National Physical Laboratory, is designed to stabilize precision machine tools and related equipment against external mechanical or thermal disturbance.

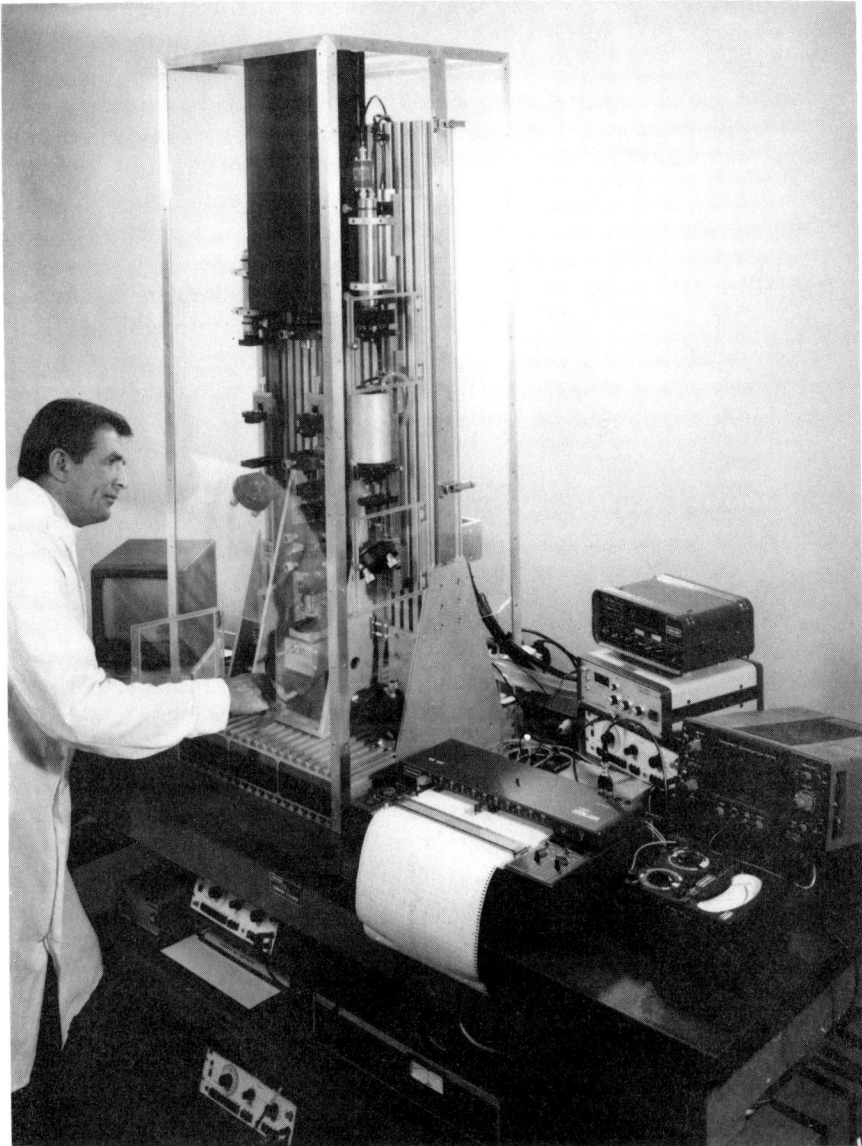

Figure 27.8.   The NPL-designed scanning optical interferometer. The interferometer is shown here being used to measure the subnanometre surface profiles of Zerodure ring laser gyro mirrors.

diameter of the probe beam. The new instrument is being further developed by the Cranfield Unit of Precision Engineering for on-line inspection of the surfaces produced by fine diamond turning. Figure 27.8 shows the interferometer being using to measure the sub-nanometre surface profiles of Zerodure ring laser gyro mirrors.

The projects mentioned above are examples of work carried out essentially within NPL. However, for developments in measurement technology to be relevant and effective, it is essential to secure the direct involvement of industry, both in planning and practice, at the earliest possible stage. Nanotechnology is one of a series of key areas of technology where Government has sought to stimulate collaboration between industry and science-based partners, through the DTI's LINK initiative. As well as cooperating with UK industry on a variety of measurement projects, NPL is the national coordinating centre for the LINK programme in nanotechnology.

International cooperation

The scale and sophistication of today's technology has made increased international cooperation a necessity for large industrial projects: it is the only way small and medium-sized countries can seek to compete with the industrial superpowers. The measurement industry has not been immune from similar pressures. It has become increasingly difficult for individual national metrology institutes to justify going-it-alone with large new projects on measurement standards or techniques. Even in well established measurement fields, the wisdom of pooling resources has become increasingly evident.

There has always been a considerable degree of cooperation between the world's major metrology institutes, mainly in the form of intercomparison of standards and exchange of experts. The last couple of years have seen a particular intensification of this cooperation within the Western European sphere. In 1987 an MoU on European Collaboration on Measurement Standards (EUROMET) was established by the national metrology institutes of western Europe. The agreement involves institutes within all western European nations (save Iceland), as well as the Commission of the European Communities (CEC).

The main types of collaboration envisaged under EUROMET are: coordination of research on new measurement standards and methods; sharing of major experimental and other facilities; provision of recognized European primary calibration facilities or primary standards by one member state for another covering certain physical quantities where economic considerations do not justify facilities being provided in each individual country.

In the two years since the EUROMET agreement was established, some 200 projects have been put forward for bilateral or multilateral collaboration, many of which have already moved towards implementation. In addition, moves are well under way for recognizing certain national metrology institutes as centres for providing selected European primary calibration facilities.

In a parallel development, European specification, certification, quality assurance and testing organizations have conducted intensive discussions, aimed at achieving Europe-wide rationalization within their fields. An ultimate aim is the harmonizaton of European product specifications, certification and assesssment procedures, and labora-tory accreditation criteria. Significant progress has been made in the last named area. Once again the CEC has been a party to the discussions: rationalization of European measurement and quality assurance arrangements is seen as a key element in achieving the Commission's aim of a Single European Market.

Both measurement and quality assurance, then, are areas of considerable current national and international activity. It seems likely that the remaining years of this century will see a growing commonality and pooling of resources and methods in these fields, initially within Europe but increasingly throughout the world. Hopefully this will lead to the more effective use of measurement and quality assurance as vehicles for international trade (rather than obstacles, as has occasionally happened in the past), while preserving the level of assurance necessary to safeguard the interests of the individual citizen.

28 Functional Testing

Geoffrey Leaver

The requirements of any product or service differ widely depending on whether one is the supplier or the user. The user requires *'fitness for purpose'* (will the product or service 'perform'?) The supplier on the other hand can only work to a 'specification' and in his terms quality must be defined as *conformance to specification*.

An inspector or tester, provided with the product, specification, measuring equipment and skill can adequately assess conformance to specification but may not be in a position to judge fitness for purpose. It is thus not uncommon for products to be supplied because they 'comply with specification' even though they may not meet the customer's requirements (indeed the question of fitness for purpose may not even be raised unless the product fails to comply with specification).

It is obviously important to distinguish between functional requirements (those which relate to use) and non-functional requirements (those which allow the functional requirements to be met). Functional requirements are aimed at such aspects as ensuring performance, meeting health and safety requirements, and ensuring agreed lifetimes, etc. Non-functional requirements provide the means to the end (i.e. they enable manufacture or supply).

Functional testing is therefore carried out to verify that a product will perform under its operating conditions for a given length of time. Such testing may be conducted on the finished product or system (which is the major interest for the user) and at intermediate stages, such as at component or sub-assembly level (which may be of significant economic value to the producer).

The requirements can be divided into three main areas:

1. *Performance* These requirements, specific to the product, are defined qualities or quantities such as the expected light output from an electric luminaire, the output capacity and stability of a generator, and so on.
2. *Environmental conditions* These requirements cover such things as the temperature range, humidity, vibration, presence of corrosive or other harmful substances to which the product is likely to be exposed during its stored or operating life.
3. *Time requirements* These are the expected lifetime requirements for the product, usually relating to operating life but also, in many cases, the storage or shelf-life. Thus an electric lamp bulb may have a quoted life of 1200 hours under typical conditions, an automobile engine could have a target life of 100 000 hours before major overhaul and an exhaust silencing system could have an expected life of three years.

Each of these factors will vary between individual units of the same product and steps are necessary to determine the requirements, estimate the variation (determining the distribution) and finally testing to verify that the product can meet the requirements.

In many cases it is unrealistic, timeconsuming and extremely costly to 'test to destruction' over the lifetime of a product and accelerated testing is commonly used by applying excessive stresses or exaggerated environmental conditions to deliberately accelerate the effects.

Before testing it is necessary to define the actual requirements, and to distinguish between what is to be expected of the product or service (the design requirements) and how well the product or service actually achieves the design requirements (this degree of achievement being the conformance or production requirements).

Design testing is directed towards the approval of a design. The tests are conducted to determine whether an item is capable of meeting the requirements of the product specification.

Production testing (or conformance testing) is directed towards the approval of production. It is intended to determine whether the units, as produced, actually do meet the requirements of the product specification.

Fitness for purpose

For modern products, attainment of fitness for purpose involves striking a balance between many competing factors. Costs and other information must be obtained as necessary in such areas as:

1. Minimum functional requirements.
2. Maximum environmental expectations.
3. Cost limitations.
4. Safety requirements.
5. Reliability requirements.

Minimum functional requirements

What performance does the customer have a reasonable right to expect under specified conditions of use? This information can be obtained by market research (prior to design), field trials (during design finalizing stage) or feedback from customers (after supply).

The minimum functional requirements should be set out clearly in the functional specification, which describes in detail the characteristics of the product with regard to its intended capability. This specification should, as far as possible, be written in quantitative terms giving the limits of acceptability.

Maximum environmental expectation

Environmental factors have to be considered from two viewpoints. These are:

1. Discovering or predicting what the environmental conditions will be.
2. Testing to ensure that the product can cope with these conditions (which might include temperature, speed, acceleration, pressure, humidity, vibration, altitude and many other factors).

Cost limitations

The product design will have certain restrictions imposed by the final price (and overall cost) of the product or service supplied and it is necessary to clearly define the intended market. What sector of the market are we aiming for:

- The leather bound or paperback book buyer?
- The 'designer label' or the 'mass market'?
- The long lifetime or the 'disposable'?

Safety requirements

Safety is defined as 'the freedom from *unacceptable risks* of personal harm'. It must be realized that there is no known way of attaining absolute safety and there will always be a degree of risk whilst any hazard is present.

A *hazard* is a set of conditions in the operation of a product or system with the potential for initiating an accident sequence. Hazards can be classified in a number of ways, including:

(a) *catastrophic*, causing death, severe injury to personnel, or total loss of product;
(b) *critical*, will cause personal injury or major product damage unless immediate corrective action is taken;
(c) *controlled* or marginal, can be overcome without injury to personnel or major product damage;
(d) *negligible*, will not result in personal injury or product damage.

A *risk* is the combined effect of the probability of occurrence of an undesirable event and the magnitude of the event. It can be defined in terms of the probability of occurrence of a hazard or the effect of this occurrence.

Although absolute safety can not be attained, it must be realized that legally a manufacturer or supplier must show that all possible steps to minimize the risk of hazards are taken.

Reliability requirements

Reliability is the ability of an item to perform a required function under stated conditions for a stated minimum period of time.

Purchasers need to be told not only how a product should be used and maintained and what the expected initial performance will be. There is also a requirement to assess how long the product will continue to function and what will be its chance of failure.

Reliability sets an objective or a requirement of a product from its inception to the end of its working life. In those products where reliability is of prime importance, quantitative requirements should be included in the functional specification.

Failure

Failure is defined as 'the termination of the ability of an item to perform a required function'. In practice some kinds of failure are more important than others. It is necessary to distinguish between these — they can be classified by cause, as follows:

- *Misuse failure* — attributable to the application of stresses beyond the stated capabilities of the item.
- *Inherent weakness failure* — the item fails when it is subjected to stresses within the stated capabilities of the item.
- *Wear-out failure* — failures which have increasing probability of occurrence with time.

Testing for reliability

Reliability tests are conducted to verify that a product will work under operating conditions for a given length of time. Results are assessed on failures accumulated during the testing. The emphasis is usually placed on:

1. The component and individual parts level.
2. The complete system or assembly level.

Tests focus on three elements. These are:

1. The performance requirements. These are specific to the product, and tests must be conducted to verify that the product can withstand the expected stress for the required time period.
2. Environmental conditions. Testing may well be needed to determine the conditions, before conducting tests to verify that the product can operate and withstand these conditions for the required period.
3. Time requirements.

One common form of reliability testing, allowing reduced costs, is accelerated testing. The products are made to perform at abnormally high stress or environmental levels in order to make them fail earlier. Great care is needed in correlating accelerated test results with those expected under normal service conditions.

For any reliability testing to be valid it must provide statistically significant results. Special problems can arise in such cases as:

- A requirement for extremely high reliability (a low failure rate, or a high mean time between failures).
- A requirement for an extremely long life.
- High cost or shortage of test samples.

There are two basic types of error in evaluating significance, namely that of rejecting an acceptable item or that of accepting a rejectable item. Both of these risks are present in any sample testing.

The sample size taken depends on the chosen sampling risks, the size of the smallest time difference which is going to have to be detected and the amount of variation in the characteristic being measured.

In general, the higher the sample size (or greater the number of tests) relative to the standard to be attained, the greater the validity of the testing. For example, if there is an objective of a maximum of one defective component per million produced, a sample of only 100 would have a low validity. On the other hand, if the target is that a minimum of 90 per cent of trains shall arrive on time, then a sample of 100 could yield a significant result.

Although increasing the sample size or number of tests improves the precision of estimates obtained, this improvement does not usually vary linearly according to the number of tests. Doubling the number of tests, for example, does not double the precision. Also, the degree of precision obtained is not dependent simply on the size of the sample chosen in relation to the total batch size. The size of the total batch itself affects the result. This is illustrated in the following example, taken from ISO Standard 2859, inspection level 2. Table 28.1 shows the sample size needed to obtain the same level of testing for three different total batch sizes.

Table 28.1.
Samples size needed for the same level of testing for different total batch sizes.

Batch size	Sample size	Sample size as percentage of batch size
40	8	20.0
800	80	10.0
400 000	800	0.2

Two safeguarding approaches to improve reliability

1. *Derating* A margin of safety is built into the design so that components and systems are operated well below their specified limits. For example, the use of a capacitor rated at 3000 volts in an

application where actual level is only 200 volts.

2. *Redundancy* This is the case where the designer provides more than one means for accomplishing a given task in such a way that, should one method fail, the system will still operate. An example is the multi-engined aircraft: if one engine fails the aircraft should still be able to land safely.

Defects

Defects, or defectives, relate to items that do not comply with the specified requirements, where the non-compliance is the responsibility of the manufacturer or supplier. Defects can be classified according to their degree of seriousness, as follows:

1. *Critical* A defect which is likely to result in hazardous or unsafe conditions for individuals using, maintaining or depending on the product. A critical defect is also one which will cause the failure of a major product. As an example, the failure of a car steering mechanism would be classed as a critical defect.
2. *Major* A defect which, although not critical, will result in failure or will significantly reduce the performance of the product. Thus a defect causing a car engine to fail would be classed as major.
3. *Minor* A defect which will not appreciably affect the use of the product. Staying with the automobile industry for our examples, a slight paint blemish on a car could be classed as a minor defect.

Defects can also be classified in terms of cost. It must be remembered here that costs of consequential damage can go well beyond the costs of parts and labour for repairing the defect itself. For example, if a lorry carrying components breaks down on a delivery run to a customer, the user's costs might include (in addition to the repair costs) the value of the lorry while it is out of action, the driver's pay and the customer's lost factory production time caused by late delivery of the components.

Other examples include the breakdown of a deep freeze cabinet (in which the contents may have to be scrapped) and the costs of making alternative arrangements when a car breaks down.

Normal legal responsibility concerning defects is twofold:

1. General disclaimers in cases of injury to human beings are usually not valid.
2. Disclaimers on consequential monetary loss not involving safety are usually upheld.

Measurement

Product conformance is determined by measurements made by test equipment and it is necessary to have sufficient knowledge of the equipment to be sure that the results are valid (i.e. sufficiently accurate and precise for the required purpose).

Any error in measurement has a direct bearing on the ability to judge conformance and a clear understanding of the meaning of the measurements requires an understanding of the nature of the measurement error.

Accuracy

If a number of measurements are made on a product the mean of these measurements is calculated and this mean is compared with the true value; the extent to which this measured mean agrees with the true value is a measure of the accuracy of the equipment used.

The difference between the measured mean and the true value is the error, which can be either positive or negative and is the extent to which the equipment is out of calibration. The equipment can still be considered accurate if the error is less than the tolerance or maximum allowable for that grade of instrument.

Precision

Irrespective of the accuracy of calibration, an instrument will not give identical readings on repeat readings even when making a series of measurements on a single unit. Instead there will be a scatter of readings and the dispersion, or spread of these readings is a measure of the precision (irrespective of the relationship with the true value).

In measurements it is necessary to have both adequate accuracy *and* precision but it should be appreciated that recalibration will normally improve the *accuracy* of an instrument but will not change the *precision*.

There are many sources of measurement error which can be attributed to the operator (differences in skill levels, experience or technique of different operators), attributed to the test equipment (variations due to drift caused by changes in environmental conditions, backlash, wear, etc.) or attributed to the test procedure (where several different procedures are available).

The overall measurement error is, of course, the result of all the contributing errors. The *observed* error can be expressed in the form:

$$S_o^2 = S_a^2 + S_b^2 + S_c^2 \ldots$$

where S_o is the observed error and S_a, S_b, S_c and so on are the individual contributing errors. In a measurement system, the observed variation (S_o) will comprise the *product* variation (S_p) and the *system* variation (S_s). The relationship is of the form:

$$S_o^2 = S_p^2 + S_s^2$$

which can be expressed as

$$S_p^2 = S_o^2 - S_s^2$$

It is apparent that if the variation due to the system is less than 10 per cent of the observed variation, then the effect on the product will be less than 1 per cent. That is the basis of the commonly accepted practice of specifying that the measuring instrument should be capable of distinguishing to an accuracy of 10 per cent of the required product tolerance.

Calibration

In publishing results, it is necessary to make clear the extent of possible errors and it is essential to be able to demonstrate that the equipment used is capable of providing precise measurement before any assurance of conformance can be given. This requirement means that the measuring equipment used must be capable of an accuracy higher than that specified for the product.

Any measuring equipment has at some time been adjusted or graduated to the required accuracy within known limits (usually as one of the final steps during its manufacture). Unfortunately this by itself is insufficient as all measuring and test equipment is subject to change caused by wear, damage, etc., and it is necessary to check at a predetermined frequency.

Ideally an instrument should be checked immediately before and after each occasion of use. The pre-check will prevent a faulty instrument from being used and thus producing incorrect results, whilst the post-check will detect if any changes have occurred during the period of use. This, however, is a policy of perfection being both time consuming and expensive. Stable equipment can, in the absence of damage, normally be relied upon for periods measured in months, and checking equipment at regular intervals provides a good assurance that measurements taken are satisfactory.

With any test equipment it is necessary, therefore, to establish a calibration procedure that will detect any deterioration beyond tolerable levels of accuracy. This needs a calibration schedule to determine when each piece of equipment must be reassessed to ensure that it is still maintaining its required accuracy. There are generally three possible methods of determining calibration schedules:

1. *Time* Calibration on the basis of fixed calendar times or intervals, such as 1 week, 3 months, annually and so on.
2. *Usage* Calibration based on the amount of actual usage which the instrument has received, such as the number of units of product measured. Recalibration times can be determined by recording clerically the number of times the equipment has been used, or by automatic counting or inbuilt computer programming.
3. *Hours* This is calibration according to the number of hours for which the measuring equipment has been operated. For electrical equipment, for example, this may simply be a matter of metering the actual time for which the equipment has been drawing current.

In any calibration system it is important to measure and record the results before any recalibrating adjustments are made. This is the only way in which drift can be measured, and used as a basis for adjusting calibration periods sensibly.

Testing

Testing may be one of two basic types:

1. *Condition termination tests* where the testing is continued until failure or some predetermined change of state occurs.
2. *Fixed time sequence testing* which is based on specified acceptable values of the characteristics being assessed.

Testing to expose design weaknesses should be planned to generate failures. Weaknesses are only demonstrated by failure and therefore a test that generates no failures has provided no information on which to base improvements. Tests therefore should be as severe as is compatible with the planned operation of the products.

Once the design has been established the actual performance parameters are specified and fixed time or sequence testing is used to monitor the continuing product conformance. The aims of a test programme generally are to:

1. Ensure that the item meets the specified performance or operational requirements.

2. Minimize manufacturing faults and defective parts.
3. Highlight systematic errors so that design deficiencies can be overcome.
4. Provide information which can be fed back to design as part of an improvement plan.

Whilst the performance requirements under normal or anticipated conditions of operation may be readily specified and tested for an item as produced, in certain cases this may be of limited value since subsequent operations including packaging, transportation, installation/commissioning and usage may all have an effect on subsequent field performance. In such cases it is necessary to specify clearly and test for these conditions, which may include:

- *Packaging* Protection of the product during handling, transport and storage. This may require special attention, such as verifying the effectiveness of rustproofing of steel, or the shielding of sensitive electronics components.
- *Transportation* Tests to check that damage will not occur due to temperature, humidity, vibration, shock, sabotage, etc.
- *Storage* Testing to ensure that shelf-life is determined and specified and that the product is clearly dated.
- *Installation, commissioning and handover* Special facilities and tests may have to be specified to support commissioning and to demonstrate the product to the customer before handover.
- *Usage* Problems can arise when the user fails to observe the operating instructions, or overstresses or fails to maintain the product. Tests may be necessary to determine the consequences of forseeable misuse.

Ideally testing should compare actual service performance with users' service needs and the most significant aspect is the need for the manufacturer to find out the actual usage which takes place. There are numerous sources of such information such as direct observation, complaint analysis, positive feedback, etc., and it is essential to ensure that all such data is used and incorporated into the functional specification and hence into the functional test programme.

It is not always possible or economical to test complete systems; it may be necessary to test components and subassemblies and hence predict the behaviour of complete systems.

In a similar way, testing under normal or anticipated operating conditions can be unrealistically timeconsuming or expensive and accelerated testing may be carried out, whose primary purpose is to provide failures and/or performance data more quickly than if the item were tested under normal conditions. To be valid, an accelerated test should not alter the modes of failure, and the relation between the accelerated data must be understood. In accelerated testing, the stresses applied are more severe than those encountered in normal use in order to speed up the ageing process and may be applied either as constant stress or step stress. Care must however be taken when predicting performance under normal conditions from results obtained under exaggerated conditions since different factors may come into play.

Automation of testing

Automated inspection and testing is designed to reduce costs, improve efficiency, reduce time, overcome manpower shortages, increase accuracy and eliminate human monotony.

Commonly automation involves substantial investment in capital equipment and there are drawbacks with automated testing which need to be overcome. Its use, however, is rapidly increasing and for very good reasons and just as computer-aided design (CAD) and computer-aided manufacture (CAM) are widely used, computer-aided testing (CAT) and computer-aided inspection (CAI) are becoming more and more widely adopted.

When examining the possibility of automatic test equipment it is necessary to consider many aspects including an awareness that any automated process requires:

- Criteria which can be expressed exactly (numbers).
- Decisions which can be made in advance (what happens if?).
- Repetitive nature.
- Decisions must be right or wrong, good or bad, etc.
- A high degree of order.

In addition it is necessary to consider the cost of automated testing and the economic justification of its introduction, comparing the anticipated benefits in time-saving or improved information with the capital cost of the equipment together with the cost of obtaining, maintaining and protecting the software.

Once all these factors have been resolved, automatic test equipment offers many advantages in terms of speed and the number of parameters which can be evaluated. The limiting factor in speed of test may indeed be the time taken in positioning the item in the test equipment.

Automatic test methods can generate a tremendous amount of data of varying degrees of usefulness and it is essential to identify the information which is really needed for evaluation. Only data which are required should be processed, whereas there is a danger of processing all data for no other reason than that they are available.

Both attribute and variables data require processing. Attribute data are used to identify major defect types, determine yields, classify into different grades, etc. Variables data may be processed for analysis and presented in various statistical forms (such as distributions, central tendency, etc.).

Two needs must be satisfied when testing is automated; the inspection itself and the calibration of the test equipment. Automatic testing may be used on high volume production lines to provide go/no-go answers. When multiple properties are measured or the product must be sequenced through a variety of environmental conditions or monitored over time, computer systems can continually follow the product under test and it is possible therefore to combine data collection as well as exception reporting with automatic testing.

Test procedures

Test procedures are usually tailor-made for a specific product type. They would normally include some or all of the following:

- *Scope* The product to be tested must be identified by name or by a specific reference number.
- *Field of application* The intended usage of the procedure itself and of the item which is its subject. Sufficient information should also be given of any secondary or partly applicable uses.
- *References* Other relevant standards, procedures or other documents.
- *Definitions* All specialized terms used must be defined, following the relevant international standards.
- *Responsibilities* The responsibility for conducting the testing and for determining the subsequent course of action must be defined.
- *Purpose and context of use* This part describes the role that the item is intended to perform. Environmental conditions and other factors associated with the performance of the item in service must be listed.

- *Equipment* Equipment to be used for the testing should be listed, together with acceptable alternatives, where these are applicable.
- *Performance requirements* Each performance requirement should be defined in terms of a function which is to be fulfilled, together with the physical, chemical or mechanical property on which assessment or verification can be assessed. Wherever possible, terms and expressions capable of quantification should be used in accordance with any applicable international standard. Requirements should be listed so that those which always apply are distinguished from those which apply only under certain circumstances.
- *Method of assessment or verification* For each performance requirement, this part will describe fully (or cross refer to) the means by which the achieved performance of the product will be assured or verified and, in addition, the means for predicting the performance over time. Cross reference should be made to international standards wherever possible.
- *Performance values* For each performance requirement must be stated the upper and lower acceptable performance values or grades against which the product will be required to perform. The relationship of the values or grades to the purpose and context of use should be indicated.
- *Frequency of testing* This part defines the frequency of testing, which may be based on time or quantity.
- *Follow-up action* The procedure for action to be taken in the case of either acceptance or rejection should be defined.

Test procedures within a company may conveniently be drawn together into a test and inspection procedures manual. This, typically, may contain:

- Authorization, by the responsible person or department.
- List of contents, with amendments.
- Statement of responsibilities and authorities.
- General policy on the classification of defects.
- Sampling plans.
- Copies of test reporting forms.
- Procedure for identification and labelling of the product and its test status.
- Non-conformance procedure.
- Individual product test procedures (either included in the manual or referenced from it).

Test specifications are derived from design documents, and they cannot be fully defined until the following questions have been resolved:

1. What constitutes acceptable performance? The need is to define the purpose of the product or service and to specify the conditions which must prevail for this purpose to be considered as having been met. When the purpose is defined in detail it becomes clearer which failures will impair the performance and which will not.
2. What are the loads or stresses to which the item will be subjected during its life? Many failures result from misunderstandings between the designer and the user. For example, a component may be designed for continuous operation at 150° C with intermittent exposure to temperatures of 180° C. But what does this term 'intermittent exposure' mean in this case? What happens if, on occasions, the temperature rises to 200° C?
3. What are the reliability targets? These should be specified in quantifiable terms (for example, a failure rate not exceeding 1 per cent per annum, or a specified mean time between failures).

In some cases the customer may specify these requirements but, in many other cases, the manufacturer or supplier must take the initiative in establishing specifications.

Test strategy

A major quality problem on assembled products has been inadequate expertise among field service engineers. In addition to improvements in product designs to achieve greater reliability, there has been a vast increase in the use of modular construction, in which subassemblies or modules are designed for easy removal and replacement. Thus a failure in a television set or a computer (as examples) can usually be dealt with by the speedy replacement of one or more modules on site and, where possible, repairing the defective modules later at a factory or service workshop.

This use of modular construction also has benefits for the manufacturer, since subassemblies can be tested and accepted on the basis of defined criteria before they are built in to the total assembly or system.

During the design stages of a new or modified product the system, subsystems and units must be precisely defined in terms of their functional requirements and the conditions which constitute acceptable or unacceptable performance. At this stage the interfaces between the various components must also be clearly defined.

The critical parts must be identified. These can be defined as those which:

- have a high population in the product;
- have a single (or unreliable) source of supply;
- have to function within unusually tight limits;
- would have serious consequences in the case of failure;
- are unproven owing to lack of data.

For each critical part, it is necessary to list all the factors which are relevant to its performance or its reliability such as the actual functions, ratings, internal environment and stresses, expected external

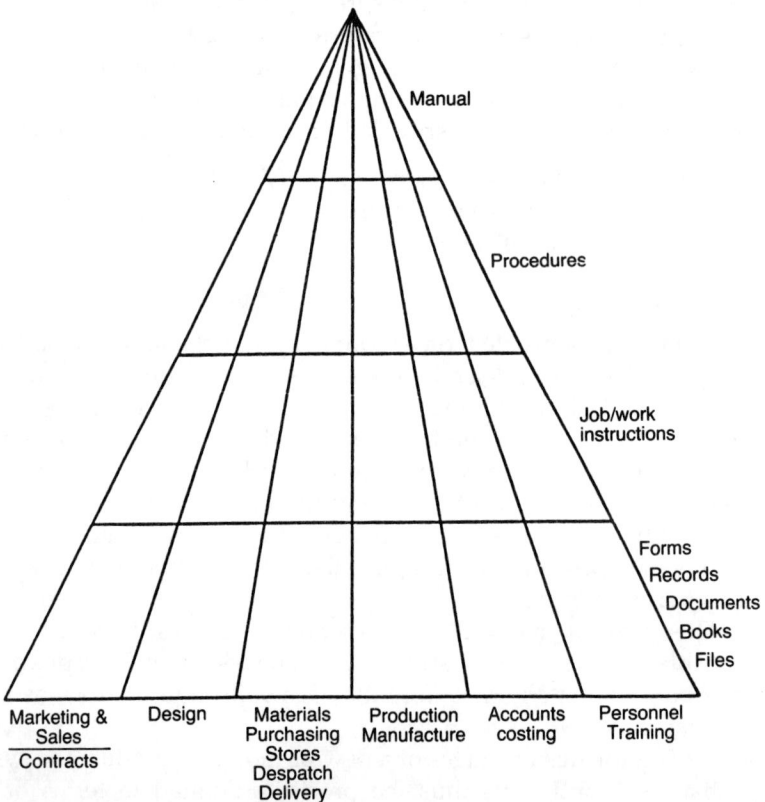

Figure 28.1.   System documentation.

environments and stresses, and the actual duty (operation time) cycle.

Once the requirements for each component and/or assembly have been defined and specifications and procedures written, testing can be conducted on a bottom-upward basis. This approach will ensure that the satisfactory operation (or non-conformance) of each module is discovered at the earliest possible stage. Integration of accepted modules into the main assembly should then be followed by a final functional test to ensure that the complete product or system meets the test specification — and hence the design requirements.

Procedures in relation to the quality system

Where quality assurance and total quality management philosophies are practised, these test and inspection procedures form an integral part of the overall quality system documentation. A typical system documentation would be arranged as shown in Figure 28.1.

Further reading

Knowles, R., *Automatic Testing Systems and Applications*, McGraw-Hill, Maidenhead 1976.

29 Managing Non-conformances

Ray H. Spencer

Even with well defined requirements and capable systems or processes, there are occasions when items or services do not conform to specified requirements. In such cases, a decision is required. The way a business manages such decisions will say more about its approach to quality than any quality policy statement ever could. It provides the acid test for commitment and integrity.

This chapter examines the pitfalls and the opportunities presented by non-conformance, the distinction between non-conforming and defective, the process for managing non-conformance and how to use it as a springboard for improvement in the quality of products, processes and systems.

The pitfalls and the opportunities

In the absence of a well defined system for dealing with non-conformance, there are a number of hazards which will emerge, sooner or later. Whether non-conformance occurs frequently or infrequently, it is likely to threaten schedules or output. Consequently, a decision on action will often be required urgently. As the performance of many functions is measured in terms of schedule or output, it is hardly surprising that the risks or consequences of non-conformance will be played down in certain quarters. A question frequently asked when a non-conformance occurs is 'can it be used?' It is a perfectly reasonable question, but dangerous if answered by the wrong person, for the wrong motives. Particularly dangerous, if someone else will bear the consequences.

The individual most frequently called upon to make the final decision is the quality manager and in so doing is seen by many as having total responsibility for anything which happens from that point on. The quality manager must therefore take full account of the risks and consequences. If the quality manager is intimidated by peer or higher pressure, the situation will be exploited, with the inevitable and serious consequences of returns, liability claims and lost sales. However, if undue caution prevails, those whose targets suffer unnecessarily will be quick to point out the costs incurred by scrap, rework, repair, rescheduling, inventories, later deliveries, cancellations, etc. Even where the quality manager attempts to take the middle ground, if the facts and opinions of those who are qualified or authorized to provide them are not fully taken into account, decisions could be questionable or appear inconsistent.

It may seem that the quality manager just cannot win. There are indeed many ways of losing, but the surest way of performing effectively is to employ an approach which is well defined, consistent and provides the opportunity for all relevant facts and opinions to be considered in decision-making. In this way, although non-conformance will still be a problem when it occurs, the process will be viewed as a positive means of averting more serious problems and as an opportunity for triggering longer term improvements.

For the quality manager, a systematic approach offers the following benefits.

1.   Commitment, based on the involvement of others in the decision process.
2.   Credibility, based on objective and consistent decisions.
3.   Trust, based on openness with users.
4.   Visibility, of non-conforming performance.
5.   Peace of mind, from employing a rational decision process.

For the business as a whole, the approach provides:

1.   Understanding of requirements.
2.   Identification of causes and preventive measures.
3.   Knowledge, which can be applied in future designs.

4. Quality improvements, based on problem resolution.
5. Increased profitability, stemming from quality improvements.

Definitions

Before discussing the management of non-conformance, it is worth considering the distinction between non-conforming and defective; terms which are often confused.

Non-conforming
A unit or service is non-conforming when at least one quality characteristic causes a specified requirement not to be met.

Defective
A unit or service is defective when at least one quality characteristic causes a failure to satisfy an intended purpose.

In simpler terms, non-conforming means 'specification not met' and defective means 'intended purpose not achieved'. It is a subtle but important distinction.

Specifications and standards

When considering any item which is potentially non-conforming or defective, it is necessary to make reference to existing specifications or standards used to define acceptability.

Specifications relate to products, processes or services and are normally specific to an individual product, process or service, defining performance, reliability, capability, service, etc.

Standards can also relate to products, processes or services, but are often applicable to a range of products, processes or services. They can be internally generated by a department or business, or they can be developed by trade associations, professional bodies, buying groups, government institutions, military agencies or international standards organizations. Some examples are:

American National Standards Institute	ANSI
British Standards Institution	BSI
Deutsche Institüt Normenausschuss	DIN
United States Military	MIL

International Electrotechnical Commission   IEC
International Organization for Standardization   ISO

It is important that specifications clearly define the boundaries of acceptability. This may appear obvious, but many issues relating to non-conformity will be centred on interpretation or opinion of acceptability rather than whether the current specification or standard truly represents the criteria to determine fitness for purpose.

Subjectivity

Subjectivity means, 'dependent on personal taste or views'. Where no definition of acceptability exists, subjectivity thrives, with much uncertainty, inconsistency and conflict resulting. Operators may set lower standards than inspectors, suppliers may disclaim liability for rejections, the intended purpose may or may not be affected and customers may or may not find results acceptable.

All too often, local authorities become established, making decisions based on their views, without reference to the design authority, the sales department or the customer. Their views may be based on past experience and their decisions may be good in many instances. They will certainly be valued by certain functions, like production, who have a high regard for quick and largely painless decision-makers.

Even where the design authority or the customer is consulted on acceptability, unless standards are established, limits of acceptability clearly defined and the conditions for accepting non-conformance known, it is probable that the same problem will occur time and time again.

Precedent

Using a previous case to serve as an example to be followed has obvious merit, but also has certain limitations when applied to non-conformance.

Providing the circumstances and consequences of the previous case are understood and defined, the approach is sound. The danger is that something which is all right in one set of circumstances may not be all right when, for instance, mating parts are produced to a different size within their tolerance range. Also, something which is functionally acceptable immediately may in time cause a major reliability problem. Until the problem becomes apparent, precedent will incorrectly suggest that such a non-conformity is acceptable. A full investigation by the design authority at the outset would almost certainly have alerted all to the reliability risk.

Precedent can also encourage others to assume that because something was accepted previously, it will always be all right and there is no need to report or gain approval for the same condition on future occasions.

Attitude

The attitude to non-conformance can vary greatly according to circumstances. The major threats to rational decisions are:

(a)   lack of information, and
(b)   conflicting priorities.

The former is often a direct result of the latter.

When a non-conformance occurs, an unplanned condition has occurred. The consequences are often unknown, may or may not be serious, but will certainly involve time being spent on investigation and may even result in starting again. Either way, the planned condition is threatened and a strong bias towards accepting the non-conformance can develop. There is also a strong temptation for some to turn a blind eye if there is a chance that the deviation will not be noticed, or will not be traceable to an individual.

Even when non-conformance is identified, the possibility of a problem resulting can be made to appear insignificant in comparison with non-achievement of the plan; particularly by the person responsible for the plan (e.g. project managers faced with missed schedules, production managers faced with reduced output, designers faced with late new model introductions, materials managers faced with increased inventories, sales managers faced with lost follow-up orders and general managers faced with bad results at crucial periods). They can provide formidable opposition to the diligent quality manager who is only protecting the business from damaging its well being. Failure to accept non-conformance in the wrong environment can be made to seem like a far greater crime than causing non-conformance.

The reason for such situations developing is often due to the overall attitude of a business towards responsibility. Such attitudes stem from the view that a quality manager alone is responsible for quality, a production manager alone is responsible for output, the sales manager alone is responsible for sales, etc., and may the best man win. Sadly, no one wins and overall the business suffers. In such businesses, the only time non-conformance is reviewed or approved is when a concession is required.

Objectivity

To make decisions which are not influenced by personal feelings, opinions or conflicting priorities, they must be viewed objectively. In effect, this means assessing facts and quantifying results. All characteristics considered must in some form be measurable. This is not always easy, but if it cannot be measured, how can it be determined whether or not it is acceptable?

In practical terms, measurement of length, weight, speed, electrical current, etc., is generally quite straightforward, employing some form of measuring instrument. Problems occur where instruments do not exist, or would be difficult to conceive (as for instance with paint finish and solder joints). In such situations, it is necessary to conduct capability studies to establish the range and frequency of occurrence of variable conditions and then develop standards which demonstrate the limits of acceptability. Such standards can be in the form of charts, samples, sketches, photographs and many more.

Once a basis for measurement has been established, debate will change from whether the item is acceptable to whether the standard is acceptable. It may take some time to establish the right level, but at least any changes required can be controlled and managed in an orderly and cost effective manner.

Process

The process for dealing with non-conformance varies with the size and nature of a business. At one end of the scale there is a need for detailed procedures, regular reviews, nominated representatives, approval rules, fixed timescales and the maintenance of detailed records. In a very formal system, the body conducting these activities is often termed a Material Review Board (MRB). The MRB may consider all non-conforming material, or only purchased material. At the other end of the scale there may be outline procedures operated on an *ad hoc* basis, with little documentation involved. However, whichever approach is most appropriate, the process needs to consider the following aspects relating to non-conformance, no matter how informally.

1. Discovery.
2. Identification.
3. Segregation.
4. Analysis.
5. Approval.
6. Documentation.
7. Disposal.
8. Closeout.
9. Tracking.

An outline of the stages involved in the management of non-conformance is illustrated in Figure 29.1.

Discovery

Non-conformance, whether discovered at incoming inspection, in-process, at final test or inspection, or as returns from customers, must be investigated to reach a clear decision on what needs to be done with the items concerned and what action must be taken to prevent recurrence. To achieve this, a document or computer record is raised to record occurrence, define conditions, identify how to dispose of the items and giving reference to documents initiating further actions required. Such a form is often called a non-conforming material report. For the remainder of this chapter, this will be abbreviated to NMR. An example is shown in Figure 29.2.

Information entered at the discovery stage is typically:

1. Material or part number, issue and description.
2. Specified and actual result (deviation).
3. Quantity or ratio of non-conforming items.
4. Batch or order number.
5. Originator's name and the date raised.

The NMR is normally initiated by the quality function and then used for input and approval as described later. Dependent on the approach adopted and the urgency of the situation, the NMR may be distributed,

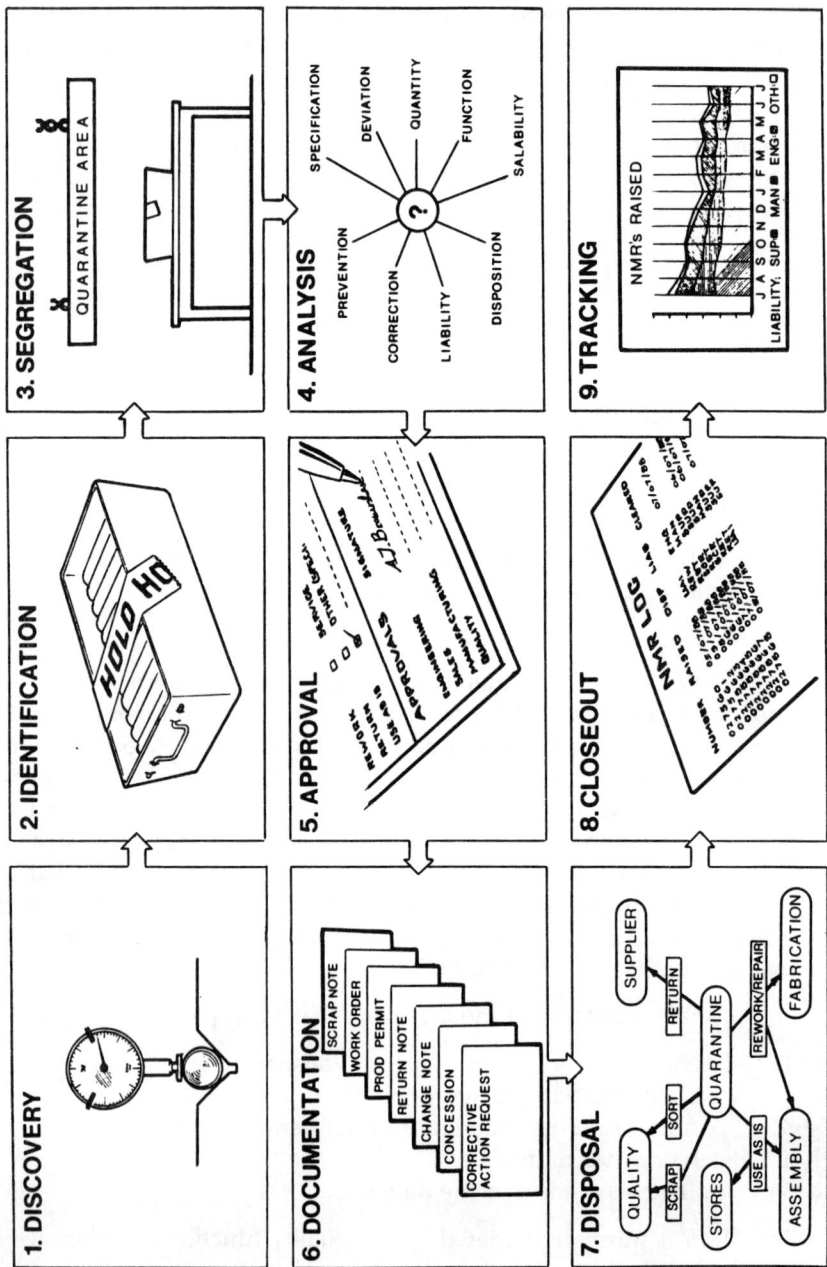

Figure 29.1.   The stages of non-conformance management.

614

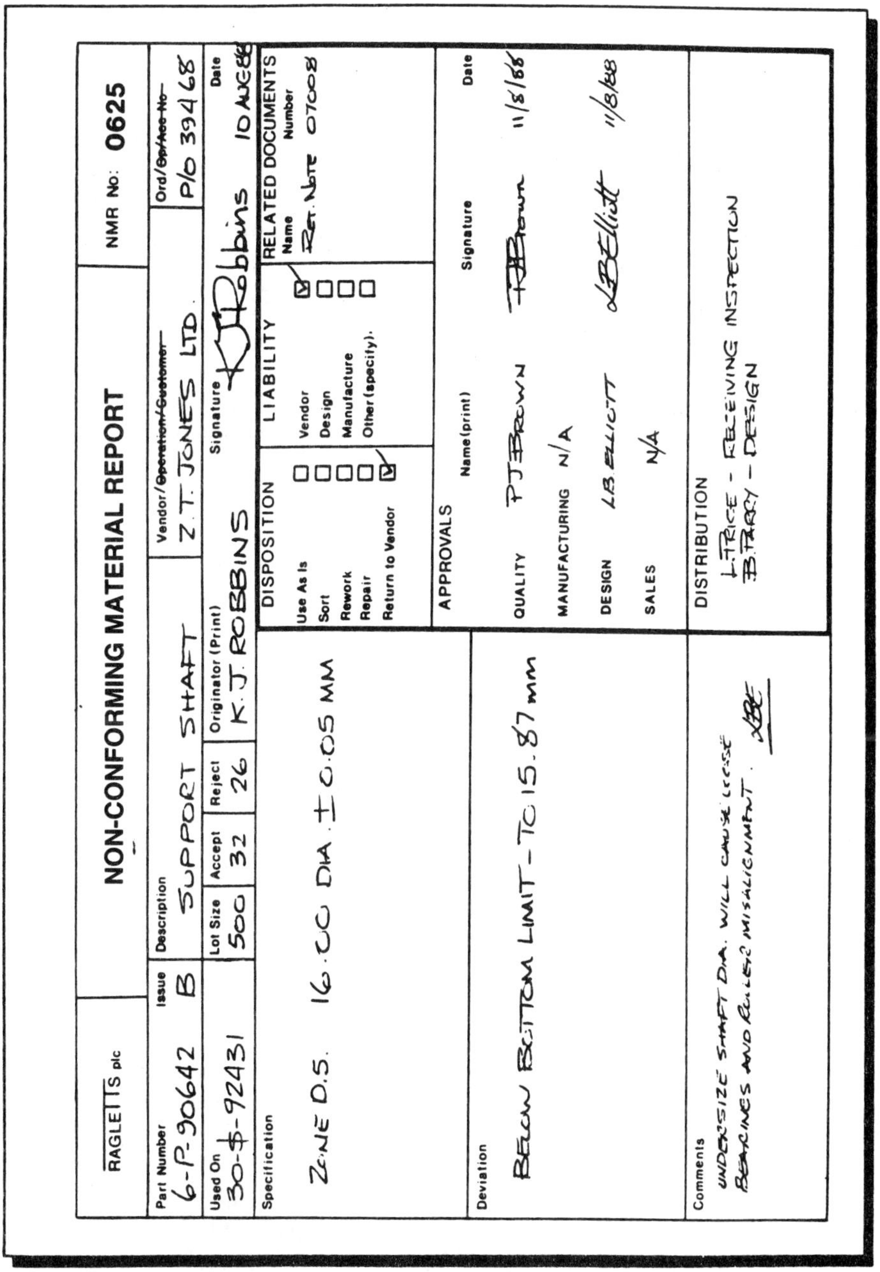

RAGLETTS plc		NON-CONFORMING MATERIAL REPORT		NMR No: **0625**

Part Number	Issue	Description	Vendor/Operation/Customer	Ord/B/Acc to
6-P-90642	B	SUPPORT SHAFT	Z.T. JONES LTD.	P/O 39468

Used On	Lot Size	Accept	Reject	Originator (Print)	Signature	Date
30-$-92431	500	32	26	K.J. ROBBINS	KJRobbins	10 AUG 88

Specification

ZONE D.5.   16.00 DIA. ± 0.05 MM

DISPOSITION

		LIABILITY	
Use As Is	☐	Vendor	☒
Sort	☐	Design	☐
Rework	☐	Manufacture	☐
Repair	☐	Other (specify).	☐
Return to Vendor	☒		

RELATED DOCUMENTS

Name	Number
☒ Rej. Note	07008
☐	
☐	

Deviation

BELOW BOTTOM LIMIT - TO 15.87 mm

APPROVALS

	Name(print)	Signature	Date
QUALITY	PJ BROWN	PJBrown	11/8/88
MANUFACTURING	N/A		
DESIGN	L B ELLIOTT	LBElliott	11/8/88
SALES	N/A		

DISTRIBUTION

L.PRICE - RECEIVING INSPECTION
B.TRACY - DESIGN

Comments

UNDERSIZE SHAFT DIA. WILL CAUSE LOOSE
BEARINGS AND ROLLER MISALIGNMENT. JBE

Figure 29.2.   A typical non-conforming material report.

615

hand-carried or held pending a meeting of individuals involved in the decision process.

Identification

Upon discovery of the non-conforming material, whether the level or extent is known or not, it is important that all such material is identified as being, or suspected of being, 'Non-conforming material — DO NOT USE'. Wording and methods can vary, but commonly red labels or lettering are used in the following forms:

- tote box label inserts;
- adhesive tape;
- tie on labels;
- sign plates.

Segregation

Having clearly identified material as non-conforming, it is necessary to segregate that material from all other material until a decision has been reached on disposition. Such an area is often called a quarantine area, with access restricted to quality staff for placement and disposal of material.

Analysis

The first stage of analysis is to determine whether the item is truly non-conforming, defective or both. This involves examining drawings, specifications, standards, job instructions or purchase orders to decide whether requirements have been met, or not, and whether requirements are adequately defined. This stage is normally conducted by the quality function.

The second stage of analysis is to determine the extent of non-conformance, in two respects:

1. The maximum deviation from specification
2. The quantity or rate of items non-conforming.

This is also normally conducted by the quality function.

The third stage is to determine what effect the non-conformance or defect will have on the function or saleability of the product. Where function is in question, the design authority must be consulted. Sometimes the internal design authority will have sufficient knowledge of the application to do this, but where the application by a customer is unknown, it will be necessary to consult the customer. Where appearance rather than function is in question, it will be necessary to consult the customer or, for consumer products, the sales function, to assess whether the condition will affect saleability.

The fourth stage of analysis considers what can be done with the items (i.e. disposition). The major factors affecting disposition are urgency and feasibility. The materials or sales function identify how urgently the items are required and the vendor or the manufacturing planning function identify what is feasible in terms of repairing or reworking materials. The major options available are:

- return to supplier
- sort, then rework, repair or scrap.

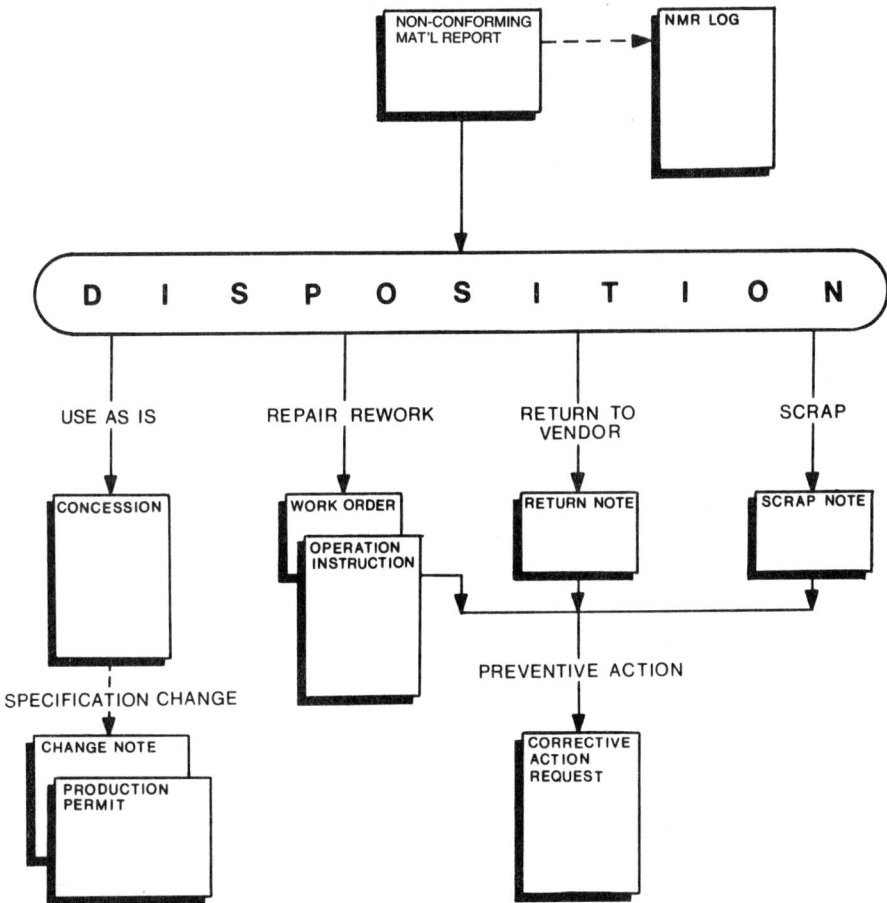

Figure 29.3.   **Documents used, dependent upon disposition.**

The fifth and final stage of analysis is to detemine who is responsible for causing the non-conformance or defect (i.e. liability). This is not necessarily the same as deciding who takes corrective action. Often, the production function or vendors take short term actions pending a tooling or design change. Liability is normally self-evident but, where any doubt exists, the quality function makes the final decision.

Approval

Approval involves completing the NMR to indicate disposition, liability and actions required, which affected parties sign to signify their approval. This may involve a meeting of nominated representatives, it may involve walking the NMR around to those concerned or (in a very small business) it may be a single individual who completes the document to record occurrence, disposition and liability.

The responsibility for obtaining approval and overall control of the process is normally held by the quality function. Where nominated representatives are used and they are unable to reach agreement, an elevation process must be defined, which ultimately involves the chief executive if necessary.

Documentation

As a result of analysis and approval of disposition, liability and actions agreed, documents (of the type listed below) are raised to initiate the actions.

Disposition	*Documents*
Use 'as is'	Concession
Rework/scrap	Work order
Scrap	Scrap note
Return to supplier	Return note
Action	
Corrective action	Corrective action request
	Tool order
	Operation instruction
Specification change	Engineering change note
	Production permit

A brief outline of the purpose of each document is given below and the use of documents depending upon the disposition assigned, is shown in Figure 29.3.

Concession
A written authorization prior to use or release of a quantity of items produced which do not conform to the specified requirements (see Chapter 10).

Work order
An order for repair or rework or any other form of corrective action which is additional to the standard work content.

Scrap note
Authorization to dispose of material which cannot be reworked, repaired, or used for any other purpose.

Return note
Notification to a vendor of the reason for returning material. This document sometimes incorporates the corrective action request document.

Corrective action request
A request for the individual or area deemed liable for a non-conformity to define the cause, corrective action and measures to prevent recurrence.

Tool order
An order for new or modified tooling.

Operation instruction
A written instruction detailing materials, methods and tooling required to perform an operation, which usually also includes diagrams or sketches and makes reference to key points of attention.

Engineering change note
An authorization for a permanent change to a specification or drawing. How this is achieved is covered in detail in Chapter 10.

Production permit
A written authorization prior to production or provision of a service, to depart from specified requirements for a specified quantity or period of time (see Chapter 10).

Disposal

Upon receipt of the approved NMR, the quality function will release the material for disposal as agreed.

Closeout

The quality function ensures that materials are only used as approved on the NMR and that follow-up actions for correction or prevention are implemented. For rework or repair this may involve the reinspection of the items.

Tracking

Records of NMRs raised are maintained by the quality function to determine whether actions taken are effective in reducing the number of non-conformances. The overall effectiveness can be determined by plotting the quantity of NMRs raised weekly or monthly, and this can be further broken down to show liability or major types of non-conformance. The subject is covered further in this chapter under trend analysis.

Costing

Non-conformance can be very costly when the impacts of lost sales, customer returns, production losses, processing and documentation are all taken into account. However, there is little benefit in establishing yet another system to show what these costs are. The key statistics affecting the business will almost certainly be tracked in other forms, such as supplier returns, line failures, unplanned work (repair/ rework), production output and efficiency, sales, scrap costs, etc. All of these performance factors can be improved by employing a non-conformance management process without establishing a separate system for costing non-conformance.

Controls

An important aspect leading to the reduction of non-conformance is to ensure that all occurrences are exposed when they occur. Only when this happens can effective and cost-effective action be taken to prevent recurrence. To make sure this happens, it is necessary to consider the major sources of non-conformances and the key areas of exposure.

Sources of non-conformance

Some of the many sources of non-conformance are:

- design
- manufacturing planning
- suppliers
- material supply
- fabrication
- assembly
- test/inspection
- warehousing
- transportation
- customers

This offers a wide range of possibilities, but generally the discovery of non-conformances will occur in one of four areas:

1. Incoming inspection.
2. In-process.
3. Final test/inspection.
4. Customer returns.

At each of these stages it is necessary to have the means to initiate the process. In large businesses each area may operate independently, with the overall coordination of tracking handled by a central quality function. In smaller businesses the entire process will be administered by the quality function or a single representative, but the same pattern will emerge.

Incoming inspection

Purchased material is generally inspected because there has been a history of problems or because insufficient confidence has been established to discontinue inspection. The function is therefore looking for non-conformance, often on a sample basis and generally on selected key parameters or characteristics only. For this area to be effective, it is essential that all parameters or characteristics are inspected on the entire sample quantity. There is often a strong temptation to discontinue inspection when sufficient non-conformities or defects have been found to reject the batch. The danger in doing this is that different non-conformities or defects may be missed which could have been exposed to the vendor. The vendor will almost certainly consider only the reasons for rejection, with the result that previously unidentified non-conformities will cause further

RAGLETTS plc	**CORRECTIVE ACTION REQUEST**	No: **00172**

SECTION 1	Issued to:	Please complete Section 2 of this form and return to the originator at the address shown below, by:

	Day	Month	Year

Part No   Issue   Description

Ord Job No   NMR No

Statement of Problem

Originator (print)   Signature   Date

SECTION 2	Cause of Problem

Remedial Action

Completed By (print)   Signature   Date

Ragletts plc, The Quality Department, 12, Cannon St., Clagbury, Goodshire GS99 1ZE

Figure 29.4.   A typical corrective action request form.

rejections, with delays, disruption and disputes adding to the mounting chaos. Where batch sizes are relatively small and parts are urgently required, it is advisable to sort the entire batch to clear the acceptable items. In some situations the vendor may be requested to do the sorting.

Another important aspect relating to vendor non-conformance, is the need for the vendor to identify clearly the cause and the action being taken to prevent recurrence. To trigger and track this activity, many companies issue a corrective action request (CAR) form to suppliers and ensure that a satisfactory response is received. An example is shown in Figure 29.4. As mentioned earlier, the CAR is sometimes incorporated into the return note. The form provides a good vehicle for initiating corrective and preventive action by a supplier but, in the final analysis, the proof of success is provided by future conforming deliveries.

In-process
Non-conformance discovered in-process is often the result of a clear defect or failure which hampers or prevents further production. The main danger here is that the production department may view the loss of production, rather than the non-conformance, as the major problem and resort to measures which allow production to continue in spite of the non-conforming condition. However, the 'fix' may not be acceptable for future production stages, for intended purpose or for the long term reliability of the end product.

The reason production departments take such action is often the result of frustration at the time taken in coming up with an approved solution using the formal route. It is therefore important that in-process problems have adequate support and are addressed on a high priority basis, but equally important that production only resumes on an approved basis. This can sometimes mean that finished or partly finished production needs to be quarantined pending clearance or rework.

Non-conformance which affects output will clearly receive a high profile, but there are also infrequent or isolated cases of non-conformance which can all too easily be ignored. They may not have the same urgency as the 'line stoppers', but will still generate waste and if not investigated will cause an opportunity for improvement to be lost. To prevent this happening, it is necessary to provide operators with a collection area for parts or items which have failed or are unusable. Such parts can then be collected by the line supervisor or inspector hourly or daily, or at whatever frequency is considered appropriate and manageable. The parts are then held in an in-process quarantine area pending review and allocation of disposition, liability and action required.

Final test and inspection
Non-conformance discovered at this stage is generally handled in a more uniform manner than is normally the case in-process. Like the incoming inspection area, this area is looking for non-conformance

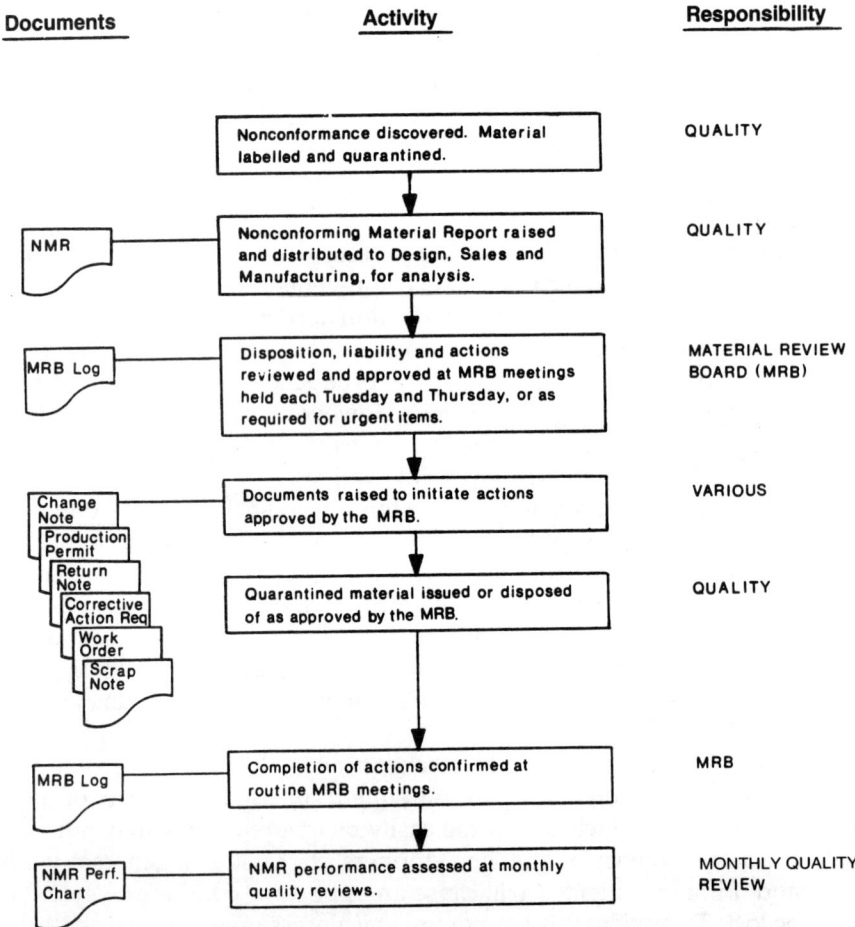

Documents	Activity	Responsibility
	Nonconformance discovered. Material labelled and quarantined.	QUALITY
NMR	Nonconforming Material Report raised and distributed to Design, Sales and Manufacturing, for analysis.	QUALITY
MRB Log	Disposition, liability and actions reviewed and approved at MRB meetings held each Tuesday and Thursday, or as required for urgent items.	MATERIAL REVIEW BOARD (MRB)
Change Note / Production Permit / Return Note / Corrective Action Req / Work Order / Scrap Note	Documents raised to initiate actions approved by the MRB.	VARIOUS
	Quarantined material issued or disposed of as approved by the MRB.	QUALITY
MRB Log	Completion of actions confirmed at routine MRB meetings.	MRB
NMR Perf. Chart	NMR performance assessed at monthly quality reviews.	MONTHLY QUALITY REVIEW

Figure 29.5.   Example of an outline non-conformance management procedure.

prior to giving approval for release of production output. As the final stage before shipment, the area often comes under intense pressure to release items. When production have missed their timescales, final test or inspection can be urged to forgo or reduce the level of inspection, non-conformities are played down and the dispatch department anxiously awaits clearance for shipment.

It is vitally important that final test and inspection are conducted as specified, and that non-conforming items receive full review and approval. When supplying items or services to a customer specification, this may include customer approval.

The quality function normally liaises with the customer on such matters, often with support from specialist technical or engineering functions, as required.

Customer returns

Certainly not all customer returns are due to non-conformance but, if the reason for return is not immediately clear, it is prudent to assume that it is until evidence is found to the contrary.

In some businesses, customer returns are handled by a service department and in others, by the quality function. Whichever it is, the same process should be applied as for all other sources of non-conformance.

The actions resulting from customer NMRs relate not only to corrective or preventative actions, but also need to consider customer settlements and responses. Such action will be dependent upon the findings, which may reveal contributory negligence, false claims, inadequate specifications or possibly, potentially serious reliability or safey issues which require more major investigations. Whatever the outcome, the response to the customer, even if handled by the quality function, need to have the full knowledge and approval of the sales function.

Approval rules and responsibility

To ensure clarity of responsibility and actions, it is necessary to prepare at least an outline procedure which shows what has to be done and by whom. An example is shown in Figure 29.5.

Implementation

Where no formal non-conforming material system exists, the costs incurred by not having such a system need to be established before ·
any attempt is made to convince others that such a system is required.

To do this, an assessment of the occurrence of non-conformance must be made. This can be done using existing data, where available, or by monitoring key stages for a period of (say) a month. From the occurrence, an estimate of the financial impacts can be made. This is best done by considering the following elements of cost:

- failure (scrap, rework, repair);
- appraisal (sorting, purging);
- returns (refunds, claims);
- recovery (lost production);
- sales (lost orders, goodwill, etc.).

It will be difficult to put a figure on some items, particularly on sales. In such cases it would be advisable not to provide a figure that cannot be supported: better to state that such losses are inevitable, but not possible to include in the financial analysis. The remaining costs should provide ample justification for the modest implementation costs.

Having established the costs incurred by not having an effective system, an outline of the system most suitable for the business should be costed. The costs will be split into:

- implementation costs (documentation, hardware, software);

- continuing costs (manpower, meetings, etc., additional to existing levels).

The benefits of the system must then be estimated. As the major benefits will result from the progressive elimination of recurring non-conformities, it has to be estimated how many could be eliminated in, say, a twelve month period. Benefit forecasts should not be overstated. Often the effect of corrective or preventive action takes months, not all actions are totally effective, and new problems crop up. A modest but achievable target which justifies the outlay within a reasonable period is sufficient.

Having prepared and costed the case for implementation, it then remains to sell it to those who will have to authorize and work it. The timescale for addressing objections and overcoming them can take weeks or months in larger businesses. Before implementation, the approved process must be clearly explained to users. A trial run in a selected area is a good way of ironing out any flaws before full implementation.

As with all systems, when fully operational it should be reviewed for efficiency and effectiveness and improved if necessary. To be able to demonstrate the effectiveness, it will be necessary to track and report the benefits claimed.

Improvements

Whatever the prime purpose is for any system or process, it must contribute to the profitability of a business. The non-conformance process is basically a reactive one. At incoming inspection, in process and at final test or inspection, it ensures that the business does not incur heavy costs at a later date as a result of non-conformance exposed today, and it triggers action to prevent further occurrences. The process also provides good data and active support to improvement processes within a business.

Corrective actions

Short term corrective action can range from action to recover a situation (e.g. rework or repair) to interim measures aimed at reducing the risk of recurrence, pending a long term solution which eliminates the risk of recurrence (e.g. increased inspection, visual aids, operator instructions). Interim measures tend to be reversible changes: i.e. there is no guarantee that the condition will not return.

Long term actions are measures which are intended to solve the problem once and for all, for a particular non-conformity. Such measures include design changes, method changes, process capability improvements, automatic adjustments, tooling and 'foolproofing'. They tend to address the cause rather than the symptom and are, in the main, irreversible.

Trend analysis

One of the most useful aspects of managing non-conformance effectively is the ability to confirm improving or deteriorating trends from analysis of NMRs raised. Useful indicators include:

- overall non-conformance rate;
- customer non-conformance rate;
- purchased material non-conformance rate.

The trends provide a source of data for selecting improvement projects and a means for determining their effectiveness.

Overall non-conformance rate

By tracking the total number of NMRs raised on a weekly, monthly or quarterly basis, the overall performance of a business in terms of non-conformance can be seen at a glance. Further analysis, for instance by liability, can reveal the areas which are causing most non-conformances.

Customer non-conformance rate

Tracking customer return NMRs will not provide an absolute figure for customer or field performance, as many customers do not return or complain about every aspect which is displeasing to them. They tend to buy the goods or services elsewhere the next time, when the displeasure becomes unbearable. However, a measure of non-conformance does provide an indicator of whether customer or field perception is getting better or worse.

Purchased material non-conformance rate

This measure should not be confused with vendor rating. NMRs which are vendor liability can be used as one of the inputs which contribute to vendor performance and rating, but when all NMRs approved for purchased materials are considered, it will be seen that liability is often not the supplier's. It does, however, provide a total measure on purchased materials and does focus attention on areas which need attention with individual suppliers or internal departments.

Cost reductions

The inevitable consequence of a well managed system to deal with non-conformance will be a dramatic reduction in the costs incurred in many areas of the business. Reductions in the number of design changes, process deficiencies, operator errors, supplier returns, repairs, rework and remakes, stemming from the avoidance of problems identified previously, are just a few of the many tangible benefits which will result.

Design and process capabilities

It is not intended that a non-conforming material process should expose fundamental design and process problems; design reviews and process capability studies, together with preproduction build activity, should do this. Nevertheless, the process will expose less obvious facets of design shortcomings and limitations of process capability or methods.

Future designs

NMRs can be a useful source of information to designers of products, processes and services. Although they are probably aware of NMRs which have design liability in the form of change notes, the knowledge of problems experienced by suppliers, manufacturing departments and users can enable designers to consider solutions that will avoid or limit such possibilities in the future. It can also ensure a clearer and more realistic definition of requirements based on a better appreciation of problems and knowledge of process capabilities. To convert this knowledge into action, designers should revise standing orders or design rules to take account of past non-conformance.

Finally, it cannot be overlooked that the management of non-conforming material is not the most stimulating area of quality management. In spite of measures taken in design, planning, manufacturing and throughout the business, this process is all about facing up to the fact that specifications or standards have not been achieved. If handled badly, all the earlier measures taken will count for little. But, if handled well, the process will serve as a foundation on which all other activities can depend and flourish.

To err is human. To learn from errors made and to take action to prevent them happening again is both sensible and profitable.

Further reading

Feigenbaum, Armand V., *Total Quality Control*, 3rd ed. McGraw-Hill, New York, U.S.A., 1988.

Juran, J.M. and Gryna, Frank M. Jr., *Quality Planning and Analysis*, 2nd ed., McGraw-Hill, New York, U.S.A., 1980.

Juran, J.M., Gryna, Frank M. and Bingham, R.S., *Quality Control Handbook*, 3rd ed., McGraw-Hill, New York, U.S.A., 1974.

Index